THE WORLD OF WORDS

A LANGUAGE READER

We have taken our title from John Florio, who is renowned as a translator of the *Essays* of Montaigne and who in 1598 published an Italian-English dictionary called *A Worlde of Wordes*. His phrase evokes the idea that exploring the domain of language can create the same kind of excitement as does the discovery of new lands and new experiences.

❧ ❧ ❧

THE WORLD OF WORDS

A LANGUAGE READER

Edited by BARNET KOTTLER

and MARTIN LIGHT

PURDUE UNIVERSITY

HOUGHTON MIFFLIN COMPANY · BOSTON

New York   Atlanta   Geneva, Ill.   Dallas   Palo Alto

CONTENTS

6 | LANGUAGE AND LITERATURE 357

INTRODUCTION

The essays in this collection describe, illustrate, and dramatize the interplay between language and life from various personal, historical, social, and cultural perspectives. Nothing else separates man from animals as speech does. Though animals communicate, only man has an elaborate system of voiced sounds for a multitude of situations. These sounds and the system that gives them order differ from society to society, so that, as Edward Sapir has said, the process of learning to walk would be the same for a child in his native environment or in an alien one, but his speech in one would be at complete variance with his speech in the other. Because language is deeply a part of all of life, the readings in this book envelop a wide variety of human activities. We use language and respond to it all the time but in many different ways. We shout, we taunt, we argue, we speak affectionately, we curse, we read and debate and give orders, we write letters, examinations, and essays. We respond to popular song, to jokes, to the schoolyard yell, to advertising, to political oratory, to the novel, to poetry.

Another way to categorize our involvements with language is to use the term "speech community." Each person belongs to many speech communities — that is, each of us has a language for participating in the activities of one or another of the groups to which he belongs. One community can be as large as that shared by all the speakers of "English." Another can be as small as that of two children who share their own secret language. To some extent we shift languages as we move from home to church, from classroom to playing field, from hobby to business, from science laboratory to literature class, from Ozarks to California, from youth to old age. We have a jargon for baseball, for woodworking, for sewing; a regional dialect; an informal slang; and a self-conscious diction for formal occasions. This book explores many of the speech communities listed above and suggests approaches to others not dealt with directly. These essays display delight in pun and metaphor, the scholar's fascination with the history of words, the scientist's giant effort to entrap vast knowledge in an unambiguous shorthand of exact words, the hobo's slang, the words of jazz cracking like rim-shots, the gang's special language flashing aggressively like shiny jackets, the conniving and excluding language of the underworld, the politician's cautious befuddlements, the advertising man's carefully-planned ambiguities, and the literary artist's journey to the outer edges of experience, even to the place where words fail him.

Fundamental to an understanding of language is recognition of change. Language must constantly renew itself. Because the educated man must know the traditions of his civilization, he should review the history of words and their changes. We examine the principles upon which our language creates new meanings and new words. Poets rejuvenate words, often on the basis of hidden etymology, or they move words about, making verbs out of nouns. But popular speech finds new words, too.

Some of the essays in this book are by professional students of language who describe the various ways in which our understanding of the nature and development of language contributes to our understanding of the lives we lead and the world in which we live. Other essays are by men whose study of the general human condition forced them into a confrontation with language.

We believe these essays will prove illuminating, exciting, amusing, and disturbing. But we believe that whatever his reaction, the reader will experience a growing sensitivity to language. He will listen to words with a keener ear, he will look at words with a sharper eye, and he will think about words with a more reflective and critical mind. He will discover how much language he knows, why he hardly uses much that he knows, and why what he does use, he uses only in certain ways. We hope that he will be led to rediscover language that he has forgotten he knows and that can once again have meaning and value for him. That is why we begin by asking him to recall the language of childhood. Discovery and sensitivity will lead to more supple, versatile, and comfortably self-conscious use of language — to more expressive, more precise, more honest writing. In this book the reader will find some generalizations about language and society, but he will also find a multitude of examples, much particularization, and a great deal of evidence, for these essayists work close to their subjects. The essays are models of good writing, moving between concreteness and abstraction to make good argument.

This collection is divided into six sections. The first focuses on the personal involvement with language. The second steps back to get an historical perspective on language but comes forward again to see language as it is being changed and made in our times. The third section emphasizes the importance of language in our social relationships, those groupings by class, by region, and by education which help define our identities. The fourth section deals with slang and argot. The fifth ranges widely over many aspects of our culture, revealing how they can be better understood by examination of language. Finally in the sixth section, we read how those who use words most creatively — the essayists, poets, and novelists — demand from us, if we wish to appreciate them fully, a creative and critical response to their language.

Lafayette, Indiana

Barnet Kottler
Martin Light

We wish to acknowledge the help given us by

our families during our work on this book.

That part of an anthology which editors can

properly dedicate, we dedicate to

Sylvia Kottler and Dorothy Light.

B.K. / M.L.

THE WORLD OF WORDS

A LANGUAGE READER

1 ✒

THE PERSONAL RESPONSE
TO LANGUAGE

When does our awareness of language begin? For each of us the answer probably differs somewhat, but for most people awareness begins in the family, when we hear our names and some simple sounds associated with father, mother, toys, food, games, rhymes, and song. Few of us can recall these beginnings clearly, though some of us can observe them now in children we know. Helen Keller, however, has been able to remember her own first consciousness of the fact that there even was such a thing as "language." She can recall learning her first words because she knew no words until she was seven years of age. The first section of this book opens, then, with Helen Keller's discovery that everything has a name. Each essay that follows takes its focus in the personal response to language.

Naming was one of the earliest rituals our parents performed for us — through no choice of our own. What sense of appropriateness, what tradition, what response to fashion went into our naming? A name records not only family history but some fragment of the history of nations as well. Of the larger significances of names, Otto Jespersen, the renowned Danish linguist, has written: "To children and savages . . . there is something magical or mystical in a name. It is something that has power over things and is bound up with them in a far more intimate manner than we are wont to imagine." Among some Indians, for instance, uttering the name of the dead is taboo. Some tribes permit the child to name himself; others require that a name be kept secret. Children taunt and jeer with names. The taunter knows the force of names; the taunted reassures himself against magic by replying that names can never hurt. But naming can effect symbolic possession or destruction, as in voodoo.

1

Of the speech communities that touch us most closely, two have special importance: the family and the school. The family may have its own secret language, nicknames, and words of love, as well as a family tone of voice and non-verbal ways of communicating, like signals, whistles, and gestures. From a study of household language may emerge a larger picture of the unique quality of our family experience. Outside the family, the school becomes the most important influence on the child's language. The schoolroom and the schoolyard are separate places linguistically — one a place of rules and correctness, the other a place of emotion, spontaneity, and unconcern for rules. The Sandburg reminiscence and the selection from the Opies' collection of children's lore present only a small portion of the immense storehouse of the language of children. A schoolyard is not a quiet place; there are few games without shouts. Each of us needs the release that comes from spontaneous language, but we can also respect the decorum of rules. The classroom and the yard enrich each other.

The essay by Thomas Wolfe points ahead to this book's final section on style and literature, but it stands here as a personal account of the way language can become the daemon of one's life. Wolfe wrote, "I saw that I must find for myself the tongue to utter what I knew but could not say." For Wolfe, words are a way of encompassing the whole of human experience. For him they would "open the door" — as surely they may for each of us also.

Helen Keller

EVERYTHING HAS A NAME

𝕶𝕶

Deaf and blind from the age of a year and a half, Helen Keller had no language at all until she was seven. She had touched things, but had not known that words went with them. The following passage describes the occasion of learning her first word; she recalls her discovery that every palpable thing has a name. In his play and movie The Miracle Worker, William Gibson dramatized the kind of savagery that existed in Miss Keller before her teacher Anne Sullivan helped her to accept the gift of language. Words awakened Miss Keller to the world because language enables one to find and express relationships; to give thoughts their embodiment and feelings their articulation.

The most important day I remember in all my life is the one on which my teacher, Anne Mansfield Sullivan, came to me. I am filled with wonder when I consider the immeasurable contrast between the two lives which it connects. It was the third of March, 1887, three months before I was seven years old.

On the afternoon of that eventful day, I stood on the porch, dumb, expectant. I guessed vaguely from my mother's signs and from the hurrying to and fro in the house that something unusual was about to happen, so I went to the door and waited on the steps. The afternoon sun penetrated the mass of honeysuckle that covered the porch, and fell on my upturned face. My fingers lingered almost unconsciously on the familiar leaves and blossoms which had just come forth to greet the sweet southern spring. I did not know what the future held of marvel or surprise for me. Anger

Reprinted from *The Story of My Life* by Helen Keller, published by Doubleday & Company. Title supplied by the editors.

and bitterness had preyed upon me continually for weeks and a deep languor had succeeded this passionate struggle.

Have you ever been at sea in a dense fog, when it seemed as if a tangible white darkness shut you in, and the great ship, tense and anxious, groped her way toward the shore with plummet and sounding-line, and you waited with beating heart for something to happen? I was like that ship before my education began, only I was without compass or sounding-line, and had no way of knowing how near the harbour was. "Light! give me light!" was the wordless cry of my soul, and the light of love shone on me in that very hour.

I felt approaching footsteps. I stretched out my hand as I supposed to my mother. Some one took it, and I was caught up and held close in the arms of her who had come to reveal all things to me, and, more than all things else, to love me.

The morning after my teacher came she led me into her room and gave me a doll. The little blind children at the Perkins Institution had sent it and Laura Bridgman had dressed it; but I did not know this until afterward. When I had played with it a little while, Miss Sullivan slowly spelled into my hand the word "d-o-l-l." I was at once interested in this finger play and tried to imitate it. When I finally succeeded in making the letters correctly I was flushed with childish pleasure and pride. Running downstairs to my mother I held up my hand and made the letters for doll. I did not know that I was spelling a word or even that words existed; I was simply making my fingers go in monkey-like imitation. In the days that followed I learned to spell in this uncomprehending way a great many words, among them *pin, hat, cup* and a few verbs like *sit, stand* and *walk*. But my teacher had been with me several weeks before I understood that everything has a name.

One day, while I was playing with my new doll, Miss Sullivan put my big rag doll into my lap also, spelled "d-o-l-l" and tried to make me understand that "d-o-l-l" applied to both. Earlier in the day we had had a tussle over the words "m-u-g" and "w-a-t-e-r." Miss Sullivan had tried to impress it upon me that "m-u-g" is *mug* and that "w-a-t-e-r" is *water,* but I persisted in confounding the two. In despair she had dropped the subject for the time, only to renew it at the first opportunity. I became impatient at her repeated attempts and, seizing the new doll, I dashed it upon the floor. I was keenly delighted when I felt the fragments of the broken doll at my feet. Neither sorrow nor regret followed my passionate outburst. I had not loved the doll. In the still, dark world in which I lived there was no strong sentiment or tenderness. I felt my teacher sweep the fragments to one side of the hearth, and I had a sense of satisfaction that the cause of my discomfort was removed. She brought me my hat, and I knew I was going out into the warm sunshine. This thought, if a wordless sensation may be called a thought, made me hop and skip with pleasure.

We walked down the path to the well-house, attracted by the fragrance of the honeysuckle with which it was covered. Some one was drawing water and my teacher placed my hand under the spout. As the cool stream gushed over one hand she spelled into the other the word *water*, first slowly, then rapidly. I stood still, my whole attention fixed upon the motions of her fingers. Suddenly I felt a misty consciousness as of something forgotten — a thrill of returning thought; and somehow the mystery of language was revealed to me. I knew then that "w-a-t-e-r" meant the wonderful cool something that was flowing over my hand. That living word awakened my soul, gave it light, hope, joy, set it free! There were barriers still, it is true, but barriers that could in time be swept away.

I left the well-house eager to learn. Everything had a name, and each name gave birth to a new thought. As we returned to the house every object which I touched seemed to quiver with life. That was because I saw everything with the strange, new sight that had come to me. On entering the door I remembered the doll I had broken. I felt my way to the hearth and picked up the pieces. I tried vainly to put them together. Then my eyes filled with tears; for I realized what I had done, and for the first time I felt repentance and sorrow.

I learned a great many new words that day. I do not remember what they all were; but I do know that *mother, father, sister, teacher* were among them — words that were to make the world blossom for me, "like Aaron's rod, with flowers." It would have been difficult to find a happier child than I was as I lay in my crib at the close of that eventful day and lived over the joys it had brought me, and for the first time longed for a new day to come.

Noah Jonathan Jacobs

NAMES TO CONJURE WITH

彡彡

In the preface to the book from which the following essay comes, Mr. Jacobs calls our attention to the remarkable Biblical myth in which God gave Adam a language. God brought the beasts and fowls to Adam, as the Bible says, "to see what he would call them; and whatsoever Adam called every living creature, that was the name thereof." Mr. Jacobs points out that "with these names man drew a line . . . between the lower animals and himself." Mr. Jacobs is both amused and impressed by man's concern for the appropriate naming of things. We may receive our personal names for good or trivial reasons; we are sensitive about the misspelling or mispronunciation of our names; we like our own names or we dislike them. James Baldwin believed that he had epitomized the American Negro's dilemma of personal and social identity in the title of his book Nobody Knows My Name.

In the joust with the Devil man and God united their efforts in a student-teacher relationship against a common enemy. They had not yet entered into a genuine personal relationship. This involved a ceremonious exchange of first names as customary in order to make informal dialogue possible. Both God and man have two names. The surname *Adam* refers to man's natural history, his past legacy and his involvement in an impersonal process; his first name, also *Adam* in this case, refers to his unique qualities

Reprinted with permission of The Macmillan Company from *Naming-Day in Eden* by Noah Jonathan Jacobs. © Noah Jonathan Jacobs 1958.

as an individual, and points to the future. It is used to arouse him from his lethargy and summon him to his overarching human self. God also has two names. As *Elohim* He is the God of Nature who created the world and dispenses justice; as *Yahve* (the ineffable Name) He is the God of mercy who answers those who call upon Him in truth. The heresy of Marcionism holds that these two names refer to two different gods and that Jesus spoke only with the second. The Lord *our* God, however, is One and his *Name* is One.

This circumstance was understood by Adam for when, according to a traditional account, God, desirous of establishing closer relations with man, asked Adam to name Him (a request man could neither evade nor decline), Adam, quoting Scripture, complied: "It is fitting for Thee to be called *Adonai* since Thou art Lord of all Thy creatures, for it is written 'That is my name,' which means, that is the name by which Adam called me." This request was an immense concession on the Lord's part, for He was ordinarily loath to have His name revealed, preferring to appear under pseudonyms. But He had confidence in Adam as a name giver, for during the Review he gave names which have received universal approval. Years later when Moses inquired after the divine Name, he was rebuked by the Lord, who showed him His back parts. Pious commentators have taken this awkward passage as a lesson in divine instruction in the art of binding phylacteries to the back of the head. Despite this generous interpretation, however, the intent of the gesture is plain. Adam was the namer par excellence. He also gave himself a name: "It is fitting that I be called Adam because I come from the earth, *adamah.*" This was Adam's first pun (Lat. *homo* from *humus*, earth, suggested by St. Isidore, would have been equally apt), and he seemed to be enjoying his role as namer.

Despite our rejection of the superstitious views of our benighted ancestors, we have not altogether discarded the belief in the virtue of names, except that our motives are more practical than moral. The sound and form of the names parents give to the newly born are not lightly negotiated and often rise to the heights of prophetic vision. If these names are found to be unsuitable in later life, they are frequently changed for business or social reasons and a name adopted which gives its owner an air of superior culture associated with the upper classes. A fruitful area of study for the student of the contemporary social scene is to be found in the name changing of immigrants, social climbers and cinema stars. This latter group, which occupies a prominent place in the public eye, might ponder the Freudian suggestion that it adopt names which lend themselves to erotic or slightly lewd connotations, perhaps names such as Joy, Bottome, Wetmore, Philpot, Bastert, Smalbehynd, and so forth.

The custom of changing names has been resorted to from time immemorial, although for reasons which appear to our practical age irrelevant.

A number of biblical characters changed their names to correspond to the changed nature of their condition, as Abram to Abraham, Jacob to Israel, Naomi (*sweet*) to Mara (*bitter*). Pythagoreans were wont to exchange names in the belief that they would thus be able to share their mutual virtues. In Jewish tradition to this day the name of a person who is critically ill is sometimes changed in order to confuse the Angel of Death. For the same reason an infant born into a family in which other infants have been lost is left unnamed, being referred to as *Alter*, the old one, until after marriage, when he is given the name of one of the patriarchs. Some historical characters have received new names as a reward for some heroic exploit, as Siegfried or Victoria. Others had names bestowed upon them for some intellectual achievement, as some Hebrew authors in the Middle Ages who were named after the titles of their books: Joseph Caro was called Bet Josef and Jacob ben Asher became Baa'l ha-Turim. Famous men among the Greeks often received a nickname because of some distinguishing trait: Sophocles was known as *The Bee* because of the honeyed sweetness of his diction, Chrysostom as *The Light* because of his great learning, Chrysippus of Tarsus as *The Column of the Portico* because of the subtlety he displayed in the disputes at the Academy. This figure of speech, known as synecdoche, is a common form of appellation in the modern underworld, with an expected emphasis on the physical: *The Body, The Voice, Legs, Fingers, Greasy Thumb,* and so on. Synecdoche degenerates into tapinosis when an invidious or repugnant personal trait is made conspicuous by comparing a person to some base inanimate object which is calculated to detract from his dignity, as: *highbrow, egghead, sap, screwball, tightwad, battleax, ham, heel, scab, deadpan, wallflower.* The comic effect of these words is due to the excessive prominence given to the material and the inanimate over the spiritual.

The virtue of name punning, inaugurated by Adam, has persisted throughout the ages. Solemn inferences have been drawn from a pun on a name. The Bible takes special delight in such puns. The root meaning of Jacob is *heel* in the literal and in the slang sense, for Jacob emerged from the womb holding Esau's heel and later dished him out of his birthright. The Catholic Church is founded on the double meaning of the Greek name Peter. The most famous pun in literature is the one made by Ulysses when he outwitted Cyclops by calling himself *Noman.* Nor did a later age find name punning repugnant. It is a common form employed in the mottoes emblazoned on coats-of-arms. A chapel in Westminster Abbey which bears the name of Bishop Islip is adorned with a rebus showing an eye and a lad slipping from a tree, inscribed with the words "I slip." In two of his sonnets Shakespeare rings all the changes on his Christian name Will. Charles Lamb, for whom "a pun was as perfect as a sonnet," spoke of himself on one occasion as Lamb-punning (lampooning). The poet Donne outdoes himself with:

> When thou hast done, thou hast not done,
> For I have more. . . .
> And having done that: Thou hast done,
>   I fear no more.

The addiction to punning is so ingrained in our nature that the noblest of men have not shrunk from playing with their names even on their death-beds. The last defiant words of Huss at the stake were: "You may burn Huss [goose] now, but Luther [swan] will come." Rabelais found time before dying to deliver himself of the following: "Put me on my [*domino*] robe for I am cold; besides I would die in it" (Beati qui in *Domino* moriuntur). Thomas Hood, the most prolific of all the English punsters, had the presence of mind *in articulo mortis* to concoct his last pun: "Now the undertaker will earn [urn] a livelihood [lively Hood]." Several irrepressible punsters, pressed for time, have had their last witticism placed posthumously on their tombstones. Thus, the tomb of a certain Mr. Knight bears the simple inscription "Good Knight!" and the epitaph of a Mr. Partridge reads:

> What! kill a Partridge in the month of May!
> Was that done like a sportsman? eh, Death, eh?

Literary men are not averse to malicious or trivial punning. Luther carelessly wrote the name of one of his numerous enemies, Dr. Eck, as one word *Dreck* (filth). Disraeli was known to intimates as Dizzy and John Keats as Junkets. Stirling Coyne, the great dramatist, was nicknamed Filthy Lucre. The feeble pun "Anne ascended to the throne of her Anne-cestors" has been attributed to Hume. If the accusation is true, it is unworthy of the great philosopher. No one stooped lower in this regard than Dean Swift, who did not shrink from such mutilations as: seizer (Caesar), laid a couple of eggs (Leda), kill ease (Achilles), airy stuff (Aristophanes), and so on. English with its wealth of homonyms and haphazard spelling lends itself to such verbal enormities. Writers are more scrupulous in choosing appropriate names for the characters in their productions. Among the ancients Euripides was known as "the etymologizing tragedian" because of his addiction to name punning. Ben Jonson, Racine, Smollett and Gogol had an eye for the physical or moral peculiarities of their characters, for whom they found apt names. But it was Charles Dickens who, by the elaborate use of vowel symbolism, developed this art of name giving into a literary sophistication. Thus, the short *i* in a name would denote a tender or timid quality (Fips, Grig, Sniggs), the dark *u* solemn or clumsy traits (Muff, Bumble, Buzfuz), the *u* plus the *i* a mixture of both (Nupkins, Spruggins). A descriptive name could be formed by prefixing a solitary consonant (Smangle), by omitting an initial letter (Cratchit), by adding a suffix (Snagsby) or by merely changing a vowel sound (Drood, *dread*). Dickens ransacked birth and death records for suitable suggestions. His most genial invention was his name for Grandfather Smallweed, a gentleman who had to be beaten periodically, like a pillow, to have his human shape restored.

Formerly, names were given for sensible reasons. A physical trait, however unlovely, might suggest the infant's name: Oedipus (swell-foot), Boccaccio (big mouth), Calvin (bald), Varus (bowlegged), Crassus (fatty), Cincinnatus (curly), Cicero (chick pea), derived from an unpleasant excrescence on the Roman orator's nose. A name could be conferred because of some adventitious circumstance. Odysseus was so named because his grandfather Autolykos arrived at the christening "full of wrath"; Brutus received his name because he successfully escaped Tarquin's malignancy by affecting idiocy. Or, if small things may be compared to great, the name Noah (Heb. comfort) was appended to the author of these pages in honor of the Patriarch whose activities, as recorded in the early chapters of Genesis, constituted the required liturgical reading during the week of his birth. Such names, derived from apparently irrelevant circumstances, often express the wish that their literal meaning might be fulfilled or the hope that they may later prove to have been appropriately chosen. There are instances in history where the very reverse has happened. The bearer of the name Law swindled the government, Blunt was a man of uncommon sharpness and Boniface a fellow with an extraordinary amount of cheek. Edward Freely, the confectioner in George Eliot's *Romola*, had a generous-sounding name and yet was a man whose impulses were restrained and whose life was governed by the sound business principle "that the desire for sweets and pastries must only be satisfied in a direct ratio with the power to pay for them." Similarly, Erasmus Holiday, the schoolmaster in *Kenilworth*, owed his Christian name to a secret presentiment in his mother's mind that in the babe a hidden genius lay dormant which one day would lead him to rival the fame of the great scholar of Amsterdam; and he bore the surname Holiday, quasi *lucus a non lucendo*, as his students were inclined to think, because he granted so few holidays. Our own poet Tristram Coffin (lugubrious sarcophagus) is, *per antiphrasin*, the most incurable optimist in the profession.

A large number of names, however, have proved to be surprisingly apt. Consider the name Hammering Henry Armstrong, the pugilist who held three world boxing titles simultaneously! Repeat aloud the name Phineus P. Quimby, the watchmaker who cured Mary Baker Eddy! Could a *watchmaker* be more strikingly named? Not unless it were Thomas Tompion, the famous English clockmaker, in whose stately name we hear not only the ponderous tickings of the mute alliterative *t*'s but the chiming of the abrupt labial nasals as well. No wonder he was buried in Westminster Abbey! Then there are Titus Oates, a man of straw, who deserved to be thrashed, and a certain Dr. Tongue whose name fitted him to a *T*, for he was an uncommonly slippery fellow and always in a pickle. It seems that the gingival *T*, although a pure mute with no sound of its own, is excellent as the initial letter of famous names (Tacitus, Tintoretto, Turgeniev, Talleyrand, Torquemada and Torquato Tasso) and certain professions:

> It seem as if Nature had curiously planned
>> That our name with our trades should agree.
> There Twining, the Tea-man, who lives in the Strand,
>> Would be whining if robbed of his T.

The clearest case of predestination, however, is the name Rumhole, which belongs to the owner of a London pub.

The character who has suffered most from the ravages of punning is, beyond all doubt, Ajax. In Sophocles' play by that name the hero in a desperate mood is driven to pun on his own name, which in Greek has the same sound as the common interjection of sorrow or woe:

> Ay me! Whoe'er had thought how well my name
> Would fit my misery? Aye me! Aye me!

It is an additional unfortunate circumstance that this Greek hero who died of vexation should bear a name that is phonetically equivalent to the older English word for privy. We still find it so used by Lear's Kent who, while scuffling with one of the servants, is moved to exclaim: "I will tread this unbolted villain into mortar, and daub the walls of a jakes with him." The word is now obsolete, and others have sprung up to replace it. But in former times when the word was current it captured the etymological imagination of ordinary folk for whom it called up the vision of an old man groaning on the toilet (Ajax = age aches). It is recorded that a certain Jaques Wingfield was overcautiously introduced in court as Privy Wingfield. This unfortunate similarity of sound induced Sir John Harington, the English translator of Ariosto, to write his famous *Metamorphosis of Ajax*, with an appendix bearing the title *Ulysses on Ajax*. The alleged purpose of this cloacinean satire, the first Rabelaisian specimen of which our language can boast, was to describe a species of water closet which the author had erected near Bath. Prurient readers who are diverted by such facetiae can find this stale subject refreshed by a contemporary writer, Reginald Reynolds, who in his book *Godliness and Cleanliness* duly acknowledges his debt to Harington. Ajax is the prototype of the bearers of punnable names. But we are all sensitive to our names and resent having them tampered with. Goethe in his *Autobiography* relates how as a young man he was infatuated with his own name, how he wrote it everywhere and how its very sound awed him and how he resented the clever plays on his name in a sonnet published by Friedrich Schlegel. This innocent raillery so irked Goethe that he rebuked the perpetrator in the following revealing words: "I dare say it was unseemly in him to permit himself a jest at the expense of my name. A man's name is not, as it were, a mantle thrown over his shoulders, that can be yanked and plucked at will. It is rather a perfectly fitting garment, nay, a veritable skin grown on him and which can be mutilated only with injury to the man himself."

The deliberate distortion of a name is often intended to harm the owner (Ibsenity, for example). Sometimes the name is used as an epithet and then gradually converted into a common noun. At first a name may be used to refer to some distinguishing trait, as: "Rousseau was the Newton of the ethical world"; "Thomas is but Aristotle sainted"; "Theodore Roosevelt was a combination of St. Paul and St. Vitus." Then the proper name may be emphasized by being repeated in a pregnant sense, a figure of speech called ploce, as: "In that battle Caesar was Caesar, Cicero continued to be Cicero," where the characteristic qualities of bravery and eloquence implicit in the respective names emerge. To names less known an adjective or qualifying phrase is appended, as: *a doubting Thomas, a dumb Dora, a simple Simon, a Holofernes of folly, a Gogmagog of nonsense.* If widely used, the name assumes the function of an adjective, as: *Melba toast, Sacher Torte, Molotov cocktail;* or, *Spinozan, Socratic, Dantesque, Platonist, Jacobite, Hobbist* or *Hobbian, Pepysian* (pronounced Peepsian) and *Shavian* (to rhyme with Fabian). Fictional characters have given us *Pickwickian, Pecksniffian, Micawberish* and *Shandean.* From the German we have *Wagnerian* and *Nietzschean* but Heine and Schopenhauer have resisted adjectival endings, as have the French names Rousseau and Montaigne. The Russians have succeeded in making an adjective of Mark Twain (*marktvénovski*) and the Germans with less success a verb of Friedrich Nietzsche (*sich befriedrichnietzschen lassen*).

In the last stage of this hypostatization the salient quality in the word becomes dominant and assumes a separate existence as a generalized common noun written with a small letter, which may function also as an adjective or verb, its origin all but forgotten. Thus, we have the nouns *dunce* (Duns Scotus), *saxophone* (Adolphe Sax of Belgium), Fr. *gringalet,* a shrimp of a man (from Gringalet, a clown of the seventeenth century), *sadism* (Marquis de Sade, born 1740, infamous for his crimes and the character of his writings), *masochism* (Leopold von Sacher-Masoch, Austrian novelist, who described this affliction); common nouns from the Bible: *simony, onanism, jezebel;* animal names derived from proper nouns: *jackdaw* (Jack), *rabbit* (Robert), *magpie* (Margaret), *parrot* (diminutive of Peter); proper names transferred to the names of flowers: *begonia* (Bégon, governor of Santo Domingo), *dahlia* (Andreas Dahl, Swedish botanist), *camellia* (Josef Kamel, a Jesuit priest), *lobelia* (Matthias de L'obel, Flemish scholar), *gloxinia* (B. P. Gloxin, German botanist), *zinnia* (J. G. Zinn, professor of medicine at Göttingen); adjectives derived from the gods of mythology: *jovial, mercurial, saturnine, venereal, aphro-*

disiac, protean, erotic; the verbs *hector, out-herod, bowdlerize, tantalize*; adjectives derived from fictional characters: *quixotic, gargantuan, euphuistic, dryasdust*; and words of saintly origin: *maudlin* (Magdalene), *nickel* (St. Nicolaus), *dago* (St. Diego), *maumet* (Mohammed), *tawdry* (St. Audrey), *petrel* (St. Peter), *pantaloons* (St. Pantaleone), *cereal* (the Roman goddess Ceres, protector of crops), *opportune* (Portunus, the Roman God of ports), and *ladybug* (bug of our Lady).

This scrupulous concern for fitting names is not shared by most men today. We tend to regard a name as an arbitrary designation, simply a meaningless mark which enables it to be made the subject of discourse, but which in no way indicates the attributes belonging to the bearer. A proper name is a word which identifies its object by virtue of its sound alone, unassisted by considerations of associated meanings. The mind is stopped by the sensible externals of sound before it could arrive at the meaning. Wellington did not conquer India because of his resonant, aggressive name. Had Napoleon borne the cognomen Klotz or had George Washington sustained the appellation Izod Flopson, those unamiable names would now be uttered with reverence. Is Klopstock, the German Milton, too dull a name to resound through the ages? Fame does not love only high-sounding names. Those who hold this "convention theory" are impervious to the fascination of names.

An extreme measure in this direction was taken in ancient Greece by Diodorus who defiantly called his slaves by the names of the Greek particles. A name is a label, and there is no necessary correspondence between it and its owner — an evil person can have a beautiful name, as Delilah; or an ugly name, as Jezebel; and good people can have beautiful names, as David; or ugly names, as Habakkuk. To those who cannot resist reading their prejudices into names, who strive to discover the workings of the mind in the physiognomy of a name and fancy they see angles in Izaak Walton's face, Paulus Silentiarius directed his bitter epitaph:

> My name, my country — what are they to thee?
> What, whether base or proud, my pedigree?
> Perhaps I far surpassed all other men,
> Perhaps I fell below them all; what then?
> Suffice it, stranger! that thou seest a tomb;
> Thou know'st its use; it hides — no matter whom.

Allen Walker Read

FAMILY WORDS IN ENGLISH[1]

✍✍

Professor Read explores the language of one of the smallest but most vital of the speech-communities we belong to — the family. Its vocabulary encircles the children of the household first of all — with nicknames, names for pets and toys, and the coinages and mispronunciations that get fixed into the family pattern of communication. It might also involve a private language between two people: for instance, Jonathan Swift wrote an intimate and affectionate "little language" in his letters called Journal to Stella. Reminiscing about childhood can bring to the surface several examples of family words, which in turn can suggest something of the unique nature of each family structure.

Students of language have long been aware that every speaker participates in a number of overlapping speech communities. The broadest speech community is that using 'the language' itself. In the case of English, this is the body of speakers not only in the home area of the British Isles but in the far-flung regions where English has been carried. Then there are speech communities of descending size, on the basis of geography, social class, education, occupation, ceremonial activities, recreational interests, and so on, until one reaches the fundamental speech community, the family.

The linguistic importance of the family has been somewhat obscured by

[1] This article is the revised version of a paper which was read on December 2, 1961, at the Seventh Annual National Conference on Linguistics sponsored by the Linguistic Circle of New York.

From *American Speech*, XXXVII (February, 1962), pp. 5–12. **Reprinted by permission of Columbia University Press.**

the practice of linguists of referring to 'child language' or 'nursery words' as if the young age group were an entity.[2] Truly enough, there is a remarkable homogeneity in the language of the nursery and of young children, and its terms are widespread over the entire English-speaking world. The family group, however, comprises not only the children but several generations in communion with one another. As Jespersen has wisely acknowledged, 'the truth of the matter is that a child is normally surrounded by people of all ages and learns its language more or less from all of them, from Grannie down to little Dick from over the way . . .'[3]

A number of observers have pointed out the importance of the family as a unit for linguistic purposes. The earliest of these statements is from the mid-seventeenth century, by the Duchess of Newcastle, who wrote in 1653: 'And not onely every *Shire* hath a severall *Language*, but every *Family*, giving *Marks* for things according to their *Fancy*.'[4] In 1913 George Philip Krapp commented: 'Certain forms of speech will be used only among the members of the family in their family relations, and these will often be the very forms which give the group its deepest sense of intimacy and unity.'[5] Eric Partridge in 1933 supported this point of view, saying:

> All families, if they are more than a mere collocation of related individuals, if they often meet together, and especially if they prefer their own company to that of others, have their own private slang; some few an extensive vocabulary, most a score or a dozen or even fewer words and phrases. Occasionally a stranger will hear a complete sentence that obviously means something quite different.[6]

In 1937 the Irish archeologist R. A. Stewart Macalister expressed his agreement, as follows:

> Probably every family, even of moderate size, has a more or less extensive vocabulary of current words and phrases, the sources of which may have been forgotten — may even never have been known to the junior members — but which are quite comprehensible in the household, though totally unintelligible outside.[7]

[2] Thus Otto Jespersen, in *Language* (London, 1923), pp. 161–88, has devoted a long section to the topic, 'The Influence of the Child on Linguistic Development.' The extensive literature of this field can be consulted by means of Werner F. Leopold, *Bibliography of Child Language* (Evanston, Ill., 1952).

[3] *Op. cit.*, p. 165. Cf. Charles F. Hockett, 'Age-grading and Linguistic Continuity,' *Language*, XXVI (1950), 449–57. The notion of the family, as typically found in the United States and even in England, would, I think, require some modification of his 'proposition 2,' p. 449: 'The most important environmental force shaping the emerging dialect of a child is the speech of other children.'

[4] Margaret (Lucas) Cavendish (Duchess of Newcastle), *Poems, and Fancies* (London, 1653), sig. A6 recto.

[5] 'Standards of Speech and Their Value,' *Modern Philology*, XI (1913), 59.

[6] *Slang To-day and Yesterday* (London, 1933), p. 148.

[7] *The Secret Languages of Ireland* (Cambridge, England, 1937), pp. 91–92.

In 1945 Logan Pearsall Smith made a 'collection of words privately invented by some groups and families,' and he proposed to put it into print, but I have not heard that this was done.[8]

In this article I present examples of words that have had their currency within family limits. Here we can see to good advantage the effervescing of language creation. My material is drawn from a variety of sources: oral reports from friends and students, autobiographies and reminiscences, and in some cases fictional accounts that report family situations with an attempt at verisimilitude.

Let us first take up some expressions that involve figurative speech, chiefly metaphorical leaps in the naming of things. In a New York family, according to a student, parsnips are known as 'white carrots' and pepper as 'black salt.'[9] The English novelist G. B. Stern reminisced from her youth concerning *squashed flies*: 'What biscuits did you have at your nursery tea-table? We had "squashed flies." Garibaldis was their statelier name.'[10] In the family of Henry Beckett, a New York journalist, an airplane was called a 'bird-bus,' from the coinage of his daughter Martha, and the American Museum of Natural History was 'the bone house.'[11] William Holt, an English broadcaster, has reported an animal known as a 'Yukon,' invented by his daughter:

> She had invented fanciful animals which were suggested to her by new words and names which she had heard or had come across when reading. Animals such as 'Yukons.' She really believed at one time that there was such an animal. The word 'fetlock' provided her with a useful collective noun for associating with Yukons — 'a fetlock of Yukons.' When I probed her with questions as to where her idea of a 'Yukon' had come from she told me she had seen a book being loaded on to one of my motor libraries, called *The Call of the Yukon*, and I have no doubt that she distinctly heard its peculiar cry.[12]

From the ebullient Mitford family, among the daughters of Lord Redesdale, Jessica has reported: 'It was easy to make her huge blue eyes brim with tears — known as "welling" in family circles.'[13] The family of the famous poet A. E. Housman used the coinages that he invented in childhood play. As his brother Laurence Housman described them:

> Alfred, the eldest of us, and always our leader, invented three new instruments of war — the Bath Bridge, the Martin Luther, and the Flying Torpedo; outwardly quite homely objects of garden use, but imagina-

---

[8] Robert Gathorne-Hardy, *Recollections of Logan Pearsall Smith* (London, 1949), p. 224.

[9] From a report written by Catherine White.   [10] *English Digest*, Dec., 1941, p. 68.

[11] New York *Post*, March 5, 1950, p. 32/1. In another New York family, that of Frederic Fredman, *pooh-pooh-head*, coined by a daughter, is a term of derogation used about adults.

[12] *I Still Haven't Unpacked* (London, 1953), p. 227.

[13] Jessica Mitford, *Hons and Rebels* (London, 1960), p. 14.

tively endowed with terrific powers of destruction. The Bath Bridge, a mere drainpipe to look at, was designed to swallow lighted tallow candles at one end, and send them rushing out in fire at the other. We got some candle-ends, and tried the experiment; but only a melting mess and no fire came of it. The Martin Luther was a species of gatling gun which never gatled, being nothing more than a semicircle of wood with a ground-stake, for the running of bird-lines; the Flying Torpedo was a stump of wood which he threw. But if they failed to do much execution, the names made us happy, for Alfred was always able to make us believe that his word-inventions had a meaning, and that the meaning was good.[14]

Let us turn next to instances in which devices of word coinage are illustrated. The verb *to gramp*, a back formation meaning 'to blow like a grampus,' can be given. W. E. Collinson has said of it: 'This is a good instance of an individual's creation becoming a family word.'[15] The process of analogy accounts for *drinkative*. As a writer of 1942 has recounted: 'A family I know has invented a word (I think) which always pleases me — "drinkative" — less objectionable than "drunken." It is probably based upon "talkative." '[16]

The change from one part of speech to another was reported by a New Englander in 1908:

There is hardly a family but has some expressive improvised word. In my own family 'humbly' reigns supreme. This is not the adverb of current usage, but an adjective, and a cross between 'humble' and 'homely'; and it was first used to describe our washwoman, who takes such pride in her humbleness, and is of such a superlative weatherbeaten homeliness, that she needed something special to express her personality. . . . 'Humbly' she is, and as 'humbly Mrs. Wheeler' she will be known in our family, while the brother who invented the word quite puffs himself up about it.[17]

Folk etymology is illustrated by the formation *suppertash* in place of *succotash*, used by a child and carried on by the family.[18]

Blending, or the formation of portmanteau words, is found in other families. Louise Pound has recorded the following: 'The mind, hesitating between *swindle* and *wheedle*, compromises on *sweedle*. When the result pleases the coiners, it sometimes continues in family use, as *sweedle* in the case of a Nebraska family.'[19] Herbert Quick, the Iowa novelist, in *Vandemark's Folly* of 1922, put into the fictional narration of an old Iowa pioneer

[14] *The Unexpected Years* (Indianapolis, 1936), p. 19.
[15] *Contemporary English: a Personal Speech Record* (Leipzig, 1927), p. 118.
[16] *Notes & Queries*, CLXXXII (1942), 77.
[17] 'Improvised Words,' *Atlantic Monthly*, CII (1908), 714.
[18] Reported by Jerome Wyckoff, now science writer for the Golden Press.
[19] *Blends: Their Relation to English Word Formation*, 'Angl. Forsch., LXII' (Heidelberg, 1914), p. 21. She had earlier recorded the word in *Dialect Notes*, III (1911), 548.

the following sentence: 'I remembered, though, how she had skithered back to the carriage.'[20] Then he added a footnote to *skithered*, attributed to an educated granddaughter of the pioneer:

> A family word, to the study of which one would like to direct the attention of the philologists, since traces of it are found in the conversation of folk of unsophisticated vocabulary outside the Clan van de Marck. Doubtless it is of Yankee origin, and hence old English. It may, of course, be derived according to Alice-in-Wonderland principles from 'skip' and 'hither' or 'thither' or all three; but the claim is here made that it comes, like monkeys and men, from a common linguistic ancestor.[21]

Compton Mackenzie, in a novel of 1926, *Fairy Gold*, portrayed an isolated family on a small island off the coast of Cornwall in which three children used a number of blends in talking with one another, for example: 'We can't go on being glumpy about it,'[22] where *glumpy* combines *gloomy* and *grumpy*; or 'I'm sorry if I was uffish,'[23] where *uffish* combines *uppish* and *selfish*; or 'You are a silly sloach,' where *sloach* combines *slow* plus *coach*.[24]

The cleverest of all the family words that have come to my attention is one from Scotland: a celebration of Burns's birthday, at which haggis was served, was known by the 'sandwich' formation *Walp-haggis-nicht!*[25]

Other family words represent distortions that are hard to analyze. One of these, *squiblums*, was described by Lois I. Woodville, of Oswestry, Shropshire, as follows:

> One of our household words is 'squiblums.' This was first heard at a pantomime when the ugly sisters of Cinderella sought to gain entry to Prince Charming's ball. The footmen at the door asked to see their 'tickets, credentials or the equivalents.' The word 'equivalents' degenerated into 'squiblums,' and I am sure it must have been the only part of the pantomime we clearly remembered. From then on, before one could expect to gain entry, one or another member of the family would demand, 'Where's your squiblums?' And, before opening the door to another member of the family it's common practice to ask for 'Squiblums, squiblums, please?'[26]

[20] *Vandemark's Folly* (Indianapolis, 1922), p. 143.
[21] *Ibid.* Cf. the discussion by A. G. Kennedy in *American Speech*, II (1926), 155.
[22] *Fairy Gold* (New York, 1926), p. 38.   [23] *Ibid.*, p. 195.
[24] *Ibid.*, p. 322. I adopt here the interpretations given by Partridge, *op. cit.*, p. 281.
[25] Collinson, *op. cit.*, p. 118, footnote. For the category 'sandwich word,' see Harold Wentworth, ' "Sandwich" Words and Rime-caused Nonce Words,' *West Virginia University Bulletin: Philological Studies*, III (1939), 65–71.
[26] *Christian Science Monitor*, June 8, 1956, p. 17/4. Note also, *ibid.*, May 9, 1956, p. 17/8, the report of D. Elizabeth Weatherbee, of Attleboro, Mass.: 'Bettie, aged seven, just bubbling over with high spirits, had been entertaining the family for some time when her mother said laughingly, "What *does* make you do and say those things?" "Oh, I don't know," said Bettie airily. "I guess I'm just feeling *agnipocus!*" It has been

Angela Thirkell, in a novel of 1954, recorded the following: 'When Laurence — my eldest brother — was a little boy he used to get his words muddled and he called gold-beaters' skin Peter Goatskin, so the whole family called it that.'[27] And a Sussex family employed *sittybah* for 'good-bye,' derived from the local dialectal way of saying *see yer ter-morrah.*[28] In one American family the word *pumpernickel* was habitually altered to [knʌŋknknʌŋkl] and *whistle* became [hwɔrsl].[29] In another family string beans are always 'strim bims,' and the name *alligator* for 'elevator' has been adopted by all members.[30]

Fairly mysterious is the word *hoosh-mi,* from the royal family of England. As the Queen's former nanny, Marion Crawford, has chronicled:

> The pram . . . remained in purdah for some years together with . . . the hoosh-mi dish. 'Hoosh-mi' is a pleasant word made up by [Princess] Margaret for the nursery mixture of chopped meat, potato and gravy, all 'hoosh-mied' up together and spoon-fed to its victim. Later the word was to become part of the schoolroom vocabulary, and a mix of any kind was always known as a hoosh-mi.[31]

Its use is illustrated in a later passage by the nanny: 'Margaret . . . has a large round table on which can always be found a lavish clutter. Letters, invitations, dance programs, greeting telegrams — in short, a hoosh-mi.'[32] Thus this manifestation of 'family words' reaches even into the English royal family.

Many types of word formation are illustrated in a family vocabulary of about a dozen items provided by Meredith Starr, the English author and philosopher. These are as follows:

> *Cobs,* tea (the meal); *Don Johns,* onions; *droomers,* bedroom slippers, by way of *bedroomers; expud,* not nice, rejected, uncomfortable (but usually of food); *flimmick,* to throw away; *jimkins,* jam; *miffy,* stale (of food gone mouldy); *Samuel Widgeons,* sandwiches; *woozles!,* an exclamation when anything goes wrong; *yarrup!,* when it goes still more wrong; *Ye cods and cuttle fishes!,* from *Ye gods and little fishes!*[33]

Another favorite type of family expression is the alphabetical abbreviation or acronym. One immediately thinks of *F.H.B.,* for 'Family Hold

---

our "household word" ever since.' Also, *ibid.,* June 7, 1956, p. 17/8, the report of Henrietta Baucom, of El Reno, Nevada: 'Roy was three when he was given a bag of glass marbles. He was much pleased with them and came running to me to display them. I commented that he had quite a few. "No, mother," he said, "I have quite a much!" Now this family always has "quite a much" — never "quite a few." '

[27] *What Did It Mean?* (London, 1954), p. 98.   [28] Partridge, *op. cit.,* p. 148.
[29] Jerome Wyckoff, cited above.
[30] Reported by Dr. Janet Kennedy, New York psychiatrist.
[31] *The Little Princesses* (New York, 1950), p. 34.   [32] *Ibid.,* p. 237.
[33] Given by Partridge, *op. cit.,* p. 148.

Back' as a warning when an article of food is low but guests are not supposed to know it. Quite probably this arose as a family expression, but it broke into general usage many generations ago. I remember it from my boyhood as a subject of joking, and Partridge has marked it as from the mid-nineteenth century.[34] It may well be, however, that the companion expression M.I.T.K., meaning 'More in the Kitchen,' has been limited. The English publisher Ernest Benn told of it in reminiscences of 1949; when unexpected guests were brought home to tea or dinner, the signal F.H.O. for 'Family Hold Off' sometimes had to be passed, but this would bring the prompt response from an irresponsible junior, 'M.I.T.K.'[35] Another acronym was recorded by Christopher Morley in 1942 — T.E.T. As he wrote: 'Aunt Bee cautioned Jeff with an esoteric allusion. "Geoffrey, remember T.E.T." . . . Jeff remembered: T.E.T. was a private mnemonic for Temper, Excitement and Tongue.'[36] Compton Mackenzie's family on the island off Cornwall used N.A.N.P., as follows: ' "Just tell him to bart out of it for good and all, because he's an N.A.N.P." "A what?" "A Not-a-Nice person." '[37]

Let us turn now to expressions that have their origin in chance incidents that have taken place in a family. Thus You ought to see my aunt had currency in an American family, as recorded in 1924 by Harry G. Paul:

> In another home a dull servant once said, 'If you think I am foolish, you ought to see my aunt'; from this grew a custom of the various members of the family censuring themselves for any unwise act by repeating 'You ought to see my aunt,' an expression which sometimes astonished and puzzled any stranger who happened to hear it.[38]

When Eleanor Roosevelt was traveling in England with her family in 1929, a family term for a disease arose. As she described it: 'In London, Franklin, junior, developed for the third time that year a curious illness which we came to call "Franklin pox," but the doctor insisted that it was German measles. It was over in two days and did not interfere very much with our sightseeing.'[39]

From an Irish family is recorded the idiomatic phrase, to sing the hundredth psalm. As Macalister explained it in 1937:

> How could any non-initiate guess that 'to sing the hundredth psalm' meant 'to fetch a glass of water' — as it does in a family known to me? If he be admitted to the domestic arcana so far as to learn the phrase and its meaning, how could he guess the nexus between the two ideas — a chance remark made upon a midsummer day, that to allow the heated water to run off from the cold-water tap took about as long a time as it would take to perform the act of piety specified?[40]

[34] A Dictionary of Slang and Unconventional English (London, 1937), p. 261.
[35] Happier Days (London, 1949), p. 125.   [36] Thorofare (New York, 1942), p. 327.
[37] Fairy Gold, p. 331.   [38] Better Everyday English (Chicago, 1924), p. 79.
[39] This I Remember (New York, 1949), p. 58.   [40] Secret Languages, p. 92.

Again from the Housman family comes another term. In Laurence Housman's reminiscences of his youth in the Midlands, he recorded *Yorkshire-pudding bell*:

At one o'clock on Sundays a bell was again rung — why, I cannot imagine; but to that ringing we gave a domestic name and meaning of our own — 'the Yorkshire-pudding bell' we called it; Yorkshire pudding being, on three Sundays out of five, or thereabouts, the most popular feature of the midday meal.[41]

Sometimes a family phrase results from exposure to a foreign language. When William Dean Howells and his family were traveling in Germany, they were much amused by the description of a variety show in Würzburg as a *decentes Familienprogramm*. The daughter, Mildred Howells, stated that this then 'had become a family phrase.'[42] When Howells later described a village fair in Cornwall, he wrote: 'A small fair, with swings and games . . . was going on in a pasture next the house. Very *"decentes familienprogramm."* '[43] The same family adapted the German *Hoheit* into *high-hote*, as Mildred Howells explained: ' "High-hotes" was a reversal of the German *Hoheit* that Howells had invented at Carlsbad, and which had become a family word for the nobility.'[44] As Howells wrote in a letter of April 12, 1904, from London, to his wife, on visiting the National Portrait Gallery: 'It is prodigious, and full of high-hotes of every age and degree.'[45]

Another fruitful source of family words is the naming of various rooms of a house. Robert Haven Schauffler in 1925 recorded the following: 'Children, too, have a sure instinct at times for word coining. I know some who christened their play-room "The Squealery." '[46] In a family in Essex, the water closet was called 'the Euphemism.' This arose from the time when a party of visitors came and one delicate-minded lady asked in a whisper, 'May we, to use a euphemism, wash our hands?' Thereafter the lavatory was always referred to as 'the Euphemism.'[47] In the Mitford family, Lord Redesdale's study was known as the 'Closing Room.' His daughter Jessica explained how this arose:

My father's study had once been known by the more usual terms for such rooms — library, business room, smoking room — but I pointed out to Farve that since he spent virtually his entire life within its walls, one day, inevitably, his old eyes would close there, never to open again. Thus it came to be called the Closing Room, even by the servants.[48]

[41] *Unexpected Years*, p. 17.
[42] *Life in Letters of William Dean Howells*, ed. Mildred Howells (Garden City, N.Y., 1928), II, 272.
[43] Letter of September 17, 1909, *ibid.*, II, 273.   [44] *Ibid.*, II, 190.
[45] *Ibid.*, II, 191.   [46] *Peter Pantheism* (New York, 1925), p. 60.
[47] Ethelind Fearon, *The Fig and Fishbone* (London, 1959), p. 110.
[48] Mitford, *op. cit.*, p. 21.

The term *glory hole* has been recorded as the name of a catch-all closet,[49] a development from the sailor's term; but this apparently has spread to many families. In the William Dean Howells family, the library, which was housed in a barn, was known as the 'barnbury.'[50]

The terms such as I have been citing are of small use to the lexicographer. He would not wish to include them in his inventory, unless they could be shown to have broken into wider currency.[51] Nevertheless, such material should be watched by the lexicologist for its value in showing tendencies in the language. The family is the matrix in which we see the bubbling up of linguistic experimentation.

Jespersen has pointed out that there are dangers in the indulgence that a family may show to the experiments of a child. As he said,

> It would not do, however, for the child's 'little language' and its dreadful mistakes to become fixed. This might easily happen, if the child were never out of the narrow circle of its own family, which knows and recognizes its 'little language.' But this is stopped because it comes more and more into contact with others — . . . as the child becomes a member of a social group larger than that of his own little home.[52]

Nevertheless, it surely is desirable for the child to have an opportunity for free linguistic play, to try out analogies in a sympathetic atmosphere. The family serves as this experimental arena. One of the greatest gifts that can come to a speaker of a language is the sense of freedom to move about among the possible patterns that the language provides for him. This feeling of 'at-home-ness' develops and flowers in the family circle.

[49] Cf. *Better Everyday English*, p. 79: 'Thus a certain family habitually designates a particular catch-all closet under the stairs as the *glory-hole.*'

[50] Howells, *op. cit.*, II, 214.

[51] The breadth of currency is often difficult to ascertain. Thus the actor George Arliss (born 1868) in his autobiography, *Up the Years from Bloomsbury* (Boston, 1927), p. 8, wrote of the word *daggs*: 'But we had been doing "daggs." Referring to the Oxford Dictionary I do not find the word "daggs" recorded. Perhaps it belonged to our family (there are family words), or perhaps it was schoolboy slang that is no longer in vogue; I certainly do not ever remember seeing it written or printed before. But to do daggs is not only to dare, but to do the thing first yourself and then dare the others to do it. We had done every kind of daggs (there is no singular to daggs) that we could think of: stood on our heads at the end of the sofa, walked once across the room on our hands, crawled head downwards over the banisters — we were all just about the age that has tired of the more conventional methods of locomotion.' However, the *EDD* (1900) listed *dag* with the meaning, 'A daring feat amongst boys,' together with references from Cheshire (1884), the West Midlands, and western Somerset (1886); the Opies did not come upon it for *The Lore and Language of Schoolchildren* (Oxford, 1959).

[52] Jespersen, *op. cit.*, p. 144. Cf. also M. M. Lewis, *Language in Society* (New York, 1948), p. 34: 'Within the family the child has normally been understood even though his language has been imperfect — his half-spoken words, his gestures, even his silences have been correctly interpreted.'

Carl Sandburg

KID TALK—FOLK TALK

✍✍

*In his autobiography Carl Sandburg, the poet, folk singer, historian,
and novelist, says that as a child he learned Swedish words at home
before he learned English ones. Early experience in language does
expose many children to a foreign tongue spoken by an older generation in the family. In the reminiscence that follows, Mr. Sandburg
records the talk of the children of his neighborhood in Galesburg,
Illinois, in the 1880's. It is a collection of superstitions, tall tales,
jokes, and riddles. Some of them seem peculiarly local and even anti-
quated, but many are still repeated by children today. This essay is
inhabited by the clear-eyed, wry, amused personality of Mr. Sandburg,
who used some of the same kind of material in his work significantly
called* The People, Yes.

Kid talk would run to why women wore bustles, why they wore tight-laced
corsets, why a woman with a pretty face would hide it with a black veil.
When a young woman crossed a muddy street we watched whether she
lifted her skirt high enough for us to see what her legs were like.

We watched to see if Friday the thirteenth was unlucky and couldn't
see it. We heard it was bad luck to step over a broom or to walk under a
ladder, so some kids went stepping over brooms and walking under ladders
to see what would happen and nothing did. When night came and the
moon was up the same kids would look at the moon over the left shoulder
to see if it would bring bad luck. None of us ever broke a looking glass, so
we couldn't tell if that would bring bad luck for seven years. Some of us did

23

try to make the warts on our hands go away. I took a string and tied four knots in it, one knot for each of my four warts. I buried the string under a maple tree in the light of a full moon. It was many weeks before my warts went away and I didn't believe the string and the moon had helped. One kid said that when an uncle of his had a bad cold he would kiss a mule on the nose and the cold went away. I heard that when new shoes squeak it is a sign they are not paid for. I had more than one pair of new shoes that squeaked and I was sure they had been paid for, so I knew that one was a fake.

Us kids did our talking with the rest of the town about the "Water Works" and the dirty yellow water with the bad smell that came out where they had faucets. The tower stood on the north side next to the Q. tracks, privately owned. The city got disgusted with it, dug its own artesian well, and has kept its own water system ever since.

We talked too of the rubber-factory fire. On a pasture east of Farnham Street near the path where we walked to the swimming hole we saw the three-story factory go up. A fire broke out a year or two later, and several girls had bad burns from their clothes catching fire as they ran downstairs. One young woman died from her third-floor leap to the ground. Whenever we passed the gutted building and its black walls we talked about why they hadn't put fire escapes on the second and third floors. Some of us got jobs knocking plaster off the black burnt bricks, and a boy might bust out any time, "They ought to have had fire escapes."

The saying was, "If you see a white horse spit quick over a little finger and if none of the spit falls on your finger you will meet a redheaded girl." There were kids who claimed it worked. I spit clean and dry more than once and the redheaded girl didn't show up. Another saying was, "If you see a redheaded girl look for a white horse." We tried that and the white horse didn't show up, one kid busting out, "Oh, the hell with white horses!"

In 1884 when a kid called me a mugwump I called it back at him. From the grownups we learned of high-up Republicans who didn't like Blaine's record, couldn't trust him, and were going to vote for Cleveland. The regular Republican Blaine men called these others "mugwumps." I heard a Blaine Republican say, "A mugwump is a man who sits with his mug on one side of the fence and his wump on the other."

When you didn't believe a fellow you might tell him, "Don't hand me that guff," or "I've heard that guff before." It was slang and "guff" was chatter and you were "spreading it on too thick." Politicians, salesmen, book agents, auctioneers, spielers, had "a line of guff." Later a farm machine came along that sent manure flying and spread it even over the soil, and a man talking too big was called a "manure-spreader." Of a man hoping for money to put through a scheme he had in mind they would say, "He's trying to raise the wind." All he needed to blow him and his scheme into motion was a good wind.

Us kids talked about how silly was the rhyme and who was so silly as to start it:

It is a sin
To steal a pin.

We believed that anybody who had one pin had a dozen or fifty or a hundred more and it was no sin to steal "a pin," "one single little pin."

Early we heard, "You can trust him as far as you can fling a bull by the tail" and "You're all right but your feet stink," which might get the answer, "I'll give you a brick house — one brick at a time." "You don't know whether you're comin or goin" was easier to take than "If I was as ugly as you, I'd sue my father and mother." A newly married couple "got hitched" and if they separated they "split the blanket."

Going home from Grammar School one boy said, "You're not such a muchness" and the other, "You're not much of a suchness." I forget where they went from there. Whatever it was they were too smart to fight about it.

In the late 1880's, on parting of an evening, we would say, "Good night, sleep tight, and don't let the bedbugs bite." Later this was considered babyish, which wasn't the case with what we learned from the old soldiers and marched to:

Left, left, I had a good home and I left,
Right, right, right back home to my wife and children.

Early us kids learned there was no use being sent for "a left-handed monkey wrench." The carrier boys at the *Republican-Register* learned from the printers about "type lice." You were told the lice were small and you put your head down close to see them. Then something squeezed and water spurted up into your face — and you tried to be on hand when a new boy put his head down to see "type lice."

Like grown men, on a payday we said, "This is the day the ghost walks." We said of a stingy boy, "All you get from him you can put in your eye." Or if a fellow promised to do something for you and you didn't expect he would, you said, "Yes, he'll do it — in a pig's eye." We tried to picture the man we heard of, "busy as a paperhanger with the hives," and the fellow who was "quiet as two skeletons wriggling on a tin roof." Hustling on a job we liked to say, "Get out of my way, I'm busy as a cranberry merchant," a smart saying and you said it even though you had never seen a cranberry merchant nor heard why a cranberry merchant is busier than other merchants.

I knew the fellow, and from what happened to him afterward John Kerrigan was strictly correct in saying, "He's so slick one of these days his feet are goin to slide out from under him."

He wasn't one of us but he could have been, the boy hitting the top of his head with a rock. A man asked why he was doing such a fool thing and the boy said, " 'Cause it feels so good when I stop."

They told it about Brown's Hotel and a traveling man who ate corn on the cob, one ear after another, till the waitress had brought him a dozen and more and then: "Don't you think you would save money if you went over and boarded at Andy Dow's livery stable?"

A man on Main Street was saying the mayor refused to renew the license of a certain saloonkeeper: "He tells us he can't give any more favors to the saloon crowd. Think of it, and him in his life has drunk enough whisky to float a battleship!"

When it wasn't clear how a man was making his living you might hear, "He's living on the interest of his debts." One year we often saw turning the corner of Berrien and Chambers a tall heavy-set man in a gray suit, double-breasted coat, and he walked easy and cool. He was gorilla-built and iron-jawed. The talk was that he was a gambler and you could find him any afternoon or night down on the Public Square over a saloon dealing the cards till midnight or daybreak. We knew where he lived, with relatives who worked for the Q., but we never heard of his having a job except dealing at card games. Once a kid said, "Here comes the gambler," and another, "Wouldn't it be fun to hear him talk about his work!" and another, "He could tell about the suckers all right!"

In below-zero weather Mart and I were hurrying along Main Street about eight o'clock one morning. At the northeast corner of Kellogg and Main we saw a load of wood piled high on a wagon. The horses had no blankets and were champing. The driver sat high on his wood. Ahead of us we saw the butcher, Sam Swanson, stop and call to the man, "What do you think you're doing up there?" The man stopped beating his chest with his mittens and laughed as though it was the funniest thing in the world that morning: "I'm a tough sonofabitch from Old Henderson — do you want any wood?" Year after year Mart would keep asking me if I remembered it as though I might have forgotten.

The boy John Siebert had picked it up somewhere and when you said "Hello, John" to him he snapped back, "Hello yourself, and see how you like it."

John also liked to plump it straight at you, "That's what you *say* but how do I *know?*"

Charlie Hall taught a Sunday-school class and belonged to the Y.M.C.A. Driving a milk wagon for a small Jersey dairy, he wouldn't say "darn" or "doggone" to his old slow horse, those words too close to "damn." We heard him bark at the bonerack, "Get up there, Sinnania, what in all getout do you think you're doing? You diggle-depiggledy slowpoke, you're slower than molasses in January."

If he had a fall John Kerrigan might say, "The sidewalk flew up and hit me in the face." If you owed him a nickel or a dime he would say, "We'll write it in the dust and let the rain settle it." Then he might add, "You don't owe me nothin, paregorically speaking." You can never tell what a plumber's apprentice will bring away from working with master plumbers.

We heard of Horace Greeley making a correction: "I did not say that every Democrat is a saloonkeeper. I said that every saloonkeeper is a Democrat."

We said "Cheap at half the price" before we heard what the price was. We might say, "My ears are burning, someone is talking about me," when our ears weren't burning. A boy called another a liar and heard, "You're a double liar" and snapped back, "You're a double-double liar." They were learning the multiplication table.

We brought home to the folks the one about the Irish hod-carrier who said his work wasn't hard. "All I do is carry the bricks in me hod up the ladder to the man at the top and he does all the work."

A Norwegian told me his mother sent him to a store to get something and he came home saying he forgot what she sent him for. She sent him again with the words, "What you don't keep in your head your feet must make up for, my little man." When he ate with his fingers and his grandmother told him to eat with his fork, he said, "Fingers were made before forks," and she cornered him, "But not *your* fingers."

The best ball team the Seventh Ward had for several years didn't want a fancy name and called themselves the "Seventh Ward Red Mugs."

John MacNally met a hobo near the Q. switchyards, a New York Bowery boy who said, "Kuh-hay Cull, wot's duh chance fer duh next cab over duh rails — huh?" We practiced on that.

I went into Danny Flynn's saloon selling the *Sporting News*. They were crowding around a man knocked to the floor by a big husky. They asked the husky why he hit the man. He said, "I don't like his haircut." I saw it was a new and fancy haircut the man had. I saw friends of the big husky leading him out of the saloon and trying to explain to him that he oughtn't to knock a man down on account of his haircut.

In the two-bit gallery of the Auditorium I stood up to stuff into my pants my shirt that had wriggled up. A man in the seat behind poked me, saying: "Is your father a glass blower?" It then came over me that I was between him and the stage and he couldn't see the show going on. I sat down feeling he had the best of it.

A young Swedish grocery clerk who was a fancy dresser kept steady company for a while with a girl who was a good-looker. When they quit going together, one kid said, "She gave it to him where the chicken got the axe."

I read stories where men in New York said, "Pull down your vest" or "Wipe that egg off your chin," but I never heard the like in Galesburg. But in both New York and Galesburg people said, "That joke is as old as the hills," or "Come off your perch." And in New York and Galesburg they were beginning to say, "Most anything can happen in Chicago and usually does."

Often in the Seventh Ward schoolyard I heard: "What's your name?" "Puttin Tain, ask me again and I'll tell you the same." or "What's your name?" "John Brown, ask me again and I'll knock you down."

If I was clumsy on a job, Mart would say, "You're as handy as that bird they call the elephant." And when he said, "I worked harder than you did," I answered, "Yes, but I got more work done." When someone in the house was slow getting started on a chore you might hear, "Can't you make yourself useful as well as ornamental?"

A man who sang baritone in a church choir on Sundays kept a store and was doing a good business. I heard another storekeeper say, "He's making money hand over fist. He's got one ear for music and another ear for money. He wasn't born last week."

I couldn't quite figure it out, a fellow saying, "I'd have a good job if only I could use myself."

They told of a young fellow saying to his girl, "Let's go to the picnic and after sundown we'll have a grass sandwich."

I was knee-high to a grasshopper maybe when I heard a neighbor woman talking about a man who moved slow and took it easy. When she said, "He's slow as molasses in January," I said to myself, "I've heard that before. I heard fellows say it about me when I didn't run fast enough to first base." But then she went on and laughed about this man who took it easy, "He'll never set a river on fire!" I saw by the way she laughed it that she knew nobody could set a river on fire, but the man she had in mind would be the last anybody could think of that might set a river on fire. I had not yet seen a river but I knew that a river was just like the Cedar Fork Creek only bigger. For days I fooled around in my mind with the picture of a man trying to set a river on fire.

The first time I heard about a man "going to hell in a hanging basket" I did a lot of wondering what a hanging basket is like and why you couldn't fall headfirst down into hell instead of making the trip in a hanging basket.

It wasn't an insult among us kids to say, "You're off your nut" or "You're dippy" or "Say, your head wasn't screwed on wrong, was it?" or "You've got bats in your belfry."

From farmers we learned, "He don't know the difference between a furrow and a farrow."

A man without enough clothes to need a trunk married a woman with a farm and money in the bank. One boy said, "He got himself tied to a hunk of tin, all right." "Yes," said another boy, "before the wedding he was thinner than an old dime." They turned out to be a pretty good couple. Us kids were like many of the grownups, talking just to be talking.

Forty ways it was drilled into us, over and over, at home and in school and on the streets, "If you don't look out for yourself nobody else will." A thousand times in a year we heard it, "Save your pennies. They will grow into dollars. Great oaks from little acorns grow. Don't waste your money. Lay by what you can for a rainy day. A little money can be a big comfort. Money talks. Even when it stinks, money talks."

There were few divorced women in the town. When a woman was mentioned as a widow, the question might come, "Grass or sod?"

Of a boy no good at singing we said, "He can't carry a tune in a basket."

We tried to tease a rubber-factory girl about a fellow she had been seen with. She said, "Aw, shut up about him. He's the least of my troubles." Of a foreman at the factory she said, "He chews the rag. Listen to him and you get lint on your lungs."

Selling my papers I heard two men on a street corner. "How are they comin fer yuh, Bud?" "I'm all to the sandpaper, Bo. Got a snootful last night but now I'm all in the clear." "Could yuh slip me a couple uh sawbucks?" "Well, I could slide yuh out one little William the Fifth. If I could finger you more I would." "Ain't the gettin been good with you?" "Next you'll be tellin me givin is better than gettin." "Well, you know I never been a Wanderin Willie." "Well, you're a hard case, the way I look at it. My guff to you is you beat it in the hay tonight. You been lickin it up an throwin it in too fast." And handing over a William the Fifth (a five-dollar bill) he said, "Do a fade now, do a fade, Bo." . . .

These sayings and stories on the streets and in the schoolyard stick in the memory like cockleburrs on a pants leg.

Iona and Peter Opie

UNPOPULAR CHILDREN
Jeers and Torments

From the Opies' collection of children's lore comes the following selection of jeers, taunts, and nicknames. Such language quickly indicates how children feel about each other. It is vigorous, irreverent, imaginative, and explosive. It can characterize its victims so pointedly that sometimes a person never forgets what he was labeled as a child. In addition to jeers, there is of course a great amount of language of happy children at happier times, as the Opies' table of contents suggests; the collection includes songs, stale jokes, riddles, jump-rope rhymes, secret codes, and so on. Though most of the examples derive from British sources, American children use such torments, too.

Nobody loves me, everybody hates me,
   Going in the garden to eat worms;
Big fat juicy ones, little squiggly niggly ones,
   Going in the garden to eat worms.

Song for the unhappy.

Somebody they dislike, 'a person with whom you are not pally', may be called (general terms): beast, clot, dreg, dumb cluck, erk, gawp, kid, monkey ('little monkey' in particular), pig, rat (usually 'dirty rat'), rogue, rotter, rotten dog, and stinker. In Kirkcaldy a bossy person is 'pawpy'. In Bishop Auckland 'Dog Harry' is a general term of reproach.

The girls gang up on 'an unfriendly person' and chant:

> I know a little girl sly and deceitful,
> Every little tittle-tat she goes and tells the people.
> Long nose, ugly face, ought to be put in a glass case,
> If you want to know her name, her name is *Heather Lee.*
> Please *Heather Lee,* keep away from me;
> I don't want to speak to you, nor you to speak to me.
> Once we were friends, now we disagree,
> Oh, *Heather Lee,* keep away from me.
> It's not because you're dirty,
> It's not because you're clean,
> It's because you've got the whooping-cough,
> Pooh! You awful thing!

> *Versions from fifteen schools throughout Britain (much employed also for skipping).*

Compared with the piercing exactitude of the jeers for specific offences (e.g. crying and tale-bearing, hereafter), the rhymes expressing general dislike have an impersonal air. One has the feeling, often correct, that the children are being rude just for the fun of being rude. The recipient can take little harm from taunts such as the following:

> *Brian Johnson* is no good,
> Chop him up for fi-er wood;
> When he's dead, boil his head,
> Make it into ginger bread.

> *Versions from fifteen schools in Britain, also common in the United States.*

> God made the French,
> God made the Dutch,
> Whoever made you
> Never made much.

> *Caistor, Lincs.*

> Tiddly Winks old man,
> Suck a lemon if you can;
> If you can't suck a lemon
> Suck an old tin can.

> *Versions from eleven schools in Britain.*

> Hubbah hubbah ding ding,
> Look at the legs on that thing.
> What thing? That thing.
> Hubbah hubbah ding ding.

> *Helensburgh and Kirkcaldy.*

A particular pleasure, as has already been remarked, is to liken a companion to one of the lower orders of creation:

> Donkey walks on four legs,
> And I walk on two,
> The last one I saw
> Was just like you.

To one singing:
> Sweetly sings the donkey
> As he goes to grass,
> He who sings so sweetly
> Is sure to be an ass.

> That's the way to the zoo,
> That's the way to the zoo,
> The monkey house is nearly full
> But there's room enough for you.

> Toorally oorally oorally oo,
> They're wanting monkeys at the zoo.
> I'd apply if I were you
> And get a situation.

SPOIL-SPORTS, SOURPUSSES, SPITFIRES

The children frequently mention spoil-sports as being the people they most dislike. 'When playing games', says a 9-year-old in Dovenby, Cumberland, 'if one of the girls falls out we shout sulky puss or spoil sport or Baby baby bunting Daddy's gone a hunting for a rabbit skin to lap the baby in or Water works.' The young in Newcastle shout:

> Trouble maker, trouble maker,
> Fetch a pan and a cake we'll make of her.

To a moaner who keeps whining 'Oh dear me!' Forfar children put the question, 'Fat's dear aboot you and dirt sae chaip?' A peevish person is referred to as a Cross-patch, Old Grousey or Grumpy, Misery, Mardy-baby, Peevy, Sourpuss, or Sulky Sue. In Glasgow, when having fun with somebody who does not take it as fun, they chant:

> Roses are red,
> Violets are blue,
> Lemons are sour
> And so are you.

A name for one 'with a grim glum face' is 'Smiler'. When someone thoroughly unwelcome turns up they comment, 'Look what the cat's brought in' or 'Look who it ain't'. When accosted by an irritating person who 'gets their goat' or 'gets their needle', they complain 'Why don't you drop dead?' (very common), or suggest: 'Go and get lost', 'Go chase yourself round the gasworks', 'Go and run round yourself', 'Go and take a running jump at yourself', 'Take a long run off a short pier', 'Walk into the sea until your hat floats', 'Go fish a brick', 'For Pete's sake wrap up', 'Pipe down', 'Take a powder' (particularly to a grumpy person), 'Suck a lemon', 'Go boil your bonce', 'Go fry your face', 'Stick your head in a gas oven' ('bucket of water', 'coal hole', &c.), 'Go and eat coke', 'Dry up and blow away'. If the person takes the hint and withdraws, they comment 'Good riddance to bad rubbish' or 'Good riddance to a dirty dish clout'.

To find out whether a child has a good or bad temper they run their finger down his back. If the finger stays cool, good temper; if the finger becomes hot, the person has a bad temper. In Radnorshire they test a child by plucking a hair from his head, and pulling their moistened finger and thumb along it; if the hair remains straight it shows a placid temper, but if it kinkles it reveals an ill temper.

A short-tempered person is spoken of as being: catty (very common), crusty, fiery, grizzly, niggled or niggly (Headington, Oxford), ratty, shirty, snappy, snooty (meaning easily irritated), and sharp-edged. Such a person, whose temper is easily provoked, may be named: Our bomb, Fire-blower, Hot pot, Pepper pot, Mulligrubs,[1] Radish, Temper puss, Spitfire (very common), or Vixen. They taunt the person: 'Now don't fly off the handle', 'Don't get in a paddy', 'Don't lose your bait' ('rag', 'rise', or 'wool'), 'Keep your hair on', 'Now, now, temper! temper!' In Aberdeen they taunt:

> *Lorna's* in a ragie
> Pit her in a cagie.[2]

CLEVER-DICKS

Their terms for the bright boy or girl show both admiration and contempt. They are willing to acclaim anyone who habitually comes top of the class without apparent effort, naming him Genius, The Brains, Miracle Man, Professor, and Topper; but they look down upon the one who has to work hard to keep first place. Such a person is a 'swotter', 'swotpot', or 'stewpot'. They snort 'You swot!' if they find him preparing work before a lesson. 'Swotting' or 'mugging up' is only considered good form if a

[1] 'Said while the teaser rubs the head of the offended person' (Pendeen, Cornwall).
[2] In the United States, where 'mad' means 'cross' or 'in a rage', the common gibe is:
> *Mary's* mad, and I am glad,
> And I know what will please her,
> A bottle of ink to make her stink
> And a nigger boy to squeeze her.

person is on the point of taking an exam. A couplet common in schools around Peterborough is:

> He that works and does his best
> Gets the sack like all the rest.

People who keep at their work are Ants, Bookworms, Slaves, Plodderoners, and Old Grindstones. A clever boy is most often styled a 'clever-dick', or, less frequently: brainy pup, brilliant bonce, cleverguts, cleverpot, cleversides, cleversticks, jingler, know-all, squelch, and (in Oxford) Brain Basil —all terms which may also, on occasions, be ironical, meaning that he is: artful, over-witty, too clever by half, a show-off, a snob, or a 'poshy guy'.

DAFTIES, FOOLS, AND DUNCES

The most common, and pertinent (and most resented), of all child-to-child abuse is saying that a person is daft in the head.

> You're daft, you're potty, you're barmy,
> You ought to join the army.
> You got knocked out
> With a brussel sprout,
> You're daft, you're potty, you're barmy.

> *Market Rasen version.*

A person who is 'wanting in the upper storey' is: bats, batty, barmy, crackers or a crackpot, daffy, dippy, dithering ('You're daft and dithering, wipe your chin and stop dribbling' — Cleethorpes), dizzy, a dope, a dopey dick, dotty, goofy or goopy, a gowk (in Scotland), a ninny, a nit-wit, nutty, potty, a pot-head ('You're daft, you're potty, you're made of treacle toffee'— Newcastle.) He is cracked, he's cuckoo, he's loco, he's nuts, he's not all there ('Yer out of your waggon' — Bishop Auckland), he's not plumb, he's off his rocket ('Off your rocket' is a development of 'off your rocker'). He is—scatty, screwy, scearie (in Perth), off his chump (head, nut, block), has a screw loose, a tile loose, is a bit touched, a bit wrong in the head, soft in the head, half baked, a stupe, and in Bishop Auckland, for some reason, a rajah.

'Don't be so nutty, you dull ass.'

Answer: 'If you're right in the head, I'll stay as I am.'

All these words imply, or are intended to imply, that the subject is not in full possession of his mental faculties; but this is not necessarily the case if he is called a fool.

> *Willie Carey* is a fool
> Like a monkey on a stool,
> When he's dead
> Lay him on a bed
> And bake his head with gingerbread.

> *Headington.*

Lydia Smith is a fool,
Like a donkey on a stool.
When the stool began to crack,
All the fleas ran down her back.

> *Alton, Enfield, Norfolk, Lydney, and
> similar versions from elsewhere.*

Joe Egg is a fool,
He tied his stocking to a stool.
When the stool begins to crack
All the beetles run up his back.

> *Market Rasen.*

Oor *Leebie* is a fule,
And a donkey at the skule.
If she had a langer tail,
I would hang her up for sale.

> *Forfar. Known to date back to 1910.*

Jean Mactaggart is a fule (or 'feel'),
She's made up wi' brose an' meal,
Brose an' meal makes her fat,
That's the way she's a cheeky cat.

> *Aberdeen.*

Tammie Ross is an ass,
For a donkey he would pass,
If he only had a tail
We would hang him up for sale.

> *Dundee.*

Being a silly fool, or behaving like a fool, may mean only that the person is acting the goat, doing idiotic things, behaving foolishly. He is — a clown, a clot, a fathead, a mutt, a muggins, an oaf, a bit of a twerp, a silly goop, a proper Charlie. He has behaved like a chump, like a donkey, or a goose, or a juggins. They say 'You fool, you must be potty to do such a thing'. They do not say that he *is* potty, but that he is behaving as if he were.

A dunce is slightly different again. He may be sane, good at games, and seldom act the fool, but he lacks scholastic abilities, he is dense, slow on the uptake, he has got a thick head.

Dunce, dunce, double D,
Doesn't know his A.B.C.

> *Market Rasen, Oxford, Ruthin, Shrews-
> bury. Also given as a popular rhyme in
> 1898 ('The English Dialect Dictionary').*

Dunce, dunce, double D,
Cannot learn his A.B.C.

> Put a cap on then you'll see
> What a silly boy is he.
>
> *Headington and Portsmouth.*

> Silly-Dick he has no brains,
> Soon he didn't have no veins.
>
> *Oundle.*

In this rhyme the fool is the dunce type:

> *Jimmy Snaps* is a fool,
> Send him to the baby school,
> Give him one, give him two,
> Tell the teacher what to do.
>
> *Kirkcaldy.*

The difference can be seen in the three terms: soft in the head, fathead, and blockhead. The significance, of course, of all terms varies according to how they are used, but someone who is 'soft in the head' is generally understood to be dippy; a 'fathead' is a fool, or someone who has done something stupid; and a 'blockhead' is someone who is dense.[3] He is a 'big-'ead' (very common), a 'thick-head', with a 'head full of lead', or 'bone from the knees up' (a Suffolk saying). He is — a clodpoll, a dim-wit, a dull-dick, a dullard, a dunderpate, a know-nothing, a numbskull, a corner-boy (or corner-girl). He is — a brainless chump, a brainless gorm, a pea-brain, or a putty-brain.

He may also be called a 'booby'; to boob something is to make a mess of it, to get it wrong, and the booby prize is awarded to the one who is bottom of the class. But booby is not the usual term for a dunce; it is more often applied to a simpleton, and the children seem to associate it with crying. A booby is a foolish cry-baby, possibly arrived at from the term 'boo-baby' and the word 'booing' for crying. . . . To warm one's hands by slapping oneself is to 'beat the booby'.

Again, it may be noted that to be a clot, a dumb clot, or a 'dumbless thing', is not necessarily to be a dunce. These epithets may be used to describe someone who has merely behaved idiotically, or who is a 'no-good', or a duffer; that is to say a person not proficient in an activity which is esteemed: no good at games, or no good at carpentry, physically awkward, a 'clumsy clot'.[4] Similarly a 'yob' (backslang for boy) has come to mean a lout. The terms 'scatterbrain', 'featherhead', 'empty vessel', are applied, in particular, to people who are vague or forgetful. A 'dilly-day-

---

[3] An inscription written in the margin of a schoolbook by an 11-year-old in 1710 has a familiar ring about it. 'Alexander Meason can write better nor Robert Barclay, but he is a blockhead at countins.' — *Notes and Queries*, 9th ser. vol. xi, 1903, p. 145.

[4] *Clot* is now common in the juvenile world, aided by the frequency with which it appeared in the balloons in the *Eagle* picture strip 'P.C. 49'.

dream' (or just 'dream'), or a 'Joseph' (after Joseph's dream) is a person who has his mind on other things. And the word 'sap', which at Eton is primarily used to castigate someone who is over-keen on his work (equivalent to 'swot'), the children define as meaning a sissy or a softy ('soft in that he does not do anything wrong'), and suggest other moist alternatives, as 'milksop', 'soppy date', a 'wet', or a 'drip'. 'What's on the bread today?' 'You with I–N–G at the end.' 'Is your hair wet? There's a big drip under it!'

CRY-BABIES

Amongst boys to use the word 'crying' is sometimes held to be almost as sissy as the act itself. A lad must say 'blubbing',[5] or 'bawling', or 'squalling', according to the custom of his school, or the district in which he lives. In southern England the usual term is 'booing', while in Scotland and the north-east of England it is often 'bubblin', hence a cry-baby is a 'bubbly baby', 'bubbly Jock', or 'mum's big bubbly bairn', just as in London the wet-faced child is a 'boo-baby' or 'booby'.

Other local terms for crying are: babbling (Whitehaven), blabbing (Lydney), blabbling (Derby), blabbering (Isle of Ely), blahing or blarting (Birmingham, Hanley, Wolverhampton), blaring (Norwich), bleating (Birmingham), moaning (the general term in Liverpool), and slobbering (Rochdale). In Welshpool the common term is 'cribbing' and a cry-baby is a 'cribber'; in Croydon they sometimes speak of 'mizzogging' and 'mizzog'; in the area of Blackburn, Bolton, Manchester, Stockport, and Halifax the term 'skriking' is common, the noun being 'skriker'; and in Dublin the usual word is 'whinging', hence 'whinger', a term also still used in Cumberland, and occasionally heard in Liverpool. In Scotland, as well as 'bubblin', they speak of 'girnin' and, of course, 'greetin', hence epithets like 'girnie bubbler', 'girnie gowk', and 'greetin-faced teenie'. 'Girnin' is also fairly general in Cumberland, and in the North Riding where it is pronounced 'gennin', while 'bubblin' is heard south to the Tees.

Some of the terms have different shades of meaning. In the West Riding the degrees of intensity are said to be firstly 'bluthering', which is quietly whimpering, then 'rooaring', and then 'skriking', which is yelling blue murder. In Fife 'grump' and 'peenger' apply more to people who are snivelling and fretful than openly sobbing. Similarly, especially in the southwest, a person is said to be 'grizzling' when he is merely whining and complaining, the brat himself being styled 'grizzle-guts' or, in Wiltshire, 'grizzle-grunt', while in the North Midlands a like condition is expressed by the word 'mardy'. . . .

---

[5] The term favoured in most private schools, including *The Fifth Form at St. Dominics* (1887) where a character is described as 'a horrid young blub-baby'. 'Blubber-face' was recently heard in Manchester, 'blubber-bib' in Bolsover, and 'blubber-puss' in Kirkcaldy.

Croydon boys have twenty names for a cry-baby: baby-bunting, blubber, boo-baby, boo-hoo, diddums, grizzle-guts, howler, leaky, Lumleyite (after a local boy), moaner, mother's little darling sissy, slobber-baby, sniveller, softy, tap, Tearful Tilly, water-can, water-hog, waterworks, and weeping willow.

Gloucestershire children comment: you babby, big baby, cuddled baby, mummy's baby, diddums do it to you, cry-a-lot, big gob, booby, poor babba, mother's blubber, mother's pet, mamma's little sugar, grizzly guts, milk sop, misery, pautey pipe, sniveller, sissy, squall-ass, spouter, and wet-eyes.

Elsewhere the weak one may carry the label: babbity (in Glasgow), baby-cake, bubbles, crybaby Joe, drip, drainpipe, fountain-spouter, jelly baby, lassie boy (Scottish border); mardy-baby, mardy bum, mard 'un, or mardy-mardy-mustard (North Midlands); Moan-a-lot or Mona Liza (Liverpool), mummy's darling boo-hoo, pansy face, softie, slaver-chops (Lancaster), squealer, suckie thumb, sugar baby, smiler, taps, titty-titty-baby (Birmingham), and District Waterworks, or Waterworks Willie.

He or she may receive the advice: 'Go back to your bottle', 'Don't make it wet on a dry day', 'Mammy have to rock you to sleep'. The dry-faced smirk to each other: 'He's got water on the brain', 'He's turned on the tap', 'Don't worry, he's just left his napkins', 'He's just fallen out of his cot'.

James Thurber

THE TYRANNY OF TRIVIA

✄✄

James Thurber, the great humorist, searches into words for us with marvelous insight. Nearly blind during much of his later life, he became painfully, yet playfully sensitive to the shapes and sounds of words. He begins by playing with letter-combinations that he sees and other people don't. He then retells his nighttime wanderings among words as he explores the mystery of the relation between sound and meaning. (*The children in the Opies' collection know about this relation too: dim-wit, dullard, dunderpate, dunce.*) In Mr. Thurber's discovery there is a suggestion that he is on the edge of metaphysics, but he stops short of taking himself too seriously. We may be alarmed, but we are left nevertheless with a sense of the wit behind it all.

An intrepid young literary explorer named Otto Friedrich recently stumbled upon the body of my work lying sprawled and unburied on the plain, and was distressed to discover that it had been ravaged by trivia. Mr. Friedrich thinks that preoccupation with trivia is unbecoming in a writer who belongs to the Solemn if not, indeed, the Sombre tradition of American letters. (How do you like it now, gentlemen?) The critic, whose findings appeared in a periodical called *Discovery*, detected what he called my need to write trivia, and shrewdly coupled it with "a constant need to make money." By trivia, the author meant the minor and the unimportant (unless I misread him, he included sex in this category), and not grammar, logic, and rhetoric, the big trivia of the dictionary definitions of the word.

I could begin by insisting that Mr. Friedrich has confused my armor with its chink, but this might lead to an intricate and turgid flow of metaphor. It is simpler to say, in another figure, that Trivia Mundi has always been as dear and as necessary to me as her bigger and more glamorous sister, Gloria. They have both long and amicably inhabited a phrase of Coleridge's, "All things both great and small," and I like to think of them taking turns at shooting albatrosses and playing the bassoon.

Some notable trivia, such as the last straw, the lost horseshoe nail, and a piece of string, became involved with larger issues, but my own, I am afraid, never rise to such heights. They consist mainly of a preoccupation, compulsive perhaps, but not obsessive, with words and the alphabet, and most of them never get into print. Their purpose is the side-tracking of worrisome trains of thought. The modern mind has many shuttles and shuntings, the principal one being, I suppose, the reading of mystery novels in bed, to shut out the terrors of the night and the world. Profound thought or plain positive thinking does not conduce to repose. Every man, laying his book aside, still has the night and the world to bypass. The late Bert Leston Taylor used to find comfort in contemplating Canopus, "a star that has no parallax to speak of." I happen to get cold up there in the immeasurable spaces of the outer constellations, and my own system of mental sedation is more mundane.

Some may ward off insomnia by reciting poetry to themselves, such as Tennyson's "The moan of doves in immemorial elms, and murmuring of innumerable bees." But this has never worked for me, because I invariably begin to take the lines of a poem apart. A friend of mine, fighting off the bells of Poe and avoiding the thickets of Eliot, manages to doze off after several repetitions of, to set it down in a long ramble, "In Xanadu did Kubla Khan a stately pleasure dome decree, where Alph the sacred river ran through caverns measureless to man down to a sunless sea." I tried that several times, discovered the solitary long O in "dome," the six consecutive words containing R, and the last seven R-less words. The dome seemed to stick up a mile above the sunless sea, the rolling Rs trickled away, and I was left stranded in a desiccation of ". . . to man down to a sunless sea."

A mariner so easily marooned in a wasteland of verse finds himself turning away from, say, the lines of Shakespeare that end ". . . how like a god" and toward the old Ed Wynn gag that begins "How would you like to die?" If you don't happen to remember it, a group of murderous gangsters, armed with everything lethal, from a hangman's rope to an enormous bottle of poison, propounded the question to the great comedian. "In Gloria Swanson's arms" was Mr. Wynn's prompt and wistful reply.

I was laughing about that ancient routine a few years ago while lying in a hospital bed, and my alarmed nurse asked me what was the matter. My solitary laughter has always alarmed my nurses, of whom I have had more than twenty since the silent artillery of time began firing at me. I told this particular nurse what I was laughing about, and she thought it over solemnly for a moment. "Well," she said finally, "to me she is every bit as attractive now as she was when I first saw her in a silent film about the French Foreign Legion." She pronounced the last word as if it were "lesion." And here I am again, in the midst of verbal trivia. Nurses' verbal trivia, however, are the very best trivia, and rank high in my collection. I remember a Canadian nurse who read aloud to me from some book or other ". . . that first fine careless rupture," and another who shook me for several long moments one day in 1940 when, in reading aloud from the "Books" department of an erudite journal, she paused to remark that there were notices of eight books about Mussolini. She had come upon, it turned out, a list of short reviews headed "Miscellany." Nurses are wonderful women and dedicated ministering angels, and they have no time to fritter away on the trivia of spelling and pronunciation.

When a patient is lying at right angles to his nurses and doctors and visitors, and considerably lower — in more ways than one — than all of them, he is in the standard posture for the onset of trivia. I have no doubt that many a dark, serious book has been conceived on a bed, but surely few of them will outlast the wonderful description of wallpaper that was born in the mind of Reginald Gardiner when he lay parallel to the floor and at right angles to everybody. The temper of the supine patient, particularly the postoperative, is capricious and unpredictable, and forms one of the best arguments for the theory and practice of minimum bed rest. My own habit, in bed at home or in the hospital, of exploring words and the alphabet acts to prevent my talking back to the wallpaper, a practice that, except in the case of the upright figure, may be more alarming than amusing.

Most of my hospitalizations were during the war years, when nurses were on twelve-hour shifts — a long time to spend alone with me, especially at night. Many nurses go on the night shift because it is supposed to be easier, but at least one of mine later asked to be transferred to day duty. Nurses, because of their tight and highly specialized vocabulary, are not very good at word games. When I told one apprehensive nurse, around midnight, that only seven capital letters are wholly or partially enclosed — A, B, D, O, P, Q, and R — she promptly printed the entire alphabet on a sheet of paper and told me that H, K, M, N, W, and X are also partially enclosed. She had, you see, set them down squarely on the lines of a sheet of ruled paper. Nurses live by rule and line, and they cannot think of anything as hanging in the circumambient mental air. Occasionally, when I hung a concept there for one of them, she would tiptoe from the room and bring in the night resident doctor. "This patient," as I used to be called with a trace of irritation, was set down as atypical, without significance or syndrome.

One night I asked my nurse if she could think of a seven-letter word in which the letter U appears three times. She sighed and said, "It's probably unusual." I told her that it was and it wasn't, and she slipped out of the room, and a short time later Dr. Conway came in. My doctors always approached my bedside with an air of bluff insincerity, sometimes humming a tune nervously, in an unsuccessful effort to imitate casualness. I asked Dr. Conway if he could find the other six-letter word in suture. "It's right up your alley, but then again it certainly isn't," I told him. An hour later he came back to say that he couldn't find it and I had to spell it out for him.

Before many days I had Dr. Conway lying awake trying to find a word in which all five vowels appear in order. Even when I told him that three of the vowels come in direct sequence he couldn't get it. Among such words, to release your own mind for more profitable researches, are "facetious" and "abstemious." Doctors go to bed — when they can, which isn't often — in the fond and sometimes desperate hope that they will be able to sleep, and the letters of the alphabet that visit their overburdened minds are cogent ones in familiar combinations, such as T.B. and E.S.P. It occurred to me that Dr. Conway, who had a hard time sleeping, might benefit by thinking dreamily of the letter Y and the soporific words for which it stands — yore and yarrow, youth and yesterday. Doctors, however, traditionally hunt for trouble, and all that Dr. Conway got out of Y was its noisy category of yammer and yell, yowl and yelp. This worried me, and I suddenly began thinking of myself as doctor and Conway as patient.

"N is probably the letter for you," I told him, "and I'm sorry I didn't prescribe it. But you know how it is; we have to proceed with each subject, or patient, by a process of trial and error. Some persons are nauseated by an injection of codeine — but react well to demerol. N should be fine for doctors of your temperament, because it is the letter of nowhere and never, novocain and nicotine and narcotic. If you drift into nightmare and night-shade instead of nightingale and narcissus, it is significant but not necessarily alarming. I worry about my doctors when they are undergoing alphabetical sedation only if they exhibit a tendency to slip too easily from nocturne and Nepenthe into some such sequelae as ninety naked night nurses." Dr. Conway seemed rather more disturbed than amused by my analysis of his association problems. "I don't know enough words beginning with N to get very far," he said.

"N doesn't have very many words," I said soothingly. "Practically nothing edible begins with N and there are almost no animals at all to keep you awake. So you won't lie there yearning for something to eat or worrying about beasts on the prowl. The newt and the narwhal cannot be said to prowl, but think of the animals that inhabit both sides of N, in M and O. The first has many creatures, from the mastodon to the mouse, and the second has an oppressively oleaginous company of oozy things, from the octopus to the oyster. But in N your consciousness is nurtured by the letter of Nineveh and Nirvana, No Man's Land and nomad, Nemo and Nod." Dr. Conway didn't say anything, he just went away. I understand that he takes sleeping pills now in order to sleep, and tries to think of nothing, including N.

I was perfectly content with my aimless wanderings in the avenues and lanes of the alphabet until Mr. Friedrich brought up the factor of value, or worth-whileness. When Dr. Alfred North Whitehead died, the *New York Times* described him as "a supreme adventurer in the realm of the mind." And now I am afraid that in its little piece about my own passing that great newspaper may refer to me as "just another vagabond in the backwoods of the imagination." This has taken the edge off my supine meanderings and given my dreams a nasty turn. In one of them I was being hunted down like a deer in a wooded wilderness. Men like Lord Bertrand Russell, another supreme adventurer in the realm of the mind, kept firing at me from cover. In something of a panic, I have recently been trying to give my nocturnal thoughts at least the semblance of importance. So far this has merely had the effect of making them a little stuffy. Whereas I used to drop off to sleep while looking for quiet characters in B, I now find myself trying to discover something significant in the curious ambivalence, the antipathy-affinity of C and M.

Most of the characters in B, to get back to them for a moment, murder sleep: the bugler, braggart, blowhard, blatherskite, barber, bowler, barker, booster, bouncer, bruiser, and so on. But their broken-bottle barroom brawling, bombast, bluster, and blockbusting bombardment of Babel and Bedlam die down when you come upon the subdued figures of the only truly quiet characters in the second letter of the alphabet — the butler, the bridegroom, and the burglar. The first night I came upon them, whispering and tiptoeing in the corridors of B, I fell asleep almost instantly. Now I lie awake for hours, staring at the ceiling, becoming more and more involved in what may easily turn out to be the utterly meaningless relationship of C and M. On the other hand, it is just barely possible that I have got the tips of my fingers on a valid and valuable discovery in the field of alphabetical relativity. I began, simply enough, with the discovery that C and M contain some of the greatest traditional antipathetical entities of fact and fiction — cat and mouse, cobra and mongoose, Capulet and Montague. From there I went on to explore certain other tragic associations of the two letters, Mary Celeste, Morro Castle, McKinley and Czolgosz, and Marat and Corday. I tried to get out of the darker side of the combination by thinking of Madonna and Child, Maurice Chevalier, and Christy Mathewson, but then I became wide awake and a little sweaty with Chamberlain and Munich, and Capitalism and Marxism, from which it was a simple mental journey to Christian and Moslem, civil and military, celibacy and marriage, church and monarchy, classical and modern, chemical and mechanical, mundane and cosmic. My mind had no sooner calmed itself with magic carpet than it leaped even wider awake with the Caine Mutiny and the Caine Mutiny Court Martial. I soon realized, as I turned on the lights and lit a cigarette, that C-M clearly militates against that relaxation of posture and thought which leads to unconsciousness. I got into dozens of conjunctions of the two letters — Mark and Cleopatra, Candida and Marchbanks, malice and charity, cow and moon, moth and cloth, mountain and climber, cadets and midshipmen, Monroe and colonization, and Custer and massacre. I began thinking of Charles Martel, who checked the Moors, but found this unrelaxing and tried to settle back in a cozy mental Morris chair. And suddenly I was in the midst of Martini cocktail, maraschino cherry, cockles and mussels, mutton chop, Château Margaux, mulled cider, Martell cognac, chocolate mousse, and Moët et Chandon. This naturally brought on cholera morbus. (Incidentally, the cholera morbus that killed President Zachary Taylor was caused by a surfeit of milk and cherries.) I don't know how I finally managed sleep; perhaps it was by thinking of the triumphs of the Count of Monte Cristo, or the whirling wheels of Monte Carlo, but my unconsciousness did not last long and my dreams were troubled. In one of them I was suddenly enfiladed by the rifle fire of the Coys and McHatfields. This distortion brought me so wide awake that I had to get up and dress.

A few nights later, having resolutely shaken C-M from my mind, I turned to S and W in the hope that the combination would be soft and winsome, soporific and wistful, but there is definitely a dark basic twist in my mental processes somewhere, for I abruptly shifted from a momentary contemplation of sweet William to storm warning, sou'wester, windstorm, waterspout, and shipwreck. I made a hasty grab for E, with its ease, ephemera, and evanescence, and then found myself, to my dismay, in the endless, eternal, everlasting, energetic enterprise and endeavor of the most restless letter of all twenty-six. Once you get into the explorations, examinations, excavations, and elaborate edifices of E, a tranquil mind is impossible. If you make the mistake of turning in desperation to D, you are even more disconcerted, for its doves, desires, and dreams give way almost at once to its terrible atmosphere of doubt, dread, decline, derangement, decay, dissolution, degradation, and its dire, dismal, disease, doom, and dusty death. If you contemplate the thousand depressing words that begin with D, you will understand why it was necessary to follow delightful and delicious with delovely in the Cole Porter song lyric. There just aren't three genuine three-syllable words that would fit into the mood of ecstasy, so one had to be invented. If from this dark, dolorous, demented, destructive, desperate, and demoniac letter you look for serenity in F, you find yourself in both the frying pan and the fire. F is the letter of falter, foozle, flunk, flop, flaw, feeble, flounder, fall, flat, and failure, of fake, fallacious, flimflam, fishy, fib, fob, foist, forgery, facsimile, and fabrication. The fox of its foxfire is not a fox, and the fire is not fire. Even its fleabane is often false. It is the flimsy, fluttery, finicky, frantic, frenetic, feverish headquarters of flibbertigibbet, fuddyduddy, fogy, fossil, fourflusher, frustrated female, and flabbergasted fussbudget. To sports it brings foul, fault, footfault, fumble, and forfeit. Its fineness and finesse have a filigree frailty, and a furry fungus blurs its focus, making it filmy, fuzzy, and foggy. When you come upon fame, family, fortune, and faith in these surroundings, they have a faint, furtive, fragile, and almost fictitious feeling. F brings the fingers to butterfingers, the fly to fly-by-night, the flash to flash-in-the-pan, and the forsaken to godforsaken. Its friend is too close to fiend for comfort, and it is not reassuring to realize that our finances and future keep such fearful, fitful, fretful, and fantastic company. F is so flagrantly flagitious and so flamboyantly flexuous that it might easily drive any patient to floccillation, or at least make him want to rush out and flense a whale with a fleam. If its fizzle doesn't get us, its fission may.

G, if you are still with me, is no longer the most gruesome, gloomy, and gory letter; its terrors have become old-fashioned with the passing of the centuries and the development of modern man. The things that go bump in G would no longer frighten even Goldilocks, for who is afraid nowadays of ghouls, ghosts, goblins, giants, gargoyles, griffins, gorgons, or Gargantua and Goliath? If you want to get hell's own heebie-jeebies, take H. This

Century of Violence has invented new words and combinations of words and thrown a greenish light on old ones to point up its hellions and horrors, and most of them begin with H: hoodlum, hooligan, heel, hooch, heroin, hitchhiker, hotrod, hijacker, holdup, hophead, hipped, hideout, hatchet-man, higher-up, hangover, hooker, homicide, homosexual, hydrogen, halitosis, hysteria, and Hollywood.

I don't know whether or not psychiatry has explored the diagnostic potential of what it would surely call, and perhaps already has, letter stimulus and word response. A simple way to measure the degree of apprehension, or *Angst*, in a patient who keeps looking over his shoulder or glancing into the sky would be the C-test or the T-test. I tried both of them on myself one night, with depressing results. All hell broke loose in each of them without warning. C has almost as many words of calm and comfort as of crisis and conflict, and the well-balanced psyche should be able to fall asleep while still in the category of anodyne, before the bells of alarm have begun to ring. I started out pleasantly and restfully one night like this: carillon, caroler, cavalcade, carriages, cobblestone, clip-clop, countryside, chickadee, candytuft, chimney corner, cricket, chessmen, cider, chestnuts. Then the trouble began, for C is the letter of catcall, curse, calumny, and contumely. I suddenly found myself in the midst of a loud-mouthed exchange of epithets and insults, from the old-fashioned cad and cockalorum up to the present-day card-carrying Communist conspirator and cockeyed Congressional-committee chairman. (If you can't fill in forty others, from clodhopper to creep, you are out of touch with your times.) The imprecations I had bumped into in C after such a serene start instantly led to creak, crack, crumple, crumble, collapse, crash, conflagration, consternation, confusion, cyclone, collision, calamity, catastrophe, cataclysm, and chaos. Anybody who can doze off while still thinking of clover, candle, comforter, clock, and chime is living in the alphabetical past, and his state of mind is probably even more indicative of derangement than my own.

There isn't a thing C can do that T cannot equal or surpass. I forget just how I started out in this promising letter of time and truth, but in a flash I was wandering among turtles and toadstools, and then I came to the tiny termite and what happened was far more terrible than the crackup in the chimney corner of C: tremble, teeter-totter, tower, tremor, tremblor, television, telephone, telegraph, transmission, topple, tumble, twist, topsy-turvy, tumult, turbulent, turmoil, thunder, tempest, tornado, tropical, typhoon, terror, tantrum, tirade, tailspin, traffic tieup, train, taxi, truck, trolley, tram, terminal, trouble, trial, tears, tribulation, torment, torture, triumph. (I don't know how that triumph got in there, but probably my consciousness had taken as much as it could.)

It is my intention to be helpful as possible to my neighbors at the corner of Dread and Jeopardy, and I suggest that they play around in P before venturing into more menacing letters. P is a rather silly letter, given to repeating itself, and to a strange assortment of games: ping-pong, polo, pool, poker, pedro, pinochle, parcheesi, pussy-wants-a-corner, post office, and pillow. The sixteenth letter of the alphabet has many pixies, great and small: Puck, Pan, Pandora, Peter Pan, Pinocchio, Pollyanna, Puss in Boots, and the Pooh. No other letter is quite so addicted to the vice of alliteration, and it is possible that no writer has ever lived who did not think up and mull over in his mind at least one title in the same category as *Pilgrim's Progress, Pippa Passes, Pied Piper, Pickwick Papers, Peterkin Papers, Pride and Prejudice, Prince and Pauper, Poet and Peasant, Pit and Pendulum, Peacock Pie, Potash and Perlmutter,* and so on, and on, and on, back through the ages. I once made up a little man named Pendly in the early years of my constant need to make money, and for some reason or other, no longer clear to me, I invented the name of a make of automobile in the same story. Naturally, I fell into the facile trap of repeating the P in the title of the story, which came out "Mr. Pendly and the Poindexter." It is because of this confounded tendency that our language is spotted with such expressions as pooh-pooh, pitter-patter, pish-posh, pompon, pretty please, postprandial, party politics, pumpkin papers, pink pills, pale people, pip-pip, pawpaw, papa, and the awful like.

In conclusion — all this thin slicing is getting us nowhere — easily the most fecund and probably the least frightening combination of letters is S-P. I have been working on it for years, off and on, and it has taken me from Stony Point to Seven Pines and from swimming pool to South Pacific with hundreds of stopoffs along the way. To games, for example, it has given southpaw, screen pass, short putt, set point, shot put, Sunday punch, and "sorry partner." Nothing has leaped out of this union to scale my pajamas off or to keep me awake very long. Right now, however, I am finding it a somnolent experience to wander in W, with its wilderness, Wonderland, wabe, wildwood, and Woodland of Weir. If you're lucky you can stay with nothing worse than witches and warlocks until the sandman gets you.

Pleasant dreams.

Thomas Wolfe

THE LANGUAGE THAT I SEEK

≥≤

The legend of Thomas Wolfe, the author of Look Homeward, Angel, *is of the giant who poured out great quantities of words that had to be cut, reshaped, and organized into novels by his editors. He ached with the whole memory of his life and ached to find a language to express it. In the following passage, taken from* The Story of a Novel, *Wolfe recalls how in Paris one summer he began to recreate the record of everything he had known. Words were palpable for Wolfe. And each of the authors in this book — scholar, lexicographer, novelist, poet — takes some delight (if not always Wolfe's effusive passion) in examining, turning, handling words.*

The quality of my memory is characterized, I believe, in a more than ordinary degree by the intensity of its sense impressions, its power to evoke and bring back the odors, sounds, colors, shapes, and feel of things with concrete vividness. Now my memory was at work night and day, in a way that I could at first neither check nor control and that swarmed unbidden in a stream of blazing pageantry across my mind, with the million forms and substances of the life that I had left, which was my own, America. I would be sitting, for example, on the terrace of a café watching the flash and play of life before me on the Avenue de l'Opéra and suddenly I would remember the iron railing that goes along the boardwalk at Atlantic City. I could see it instantly just the way it was, the heavy iron pipe; its raw, galvanized look; the way the joints were fitted together. It was all so vivid and concrete that I could feel my hand upon it and know the exact dimensions, its size and weight and shape. And suddenly I would realize that I had never seen any railing that looked like this in Europe. And this utterly familiar, common thing would suddenly be revealed to me with all the wonder with which we discover a thing which we have seen all our life and yet have never known before. Or again, it would be a bridge, the look of an old iron bridge across an American river, the sound the train makes as it goes across it; the spoke-and-hollow rumble of the ties below; the look of the muddy banks; the slow, thick, yellow wash of an American river; an old flat-bottomed boat half filled with water stogged in the muddy bank; or it would be, most lonely and haunting of all the sounds I know, the sound of a milk wagon as it entered an American street just at the first gray of the morning, the slow and lonely clopping of the hoof upon the street, the jink of bottles, the sudden rattle of a battered old milk can, the swift and hurried footsteps of the milkman, and again the jink of bottles, a low word spoken to his horse, and then the great, slow, clopping hoof receding into silence, and then quietness and a bird song rising in the street again. Or it would be a little wooden shed out in the country two miles from my home town where people waited for the street car, and I could see and feel again the dull and rusty color of the old green paint and see and feel all of the initials that had been carved out with jackknives on the planks and benches within the shed, and smell the warm and sultry smell so resinous and so thrilling, so filled with a strange and nameless excitement of an unknown joy, a coming prophecy, and hear the street car as it came to a stop, the moment of brooding, drowzing silence; a hot thrum and drowsy stitch at three o'clock; the smell of grass and hot sweet clover; and then the sudden sense of absence, loneliness and departure when the street car had gone and there was nothing but the hot and drowsy stitch at three o'clock again.

Or again, it would be an American street with all its jumble of a thousand ugly architectures. It would be Montague Street or Fulton Street in Brooklyn, or Eleventh Street in New York, or other streets where I had lived; and suddenly I would see the gaunt and savage webbing of the elevated structure along Fulton Street, and how the light swarmed through in dusty, broken bars, and I could remember the old, familiar rusty color, that incomparable rusty color that gets into so many things here in America. And this also would be like something I had seen a million times and lived with all my life.

I would sit there, looking out upon the Avenue de l'Opéra and my life would ache with the whole memory of it; the desire to see it again; somehow to find a word for it; a language that would tell its shape, its color, the way we have all known and felt and seen it. And when I understood this thing, I saw that I must find for myself the tongue to utter what I knew but could not say. And from the moment of that discovery, the line and purpose of my life was shaped. The end toward which every energy of my life and talent would be henceforth directed was in such a way as this defined. It was as if I had discovered a whole new universe of chemical elements and had begun to see certain relations between some of them but had by no means begun to organize the whole series into a harmonious and coherent union. From this time on, I think my efforts might be described as the effort to complete that organization, to discover that articulation for which I strove, to bring about that final coherent union. I know that I have failed thus far in doing so, but I believe I understand pretty thoroughly just where the nature of my failure lies, and of course my deepest and most earnest hope is that the time will come when I shall not fail.

At any rate, from this time on the general progress of the three books which I was to write in the next four and a half years could be fairly described in somewhat this way. It was a progress that began in a whirling vortex and a creative chaos and that proceeded slowly at the expense of infinite confusion, toil, and error toward clarification and the articulation of an ordered and formal structure. An extraordinary image remains to me from that year, the year I spent abroad when the material of these books first began to take on an articulate form. It seemed that I had inside me, swelling and gathering all the time, a huge black cloud, and that this cloud was loaded with electricity, pregnant, crested, with a kind of hurricane violence that could not be held in check much longer; that the moment was approaching fast when it must break. Well, all I can say is that the storm did break. It broke that summer while I was in Switzerland. It came in torrents, and it is not over yet.

I cannot really say the book was written. It was something that took hold of me and possessed me, and before I was done with it — that is, before I finally emerged with the first completed part — it seemed to me that it had done for me. It was exactly as if this great black storm cloud I have spoken of had opened up and, mid flashes of lightning, was pouring from its depth a torrential and ungovernable flood. Upon that flood everything was swept and borne along as by a great river. And I was borne along with it.

There was nothing at first which could be called a novel. I wrote about night and darkness in America, and the faces of the sleepers in ten thousand little towns; and of the tides of sleep and how the rivers flowed forever in the darkness. I wrote about the hissing glut of tides upon ten thousand miles of coast; of how the moonlight blazed down on the wilderness and filled the cat's cold eye with blazing yellow. I wrote about death and sleep, and of that enfabled rock of life we call the city. I wrote about October, of great trains that thundered through the night, of ships and stations in the morning; of men in harbors and the traffic of the ships.

I spent the winter of that year in England from October until March, and here perhaps because of the homely familiarity of the English life, the sense of order and repose which such a life can give one, my work moved forward still another step from this flood tide chaos of creation. For the first time the work began to take on the lineaments of design. These lineaments were still confused and broken, sometimes utterly lost, but now I really did get the sense at last that I was working on a great block of marble, shaping a figure which no one but its maker could as yet define, but which was emerging more and more into the sinewy lines of composition.

From the beginning — and this was one fact that in all my times of hopelessness returned to fortify my faith in my conviction — the idea, the central legend that I wished my book to express had not changed. And this central idea was this: the deepest search in life, it seemed to me, the thing that in one way or another was central to all living was man's search to find a father, not merely the father of his flesh, not merely the lost father of his youth, but the image of a strength and wisdom external to his need and superior to his hunger, to which the belief and power of his own life could be united.

Yet I was terribly far away from the actual accomplishment of a book — how far away I could not at that time foresee. But four more years would have to pass before the first of a series of books on which I was now embarked would be ready for the press, and if I could have known that in those next four years there would be packed a hundred lives of birth and death, despair, defeat, and triumph and the sheer exhaustion of a brute fatigue, I do not know whether or not I could have found the power within myself to continue. But I was still sustained by the exuberant optimism of youth. My temperament, which is pessimistic about many things, has always been a curiously sanguine one concerning time, and although more than a year had now gone by and I had done no more than write great chants on death and sleep, prepare countless notes and trace here and there the first dim outlines of a formal pattern, I was confident that by the spring or the fall of the next year my book would somehow miraculously be ready.

So far as I can describe with any accuracy, the progress of that winter's work in England was not along the lines of planned design, but along this line that I have mentioned — writing some of the sections which I knew would have to be in the book. Meanwhile what was really going on in my whole creative consciousness, during all this time, although I did not realize it at the moment, was this: What I was really doing, what I had been doing all the time since my discovery of my America in Paris the summer before, was to explore day by day and month by month with a fanatical intensity, the whole material domain of my resources as a man and as a writer. This exploration went on for a period which I can estimate conservatively as two years and a half. It is still going on, although not with the same all-absorbing concentration, because the work it led to, the work that after infinite waste and labor it helped me wonderfully to define, that work has reached such a state of final definition that the immediate task of finishing it is the one that now occupies the energy and interest of my life.

In a way, during that period of my life, I think I was like the Ancient Mariner who told the Wedding Guest that his frame was wrenched by the woeful agony which forced him to begin his tale before it left him free. In my own experience, my wedding guests were the great ledgers in which I wrote, and the tale which I told to them would have seemed, I am afraid, completely incoherent, as meaningless as Chinese characters, had any reader seen them. I could by no means hope to give a comprehensive idea of the whole extent of this labor because three years of work and perhaps a million and a half words went into these books. It included everything from gigantic and staggering lists of the towns, cities, counties, states, and countries I had been in, to minutely thorough, desperately evocative descriptions of the undercarriage, the springs, wheels, flanges, axle rods, color, weight, and quality of the day coach of an American railway train. There were lists of the rooms and houses in which I had lived or in which I had slept for at least a night, together with the most accurate and evocative descriptions of those rooms that I could write — their size, their shape, the color and design of the wallpaper, the way a towel hung down, the way a chair creaked, a streak of water rust upon the ceiling. There were countless charts, catalogues, descriptions that I can only classify here under the general heading of Amount and Number. What were the total combined populations of all the countries in Europe and America? In how many of those countries had I had some personal and vital experience? In the course of my twenty-nine or thirty years of living, how many people had I seen? How many had I passed by on the streets? How many had I seen on trains and subways, in theatres, at baseball or football games? With how many had I actually had some vital and illuminating experience, whether of joy, pain, anger, pity, love, or simple casual companionship, however brief?

In addition, one might come upon other sections under some such cryptic heading as "Where now?" Under such a heading as this, there would be brief notations of those thousands of things which all of us have seen for just a flash, a moment in our lives, which seem to be of no consequence whatever at the moment that we see them, and which live in our minds and hearts forever, which are somehow pregnant with all the joy and sorrow of the human destiny, and which we know, somehow, are therefore more important than many things of more apparent consequence. "Where now?" Some quiet steps that came and passed along a leafy night-time street in summer in a little town down South long years ago; a woman's voice, her sudden burst of low and tender laughter; then the voices and the footsteps going, silence, the leafy rustle of the trees. "Where now?" Two trains that met and paused at a little station at some little town at some unknown moment upon the huge body of the continent; a girl who looked and smiled from the window of the other train; another passing in a motor car on the streets of Norfolk; the winter boarders in a little boarding house down South twenty years ago; Miss Florrie Mangle, the trained nurse; Miss Jessie Rimmer, the cashier at Reed's drug store; Doctor Richards, the clairvoyant; the pretty girl who cracked the whip and thrust her head into the lion's mouth with Johnny J. Jones Carnival and Combined Shows.

"Where now?" It went beyond the limits of man's actual memory. It went back to the farthest adyt of his childhood before conscious memory had begun, the way he thought he must have felt the sun one day and heard Peagram's cow next door wrenching the coarse grass against the fence, or heard the street car stop upon the hill above his father's house at noon; and Earnest Peagram coming home to lunch, his hearty voice in midday greeting; and then the street car going, the sudden lonely green-gold silence of the street car's absence and an iron gate slamming, then the light of that lost day fades out. "Where now?" He can recall no more and does not know if what he has recalled is fact or fable or a fusion of the two. Where now — in these great ledger books, month after month, I wrote such things as this, not only the concrete, material record of man's ordered memory, but all the things he scarcely dares to think he has remembered; all the flicks and darts and haunting lights that flash across the mind of man that will return unbidden at an unexpected moment: a voice once heard; a face that vanished; the way the sunlight came and went; the rustling of a leaf upon a bough; a stone, a leaf, a door.

It may be objected, it has been objected already by certain critics, that in such research as I have here attempted to describe there is a quality of intemperate excess, an almost insane hunger to devour the entire body of human experience, to attempt to include more, experience more, than the measure of one life can hold, or than the limits of a single work of art can well define. I readily admit the validity of this criticism. I think I realize as well as any one the fatal dangers that are consequent to such a ravenous desire, the damage it may wreak upon one's life and on one's work. But having had this thing within me, it was in no way possible for me to reason it out of me, no matter how cogently my reason worked against it. The only way I could meet it was to meet it squarely, not with reason but with life.

It was part of my life; for many years it was my life; and the only way I could get it out of me was to live it out of me. And that is what I did. I have not wholly succeeded in that purpose yet, but I have succeeded better than I at one time dared to hope. And now I really believe that so far as the artist is concerned, the unlimited extent of human experience is not so important for him as the depth and intensity with which he experiences things. I also know now that it is a great deal more important to have known one hundred living men and women in New York, to have understood their lives, to have got, somehow, at the root and source from which their natures came than to have seen or passed or talked with 7,000,000 people upon the city streets. And what finally I should most like to say about this research which I have attempted to describe is this: That foolish and mistaken as much of it may seem, the total quality, end, and impact of that whole experience was not useless or excessive. And from my own point of view, at least, it is in its whole implication the one thing I may have to tell about my experience as a writer which may be of some concrete value to other people. I consider this experience on the whole the most valuable and practical in my whole writing life thus far. With all the waste and error and confusion it led me into, it brought me closer to a concrete definition of my resources, a true estimate of my talents at this period of my life, and, most of all, toward a rudimentary, a just-beginning, but a living apprehension of the articulation I am looking for, the language I have got to have if, as an artist, my life is to proceed and grow, than any other thing that has ever happened to me.

I know the door is not yet open. I know the tongue, the speech, the language that I seek is not yet found, but I believe with all my heart that I have found the way, have made a channel, am started on my first beginning. And I believe with all my heart, also, that each man for himself and in his own way, each man who ever hopes to make a living thing out of the substances of his one life, must find that way, that language, and that door — must find it for himself as I have tried to do.

2 | ✍

WORDS AND HISTORY

The essays in Section 1 dealt with language as a reflection and embodiment of personal history. Now we look at language as an expression of national history. The developments in the language, particularly deletions from and additions to the lexicon, stand as a record of the life of a nation and its people.

History is the account of events that result in political and social changes. The invasion of England by the Germanic tribes beginning in the middle of the fifth century, the coming of Christianity to England in 597, the Scandinavian incursions from the end of the eighth to the beginning of the eleventh century, the Norman Conquest in 1066 — these are some of the major events in the early history of the English-speaking people which demanded and received a linguistic response. Latin was the language of worship, so the English borrowed *altar, hymn, mass,* and *psalm.* The earliest Scandinavian words that made their way into English bore the mark of marauders, and most of these words have not survived. It is rather from the later period of peaceful amalgamation of the Danes and the English that we get such Scandinavian loanwords as *broth, egg, fellow, sister, skill,* and *skirt.*

The most dramatic events result in the most sharply outlined intersection of history and language. Two scholars, Hans Sperber and Robert Estrich, offer a theory that some changes occur because of emotional pressure, which they illustrate with two fully elaborated examples, one from political revolt, the other from the Civil War. And Eric Partridge's essay on the language of World War II makes us conscious of the new meanings now emerging for words like *pacification* and *escalation.*

But history also involves men's attitudes, habits, prejudices, and enthusiasms. The list of compound words with *self* (*self-esteem, self-*

pity) that grew steadily in the English language from the end of the sixteenth and throughout the seventeenth century does not memorialize any datable event. These words testify to a sense of a new way of considering man and his place in the world. Similarly, the prolific use in America of the suffix *-ize* meaning "to make" (*glamorize, sanitize, vitalize, personalize*) tells us something about American confidence in our unlimited "know-how." This kind of history of men's minds as described in the essays by Owen Barfield and Thomas Pyles leads Salvador de Madariaga to assert that "Languages are the most direct expression of national character."

Such historical dictionaries as *The Oxford English Dictionary* (*O.E.D.*), *A Dictionary of American English* (*D.A.E.*), and *A Dictionary of Americanisms* (*D.A.*) contain the history of the evolution of our vocabulary. To compile such a dictionary, lexicographers gather thousands upon thousands of citations from the other repositories of our history — official documents, letters, newspapers, books — to build up layer by layer the complete history of a word. And in the successive layers, just as geologists find the history of the earth in the strata of rock, we find imbedded the history of a people.

Paul Roberts

SOMETHING ABOUT ENGLISH

✍✍

Because language is nothing without a context, in order to sketch a history of the English language, Paul Roberts had also to write a brief history of England and its people. The early years tell the story of invasions and conquests by Romans, Angles, Saxons, Danes, and, later, Frenchmen, who brought their language and ideas. New forces thrust new words into English. Other developments, such as changes in sound and grammar, occurred over long periods of time and cannot always be causally and dramatically connected with the history of events. Mr. Roberts' essay will give you a sense of the 1400-year history of English, its periods and its evolution. This material will also help you to use the large historical dictionaries with better understanding. In subsequent essays in this section, you will learn how the recent history of language interacts with current events.

Historical Backgrounds

No understanding of the English language can be very satisfactory without a notion of the history of the language. But we shall have to make do with just a notion. The history of English is long and complicated, and we can only hit the high spots.

The history of our language begins a little after A.D. 600. Everything before that is pre-history, which means that we can guess at it but can't prove much. For a thousand years or so before the birth of Christ our linguistic ancestors were savages wandering through the forests of northern Europe. Their language was a part of the Germanic branch of the Indo-European family.

At the time of the Roman Empire — say, from the beginning of the Christian Era to around A.D. 400 — the speakers of what was to become English were scattered along the northern coast of Europe. They spoke a dialect of Low German. More exactly, they spoke several different dialects, since they were several different tribes. The names given to the tribes who got to England are *Angles, Saxons,* and *Jutes.* For convenience, we can refer to them all as Anglo-Saxons.

Their first contact with civilization was a rather thin acquaintance with the Roman Empire on whose borders they lived. Probably some of the Anglo-Saxons wandered into the Empire occasionally, and certainly Roman merchants and traders traveled among the tribes. At any rate, this period saw the first of our many borrowings from Latin. Such words as *kettle, wine, cheese, butter, cheap, plum, gem, bishop, church* were borrowed at this time. They show something of the relationship of the Anglo-Saxons with the Romans. The Anglo-Saxons were learning, getting their first taste of civilization.

They still had a long way to go, however, and their first step was to help smash the civilization they were learning from. In the fourth century the Roman power weakened badly. While the Goths were pounding away at the Romans in the Mediterranean countries, their relatives, the Anglo-Saxons, began to attack Britain.

The Romans had been the ruling power in Britain since A.D. 43. They had subjugated the Celts whom they found living there and had succeeded in setting up a Roman administration. The Roman influence did not extend to the outlying parts of the British Isles. In Scotland, Wales, and Ireland the Celts remained free and wild, and they made periodic forays against the Romans in England. Among other defense measures, the Romans built the famous Roman Wall to ward off the tribes in the north.

Even in England the Roman power was thin. Latin did not become the language of the country as it did in Gaul and Spain. The mass of people continued to speak Celtic, with Latin and the Roman civilization it contained in use as a top dressing.

In the fourth century, troubles multiplied for the Romans in Britain. Not only did the untamed tribes of Scotland and Wales grow more and more restive, but the Anglo-Saxons began to make pirate raids on the eastern coast. Furthermore, there was growing difficulty everywhere in the Empire, and the legions in Britain were siphoned off to fight elsewhere. Finally, in A.D. 410, the last Roman ruler in England, bent on becoming emperor, left the islands and took the last of the legions with him. The Celts were left in possession of Britain but almost defenseless against the impending Anglo-Saxon attack.

Not much is surely known about the arrival of the Anglo-Saxons in England. According to the best early source, the eighth-century historian Bede, the Jutes came in 449 in response to a plea from the Celtic king,

Vortigern, who wanted their help against the Picts attacking from the north. The Jutes subdued the Picts but then quarreled and fought with Vortigern, and, with reinforcements from the Continent, settled permanently in Kent. Somewhat later the Angles established themselves in eastern England and the Saxons in the south and west. Bede's account is plausible enough, and these were probably the main lines of the invasion.

We do know, however, that the Angles, Saxons, and Jutes were a long time securing themselves in England. Fighting went on for as long as a hundred years before the Celts in England were all killed, driven into Wales, or reduced to slavery. This is the period of King Arthur, who was not entirely mythological. He was a Romanized Celt, a general, though probably not a king. He had some success against the Anglo-Saxons, but it was only temporary. By 550 or so the Anglo-Saxons were firmly established. English was in England.

Old English

All this is pre-history, so far as the language is concerned. We have no record of the English language until after 600, when the Anglo-Saxons were converted to Christianity and learned the Latin alphabet. The conversion began, to be precise, in the year 597 and was accomplished within thirty or forty years. The conversion was a great advance for the Anglo-Saxons, not only because of the spiritual benefits but because it reëstablished contact with what remained of Roman civilization. This civilization didn't amount to much in the year 600, but it was certainly superior to anything in England up to that time.

It is customary to divide the history of the English language into three periods: Old English, Middle English, and Modern English. Old English runs from the earliest records — i.e., seventh century — to about 1100; Middle English from 1100 to 1450 or 1500; Modern English from 1500 to the present day. Sometimes Modern English is further divided into Early Modern, 1500–1700, and Late Modern, 1700 to the present.

When England came into history, it was divided into several more or less autonomous kingdoms, some of which at times exercised a certain amount of control over the others. In the century after the conversion the most advanced kingdom was Northumbria, the area between the Humber River and the Scottish border. By A.D. 700 the Northumbrians had developed a respectable civilization, the finest in Europe. It is sometimes called the Northumbrian Renaissance, and it was the first of the several renaissances through which Europe struggled upward out of the ruins of the Roman Empire. It was in this period that the best of the Old English literature was written, including the epic poem *Beowulf*.

In the eighth century, Northumbrian power declined, and the center of influence moved southward to Mercia, the kingdom of the Midlands. A century later the center shifted again, and Wessex, the country of the West Saxons, became the leading power. The most famous king of the West Saxons was Alfred the Great, who reigned in the second half of the ninth century, dying in 901. He was famous not only as a military man and administrator but also as a champion of learning. He founded and supported schools and translated or caused to be translated many books from Latin into English. At this time also much of the Northumbrian literature of two centuries earlier was copied in West Saxon. Indeed, the great bulk of Old English writing which has come down to us is in the West Saxon dialect of 900 or later.

In the military sphere, Alfred's great accomplishment was his successful opposition to the viking invasions. In the ninth and tenth centuries, the Norsemen emerged in their ships from their homelands in Denmark and the Scandinavian peninsula. They traveled far and attacked and plundered at will and almost with impunity. They ravaged Italy and Greece, settled in France, Russia, and Ireland, colonized Iceland and Greenland, and discovered America several centuries before Columbus. Nor did they overlook England.

After many years of hit-and-run raids, the Norsemen landed an army on the east coast of England in the year 866. There was nothing much to oppose them except the Wessex power led by Alfred. The long struggle ended in 877 with a treaty by which a line was drawn roughly from the northwest of England to the southeast. On the eastern side of the line Norse rule was to prevail. This was called the Danelaw. The western side was to be governed by Wessex.

The linguistic result of all this was a considerable injection of Norse into the English language. Norse was at this time not so different from English as Norwegian or Danish is now. Probably speakers of English could understand, more or less, the language of the newcomers who had moved into eastern England. At any rate, there was considerable interchange and word borrowing. Examples of Norse words in the English language are *sky, give, law, egg, outlaw, leg, ugly, scant, sly, crawl, scowl, take, thrust.* There are hundreds more. We have even borrowed some pronouns from Norse — *they, their,* and *them.* These words were borrowed first by the eastern and northern dialects and then in the course of hundreds of years made their way into English generally.

It is supposed also — indeed, it must be true — that the Norsemen influenced the sound structure and the grammar of English. But this is hard to demonstrate in detail.

A Specimen of Old English

We may now have an example of Old English. The favorite illustration is the Lord's Prayer, since it needs no translation. This has come to us in several different versions. Here is one:

Fæder ure þu ðe eart on heofonum si þin nama gehalgod. Tobecume þin rice. Gewurðe þin willa on eorðan swa swa on heofonum. Urne gedæghwamlican hlaf syle us to dæg. And forgyf us ure gyltas swa swa we forgyfaþ urum gyltendum. And ne gelæd þu us on costnunge ac alys us of yfele. Soðlice.

Some of the differences between this and Modern English are merely differences in orthography. For instance, the sign *æ* is what Old English writers used for a vowel sound like that in modern *hat* or *and*. The *th* sounds of modern *thin* or *then* are represented in Old English by þ or ð. But of course there are many differences in sound too. *Ure* is the ancestor of modern *our*, but the first vowel was like that in *too* or *ooze*. *Hlaf* is modern *loaf*; we have dropped the *h* sound and changed the vowel, which in *hlaf* was pronounced something like the vowel in *father*. Old English had some sounds which we do not have. The sound represented by *y* does not occur in Modern English. If you pronounce the vowel in *bit* with your lips rounded, you may approach it.

In grammar, Old English was much more highly inflected than Modern English is. That is, there were more case endings for nouns, more person and number endings for verbs, a more complicated pronoun system, various endings for adjectives, and so on. Old English nouns had four cases — nominative, genitive, dative, accusative. Adjectives had five — all these and an instrumental case besides. Present-day English has only two cases for nouns — common case and possessive case. Adjectives now have no case system at all. On the other hand, we now use a more rigid word order and more structure words (prepositions, auxiliaries, and the like) to express relationships than Old English did.

Some of this grammar we can see in the Lord's Prayer. *Heofonum*, for instance, is a dative plural; the nominative singular was *heofon*. *Urne* is an accusative singular; the nominative is *ure*. In *urum gyltendum* both words are dative plural. *Forgyfaþ* is the first person plural form of the verb. Word order is different: "urne gedæghwamlican hlaf syle us" in place of "Give us our daily bread." And so on.

In vocabulary Old English is quite different from Modern English. Most of the Old English words are what we may call native English: that is, words which have not been borrowed from other languages but which have been a part of English ever since English was a part of Indo-European. Old English did certainly contain borrowed words. We have seen that many borrowings were coming in from Norse. Rather large numbers had been borrowed from Latin, too. Some of these were taken while the Anglo-Saxons were still on the Continent (*cheese, butter, bishop, kettle,* etc.); a larger number came into English after the Conversion (*angel, candle, priest, martyr, radish, oyster, purple, school, spend,* etc.). But the great majority of Old English words were native English.

Now, on the contrary, the majority of words in English are borrowed, taken mostly from Latin and French. Of the words in *The American College Dictionary* only about 14 percent are native. Most of these, to be sure, are common, high-frequency words — *the, of, I, and, because, man, mother, road,* etc.; of the thousand most common words in English, some 62 percent are native English. Even so, the modern vocabulary is very much Latinized and Frenchified. The Old English vocabulary was not.

Middle English

Sometime between the years 1000 and 1200 various important changes took place in the structure of English, and Old English became Middle English. The political event which facilitated these changes was the Norman Conquest. The Normans, as the name shows, came originally from Scandinavia. In the early tenth century they established themselves in northern France, adopted the French language, and developed a vigorous kingdom and a very passable civilization. In the year 1066, led by Duke William, they crossed the Channel and made themselves masters of England. For the next several hundred years, England was ruled by kings whose first language was French.

One might wonder why, after the Norman Conquest, French did not become the national language, replacing English entirely. The reason is that the Conquest was not a national migration, as the earlier Anglo-Saxon invasion had been. Great numbers of Normans came to England, but they came as rulers and landlords. French became the language of the court, the language of the nobility, the language of polite society, the language of literature. But it did not replace English as the language of the people. There must always have been hundreds of towns and villages in which French was never heard except when visitors of high station passed through.

But English, though it survived as the national language, was profoundly changed after the Norman Conquest. Some of the changes — in sound structure and grammar — would no doubt have taken place whether there had been a Conquest or not. Even before 1066 the case system of English nouns and adjectives was becoming simplified; people came to rely more on word order and prepositions than on inflectional endings to communicate their meanings. The process was speeded up by sound changes which caused many of the endings to sound alike. But no doubt the Conquest facilitated the change. German, which didn't experience a Norman Conquest, is today rather highly inflected compared to its cousin English.

But it is in vocabulary that the effects of the Conquest are most obvious. French ceased, after a hundred years or so, to be the native language of very many people in England, but it continued — and continues still — to be a zealously cultivated second language, the mirror of elegance and civilization. When one spoke English, one introduced not only French ideas and French things but also their French names. This was not only easy but socially useful. To pepper one's conversation with French expressions was to show that one was well-bred, elegant, *au courant*. The last sentence shows that the process is not yet dead. By using *au courant* instead of, say, *abreast of things*, the writer indicates that he is no dull clod who knows only English but an elegant person aware of how things are done in *le haut monde*.

Thus French words came into English, all sorts of them. There were words to do with government: *parliament, majesty, treaty, alliance, tax, government*; church words: *parson, sermon, baptism, incense, crucifix, religion*; words for foods: *veal, beef, mutton, bacon, jelly, peach, lemon, cream, biscuit*; colors: *blue, scarlet, vermilion*; household words: *curtain, chair, lamp, towel, blanket, parlor*; play words: *dance, chess, music, leisure, conversation*; literary words: *story, romance, poet, literary*; learned words: *study, logic, grammar, noun, surgeon, anatomy, stomach*; just ordinary words of all sorts: *nice, second, very, age, bucket, gentle, final, fault, flower, cry, count, sure, move, surprise, plain.*

All these and thousands more poured into the English vocabulary between 1100 and 1500, until at the end of that time many people must have had more French words than English at their command. This is not to say that English became French. English remained English in sound structure and in grammar, though these also felt the ripples of French influence. The very heart of the vocabulary, too, remained English. Most of the high-frequency words — the pronouns, the prepositions, the conjunctions, the auxiliaries, as well as a great many ordinary nouns and verbs and adjectives — were not replaced by borrowings.

Middle English, then, was still a Germanic language, but it differed from Old English in many ways. The sound system and the grammar changed a good deal. Speakers made less use of case systems and other inflectional devices and relied more on word order and structure words to express their meanings. This is often said to be a simplification, but it isn't really. Languages don't become simpler; they merely exchange one kind of complexity for another. Modern English is not a simple language, as any foreign speaker who tries to learn it will hasten to tell you.

For us Middle English is simpler than Old English just because it is closer to Modern English. It takes three or four months at least to learn to read Old English prose and more than that for poetry. But a week of good study should put one in touch with the Middle English poet Chaucer. Indeed, you may be able to make some sense of Chaucer straight off, though you would need instruction in pronunciation to make it sound like poetry. Here is a famous passage from the *General Prologue to the Canterbury Tales*, fourteenth century:

> Ther was also a nonne, a Prioresse,
> That of hir smyling was ful symple and coy,
> Hir gretteste oath was but by Seinte Loy,

And she was cleped Madame Eglentyne.
Ful wel she song the service dyvyne,
Entuned in hir nose ful semely.
And Frenshe she spak ful faire and fetisly,
After the scole of Stratford-atte-Bowe,
For Frenshe of Parys was to hir unknowe.

Early Modern English

Sometime between 1400 and 1600 English underwent a couple of sound changes which made the language of Shakespeare quite different from that of Chaucer. Incidentally, these changes contributed much to the chaos in which English spelling now finds itself.

One change was the elimination of a vowel sound in certain unstressed positions at the end of words. For instance, the words *name, stone, wine, dance* were pronounced as two syllables by Chaucer but as just one by Shakespeare. The *e* in these words became, as we say, "silent." But it wasn't silent for Chaucer; it represented a vowel sound. So also the words *laughed, seemed, stored* would have been pronounced by Chaucer as two-syllable words. The change was an important one because it affected thousands of words and gave a different aspect to the whole language.

The other change is what is called the Great Vowel Shift. This was a systematic shifting of half a dozen vowels and diphthongs in stressed syllables. For instance, the word *name* had in Middle English a vowel something like that in the modern word *father*; *wine* had the vowel of modern *mean*; *he* was pronounced something like modern *hey*; *mouse* sounded like *moose*; *moon* had the vowel of *moan*. Again the shift was thoroughgoing and affected all the words in which these vowel sounds occurred. Since we still keep the Middle English system of spelling these words, the differences between Modern English and Middle English are often more real than apparent.

The vowel shift has meant also that we have come to use an entirely different set of symbols for representing vowel sounds than is used by writers of such languages as French, Italian, or Spanish, in which no such vowel shift occurred. If you come across a strange word — say, *bine* — in an English book, you will pronounce it according to the English system, with the vowel of *wine* or *dine*. But if you read *bine* in a French, Italian, or Spanish book, you will pronounce it with the vowel of *mean* or *seen*.

These two changes, then, produced the basic differences between Middle English and Modern English. But there were several other developments that had an effect upon the language. One was the invention of printing, an invention introduced into England by William Caxton in the year 1475. Where before books had been rare and costly, they suddenly became cheap and common. More and more people learned to read and write. This was the first of many advances in communcation which have worked to unify languages and to arrest the development of dialect differences, though of course printing affects writing principally rather than speech. Among other things it hastened the standardization of spelling.

The period of Early Modern English — that is, the sixteenth and seventeenth centuries — was also the period of the English Renaissance, when people developed, on the one hand, a keen interest in the past and, on the other, a more daring and imaginative view of the future. New ideas multiplied, and new ideas meant new language. Englishmen had grown accustomed to borrowing words from French as a result of the Norman Conquest; now they borrowed from Latin and Greek. As we have seen, English had been raiding Latin from Old English times and before, but now the floodgates really opened, and thousands of words from the classical languages poured in. *Pedestrian, bonus, anatomy, contradict, climax, dictionary, benefit, multiply, exist, paragraph, initiate, scene, inspire* are random examples. Probably the average educated American today has more words from French in his vocabulary than from native English sources, and more from Latin than from French.

The greatest writer of the Early Modern English period is of course Shakespeare, and the best-known book is the King James Version of the Bible, published in 1611. The Bible (if not Shakespeare) has made many features of Early Modern English perfectly familiar to many people down to present times, even though we do not use these features in present-day speech and writing. For instance, the old pronouns *thou* and *thee* have dropped out of use now, together with their verb forms, but they are still familiar to us in prayer and in Biblical quotation: "Whither thou goest, I will go." Such forms as *hath* and *doth* have been replaced by *has* and *does*; "Goes he hence tonight?" would now be "Is he going away tonight?"; Shakespeare's "Fie, on't, sirrah" would be "Nuts to that, Mac." Still, all these expressions linger with us because of the power of the works in which they occur.

It is not always realized, however, that considerable sound changes have taken place between Early Modern English and the English of the present day. Shakespearian actors putting on a play speak the words, properly enough, in their modern pronunciation. But it is very doubtful that this pronunciation would be understood at all by Shakespeare. In Shakespeare's time, the word *reason* was pronounced like modern *raisin;* face had the sound of modern *glass;* the *l* in *would, should, palm* was pronounced. In these points and a great many others the English language has moved a long way from what it was in 1600.

Recent Developments

The history of English since 1700 is filled with many movements and countermovements, of which we can notice only a couple. One of these is the vigorous attempt made in the eighteenth century, and the rather half-hearted attempts made since, to regulate and control the English language. Many people of the eighteenth century, not understanding very well the forces which govern language, proposed to polish and prune and restrict English, which they felt was proliferating too wildly. There was much talk of an academy which would rule on what people could and could not say and write. The academy never came into being, but the eighteenth century did succeed in establishing certain attitudes which, though they haven't had much effect on the development of the language itself, have certainly changed the native speaker's feeling about the language.

In part a product of the wish to fix and establish the language was the development of the dictionary. The first English dictionary was published in 1603; it was a list of 2500 words briefly defined. Many others were published with gradual improvements until Samuel Johnson published his *English Dictionary* in 1755. This, steadily revised, dominated the field in England for nearly a hundred years. Meanwhile in America, Noah Webster published his dictionary in 1828, and before long dictionary publishing was a big business in this country. The last century has seen the publication of one great dictionary: the twelve-volume *Oxford English Dictionary*, compiled in the course of seventy-five years through the labors of many scholars. We have also, of course, numerous commercial dictionaries which are as good as the public wants them to be if not, indeed, rather better.

Another product of the eighteenth century was the invention of "English grammar." As English came to replace Latin as the language of scholarship it was felt that one should also be able to control and dissect it, parse and analyze it, as one could Latin. What happened in practice was that the grammatical description that applied to Latin was removed and superimposed on English. This was silly, because English is an entirely different kind of language, with its own forms and signals and ways of producing meaning. Nevertheless, English grammars on the Latin model were worked out and taught in the schools. In many schools they are still being taught. This activity is not often popular with school children, but it is sometimes an interesting and instructive exercise in logic. The principal harm in it is that it has tended to keep people from being interested in English and has obscured the real features of English structure.

But probably the most important force on the development of English in the modern period has been the tremendous expansion of English-speaking peoples. In 1500 English was a minor language, spoken by a few people on a small island. Now it is perhaps the greatest language of the world, spoken natively by over a quarter of a billion people and as a second language by many millions more. When we speak of English now, we must specify whether we mean American English, British English, Australian English, Indian English, or what, since the differences are considerable. The American cannot go to England or the Englishman to America confident that he will always understand and be understood. The Alabaman in Iowa or the Iowan in Alabama shows himself a foreigner every time he speaks. It is only because communication has become fast and easy that English in this period of its expansion has not broken into a dozen mutually unintelligible languages.

Owen Barfield

MODERN ENGLAND

κ̄κ̄

We move now from a history of the language to a more detailed picture of history in the language. Mr. Barfield looks hard at words, sometimes singly but most often in related clusters, and finds in the origins, time, and circumstances of their appearance an eloquent record of developments in intellectual, political, and social history. The English love of sport, for instance, from the sixteenth century on, has had a continuous effect on language: *allure* and *haggard* from hawking, *retrieve* and *run riot* from hunting, and *crestfallen* from cockfighting. Similarly, the American passion for sport has enriched our vocabulary.

The English language has been facetiously described as 'French badly pronounced.' At the death of Chaucer, and for nearly a hundred years afterwards, this description would have been very nearly a true one. Apart from the adoption of a few Latin words, changes seem to have been few and insignificant during the fifteenth century, and we may assume that, for the

Reprinted from *History in English Words* by Owen Barfield, by permission of the author and Faber and Faber Ltd., Publishers. A paperback edition of this book has recently been published in the United States by Wm. B. Eerdmans.

first half of it at any rate, the Hundred Years' War was occupying too many of our energies to leave much time for cultural growth. Nevertheless, from developments such as those which have been pointed out in some of our legal terminology we can feel something of the way in which the genius of the English language was steadily, if slowly, reasserting itself and claiming its right to a separate personality. At the Reformation, when England finally shook herself free from the dangerous embraces of the Holy Roman Empire, the period of excessive French influence came to an end. The general effect of Protestantism on our language, subtle and profound as it has been, will be dealt with later,* but the Reformation cannot be passed over here without recording one instance in which a word — perhaps a misunderstood word — has had extraordinarily lasting results. It is the confusion of the English *Sunday* with the Jewish *Sabbath*[1] and the consequent fastening upon that day of rest of many of the sombre inhibitions entailed by Sabbatic Law.

There is, however, another historical event which had a far more universal and direct bearing on English words, and that is the Revival of Learning. The new intercourse with the ancient literatures of Greece and Rome naturally brought into English a positive stream of 'literary borrowings'. At first these were mostly Latin words. If we try to imagine an English from which such words as *accommodate, capable, capacious, compute, corroborate, distinguish, efficacy, estimate, experiment, insinuate, investigate,* and a host of others equally common are as yet absent, we may partly realize what an important part was played by the Renaissance in producing the language in which we speak and think. There is indeed good evidence that the stream of new words flowed too fast at this time for ordinary people to keep up with it. For instance, many of the Latin words that were borrowed have since fallen out of use. At the beginning of the seventeenth century Francis Bacon, who is not a fantastic writer, was using such unfamiliar expressions as *contentation, contristation, digladiation, morigeration, redargution, ventosity,* . . . and somewhat before this, when the Classical influx was at its height, it was conspicuous enough to call forth several amusing parodies. We remember Shakespeare's Holofernes in *Love's Labour's Lost,* and Sir Thomas Wilson includes in his *Arte of Rhetorike* a fictitious letter applying for a church benefice, in which he satirizes as follows the Klondyke rush after fashionable Latinity:

'Pondering, expending, and revoluting with myself, your ingent affability, and ingenious capacity for mundane affairs: I cannot but celebrate and extoll your magnifical dexterity above all other. For how could you have adepted such illustrate prerogative, and domestical superiority, if the fecundity of your ingeny had not been so fertile and wonderful pregnant? . . .'

---

* *Editors' Note:* Mr. Barfield discusses this in chapters 8 and 9 of his book.
[1] First found with the meaning of *Sunday* in an edict of the Long Parliament.

Now this outcrop of linguistic parody is significant for other reasons too. It reminds us that the English language had at last become 'self-conscious'. In former times the struggle between different ways of saying the same thing, between the old and the new, the native and the foreign, had generally worked itself out under the surface, amid the half-conscious preferences of the mass of the people. Thus, the old English translators who rendered the Latin 'exodus' as *outfaring* and 'discipulus' (disciple) as *learning-boy*, were not consciously trying to keep the Latin words out; nor did the fourteenth-century author of a book, which he called the *Againbite of Inwit*, have any academic horror, as far as we know, of the new Latin borrowings *remorse* and *conscience*, with one of which, at least, he must have been familiar. The same may be said of Wyclif, who translated 'resurrectio' *againrising* and 'immortalitas' *undeadliness*. These old writers anglicized because it came natural to them to anglicize, just as the next generation began to prefer the Latin words. But it was not so in Italy, nor in France, in both of which countries poets had long ago written careful treatises on the beloved medium of their art, their native language. And now, after the Revival of Learning, in England, too, scholars and literary men began to notice such things. Counterbalancing the enthusiasm for Latin and Greek, there arose a 'Purist' movement of just the kind which has had such a powerful effect on the development of modern German. People tried to expel all 'foreign' words from the language; Sir John Cheke began a translation of the New Testament in which none but native words were to be used; and we find in his *Matthew moond* for *lunatic*, *hundreder* for *centurion*, *frosent* (from-sent) for *apostle*, *crossed* for *crucified*, *freshman* for *proselyte*, and many other equally odd-sounding concoctions. To look back in this way on the uncertainty and chaos which reigned at the beginning of the seventeenth century is to intensify our admiration for the scholarship and poetic taste displayed by the devout compilers of the Authorised Version.

If we were to look for another symptom of this sometimes pedantic self-consciousness, we could find it in the modern way of spelling *debt* and *doubt*. The old orthography, *det* and *dout*, is a perfectly correct English rendering of the French words from which they are taken, but the scholars of the Renaissance, anxious to show the ultimate derivation from the Latin stems 'deb' and 'dub', inserted an entirely unnecessary 'b' into the words, and there it has stayed ever since. Sometimes, too, these Elizabethan dons made learned howlers, as in the now abandoned spelling *abhominable*, which arose from a quite false idea that that adjective is derived from the Latin 'ab' (from) and 'homo' (man).

One can also get a curiously vivid sense of the way in which new Latin words had been streaming into the language during the sixteenth century from Bacon's literary style. He is so fond of placing a Latin and an English word side by side, in order to express what is virtually a single idea, that two consecutive pages of the *Advancement of Learning* supply no less than ten examples of this habit. Among them are *immoderate and over-weening, action and business, charge and accusation, eloquence and speech*. To understand the exact effect which this kind of writing must have had on the ears of his contemporaries we must try to realize the faintly novel and difficult sound with which many of these Latin syllables would still be ringing. No such effort is required, however, to comprehend the way in which this deliberate duplication must have helped to familiarize English people with the sound and meaning of the new words.

Very soon the Greek language too began to be drawn upon, though never to quite the same extent as Latin. Thus, English of the fifteenth century must also be thought of as a language in which hundreds of familiar words like *apology, apostrophe, bucolic, climax, drama, emphasis, encyclopedia, epidemic, epilogue, episode, hypothesis, hysterical, paragraph, parallel, paraphrase, physical*, do not yet exist, for these are all examples of words which came in with the Renaissance.[2] The number of technical terms of art and literature is particularly noticeable, and it was now that the foundations were laid of that almost automatic system whereby a new Greek-English word is coined to mark each advance that is made in science, and especially in technics. *Automatic* is itself an example, and it is hardly necessary to add *chronometer, dynamo, magneto, metronome, tele-scope, theodolite, thermometer, . . .*

But though the stern lovers of their native tongue were thus hopelessly outclassed, yet the mere existence of the conservative feeling which they tried to voice must have acted as a useful brake on the too indiscriminate adoption of new words. The English language was, in fact, settling down. It was in the future to receive countless additions — never to change its very essence as it had done in the thirteenth and fourteenth centuries. And thus, as we look on towards the modern period, we find only fewer and more scattered historical vestiges. But if we can no longer expect etymology to tell us anything approaching to a complete and coherent tale, it will nevertheless still light up for us from different angles different little portions of that dark, mysterious mass, the past.

By the sixteenth century, for example, that peculiarly English characteristic, the love of sport, had already begun to make its mark on the language. *Sport* itself is an abbreviation of 'disport', a French word meaning 'to carry oneself in a different direction from that of one's ordinary business'. It is interesting to observe how both the form and meaning of the English word have diverged from their origin, and how they have since

2 Two of the words quoted are first found, according to the *Oxford Dictionary*, in Sir Thomas More, one (*apostrophe*) in the text and the other in the title of his *Apologie of Syr Thomas More, Knyght*, 'made by him, after he had geven over the Office of Lord Chancellor of Englande'. It is not surprising that the creator of a European success like the word *Utopia* should have had a fine taste in real Greek words too.

been reborrowed into French and most of the other languages of Europe. Italian tailors will even use the term to describe a roll of loud check cloth! Of the older sports, hawking has given us *allure, haggard, rebate,* and *reclaim.* The Latin 'reclamare' had meant 'to cry out against' or 'to contradict'; it was only in hawking that it acquired its present sense of 'calling back' from the cries that were uttered to summon the hawk back to the wrist. *Allure* is from the old *lure,* an apparatus for recalling the birds, and *haggard* is a word of obscure etymology which was used of a wild hawk. *Forte* and *foible* are old fencing terms, describing the strong and weak (*feeble*) points of a sword. *Couple, muse, relay, retrieve* (French 're-trouver'), *run riot, ruse, sagacious, tryst,* and *worry* we owe to hunting, as also the development of the Latin 'sentire' into the English word *scent.* Of these the most interesting are perhaps *muse,* which is supposed to be derived from the same word as *muzzle,* and *ruse,* another form of *rush.* The hounds were said to 'muzzle' when they sniffed the air in doubt about the scent, and a *ruse* was a doubling of the hunted animal on its own tracks. *Rove* (but not *rover*) is from archery, meaning in the first place 'to shoot arrows at an arbitrarily selected target'. *Bias, bowl over,* and *rub* in the phrase 'there's the rub' are from bowls, *crestfallen* and *white feather* from cockfighting, and *chess, check, checkmate, cheque,* and *chequer* come to us through the Arabian from Persian, the central word being a corruption of the Persian 'Shah mat', meaning 'The Shah (the King) is dead'. It is not so generally known that the varied meanings of *all* these words are metaphors taken either from the game or from the board on which it is played.

The more modern sports do not yet seem to have provided us with many new words, but there is a promising tendency to transmute some of their technical terms into lively idiom. In this way we can use, for example, to *sprint,* to *put on a spurt,* the *last lap, clean bowled,* to *take his middle stump,* to *skate on thin ice,* to *kick off,* to *tee off, one up,* . . . ; and modern games have also been instrumental in preserving from oblivion the odd old French word *bisque,* of unknown origin, which came over to England with the now nearly obsolete game of tennis, as well as the French-Scottish *caddie.*

When we hear a golfer use this word, when we hear a Scotch person ask for an *aschet,* instead of a dish, or see the queer expression *petticoat-tails* on a tin of Edinburgh shortbread, we are taken back to the close connection between the French and Scottish Courts which existed in the days of Mary Stuart. For *caddie* is a corruption of the French 'cadet' (younger son), whence also modern English *cad* and *cadet*; *aschet* is a form of the French 'assiette'; and *petticoat-tails* a corruption of 'petits gateaux' (little cakes).

Another phenomenon of history which is very faithfully preserved in the English language is our long-standing and not always creditable nautical relations with the Dutch. From the fourteenth to the seventeenth century Dutch sea words continued to trickle into the language, the fourteenth seeing the arrival of *bowsprit* and *skipper*, the fifteenth of *freight, hoy, keel, lighter, pink, pump, scout, marline*, and *buoy*, the sixteenth of *aloof, belay, dock, mesh, reef, rover*, and *flyboat*, while the seventeenth century, when Van Tromp nailed his broom to the mast, the Dutch fleet sailed up the Medway, and William of Orange sat upon the English throne, gave us *avast, bow, boom, cruise, cruiser, gybe*, and *keelhaul*. Besides these maritime words English possesses certain military memories of the Dutch. *Freebooter* goes back to the war with Spain in the reign of Elizabeth, and *cashier, domineer, drill, furlough*, and *onslaught* are also among the words brought back from the Low Countries by English soldiers. A particularly freakish Dutch borrowing is the apparently English *forlorn hope*, which is in reality a popular corruption of the Flemish 'verloren hoop', a phrase that has nothing to do with hope and means a 'lost expedition'.

The Spanish words in the English language, like the Dutch, are few in number, but often full of history. Those which came originally from Arabic — the most interesting of all — will be dealt with in another chapter. We received them for the most part through the French. *Alligator,*[3] *chocolate, cocoa*, and *tomato*, which come through Spanish from Mexican, commemorate the Spanish conquest of Mexico, and *breeze* is a sixteenth-century adaptation of the Spanish 'briza', a name for the north-east trade wind in the Spanish Main. Of the other words which come to us through Spanish *cannibal, hammock, hurricane, maize*, and *savannah* are Caribbean, while *canoe, potato*, and *tobacco* are South American. *Cannibal*, like the names *West Indies* and *Indian* (meaning 'aboriginal inhabitant of America'), hides a more detailed history. It was brought back by Christopher Columbus, who believed, when he reached the islands of the Caribbean Sea, that he had sailed right round the world, back to the east coast of India. The name 'Caniba' — a variant of 'Carib' or 'Caribes' — he took as a proof that the inhabitants were subjects of the Grand Khan of Tartary.

We can see, then, how the new impulse towards travel and exploration which followed the Renaissance left behind, when it ebbed, many exotic and exotic-sounding words whose etymologies can tell us not a little of the nationality of those adventurous mariners who led the way to the East and to the new world. The Spaniards were not the only explorers. The Indian words *coolie* and *curry* come to us through Portuguese; *banana* and *negro* reached us from Africa, possibly by the same route; and *cocoanut* is from the Portuguese 'coco', a bugbear or bogy — alluding to the nut's monkey-like face. *Drub* — once used only of the bastinado — is thought to be an Arabic word brought back by suffering Christians from the Barbary States. *Amuck, bamboo*, and *cockatoo*, come from Malayan through Portuguese, and *caddy* (the receptacle) from Malayan direct. *Moccasin, tomahawk,*

[3] A corrupted form of 'al-lagarto' — 'the lizard'.

and *hickory* are among the words sent back to us by the seventeenth-century English settlers in North America. *Taboo, tattoo,* and *kangaroo* came home with Captain Cook from the Pacific.

Meanwhile, the civil and political history of England has been growing steadily. *Political, politics, politician,* and *parliamentary* first appear in the sixteenth century, and *Cabinet Council* seems to have been introduced at the accession of Charles I. *Cabal,* one of the few Hebrew words in the English language, probably owes it familiarity to two historical events. It was applied in Charles II's reign to a small committee of the Privy Council, also known as the 'Committee for Foreign Affairs', which afterwards became the Cabinet; moreover, a little later on it happened that the names of the five Ministers who signed the Treaty of Alliance with France against Holland were Clifford, Arlington, Buckingham, Ashley, and Lauderdale. Their initials thus arranged spell the word *cabal,* which was humorously used to describe them. Another far commoner expression which dates back to the Civil War is the phrase 'the *army*'. It reminds us that we had no standing army until after the foundation of the Parliamentary Forces. *Cavalier* and *Roundhead* are words which carry their history, so to speak, on their sleeves. They were both coined as terms of abuse, and among other uncivil relics of the Civil War which have found a more extended application, *fanatic* and *Puritan* were invented by the Royalists and *malignant* by the Roundheads. *Independent* and *independence* are also Puritan words, and the useful *demagogue* first appeared in the *Eikon Basilike,* the famous pamphlet in defence of the Crown, which Milton answered with his *Eikonoklastes.* The expression *to send to Coventry* is probably a gift from the rebellious citizens of Birmingham, who, according to Clarendon, frequently 'rose upon small parties of the King's' and either killed them or sent them, as prisoners, to Coventry, which was a Parliamentary stronghold.

Spite, which always loves a rich vocabulary, is also the father of those venerable labels *tory* and *whig.* The old Celtic word *tory* was first applied in the seventeenth century to the unfortunate Irish Catholics, dispossessed by Cromwell, who became savage outlaws living chiefly upon plunder; after that it was used for some time of bandits in general, and at the close of James II's reign the 'Exclusioners' found it a conveniently offensive nickname for those who favoured the succession of the Roman Catholic James, Duke of York. Thus, when William of Orange finally succeeded in reaching the throne, it became the approved name of one of the two great political parties in Great Britain. *Whig* is a shortened form of *whiggamore,* a name given to certain Scotchmen from the word *whiggam,* which they used in driving their horses. It was first used of the rebellious Scottish Covenanters who marched to Edinburgh in 1648; then of the Exclusioners, who were opposed to the accession of James; and finally, from 1689 onwards, of the other great political party or one of its adherents.

That the seventeenth century saw the true genesis of many of our commercial and financial institutions is suggested by the fact that their names first appear at this time. Such are *capital*, which is a doublet of *cattle* — the very oldest Aryan form of wealth — *commercial, discount, dividend, insurance, investment*, and lastly the modern meaning of *bank*, which, like the names of so many protective and responsible institutions — the *Assizes*, the *Bench*, the *Consulate*, the *Council*, the *Chair* at a public meeting, a *Seat* in Parliament, and the *Throne* — is based etymologically on what may well be one of the oldest and safest of human occupations. The old Teutonic word which subsequently became modern English *bench* was adopted into Italian, probably from the Teutonic Lombards of northern Italy, in the form 'banco'. It soon acquired the special sense of a money-changer's 'bench' or table and found its way, together with the object it represents, into most of the countries of Europe. Thus, like the name *Lombard Street*, the little word carries us back with it to the origin of banking in northern Italy and to Edward I's substitution of Italian *bankers* for Jewish moneylenders. *Bankruptcy, currency*, and *remittance* appeared in the first half of the eighteenth century, and in the second *bonus, capitalist, consols*, and *finance*. The history of *finance* is again interesting. The word goes right back to the Latin 'finis' (end). When it first appeared in English, it had the sense of a 'fine' or forfeit, but its modern significance was developed in eighteenth-century France among the tax-farmers or 'financiers', as they were called, to whom the king delegated the duty of collecting his taxes. As time went on, these shrewd individuals amalgamated into a sort of limited company, which, by a judicious application of the principles of usury, gradually gained more and more control over the revenue, until 'toutes les finances du royaume', as Voltaire says, 'dépendirent d'une compagnie de commerce'. In England the phrase *Bank of England* first appears in 1694, describing a body of individuals associated for the purpose of lending money to the Government; and about thirty years later this still (1953) outstanding loan began to be known as the *National Debt*.

From the beginning of the eighteenth century commercial and financial considerations seem to have played a steadily increasing part in determining the nation's policy. Horace Walpole is the first person known to have used *speculation* in the sense of buying and selling stocks and shares; and *budget* (a little bag or pocket) may owe its modern political meaning to a pamphlet sarcastically entitled *The Budget Opened*, in which his brother Robert's financial policy received some severe handling. *Prime Minister* also takes us back to Sir Robert Walpole, to whom it was applied with derisive innuendo, for it had in those days more the sense of 'Grand Vizier' or despot's tool. In the old-fashioned *nabob*, as a synonym for '*plutocrat*', we have a memory of the latter days of the East India Company when the squandering of large sums of money in London, often rounded off a life of empire-building in Bombay or Calcutta. The dictionary suggests, however, that later generations of Anglo-Indians preferred to bring back with them less questionable impedimenta, such as *pyjamas* and *shampoo*.

The phrase, the *Rights of Man*, takes us back to the American Declaration of Independence. The borrowing of *aristocrat* and *democrat* from French, the French word *guillotine*, and the appearance in English of *revolutionize* and *terrorize* are enduring relics of the French Revolution, and the word *sectional*, which came in in the nineteenth century, is closely bound up with the history of France, for it is derived (together with the geographical use of *section*) from the division of France into electoral sections under the Directory. The military meaning of *conscription* goes back to the France of the same period. To the campaigns in the Soudan we owe *zareeba*, and to the Boer War the Dutch words *kopje* and *spoor*. The 1914 War has left us the anonymous *stunt* and *gadget* (small mechanical contrivance), and the French *camouflage*, and President Wilson's *self-determination* has probably been added to half the languages of the world, while the expressions *eyewash*, to *scrounge* (meaning to 'steal'), to *get the wind up*, to *go west*, and possibly to *swing the lead* (to be idle at somebody else's expense), are idioms which may or may not take a permanent hold. In the second European War the Air Force has shown itself more 'fertile and wonderful pregnant' in the field of vocabulary than the Army. But it is too early yet to say whether *stooge* and *stooging*, *kite* (for aeroplane), *gen*, *bods*, and the rest of them will rise above the status of slang. . . .

Thomas Pyles

LATER AMERICAN SPEECH
Coinages and Adaptations

ﯹﯹ

When the English language traveled from Britain to America, it had to adapt itself to a new world. For many settlers America appeared to be an Eden. In an earlier chapter of his book, Professor Pyles details how the settlers found and borrowed new words to describe the *Terra Americana* — animals, flowers, and topographic features which they had never seen before and which had to be named. Thus, here in the New World was reenacted that mythic exercise which Noah Jacobs told of in *Naming-Day in Eden.* The coming of the nineteenth century, according to Pyles, marked the "beginning of an indigenous *psyche Americana* which is strikingly reflected in the flood of Americanisms. . . ." In the essay "What Is American about America?" John A. Kouvenhoven lists the following among a dozen items that define the character of our culture: the skyscraper, the model-T Ford, jazz, comic strips, soap operas, assembly-line production, chewing gum. These are American creations expressive of our civilization, and Americans invented words to name them.

T he War of 1812 and the appearance on the American scene of the frontiersman — both in the flesh and as a national symbol — mark the beginning of an indigenous *psyche Americana* which is strikingly reflected in the flood of Americanisms originating in the nineteenth century. The gaudy pageant of American history in that era — the standard of living, science, politics, morals, taste, in short America's contribution to civilization such as it has been — emerges from a bare list of such Americanisms. The dates in parentheses in the list which follows are those of the earliest citations for the words in M. M. Mathews's *Dictionary of Americanisms*:

cocktail (1806)	blockade-runner (1863)
gerrymander (1812)	boys in blue (1866)
spoils "political system" (1833)	apartment house (1876)
bowie knife (1836)	rustler "cattle thief" (1882)
gold fever (1847)	nickelodeon (1888)
bloomers (1851)	Anti-Saloon League (1892)
coeducation (1852)	basketball (1892)
filibuster (1853)	stogy (1893)
pay dirt (1856)	mortician (1895)
brownstone front (1858)	gangster (1896)

The America of our own century is similarly mirrored in the next list, which gives the merest sampling of twentieth-century Americanisms, arranged in roughly chronological order. The reader of mature years who is acquainted with the "American way" will have no difficulty supplying an approximate, and in many instances an exact, date for the earliest appearance of the words which follow:

big stick	superhighway
sundae	auto court
Rotarian	Technicolor
Liberty Bond	G.I.
companionate marriage	bobbysox(er)
Hays Office	Dixiecrat
dust bowl	stratocruiser
studio couch	dianetics

Words as a rule cannot fail to tell us something about the people who use them or have used them, and every one of these randomly chosen Americanisms is redolent of some aspect of American history, American life, or the American character. To tell the story behind them all would require a work of far greater magnitude than the present volume. Here it will be possible to touch upon only a few.

Stogy, for instance, calls to mind the Conestoga wagon and the part it played in the amazing westward push early in the nineteenth century. The vehicle and its name were in use as early as the mid-eighteenth century, but seem not to have been much known outside Pennsylvania until the 1800s. *Conestoga* was the name of an Iroquoian tribe, now long extinct; the tribal designation was applied to a valley in Lancaster County, Pennsylvania, where the large covered wagon which was the principal means of westward transportation before the introduction of railroads seems to have originated. The early Conestoga wagoners rolled long cigars for smoking on their trips, and such a cigar was called a *conestogy* (which is merely the earlier pronunciation of *Conestoga,* like *Iowy* for Iowa); this was subsequently clipped to *stogy.* The *prairie schooner* was a later development of the Conestoga wagon, built on a somewhat smaller scale.

Gerrymander is only one of a prodigious number of Americanisms that have grown out of our national politics. The eighteenth century gave us *caucus* and a few others, but it was the nineteenth century which really saw the full flowering of a distinctively American political life. It is an unhappy circumstance that much of the vernacular of American public life is suggestive of chicanery and deception; the historian's lot is far from being a happy one if he also happens to be an idealist.

Gerrymander, originally used as a noun but within a year of its coinage converted into a verb, is a blend of *Gerry* and *salamander.* The *Gerry* comes from the name of Elbridge Gerry, a staunch anti-Federalist who was in the course of a long career in politics a member of the Continental Congress, a delegate to the Constitutional Convention, a member of Congress, Governor of Massachusetts, and Vice-President of the United States. In 1812, while he was Governor of Massachusetts, his party, in an attempt to perpetuate its power, divided the state into electoral districts with more regard for politics than for geography. It happened that a district in Essex County somewhat resembled a salamander. When head, wings, and claws were added by Gilbert Stuart, the celebrated painter, to a map, the result was by a stroke of genius called a *gerrymander.* Within a year this attractive and ingenious linguistic novelty was being used throughout the country to describe what had already become a favorite though nameless device of the party in power. Towards the end of the century the word was adopted by the English, who have used it without much consciousness of its American origin.

The *spoils system* was introduced into our government during Andrew Jackson's administration. Strictly speaking, the term denotes the practice of making political appointments on the basis of party service rather than merit, though it has come to be used more broadly for any improper use of public office for political or even personal purposes. Old Hickory's slogan "to the victors belong the spoils" continued to be the accepted rule of political conduct until the introduction of the present civil service laws put a stop to many of the evils inherent in the spoils system.

Filibuster is old in British English as a modification of Spanish *filibustero,* which had in turn been taken from Dutch *vrijbuiter* "freebooter," but the word acquired a new meaning in the United States around the middle of the nineteenth century, when it came to be applied to those American adventurers and soldiers of fortune who engaged in the expeditions against Cuba under General Narciso López, most of them recruited from Louisiana, Mississippi, and Kentucky and many of them, as the New York *Courier and Enquirer* put it, not free and noble souls, but rather "men whom rascality has outlawed, men whom society . . . kicks out with contempt." *Filibuster* soon came to be used as a verb in the figurative sense "to use delaying or obstructing tactics in a legislature." And thus another political Americanism was born.

The most famous of all Americanisms, *O.K.*, grew out of a presidential race, according to the most widely accepted theory of its origin — if indeed a story so well documented must be called a theory. *O.K.* has gained lodgment in practically all civilized languages as well as in a few uncivilized ones. In the course of its hardy existence it has acquired practically every grammatical function; it may be used as an adjective ("His account was O.K."), a noun ("He got my O.K."), an adverb ("He did the job O.K."), and a verb ("O.K. this for me").

The origin of the expression, which began as a political slogan more than a century ago, seems to have been quickly forgotten in the hubbub which was American politics in the first half of the nineteenth century. Beginning shortly after its introduction, numerous theories of its origin have been advanced, many of them ably testifying to the ingenuity of their proponents and some of them quite engaging indeed. Mencken discusses fully these various theories, so that the account which follows must of necessity seem to lean heavily upon his résumé, as indeed it does.

A story which is both charming and plausible, and which would be altogether acceptable were it not for certain details having to do with chronology, derives *O.K.* from the passionate effusion of a semiliterate sign painter whose political sentiments do him more credit than does his orthography or, for that matter, his grammar. According to the story, this devotee of demos painted in large letters the legend "The People is Oll Korrect" on a streamer which was used in a Whig demonstration on September 15, 1840, in Urbana, Ohio. This was during the famous "Log Cabin Campaign" of General William Henry Harrison, the Whig candidate for the presidency, who was running against the Democratic incumbent, Martin Van Buren. The tale runs that Harrison's supporters were so taken by the sentence that they used it as a political slogan, underscoring the quaintness of *Oll Korrect* by reducing it to *O.K.* Unfortunately for this attractive theory, it was discovered in 1934 that *O.K.* had appeared in the Columbus *Ohio Statesman* on September 11, four days before the Harrison rally in question — and subsequent researches in files of yellowing newspapers have revealed a good many earlier occurrences of the mysterious letters.

Some have identified *O.K.* with a Choctaw word meaning "it is so." President Woodrow Wilson was "sold" on the Choctaw origin to such an extent that he always took the trouble to write out *okeh*, as he thought the Indian word should be written, as his mark of approval, eschewing the more common *O.K.* because, though amply justified by usage, it was not in his opinion correct. The supposed Choctaw spelling is also used as a trade name by the manufacturers of a popular brand of phonograph records.

Other theories which have been advanced from time to time have a certain entertainment value and are given here only for that reason. It has been proposed, for instance, that the *K* stand for *Keokuk*, the name of the Sac Indian chief for whom the city in Iowa was named. According to the story, this aboriginal worthy was affectionately called *Old Keokuk*, and, inasmuch as he had aided the Americans at the time of the Black Hawk War, he was quite definitely "all right"; hence the initials of *Old Keokuk* came to be used in the sense "all right."

Still other proposed etymologies derive *O.K.* from the name of a firm of biscuit manufacturers, the Orrins-Kendall Company, who supplied the War Department with their product during the Civil War and who stamped their boxes with their initials; from the name of one Obadiah Kelly, a freight agent who affixed his initials to bills of lading; from *Aux Cayes*, the name of a Haitian port from which the best rum known to the American colonists used to be shipped; from a signal supposedly used by early telegraphers; from an archaic English word variously spelled *hoacky, horkey, hawkey,* and *hockey,* apparently a corruption of *hock tide,* a festival marking the end of the harvesting season; and from *aux quais* (in effect, "I'll meet you down at the wharves"), a phrase thought to be used in Revolutionary War times by French sailors making dates with American girls. Nor are these all. Other theories set forth Greek (ὅλα καλὰ), Latin (*omnia korrecta*), Norwegian, Danish, and even Finnish etyma — all more or less ingenious, be it said, and all indubitably wrong.

On March 30, 1840, the New York *Herald,* the most prestigious Whig journal of that day, attributed the then strange expression *O.K.* to Andrew Jackson in an effort to cast ridicule upon his cultural attainments. The paper reported that, while he was still President, Jackson had said, after examining some documents purporting to expose the skulduggery of his favorite, Postmaster General Amos Kendall, "Mark on them *O.K.*," which letters he thought to be the initials of *all correct.* It is to this political canard, which was widely accepted as true at the time, particularly by enemies of Jackson and of the Democratic party, that *O.K.* owes its present meaning of "all right," though, as we shall see shortly, that was not its original meaning at all.

It was Allen Walker Read, of Columbia University, one of the world's most indefatigable readers of old newspapers, who set forth what is evidently the true story of *O.K.* in an article "The Evidence on *O.K.,*" published in the *Saturday Review of Literature* for July 19, 1941. The evidence Read has discovered shows that the term did indeed grow out of the presidential campaign of 1840, though it had no connection with the

Whig rally in Urbana, Ohio, on September 15. Far from it — it was not a Whig slogan at all, but a Democratic one. And a senseless slogan was *all* it was in the beginning; it took the false Jackson story to give it a meaning.

Martin Van Buren, who was Jackson's successor and who was, after the manner of politicians, panting after a second term as president in 1840, was a native of a village in eastern New York called Kinderhook. It seems perfectly clear now that O.K. began its hardy existence as nothing more mysterious than an abbreviation formed from the initial letters of *Old Kinderhook*. Throughout his career Van Buren's name was associated with that of his native village: he had been called the Kinderhook Fox by his enemies in the days of the "Albany regency," and it is not particularly surprising that his partisans should also have seized upon the name of the little village — perhaps in retaliation — and have called him the Magician of Kinderhook, the Sage of Kinderhook, and the Wizard of Kinderhook. In any case, *Old Kinderhook* became in time a sort of rallying cry for the Democrats in the days of Van Buren's power.

Read's evidence is to the effect that O.K. first appeared in print in the New York *New Era* on March 23, 1840 (a week before the libel on Jackson's spelling) as part of the name of an organization — the O.K. Club — made up of supporters of Van Buren in his campaign against General Harrison. Even in the light of Van Buren's well-known connection with Kinderhook, those who were not "in the know" were apparently mystified by the letters. Their true explanation appeared in the same newspaper on May 27th of the same year, when it was pointed out that they were "significant of the birthplace of Martin Van Buren, Old Kinderhook," but it seems to have made little impression at the time. The Jackson story had already appeared in the *Herald* and had captured the public fancy; the truth simply could not compete with the more romantic lie.

Beginning, then, as the name of a political organization dedicated to advancing by hook or by crook — such was the deplorable state of American political ethics in those unenlightened days — the political interests of Martin Van Buren of Old Kinderhook, O.K. was shortly to be used as a war cry by the Locofocos, as the unwashed members of the radical wing of the Democratic party called themselves. The O.K. Club, like other political clubs of the day, seems to have been composed largely of rowdies and bullies, and, on March 27, a group of these ruffians raided a Whig mass meeting in Masonic Hall. According to the report appearing in the *Herald* on the following day, "about 500 stout, strapping men" marched to the meeting place, where "the word O.K. was passed from mouth to mouth, a cheer was given, and they rushed into the hall upstairs, like a torrent." The mysterious battle cry spread rapidly, acquiring a sense quite different from its original one — which, as we have seen, was very little sense at all — as a result of the appearance of the Jackson story in the same paper only three days after the ascent of the gallant 500 upon the Whigs. Before very long O.K., meaning "all right, all correct" had spread all over the country, soon losing all connection with the Democratic party, even though commonly attributed to Jackson. Even the Whigs themselves, by a bitter irony, came to make use of the expression.

Despite the very convincing ring of the case built up by Read, it is yet possible, if only barely so, that there are genuinely earlier occurrences of our O.K. than that of March 23, 1840. If so, we should have to set aside the *Old Kinderhook* explanation as given in the *New Era* of May 27th as a newspaper writer's fabrication of an etymology after the fact, or else assume that the O.K. Club was using an earlier expression meaning "all right" with the additional connotation of *Old Kinderhook*. If this should be the case, one wonders where the members of the club dug up the expression, for it was obviously not in general use before 1840.

Improbable as such assumptions are, the annoying fact remains that there is one further bit of evidence which must be taken account of — that of the *Travel Diary* of William Richardson, written in 1815, in which the following entry occurs: "Arrived at Princeton, a handsome little village, 15 miles from N. Brunswick, o k & at Trenton, where we dined at 1 P.M." This has been accepted by some as a genuine pre-1840 occurrence of O.K., but Read suggests, in a note in *American Speech* for April, 1941, that Richardson's apparent *o k* is really two other letters, *a h*. According to Read's explanation, Richardson, who had revised the passage considerably already — the manuscript shows deletions and insertions — started to write "a handsome little village" after "N. Brunswick," but after writing the first two letters (*a h*) discovered that he had used the same phrase in describing Princeton: he went no further but neglected to cross out the two letters he had written.

If this explanation or something similar to it is not correct, then we actually have here an occurrence of O.K. twenty-five years before that in the *New Era* of March 23, 1840. It is possible that an O.K. of unknown origin was indeed in use before 1840, but it is obvious from the *New Era's* explanation of May 27th to the effect that the term was "significant of . . . Old Kinderhook" that it had all the freshness of a new coinage at that time, and the same is indicated by the Jackson anecdote in the *Herald* which apparently furnished a meaning for it.

This Americanism became naturalized in England a long time ago. Today O.K. is used about as freely in England as in America, though it was not until 1935 that the London *Times* admitted the expression as a permanent addition to the English word stock. In the same year the Judicial Committee of the Privy Council ruled that O.K. was even permissible on legal documents to indicate that the details therein were correctly given This was two years after O.K. had been included in the Supplement to the great *Oxford English Dictionary*. Lord Beaverbrook's report of the Moscow

Conference indicates that the wheel is come full circle: as Stalin's demands were read out item by item, Beaverbrook indicated Britain's agreement by O.K. (or *okay*, as he spells it); the American representative, Mr. W. Averell Harriman, rejecting his country's noble contribution to language, contented himself with saying *agreed* if the item concerned the United States.

The familiar *buncombe* — usually spelled *bunkum* nowadays — arose out of American political life. Bartlett (2nd ed., 1859) uses a spelling *buncome* (along with *bunkum*) and quotes Thomas C. Haliburton, the Nova Scotian judge who wrote the once famous Sam Slick books, as defining the word, "which is now as well understood as any in our language," as follows (Haliburton is speaking in the character of Slick, a Yankee clock pedlar):

> Our free and enlightened citizens don't appreciate silent members [of Congress]; it don't seem to them as if Squashville, or Punkinsville, or Lumbertown was right represented, unless Squashville, or Punkinsville, or Lumbertown makes itself heard and known, ay, and feared too. So every feller, in bounden duty, talks, and talks big too, and the smaller the State, the louder, bigger, and fiercer its members talk. Well, when a crittur talks for talk sake, just to have a speech in the paper to send to home, and not for any other airthly puppus but electioneering, our folks call it Bunkum.

The phrase *talking for Buncombe*, now obsolete, throws light on the word in question. It is explained in John H. Wheeler's *Historical Sketches of North Carolina* (1851), as quoted by Bartlett. Wheeler relates that "several years ago" (presumably during the Sixteenth Congress, 1819–21) the member from the district of North Carolina which included Buncombe County "arose to address the House, without any extraordinary powers, in manner or matter, to interest the audience. Many members left the hall. Very naïvely he told those who remained that they might go too; he should speak for some time, but 'he was only talking for Buncombe.' "

The term caught on rapidly, in the insane way that such terms frequently capture the public fancy, and by the middle of the century was being used in England as well as in America. It has given birth to *bunk* ("The worst bunk ever written," said the Duke of Windsor of published rumors of a marital rift, as reported by the Associated Press on March 16, 1951), *to debunk*, and *bunco* "a swindle, confidence game, misrepresentation." *Hokum*, according to the supplement to the *Oxford English Dictionary*, is a blend of *hocus-pocus* and *bunkum*.

A detailed treatment of all the Americanisms which in one way or another have application to American political life would require a volume to itself. It must here suffice to make brief mention of a few more and pass on to other areas. It will doubtless surprise many to learn that *New Deal* was not originated by the late F.D.R. — actually it is more than a century old — although he was certainly largely responsible for its popularization and for its identification with the policies and measures he advocated. Nor was *forgotten man* a Rooseveltism; there is an odor of cynicism in Roosevelt's appropriation of it, for it appears in 1883 as the title of a speech by William Graham Sumner, the brilliant American economist and sociologist whose political philosophy was diametrically opposed to all the New Deal stood for. The Roosevelt administration did, however, give birth to a good many new combinations, for instance, *economic royalist, court-packing, good neighbor policy, brain trust,* and to such horrible jargon as *coördinator, expediter, directive, "must" legislation, to process, to finalize,* and *bottleneck.* It is saddening to have to report that *graft* as a political term is an Americanism. . . .

The fact that *nickelodeon, mortician,* and *gangster* occur in the nineteenth century will probably occasion some surprise. *Nickelodeon* meant originally any show making an admission charge of five cents, but by 1908, with the development of cinematography, it had come to mean a motion picture show to which the admission charge was a nickel. With the raising of this charge and the erection of the flamboyant "supercolossal" movie palaces of our own day, *nickelodeon* has come to have only a historical interest as far as the motion picture industry is concerned. The word was revived, however, about fifteen years ago to designate a juke box, for which it is already ceasing to be appropriate: in the classier "joints" one can now hear only three records for a quarter.

Though *mortician* first occurs in the mid-1890s, it was not widely used for more than twenty years thereafter; its resuscitation seems to have occurred when the National Selected Morticians was organized in 1917. The linguistic virtuoso who coined the word did so by taking the first syllable of *mortuary* (ultimately Latin *mort-* "death") and affixing to it *-ician,* obviously suggested by *physician.* May he receive his reward in heaven, for he has deprived the grave of much of its victory. As for the analogy to *physician,* it is interesting to note that for a while, around the time of the Civil War, American undertakers assumed the title *Dr.,* but, strange as it seems when we consider the ease with which that title is borne today by virtually all other practitioners upon the human anatomy, they soon abandoned it. The National Selected Morticians also agitated for other verbal reforms: *coffin* to be supplanted by *casket, body* by *patient, undertaking establishment* by *reposing room, slumber room,* or *chapel,* and *hearse* by *casket coach.*

The beauty parlor operators, not to be outdone, followed the example of the morticians and gave *beautician* to a grateful world; considerably later an association of shoe repairers in Texas adopted the term *shoetrician* in the title of their organization, though it seems not to have caught on in other parts of the country, where *shoe rebuilder* is deemed of sufficient dignity to designate one who keeps shoes in repair. During the mid-Prohibition era H. L. Mencken coined *bootician* as a term for a bootlegger with a high sense of the ethics of his profession. Seeking for a term which would impress upon the public mind the high integrity of all their endeavors, the real estate salesmen were somewhat more original. They withstood the temptation of *realtician* and came up, as everyone knows, with *realtor*.

Although it occurs much earlier, *gangster* did not actually have much of a vogue until the so-called *gangster era*, a concomitant of the thirteen long years of wide-scale immorality which crowned the dedicated efforts of the Anti-Saloon League. *Gangster* has given rise to *gangsterdom* and probably furnished the model for *gagster* "comedian." . . .

The etymology of *highball*, like that of *cocktail*, is something of a mystery. The theory has been advanced that the word comes from the lingo of bartenders in the '90s, who supposedly called a glass a *ball*. If this could be established as a fact, we should have a plausible etymology, for the *high* is amply explained by the size of the glass, which is necessarily higher than that used for a straight (British *neat*) whiskey.

Professor I. Willis Russell has shown, in *American Speech* for February, 1944, that *highball* is a term used by railroaders to denote a signal to go ahead, to go fast, or to go full speed. It is likely that the use of the term to denote the drink is related to this use in railroading. Professor Leo Spitzer later pointed out in a note appearing in the same journal (February, 1945) a parallel semantic development in French, in which *rapide* "express train" is an argot term for "vin qui saoule [intoxicates] rapidement." *Électrique* and *brutal*, also used to designate fast trains, have been transferred likewise to wine which does its job rapidly: the authority quoted by Spitzer goes on to say, "the fact that a *rapide* train, sometimes *électrique*, is called *brutal* leads one to see the same idea in the same adjectives applied to wine, the idea of speed" — the drink being the vehicle which takes one speedily from reason to unreason in this metaphorical use of the adjectives. Similarly, *train direct* is an argot term both for a liter of wine and for a glass of absinthe, and *wagon* "railway car" for a large glass of wine. Spitzer concludes that "evidently American railroad terms must have had the same radius of expansion as did the French": the American highball speeds up the trip to intoxication just as do the wines called *rapide, brutal, direct,* and *électrique* in French.

About all that we can say with any certainty about *cocktail* is that it is an Americanism which has traveled all over the civilized world and has to some extent revolutionized drinking habits wherever it has gone. Many theories of its origin have been set forth. Christopher Morley once suggested that it originated in an American bar where it was customary to empty the last ounce or so of liquors into a bottle, the cork of which was decorated with a cock's feathers. Whether this etymology came to him by divine afflatus or he had evidence of any sort for it deponent saith not.

A more plausible story is that reprinted by Mencken in *Supplement One* from the house organ of the Roosevelt Hotel in New Orleans, the *Roosevelt Review*. It tells of a hospitable apothecary, Antoine Amédée Peychaud (the inventor of Peychaud bitters), who served a drink to his fellow Masons after lodge meetings consisting of sugar, water, cognac, and his own bitters. The mixture was offered in a *coquetier* (egg cup), pronounced *cocktay* by those of his guests who did not speak French. Folk etymology would account for *cocktay* becoming *cocktail*. This story is so pleasant, so apt, and so circumstantial that one wishes there were better authority for it. Other theories are that *cocktail* is from French *coquetel*, a mixed drink associated with the region of Bordeaux and supposedly introduced into America by French officers at the time of the Revolutionary War, and that it is from *cock-ale*, described by Captain Grose in his *Classical Dictionary of the Vulgar Tongue* as a "provocative drink."

There are other drinking terms of an auxiliary nature of which patriots may be proud: *stick* "a portion of liquor," *pony* "a small glass for liquor or the amount of liquor such a glass will hold," *finger, jigger, shot in the neck* (which later became *shot in the arm*), and *snifter*. *Hard liquor* is itself an Americanism; the English still prefer to say *spirits*. Also of American origin are *schooner* "tall glass, usually for beer," *to set 'em up, to rush the growler, bracer, barrelhouse, family entrance, eye opener, bender, red-eye,* and *to liquor up*. *Hooch* and *firewater* are of Indian origin, the latter term being supposedly an English rendering of the Indian term for strong liquor. The use of *rum* to refer generically to all alcoholic drinks is an Americanism, confined nowadays pretty much to the Drys; it dates from the early days before whiskey was widely known in this country, when rum was the colonists' favorite strong drink.

Saloon to designate a place for the sale of alcoholic beverages to be drunk on the premises was originally a euphemism in American English, for the word is ultimately from French *salon* "drawing or reception room." The word in its English modification came in time to have such unsavory connotations for the virtuous that, with the repeal of Prohibition, it was not revived; *tavern* is probably the most widely used of a number of terms which have supplanted it.

Barroom, bootleg(ger), and *moonshine* "illicit whiskey" are all Americanisms. The second word derives from the practice of concealing flat bottles of illegal liquor in the leg of the boot. *Moonshine*, listed in Grose's *Dictionary* with the meaning "white brandy smuggled on the coasts of Kent and Sussex" — it may also mean gin in Yorkshire — came to us by way of England, but was first applied to whiskey in this country. The fact that the earlier British use was confined to white or colorless liquors suggests a possible origin of the term, though it is more likely that the American extralegal whiskey was so called because it was made, and frequently sold as well, by the light of the moon, that is, at night. . . .

The word stock of American English increases at a dizzying rate of speed. In an attempt to record for lexicographical purposes our rapidly expanding vocabulary, I. Willis Russell, with the aid of enthusiastic assistants, conducts from time to time in *American Speech* a department "Among the New Words." Since 1945 he has recorded such new additions to our vocabulary as the following, to choose at random: *balding, name calling, jampacked, tourist court, bebop, spelunker* "cave crawler," *tape recording, TV, soap opera, VIP* "very imporant person," *Oscar* "statuette awarded for excellency in the movie industry," *to baby sit, aeropolitics, to double park, free wheeling, giveaway (show, program), radioastronomy, straw hat (theater, circuit), eager beaver, escort carrier, POW, jet* (short for *jet-propelled plane*), *aerosol bomb, atomic age, denazification, genocide, prefab, ruptured duck* "discharge button given G.I.'s," *stateside* "relating to the United States," *take-home pay, terminal leave, top secret, to cook with gas (electricity, radar)* "to get somewhere, as in 'Now you're cooking with gas'," *bobbysox (er), hot rod, psychodrama, spot check, rat race, Republocrat,* and *xerography* — to which the reader may be able to add a good many more from his own observation.

Terms like *bobbysox, bebop,* and *eager beaver* will impress the serious as being somewhat frivolous; *expediter, to process,* and *to implement* will seem "corny" to the cynical and sophisticated; but along with these, there are very substantial recent contributions, such as *genocide, radioastronomy,* and *aeropolitics,* which are altogether worthy to take their place beside such older Americanisms as *linotype, electrocute* (a blend of *electric* and *execute,* this may now be used to mean "to kill accidentally by electric shock," as in "Lineman Electrocuted When He Touches Live Wire"), *anesthesia, urinalysis, appendicitis, hydrant, gorilla, race suicide, typewriter, automobile, tularemia, moron, rotogravure, phonograph, telegram,* and *to demoralize.*

To baby sit is formed from *baby sitter,* a compound noun having here been made by back formation into a verb. *Bratting* has made some headway, probably mostly within the "profession," as a synonym for *baby sitting.* But such lighthearted terms to designate an activity which is a sign of the times in which we live would never be deemed appropriate by a government agency, and sure enough, the United States Employment Service office in at least one of our cities (Lincoln, Nebraska) has registered practitioners as *child monitors.* . . .

A large number of the cited recent additions have first appeared in *Time,* which has also been fecund in its original contributions to the American word stock. It specializes in such creations as *cinemactress, steelionaire, radiorator, stripteuse, millionheiress,* and *socialite.* Of these, the first three are blends (*cinema actress, steel millionaire, radio orator*) and the last three puns (*strip tease, millionairess, social light*). Other recent "makers" of American English are Gelett Burgess (*bromide* "platitude, also a person given to platitudes" and *blurb*), Jack Conway (*yes man*), Walter Winchell (*infanticipate*), Will Irwin (*highbrow* and probably *lowbrow*), Bob Burns (*bazooka*), Philip Wylie (*momism*), Sinclair Lewis (*babbitt, hobohemia, philanthrobber*), and H. L. Mencken (*bootician, booboisie, Bible Belt* and *ecdysiast* "strip teaser").

Blends such as *motel, twinjector, libratory, radarange, daffynition, skinjury* (from the advertisement of a medication for cuts and burns), *Dixiecrat, Chicagorilla,* and *psychiatricky* (a recent coinage of *Time* to describe the ending of a film) are very frequent nowadays. Many of them are nonce usages, and a bare list might be expanded for pages. The process is, of course, not at all new, and its very lack of subtlety probably accounts for its popularity; moreover, it is very easy to perform.

There has probably never been such fertile creation and wide use of acronyms as at present. *Acronym,* itself a new word formed from Greek *akros* "tip" and *onyma* "name" — probably of American coinage, by the way — means a word made from the initial letters of other words: examples are *radar* (*ra*dio *d*etecting *a*nd *r*anging), *Care* or CARE (*C*oöperative for *A*merican *R*emittances to *E*urope), *Unesco* (*U*nited *N*ations *E*ducational, *S*cientific, and *C*ultural *O*rganization), *loran* (*lo*ng *ra*nge *n*avigation), and *teleran* (*tele*vision *ra*dar *a*ir *n*avigation). It is likely that the colloquial name of the women's branch of the Royal Navy, the *Wrens* (*W*omen's *R*oyal *N*aval *S*ervice) furnished the model for the use of such American acronyms as *Wac* (*W*omen's *A*rmy *C*orps), *Wave* (*W*omen's *A*ppointed *V*olunteer *E*mergency *S*ervice), *Wasp* (*W*omen's *A*ir Force *S*ervice *P*ilots), and *Spar* (*S*emper *Par*atus, the motto of the Coast Guard). In the case of *Wave* (and also probably of *Care* and others as well), it is apparent that the natural process was reversed in that the acronym preceded the full name of the organization, which was made to fit. How otherwise to explain the cumbersome and inept full form of *Wave* or the forced use of *Coöperative* in the expansion of *Care*? A great number of trade names also are acronyms: *Amoco, Sunoco, Socony, Alcoa, Nabisco,* etc.

The use of initial letters to designate governmental agencies became a commonplace during the New Deal, as in *NRA* (originally *NIRA*), *AAA, HOLC, CCC, FERA, NLRB, OPA, RFC, OWI, WLB, ODT,* and others, which gave rise to Al Smith's scornful designation *alphabet soup.* The phenomenon was by no means unknown before as in *O.K., W.C.T.U., P.D.Q., I.W.W., G.A.R., G.O.P., C.O.D., B.V.D., F.F.V.,* and (*on the*) *Q.T.,* all of which antedate the New Deal by a good many years. Other recent examples are *ASCAP* (also, perhaps usually, an acronym, pronounced *ass cap*), *CIO, AFL, NAACP, TV, FM, IQ, M.C.* (which in the sense "master of ceremonies" may be converted into a verb, usually written *emcee*), and, very recently *LP* (*long-playing*) and *ACTH* (*adreno-corticotropic hormone*). Writers of advertising copy have made *B.O.* a constant dire threat to the social, economic, and erotic advancement of the American people. *P.O.* (*perspiration odor*), a subspecies of *B.O.*, constitutes a relatively minor menace to bourgeois euphoria. *TB* and *PJs* (*pajamas*) differ from the preceding in that they are abbreviations of single words. *A.W.O.L.* is usually an acronym in military use, pronounced *ay wall.* *V.P.* for *vice-president* has recently given rise to *veep*, originally applied to Alben W. Barkley, but now frequently used to designate any vice-president.

Words have circulated among the various functional categories — an ancient linguistic phenomenon by no means confined to American English, or even to English, though such conversions are especially notable in American English because of the very frequency with which they occur. Thus, nouns become verbs — a mighty flock of them, such as *to audition, to program, to accession, to package, to proposition, to vacation, to park* (also *to double park*), *to date* "to make an appointment with one of the opposite sex" (also *to double-date* "to date in couples"), *to burp* (transitively "to cause an infant to emit a belch after feeding by holding it over the shoulder and patting its back," (intransitively) "to make the digestive noise suggested by the word," *to contact, to clearance, to wow* (the noun *wow* being formed from the exclamation of enthusiasm), *to solo, to needle* "to give verbal digs," *to thumb* (*a ride*), *to service* and dozens of others. Intransitive verbs may become transitive, as in *to operate a patient, to sleep two people* (from an advertisement of a studio bed). New verbs may be made from clipped forms of nouns, including back formations: *to razz* (from *raspberry*, slang for a vulgar noise made with tongue and lips to indicate disapproval, also known as a *Bronx cheer*), *to emote, to typewrite, to perk* (*coffee*), *to enthuse* (which is from the nineteenth century and which may not be an Americanism, though it probably is), *to phone*, and such complexities as the previously mentioned *to baby sit*, as well as *to soda jerk* and *to practice teach.*

With equal ease verbs may be converted into nouns: *release* "permission to publish, sell, or exhibit," *cut* "reduction, (colloquially) failure to attend class, (slangily) share," *combine.* Nouns become adjectives, or practically so, in *air tragedy, cover girl*, and *armament race*; and adjectives become nouns, as in *lovelies* "show girls," *formals* "formal dresses," *informals* "stationery of less than standard size, usually bearing the user's name, initials, or monogram, and sometimes the address as well," *falsies* (with hypocoristic suffix) "artificial breasts, usually of sponge rubber," *tropicals* "lightweight suits or trousers," *casuals* "shoes for informal wear," *separates* "skirts and shirts worn by girls," *personal* "brief newspaper article about a particular person," *dry* "prohibitionist," *wet* "antiprohibitionist," *commercial* "commercially sponsored radio or television program or, more usually, sales talk on such a program," *short* "short moving picture subsidiary to the featured picture," *briefs* "women's skimpily cut underwear," and *scanties*, practically the same as briefs.

A very prominent characteristic of current American English, though the practice is by no means new or American, is the combination of verb and adverb to form a new verbal idea, in effect a new verb: *to call down, to check up, to scare up, to stand for* "to tolerate," *to go for* "to be enthusiastic about," *to try out, to make out* "to succeed," *to bawl out, to slip up, to rope in.* Some of these verb-adverb combinations have made themselves thoroughly at home in British English. Nouns frequently grow out of such verbal combinations: *setup, checkup, pushover, cutback, kickback, breakdown* "analysis," *drive-in, smash-up* "wreck," *slowdown, buildup, hookup, comeback* "snappy answer," *sit down, walk-up* "apartment house without elevator," *pin-up.* The last three of these may be used as adjectives, as in *sit-down strike, walk-up apartment, pin-up girl.* Some of the combinations cited have been in general English use for a long time (for instance, *breakdown* and *smash-up*), but have acquired new senses, or perhaps have been coined anew, in American English. *Pin-up* has made its way into French (and doubtless other Continental languages as well), according to B. Mathieu, writing in the *New Yorker* of November 4, 1950; it is used of any pretty woman, or one who is in the public eye, pictures of Mistinguett frequently carrying the caption *La vieille pin-up.*

Clipping is an old process; it was old, in fact, when Jonathan Swift inveighed against it, and it has contributed a great many words to the standard language — *mob,* for instance, which the Dean objected to as a clipped form of Latin *mobile vulgus,* and which now may appear in the most formal of contexts. Clipped forms which have arisen in America are *gas* (for *gasoline*), *photo, pep, bike, ad, bunk, auto, prof, taxi, tux, con* (for *confidence* as in *con man, con game*), *fax* (*facsimile newspaper*), and *Jax* (local for Jacksonville, Florida, also the name of a brand of beer made there). *Movie,* and, by analogy with it, *talkie,* are clipped forms with hypocoristic suffix.

Recent American English has made considerable use of prefixes and suffixes, like *de-* and *-ette,* word elements like *para-* and *-burger* which may be affixed in the manner of true prefixes and suffixes, and compounding elements like *-happy* and *-buster.* All these will here be discussed together for convenience's sake. *Para-* dates from World War II, occurring in *paratroops, paratrooper, parabomb, para-medic,* and *parashot.* These, like the *-burger* combinations (and others as well) may have begun as blends (*parachute troops* becoming *paratroops, cheese* and *hamburger* becoming *cheeseburger*); if so, it did not take long for the *para-, -burger,* etc., to be felt as free word elements capable of being affixed to other words. *De-* occurs in American *debunk;* it may be freely used in both British and American English, and it is difficult to say whether *dewax, defrost,* and the like are Americanisms or not. *Super-* has had a great vogue, occurring in such Hollywoodisms as *superfilm, supercolossal,* in *superhighway* and *super-*

market, and in *Superman,* the name of the comic strip character, who probably has no connection whatever with Shaw's *Man and Superman* or Goethe's *Übermensch. Super* used alone is slang on a somewhat juvenile level ("Superman's sure super today"), as is the riming *super-duper* "extra super." *Anti-* is much more frequent in American usage than in British and has been so since the eighteenth century. The prefix was used alone (with a pun on *Aunty*) as the name of the gaunt, bombazine-clad female prohibitionist depicted by the cartoonists in the days before Repeal. *Semi-* is likewise used more in America than in England: American English prefers the more pompous Latinate *semiannual* to *half-yearly.* H. W. Horwill in *Modern American Usage* says that a jubilee in America always becomes a *semicentennial,* and goes on to point out the looseness of meaning of *semi-* in American usage, in which it is frequently the equivalent of *partly, largely,* or *approximately* rather than *half. Near-,* as in *near-beer, near-silk,* and *near-leather,* came to acquire all the derogatory connotations of *imitation,* for which it was a euphemism in the beginning. It has lost ground in recent years. What used to be called *near-leather* would nowadays be called *simulated leather.*

Among the true suffixes, *-ize* has probably been as prolific as any, particularly in advertising writing and Federalese: *glamorize, sanitize, motorize, vitalize, finalize, personalize* "mark with the buyer's name, initials, or monogram, as *personalized stationery, underwear, luggage, bath towels,* etc.," *winterize* "prepare or equip for the winter, as a car," *sanforize* "preshrink by a special process" (from the name of *Sanford* L. Cluett, inventor), *tenderize, customize, comfortize* ("let us comfortize your shoes"), and a host of other verbs. Also widely used is *-ette:* it may be either diminutive (*kitchenette, dinette, bathinette, superette* "small super market") or feminine (*farmerette, conductorette, usherette, guidette, Rockette* "member of dancing chorus in Rockefeller Center's Radio City Music Hall," *tusslerette* "lady wrestler," *Hularette* "hula-dancing chorus girl in girl-show *A Night in Hawaii,*" and *drum majorette.*) After John Philip Sousa, the booteed, swivel-hipped drum majorette is probably America's greatest contribution to band music; it is likely that only America, its sexual mores conditioned to a large extent by the cinematic convention of almost irresistibly alluring yet untouched femininity, could in all naïveté have insinuated this glamorized symbol of sex into martial music. Nowadays marching bands must have as a rule not merely one drum majorette, but a whole corps of them, flanked (metaphorically speaking) by subsidiary Corybantes called *twirlers.*

Among other suffixes widely used are *-ee* (*donee, returnee, draftee, trainee, selectee, giftee, forgettee, addressee, baby sittee*), *-eer* (*racketeer, blacketeer* "black market racketeer," *donuteer* "girl who served many doughnuts in a USO canteen in Champaign, Illinois," *fashioneer, junketeer, fountaineer* "soda jerk," *vacationeer, fictioneer, budgeteer, chariteer* "professional beggar for charity," *oilateer* "gas-station attendant," *upper-bracketeer, gadgeteer, sloganeer*), *-orium* (*odditorium, lubritorium* "place where cars are greased," *pantatorium* "place where pants are pressed," *shavatorium, barberatorium, shoetorium, corsetorium, spaghettorium, pastorium*), *-ine* (*dudine* "girl on dude ranch," *chorine* "chorus girl"), *-ster* (*gangster, mobster, roadster, pollster, schoolster* "pupil," *Jeepster* "type of sports car"), *-dom* (*gangdom, gangsterdom, mobdom, fandom, moviedom, filmdom*), and *-ery* (*hashery, beanery, shoe-fixery* and, from the eighteenth century, *printery* and *grocery*, with *groggery, bakery*, and *bindery* appearing early in the nineteenth). The suffix *-eer* acquired derogatory connotations from *profiteer* and *patrioteer*, both British coinages of the twentieth century. In many of the Americanisms with this suffix, however, it is notable that there is no such connotation; only *racketeer* and *blacketeer*, perhaps *fictioneer*, have it among the examples cited. Certainly *toileteer* "plumber specializing in the installation and care of water closets" has nothing pejorative about it, nor has its synonym *flushologist*, both of which appeared in the four-column newspaper advertising "spread" of a plumbing supply company in Jacksonville, Florida. *Odditorium* was probably an independent coinage of the late Robert L. ("Believe It or Not") Ripley, with whom the word is invariably associated, though an earlier British use has been unearthed. *Pastorium* is used in all seriousness by members of the Baptist fold for *parsonage*.

Word elements freely used in combinations are *-burger* and *-furter*, both of which, because of their foreign origin, will be discussed in the following chapter. The *-wich* has been taken from *sandwich* and used in much the same way as *-burger* and *-furter*, though not so widely as the former: *duckwich* and *turkeywich* have been cited in the pages of *American Speech* in recent years and *Spamwich* was for a time fairly common, but this is a poor showing indeed compared with the prodigious offspring of *-burger*. *Cavalcade* furnished the popular word element *-cade: motorcade, autocade, musicade, aquacade*, and a number of similar combinations have frequently achieved the dignity of print. *Icecapade* "skating show" is doubtless a blend of *ice escapade*, but may well have been suggested by the numerous *-cade* words with which it rimes. *-Mobile* occurs in *bookmobile* "traveling library," *clubmobile, snowmobile, skimobile, foodmobile, bloodmobile* "traveling blood bank," *chowmobile* "canteen type of trailer," *whoopmobile* "bus to pick up New Year's Eve celebrants unable to drive their own cars," *jeepmobile* "bookmobile on a jeep," and *vetmobile* "midget auto constructed for a veteran paralyzed from the waist down."

The earliest *-buster* combinations are probably *bronco-buster, trust-buster*, and *belly buster*, all occurring in the latter years of the nineteenth century. Since then, the following, along with many others, have appeared: *gang-buster, racket buster, union-buster, factory buster* "six-ton missile," *button-buster, block-buster, atom-buster, par-buster* (in golf). Combinations with *-crazy, -happy, -wise, -conscious, -struck,* and *-minded* are freely made: *girl-crazy* (and *boy-crazy*), *stir-crazy* "too long in prison," *stage-crazy; slap-happy, bark-happy* (of watchdogs), *fight-happy, stripe-happy* (of a soldier itching for promotion), *trigger-happy; marketwise, stylewise, budgetwise, fightwise; social-conscious, class-conscious, race-conscious, profit-conscious; girl-struck* (and vice versa), *stage-struck, movie-struck; social-minded, security-minded, federation-minded* — these are the merest sampling.

Most of the processes which have been discussed in this chapter are, as has been pointed out, not new, nor are they exclusively American. But the freedom with which they are employed and the attitude towards life they sometimes mirror may certainly be regarded as characteristic of the America of our times. Along with much that is silly, much that is churlish and tasteless, and much that is nauseatingly arch, we have encountered much that is vigorous and vital and wonderfully apt. That American English has been inventive and resourceful no one who has examined the evidence could ever gainsay, nor is it disputable that it has struck fire more often than it has missed: the amazing number of Americanisms that have been adopted by the mother country — not that we should be too much impressed by this — is merely an indication of the American talent for saying things pungently and expressively. What is fittest in language has a way of surviving, as the admirable *O.K., the real McCoy, highbrow, crook, lengthy, haywire, panhandle, roughneck, Annie Oakley,* and *bawl out* — to mention only a few of the finer linguistic growths to spring from our soil — have done. What is graceless or fraudulent or ponderously "cute" — heaven knows sufficient examples have been cited in the course of this volume — ekes out a banal and colorless existence among the silly, the sentimental, and the addlepated, whose name is legion but whose influence is fortunately small.

In its vocabulary American English has indeed manifested the daring, the boldness, and the initiative which have so often been attributed to it on other, and usually irrelevant, grounds. Here there has been and is a warmth, an enthusiasm, a youthfulness of spirit that all the awesome powers of all the teachers and all the textbooks have failed to blight.

M. M. Mathews

REVIEW OF LEXICOGRAPHIC METHODS

ﰥﰥ

Where does one get the material to write about the histories of words? The primary sources must be the dictionaries. The thirteen sample entries gathered by M. M. Mathews, himself a distinguished lexicographer, reveal not only what vast differences in the kinds and amount of information appear in various dictionaries, but also how the full entries with their many citations and dates show the life-history of a word.

Dictionaries are by no means modern creations, but at the present time they possess features that may fairly be referred to as modern — features that were not even thought of when the first dictionaries appeared.

A good method for (1) showing how dictionaries have become what they are at present, and for (2) indicating the directions in which further developments will have to be made, is to take some common word and show its treatment at the hands of successive lexicographers from very early times to the present. The word *fraternity* is a good one for this purpose. How it has been dealt with in dictionaries from the beginning of the seventeenth century to the present time may be shown as follows.

(1) 1604 Cawdrey

Fraternitie, brotherhood.

Reprinted from *A Survey of English Dictionaries* by M. M. Mathews by permission of the Clarendon Press, Oxford.

(2) 1616 Bullokar

Fraternitie. A brotherhood.

(3) 1658 Phillips

Fraternity (lat.) a brother-hood, also a company of men entered into a firm bond of society, or friendship.

(4) 1754 Martin

Frate'rnity, 1 brotherhood; 2 society, or company.

(5) 1755 Johnson

Frate'rnity, n.s. [*fraternité*, French; *fraternitas*, Latin].
1. The state or quality of a brother.
2. Body of men united; corporation; society; association; brotherhood.

'Tis a necessary rule in alliances, societies, and *fraternities,* and all manner of civil contracts, to have a strict regard to the humour of those we have to do withal. *L'Estrange's Fables.*

3. Men of the same class or character.

With what terms of respect knaves and sots will speak of their own *fraternity. South's Sermons.*

(6) 1789 Sheridan

Fraternity, fra¹ teŕ¹ ni¹ ty¹, s. the state or quality of a brother; body of men united, corporation, society; men of the same class or character.

(7) 1826 Walker

Fraternity, fra-teŕ-ne¹-te¹, s. The state or quality of a brother; body of men united, corporation, society; men of the same class or character.

(8) 1828 Webster

Fratern'ity, n. [L. *fraternitas.*] The state or quality of a brother; brother hood.
2. A body of men associated for their common interest or pleasure; a company; a brotherhood; a society; as the *fraternity* of free masons.
3. Men of the same class, profession, occupation, or character.

With what terms of respect knaves and sots will speak of their own *fraternity. South.*

(9) 1836 Richardson

Frate'rnal, Frate'rnity, Frate'rnize, v., Fraterniza'tion, Frate'rnizer. Fr. *Fraternel;* It. *Fraternale;* Sp. *Fraternal;* Lat. *Fraternus;* from *frater,* a brother. The Northern word is probably the root of the Latin: by the literal changes, b, p, ph, f.

To *fraternize,* is a word revived, not created, during the French Revolution. Cotgrave says,

'*Fraternizer,* — to *fraternize,* concur with; be near unto, agree as brothers.'

Fraternal, — of or pertaining to brothers or brethren, to brotherhood; to those united or conjoined as brothers or brethren; brotherly.

With [him] were the templers, & ther *fraternite.*
Fals in alle maners, so tellis the storie me. *R. Brunne,* p. 188.
Thauh he be founde in *fraternite* of all fyve ordres. *Piers Plouhman,* p. 165.
A webbe, a deyer, and a tapiser,
Were alle yclothed in a livere,
Of a solempne and grete *fraternite.* — *Chaucer. Prologue.*
I would be loth to be judged by the only brethren and systers of the false *fraternitie.* — *Sir T. More, Workes,* p. 851.

Thus from the Laureat *fraternity* of Poets, riper years and the ceaseless round of study and reading, led me to the shady spaces of Philosophy; but chiefly to the divine volumes of Plato, and his equal Xenophon. *Id. Apology for Smectymnuus.*

And that M. Furius should ordain a guild, or *fraternitie* out of those that dwelt in the hil of the Capitoll, for the celebration of those plaies. —*Holland. Livivs,* p. 211.

It is also worth our while to consider with what terms of respect and commendation knaves and sots will speak of their own *fraternity.* —*South,* vol. ii, ser. 6.

Their first charter in which they are styled Peyntours, was granted in the 6th of Edward IV., but they had existed as a *fraternity* long before. *Walpole. Anecdotes of Painting,* vol. i, c. 4.

(10) 1847 Craig

Fraternity, fra-ter′-ne-te, s. (*fraternitas,* Lat.)

The state or quality of a brother; brotherhood; a body of men associated for their common interest or pleasure; a corporation; a company; a society; men of the same class, profession, occupation, or character. In Roman Catholic countries, the word *fraternity* is applied to certain societies which have certain prescribed religious duties and formalities to attend to — as that of the Rosary, who communicate every month, and repeat the rosary continually; of the Scapulary, whom the blessed Virgin, according to the sabbatical bull of Pope John XXII, has promised to deliver out of hell the first Sunday after their death; of St. Francis's Girdle, of St. Austin's Leathern Girdle, &c., &c. The Archfraternity of Charity, instituted by Pope Clement VII., distributes bread every Sunday among the poor, and gives portions to forty poor girls on the feast of St. Jerome, their patron. The Fraternity of Death bury the unclaimed and abandoned dead.

(11) 1860 Worcester

Fra-teŕ ni-ty, *n.* [L. *fraternitas*; It. *fraternita*; Sp. *fraternidad*; Fr. *fraternité.*]

1. State or quality of a brother. *Johnson.*
2. A body of men united for mutual interest or improvement; a society; an association; a brotherhood; as 'The Masonic *fraternity*'.
3. Men of the same occupation, class, or character.

'The . . . *fraternity* of poets.' — Milton

(12) 1889 *Century Dictionary*

fraternity (frā-tėr′ ni-ti), *n.*; pl. *fraternities* (-tiz). [⟨ME. *fraternite*, ⟨OF. *fraternite*, F. *fraternité* = Sp. *fraternidad* = Pg. *fraternidade* = It. *fraternità*, ⟨LL. *fraternita*(t-)*s*, a brotherhood, a fraternity, ⟨L. *fraternus*, brotherly, ⟨*frater* = E. *brother*: see *fraternal*, *friar*, *brother*.] 1. The relationship of a brother; the condition of being a brother or of being brothers; brotherhood. *E. Phillips* 1706. Hence — 2. That mutual interest and affection which is characteristic of the fraternal relation; brotherly regard and sympathy for others, regardless of relationship by blood; brotherhood in general.

For you I have only a comrade's constancy; a fellow-soldier's frankness, fidelity, *fraternity*, if you like; a neophyte's respect and submission to his hierophant; nothing more. *Charlotte Brontë*, Jane Eyre, xxxiv.

The first aspect in which Christianity presented itself to the world was as a declaration of the *fraternity* of men in Christ. *Lecky*, Europ. Morals, ii. 19.

3. A body of men associated by some natural tie, as of common interest or character, of common business or profession, or by some formal tie, as of organization for religious or social purposes; a company; a brotherhood; a society; as, a *fraternity* of monks; a college *fraternity*.

In ye begynnyng it is ordeynede yat yis *fraternite* shal be holden, at ye Chirche of seint Botulphe forsayde, on ye sonday next folowande ye Epiphany of oure lorde. *English Gilds* (E.E.T.S.), p. 15.

With what terms of respect knaves and sots will speak of their own *fraternity! South*, Sermons.

Their first charter, in which they are styled Peyntours, was granted in the 6th of Edward IV., but they had existed as a *fraternity* long before. *Walpole*, Anecdotes of Painting, I. iv.

The constitutions of many college *fraternities* are now open to the inspection of faculties; the most vigorous publish detailed accounts of their conventions and social gatherings. *The Century*, xxxvi. 759.

4. Specifically, in the *Rom. Cath. Ch.*, an organization of laymen for pious or charitable purposes, as the special worship of Christ, the honor of the Virgin Mary or of particular saints, the care of the distressed, sick, or dead, etc. Also called *confraternity*, *gild*, or *sodality*. = Syn. 3 and 4. Association, circle, sodality, league, clan.

(13) 1898 *Oxford English Dictionary*

Fraternity (frătɔr,nĭtĭ). [a. OF. *fraternité*, ad. L. *frāternitāt-em*, f. *frāternus* pertaining to a brother: see Fraternal and -ity.]

1. The relation of a brother or of brothers; brotherhood.

1390 Gower *Conf.* II. 186 In the virgine, where he [the godhede] nome Oure flesshe and verray man become Of bodely fraternite. 1582 Bentley *Mon. Matrones* ii. 22 O my brother what fraternitie! O my child what delectation! 1659 Pearson *Creed* (1839) 40 If sons, we must be brethren to the only-begotten: but being he came not to do his own will, but the will of him that sent him, he acknowledgeth no fraternity but with such as do the same. 1669 Gale *Crt. Gentiles* i. i. ii. 12 A Phenician Fable touching the Fraternitie of al men made out of the Earth.

2. The state or quality of being fraternal or brotherly; brotherliness.

1470–85 Malory *Arthur* xvi. iii, Therfor was the round table founden and the Chyualry hath ben at alle tymes soo by the fraternyte whiche was there that she myght not be ouercomen. 1598–9 E. Forde *Parismus* i. vi. (1636) 34 Those Out-lawes . . continued a great fraternity amongst them. 1605 Bacon *Adv. Learn.* ii. To the King § 13 There cannot but be a fraternitie in learning and illumination relating to that Paternitie which is attributed to God. 1793 Burke *Conduct of Minority* § 35 To substitute the principles of fraternity in the room of that salutary prejudice called our Country. 1844 Thirlwall *Greece* VIII. 255 It was a treaty of friendship, fraternity, and alliance. 1875 Jowett *Plato* (ed. 2) III. 106 Equality and fraternity of governors and governed.

†3. A family of brothers. *Obs. rare.*

a 1635 Naunton *Fragm. Reg.* (Arb.) 23 When there is an ample fraternity of the bloud Royall, and of the Princes of the Bloud. *Ibid.* 40 Between these two Families, there was . . no great correspondencie . . there was a time when (both these Fraternities being met at Court) there passed a challenge between them.

4. A body or order of men organized for religious or devout purposes.

Letters of fraternity: letters granted by a convent or an order to its benefactors entitling those named in them to a share in the benefits of its prayers and good works.
c 1330 R. Brunne *Chron.* (1810) 188 With [þam] were þe templers, & þer fraternite. 1362 Langl. *P. Pl.* A. viii. 179 Thauh thou be founden in fraternite a-mong the foure ordres. *c* 1380 Wyclif *Wks.* (1880) 12 ʒif þei maken wyues and oþer wymmen hure sustris bi lettris of fraternite. 1401 *Pol. Poems* (Rolls) II. 29 Why be ye so hardie to grant by letters of fraternitie to men and women, that they shall have part and merite of all your good deedes? *a* 1512 Fabyan *Will* in *Chron.* Pref. 5 To the fraternytie of our Lady and seynt Anne, wᵗin the said church xii d. 1653 H. Cogan tr. *Pinto's Trav.* xxvii. 105 Like unto the fraternity of mercy among the Papists, which onely out of charity . . do tend those that are sick. 1703 Maundrell *Journ. Jerus.* (1732) 70 Each Fraternity have their Altars and Sanctuary. 1788 Priestley *Lect. Hist.* iv. xxv. 193 In each mitred abbey of the order of St. Benedict, some persons of the fraternity

were appointed to register the most considerable events. 1851 D. WILSON *Preh. Ann.* (1863) II. IV. viii. 398 The first recluses and monks who established religious fraternities in Scotland.

5. A body of men associated by some tie or common interest; a company, guild.

c 1386 CHAUCER *Prol.* 364 An Haberdassher and a Carpenter . . clothed in o liveree, Of a solempne and greet fraternitee. 1389 in *Eng. Gilds* (1870) 4 Eche broþer oþer suster þᵗ ben of þe fraternite . . schal ȝeue somwhat in maintenance of þe bretherhede. 1433 *E. E. Wills* (1882) 95 The fraternyte of my crafte of cokes. 1483 CAXTON *Cato* 2, I William Caxton . . of the fraternyte and felauship of the mercerye. 1611 CORYAT *Crudities* 13 This dooth the fraternity of the shoemakers carry in solemne procession. *a* 1674 CLARENDON *Hist. Reb.* xv. § 15 Fraternities enter'd into there for the better carrying on that Plantation. 1762 H. WALPOLE *Vertue's Anecd. Paint.* I. iv. 59 Their first charter in which they are styled Peyntours, was granted in the 6th of Edward IV, but they had existed as a fraternity long before. 1851 D. WILSON *Preh. Ann.* (1863) II. iv. viii. 442 The ancient . . fraternity of Free Masons. 1870 YEATS *Techn. Hist. Comm.* 358 Scarcely a town of importance . . in Italy was without its fraternity of goldsmiths.

attrib. 1671 EVELYN *Diary* 21 Sept., I din'd in the City, at the fraternity feast in yron-mongers Hall.

6. A body of men of the same class, occupation, pursuits, etc.

1561 AWDELAY (*title*), The Fraternitye of Vacabondes. 1653 WALTON *Angler* i. 5 *Auceps.* Why Sir, I pray, of what Fraternity are you, that you are so angry with the poor Otter! *Pisc.* I am . . a Brother of the Angle. 1686 N. Cox *Gentl. Recreat.* v. (ed. 3) 44 Some ignorant Grooms . . think they are able to give Laws to all their Fraternity. 1712 HENLEY *Spect.* No. 396. ⟨ 2 The Fraternity of the People called Quakers. 1793 BURKE *Conduct of Minority* § 25 The French fraternity in that town. 1838 *Murray's Handbk. N. Germany* 91 Calais is one of those places where the fraternity of couriers have a station. 1858 FROUDE *Hist. Eng.* III xv. 269 [Henry] was . . ardently anxious to resume his place in the fraternity of European sovereigns.

This list of successive entries possesses some interesting features. The most striking thing about it is the increasing fullness of treatment that characterizes the later dictionaries. Later dictionaries improve upon earlier ones, not only in completeness of treatment, however, but also in accuracy. For example, Johnson (see entry 5 above), in giving the source of *Fraternity* was content to give the Latin word from which it comes, but in the O.E.D. (see entry 13), the more exact information is given that the English word is ultimately derived from an oblique case of the Latin word. This gain in accuracy is also noticeable in the use of illustrative citations. A comparison of Johnson's illustrative excerpts with those found in the O.E.D. shows quite well the gain in specificness.

Benjamin Martin, whose dictionary is cited in 4 above, was a lexicographer whose work is characterized by the care taken in it to differentiate the various meanings of words. Martin distinguished eighteen 'significations', as he called them, possessed by the verb *set*. The first edition of his dictionary was published in 1749. Entries 6 and 7 show early attempts at indicating pronunciation by using numbers which referred to a table of sounds. Entry 10 shows that Craig's dictionary had some encyclopedic features, though these occur only rarely in it.

A close examination of these specimen treatments shows that a meaning of *Fraternity* quite common in the United States did not attract the attention of lexicographers till comparatively recent times. In *The Century* (see number 12 above), the fact is pointed out that the word sometimes refers to a 'college *fraternity*', and one citation, the date of which is 1888, is given to illustrate that meaning. In later American dictionaries, like the *New Standard* and the *New International,* this meaning receives generous notice. As a matter of fact, the word is used in the United States more often than not to refer to Greek letter societies in colleges and universities. In 1776 the first society of this kind was organized at the College of William and Mary in Virginia. It is clear that from the very beginning the members referred to the organization as a society or as a fraternity, using the two terms quite indifferently, as is shown by recently collected examples of the use of *fraternity* from 1777 onwards.

For three-quarters of a century, however, college men were not very numerous in the United States, and naturally fraternity men were not much in evidence. The result was that *fraternity* in the sense of a Greek letter society, was, generally speaking, confined to a small group, and failed to penetrate thoroughly into common use. In time fraternity men became numerous, the proceedings of their organizations were printed, and the developed sense of *fraternity* finally gained recognition at the hands of lexicographers.

During the years that dictionaries have been evolving into such works as they are to-day, changes have taken place in the methods of compiling them. Unfortunately not much is known about the methods employed by the earliest dictionary makers. . . .

As a rule, the first step taken in preparing the material for a dictionary is to prepare a 'slip' for each word to be dealt with — a 'slip' being a piece of paper approximately four inches by six inches in size. The kind of information placed on the slip depends upon the purpose and scope of the contemplated dictionary. Nearly all the slips used in preparing a dictionary on historical principles contain the 'catch word', written in the upper left-hand corner, and a passage from some book, newspaper, &c., illustrating the use of the 'catch word'. The source of the passage, the author's name, when known, the date, and the page on which the extract is found are given in some such fashion as shown on the following specimen slips:

Tomahawk, n.

1809 A. Henry, *Travels*, 41.

They walked in single file, each with his tomahawk in one hand, and scalping knife in the other.

Tile-fish, n.

1898 *Boston Record*, 16 Aug. 4/2.

The U.S. fish commission has located a school of 'tile-fish' off Cape Cod. This valuable food fish was first discovered in 1879. . . . The fish taste like cusk and are very edible. They range from 6 to 50 lb. in weight and can be roughly classed as between channel bass and codfish.

The extract in specimen two is longer than necessary for a dictionary entry, but the entire passage is worth giving because it contains information that may be of use to the editor when he writes the definition of tile-fish.

When a sufficiently large number of slips have been provided and arranged in alphabetical order, the work of editing them may be begun. The slips that contain passages illustrating the same meaning of the word concerned are arranged in the order of their dates and placed together. When this preliminary arrangement has been made for a word in all its meanings, additional slips are prepared, showing the spelling, pronunciation, etymology, and definitions of the word. These slips are then inserted in their proper places.

The editing of a dictionary is work that demands the best care of a capable scholar, but collecting material in slip form can be done by any one with sufficient leisure. Word hunting is an interesting pastime, and the interest which it possesses led hundreds of voluntary readers to supply hundreds and thousands of slips to the editors of the O.E.D. for their use in compiling that dictionary.

Ernest Weekley

LIVES OF WORDS

✍✍

"... according to the Oxford Dictionary ..." Here are three demonstrations of scholarly and imaginative use of the rich resources of an historical dictionary to reconstruct the course of the changing meanings and uses of words. Citations illustrate the chronological stages in each word's life-history, but it takes an inquiring mind like Mr. Weekley's to provide the connections and suggest larger implications. Compare what Mr. Weekley has created to the entries from the O.E.D. which follow his discussions.

BLACKMAIL

An interested foreigner, trying to glean from the daily Press some idea of "England, its people, polity and pursuits," might be excused for coming to the conclusion that one of the chief interests of the more leisured class is *blackmail,* active or passive.[1] The word and the thing are now so common, that it is difficult to realize that the practice, at any rate in its most efficient form, is essentially a contemporary feature of social progress. The Oxford Dictionary's first quotation for *blackmail* in a sense approaching that now current is from Macaulay's essay on Clive. The Dictionary's definition, formulated in 1888, runs, "any payment extorted by intimidation or pressure, or levied by unprincipled officials, critics, journalists, etc., upon those whom they have it in their power to help or injure." If this definition were to be rewritten in the light of the latest research, I imagine that the "officials, critics and journalists" would take second place, and the "etc." would come into their own. The scale of the science has also been

---

[1] This article appeared in the Observer at a time when two amazing blackmail cases filled the greater part of the daily papers.

Reprinted from *Words Ancient and Modern* by Ernest Weekley (London: John Murray, Inc., 1958), by permission of the publisher.

so intelligently enlarged that the trifling baksheesh with which the 19th-century blackmailer was satisfied would hardly pay the postal expenses of a modern operator.

So far as the Oxford Dictionary records go, it would seem that the practice of extorting money by the threat of damaging publicity was first developed in the United States. At any rate, the earliest quotation for the word *blackmailer* is from the New York Herald (1868). English travellers in the past have mostly used it in reference to the tribute levied by Arab sheikhs and other Eastern potentates for permission to pass through their territory unharmed.

There is a very considerable gap between the contemporary applications of the word and its earliest use as a respectable legal term. Like so much of our administrative vocabulary, *mail* is a Viking word. It is found in various forms in all the Teutonic languages (Old Norse *māl*, Anglo-Sax. *mæthel*, Old High Ger. *mahal*, Goth. *mathl*), with the general idea of meeting, speech, agreement, contract, etc., and is copiously recorded in English, from the 11th century onward, in the sense of payment, tax, rent. But it has always been especially a North Country word, preserving its proper sense only in Scotland, where a rent-paying tenant is still in some districts a *mailer*.

There are also compounds descriptive of the type of tenancy, such as *grass-mail* and *land-mail*, or of the method of payment, such as *silver-mail* and *black-mail*. We do not know the original meaning of the latter. Camden conjectured that the *black* referred to copper coin, and the fact that we find *white-rent* used as equivalent to *silver-mail* lends some plausibility to this view. But the accepted legal sense of *black-mail* was, according to the Oxford Dictionary, "rent reserved in labour, produce, etc., as distinguished from *white-rents*, which were reserved in *white money*, or silver."

Such dues usually come to be regarded as oppressive and extortionate, and the forbidding adjective *black* would not help to make the word popular. So it was adopted, no doubt by the victims, as the name for the tribute exacted from farmers and landholders by the freebooters of the Border and the Highland chiefs neighbouring on the Lowlands. The system was, compared with modern blackmailing, quite straight business. The bandit undertook, in consideration of an annual contribution, to guarantee the contributor against the exactions of all other bandits. If he failed to do so, he felt as humiliated as the Arab chief who allows travellers who have paid him for safe-conduct to be massacred by marauders trespassing on his territory. In other words, there was a *quid pro quo*, and the blackmailer did not adopt towards his public the "heads I win, tails you lose" policy of a modern trust or trade union.

The contemporary currency of the word remains a problem. As a Highland industry *blackmail* died out after the Forty-five, and in England much earlier. Rose Bradwardine informed Edward Waverley that not the boldest Highland cateran would "steal a hoof from anyone that pays blackmail to Vich Ian Vohr," and, in reply to his puzzled "And what is blackmail?" gave him the classic definition of the term: "a sort of protection-money that Low-country gentlemen and heritors, lying near the Highlands, pay to some Highland chief, that he may neither do them harm himself, nor suffer it to be done to them by others" (Waverley, ch. 15). But Scott, writing in 1829, found it necessary to add one of his historical Notes on the subject. It is quite probable that the revival of this archaic word was due, like that of so many others, to the popularity of the Waverley Novels.

DISEASE

Our mental reaction to the sound of a word has little to do with its musical quality or its etymological meaning. It is almost entirely a question of association. There is hardly a more repellent word in English than *disease*, though it has no more intrinsic horror in it than *discomfort*, which has become weakened just as *disease* has become strengthened: "The abhomynacioun of discomfort that is said of Danyel the prophete" (Wyclif, Matt. xxiv. 15).

The history of *disease* illustrates the inevitable fate of the euphemism, its gradual acquisition of a sense more unpleasant than that of the older term which it was intended to avoid. When we wish to describe what is *nasty* or *dirty*, we forsake these old words, once much stronger than now, and try to express our feelings more fully with *disgusting* and *unsavoury*, mere euphemisms which mean no more than distasteful. The extreme of human depravity is expressed in *infamous*, and any number of the most desolating epithets can be coined by the use of that amazing *un-* which we can prefix to nearly every adjective in the language: "We have our profound and powerful particle in our *undone, unloved, unforgiven*, the *un-* that summons in order that it may banish, and keeps the living word present to hear sentence and denial" (Alice Meynell).

To return to the word *disease*, the Anglo-Saxon was unaffectedly and unashamedly *sick*. Early Mid. English borrowed from Old Norse the word *ill*, with the general sense of evil which it still has in "ill weeds grow apace," "it's an ill wind that blows no one good," etc. In the 15th century this began to compete with *sick*, though it is not used in the Bible in this sense, and in Shakespeare is usually semi-adverbial ("to look ill," etc.). As the older *sick* came to denote one particular symptom of bodily discomfort, it was gradually expelled from the polite vocabulary in the general sense of bad health, except in the literary style, in the United States, and in such compounds as *sick-list*. When a word expressive of mere indisposition was needed, *disease* naturally presented itself.

It is an old word in English, having been borrowed c. 1300 from Old Fr. *desaise*, and, as late as the 16th century, it was still used in its etymological sense: "Thy doughter is deed: why deseasest thou the master eny further" (Tyndale, Mark v. 35). Where we should now speak of being a little indisposed or unwell, Wriothesley, in his Chronicle (1553), speaks of Edward VI as "a little diseased from catching cold." But, before the century was out, *disease* was being used of dangerous maladies, and in 1602 Shakespeare wrote:

> Diseases desperate grown,
> By desperate appliance are relieved.
> (Hamlet, iv. 3.)

So the 18th century, in search of a word to describe a state of health for which *diseased* had become, by association, too strong, introduced *unwell*, already long familiar in Scotland and Ireland. It appears that it was Lord Chesterfield who gave polite currency to the new euphemism, so gracefully used in our own times by Private Mulvaney: " 'Let me out, bhoys,' sez I, backin' in among thim. I'm goin' to be onwell' " (With the Main-Guard).

MAGAZINE

An intelligence test on a hundred modern children would, I suppose, show, as the immediate reaction of 99 per cent. to the sound of this word, the mental picture of a paper cover adorned by the figure of a shapely damsel, in a costume, or lack of costume, more or less appropriate to the season. This literary sense of the word is, however, only about two centuries old, and the shapely damsel, still absent from the serious and historic magazines, is merely a symptom of the wider appeal which results from the existence of an educated democracy.

A *magazine* is a store-house, now usually associated with gunpowder, but in the 16th century with any kind of goods. Fr. *magasin* is still a warehouse, though, from being applied to the great multiple stores, it has come to be a polite substitute for *boutique*, a shop.

Magazine, like *arsenal* (It. *arsenale*, Arab *al-sinaah*, the workshop), is a reminder of the power once exercised by the Arabs over the Mediterranean. It is Arab. *makhazīn*, the plural of *makhzan*, a warehouse, from *khazana*, to store up. It reached us via Fr. *magasin* or It. *magazzino*. Sp. *almacén* preserves, like many other Spanish words, the Arabic definite article *al*. Torriano has "*magazzino*: a ware-house, a store-house, a magazine," and "*magazzino d'artegliaria*: an arsenall or store-house for artillerie," a sense which eventually became predominant in English.

Introduced by the 16th-century travellers and merchant-venturers, the word was, as early as Ben Jonson, used in the figurative sense of treasury, intellectual wealth. In 1731 appeared the first number of The Gentleman's Magazine, described in the Introduction as "a monthly collection to treasure up, as in a magazine, the most remarkable pieces on the subjects above-mentioned." This was imitated in the names of later rival publications, so that *magazine* eventually became a vague term for a periodical.

The more purely literary *review* is of earlier date. Apparently the title was first used in English by Defoe, who began the publication of The Review when in prison in 1704 and continued it till its suppression in 1713. The Annual Register (established in 1758) aimed at "uniting the plan of the magazines and that of the reviews."

EXAMPLES FROM THE

Oxford English Dictionary

Black mail. Also **black-mail, blackmail.** [f. MAIL = rent, tribute.]
1. *Hist.* A tribute formerly exacted from farmers and small owners in the border counties of England and Scotland, and along the Highland border, by freebooting chiefs, in return for protection or immunity from plunder.
1552 ABP. HAMILTON *Catech.* (1884) 98 Quhay takis ouer sair mail, ouer mekle ferme, or ony blake maillis, fra thair tennands. *c* **1561** R. MAITLAND *Thievis Liddesd.* vi, Commoun taking of blak maill. **1567** *Scot. Act Jas. VI*, (1597) xxi, Diuers subjects of the Inland, takis and sittis vnder their assurance, payand them black-maill, and permittand them to reif, herrie, and oppresse their Nichtbouris. **1601** *Act* 43 *Eliz.* xiii, Sundry of her Maiesties louing Subiects within the sayd [4 northern] Counties..have been inforced to pay a certaine rate of money, corne, cattell, or other consideration, commonly there called by the name of Blacke maile. **1707** *Addr. fr. Cumbrld.* in *Lond. Gaz.* No. 4334/2 There is, now, no Debatable Land to contend for; no Black Mail to be paid to the Leaders of the Robbers, as a Ransom. **1768** BLACKSTONE *Comm.* IV. 263. **1814** SCOTT *Wav.* l. 222 The boldest of them will never steal a hoof from any one that pays black-mail to Vich Ian Vohr. **1875** STUBBS *Const. Hist.* II. xvi. 344 Preferring to pay blackmail to the Scots.
2. By extension : Any payment extorted by intimidation or pressure, or levied by unprincipled officials, critics, journalists, etc. upon those whom they have it in their power to help or injure.
1840 MACAULAY *Clive, Ess.* (1854) II. 503 Even the wretched phantom who still bore the imperial title stooped to pay this ignominious black-mail. **1860** MRS. HARVEY *Cruise Claymore* II. 216 Arabs infesting the country, and levying blackmail on all passers-by. **1863** LONGF. *Birds Killingw.* 36 Marauders who, in lieu of pay, Levied black mail upon the garden beds.
†3. *Law.* Rent reserved in labour, produce, etc., as distinguished from 'white rents,' which were reserved in 'white money' or silver. *Obs.* (Coke's and Blackstone's explanation of *redditus nigri*, which Camden appears to have taken for rents in 'black money' or copper.)
1605 CAMDEN *Rem.* 205 Black money (what that was I know not, if it were not of Copper, as *Maill* and *Blackmaill*). **1642** COKE *Inst.* II. *Magna Ch.* viii, Work-days, rent cummin, rent corn, etc. .. called *Redditus nigri*, black maile, that is, black rents. **1768** BLACKSTONE *Comm.* II. 42.

Black-mai·l, *v.* [f. prec.] *trans.* To levy black mail upon ; to extort money from by intimidation, by the unscrupulous use of an official or social position, or of political influence or vote.
1880 L. OLIPHANT *Gilead* ix. 265 The sheikh .. black-mails travellers. **1882** W. WEEDEN *Soc. Law Labor* 176 The chief .. would protect and blackmail him.
Hence **Blac.x-mai·ler, Black-mai·ling** *vbl. sb.* and *ppl. a.* (modern words referring chiefly to the levying of BLACK-MAIL in sense 2.)
1868 *N. York Herald* 24 Apr., The Quixotic enterprise of the lobbyists and blackmailers. **1879** J. HAWTHORNE *Laugh. Mill* 108 Were I to lose all my fortune, I could, by turning black-mailer, ensure a permanent income twice as large. **1884** *Pall Mall. G.* 27 Feb. 4/1 Introducing a system of blackmailing even worse than that which prevailed before. **1884** *Harper's Mag.* Mar. 567/1 The black-mailing vixen.

Disease (dizī·z), *sb.* Forms: 4 **deses, deisese, disseease, dishese,** 4–5 **disese, -sese, desese, dysese,** 5 **disess, -cese, -ees**(e, **-sesse, -easse, desesse, -eas, -eyce, dyses, -esse, -hese, -sese, -ase, -easse, -eze, -zese, -eysse,** 5–6 **dysease, -sease,** *Sc.* **diseis,** 6 **desease, disseyse, dysseasse,** *Sc.* **dises,** :– **disease.** [ME. *di-, desese,* a. AF. *disease, desaese* (Stat. Rich. II), OF. *desaise, -ayse* (14th c. in Godef.), f. *des-,* DIS- 4 + *aise* EASE *sb.*]
†1. Absence of ease ; uneasiness, discomfort ; inconvenience, annoyance ; disquiet, disturbance ; trouble. *Obs.*
In later use, generally with distinct reference to the etym. elements of the word : cf. DISEASE *v.* 1.
c **1330** R. BRUNNE *Chron.* (1810) 166 Go and mak his pes, or he do þe more stoure, And þou to þi deses may haf þe frute and floure. **1388** WYCLIF *John* xvi. 33 In the world 3e schulen haue disese. *c* **1410** LOVE *Bonavent. Mirr.* xxvii, His disciples were in the see in grete disese. *c* **1450** *Merlin* 54 Thei shull haue grete dissesse for lakke of water. *a* **1547** SURREY in *Tottell's Misc.* (Arb.) 22 Till thou know my hole disseyse my hart can haue no rest. **1615** CHAPMAN *Odyss.* IV. 1088 Doth sleep thus seize Thy powers, affected

with so much dis-ease? **1623** LISLE *Ælfric on O. & N. Test.* Ded. xxiii, Some grudge of old disease, Which will enforce us fortifie our townes.

† b. A cause of discomfort or distress; a trouble. an annoyance, a grievance. *Obs.*

c **1386** CHAUCER *Nun's Pr. Prol.* 5 It is a greet disese, Where as men han been in greet welthe and ese, To heeren of hire sodeyn fal. **1443** *Paston Lett.* No. 36 I. 49 Sende me a letter as hastely as ȝe may, yf wrytyn be non dysesse to yow. *a* **1667** JER. TAYLOR *Serm.* xxv. § 5 Wks. 1847–54 IV. 641 The disemployed is a disease, and like a long sleepless night to himself, and a load to his country. **1712** PRIDEAUX *Direct. Ch.-wardens* (ed. 4) 59 [It] is only for their own ease, and that must not be made a dis-ease to the rest of the Parish.

† c. Molestation. *To do disease to*, to molest.

c **1400** MAUNDEV. (Roxb.) xxi. 98 Nedders and oþer venymous bestez of þat cuntree duse na diseese to na straungers ne pilgrimes. *c* **1440** *Gesta Rom.* II. xxvi. (1838) 353 The Emperour comaundede, that no man shulde dispoile the ymages.. ne to hem do no disease. **1493** *Festivall* (W. de W. 1515) 71 To praye for his enemys and them that.. dyde him dysease.

2. A condition of the body, or of some part or organ of the body, in which its functions are disturbed or deranged; a morbid physical condition; 'a departure from the state of health, especially when caused by structural change' (*Syd. Soc. Lex.*). Also applied to a disordered condition in plants.

(A gradual restriction of sense 1, in early use only contextual: cf. the similar use of 'trouble' in dialects.)

a. *gen.* The condition of being (more or less seriously) out of health; illness, sickness.

1393 GOWER *Conf.* III. 35 He was full of such disese, That he may nought the deth escape. *a* **1400–50** *Alexander* 2549 He was fallen in a feuire.. þai.. said ilkane to othire: Be is disese to ser Darie and his dukis knawen, He sall vs. surely encounbre. **1555** EDEN *Decades* Pref. to Rdr. (Arb.) 53 Least thy disease become vncurable. **1727–46** THOMSON *Summer* 1035 The dire power of pestilent disease. **1788** GIBBON *Decl. & F.* I. (1846) V. 10 The legions of Augustus melted away in disease and lassitude. **1875** H. C. WOOD *Therap.* (1879) 21 Disease often fortifies the system against the action of remedies. **1879** E. GARRETT *House by Works* II. 42 Suppressing disease instead of curing it.

b. An individual case or instance of such a condition; an illness, ailment, malady, disorder.

1526 *Pilgr. Perf.* (W. de W. 1531) 38 Cured many diseases or sycknesses. **1552** LATIMER *Serm. & Rem.* (1845) II. 67 [The burial ground being within the city] be the occasion of much sickness and diseases. **1602** SHAKS. *Ham.* IV. iii. 9 Diseases, desperate growne, By desperate appliance are releeued. **1671** MILTON *Samson* 618 My griefs.. pain me As

a lingering disease. **1765** A. DICKSON *Treat. Agric.* viii. (ed. 2) 83 The diseases of plants we may possibly do something to prevent, but we can do little to remove. **1847** EMERSON *Repr. Men, Montaigne* Wks. (Bohn) I. 343 To entertain you with the records of his disease.

c. Any one of the various kinds of such conditions; a species of disorder or ailment, exhibiting special symptoms or affecting a special organ.

Often with defining words, indicating its nature, or derived from the name of a person who has suffered from it, or of the physician who first diagnosed it: e.g. *Addison's disease*, a structural disease of the suprarenal capsules, resulting in anæmia and loss of strength, and commonly characterized by a brownish-olive discoloration of the skin (see BRONZED 4); first described by Thomas Addison (1793–1860). *Bad disease, foul disease*, names for syphilis (*Syd. Soc. Lex.*). BLUE *disease*, BRIGHT'S DISEASE, FISH-SKIN *disease*, FOOT-AND-MOUTH DISEASE, FRENCH *disease*, POTATO *disease*, etc.: see these words.

1460–70 *Bk. Quintessence* 18 Oure quinte essence auri et perelarum heelith þese disesis. **1555** EDEN *Decades* 230 The disease of saynt Iob whiche wee caule the frenche poxe. **1651** HOBBES *Leviath.* II. xxix. 173 A Disease, which resembleth the Pleurisie. **1725** N. ST. ANDRÉ in *Lond. Gaz.* No. 6349/1 The .. Woman had the Foul Disease. **1727–51** CHAMBERS *Cycl., Diseases of plants* .. Mildew, a kind of epidemical disease. **1799** *Med. Jrnl.* II. 183 The diseases of human teeth and bones. **1836** *Penny Cycl.* VI. 93/2 Cabbages are subject to a peculiar disease .. called clubbing. **1885** *Law Times* LXXIX. 161/2 The mare was suffering from no catching disease.

3. *fig.* A deranged, depraved, or morbid condition (of mind or disposition, of the affairs of a community, etc.); an evil affection or tendency.

1509 HAWES *Past. Pleas.* XVI. xlviii, A, a ! said Counseyle, doubte ye never a dele, But your disease I shal by wysdome hele. **1597** SHAKS. *2 Hen. IV*, I. ii. 138 It is the disease of not Listning, the malady of not Marking, that I am troubled withall. **1607** ROWLANDS *Famous Hist.* 57 Ambitious pride hath been my youths disease. *a* **1661** FULLER *Worthies, Warwicksh.*, Bad Latin was a catching disease in that age. **1785** FRANKLIN *Lett.* Wks. 1840 VI. 526 The common causes of the smoking of chimneys.. the principles on which both the disease and the remedy depend. **1844** EMERSON *Lect., New Eng. Ref.* Wks. (Bohn) I. 266 The disease with which the human mind now labours is want of faith.

4. *Comb.*, as *disease-germ, -maker*; *disease-causing, -resisting, -spreading*, etc.. adjs.

1865 TYLOR *Early Hist. Man.* vi. 128 In the New Hebrides, there was a colony of disease-makers. **1883** *Chamb. Jrnl.* 27 What is known .. in regard to the nature of disease-germs. **1886** *Athenæum* 7 Aug. 178/1 The coffee tree is the patient, the fungus .. is the disease-causing agent. **1890** *Daily News* 22 Oct. 5/4 The disease-resisting potatoes.

Robert M. Estrich • Hans Sperber

CHANGE OF MEANING

✍✍

Here are two studies in depth ("Loco-foco" and "copperhead") as illustrations of one theory to explain change of meaning. Professors Estrich and Sperber try to recover and recreate the full circumstances which generated sufficient emotional pressure to gain mass acceptance for a new meaning of an old word. "Collective preparedness" must precede change. It is not surprising that the moments which they can recreate most fully come from our political history (compare Pyles' essay), for as de Tocqueville noted, as early as 1835, we are a most passionately political nation.

Meaning, as well as every other feature of language, is subject to constant fluctuations. The same meaning never occurs twice. Even a commonplace phrase like "my daughter" has not the identical significance today that it had yesterday. The short intervening space of time has brought with it certain changes in her growth, in her knowledge, in her attitude toward persons and things, as well as in my attitude toward her. Accordingly, the meaning of today's "my daughter" can be defined as "my daughter as she was yesterday plus all the changes that have occurred during the last twenty-four hours."

However, in speaking of changes of meaning, we do not, in general, think of these minor fluctuations but, rather, of certain phenomena on a larger scale that become apparent if we confront modern vocabularies with earlier stages of the same language. Discounting certain phonetic changes, we consider our "meat" to be the same word as Middle-English *mete*, which means "food"; we identify "cheek" with Anglo-Saxon *ceace* "jaw"; and "starve" with Anglo-Saxon *steorfan*, which means "to die." On the basis of these identifications, we pronounce these words to have undergone not mere occasional fluctuations of meaning but established and general changes of meaning. It is the task of the linguist, of course, to attempt an explanation of these changes.

In view of the frequent occurrence of misunderstandings, some authors have advanced the opinion that change of meaning, as we observe it in comparing the different periods of language, is largely due to misapprehension.

It must be admitted that several cases on record appear to support this theory. If the following report is trustworthy, the word *yegg* has come by its present meaning, "a burglar or safebreaker," by way of a misunderstanding:

> In speaking of the cook ovens [in the Chinatown of San Francisco] I may say that it was there the word "yegg" originated. It has not yet been locked in the dictionary, but it has a place in our language and it's about time its derivation was settled once and for all. It is a corruption of "yekk," a word from one of the many dialects spoken in Chinatown, and it means beggar. When a hypo or beggar approached a Chinaman to ask for something to eat, he was greeted with the exclamation, "yekk man, yekk man."
>
> The underworld is quick to seize upon strange words, and the bums and hypos in Chinatown were calling themselves yeggmen years before the term was taken out on the road and given currency by eastbound beggars. In no time it had a verb hung on it, and to yegg meant to beg.
>
> The late William A. Pinkerton was responsible for its changed meaning. His business consisted largely of asking questions and necessarily he acquired much misinformation. A burglar with some humor fell into Pinkerton's hands and when asked who was breaking open the country "jugs" he whispered to the detective that it was the yeggs. Investigation convinced Pinkerton that there were a lot of men drifting about the country who called themselves yeggs. The word went into a series of magazine articles Pinkerton was writing at the time and was fastened upon the "box" men. Its meaning has since widened until now the term "yegg" includes all criminals whose work is "heavy."[1]

Derring-do, now used as an archaic word for reckless courage, is a well-attested example of change of meaning due to misunderstanding. The history of the change begins with *Troilus and Criseyde*, where Chaucer says:

[1] Jack Black, *You Can't Win* (New York: The Macmillan Company, 1927), p. 172. *Yegg* is not listed in the *American English Dictionary*. The *Oxford English Dictionary*, clearly as an unsupported hypothesis, remarks that it is "said to be the surname of an American burglar and safebreaker."

> And certeynly in storye it is yfounde,
> That Troilus was nevere unto no wight,
> As in his tyme, in no degree secounde
> In durryng don that longeth to a knight.[2]

Here *durryng don* (of which *derring-do* is only a spelling variation) is no noun but a verbal combination: "He was second to none in daring to do what belongs to a knight." Spenser, however, who frequently borrowed from Chaucer in order to give an old-time coloring to his style, did not understand the grammatical structure of this passage, even though Chaucer in this same stanza repeats the phrase in the infinitive — *to durre don*, "to dare to do" — in a way which might have enlightened his follower. Spenser derived a noun from it, which in its turn was taken up by others:

> So from immortall race he does proceede,
> That mortall hands may not withstand his might,
> Drad for his derring doe and bloudy deed;
> For all in blood and spoile is his delight.[3]

That in this case the change of meaning is complicated by a change of grammatical function does not materially alter its character.

The classical example of semantic change caused by misunderstanding is offered by the history of *weird*. Holinshed, to whom Shakespeare is indebted for the plot of *Macbeth*, says of the witches who prophesied Macbeth's future greatness that

> . . . the common opinion was, that these women were either the weird sisters, that is (as ye would say) the goddesses of destinie, or else some nymphs or feiries, indued with knowledge of prophesie by their necro-manticall science, because euerie thing came to passe as they had spoken.[4]

Holinshed's explanation that the weird sisters are the goddesses of fate is quite correct. *Weird* is a Northern form of Old English *wyrd*, fate, destiny. Shakespeare took over the word as it was. He probably understood it correctly, for he also speaks of the "weird women" as giving promises. To judge from the citations in the *Oxford English Dictionary*, later generations were either vague about the meaning of the word and hence did what we regularly do when confronted with an unfamiliar word — guessed at its sense from the character of the persons and situations involved; or else the suggestive connotations of *weird* extended themselves even over its known primary meaning. At any rate, as a result apparently of its use by such romantic poets as Shelley the word came to be an equivalent of *uncanny, strange,* even *odd* and *unusual.*

---

[2] Chaucer, *Troilus and Criseyde*, Book V, lines 834–837.
[3] Spenser, *The Faerie Queene*, Book II, canto iv, stanza 42.
[4] *Holinshed's Chronicle As Used in Shakespeare's Plays*, Everyman's Library, p. 211.

In acknowledging that some words have, and others may have, developed new meanings by way of faulty understanding, however, we have not admitted that this is the normal way in which new meanings come into existence. It is easy to see that all three examples have one thing in common: the men from whom the words were learned and those who, by insufficient understanding, altered their meanings belong to entirely different speech communities. One might almost say that we are dealing with incorrect translations from a foreign language. This is certainly not an exaggeration in the case of "yegg," borrowed from English-speaking Chinese, although willful deception appears to have been added to the normal difficulties of understanding. But it is also true in a certain sense of our relation to earlier writers in our own language, many of whose words are as unfamiliar to us as foreign idioms.

Since all our examples are of an exceptional character, it would be extremely hasty to conclude from them that changes of meaning under more normal circumstances, i.e., if the speaker or writer belongs to essentially the same speech community as the listener or reader, must necessarily follow the same pattern. In many a case, semantic change has taken place in which lack of understanding has played no part at all. We follow our usual method of discussing one or two examples of which we have detailed knowledge before attempting to establish a theory.

Until October 29, 1835, the word *Loco-foco* meant just one thing: a friction match. The word was an artificial trade name given to a certain brand of matches and probably designed to suggest something easily set afire, with Latin *locus*, "place," "spot," and Italian *fuoco*, "fire," furnishing the material for the coinage.

On this very day, however, something happened which caused the word to develop a new meaning that finally superseded the original one. At a Democratic party meeting in New York the assembly was presented with a prepared list of candidates for political offices which its sponsors, the group known as the Tammany Society, expected to pass in a hurry before any opposition could be voiced. The left-wing faction of the party, a group known as the Equal Rights Democrats, had been warned of the planned maneuver and prepared a countermove. All at once they unfurled banners inscribed with the names of opposition candidates, and the tumult that ensued grew so violent that the Tammany men found it wise to attempt to break off the meeting — in vain — by turning off the gas. Loco-foco matches and candles were lit, the meeting was continued, and the Equal Rights ticket was passed:

> The morning of the 30th of October, 1835, was a joyous one to the readers of the Whig press in the city. Descriptions, both grave and ridiculous, were given of the scene of the previous evening in Tammany Hall, and great were the exultations over the divisions in the ranks of the Democracy. The Courier and Enquirer took the lead in this labor

of love, and bedubbed the anti-monopolists with the name of Loco-Focos. But the Whig press, true to its natural dislike of real democracy, took sides with the monopolists; at least so far as to abuse the friends of Equal Rights without stint or conscience. On the other side, the New York Times, the cherished organ of the oldest and wisest of the monopoly Democracy, lifts up its voice in mingled tones of shame, chagrin, and denunciation. . . . But this was not all; for it undertook the Herculean task of castigating the whole of the Equal Rights democracy. That the reader may be enabled to form some idea of the glorious feats of this protégé of the "thirty-six fathers," its epithets are extracted, leaving the imagination to supply the context which was equally classic, moral and instructive. *"Disorganizers" — "Intruders" — "Revolters" — "Agrarians" — "Working Men's faction" — "Rowdies" — "Odds and Ends of extinct party" — "Eleventh hour Democrats" — "Sweepings and remnants of all recent factions" — "Renegade anti-Masons" — "Pests of party" — "Bad factionists" — "Fanny Wright men" — "Noisy brawlers" — "Political nuisances" — "Loco-Foco party" — "Carbonari" — "Infidels" — "Pledge spouters" — "Resolution mongers" — "Small fry of small politicians" — "Small lights" — "Fire flies of faction" — "Unclean birds" — "Jack o'Lanterns who shine in an unhealthy atmosphere" — "Noisy discontented politicians" — "Scum of politics" — "Knaves" — "Political cheats and swindlers" — "The Guy Fawkes of politics"*!!![5]

It becomes clear at once that this overnight change of *Loco-foco* from the name of a match to that of a political party is not based on a misunderstanding. It would be absurd to think that some people, in speaking of the meeting, refer to the matches as "Loco-focos," while others, unfamiliar with this trade name, made the wrong guess that the word referred to the Equal Rights party. Even without Byrdsall's express statement, it would be impossible to doubt that the first persons to use the new meaning intended to create a new nickname for political opponents. The mechanism of this process is, of course, entirely different from that of a misunderstanding. A change of meaning based on misunderstanding takes place if A uses a word in its traditional ("correct") meaning while B, unfamiliar with the word, has to guess at its sense from the context and guesses wrong. In the case of *Loco-foco* the persons who gave it its new meaning used it intentionally in an untraditional sense but were nevertheless understood correctly, i.e., as they had intended to be understood. Everyone of their readers knew at once that the Equal Rights party, not safety matches, was alluded to.

Changes of this type are extremely frequent. While it should take much labor to collect as many as a dozen examples in which the new meaning is clearly due to misunderstanding, any number of occurrences could be cited

[5] F. Byrdsall, *The History of the Loco-Foco or Equal Rights Party* (New York: Clement & Packard, 1842), pp. 28–29.

that were inaugurated by a speaker's voluntary decision to deviate from the traditional meaning of a word and were completed by the hearer's ability to understand the new meaning although, up to the critical moment, the word meant to him something different. This, then, is a type of semantic change that can be considered normal, while changes based on misunderstanding are decidedly exceptional.

From here on, our discussion must proceed along lines similar to those we followed in investigating the nature of phonetic changes and speech communities. To begin with, the innovation is a merely individual act: it consists simply in the fact that some person decides to use an old expression in a context in which it has not been used before, thereby transferring it into a new sphere of vocabulary, say from technology into politics. However, if this personal speech act is to result in a generally accepted change of meaning, it is necessary not only that the speaker be understood according to his intentions but also that a large number of other persons be prepared to take their cue from him and to incorporate the new meaning in their own speech. If the second step is not taken, the innovation remains a matter of personal style, a characteristic of language as used by a certain individual; as such it may be interesting enough, but it can hardly be considered a concern of the linguist in his dealings with the general development of language. If, on the other hand, the new expression is adopted by a sufficient number of imitators, then each imitation helps to establish the new meaning until what has started as a personal deviation from general speech habits becomes a new element in the common vocabulary. The completion of such semantic changes will necessarily go hand in hand with a decrease in the frequency of the word or words which, before the new expression was introduced, had the exclusive privilege of designating the idea, now partially (sometimes exclusively) annexed by the newcomer. Every case in which an Equal Rights Democrat was called a "Loco-foco" must evidently have reduced the number of occurrences of the former expression. Thus there exists an intimate connection between the problem of new meanings and the question of why well-known and apparently necessary words can become extinct.

It is now clear that two things are essential in order fully to understand a change of meaning. (1) If we know the originator of the change, then there is sense in the question: What caused him to deviate from common usage and what made him choose just this one word as the object and the means of his innovation? If he is a writer, we will study his works with a view of finding other new words and meanings introduced by him and of establishing certain tendencies of his linguistic productivity, thereby trying to contribute to the knowledge of his individual psychology. . . . It is true that in most cases the originator of a semantic change is unknown, but even so, we can often define the group of persons within which a certain change of meaning must have begun. It is, then, just as likely to prove a valuable guide to an understanding of the speaking and thinking habits of the groups from which it emanates, as the individual changes introduced by an author are a guide to his personality.

(2) As soon as the origin of a new meaning has been established, we must try to answer the question: By what qualities of the word and needs of the community was it raised from the status of an individual peculiarity of speech to an acknowledged element of the vocabulary of a whole speech community? That a new word or meaning has made its appearance in a certain language is not, of course, proof of its having ever been generally accepted. Speech innovations of every sort are constantly cropping up, but in most cases they do not influence the formation of the common vocabulary. We hear them and forget about them almost immediately. Even if they are striking enough to force themselves upon our attention, we may not be prepared to incorporate them with our own stock of words and phrases. Everything that is new in language has to overcome a large measure of inertia, if not of hostility, before it can be accepted, and we must not forget that the introduction of a new word into the speech of a large community presupposes its acceptance by millions of individual speakers. If, therefore, in opposition to the generally conservative attitude of the large majority, a considerable number of persons not only notice a new expression but decide to make active use of it, then the individual reactions of all persons participating in this process of acceptance must be directed by some unifying influence that makes the millions all take the same favorable attitude toward the innovation. In other words, the attitude of the speech community must be one of collective preparedness — *kollektive Bereitschaft*, as a Swiss scholar, Gustav Bally, has aptly termed it.[6] To explain the success of a new word is, therefore, equivalent to showing up the factors that created this collective preparedness.

The case of *Loco-foco* is very revealing even in this respect. A community in a state of high political tension gets the news of the dramatic meeting in which the Loco-foco matches played such an important part. Every newspaper not only gives the factual report but expresses its opinion about what has happened. Thousands of citizens discuss it in their private conversation. In view of all this, the official name of Equal Rights party becomes insufficient. Even if the discussion were carried on in cold blood and in a spirit of impartiality, it would become a tedious thing to repeat that name every time the party has to be mentioned, and any newly invented name would probably be gratefully accepted as alleviating the necessity for endless repetitions. As it is, the discussion is far from being dispassionate. The enemies of the party in particular are full of excitement and anger over the successful trick, and a veritable flood of abusive terms directed against the Equal Rights party is the result. Byrdsall has done

[6] Gustav Bally, "Psychologische Phänomene im Bedeutungswandel," *Sprache und Dichtung*, XXX (Bern: 1924), 8 ff.

us the service of collecting a list of these terms from one of the contemporary papers. Had he failed to do so, we would still have guessed that just such an orgy of abuse must have followed the incident, and it would have been the duty of the investigating linguist to verify this suspicion.

After the first excitement has subsided, the need for a multitude of expressions for the same thing is of course reduced. But while it lasts, everybody has heard them, and some of them may have become so familiar to all of the speech community that they will survive; not, however, wholly unchanged, because the more they are used the weaker will become their derogatory power. From terms of abuse they will, very likely, change into comparatively neutral everyday words.

In this process a secondary change of meaning will frequently develop. Once on the march, a new word is not likely to stop at the exact boundary line of the meaning it was originally intended to express. Loco-foco was intended as a nickname for the Equal Rights Democrats only. Very soon, however, it became used against Democrats in general, no matter what wing of the party they adhered to. The following passage is from a late but very vivid account of the campaign of William Henry Harrison:

> They [the Whigs] peremptorily refused to designate their opponents any longer by their ancient title of "Democrats." They said it was too sober, too grave — the very sound made them melancholy; and they never applied the word "democrat" to their adversaries again. They called them "Loco-focos" — said there was something light as well as sulphurous about that name which pleased them; and ever afterwards they refused to recognize their adversaries by any other title. Their coat of arms was a log cabin, with the string of the doorlatch upon the outside, a jug of hard cider, a 'coon *rampant*, regarding with a sardonic grin a "loco-foco" *couchant*.[7]

The reasons the word showed such power of expansion, not only over *Democrat* but over all the competitors listed by Byrdsall, are probably only in part recognized by Williams. In addition, it is strongly abusive only during the first period of its existence and later, therefore, had better chances of adoption by neutral persons and even by the members of the party. Still, it was closely associated with the idea of fire and therefore recommended itself to the enemy parties who, by a slight twist of meaning accomplished by a few well-chosen adjectives, could easily make it suggest that the persons so designated were dangerous political incendiaries. Notice that accusations of "incendiarism" are extremely common in the political debates of those days and that other epithets in Byrdsall's list likewise allude to various fiery phenomena: "Fire flies of faction," "Jack o'Lanterns who shine in an unhealthy atmosphere," "The Guy Fawkes of politics." Not the least important reason for the success of *Loco-foco* is probably the

[7] James Williams, *The Rise and Fall of "The Model Republic"* (London: R. Bentley, 1863), pp. 278–279.

sound effect of the word, originally calculated by the inventors of the matches so designated to arrest the attention of the public, but no less useful to those who wanted to make the term serve their political intentions. And, of course, we must remember that, among all its competitors, *Loco-foco* stood out as the one word having the closest relation to the event that had caused all the emotion.

Very probably, this analysis is far from complete, but it will suffice to bring out a few important things. Here are some of the most obvious inferences:

There exist changes of meaning in which misunderstanding has no, or no appreciable, part.

The phenomenon is closely connected, on the one hand, with that of competition between words of similar function; on the other, with the fact that important ideas are likely to develop an abundance of synonyms.

Emotional elements are of supreme importance to the whole process.

Some time during the year 1861, at the height of the remarkable vogue of name-calling that preceded, accompanied, and followed the Civil War, the abusive vocabulary of the Unionists was enriched by the introduction of the name *copperhead* for such Northern Democrats as were in sympathy with the South. Until then the word had been the name of a venomous snake, and like other words of its group, as for instance, *snake, reptile, adder,* it had occasionally been applied with derogatory meaning to human beings. From the examples listed in the *Dictionary of American English,* it appears that it had been used to describe, in turn, Indians, Dutch settlers in New York, Presbyterians, and red-headed persons, this last use being perhaps a reflection of the old prejudice that ascribed red hair to Judas — or perhaps merely a slighting metaphor based on the color of copper. None of these applications appears to have survived the Civil War; whoever first used the word in its new political sense may, therefore, be said to have originated a permanent change of meaning. The new phase in the history of the word seems to begin with its use in the Detroit *Free Press* of May 5, 1861:

> These neutral papers are always deceptive. In some parts of the country they go by the name of rattlesnake papers; but a friend suggests to us that they ought to be called Copperheads — because the first named reptile always gives notice before he bites, whereas the neutral papers never show their colors before they apply their fangs.[8]

[8] Detroit *Free Press*, May 5, 1861, quoted in *Journalism Quarterly*, XVI, 345. We wish to record one use prior to the Civil War in which *copperhead* clearly refers to the Democratic party. The Ohio State *Journal* of February 4, 1857, in speaking of the Cadiz [Ohio] *Sentinel says*, "This paper is locofocoish of the most intensified copperhead stripe." It seems to us now that this use is isolated. In any case, it does not change the fact that a new epoch in the history of the word starts with the use of the Detroit *Free Press.*

It is not surprising that the name of this "friend," if, indeed, he is any-thing more than a fiction of the writer, is forgotten. What he did is really very little; finding a new use for an old word is certainly no achievement deserving immortality. Not what the innovator did but what his con-temporaries did with his innovation is what really matters. Thanks to the painstaking investigations of Albert Matthews[9] and of Paul S. Smith,[10] we know that the new expression met with success — not, it seems, immedi-ately, but as soon as the approaching elections of 1862 intensified the politi-cal struggle in the North and consequently the search for new emotional words. At first the word appears to have been limited to the Middle West. The Cincinnati *Gazette* has it on July 30, 1862, the Chicago *Tribune* on August 3 and 5, the Cincinnati *Commercial* on August 21. The Columbus *Crisis* of October 22 quotes it from the Ashland *Union*. By January, 1863, the word is in almost daily use in the Chicago *Tribune*. Matthews gives quotations from this paper of January 6, 7, 8, 9, 10, 15, 22, and so on. During the same month, if not earlier, it invaded the East. A cartoon in *Harper's Weekly* shows Vallandigham and other Peace Democrats apply-ing for admission to Jefferson Davis' residence in Richmond and being refused by a colored servant with the words, "He [Davis] haven't got no friends at the Norf; and when he wants any, he won't choose'em among de Peace Sneeks." If the pun is not obvious, the title of the cartoon, "Re-ception of the Copperheads at Richmond" makes it so. On February 13, the New York *Times* has an editorial called "The Western Copperheads." The following day, the New York *Tribune* writes about the "Copperhead Conspiracy." From then on, the word is in universal use.

The best proof that a political catchword is taking effect is usually found in the reactions of the persons against whom it is directed. As long as a new slogan produces no large-scale repercussions, it can safely be ignored. Not before its sting is felt will the attacked party be compelled to take countermeasures. A common one consists in a ready acceptance of the abusive term, for, if used by a speaker about himself, it loses much of its poison. As early as February 14, 1863, in a speech delivered in Newark, New Jersey, one of the leading Northern Democrats, Vallandigham, tried this method: "There are others here from the Northwest, all 'Butternuts,'[11] 'Copperheads' like myself. (Cheers)"

Somewhat later a more subtle attempt was made to neutralize the aggres-sive force of *Copperhead*. A certain type of copper penny with a feminine head representing the Goddess of Liberty was adopted as a party badge — a visible expression of the idea that the Copperheads were the real cham-pions of freedom. Surely a clever countermove and, by its very failure, a stringent proof of the power of the new slogan.

[9] *Publications of the Colonial Society of Massachusetts*, XX, 205 ff.

[10] *American Historical Review*, XXXII, 799 ff.

[11] "Butternut" is another nickname for the Northern Democrats. Its history is treated in Matthews' paper.

Thus it appears that both friend and enemy contributed to the rapid spread of the new word. The reason that we found it necessary to illustrate this process by so many quotations and references follows from what we have already said: the invention of a new word or meaning of a word is only a first impulse. As far as the history of a language, as distinct from individual style, is concerned, the second stage is by far the more important. It consists in the acceptance of the new mode of speech by all, or at least by a large part, of the speech community. It is in the description of this second stage that so many otherwise valuable studies in word history fail. Therefore we have preferred to brave the common charge that philologists habitually delight in the accumulation of trifling detail rather than stint the description of an essential process. Only by presenting a large number of instances could we show the existence of that "collective preparedness" which explains why a word invented by one man became, within scarcely more than one year, the common property of millions. Why that preparedness existed is evident from the state of public feeling during this period. The attitude of a Northern majority against such persons in their midst as sympathized with secession had become increasingly bitter. Terms like *Northern Democrat* or *Peace Democrat*, although describing the minority in a logically adequate way, were incapable of expressing the hostility of which this group was the object. Thus there had arisen a discrepancy between the traditional vocabulary as it was before *Copperhead* was put into circulation, and the need of expression existing in a group numerically and politically dominant. This linguistic vacuum was bound to be filled by any new word offered by some creative person, provided it characterized the dissenting party in an adequately unpleasant way.

We have already pointed out that the emotional connotations of a word form part of its biography. Passages like the following provide useful evidence:

> The Copperhead is described by naturalists as "An American venomous serpent, the most dangerous after the rattlesnake. . . ." The rattlesnake, with all its venom, has one virtue — it never strikes without warning. . . . Your copperhead is no such chivalrous foe; for he hides in the grass, silent and treacherous, springs upon you unawares. . . . No rattle. no hiss, but a lurking watchfulness and a leap at your throat. . . . There is a remarkable fitness in the name — let the traitors be called "Copperheads."[12]

Now this is the same idea as that expressed in the passage quoted above from the Detroit *Free Press*, but nobody can fail to see the increased virulence of this second version. A still higher note of indignation is struck in Bret Harte's poem *The Copperhead* (1864). We quote all of it in order not to spoil its effect of abusive contempt:

[12] New York *Tribune*, February 16, 1863, quoted in Matthews, *op. cit.*, p. 231.

There is peace in the swamp where the Copperhead sleeps,
Where the waters are stagnant, the white vapor creeps,
Where the musk of Magnolia hangs thick in the air,
And the lilies' phylacteries broaden in prayer.
There is peace in the swamp, though the quiet is death,
Though the mist is miasma, the upas-tree's breath,
Though no echo awakes to the cooing of doves, —
There is peace: yes, the peace that the Copperhead loves.

Go seek him: he coils in the ooze and the drip,
Like a thong idly flung from the slave-driver's whip;
But beware the false footstep, — the stumble that brings
A deadlier lash than the overseer swings.
Never arrow so true, never bullet so dread,
As the straight steady stroke of that hammer-shaped head;
Whether slave or proud planter, who braves that dull crest,
Woe to him who shall trouble the Copperhead's rest!

Then why waste your labors, brave hearts and strong men,
In tracking a trail to the Copperhead's den?
Lay your axe to the cypress, hew open the shade
To the free sky and sunshine Jehovah has made;
Let the breeze of the North sweep the vapors away,
Till the stagnant lake ripples, the freed waters play;
And then to your heel can you righteously doom
The Copperhead born of its shadow and gloom!

An attempt to trace the history of *Copperhead* from the time of the Civil War to the First World War, when it had a sporadic revival as a synonym of *pro-German*, would involve too complex a study. All we wish to point out here is that during the Reconstruction period the word underwent a secondary change of meaning to the extent that it became more and more a synonym of Democrat, used, of course, only abusively. Both the derogatory character of the word and the expansion of its meaning become clear from an episode in Congress (1870), when Blaine discussed the consequences of admitting a congressman from Tennessee accused of having supported the Confederate Constitution.

[Mr. Blaine] . . . If the Committee of Election shall report that he is ineligible on that account, why of course then this copperhead competitor by this construction comes immediately in.
Eldridge. — I rise to a question of order. I insist that the term copperhead is not parliamentary.
Mr. Blaine. — I recall the word. I never used it before in a debate here. I will say his Democratic competitor.
The Speaker overruled the point of order on the ground that he was

not speaking of any gentleman in the House, but Mr. Blaine refused to be thus upheld: "I did not withdraw the word as a question of order. I should have told the gentleman that he had made no point of order. As a question of taste I confess that I have transgressed, and as a question of taste I change the word. It was in bad taste, as it always is, to use offensive political epithets in debate."[13]

This same change is further documented by the following quotation which we cannot date exactly but which probably comes from Cleveland's first term:

Rev. N. W. Cleveland, brother of the President, complains in the papers that his parishioners call him a "copperhead," and even insinuate that a man cannot be both a Democrat and a consistent Christian.[14] . . .

[13] Gail Hamilton (Mary Abigail Dodge), *Biography of James G. Blaine* (Norwich, Conn.: Henry Bill Publishing Co., 1895), p. 198.
[14] *The Complete Works of Brann the Iconoclast* (New York: The Brann Publishers, Inc., 1919), V, 51.

Eric Partridge

THANKS TO THE WAR . . .

ᘓᘓ

As we have seen in the essay by Estrich and Sperber, if political events can act as a stimulant for word-making, then times of war would be expected to yield rapid change and many additions to the lexicon. This is Mr. Partridge's point. His title is, of course, ironic; we would gladly forgo these new words if we could avoid war. Since Mr. Partridge wrote his essay we have been engaged in a cold war and two hot

Reprinted from *Words at War: Words at Peace* by Eric Partridge (London: Frederick Muller Ltd., 1948) by permission of the publisher.

ones. Reading "Thanks to the War . . ." provokes us to ask what changes in meaning and what new words recent events have thrust forward.

War is a powerful excitant, perhaps the most rapidly effectual excitant, of language. It quickens and enlivens, enriches and invigorates language as much in the 20th century as exploration and travel used to do in the 16th–17th centuries. That is not a justification, it is an inevitable result, of war — at least of any modern war that has lasted more than a few months.

In the war of 1939–45, as in that of 1914–18, the fighting Services have experienced a far more extensive enrichment of their vocabularies, whether technical or unconventional, than the civilian or social services have experienced; many Service terms, however, soon find their way into the civilian vocabulary. 'In the Services, the men [and the women] live — or should live — a more exciting life; they deal with new equipment and various weapons; do things they've never done before . . . ; many of them visit strange countries; many become engaged in a service that is actually instead of nominally active; all of them mingle in such a companionship as they have never had before they enlisted and will never again have, once they quit the Service.

'Such conditions inevitably lead to a rejuvenation of language — to vividness — to picturesqueness — to vigour; language becomes youthful, energetic, adventurous.' (From the introduction to *A Dictionary of R.A.F. Slang.*) But civilians have, in the recent 'spot of bother', been involved as never before: to pass through a *blitz* is unpleasant; yet, as an old lady of the East End remarked in December 1940, 'it does take your mind off your worries'.

The words that are to be briefly treated here have been selected to fit a chronological arrangement. Some of them refuse to fit. Nevertheless, they do belong where I've put them, whenever or wherever else they may assert themselves — as words have a way of asserting themselves. But it is only a selection.

The Spanish Civil War, lasting from July 18, 1936, to April 4, 1939, constituted, although only the Axis powers seem to have been aware of the fact, that rehearsal, that Martian pre-view, of the impending World War which has been admirably related in J. Alvarez del Vayo's *Freedom's Battle.* The original *Fifth Column* consisted in the Franco sympathizers within Madrid and it was General Mola who, leading four columns of troops against the city, thus described them in a wireless address; hence, *fifth column*, 'secret subverters and sympathizers', any one of them being a *fifth-columnist*. In that stylistic exemplar of compression, *The Civilization of Spain*, Professor J. B. Trend spoke of Philip of Spain's sympathizers in pre-Armada England as 'a "fifth column"'.

Far closer attention was paid, in Great Britain, to the Hitler-generated 'alarums and excursions': the days of *Weltpolitik* and *Machtpolitik* (the latter more usual in its translation, *power politics*), of *encirclement* and *protective custody*, of *appeasement* and *peace in our time*, and of *Rassentheorie* with its perversions of *Aryan* and *Semitic*. But into that Jungian maelstrom of Teutonic delusion and British procrastination I prefer, uncontroversially, to refrain from plunging; the hysteria of the *Herrenvolk* does not appeal to me, nor yet the other thing. If you, however, wish to plunge, then take, as companions, Walter Theimer (hereinafter mentioned) and the R. G. Collingwood of *The New Leviathan*.

On September 1 (merely confirmed by September 3), 1939, many of us said, 'This is it!' and on September 4, we bought *black-outs* for the windows; we became experts in the art of *blacking-out*. Rather earlier was the aviators' *black(-)out*, noun and verb, '(to experience) a temporary loss of consciousness, especially during a long powerdive', but it was only in 1940 that this technical sense became public property. For some eight months, the self-deluders spoke of 'the *phoney* war' (*phoney* being American slang from the American underworld, earlier the English underworld) and restored that expressive word to the British vocabulary. But, Hitler ready, the storm broke — where no storm had been feared by the credulous. Nations fell. Thanks, in the main, to the *quislings*. Rarely has a word so quickly and so firmly grasped the world's imagination as this common-propertying of the Proper Name, 'Vidkun *Quisling*'. This Norwegian ex-Army officer, turning politician, turning traitor, was executed in 1945 at the age of fifty-eight, but not before he had, in April, 1940, done his country a great wrong. *The Little Oxford Dictionary*, 3rd edition, 1941, classified it as slang, but by — indeed, well before — the end of the year it had been admitted to Standard English.

Within a month of Quisling's manifested treachery, we had another neologism — 'to *Rotterdam*', to which the bombing of Britain added 'to *Coventrate* (better, *coventrate*)'. Whereas the former term means 'to obliterate — or attempt to obliterate — a vital portion — a clearly indicated area — of a city', the latter means 'to (attempt to) destroy an entire city', as citizens of Coventry are unlikely to forget.

A notable element in German efficiency was that of the *Panzerdivision* or, as we know it, *Panzer division*, 'armoured division'. The word *Panzer* has nothing to do with *panthers*, that idea being folk-etymology that arose from an association of not grossly dissimilar sounds and the swiftness of panthers and Panzers. Literally, *Panzer* is 'armour'; in combination it is equivalent to 'armoured'. The German word was used so much, not only in May–June 1940 but again in North Africa, that it was adopted by the troops, as in 'Here come the Panzers!' British pluck not long availed against the Germans in the spring of 1940, and at the end of May the B.E.F. had to *do a Dunkirk* in grim fact (see, above all, A. D. Divine's *Dunkirk*); the phrase was painfully repeated in connexion with the departures from Greece and Crete (see especially James Aldridge's *Signed with Their Honour* and *The Sea Eagle*), much less painfully when the Axis troops were prevented from 'doing a Dunkirk': effecting a sea-borne withdrawal against heavy odds. So ended the *Blitzkrieg* or 'lightning-war'.

But not *Blitzkrieg* itself, for in a shortened form and a different sense, it dominated the next period, the Battle of Britain and the bombing of Britain, especially *the London blitz*: August 1940–May 1941, with isolated *Baedeker raids* on places of tourist interest, especially cathedral cities, later. In *The* (New York) *Nation* of November 9, 1940, Lester V. Berrey, American scholar, in an article, 'English War Slang', wrote: 'The word that has received the greatest currency at home and abroad is *blitz*, used as both noun and verb. It carries the implication of bombardment on a much grander scale than the 1914[–1918] contribution of *strafe*, and will probably find as permanent a place in the language of war.' Like *strafe*, it has also been used derivatively, both as noun and as verb, for '(to deliver) a severe reprimand (to a person)'. For millions of people, the *blitz* has invested such simple words as *siren, alert, all-clear*, with an emotional content, a tremendous significance these words had not previously possessed, and, as to millions the Blitzkrieg had transformed *refugee* from a colourless to a dolorous word, so to millions the *blitz* has familiarized *evacuee*, which, however horrible a derivation from 'evacuated person' (itself a poor substitute for 'transferred person' or some richer term), has been forced upon us by usage. It was also during this period, latter 1940–early 1941, that *fighter* became established for 'fighter 'plane' and *bomber* for 'bomber (or bombing) 'plane', to such an extent that these are now almost the predominant senses of those two words.

To the earlier part of this period we owe the expressive *take evasive action*. Mary Welsh Monks, in her article, 'No Time for Tears', in Allan A. Michie & Walter Graebner's *Lights of Freedom*, 1941, conveniently stated that 'Fighter pilots' combat reports include "I took evasive action", and the W.A.A.F. adopted it in describing their adventures on dates. It is heard in powder rooms everywhere now' — *powder room* being an import from the United States. In 1941–42 it signified (as it still does), 'to avoid a difficulty or a danger; to depart tactfully, or prudently escape'. Since early 1943 it has also signified, 'to evade payment of a debt or the discharge of an onerous or unpleasant duty'.

Let us, before we pass to another Service and to other periods, discharge our neological debt to the Royal Air Force and its fellows, chiefly the R.A.A.F., the R.C.A.F., the R.N.Z.A.F., the R.S.A.A.F., and note a few of the inceptions made by, or because of, the Air Force. One of the most enduring is *flak*, which began as slang and as a toast ('Here's flak' — instead of *mud* — 'in your eye!'), so very quicky became jargon, or official technicality, and by late 1943 formed a reputable ingredient of the language, for 'anti-aircraft fire or guns'. Its four letters represent the initials of the elements in the German compound noun, '*Fliegerabwehrkanone*'. It took more than flak to send our bomber pilots into *a flat spin* (or fluster), which is a revival from the R.F.C. — R.A.F. slang of 1914–18. Of one who failed to return from a sortie, his companions remarked that he had *gone for a Burton*, the reference being to ale. *He's (or You've) had it!*, on the other hand, means not that 'He's copped it' but that he will have to go without something: in other words, 'He hasn't had it — and won't get it'! An ironic expression.

Such irony may be postulated to move gremlins to work the mischief that airmen have, for some years, been asserting is constantly being done by these sprites. The gremlins are reputed to be a foot high, to be diabolically mischievous, and to sit or stand about grinning and grimacing at the aircrew they have so gravely inconvenienced by interfering with the mechanism of the 'plane while it was flying. The gremlin belongs to what we might rather fatuously call 'a conscious, or deliberate, piece of folk-lore'. The origin of the term is obscure. *Webster's New International Dictionary* says, 'Perhaps from Irish *gruaimin*, ill-humoured little fellow, by confusion with *goblin*'. That is an ingenious theory, and perhaps correct; certainly there is either confusion, or a blending, with *goblin*, for the gremlin is a Puck-like imp. My own theory is that *gremlin* is a blend of *grim*acing (or *grin*ning) gob*lin*. Against the wiles of gremlins, even a Mae West is sometimes useless.

Already current in 1939 was *Mae West*, the life-jacket worn by aircrews. Beginning as slang, in reference to that famous film actress's vital buxomness, it had, by late 1942, become the official term. Earlier — probably since about 1930 — is *gen*, 'information, or instructions', and it derives not, as so often stated, from 'genuine', but from that sacrosanct phrase, 'for the *general information* of all ranks'. But *gen* has always been slang. To the deepest jargon, however, belongs *cannibalization*, 'the use of parts from various damaged or other unserviceable, or at the least no longer or not yet operational, aircraft': one 'plane eating many others.

Aircraft? 'plane? Early in 1943 the Air Ministry decreed that an *aeroplane* was now to be an *aircraft* (plural, *aircraft*) and an *aerodrome* an *airfield*. The names of aircraft hardly concern us here, but it is worth noting that whereas the Germans name their aircraft after the designers or occasionally the manufacturers, as in *Junkers* (not *Junker*), *Dornier*, *Heinkel*, *Henschel*, *Messerschmitt*, *Focke-Wulf*, we ignore our brilliant inventors and name our aircraft after physical disturbances (*Hurricane*, *Spitfire*, *Tempest*, *Typhoon*) or after cities (the bombers: e.g., *Lancaster* and *Halifax*) or, rather earlier, after national heroes long dead (*Wellington*,

Hampden) or famous places (*Whitley, Blenheim*), although once someone was happily inspired to permit a *Mosquito*, with the differentiating
plural *Mosquitos*.

But what of the Army in 1939–45? Well, in addition to a mass of jargon
(for instance, *category* debased to ineptitude and allowed to father such
undesirables as *recategorization*), it has coined, or at the least popularized,
some very effective slang words and phrases, of which perhaps the most
famous is *browned(-)off*, 'fed up', thoroughly depressed and perhaps rather
disgusted. Note that this is not a war-baby; it has been employed in the
Regular Army from certainly not later than 1930 and was in use among
R.A.F. personnel in India and at Aden since as early as 1931 or 1932. Yet
it was in the years 1939–45 that *browned off* achieved a national currency.
Despite its origination in the torrid East, the term derives, not from the
sun-browned hills or sun-scorched parade grounds, but from cookery — in
short, from those mishaps known jocularly as *burnt sacrifices* (a fertile
source of discontent among 'the men-folk of the house'). The approbatory
smashing, originally Cockney, has been disseminated by the Army, which
passed it generously to the R.A.F. (*a smashing job*, a very attractive girl)
and to the Navy (*a smashing Jenny* or Wren). The Army also allowed
the other Services the use of *stooge*, 'a learner; a deputy or stand-in; an
over-willing fellow; a third-rater'; *to stooge about*, 'to be on patrol, to cruise
about, to delay one's landing', the verb being almost solely an Air Force
usage. The origin is either the American *stool pigeon*, 'informer to the
police; hence, in the theatre, an understudy', or, as I prefer (the earliest
English sense being 'learner'), the ordinary word *student* — via *studious*
mispronounced *stoo-djus*. Also originally Army words are these three:
synthetic, 'artificial; impractical' (compare the 1914–18 *ersatz*); *snoop
around* or *about*, 'to pry'; *that shook him*, 'disturbed his equanimity, im-
paired his complacence'.

From the France of 1940–45 we have already derived *do a Dunkirk*.
Other French terms are collaborator ('Ces collaborateurs infâmes!'), *underground movement* ('le mouvement souterrain' — sometimes shortened to
'le souterrain,' as, in English, we sometimes use the shorter *underground*)*,
and *Maquis*, 'Les Maquis' being those French guerilla fighters who opposed
the Nazis in rural France, especially in the scrublands of the Central, and
the Southern, East of France. In France *maquis* is 'rough scrub, tough
scrub', adopted from *maquis* (or *makis*), 'wild bushy land in Corsica', the
original being Italian *macchie*, the plural of *macchia*, itself from Latin
macula, 'a spot, a mesh'.

The Soviet Union has contributed three terms, one directly as in 'the
scorched earth policy' of which we heard so much in the three months
following Hitler's unannounced invasion of Russia on June 22, 1941, and

---

* In, e.g., Paul Brickhill & Conrad Norton's exceptional book, *Escape to Danger*,
1946 — the best of the 1939–45 escape books.

two indirectly — by allusion to V. M. Molotov, who, born in 1890, became in 1939 the head of the Commissariat for Foreign Affairs and in May 1941 Foreign Commissar. These two are the *Molotov bread-basket*, a rack that, released from an aircraft, rotates as it falls, and scatters, one by one, its load of dozens of incendiary bombs, thus tending to produce a group-conflagration, and the *Molotov cocktail*, a bottle filled with an inflammable mixture (chiefly petrol) and fitted with a wick, or a saturated piece of rag-tape, ignited immediately before it is thrown at, e.g., a tank. *Molotov cocktail* may be the translation of a term coined by the Finns during the Russo-Finnish war.

The war with Japan (early December 1941–August 1945) has revived the popularity of *hara-kiri* — incorrectly *hari-kari* — 'suicide by disembowelment' (from *hara*, 'belly', and *kiri*, 'to cut'), practised only by other ranks and the ignobles, for nobles and officers do it ceremonially and most ceremoniously, and they call it *seppuku*. In 1914–18, when the Japanese were with us, we heard little; in 1941–45 when they were against us we heard much; of *bushido*, 'code of honour', strictly, *Bushido*, 'the Samurai code of honour'. Literally *bu-shi-do*, 'military-knight ways' — hence, the customs, 'the book of words', of the well-born soldier, the term is something of a fake, more or less invented, a few years before the Russo-Japanese war (1904–05), for the use of gullible foreigners. It is the one important Japanese contribution to Western thought in the 1940's.

The American soldiers and sailors did not 'fall' for it. But they did make two interesting additions to the language: *G.I.* (their equivalent of *Tommy*), 'an ordinary soldier', from the abbreviation *G.I.*, 'general issue', as applied to clothes and equipment; and *jeep*, that extraordinarily useful and versatile cross-country vehicle which came on lease-lend to Britain long before we welcomed the G.I.'s and which has likewise been formed from initials in this instance *G.P.*, '(for) general purposes', hence an adjective, 'general-purpose', the original form being '*a G.P. vehicle*'.

Oddly enough, the 'jeep' (official since 1943) had a precursor in the not dissimilar, ugly but efficient British utility motor-van that in 1939–43 the Army called a *doodlebug*, so named both from the *doodles* one absent-mindedly draws on pad or paper and from the resemblance this vehicle bears to a large *bug* or beetle. And so the *doodlebug*, as the V.1 or German *flying bomb* of the latter half of 1944 was called by the general population, Service and non-Service, of Britain at the time, was not, as I have seen it glamorously stated, a spontaneous, genius-attaining creation by civilians but a sense-adaptation, probably made by soldiers or airmen in South-Eastern England, of the earlier, the Army term, by way of the idea, 'a doodlebug, or a jeep, in the air'.

Objects even more unpleasant than the doodlebug were to travel the skyways. Late in 1944 and early in 1945, the same area of England was visited by numbers of projectiles known as V.2 or the *rocket-bomb*, which received no happy nickname but, much as Hitler was usually mentioned as *that man* (cleverly misappropriated by Tommy Handley), was usually referred to as *that bloody nuisance*.

Apparently the Japanese found the *atom bomb* to be something more than a nuisance. The term *atom bomb* is a shortening of the perhaps more sensible, more aptly descriptive *atomic bomb*, which, by the way, was, as a potential, being freely discussed by the Americans before they became involved in the war, as you may see for yourselves if you turn to *The Reader's* (not *The English*) *Digest* of 1941. That the word, like the thing, has come to stay, seems all too probable.

The war has ended, but war responsibilities are with us. In occupied enemy countries our troops were, at first, forbidden and later allowed to *fraternize*, which has therefore modified its meaning from 'to live, to act, as brothers with — or towards — others of one's own race' to 'doing this with members of an enemy or ex-enemy race; especially to become friendly with an enemy of the opposite sex'. The slang shape of the word is 'to *frat*', and he or she who 'frats' is a *fratter* and the practice is *fratting*.

Which reminds me that the war of 1939–45 has popularized the hitherto official or pedantic *national*, 'one who belongs to a nation', as in 'a British national — enemy nationals'. Originating, at the beginning of the present century, as a term in the theory of International Law, it has its justification in the fact that it is so very convenient, for it covers sovereign (or president) and subject, citizen and non-citizen.

Nobody can *blue-print* a living language; nobody can furnish an adequate *blue-print* of even the neologisms: such fatuities are best left to bull-dozing bureaucrats and doctrinaire departmentalists. John P. Marquand has, in *So Little Time*, 1943, said, 'He was suddenly tired of all the new words — "streamlined", "blitz", "three-point program", "blueprint" '.

J. Willis Russell

(with the assistance of Norman R. McMillan)

AMONG THE NEW WORDS

≰≰

As a demonstration that our language changes constantly and our vocabulary increases rapidly, we offer one sampling (October 1965) of "Among the New Words," a regular list and commentary that appears in *American Speech*. This interesting list shows how lexicographers collect citations, and something of the citation form and cross-referencing to *Webster's Third New International Dictionary*, (NID 3), the Oxford English Dictionary, (OED), and others.

Reference to the entry *chimp(o)naut* and the citations under-*naut* will disclose an interesting new formative element. It may have become implicit in the word *astronaut*, formed, according to the NID 3, from "*astr-* + *-naut* (as in *aeronaut*)" and defined in one sense as 'a traveler in interplanetary space.' *Aeronaut* itself is generally considered to be a borrowing from the French *aéronaute* (Gr. *aēr(o)-* + *nautēs* 'sailor'). It is defined by the OED as 'one who sails through the air, or who makes balloon ascents,' by the NID 3 as 'one that operates or travels in an airship or balloon.'

Though perhaps the astronauts began as 'travelers in interplanetary space,' they have more and more become explorers, and with the word in this connotation is almost immediately associated another, *Argonaut*, one who, if not an actual explorer, came to be considered 'an adventurer or traveler engaged in a particular quest' (NID 3, b). Hence we arrive at the use of *-naut* added to another word element to denote 'one who explores or

Reprinted from "Among the New Words," from *American Speech* (October, 1965), pp. 208–215, by permission of Columbia University Press.

investigates; that which is employed in exploration or investigation.' It is, possibly, to be described as a combining form.

Despite the fact that *plastiqueur* is apparently not yet an English word, the two citations in English publications perhaps justify its inclusion in the glossary along with *plastic bomb* and *plastic bombing*. Its formation would presumably parallel that of English agent nouns, viz., *plastique* + *-eur*. No French dictionary available to me lists *plastique* in the sense given in the etymology of *plastic bomb* in the glossary. The *Larousse Modern French-English Dictionary* (N.Y.: McGraw-Hill Book Co., 1960) has the sense 'plastic goods.'

The number of citations of *megabuck* may seem disproportionate for such a simply defined term. They are included for the light they throw on attitudes. Even after nineteen years, a writer still regards the term as slang. In this connection there comes to mind a remark that James B. McMillan once made (*Coll. Eng.*, 10:217/1) to the effect that the slang label might better be used only for "short-lived novelties."

ACKNOWLEDGMENTS: For citations, H. Alexander (1), T. L. Crowell (1), O. B. Emerson (1), E. E. Ericson (1), Rex Everage (1), Ernest H. Hawkins (2), Alice C. Kingery (1), Raven I. McDavid (2), James Macris (1), Mamie J. Meredith (7), Porter G. Perrin (7), Anne B. Russell (3), and R. M. Wallace (2). C. Beaumont Wicks contributed to the remarks on *plastiqueur*, and Charles L. Seebeck, Jr., composed the definition of *real time*.

BIODEGRADABLE, *adj.* [bio- + ¹*degrade* (cf. *v.t.* 6 and *v.i.* 4 in NID 3) + *-able*] See quots. — 1964 Texize Chemicals, Inc. "Interim Report on Operations for Six Months Ended May 2, 1964," 29 May. We are now preparing to market a remarkable new light-duty liquid detergent product that is biodegradable, referred to as a "soft" detergent. 1965 *Encyclopedia Year Book* (N.Y.: Gaché Publishing Co.) p. 357/1 BIODEGRADABLE, *adj.* Said of a detergent whose chemicals are quickly destroyed or broken down by the bacteria found in soil and water.

BIOTRON, *n.* [Cf. OEDS, s.v. *Biotron* '*Wireless Telegr.*' {1926} The biological term seems more likely to be formed by analogy with *phytotron*, as suggested by the first quot.] See quots. — 1958 *Science* 5 Sept. p. 510/3 (S. B. Hendricks and F. W. Went) The phytotron has been generally accepted as an experimental tool, comparable to telescopes, particle accelerators, fossil collections, and other tools of science. Interest in such facilities . . . has also been expressed by others experimenting with animals; thus the concept of a "biotron" developed. 1959 *New International Year Book* (New York: Funk & Wagnalls Co.) p. 544/1. 1964 N.Y. *Times* 31 May p. E7/8 Final approval has been given for the construction of a "Biotron" at the University of Wisconsin. The building will be designed for the study of living organisms in a wide variety of environments.

CHIMP(O)NAUT, *n.* [*chimp*anzee + *-naut* (see preliminary remarks and *-naut* in the glossary)] See quots. — 1961 Des Moines *Register* 30 Nov. p. 6/2 Chimpnaut Enos has said very little about his experience in orbit, but for solid information, his report is about as enlightening as those of the Russian cosmonauts at that. 1962 N.Y. *Journal-American* 14 May p. 8/5–7 (heading and subheading) [Dr. James A.] Van Allen downgrades spacemen[.] Prefers chimponauts. Tuscaloosa *News* 17 June p. 26/6–7 Because of the close similarity between chimpanzees and men, the chimponauts are expected to keep pioneering the way for man in space — perhaps all the way to the moon. 1965 *World Book Year Book* p. 546/1.

COUNTER-ESCALATION, *n.* See *escalation.* — 1965 *Newsweek* 7 June p. 55/3 However, the Soviets now begin to take a more active role in the defense of North Vietnam, simultaneously hinting at counter-escalations against the West elsewhere in the world. . . .

ESCALATE, *v.t. & i.* [Cf. *escalate* and *escalation* in *NID* 3.] See last quot. — 1964 Chet Huntley over NBC 8 June The war in Laos has been escalated. . . . Tuscaloosa *News* 27 June p. 4/2 No, it is not 1914 in the Far East. The present unacknowledged war might indeed be "escalated." But — again assuming rationality in Peking — it could hardly "escalate" too violently. *World Book Year Book* p. 608/3. 1965 Tuscaloosa *News* 15 Feb. p. 2/2 (AP) The fact that the Viet Nam crisis did not escalate into anything worse over the weekend was a reassuring factor. N.Y. *Times* 11 April p. 14E/3 "Escalate" means "step up the war," but again anybody can say, "We've stepped up the war in Asia," without giving the impression that all he knows is what he reads in the newspapers.

ESCALATION, *n.* — 1961 *Nation* 4 March p. 181/2 But wars, large or small, are fought for victory. That means you pound the enemy with every available lethal assistance, with the inevitable result — to use the fancy new term — of escalation to all-out war. Limited war is a contradiction of terms. It is an illusion of limited minds. 1965 *Newsweek* 7 June p. 54/3 Kahn's odd brand of liberalism strongly colors his latest book, "On Escalation: Metaphors and Scenarios" (*308 pages. Frederic A. Praeger. $6.95*), a searching exploration of modern nuclear strategy.

GOLDWATERISM, *n.* See *Am. Sp.* 40: 144. Add earlier quots. — 1960 *Nation* 9 July p. 25/2 (letter from Barry M. Goldwater) A bit further along Mr. Spivack asks [*Nation* 18 June p. 531/3]: "How deep is Goldwaterism? And what does it portend for the future of the GOP?" That is the end of any discussion of my Republican philosophy. What he has done here is to resort to a word — "Goldwaterism" — hoping that, without explanation, it will mean something to the general public.

HARD, *adj.* [Cf. OED, s.v. *hard, adj.*, 14.a: 'Applied to water holding in solution mineral, especially calcareous, salts, which decompose soap and render the water unfit for washing purposes' {1660–}] See quot. — 1964 N.Y. *Times* 2 Aug. p. E7/7–8 An end may be in sight to the pollution of the nation's underground water supplies by the foamy "hard" detergents. Those chemicals, which are not easily degraded by natural biological processes in the soil they pass through, have been putting heads of foam on lakes and streams, blowing as froth over the countryside and even streaming sudsily out of drinking faucets.

INNER SPACE, *n.* [Cf. *inner space,* 'the sea' (*Am. Sp.* 35: 285)] See quots. — 1958 *Sat. Rev.* 13 Sept. p. 28/2 Must this inner space continue to be peopled with imaginative dragons of strange color and dropping off places that confine the moral venture to the shallow water of one's own mainland or adjacent islands of narrow self-interest? Must the haunting emptiness of inner space isolating man from man and nation from nation continue to be the dominant theme of poet, prophet, and philosopher in our time? 1961 N.Y. *Times Book Rev.* 14 May p. 7/1–2 In "Exploring Inner Space," "a nationally known writer chose to use the pseudonym Jane Dunlap" for the purpose of relating her "personal experiences under LSD–25," lysergic acid diethylamide, a drug that induces psychotic-like reactions. 1962 N.Y. *Times* 1 July p. E7/2 (cartoon cap.) "Anybody worried about inner space?" 1963 *Friends Journal* 1 Feb. p. 53/1 Fifth, exploring "inner space" of the "beyond within" appears to be no armchair diversion for the timorous. It takes uncommon audacity to venture into the unknown. Outer space has captured the public fancy, but probing the beyond within is just as daring a pursuit as piloting a space ship, with as many rigors, demanding every ounce of a person's courage, skill, and determination. *Ibid.* 1 Nov. p. 465/1 An article in the Friends Journal of February 1, 1963, "Exploring Inner Space," by G. M. Smith, tells of a group of people who met at Pendle Hill with a Japanese Zen Buddhist to learn oriental ways of meditation. The article suggests that this sort of training might be given to groups of Friends to deepen the spiritual life of our Meetings. I would like to point out that the new depth psychology, coming to us from Europe, offers a method of spiritual growth that is more suited to our western minds. 1964 *Encyclopedia Year Book* p. 365/2 INNER SPACE. The limitless depths of the personality.

MEGABUCK, *n.* [*mega*- 'million' + *buck* 'dollar'] See quots. (Also attrib.) — 1946 London *Picture Post* 7 Dec. p. 10 They have laughingly coined the term 'megabuck' — one megabuck equals a million dollars. 1950 *Sat. Eve. Post* 18 Feb. p. 111/1 The Mark trio, which cost more than $1,000,000 — a "megabuck" or "kilogrand," as mathematicians say facetiously — work twenty-four hours a day, seven days a week. 1951 N.Y. *Times Mag.* 22 April p. 35/4–5 Megabuck: Today this unofficial term is as frequent in modern physics as its predecessor, "kilobuck," which is a scientist's idea of a short way to say "a thousand dollars." A fifty-megabuck ($50,000,000) laboratory is today a commonplace. Mega means "great" in Greek, "million" as used here. *Fortune* July p. 138 It has recently been estimated that all that would be required to build a pilot model of a completely electronic record-keeping system is one 'megabuck' — $1 million. 1952 N.Y. *Times* 21 Dec. p. E7/7 (The cosmotron cost about three and one-half "megabucks" — a megabuck being physicist's slang for $1,000,000.) 1953 Seattle *Times* 24 June p. 6 And what is a megabuck? It is a million dollars — as in the sentence, "it will cost so and so many thousand megabucks to deliver (or to prevent) an attack of X-megaton power, which may be expected to result in Y-megadeaths." 1954 *Life* 12 April p. 27 Scientists, preparing to measure the force of the explosion in megatons (1 megaton is 1 million tons of TNT), measured the cost facetiously in megabucks. 1956 N.Y. *Times* 18 Nov. p. 46/3 This, with other equipment, including the half-mile tunnel, the subterranean target building, the building for the remote control of the machine, a large administration building and a power house with a 30,000-kilowatt generator, will bring the total cost of the machine to $26,000,-000, or 26 "megabucks" in the terminology of the scientists. 1958 *New Republic* 27 Jan. p. 10 We are living in what Von Neumann called the Megabuck or

Kilogrand era. 1963 Mencken-McDavid *The American Language* (N.Y.: A. A. Knopf) p. 232 Nuclear physicists talk cheerfully of . . . the cost of apparatus in *megabucks*. . . . 1965 Tuscaloosa *News* 16 June In atomic age slang, $1 million is a megabuck.

MONOKINI, *n.* [*mono-* + bi*kini*] Skimpy bathing trunks for men. — 1964 *Time* 7 Aug. p. 36/3 Betweentimes, they had themselves a ball sunbathing at Beirut's Saint Simon Beach, she in a bikini that was utterly tutu, he in a monokini that was, as they say in London, utterly twee. 1965 *Encyclopedia Year Book* p. 357/2. *Newsweek* 7 June p. 80/1 The monokini already had gone the way of the bikini.

MOON SHIP, MOONSHIP, *n.* See quots. — 1951 Tuscaloosa *News* 21 Oct. p. 25/6 (UP) Actually, he said, there probably will be three types of space ships — a ferry or "local" ship to take man outside the atmosphere, a moon ship sent up to the artificial satellite or even built there to make the flights to the moon where another tanker might refuel it for the trip back, and deep space ships which would be built in space and stay there. 1958 *Life* 6 Jan. p. 65 The moon ship, designed for exploration trips around the moon, is composed mainly of a cluster of chemical fuel tanks. [Remainder of quot. fully describes the moon ship.] 1959 Woodford A. Heflin (ed.) *Aerospace Glossary* (Maxwell [Ala.] Air Force Base: Research Studies Institute, Air University) p. 67/2 MOONSHIP, *n.* A spacecraft designed for travel to the moon. 1964 N.Y. *Times* 16 Aug. p. 9/4 The Saturn will carry a dummy Apollo moonship into orbit for the second time.

NAB, *n.* [*n*ut + *a*nd + *b*olt] See quots. — 1963 *Life* 27 Sept. p. 37 The other idea is to outfit him with a weird, new array of tools . . . a technician . . . tries out a NAB (Nuts and Bolts) which works very much like a ZERT . . . (which see) 1964 *National Geographic* March p. 380/1–2 At right, a special wrench called nab (short for nut and bolt) allows him to apply twisting force to the bolt without moving his body. 1965 *Newsweek* 14 June p. 34/3 Some of the hardware is small, like the tool called nab (a contraction of nut and bolt), for use in weightless space.

-NAUT. See quots. and preliminary remarks. — ALUMINAUT. 1964 N.Y. *Times* 30 Aug. p. 81/1 Hamilton, Bermuda, Aug. 29 — An important new weapon will be added to man's armory for exploration and research exploitation of ocean depths on Wednesday when the Aluminaut is launched at Groton, Conn. The Aluminaut, being built by the Electric Boat Company, is 50 feet long and designed to descend 15,000 feet and travel underwater for 100 miles. In Bermuda at the moment is the father of the vessel, Louis Reynolds, chairman of the board of Reynolds Metals, owner of the submarine. BATHYNAUT. 1961 N.Y. *Times Book Rev.* 5 Feb. p. 7/5 As the deep-ship crept down into its last fathom — its dangling guide rope coiling on the red ooze, its lanterns wan in the primordial dark — the bathynauts saw a fish, not a nightmare of a creature suited to the place but a prosaic flatfish like a sole, with a pair of normal-looking and wholly unaccountable eyes. Slowly, too, Picard and Walsh shook hands. HYDRONAUT. 1961 N.Y. *Times Book Rev.* 25 June p. 20/4 *130 FEET DOWN: Handbook for Hydronauts.* By Hank and Shaney Frey. Illustrated. 274 pp. New York: Harcourt, Brace & World. $6.50. Basic information for those who wish to explore the underwater world. PLASTINAUT. [See quots. s.v. in *Am. Sp.*

39: 146.] 1964 *Missiles and Rockets* 10 Feb. p. 35/3 . . . the Air Force "plasti-naut," a plastic dummy whose tissue characteristics simulate man's, could be orbited in the early unmanned check-out of the MOL [Manned Orbiting Laboratory] to get exact radiation data. (1965 *Encyclopedia Year Book*, p. 357/2.)

NERVA, N.E.R.V.A., *n.* [See first quot.] See quots. (Also attrib.) — 1961 Seattle *Times Mag.* 2 July p. 17 Research results will be used in the fabrication of the first flyable nuclear-rocket engine, called N.E.R.V.A. (an acronym for Nuclear Engine for Rocket Vehicle Application). 1962 *Brit. Book of the Year* p. 742/2. N.Y. *Times* 7 Oct. p. E7/8 A major step in the development of NERVA, the A. E. C. states in its 1962 report to Congress, will be the initial inflight test series "which may reasonably be anticipated in the 1966–67 period." It is presently planned to test a NERVA engine in an upper-stage of a Saturn launch vehicle. The flight-test vehicle would be lifted off the ground by the chemical booster and the nuclear engine would start as the chemical booster finished firing. 1964 *Sci. News Letter* 28 Nov. p. 343/1 Tests for the Westing-house-developed NERVA reactor (Nuclear Engine for Rocket Vehicle Application) have already shown a specific impulse — the rocket equivalent of miles-per-gallon or efficiency — better than twice as great as that of equally powerful chemically-powered engines.

NEUTRON STAR, *n.* See quots. — 1952 *Time* 14 July p. 51/1 But when the excitement was over, the only thing left would be a "neutron-star": a ball of peculiar matter made largely or entirely of neutrons. 1964 N.Y. *Times* 12 Jan. p. E11/7 The new technique of rocket astronomy has disclosed what seem to be the most "solid" objects ever observed. They are thought to be stars composed entirely of closely packed neutrons, weighing from 10 to 100 billion tons per cubic inch. It has been calculated that such neutron stars must be from five to ten miles in diameter, with a weight comparable to that of the entire sun. Tuscaloosa *News* 27 April p. 1/5–6 (AP) . . . the novel experiment is designed to prove or disprove this theory: That mysterious, celestial X-rays, discovered last summer by another rocket flight, are generated "neutron stars." These are believed to be the ultimate remnants of supernovae, or exploding stars.

NUKE, *n.* [From *nuclear.*] See quots. — 1959 N.Y. *Times Mag.* 1 Feb. p. 46/3 . . . soon there may be 5-inch nuclear shells and portable Davy Crockett "nukes" for the infantryman. 1960 *Time* 4 July p. 52/1 But the nuclear sub-marines — called "nukes" — can cruise underwater for weeks at top speed. 1964 *Time* 25 Sept. p. 16/2 G . . . has described these tactical "nukes" as "conventional — any weapon carried by an infantryman or a team of infantrymen." U. S. *News & World Report* 19 Oct. p. 46 All the "tactical nukes" now are said to require a personal go-ahead from the President before they can be fired.

OP-, OP ART, *n.* See quots. — 1964 *Life* 11 Dec. p. 133 Op-art is short for "optical art," a paradoxical movement dedicated to the practice of fascinating deceptions. *Reporter* 14 Jan. p. 46/3 But they do have the beginnings of Pop Art and Op Art (Optical Art), and since a copy of *Art International* mailed from Zurich will reach Tel Aviv in ten or twelve days, there is no reason for any lag. 1965 *Sat. Rev.* 29 May p. 29/3 Though Albers has been called the father of op art, I find this an unjust label. His delicately balanced paintings are not based on obvious optical rules, nor is he trying to shock our eyes merely by illusive tricks. *Ibid.* 5 June p. 6/2 Well, we've had pop art and op art, and we suppose it's only simple computer logic to expect the next step. . . . Tuscaloosa *News* 4 July Sunday Comics ("Buzz Sawyer" by Roy Crane) What's "op" art? It's a new movement, Sir. "Op" stands for optical. It's intended to dazzle the eye and give illusion of motion.

OPSTER, *n.* [*op* art + *-ster*] — 1965 *Sat. Rev.* 29 May p. 29/3 It would seem that two older artists have been curiously misunderstood — Albers by the "opsters" and Duchamp by the "popsters."

PHYTOTRON, *n.* [*phyto-* 'plant' + *-tron* (see NID 3 and first quot. s. v. *biotron*)] See quots. and *biotron* above. — 1949 *New Words and Words in the News* (Funk & Wagnalls Co.) Supp. No. 3 Fall p. 3/1. *Newsweek* 20 June p. 54 The laboratory, called the 'phytotron,' . . . creates 'weather' by closing switches and pushing buttons on an intricate control board. 1950 *Brit. Book of the Year* p. 740/1. 1958 *Science* 5 Sept. p. 510/2–3 The first facility for the study of plant growth under a wide range of controlled conditions was constructed at California Institute of Technology in Pasadena, in 1948–49. This facility was dubbed a "phytotron" in a humorous moment, but the term was so appropriate that it has endured. The variables under control are chiefly ranges of temperature, light intensities, and cycles of these variables.

PLASTIC BOMB, *n.* [Fr. *plastique, Specif.* An explosive the consistency of putty that combines TNT and hexogen (1962 N.Y. *Times Mag.* 4 Feb. p. 10/1; *Newsweek* 5 Feb. p. 37/2)]. See etymology and quots. (Also fig.) — 1962 Douglas Edwards on CBS News 22 Jan./plæstɪk bam/. *Newsweek* 5 Feb. p. 37/2 The French language has gained several new words from the plastic bombs that rock Paris every night. *Life* 23 Feb. p. 41 (pict. cap.) The night before, the O.A.S. had flung here and there the plastic bombs that have become the dread of Paris. *Harper's Mag.* April p. 26 It is thus a kind of French "ultra" movement, lobbing ideological plastic bombs into the national marketplace. 1964 *World Book Year Book* p. 611/1.

PLASTIC BOMBING, *n.* — 1962 N.Y. *Times Mag.* 4 Feb. p. 11/1–2 A wave of plastic bombings . . . has led to widespread belief in the danger of a Fascist coup.

PLASTIQUEUR, *n.* See quots. — 1962 *Newsweek* 5 Feb. p. 37/2 The French language has gained several ominous new words from the plastic bombs that rock Paris every night. The men who plant the explosives are *les plastiqueurs.* . . . Seattle *Times* 13 May p. 8 I cannot help but wonder if "plastiqueur" may not soon find its idiomatic equivalent in Spanish and Portuguese.

PLENCH, *n.* [See quots.] See quots. — 1963 *Life* 27 Sept. p. 37 PLENCH. Combination pliers and wrench, it works like a ZERT to install or remove nuts and bolts. 1964 *National Geographic* March p. 380/1–2 Astronaut's tool kit includes new devices for making repairs in the weightless environment of space — spammer (space hammer), plench (pliers and wrench), and zert (zero reaction tool).

POLYUNSATURATE, *n.* [*poly-* + *unsaturate, n.* (NID 3 Cf. *ibid.,* s.v. *unsaturated, adj.* b: '*of a chemical compound or mixture:* used esp. of organic compounds containing double or triple bonds between carbon atoms. . . .')] See quots. — 1962 Seattle *Times Pictorial* 25 March (adv.) Polyunsaturates Make Beauty News [.] It's a face cream that contains essential polyunsaturates. That's right — polyunsaturates, the natural elements you've been reading so much about that are so important to your health. Chicago *Sun-Times* 20 July p. 28/3 Maybe, so current thinking goes, we would be better off in the long run to reduce our costly animal fats and substitute the vegetable (polyunsaturate) fats and oils. 1965 *Newsweek* 24 May p. 56/1 (adv.) Medical studies now suggest great possible advantages in diets low in saturated fats and high in polyunsaturates.

QUASAR, *n.* [*quasi*-stell*ar* object.] See quots. — 1964 N.Y. *Times* 6 Sept. p. E9/7 The recent discovery of "quasars" — objects at extreme distances radiating light and radio waves with almost incredible intensity — has revived Dr. Ambartsumian's theory. Some at the meeting suggested that there may be no essential difference between the energy source at the core of our own galaxy and that which powers the radio galaxies of the quasars. 1965 *Sci. News Letter* 2 Jan. p. 7/3 Combined optical and radio studies of the universe increased the observed number of "quasars," short for "quasi-stellar objects," to 13. Quasars are the most distant objects so far discovered in space and the most powerful sources of radiation, both light and radio waves, yet known. *Newsweek* 21 June p. 62/2 Sandage and other astronomers have found about 60 quasars — a unique class of starlike objects that give off more light and radio noise than a galaxy of 100 billion stars. N.Y. *Times* 13 June p. 1/3 They resemble the strange, recently discovered "quasars," except they are not sources of strong radio emission, and are so numerous that they should enable astronomers to determine the nature of the universe.

REAL TIME, *n.* The term used when a computer is processing data so that its results can be immediately utilized in an experiment being conducted. Also see quots. (Also attrib.) — 1959 Woodford A. Heflin (ed.) *Aerospace Glossary* (Maxwell [Ala.] Air Force Base: Research Studies Institute, Air University) p. 84/1–2 REAL TIME. Time in which reporting on events or recording of events is simultaneous with the events. *Systems Mag.* (Remington Rand) Feb. p. 17/2 (pict. cap.) The objective is data reporting on missile test flights in 'real time' (instantaneously). When the system is completed, information will be read back from a missile immediately, telling the scientists how it is reacting to speed, friction, how the guidance system is performing, and many other details. 1960 N.Y. *Times* 17 July p. 13/4 As an experiment, Air Force and Weather Bureau meteorologists attempted to use the pictures to make "real time" forecasts of the weather — forecasts fresh enough to be useful. 1961 *ibid.* 28 Feb. p. 13S The airline said it recently signed an order for two Remington Rand Univac "real time" computers and their auxiliary equipment. The term "real time" refers to computer operation that takes place simultaneously with an event, such as a sale of a seat or a change in an airliner's arrival time. Such systems are used in the control of missiles in flight. 1964 *ibid.* 22 Nov. p. 10F/3 A process computer accepts data directly from measuring devices used in industrial processes. It acts upon the data in "real time," or at a speed sufficient to make effective changes in the process. 1965 *Newsweek* 14 June p. 32/3 This "real-time flight planning" — deciding what to do according to the occasion — pleased Kraft.

REVERSE INTEGRATION, *n.* See quots. — 1954 N.Y. *Times* 30 May p. 34/5 Fisk officials cite her case as being possibly an example of "reverse integration," a phrase enunciated in the light of the recent Supreme Court decision prohibiting segregation in the public schools. There are two others at Fisk who offer comparable examples. They are white students in the undergraduate school. 1957 N.Y. *Times Mag.* 6 Jan. p. 20 (title) Reverse Integration. 1963 N.Y. *Times* 7 April p. 63/4 Hundreds of white students are attending educational institutions that were once Negro, according to the Associated Press. "Reverse integration," this development is called. Tuscaloosa *News* 8 Sept. p. 14/7 (AP) Little Rock, scene of violent integrationist movements six years ago when Negro students sought entrance to all-white schools, is the scene today of reverse integration.

RHOCHREMATICS, *n.* [See second quot.] See quots. — 1960 Seattle *Times* 15 May p. 19 The subject is "Rhochrematics — A Scientific Approach to the Management of Material Flows." *Rhochrematics, A Scientific Approach to the Management of Material Flows.* Management series, no. 2 (Seattle: Bureau of Business Research, College of Business Administration, University of Washington) p. 3 Today's business literature is replete with references to "total distribution costs," "landed cost management," and other words and phrases which refer to different aspects of the management of material flows. To avoid the stigmas and manifold impressions attached to new terms a new word broad enough to encompass those areas of business activity yet precise to the point of being exclusive in connotation has been developed. This word is Rhochrematics ["Created by Professor William C. Grummel and Mr. William Royal Stokes of the Department of Classics, University of Washington."] It comes from the Greek "rhoe" meaning to flow as a river or a stream; "chrema" meaning products, materials, or things; and the abstract ending "ics" for any of the sciences. 1961 *Advanced Management* Feb. p. 16/1 (Richard A. Johnson) Rhochrematics is defined to include the flow from raw materials, through the processing stages, to the distribution of the finished product, and was coined specifically to eliminate the confusion among terms. It incorporates all of the other concepts — to produce to satisfy the needs of the consumer — to organize the distribution of finished goods in terms of the consumer — to integrate the functions of production and marketing into an effective total system.

SHOCK FROCK, *n.* See quots. — 1964 Nashville *Tennessean* 25 June p. 15/4 (AP) The makers of Britain's first bare-bosomed cocktail dresses said yesterday they have had second thoughts about their shock frocks. 1965 Tuscaloosa *News* 13 Feb. p. 4/3 (quoting Charleston *Daily Mail*) Now comes the ultimate — the topless swim suit and the "shock frock" or (why not come right out and say it) the bare-bosom look.

SOFT, *adj.* [Cf. OED, s.v. *soft, adj.*, 25.a: 'Applied to water, such as rain or river water, which is more or less free from calcium and magnesium salts . . .' {1775–}] See quots. — 1963 *Union Carbide Stockholder News* Sept. p. 1/1 Facilities are now being built at Union Carbide's Texas City, Texas, and Institute, West Virginia, plants for producing 150 million pounds or more a year of an alkylate for making "biologically soft" detergents. Most of today's detergents resist breakdown by bacteria present in soil and water, and as a result create voluminous foam in sewage treatment systems. However, the detergents that can be produced from the new Union Carbide chemicals can be quickly destroyed or degraded in sewage systems and waterways to non-detergent-like products, which show little surface activity and do not produce foam. 1964 Texize Chemicals, Inc. 29 May [Quot. s.v. *biodegradable*.]

SOFT-LAND, *v.t.* & *i.* To land (an object) on the moon in such a manner as to prevent its being destroyed on impact. — 1960 Seattle *Times Mag.* 29 May p. 22 . . . the first lunar vehicle may be a small robot to be soft-landed on the moon within the next five years. 1963 *Family Weekly* 7 April p. 5/1 You've soft-landed on the uneroded, airless surface of the moon. 1964 *Time* 7 Aug. p. 42/3 Later, J.P.L.'s unmanned Surveyor spacecraft will soft-land on the moon. . . . 1965 *Newsweek* 21 June p. 24/3 . . . the latest Lunik probe, dispatched on Tuesday to "soft land" on the moon and perhaps steal some of the spotlight from the Gemini 4, failed to make a needed mid-course maneuver and missed its target by 100,000 miles.

SOFT LANDING, *n.* See last quot. — 1958 *Think* July p. 6/1 Moon explorations will involve three distinct levels of difficulty. The first would be a simple shot at the moon, ending either in a 'hard' landing or a circling of the moon. Next in difficulty would be a 'soft' landing. And most difficult of all would be a 'soft' landing followed by a safe return to earth. 1959 Seattle *Times Mag.* 25 Oct. p. 10 In a soft landing it is necessary to take the payload down to the surface with retro-rockets firing near the approach. . . . 1960 N.Y. *Times* 31 July p. E7/8 The Surveyor craft will be used for "soft" landings, designed to place equipment on the moon, with the craft presumably still able to function. 1965 Tuscaloosa *News* 8 July p. 7/2 In a soft landing the spacecraft comes down so slowly and gently that delicate scientific instruments are able to survive the impact and relay their measurements back to earth.

SPAMMER, *n.* [See quots.] See quots. — 1963 *Life* 27 Sept. p. 37 SPAMMER. Short for space hammer, it uses a spring which is triggered to bang away like a riveter. 1964 *National Geographic* March p. 380/1–2 [Quot. s.v. *plench.*]

SPY IN THE SKY, SPY-IN-THE-SKY, *n.* 1. See quots. — 1960 N.Y. *Times* 12 June p. 6E/2 The U–2 reconnaissance "overflights" provided, by aerial photography and tape recording of Soviet radio and radar emissions, the most important intelligence gathered by the C.I.A. The "spy in the sky" more than compensated for the very few spies on the ground that the United States has been able to infiltrate into Russia. 1961 *World Book Year Book* p. 160/2. 1963 N.Y. *Times Mag.* 10 Nov. p. 96/4 The argument about so-called "spies in the sky" serves to illustrate how military-political issues act as roadblocks to progress in reaching agreement on practical legal questions. 2. *Attrib.* See quots. — 1960 *Life* 22 Aug. p. 19/2 Still to come in 1960: more weather, navigation, communication and "spy-in-the-sky" satellites, two moon orbiters, another deep space probe, two Mercury orbital shots with mansized capsules, and three suborbital shots — the last one with a man in it. 1965 *Sat. Rev.* 22 May p. 16/2 The notorious U–2, the most effective spy ever invented, was developed, and a start was made with the spy-in-the-sky satellites — though their value may have been exaggerated.

ZERT, *n.* [See quots.] See quots. — 1963 *Life* 27 Sept. p. 37 POWER ZERT. Battery-powered wrench does work. It is anchored in place to keep it from spinning. *Ibid.* 27 Sept. p. 37 HAND ZERT. The word stands for Zero Reaction Tool, and you must squeeze the handles to turn a bolt. 1964 *National Geographic* March p. 380/1–2 [Quot. s.v. *plench.*]

3 | ✍

LANGUAGE AND SOCIAL FORCES

Language expresses social status and responds to social forces. In a mobile society like that of the United States, a person might write his autobiography in terms of the way national, religious, and racial heritage, as well as geographic, economic, and educational background, has affected his language experience. A passage from Alfred Kazin's *A Walker in the City* exemplifies the reaction of children whose parents and teachers make them conscious of language as the indicator of social position: ". . . we were somehow to be a little ashamed of what we were. . . . A 'refined,' 'correct,' 'nice' English was required of us at school that we did not naturally speak. . . . This English was peculiarly the ladder of advancement. . . . It was bright and clean and polished. We were expected to show it off like a new pair of shoes." To climb this ladder could be, as Kazin reports, a painful and humiliating process. In *Pygmalion* and *My Fair Lady* Professor Henry Higgins uses language to reshape Eliza Doolittle to an upper-class standard. But Eliza wins our admiration by the element of earthiness she retains even in her new refinement.

The debate about good and bad English goes back to the eighteenth century when the rules of English grammar were established upon the model of Latin. But from the early 1900's onward, linguists have frequently expressed doubts about the inviolability of these rules, and, during the last several decades especially, have opened wider our knowledge of the range of usages, and of the relationship between the spoken and the written language. The matter came to a climax with the appearance of the third edition of *Webster's New International Dictionary* in 1961. Reviewers of the dictionary quarreled over prescriptive and descriptive approaches to language. The result has been a broader understanding of the variability of usage,

137

and at the same time a reaffirmation by linguists that they do not support a doctrine that "anything goes." They assert the principle of appropriateness, politeness, flexibility, and effectiveness. The writer or speaker of English must be nimble and able to change his voice, like his clothing, for different situations.

Political and social events of recent years underscore the needs of a pluralistic society. One linguist has asked what the solution should be when "the children in school speak a regional dialect of Standard American English which is radically different from a regional variety of some other part of the country." Until fairly recently the notion has been to submerge differences and to apologize for them. For many people the need to be accepted as correct led to imitation of the bland and undistinguished voice of the radio announcer, with the effect of hiding individuality. But linguists have more and more felt that people can be multidialectal. Without rejection of one dialect, students can learn the standard dialect necessary for fulfillment of their educational and economic ambitions. Recognition of the advantages of standards need not conflict with respect for difference and individuality.

W. Nelson Francis

SOCIAL AND EDUCATIONAL
VARIETIES OF ENGLISH

✍✍

Bartolomeo Vanzetti's speeches and letters had simple, honest eloquence, yet he used what we call "broken English." His language
illustrates the distinction Nelson Francis and many modern grammarians and linguists make: the merely correct may also be dull; uneducated language may be eloquent. Needless to say, this is not to
recommend striving for eloquence by violating the conventions of
grammar and usage. Chances are that the language of educated people
will be effective, but it does not automatically follow. This essay gives
a broad understanding of such terms as "levels of usage," "appropriateness," "effectiveness," "varieties of English," "dialects," "standard
English," "uneducated English," and "vernacular." It should help
you to be more sensitive to language in its social context and to the
appropriate shifts in dialect and usage that each of us makes as he
enters and leaves several speech communities or writing situations.

We have already noted that there are social varieties of English, differing
in pronunciation, grammar, and vocabulary. These are the natural modes
of speech of people who differ in education and in the positions they
occupy in the social system. It is here, even more than in regional variation, that value judgments are most likely to be made. Specifically, the
dialect of educated people who occupy positions of influence and responsibility is commonly called "good English" and that of people lower on the
educational and social scale "bad English." Let us briefly investigate the
implications of these terms.

Applied to language, the adjective *good* can have two meanings: (1) "effective, adequate for the purpose to which it is put" and (2) "acceptable, conforming to approved usage." The first of these is truly a value judgment of the language itself. In this sense the language of Shakespeare, for example, is "good English" because it serves as a highly effective vehicle for his material. On the other hand, the language of a poorer writer, which does not meet adequately the demands put upon it, might be called "bad English." The second meaning of *good* is not really a judgment of the language itself but a social appraisal of the persons who use it. An expression like *I ain't got no time for youse* may be most effective in the situation in which it is used, and hence "good English" in the first sense. But most people, including those who naturally speak this way, will call it "bad English" because grammatical features like *ain't, youse,* and the double negative construction belong to a variety of English commonly used by people with little education and low social and economic status.

This second meaning of the terms *good English* and *bad English* is much more common than the first. It is easier, no doubt, to identify a dialect by certain overt items of grammar and vocabulary than it is to estimate the effectiveness of a specific sample of language. Furthermore, the notion that the language of social and educational inferiors is "bad" has been extensively taught in schools, so that even those who speak it naturally often get the idea that there is something intrinsically wrong with their language, usually without clearly understanding why. Others, of course, alter their language to make it conform more nearly to what they have been taught to consider "good." In effect, they adopt a social dialect appropriate to a higher position on the educational and social scale.

It is unfortunate that these two notions — effectiveness and social prestige — have both come to be expressed in the same terms, as value judgments of the language itself. They are not necessarily connected. What is called "bad English" in the usual sense may be highly effective in the appropriate context. Conversely, language which is socially and educationally impeccable may be most ineffective, as anyone who has listened to a dull speech can testify. It is true that on the whole the language of the more educated is likely to be more effective, since it has a larger vocabulary and somewhat more complex grammar and hence is capable of finer and more subtle shades of meaning as well as finer effects of rhythm and tone. But unless these resources are used skillfully they do not necessarily produce better language from the point of view of effectiveness. On the other hand, writers like Mark Twain, Ring Lardner, and William Faulkner have shown that vernacular or uneducated English can be used with great effectiveness in literature.

As with other kinds of variation, social levels of English shade gradually into one another. But we can recognize three main levels. At the top is **educated** or **standard English;** at the bottom is **uneducated English,** and between them comes what H. L. Mencken called the **vernacular**.[1] These have in common the larger part of their grammar, pronunciation, and basic vocabulary but are marked by significant differences in all three areas.

Educated or **Standard English** is that naturally used by most college-educated people who fill positions of social, financial, and professional influence in the community. Some people learn it as their native speech, if they come from families that already belong to this social class. Others acquire it in the course of their schooling and later by conscious or unconscious imitation of their associates. Control of standard English does not, of course, guarantee professional, social, or financial success. But it is an almost indispensable attribute of those who attain such success.

In addition to its social importance, educated English is on the whole a more flexible and versatile instrument than the other social varieties. As the language of the professions and the learned disciplines, it is called on to express more complex ideas, for which it has developed an extensive vocabulary. Its grammar, too, is more complex, and it uses longer sentences with more levels of subordination. This does not mean that it presents greater difficulties to the listener or reader, provided he is familiar with its vocabulary and grammar. But the fact that it is often used to express complicated and difficult material means that, unskillfully used, it can be vague or obscure. When its resources of vocabulary and grammar are over-exploited in the expression of simple ideas, it may become the inflated jargon sometimes called "gobbledygook":

> With regard to personnel utilizing the premises after normal working hours, it is requested that precautions be observed to insure that all windows and doors are firmly secured and all illumination extinguished before vacating the building.

This is obviously only a much elaborated expression of the request that can be more simply and effectively stated:

> If you work late, be sure to lock the doors and windows and turn off the lights when you leave.

In the first sense of the phrase "good English," this translation is good and the gobbledygook which it translates, though it contains no errors of grammar or usage, is incredibly bad.

The British version of standard English, RP, is the same for all speakers regardless of their place of origin. In America, however, there is no such thing as a single standard form of American English, especially in pronunciation. The nearest thing to it is the speech of anonymous radio and television announcers, which one linguist has aptly called "network Eng-

[1] H. L. Mencken, *The American Language*, 4th ed. (New York: Alfred A. Knopf, 1937), p. 417.

lish."[2] In contrast to the well known individual commentators, who are allowed to use their native regional pronunciation, the network announcers all use a common version of English which is in most features that of the Inland Northern area. The contrast between a routine sports announcer and Dizzy Dean is the contrast between "network English," faultless but rather dull, and a picturesque use of South Midland vernacular.

Because of its nationwide use, network English is an acceptable standard form everywhere. But it is not a prestige dialect. Educated speakers in Boston, New York, Philadelphia, Richmond, Charleston, Atlanta, or New Orleans use the dialects of their own regions in educated form. The last five Presidents of the United States are a good example of the diversity of pronunciation to be found in standard English. President Johnson speaks the educated South Midland speech of Texas. President Kennedy's Boston speech with its lack of postvocalic /r/ and its intrusive /r/ at the end of words like *Cuba*, was very distinctive. President Eisenhower's speech was a good illustration of the Middle Western variety sometimes called General American. It betrayed his Kansas origin in spite of a military career that took him to many parts of the English-speaking world. President Truman retained many of the South Midland features of his native Missouri, and President Roosevelt spoke the educated version of New York City speech, somewhat modified by his Harvard education and New England connections. Although most of these men had long careers in politics and frequently addressed nationwide audiences, each of them used the educated version of his native regional dialect.

Vernacular English is the variety naturally used by the middle group of the population, who constitute the vast majority. Their schooling extends into or through high school, with perhaps a year of college or technical school. They occupy the lesser white-collar jobs, staff the service trades, and fill the ranks of skilled labor. Many of these jobs require considerable verbal skill and have extensive occupational vocabularies. Vernacular speakers, when "talking shop," characteristically show considerable control of technical vocabulary and relatively complex grammar.

Just as jargon and gobbledygook are the result of overpretentious style in standard English, so the **hyperurbanism** or **hyperform** is in the vernacular. A hyperurbanism is a usage which results from the overcorrection of one of the supposedly "bad" (*i.e.* nonstandard) features of the vernacular. For example, the usage of pronoun case in the vernacular differs from that of standard English in several respects, one being that a pronoun subject when coordinated with another pronoun or with a noun may be the objective case:

2 William A. Stewart, in a discussion of the problem of teaching standard English to nonstandard speakers, Bloomington, Indiana, August 1964.

vernacular:	Him and Joe went.
standard:	Joe and he went.
vernacular:	You and me can do it.
standard:	You and I can do it.

The native speaker of the vernacular who aspires to speak standard learns to change this use of the objective case to the standard subjective. But this change often leads to uncertainty about pronoun case in coordination constructions elsewhere than as subject. The vernacular speaker who has learned that *you and me* is incorrect as subject is likely to be suspicious of it anywhere, so he says *between you and I,* which is just as much a violation of standard grammar as *you and me can do it.*

This is not the place for an extended discussion of the features which distinguish the vernacular from standard educated English. Many of them are identified and discussed in the standard handbooks and dictionaries of usage. . . . Since the vernacular shades gradually into educated standard, many of these items characterize only the varieties of vernacular nearest to uneducated English. Many points of usage which are condemned as non-standard by handbooks actually represent **divided usage;** that is, they are accepted and used by some standard English speakers but rejected by others. Sometimes the division is regional: a form or construction which is vernacular or uneducated in one region may be standard in another. An example is the use of *like* in such sentences as *It looks like it might rain* and *He acts like he's hungry.* This usage, condemned as nonstandard by most handbooks, is certainly standard in England and in the American South in all but the most formal style. In the American North and Midland it is probably to be classed as vernacular. At least, a recent advertising slogan that used *like* in this way stirred up considerable discussion and condemnation among those who feel responsible for protecting standard English from vernacular encroachments. In fact, some aspirants to standard "correctness" avoid the use of *like* as a subordinator entirely, replacing it with *as* in sentences like *He drove as a crazy man.* This hyperurbanism throws away the nice semantic distinction between the prepositions *like* and *as,* as in the following:

He is acting *like* a lawyer in this affair.
He is acting *as* a lawyer in this affair.

The implication of the first is either that he is not a lawyer at all or that his lawyerlike behavior is inappropriate or unwelcome. In the second, no such judgment is implied; the sentence merely states that in the affair in question his participation is limited to the role of lawyer. It is frequently the effect of a hyperurbanism to gain a supposed (but spurious) "correctness" at the expense of precision. It thus becomes an example of "bad English" in the first sense discussed above. If preciseness in communication is an important quality of language, which certainly few will deny, the hyperurbanism that blurs preciseness in the interest of a fancied correctness is a greater linguistic offense than the nonstandard vernacular usage which is accurate and clear.

The vernacular is very much with us and presumably always will be. It is the stratum of English where there develop many new features of grammar, pronunciation, and vocabulary which are ultimately accepted into standard usage. In a democratic society like that of America, it is an essential medium of communication even for the educated, who must at least understand and accept its usage, though they do not necessarily have to speak it. In fact, if they can speak it only with conscious and obvious effort, educated speakers should avoid it, for people are quick to take offense at what they consider patronizing. But those native speakers of the vernacular who have also acquired a command of educated standard English should not lose control of the vernacular, since a native command of it can be of great value on many occasions.

A practical illustration is the case of the college professor of English, a native speaker of educated English, who needed a rare part for his car. He consulted a colleague who had at one time been a garage mechanic and spoke the appropriate form of the vernacular. The colleague told him where to telephone to inquire for the part, but added "You'd better let me do the phoning; it'll cost you twice as much if you do it."[3]

Uneducated English is that naturally used by people whose schooling is limited and who perform the unskilled labor in country and city. Certain grammatical features, such as the double or multiple negative (which was standard in Chaucer's English) and the use of *them* as a plural demonstrative, are common to most regional varieties. But in other respects uneducated English shows much regional variety in all its features. An uneducated speaker may find that he has difficulty making himself understood outside his home region. Such features as past-tense *holp* for *helped* and *drug* for *dragged* have clear-cut regional distribution.[4] Likewise regional differences of pronunciation, which, as we have seen, exist on all levels, are much greater in uneducated speech. The same is true of vocabulary; the local words and expressions which more educated speakers avoid (though they may consider them picturesque and use them occasionally for special effect) persistently survive in uneducated speech. For this reason dialectological investigations like the Linguistic Survey of England often confine themselves almost wholly to uneducated, preferably illiterate, informants.[5]

[3] This anecdote is told of himself by Professor J. J. Lamberts of Arizona State University.

[4] Atwood, *Survey*, pp. 9f., 16f. [E. Bagby Atwood, *A Survey of Verb Forms in the Eastern United States* (University of Michigan Press, 1953)]

[5] Harold Orton and Eugen Dieth, *Survey of English Dialects* (Leeds: E. J. Arnold & Son, Ltd., 1962), pp. 14–17, 44. In the Linguistic Atlas of the United States and Canada, however, three types of informants — representing roughly what we have called

Uneducated English doesn't often get into writing, since its users have little occasion to write and may be semiliterate or even wholly illiterate.[6] In literary writing, uneducated speakers are often marked as such by attempts to represent their pronunciation by distorted spelling, including a liberal use of eye dialect. But a truly skillful use of uneducated English in literature suggests the level of the speaker without resorting to the rather cheap device of eye dialect. Notice in the following passage from William Faulkner's great novel *As I Lay Dying* how the nature of the speaker — an uneducated Mississippi farmer — is indicated by grammar and vocabulary, without any attempt to illustrate pronunciation at all.

It was nigh toward daybreak when we drove the last nail and toted it into the house, where she was laying on the bed with the window open and the rain blowing on her again. Twice he did it, and him so dead for sleep that Cora says his face looked like one of these here Christmas masts that had done been buried a while and then dug up, until at last they put her into it and nailed it down so he couldn't open the window on her no more. And the next morning they found him in his shirt tail, laying asleep on the floor like a felled steer, and the top of the box bored clean full of holes and Cash's new auger broke off in the last one. When they taken the lid off they found that two of them had bored on into her face.

If it's a judgment, it aint right. Because the Lord's got more to do than that. He's bound to have. Because the only burden Anse Bundren's ever had is himself. And when folks talks him low, I think to myself he aint that less of a man or he couldn't a bore himself this long (p. 68).

Here the markers of uneducated regional dialect are such grammatical items as the verb phrase *had done been buried* and the double negative in *couldn't open the window on her no more*, the lexical item *toted*, and idioms like *talks him low* and *he aint that less of a man*.

The uneducated English of this sample contrasts with the following passage from the same novel, representing the English of a country doctor from the same region:

When Anse finally sent for me of his own accord, I said "He has wore her out at last." And I said a damn good thing, and at first I would

---

uneducated, vernacular, and educated English — are used. See Hans Kurath, *Handbook of the Linguistic Geography of New England* (Washington: American Council of Learned Societies, 1939), pp. 41–44.

[6] C. C. Fries, in preparing his *American English Grammar* (New York: Appleton-Century-Crofts, 1940), found a plentiful source of uneducated written English in letters written to a government bureau whose constituents included many uneducated speakers.

not go because there might be something I could do and I would have to haul her back, by God. I thought maybe they have the same sort of fool ethics in heaven they have in the Medical College and that it was maybe Vernon Tull sending for me again, getting me there in the nick of time, as Vernon always does things, getting the most for Anse's money like he does for his own. But when it got far enough into the day for me to read weather sign I knew it couldn't have been anybody but Anse that sent. I knew that nobody but a luckless man could ever need a doctor in the face of a cyclone. And I knew that if it had finally occurred to Anse himself that he needed one, it was already too late.[7]

There are items here which are not educated standard — *wore* as past participle, for example. But the general level of the English is educated colloquial, quite different from that of the previous passage. Note especially the grammatical complexity of the last sentence.

The speaker who is confined to uneducated English finds himself under a great handicap if he wishes to improve his position in society. This is true even in his own region; it is doubly so when he moves to another dialect area, where he may find not only that his speech is a liability when it comes to getting a good job, but even that he can't make himself understood at all. Furthermore, in an age when more and more of the unskilled tasks are being done by machines, the number of jobs available to persons unable to use any but uneducated English gets smaller every year. The geographical and social mobility of our people presents a great problem to the schools, one of whose tasks is to help students acquire a kind of language which will be an asset to them rather than a handicap. The problem is especially acute in the Northern cities which have had a large influx of uneducated people from the South. It is encouraging to observe that linguists, especially dialectologists, are being called on to help with this problem. The idea is getting about that the speaker of uneducated English is better served if an attempt is made not to "correct" his language and eradicate his "bad language habits," but to extend his linguistic range and versatility by helping him acquire a new dialect that is socially more acceptable. Some educators are even experimenting with the techniques developed for teaching foreign languages, in order to emphasize that the task is the positive one of learning something new rather than the negative one of eliminating something bad. Already the results of tentative efforts of this sort are showing promise.

Helping speakers of uneducated English to a command of the vernacular or of standard English is only part of the problem, of course. There must be other kinds of training, and above all there must be tangible evidence that the effort will be worthwhile; otherwise motivation will be lacking, and without motivation learning is impossible. But in this area the informed student and teacher of language can certainly be of great social usefulness.

[7] *As I Lay Dying*, p. 37.

Albert H. Marckwardt

REGIONAL VARIATIONS

彡彡

In addition to studying the educational and social forces discussed by
Mr. Francis, we must also consider the role of place. We speak the
language of our own regions, with our local pronunciations and vocabulary. To make a linguistic atlas, field workers collect dialect variations
according to methods which Professor Marckwardt describes. He lists
words that are key indices for plotting the regions, words that will be
familiar to some people, though strange to others. His essay also
shows how regional vocabulary is tied to our nation's settlement
history.

Early travelers to America and native commentators on the language
agree on the existence of regional differences at an early period in our
national history. Mrs. Anne Royal called attention to various Southernisms
in the works which she wrote during the second quarter of the nineteenth
century, and as early as 1829, Dr. Robley Dunglison had identified many
of the Americanisms, in the glossary he compiled, with particular portions
of the country. Charles Dickens recognized regional differences in the
English he encountered in his first tour of the United States, and William
Howard Russell, reporting on Abraham Lincoln's first state banquet, at
which he was a guest, mentions his astonishment at finding 'a diversity of
accent almost as great as if a number of foreigners had been speaking
English.'

A number of other observers, however, were sufficiently impressed by the
uniformity of the language throughout the country to make this a matter

From *American English* by Albert H. Marckwardt. Copyright © 1958 by Oxford
University Press, Inc. Reprinted by permission.

of comment. De Tocqueville, in a rather extended treatment of the language of the young republic, flatly declared, 'There is no patois in the New World,' and John Pickering, along with Noah Webster easily the most distinguished of our early philologists, also remarked on the great uniformity of dialect through the United States, 'in consequence,' as he said, 'of the frequent removals of people from one part of our country to another.'

There is truth in both types of comment. People in various parts of the United States do not all speak alike, but there is greater uniformity here than in England or in the countries of Western Europe, and this makes the collection of a trustworthy body of information upon the regional variations in American English a somewhat difficult and delicate matter.

The gathering of authentic data on the dialects of many of the countries of Western Europe began in the latter decades of the nineteenth century. The *Atlas linguistique de la France* followed closely upon the heels of the *Sprachatlas des deutschen Reichs*, and the activities of the English Dialect Society were initiated about the same time. In 1889 a group of American scholars organized the American Dialect Society, hoping that the activities of this organization might result in a body of material from which either a dialect dictionary or a series of linguistic maps, or both, might be compiled. The society remained relatively small, however, and although some valuable information appeared in its journal *Dialect Notes*, a systematic survey of the regional varieties of American English has not yet resulted from its activities.

The past quarter of a century, however, has seen the development of such a survey. Beginning in 1928, a group of researchers under the direction of Professor Hans Kurath, now of the University of Michigan, undertook the compilation of a *Linguistic Atlas of New England* as the first unit of a projected *Linguistic Atlas of the United States and Canada*. The New England atlas, comprising a collection of some 600 maps, each showing the distribution of a single language feature throughout the area, was published over the period from 1939 to 1943. Since that time, field work for comparable atlases of the Middle Atlantic and of the South Atlantic states has been completed, and the materials are awaiting editing and publication. Field records for atlases of the North Central states and the Upper Middle West are virtually complete, and significant beginnings have been made in the Rocky Mountain and the Pacific Coast areas. Surveys in Louisiana, in Texas, and in Ontario are also under way. It is perhaps not too optimistic to predict that within the next twenty-five years all of the United States and Canada as well will have been covered in at least an initial survey.

For a number of reasons it is not easy to collect a body of valid and reliable information on American dialects. The wide spread of education, the virtual extinction of illiteracy, the extreme mobility of the population — both geographically and from one social class to another — and the tremendous development of a number of media of mass communication have all contributed to the recession of local speech forms. Moreover, the cultural insecurity of a large portion of the American people has caused them to feel apologetic about their language. Consequently, they seldom display the same degree of pride or affection that many an English or a European speaker has for his particular patois. Since all dialect research is essentially a sampling process, this means that the investigator must take particular pains to secure representative and comparable samples from the areas which are studied. Happily, the very care which this demands has had the result of developing the methodology of linguistic geography in this country to a very high level.

In general, the material for a linguistic atlas is based upon the natural responses of a number of carefully selected individuals representing certain carefully chosen communities, which in themselves reflect the principal strains of settlement and facets of cultural development in the area as a whole. Since the spread of education generally results in the disappearance of local or regional speech forms, and since the extension of schooling to virtually all of the population has been an achievement of the past seventy-five years, it became necessary for the American investigator to differentiate between the oldest generation, for whom schooling beyond the elementary level is not usual, and a middle-aged group who is likely to have had some experience with secondary schools. In addition, it is highly desirable to include some representatives of the standard or cultivated speech in each region, that their language may serve as a basis of comparison with the folk speech. Accordingly, in the American atlases, from each community represented, the field worker will choose at least two, and sometimes three representatives, in contrast to the usual practice of European researchers, who may safely content themselves with one. Moreover, it is equally necessary to make certain that the persons chosen in any community have not been subject to alien linguistic influences; consequently, only those who have lived there all of their lives, and preferably those who represent families who have long been identified with the area in question, are interviewed, although as one moves westward into the more recently settled areas this is not always possible.

Since complete materials are available only for the eastern seaboard and for the area north of the Ohio River as far west as the Mississippi, tentative conclusions relative to the regional variations in American English can be presented only for the eastern half of the country. The principal dialect areas presented in Kurath's *Word Geography of the Eastern United States*, are indicated on the next page.

The three major dialect boundaries, it will be noted, cut the country into lateral strips and are labeled by Professor Kurath *Northern*, *Midland*, and *Southern* respectively. The line which separates the Northern and Midland areas begins in New Jersey a little below Sandy Hook, proceeds

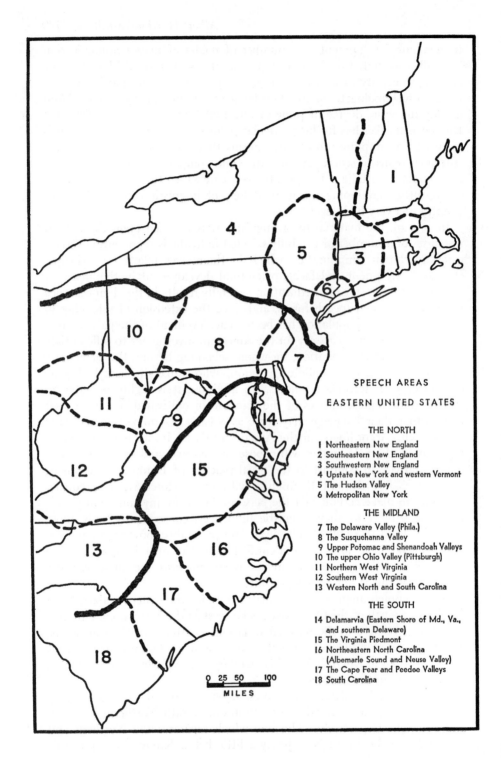

SPEECH AREAS

EASTERN UNITED STATES

THE NORTH

1 Northeastern New England
2 Southeastern New England
3 Southwestern New England
4 Upstate New York and western Vermont
5 The Hudson Valley
6 Metropolitan New York

THE MIDLAND

7 The Delaware Valley (Phila.)
8 The Susquehanna Valley
9 Upper Potomac and Shenandoah Valleys
10 The upper Ohio Valley (Pittsburgh)
11 Northern West Virginia
12 Southern West Virginia
13 Western North and South Carolina

THE SOUTH

14 Delamarvia (Eastern Shore of Md., Va., and southern Delaware)
15 The Virginia Piedmont
16 Northeastern North Carolina (Albemarle Sound and Neuse Valley)
17 The Cape Fear and Peedee Valleys
18 South Carolina

0 25 50   100
MILES

northwest to the east branch of the Susquehanna near Scranton, Pennsylvania, then goes westward through Pennsylvania just below the northern tier of counties. In Ohio the boundary dips below the Western Reserve, then turns northwest again, passing above Fort Wayne, Indiana. When it approaches South Bend it dips slightly to the southwest and cuts through Illinois, reaching the Mississippi at a point slightly above Quincy. The other principal boundary, that separating the Southern and Midland areas, begins at a point somewhat below Dover in Delaware, sweeps through Baltimore in something of an arc, turns sharply southwest north of the Potomac, follows the crest of the Blue Ridge in Virginia, and south of the James River swerves out into the North Carolina Piedmont. As we approach the lower part of South Carolina and Georgia the boundary is as yet unknown.

Even these necessarily incomplete results of the survey carried on under Professor Kurath and his associates have modified considerably our previous conceptions of the regional distribution of American speech forms. This modification is brought about principally by adding one concept and eliminating another. The concept thus eliminated has been variously known as Middle Western, Western, or General American. The older view of American dialects, reduced to its simplest terms, recognized the existence of a New England type of speech, a Southern type, and the remainder was generally blanketed by some such term as General American.

It seems clear now that what is neither New England nor Southern — which includes, of course, something between three-quarters and nine-tenths of the continental United States — is far too diverse and lacking in homogeneity to be considered a single major dialect. We know, for example, that there are a significant number of differences, both in vocabulary and in verb inflections, between the folk speech of most of Pennsylvania and that of New York state, and between Michigan and Wisconsin on the one hand, and most of Indiana and large portions of Illinois and Ohio on the other. As our information for the rest of the country becomes available, there can be little doubt that this conclusion will be strengthened.

The concept which has been added is the recognition of a Midland type of speech as distinct from both North and South. An examination of the evidence which Professor Kurath presents in his *Word Geography* leaves no doubt that the speech of this area, though it is by no means uniform, is sufficiently differentiated from both North and South to justify its classification as a major dialect area. This conclusion is supported not only by Atwood's study of the verb forms in the eastern portion of the country but by the available materials from the North Central States.

The map shown on page 150 includes also a few, but not all, of the sub-dialect areas which merit recognition. In the North the principal area is that which separates coastal New England from western New England,

New York state, and the territory to the west. In general, this boundary follows the line of the Green Mountains, the Berkshire Hills, and the Connecticut River. The Metropolitan New York area consists of a broad circle with the city itself at the center; the Hudson Valley area encompasses the original Dutch settlements in New York and northern New Jersey, spreading into northeastern Pennsylvania. The Midland area is divided into northern and southern sub-areas, the line of demarcation being just a little south of the Old National Road in Ohio, Indiana, and Illinois. Within the Southern dialect region, the Virginia Piedmont and the Delmarva peninsula constitute distinct sub-areas.

Thus far it is the lexical materials gathered in connection with the various atlas projects which have been analyzed most extensively, and as the title of Professor Kurath's work indicates, his plotting of the major dialect areas is based upon vocabulary evidence. For example, characteristic Northern expressions that are current throughout the area include *pail, swill, whiffletree* or *whippletree, comforter* or *comfortable* for a thick quilt, *brook, co-boss* or *come-boss* as a cow call, *johnnycake, salt pork,* and *darning needle* for a dragonfly. In the Midland area we find *blinds* for roller shades, *skillet, spouting* or *spouts* for eaves, a *piece* for food taken between meals, *snake feeder* for a dragonfly, *sook* as the call to calves, *armload* for an armful of wood; and one *hulls* beans when he takes off the shells. A quarter *till* the hour is a typical Midland expression, as is the elliptical *to want off,* or *out,* or *in.* The South has *lightwood* as the term for kindling, a *turn* of wood for an armful; stringbeans are generally *snap beans; hasslet* is the term for the edible inner organs of a pig, *chittlins* for the small intestine; and in this area cows are said to *low* at feeding time.

The sub-dialect areas also have their characteristic forms. In coastal New England, for instance, *pigsty* is the normal term for pig-pen, *bonny clapper* for curdled sour milk, *buttonwood* for a sycamore, and *pandowdy* for a cobbler type of dessert. Eastern Virginia has *cuppin* for a cowpen, *corn house* for a crib. *Lumber room* survives as the term for a storeroom. A grasshopper is known as a *hopper grass,* and *batter bread* is used for a soft cornbread containing egg.

As far as the sectors of the American lexicon which reflect regional differences are concerned, the matter is trenchantly summarized in Kurath's *Word Geography,* where the author points out first of all that the vocabularies of the arts and sciences, of industries, commercial enterprises, social and political institutions, and even many of the crafts, are national in scope because the activities they reflect are organized on a national basis. He then goes on to say:

Enterprises and activities that are regionally restricted have, on the other hand, a considerable body of regional vocabulary which, to be sure, may be known in other parts of the country, even if it is not in active use. The cotton planter of the South, the tobacco grower, the dairy farmer, the wheat grower, the miner, the lumberman, and the rancher of the West have many words and expressions that are strictly regional and sometimes local in their currency.

Regional and local expressions are most common in the vocabulary of the intimate everyday life of the home and the farm — not only among the simple folk and the middle class but also among the cultured . . . Food, clothing, shelter, health, the day's work, play, mating, social gatherings, the land, the farm buildings, implements, the farm stocks and crops, the weather, the fauna and flora — these are the intimate concern of the common folk in the countryside, and for these things expressions are handed down in the family and the neighborhood that schooling and reading and a familiarity with regional or national usage do not blot out.

It is not only in the vocabulary that one finds regional differences in American speech. There are pronunciation features as well. Throughout the Northern area, for example, the distinction between [o] and [ɔ] in such word pairs as *hoarse* and *horse, mourning* and *morning* is generally maintained; [s] regularly occurs in *grease* (verb) and *greasy*, and *root* is pronounced by many with the vowel of *wood*. Within the Northern area such sub-dialects as coastal New England and Metropolitan New York also show many characteristic forms; the treatment of the vowel of *bird* is only one of these, and words of the *calf, pass, path, dance* group constitute another. In the Midland area speakers fail to distinguished between *hoarse* and *horse*. Rounding is characteristic of the vowels of *hog, frog, log, wasp* and *wash*, and in the last of these words an *r* often intrudes in the speech of the not too highly educated. The vowels of *due* and *new* will resemble that of *food* rather than *feud*. In the South, *r* is 'lost' except before vowels, as it is in eastern New England and New York City but not in the Northern area generally. Words like *Tuesday, due,* and *new* have a y-like glide preceding the vowel, and final [z] in *Mrs.* is the normal form.

Among the older, relatively uneducated group and even to some extent among the middle-aged informants who have had some secondary schooling there are also regional differences in inflectional forms and syntax. For example, *hadn't ought* for 'oughtn't,' *see* as a past tense form, *clim* for 'climbed' among the oldest sector of the population, *wan't* for 'wasn't,' *be* in such expressions as *How be you?*, and the choice of the preposition *to* in *sick to his stomach* are all characteristic of the Northern area. *Clum* for 'climbed,' *seen* for 'saw,' *all the further* and *I'll wait on you* are to be found in the Midlands, whereas *belongs to be, heern* for 'heard,' *seed* as the past tense of 'to see,' *holp* for 'helped,' *might could* and *mought have* are characteristic of the South.

All of this raises the question as to how the regional forms of American English developed in our three and one-half centuries of linguistic history.

The first factor which must be taken into account is settlement history. Where did our earliest settlers come from, and what dialects did they speak? It was pointed out in Chapter 2* that at the time of the earliest settlements, English local and regional dialects were in a stronger position than they are today in that they constituted the natural speech of a greater portion of the English-speaking population and were in customary use farther up the social scale.

Moreover, it is quite unlikely that any single local settlement, even at the outset, ever consisted entirely of speakers of the same dialect. Of ten families of settlers gathered in any one place, two might well have spoken London English, three or four others one of the southern or southeastern county dialects. There would be in addition a couple of families speaking northern English and another two or three employing a western dialect. In the course of their being in constant contact with each other, compromises for the everyday terms in which their dialects differed would normally have developed, and one could reasonably expect to find a southern English term for a water receptacle, a northern word for earthworm, and a western designation for sour milk. Matters of pronunciation would eventually, perhaps after a slightly longer time, be compromised in much the same manner. Moreover, the resultant compromises for various localities would be different. In the first place, no two localities would have had exactly the same proportions of speakers of the various English dialects, and even if they had, the two localities would not have arrived at precisely the same set of compromises. Thus, early in our history we developed, at various points on the Atlantic seaboard, a number of local cultures, each with distinctive social characteristics of its own — including a dialect which was basically a unique blend of British types of speech, supplemented in its vocabulary by borrowings from the Indians and from Dutch and German neighbors.

With the beginning of the nineteenth century, three changes occurred which were to have a profound effect upon the language situation in America. First, the industrial revolution resulted in the growth of a number of industrial centers, uprooting a considerable proportion of the farm population and concentrating it in the cities. The development of the railroad and other mechanical means of travel increased greatly the mobility of the average person. The large-scale migrations westward also resulted in some resettlement and shifting, even among those who did not set out on the long trek. All of this resulted in a general abandonment of narrowly local speech forms in favor of fewer, more or less general, regional types. Some local speech forms have remained even to the present day. These are usually known as relics, particularly when they are distributed in isolated spots over an area rather than in concentration. *Open stone peach,*

* *Editors' Note:* that is, Chapter 2 of Professor Marckwardt's book, *American English.*

for example, is a relic for freestone peach, occurring in Maryland. *Smurring up*, 'getting foggy,' survives as a relic in eastern Maine and more rarely on Cape Cod and Martha's Vineyard.

Even prior to the shifts in population and changes in the culture pattern, certain colonial cities such as Boston, Philadelphia, and Charleston had acquired prestige by developing as centers of trade and foci of immigration. They became socially and culturally outstanding, as well as economically powerful, thus dominating the areas surrounding them. As a consequence, local expressions and pronunciations peculiar to the countryside came to be replaced by new forms of speech emanating from these centers. A fairly recent instance of this is to be found in the New England term *tonic* for soda water, practically co-extensive with the area served by Boston wholesalers. Professor Kurath considers the influence of these centers as second only to the influence of the original settlement in shaping the regional types of speech on the Atlantic seaboard and in determining their geographic boundaries.

Nor was the general process of dialect formation by any means completed with the settlement of the Atlantic seaboard. As the land to the west came to be taken up in successive stages (for example, western New York, Michigan, Wisconsin in the North; southern Ohio, Indiana, and southern Illinois in the Midland area) the same mixtures of speech forms among the settlers were present at first, and the same linguistic compromises had to be worked out. The same processes occurred in the interior South, in Texas, and later on in the Far West. Consequently, the complete linguistic history, particularly with respect to regional forms, of the United States will not be known until all of the facts concerning the present regional distribution of speech forms have been collected, and until these facts have been collated with the settlement history of the various areas and the speech types employed by the settlers at the time they moved in. In its entirety this would necessitate a greater knowledge of the local dialects of seventeenth-century England than we have at present.

Moreover, such environmental factors as topography, climate, and plant and animal life also play their parts in influencing the dialect of an area, just as they did in the general transplanting of the English language to America. The complexity and size of the network of fresh-water streams will affect the distribution and meaning of such terms as *brook, creek, branch,* and *river*. In parts of Ohio and Pennsylvania, for example, the term *creek* is applied to a much larger body of water than in Michigan. It is even more obvious that in those parts of the country where snow is a rarity or does not fall at all, there will be no necessity for a battery of terms to indicate coasting face down on a sled. It is not surprising that those areas of the country where cows can be milked outside, for at least part of the year, will develop a specific term for the place where this is done: witness *milk gap* or *milking gap* current in the Appalachians south of the

James River. The wealth of terms for various types of fences throughout the country is again dependent, in part at least, on the material which is available for building them, be it stones, stumps, or wooden rails.

Different types of institutions and practices which developed in various parts of the country also had their effect upon regional vocabulary. Those settlements which did not follow the practice of setting aside a parcel of land for common grazing purposes had little use for such terms as *green* or *common*. The meaning of *town* will vary according to the place and importance of township and county respectively in the organization of local government. The same principle applies equally well to foods of various kinds, which reflect not only materials which are readily available, but folk practices as well. The German custom of preparing raised doughnuts as Lenten fare survives in the Pennsylvania term *fossnocks*, shortened from *Fastnachtskuchen*.

Finally, a new invention or development introduced into several parts of the country at the same time will acquire different names in various places. The baby carriage, for example, seems to have been a development of the 1830's and '40's, and this is the term which developed in New England. Within the Philadelphia trade area, however, the article became known as a *baby coach*, whereas *baby buggy* was adopted west of the Alleghenies and *baby cab* in other regions throughout the country. Nor have we necessarily seen an end to this process. Within the last two decades the building of large, double-lane, limited-access automobile highways has been undertaken in various parts of the country, yet the terminology for them differs considerably. In eastern New York, Connecticut, and Rhode Island these are *parkways*, but *turnpikes* in Pennsylvania, New Jersey, New Hampshire, Maine, Massachusetts, Ohio, and Indiana. In New York *thruway* is used, and they are *expressways* in Michigan and *freeways* in California. These would seem to be regionalisms in the making.

It is of interest also to look at the dialect situation from the point of view of various words which are employed in various parts of the country for the same concept. One of the most interesting and instructive distributions is to be found in connection with the terms used for *earthworm*. This word is used by cultivated speakers in the metropolitan centers. *Angleworm* is the regional term in the North, *fishworm* in the Midland area, and *fishing worm* in the coastal South. *Fish bait* and *bait worm* occupy smaller areas within the extensive *fishworm* region, but are also distributed over a wide territory.

In addition, there is a large number of local terms, many of which are used principally by the older and less-educated inhabitants. The Merrimack Valley, in New Hampshire, and Essex County, Massachusetts, have *mud worm*. *Eace worm* is used in Rhode Island. *Angle dog* appears in upper Connecticut, and *ground worm* on the Eastern Shore of Virginia. *Red worm* is used in the mountains of North Carolina, and an area around

Toledo, Ohio, uses *dew worm*. Scattered instances of *rainworm* appear on Buzzards Bay in Massachusetts, throughout the Pennsylvania German area, and in German settlements in North Carolina, Maine, and Wisconsin. We have, thus, a wealth of older local terms, three distinct regional words, and the cultivated *earthworm* appearing in addition as a folk word in South Carolina and along the North Carolina and Virginia coast. Where and how did the various terms originate, and what can be determined about their subsequent history?

Earthworm itself is not an old word; it appears to have been compounded only shortly before the earliest English migrations to America. The earliest *Oxford English Dictionary* citation of the word in its present form is 1591; it appears also as *yearth worm* some thirty years earlier. The various regional terms all seem to have been coined in America; the dictionaries either record no British citations or fail to include the words at all.

The local terms have a varied and interesting history. *Mud worm* seems to occur in standard British English from the beginning of the nineteenth century on. *Eace worm*, as a combined form, goes back at least to Middle English; the first element was a term for 'bait' as early as Aelfric; it is used today in a number of southern counties in England from Kent to Gloucester. *Angle dog* is used currently in Devonshire. *Ground worm*, though coined in England, was transferred to North Carolina and Maryland in the eighteenth century. *Red worm* appears first in England in 1450 and continues through to the mid-nineteenth century, though chiefly in books on fishing, as does *dew worm*, which goes back even farther, to the late Old English period. *Rainworm*, though it appears in Aelfric as *renwyrm*, may be a reformation, even in British English, on the pattern of *Regenwurm* in German, for there is a gap of seven centuries in the citations in the *Oxford English Dictionary* and there is reason to believe that its revival in 1731 was influenced by the German form. Moreover, with but one exception, it has been cited for the United States only in areas settled by Germans.

Thus we have in the standard cultivated term one of relatively recent British formation. Apparently the regional terms were compounded in America, whereas the local terms represent survivals either of dialect usage or anglers' jargon and one loan translation. It is worth noting that the common Old English term, *angle twicce*, surviving as *angle twitch* in Cornwall and Devon, seems not to have found its way to America, and there are, furthermore, such other English formations as *tag worm, marsh worm*, and *garden worm* which have not been recorded in America.

At times, too, changes in meaning seem to have entered into the dialect situation, as is illustrated by the development of the regional terms *skillet* and *spider*, the former current in the Midland and the Virginia Piedmont, the latter in the North and in the Southern tidewater area. *Frying pan* is the urban term and is slowly supplanting the others. *Spider* was originally applied to the cast-iron pan with short legs, from which the name was presumably derived, but it was ultimately transferred to the flat-bottomed pan as well. This would seem also to explain the local term *creeper*, used in Marblehead, Massachusetts. *Skillet*, a term of doubtful etymology, first appears in English in 1403, when it was applied to a long-handled brass or copper vessel used for boiling liquids or stewing meat. It is still so used in dialects throughout England. The shift in meaning to a frying pan took place only in America, but an advertisement of 1790, offering for sale 'bakepans, spiders, skillets,' would suggest that even as late as this a distinction between the two was recognized. The examples above have been offered only as a suggestion of the various language processes which have played a part in the distribution and meaning of some of our dialect terms. It is quite obvious that no definitive conclusions about these matters can be reached until the actual facts of dialect distribution are better known than they are at present. . . .

Raven J. McDavid, Jr.

SOCIAL DIALECTS

Cause or Symptom of Social Maladjustment

Ɱ Ɱ

Profesor McDavid believes that a "person's dialect is one of his most intimate possessions." But he also knows that a dialect can be a serious linguistic handicap to the realization of full educational and economic advancement. His experience as a linguist and teacher who has moved about in the South and the North has enabled him to recognize the urgency of this dilemma and to offer direction for solving the social problem without aggravating the psychological one.

"Social Dialects: Cause or Symptom of Social Maladjustment" by Raven I. McDavid, Jr., from *Social Dialects and Language Learning: Proceedings of the Bloomington, Indiana, Conference, 1964.* Reprinted with the permission of the National Council of Teachers of English and Raven I. McDavid, Jr.

I am going to be somewhat anecdotal, but I think this treatment will lead into some of the complications that we encounter in working on social dialects, and perhaps the anecdotes will help us to realize how intricately these problems are interrelated with research, with one's own personal weltanschauung, and with one's pedagogical career and interests. Here we might make a minimal statement of the commitment of the English teaching profession as a commitment to see that in a democratic society, every citizen should have a command of the standard idiom sufficient to enable him to fulfill his intellectual potentialities, whatever kind of job, career, or ambitions he may have. Now if this sounds like one of the early phrases in Milton's "Of Education," this similarity is deliberate, since it comes from a retired Miltonist.

Let's first review the research of the last generation. It's thirty-three years since the New England field work for the Linguistic Atlas of the United States and Canada was begun. We have in this atlas the first attempt in linguistic geography to take into account the problems of social differences and the dimension of time. Those of us who have been working with the Linguistic Atlas have no illusions about having definitive answers, and no illusions that the findings of the thirties and forties are applicable to other situations that have kept on arising. In fact, from the very beginning Hans Kurath, director of the Atlas, has insisted that we needed many larger scale studies on particular problems. We simply could not cover more in the first investigation which had, as its major purpose, establishing the baselines and the general direction of apparent change in the speech of the United States.

The first suggestion, that perhaps we ought to say something to the social scientists, came from Gordon Blackwell, then chairman of sociology at North Carolina, now president of Furman University. One day when we were talking about the atlas materials, he said that we ought to have some comments in *Social Forces* so that we could at least start arguing intelligently. This conversation led to my article in the December 1946 *Social Forces*, which pointed out the direction my concern with social dialects has since taken. The intricate problem of the status indicators in South Carolina was then discussed in *American Speech*, 1948. Later came a note, based on the situation in Buffalo and elsewhere, which got into *Studies in Linguistics*.[1] In 1951, my wife and I did a paper for the American Dialect Society and the Speech Association of America at the request of Allen Walker Read on the relation of the speech of American

---

[1] Raven I. McDavid, Jr., "Dialect Geography and Social Science Problems," *Social Forces*, 25 (Dec. 1946), 165–72; "Postvocalic /–r/ in South Carolina: A Social Analysis," *American Speech*, 23 (Oct.–Dec. 1948), 194–203; "Dialect Differences and Inter-Group Tensions," *Studies in Linguistics*, 9 (Apr. 1951), 27–33.

Negroes to the speech of whites.[2] Lorenzo Turner's 20 years of investigation of Gullah along the Carolina-Georgia coast was one of the major items that we had to take into account in this paper and that everyone who starts from some of the more marginal social dialects in the United States will have to take into consideration. For a number of years since then I have been involved in working through the materials put together first by the late H. L. Mencken, and part of the problem of updating and reorganizing these statements entailed recapitulating what had been said about problems in social dialects.

I grew up in a South Carolina community where we said there were three races: white, Negroes, and cottonmill workers. Anyone who knows the situation in southern textiles knows exactly what I am talking about. Here we had white and black separated by caste lines. We also had an industrial system of the closed mill village, the closed employment situation with the company store selling, on credit, everything from contraceptives to coffins, and we had separate, segregated schools for the cotton mills. In this community we could see a number of social differences in dialects. We learned, very easily, that certain vowels were identified with the poor whites, the hillbillies, and their derivatives, the cottonmill workers. We knew that there was a rural white speech — not hillbilly — which nice but unassuming people used. We knew that, in the city, not only were there differences in white speech and Negro speech; we even learned that many of the more intelligent Negroes were bidialectal. That is, when they were speaking to the upper classes they would use one mode and when they were speaking back in the kitchen or to the yard man, they would use another. This intuitive perception is the kind of thing that one might expect from little boys playing around in grandmothers' houses and hearing things that maybe they weren't supposed to hear; they would conclude intuitively that people learn to differentiate their mode of communication according to the situation in which they were communicating and according to the people to whom they were attempting to communicate.

In the course of my pedagogical career, I was translated to Charleston across a major bundle of isoglosses and observed there another kind of dialect situation where, in many phonological matters, the urban Negro and the urban white, upper-upper, were very much alike. The city also had the strivers and strainers, in between, who were not accepted by either of these groups and were called by various inelegant terms which you will find if you study southern regional literature. On the streets, one could hear some of the varieties of Gullah from the flower sellers and seafood peddlers who would come into town. Going out in the country to fish, we often had trouble finding our way because we didn't know the language

[2] Raven I. McDavid, Jr., and Virginia Glenn McDavid, "The Relationship of the Speech of American Negroes to the Speech of Whites," *American Speech*, 26 (Feb. 1951), 3–17.

in which to ask directions properly or to ascertain what the directions were when we got them.

Later, I spent two years in Louisiana, in the center of the Cajun country. There were many local people who effectively commanded various kinds of Standard English. Unlike the situation in South Carolina, there were few poor whites who were native speakers of nonstandard varieties of English. In their place were the rural Cajuns — French-speaking poor whites. According to Wallace Lambert of McGill,[3] these people are doubly unfortunate — almost completely deculturized, illiterate in all languages; they have been made to feel that French is inferior, but have not been given a fair opportunity to learn anything approximating Standard English.

Somewhat later, after three years with the Armed Forces Language Program and two decades with the Linguistic Atlas, I found myself increasingly involved in the problems of teaching in metropolitan areas.

In the fall of 1959, preparations for the Darwin Centennial drew me into a profitable association with the Chicago Department of Anthropology. One of the first fruits of that association was an invitation to participate in a seminar in "caste and class," along with McKim Marriott and Julian Pitt-Rivers. As a scion of an old family of British landed gentry, Pitt-Rivers could evaluate the American scene objectively and dispassionately; it was illuminating for us when he remarked that, in the allegedly open society, social competition becomes keener and the unstructured markers of class increasingly important. He pointed out that the new "open society" has actually created a pattern of social segregation in the new one class neighborhoods, and particularly the one class suburbs like Levittown and Park Forest: as people move up economically they want to move away from those that they feel are economic and social threats, and toward those with whom they feel entitled to associate because of their new affluence. The flight from the central city to the suburbs is not solely white backlash, but a reflection of the fact that people in a democratic society have to keep running on the treadmill if they want to keep their place, and if they stop, they fall off and are considered failures. From these observations have come the motives for such research as the sociologically oriented dissertations of Lee Pederson[4] and Gerald Udell,[5] and the proposed dissertations of Thomas Creswell, John Dawkins, and Vernon Larsen at the University of Chicago.

So much for the theoretical background of our Chicago research. As we would like to think, these theories have been influenced by practical teaching problems in particular situations, beginning with my first teaching in South Carolina. The first striking situation where it was clear to me that

[3] Professor Lambert is the author of numerous studies on bilingualism, second-language learning, and related topics.

[4] Lee Pederson, *The Pronunciation of English in Chicago: Consonants and Vowels*, University of Chicago dissertation, 1964.

[5] Gerald Udell, *The Speech of Akron, Ohio: A Study in Urbanization*, University of Chicago dissertation, 1965.

work in social dialects was a necessity for the school system was that in southern Louisiana. Since the democratic philosophy of the state school system sought to avoid saddling students with the stigma of failure, no matter how submarginal their accomplishments, many freshmen who entered the state college with diplomas and four units of English could literally not read, write, speak, or understand English. In orthography, in grammar and pronunciation, there was a sharp divergence between the language practices of these people and of those of the dominant English-speaking culture. Moreover, it was apparent that the Negro speakers of French in southern Louisiana were more removed from standard southern Louisiana English than were the white Cajun French, because Louisiana rigidly maintained the southern tradition of separate and unequal accommodations in education and other social amenities. Clearly, in southern Louisiana, it would have been desirable to begin, at an early age, the teaching of English as a foreign language. It is ironic that these people do not appear in the census roles as speakers of foreign languages; the 1960 census indicates only the native tongue of the foreign born; presumably, everyone growing up in this country is a native speaker of English.

After World War II and several years of field work, I went to Western Reserve, in Cleveland, Ohio, a quality university with periodic illusions of football grandeur. Harrison Dillard, the great Negro hurdler, was a former student under our coach, Eddie Finnegan. As a consequence, Western Reserve attracted many Negro athletes, especially from Warren, Ohio. Warren, a town of about fifty thousand, is not large enough for educational segregation to have any particular impact on the quality of English teaching in high schools. Yet the Negro graduates from Warren High, who usually did well on the College Boards, showed in their compositions all of the grammatical features we associate with uneducated Negro speech, especially the nomadic appearance of the inflectional endings of verbs and nouns. One concluded that though the schools were not segregated, other social contacts were, since these grammatical forms could not have survived if whites and Negroes lived side by side and played together as equals.

In 1956–57 my wife taught in the Cleveland extension program of Kent State University, aimed at producing cadet teachers for the Cleveland public schools. In the program on the east side of Cleveland, the overwhelming majority of the students were Negroes. They were, as a rule, highly motivated and highly intelligent, but most of them had come with the non-standard grammar one associates with Mississippi, Alabama, etc. There were large numbers of Negroes from these states. Many of these students had to take noncredit English before they could get into freshman work. The grammatical problems were especially acute with the noncredit students, just as they have been in my wife's remedial and freshman English courses at Chicago Teachers College, South. One day she came home and said, "All week I have been trying to teach Standard English as a foreign language." This was probably the first suggestion I had that the techniques of second language teaching might be adapted to this problem. At the same time I discovered, through evening classes for inservice teachers, that the classroom teachers in Chicago are aware that the grammar of the slum Negro is a major problem. However, most teachers do not know what to do with this problem, and when they start to talk about the grammatical characteristics that distinguish Negro and white speech, professional race-men may say, "Don't mention this; this is discrimination." But among scholars concerned with the fate of our country, mentioning these features is not discrimination; we must talk about things that occur, for failure to mention them and to seek a cure will help perpetuate discrimination. Thus theoretical concern, social observation, and practical experience lie behind Pederson's dissertation and the growing cooperation with public and private groups interested in removing the educational, economic, and social handicaps of the underprivileged urban Negro. We conclude that we must remove their linguistic handicaps if our educational system is to survive. The grammatical problems are of such an order that we advance the suggestion — which Mencken had reported before the war and which my wife independently derived from her teaching experience — that in our urban slums and other areas where divergent social dialects exist, we might teach Standard English as a foreign language.

One other problem is involved here; to convey to the dominant culture a better understanding of what Standard English actually is. We must keep reminding our neighbors that Standard American English has many varieties, all good. We must remind them not to confuse what is regionally and what is socially different. And we must also realize — and make others realize — that a person's dialect is one of his most intimate possessions. We may want to give a person other modes of his language to communicate with in other situations, but we don't want to make him too self-conscious about the fact that he and his family and friends naturally use a non-standard dialect. After all, it may sometimes be to one's advantage to be able to switch back into the childhood mode, as it was to the advantage of Eugene Talmadge, a plantation owner, to be able to talk Georgia Redneck when he was on the state hustings, and it was to the advantage of Huey Long, a Louisiana Redneck, to learn Standard English so that he could communicate on the national hustings.

Vance Randolph · George P. Wilson

BACKWOODS GRAMMAR

⬱⬱

The dialect of the Ozark mountain region of southern Missouri, northern Arkansas, and eastern Oklahoma is rich in inventiveness. The mountain people are "the best talkers I have ever known," wrote Vance Randolph, who collected their songs, stories, and lore for forty years. Such people have a genuine feeling "for the vivid phrase." Indeed, according to Mr. Randolph, when the mountain people create words like *argufy* or *citified* they employ principles of word creation which are akin to those used by poets. A glance forward to Margaret Schlauch's essay (page 383) will confirm his statement. These processes give Ozark speech an authentic freshness and suggest cause for pride in local dialects.

The most conspicuous differences between the Ozark dialect and the folk-speech of the United States in general are matters of vocabulary and pronunciation, but certain other peculiarities are not altogether devoid of interest. One thing that impresses casual "furriners" is the hillman's confusion in the tense forms of the verbs. Sometimes he shows a perverse preference for the weak conjugation, rejoicing in such uncouth preterites as blowed, ketched, drawed, weeped, seed, knowed, sweared, drinked, and throwed. In other cases there is a transfer of affection from the weak conjugation to the strong, which gives such preterites as *clumb* for climbed, *div* for dived, *drug* for dragged, *het* for heated, *snuck* for sneaked, and *skun* for skinned.

The preterite of swoop is sometimes *swope*; a woman in Stone County,

Missouri, said that "a hawk *swope* down twice" to catch one of her chickens.

I have frequently heard *scrope* used as a past tense of scrape, even by graduates of the village high schools.

John Turner White, who lived near Springfield, Missouri, in the eighteen sixties, told me that his family "always used *eat* for the past as well as the present tense," but that most of their neighbors used *et* for the past tense of eat, just as the English do.

I have heard *fotch* only as the preterite and past participle of fetch. But the old-timers tell me that fifty or sixty years ago it was used in other tenses. Rufe Scott, of Galena, Missouri, remembers that his father used to say: "*Fotch* me that ax."

Mrs. Lillian Short, of Stone County, Missouri, told me about an old man who watched glumly when the soldiers marched away in 1917. "I fit in Linkhorn's war," he said, "but the folks never *wove* me goodbye." That story is still told in the Short family.

In the same category is the tale of a woman who lost her startin' of yeast. She tried to borrow from a neighbor, but the neighbor wouldn't lend. "It looks like she could have *spore* me a little," the woman said later.

The people who repeat these tales realize that *wove* and *spore* are not correct; that's why they tell the stories. I do not believe that *wove* for waved and *spore* for spared were ever really common in the Ozarks.

Mrs. C. P. Mahnkey, of Mincy, Missouri, says that she has occasionally heard *ruck* as the preterite of rake. A loaded hay wagon was driven into the barn to avoid a sudden shower, and a woman feared that her son had been *ruck off* by a low-hanging door.

The preterite and past participle of heat are nearly always *het,* but in the infinitive one sometimes hears *hotten:* "Nellie will *hotten* up the coffee whilst we're a-ketchin' the horses."

Shore is sometimes heard as the past participle of shear, as in the sentence: "Me an' Bob have *shore* ten sheep since dinner time." The preterite is usually *shirred,* which rhymes with bird.

In some sections the preterite of touch sounds like *totch* or *toch.* Jeff Davis, governor of Arkansas from 1901 to 1907, once pardoned a convicted murderer; in explaining his action to the press, he said that somebody asked the convict's little daughter if her father had killed his alleged victim. "No, he never *toch* him," the girl answered. "This reply *toch* me to the quick," said Governor Davis, "so I *toch* my hand to a pen and wrote a pardon for that father. I believe also that I *toch* the heart of that convict, his wife, and child."[1] . . .

In the free fashion of Shakespeare, the backwoodsman does not hesitate to turn a noun or an adjective into a verb. When one says "they done

[1] F. W. Allsopp, *Folklore of Romantic Arkansas* (New York, 1931), II, 330.

churched old Mis' Blackmar for card-playin'," he means that she was deprived of her membership in the church. "Don't *fault* my least young-un" means "don't blame my smallest child." One of my friends "figgered on *vealin'* two calves," adding that they would "*meat* the whole family a month, easy." Another man remarked boastingly that he could cut sufficient grass in one day to *hay* the cow all winter. "Bill just *ideals* that red-headed Heflin gal" means that he thinks very highly of her. A notorious outlaw was surrounded by officers in the woods, but managed to *eel out* somehow and escaped. The noun aunt, pronounced *ain't,* is often used as a verb; in Galena, Missouri, a woman was asked "How many time you been *aunted?*" which means "How many nieces and nephews have you?" Of a wealthy family it was said "they don't *neighbor* much with pore folks." A woman complained that her husband wouldn't work, except as a musician: "He's just *a-pleasurin'* himself fiddlin' for them dances." In Taney County, Missouri, I heard that the authorities were *jay-peein'* a friend of mine; this meant that he was being tried before a J.P., Justice of the Peace. A young girl in Pineville, Missouri, refused an elderly suitor, though he had given her some expensive presents. "Why, his whiskers is plumb white," she said scornfully. "I wouldn't *bed* with him, if he was to put candy on the trees!" A woman in Taney County, Missouri, said, "I never was one to *tea* my children," meaning that she did not treat their childish ailments with herbs, but preferred to summon a physician. The noun *hippin'*, which means diaper, becomes a transitive verb in the sentence: "Nancy, go *hippin'* that there baby."

Many good verbs are made from commonplace adjectives. Sultry is converted into a verb meaning to smother or suffocate: "I mighty nigh *sultered* down in that there holler." To *green* a man means to tease or ridicule him. "Let me *weak* that coffee for ye," said a mountain hostess, pouring milk into my cup. Much is a verb meaning to praise excessively, usually applied to the treatment of children. When one of our neighbors suddenly became insane people said, "It must have been losin' his money that *crazied* the old feller."

Such odd verbal combinations as *house-clean, horse-race,* and *hay-rake* are not uncommon. "I sure do love to *squirrel-hunt,*" remarked a prominent Arkansas lawyer. *Rabbit-hunt, fox-hunt, deer-hunt* and *turkey-hunt* are common. Even *bee-hunt,* meaning to line bees and thus locate bee-trees, is often heard in the backwoods. A boy at Sallisaw, Oklahoma, showed me a new rifle; "Let's go out and *target-practice* a while," he suggested. Near Cyclone, Missouri, the chief occupation is hacking out railroad ties and hauling them to market; asked how the natives make a living, my guide answered, "Some *tie-hacks* an' some *tie-hauls.*" A young woman in Fort Smith, Arkansas, said, "I've *school-taught* three year now, an' it's beginnin' to taste of the keg." Near Pineville, Missouri, I asked a boy to cut the grass about the cottage. "Do you-uns aim to *lawn-mow* the whole place?" he asked. By lawn-mow he meant to cut grass with the lawn-mower, rather than with the scythe or reap-hook. "If I had eddication," another Missourian remarked, "I could *bookkeep* or somethin' like that." At Cape Fair, Missouri, an old man said to me, "I *freight-hauled* for the merchants in the early days." A neighbor of ours, contemplating legal action against a man who had injured her, said, "I'm a-goin' to *law-sue* that feller." A radio announcer at Springfield, Missouri, used to advise: "Folks, whenever you *grocery-shop*, don't forget Raymey's Market!"

A lady at Pineville, Missouri, had no patience with jokes and jokers. "I love a fool," she said to a village smart-alec, "but you *over-suit* me." She did not refer to his lack of intelligence, but to his liking for practical jokes.

"They say Bill favors his Paw, but I think he *out-favors* him." This means literally that Bill looks more like his Paw than his Paw does; in other words, the father's features and characteristics are exaggerated in the son.

There is a tendency to coin verbs ending in *fy* and *ify*: *argufy* instead of argue, *speechify* instead of orate, and so on. One of Rose O'Neill's neighbors near Walnut Shade, Missouri, boasted that he could *clockify*, meaning that he knew how to repair clocks.

The hillman likes adjectives ending in *ified*. *Dressified* means particular about clothing, *fitified* means subject to fits, *citified* means urban, having the airs and manners of the city. A little boy from Massachusetts spent a summer in the Ozarks, and the local people were amused by his "*Yankee-fied* ways." A *prettyfied* woman is one provided with good clothes, a permanent wave, cosmetics, and the like. The word *holyfied*, in some of the backwoods Protestant cults, means sanctified, "possessed of the Holy Spirit." I have heard a schoolmarm speak of term papers as being *rectified* when she meant corrected, and the word *rightify* is sometimes used in the same meaning. *Jokeyfied* means habitually jocular or even clownish, sometimes in the sense of feebleminded. *Airified* means conceited, and applies to one who "puts on airs." A man in Taney County, Missouri, remarked that his mother "sure was *workified*; we couldn't git her off'n the plow till she was pretty near eighty." Uncle Jack Short, of Galena, Missouri, once remarked, "I ain't been very *eatified* the last few days," meaning that his appetite was poor. Speaking of the prospects of rain, a woman said to me, "It sure don't look very *rainified* this evenin'." Mrs. C. P. Mahnkey, of Kirbyville, Missouri, referred to a mixture of burnt whiskey and bacon grease, used as a remedy for bellyache, as "a *witchified* potion." When a man says that he's *hurtified*, he refers to a general lameness or soreness rather than a sharply localized pain. There is an old song with the line: "Madam, I have a very fine house, just newly *erectified*," meaning erected, built.[2] Cal Tinney is reported as saying that his army discharge papers

2 See my *Ozark Folksongs*, III, 53.

had finally *mister-fied* him, made him a civilian, that is.[3] Tinney was born in Pontotoc County, Oklahoma, and spent much time in the hill country.

There are some strange verbs ending in *n* or *en*. When one of our neighbors said, "That there medicine sure did *pearten* Elmer right up," she meant that it made him feel better, more lively. *Quieten* means to subside: "We'll have to wait till things kind of *quieten* down an' blow over." The preterite and past participle are *quietened*. *Belongen* is a form of belong, as in the sentence, "Them dogs *belongen* to Ab Landers." The old verb *enlargen* means to enlarge or expand; Wayman Hogue makes an Arkansas politician denounce his opponent who wants to *"enlargen* the free schools."[4]

With a taste for emphatic speech, the Ozarker is fond of attaching the intensive prefix *be* to certain participles. *Beaddled* or *beattled* means confused, addled, bewildered. *Bedaubed* and *begaumed* mean smeared, more or less covered with a liquid or semi-liquid. A man who is muddy, or stuck in the mud, is *bemired*. To describe a man as *benastied* means that he is bedaubed with some unpleasant substance, such as vomit or dung.[5] A woman at Pineville, Missouri, told me that her husband had "done got drunk and plumb *benastied* himself." . . .

[3] *Saturday Review of Literature,* June 22, 1946, p. 46.
[4] *Back Yonder,* 116.
[5] *Dialect Notes,* Vol. VI (1928), 63.

Harrison E. Salisbury

THE GANG

🍂🍂

This essay captures the special talk of one of the smallest fragments of geography — a locale with its own slang name, the "turf." Mr. Salisbury presents the language not only as interesting in itself, but as functional in the social context of the gang's dress, gestures, daily life, government. The gang on a particular turf has its own special terms, names, and significant words, showing the close relationship between what members of the gang think themselves to be and the language they use. A group can use a language to include and to exclude. Here it shows who is "in" and who is "out" — with a vengeance.

The first gang with which I got acquainted was the Cobras. None of the Cobras knows how or when the gang was started. The Cobras are an active "bopping" or street-fighting club which has its base in one of the older Brooklyn housing projects.

As far as the Cobras know, the gang was there when they began to grow up in the neighborhood or when they moved there from Manhattan or from out of town. As far as they know the gang has always been there. No Cobra can imagine his world, or any world, without a street gang. His world is a narrow one. Gang life fills it almost completely.

You can meet the Cobras any day of the week from four o'clock on in the afternoon. That is the hour when they begin to collect outside Schroeder's candy store, just across the street from the Whitman Housing Project. Winter, spring or summer you will see them in this same spot at this same hour doing the same thing — teetering back and forth, heel-to-toe, slightly loose-jointed, shoulders hunched a little, hands deep thrust in trousers' pockets, heads and chins bobbing and darting, duckfashion, eyes quick to detect any stranger moving down the street.

The Cobras are protecting their demesne — "minding our turf," in the argot of the streets. With a little time out for dinner some of them will stand on that corner until 11 P.M. of a winter's night, regardless of cold, and until 1 or 2 A.M. (unless chased away by the police) on sultry summer evenings.

"Minding our turf" is the main preoccupation of the Cobras. They live a life which touches the ordinary adult world only along the edges. Theirs is a subculture, a subsociety with its own mores, codes, ceremonies, language and interests. The Cobras do not know what goes on in the other world, nor do they care. If in some respects their way of life seemed to me to provide a grotesquerie of the adult world of nations, only a few more perceptive members possess the insight to comprehend this. For the most part the Cobras live within an impenetrable shell of their own. Theirs is a world of young people harshly buffeted by grim realities — poverty, hunger, physical hardship, danger, displacement, disease and deprivation. Beset by force and violence they escape into paranoid visions of grandeur, daydreams of demonic power, ecstasies of sadism, endless fantasies with a gun.

They erect a bizarre construction, half real, half delusionary. Within this structure they make a last-ditch stand against adult pressures and conflict beyond their immature powers to cope with or comprehend.

Here is the street gang in its most vicious flowering. Most youngsters in America, I know, do not face the struggle for survival which confronts the Cobras and strongly shapes their mores and their conduct. But the pattern of antisocial activity set by gangs like the Cobras casts a dark shadow over an ever-widening area of the nation — good neighborhoods and bad, small cities and large, New York, San Francisco and Chicago. What the Cobras do today shook-up high school seniors in Great Neck, Long Island, or Beverly Hills, California, will consciously or unconsciously imitate and reflect tomorrow.

Most of the Cobras happen to be Negro. They live, play, work and fight beside and in close relation with a "brother club," the Silver Arrows, whose membership is largely Puerto Rican. The racial divisions closely follow those of the population of the Whitman Housing Project. Geography rather than ethnic differences usually determines gang composition. "Integrated" gangs are not uncommon. Most gangs include at least a few minority race members. The Cobras and the Arrows are "tight" in the language of the street. This means that they are close allies in the treacherous, shifting sphere of the bop. The Cobras and the Arrows have many enemies. When they look beyond the boundaries of the Whitman project they see a dark and dangerous jungle populated by unknown hordes which may strike at any moment.

"You can be sure I never cross Gowanus Parkway without my piece [gun]," Chico told me. His comrades nodded sagely. "You don't know when you might meet somebody who has seen you before. Or somebody who hasn't seen you before," one added.

Within this sea of danger exist two well-known, well-identified enemies — the Rovers (Irish-Italian) and the Apaches (largely Irish), two street gangs on the perimeters of the Whitman project. The conflict between the Cobras and the Arrows, on the one hand, and the Rovers and Apaches, on the other, has roots so twisted that none of the teen-agers can tell the story straight. The enmity is as deep, bitter and tortuous as any feud in Montenegro. This spring of ever-replenishing hatred conditions the violent antisocial nature of the activity of all four clubs.

The Cobras divide themselves into two categories — Big People and Little People. This division is common to most Negro street gangs. Big People are sixteen to nineteen, for the most part. They are the core of the fighting gang. Little People are younger, ranging from nine or ten to about fifteen. The ages are approximate. There are fourteen-year-olds among the Big People. And occasionally a twenty-year-old will be found among Little People. In predominantly white gangs the divisions often are more elaborate — diapers (8–11), midgets (10–13), juniors (12–15) and seniors (15–20).

The Cobras are what social workers call a "structured" gang. That is, they have a leadership clique with titles, offices and responsibilities — a President (public policy, domestic and foreign relations, strategy), a Vice-President (Chief of Staff and Second in Command), a War Counselor (war plans, intelligence, tactics) and a Gunsmith or Armorer (weapons and logistics). The Little People have a similar top echelon but are subordinate to over-all control by the Big People.

Members of the Cobras told me that they "elect" their President. They also told me that they "vote" on decisions. Actually, there is not much democracy. It is more like a South American junta. The clique which runs the Little People generally succeeds to leadership of the Big People when age and circumstances produce a change in gang leadership.

This happens every two or three years. Arrests, casualties and desertion caused by jobs or marriage accomplish this.

The present leaders of the Cobras came to power in the summer of 1957. They had been Little People until violent tragedy made them Big People overnight. One midsummer evening the older gang members boarded a subway train, heading for downtown Brooklyn. They had been drinking heavily and started to "sound" (insult) the passengers. A train-man intervened. They wounded him badly with their switchblades and threw him off the train at the next station. Police corralled the whole group. Most were convicted and sent up for long terms in state institutions.

The Little People inherited the gang. Their first act was to change its name. The club had been called the Royal Imperials. Some years before it went under the title of the Huns. Now, the old name had acquired too much notoriety with the police. It had to be changed as a matter of defensive necessity. The members decided to call themselves Cobras because the name sounded tough. Terror value rates high in gang nomenclature. That is why there are Scorpions, Dragons (a great favorite), Vikings, Jaguars, Warriors, Huns, Demons, Comanches, Hellbenders, Sioux (pronounced Cy-ox), Tigers, Villains, Cherokees, Daggers, Stone-killers and Stompers on the streets of New York. Status value is another attribute as indicated by clubs calling themselves Viceroys, Lords, Egyptian Kings, Royal Niles, Centurians, Crusaders, Dukes, and Gents. Bloody victories in street combat have lent aura to the curiously named Bishops, Chaplains, Enchanters and Sportsmen. Probably no one will ever know why some gangs call themselves the Tims, the Jits, the Baldies or the Pigtown Lords.

When I asked a Cobra the purpose of his organization he told me that it is a social club made up of friends and good fellows. "We are," he said, "all for one and one for all." In case of danger the club provides protection and self-defense.

Protection against what? Protection of the Cobra members and their turf against any threat from the outside. The Cobra does not regard himself as a menace to anyone. But the world seems to him to be filled with menace. There is only one small island of comparative safety — his turf. On his own turf and in the presence of his own comrades he feels relatively, but only relatively, secure. Twenty-two-year-old Trigger now lives an hour's subway ride from Whitman Houses. But he comes down almost every night to be with the gang. "Man, I just don't feel safe up there in the Bronx," he says.

The Cobra does not know much about the geography of the United States. He may not even know how to get from Brooklyn to Manhattan. But there is one bit of geography which he can walk blindfold. This is his turf, the demesne the Cobras call their own. The Cobras share their demesne with the Silver Arrows. It is bounded by the limits of the housing project and is, actually, an enclave. In times of a rumble this has certain advantages (interior lines, ease of concentration for defense). But it also has grave disadvantages. Any Cobra who must leave the project for school or work is forced to walk right into enemy territory.

The boundary of the Cobra island is defined as precisely as a surveyor's map. On one perimeter, for example, the Cobra's demesne extends across the street from the Houses to include a half block occupied by a store-front church, a liquor store, a shoe repair shop, Schroeder's candy store and a bar-and-grill. On another periphery, however, the line stops at the edge of the project. The street and commercial establishments fronting the boundary are no man's land — safe enough during a "cool" but fighting ground during a rumble, an uncertain area where one side or another may at any sudden moment "jap" an unwary alien.

Security is a constant worry of the Cobras. Each has his nickname or *nom de guerre*. This is designed to prevent enemies (police, parole officers, rival gangs) from penetrating real identities and tracing participants in rumbles. But the nicknames are chosen, as well, for prowess value. Favorite *noms de gang* include Blood, Snake, Leadpipe, China, Knobby, Hatchet, Killer, Geronimo, Cochise, Diablo, Rocky, Moto, Johnny the Bop, Vice, Dice, Goat, Savage, Wolf and Saint.

Perhaps the name with the greatest status value is Kemo. Kemo was the name of a famous character in a radio serial of the late thirties. Street gang tradition has it that Kemo was the name used by one of the greatest bops in gang history — a little man, unimpressive physically, but "the fastest man in the world with a knife." Zorro, another radio and television name, is rapidly rising in popularity and status.

There are forty to fifty Cobras in all, roughly divided between Big People and Little People. About two-thirds of them are enrolled in school but many are irregular in attendance. Half of the others have jobs. Half do not.

Monk is a member of the Cobras. He is fifteen. His father died when he was three years old. His mother is a cleaning woman. She leaves the apartment a little after seven in the morning. Before she goes she tells

Monk to get up. Monk does not get up. He is supposed to be in school at eight-thirty but more often than not he skips school. It is almost ten before he drags out of bed. He cooks some French fries on the gas stove. This is breakfast. Two or three times a week this is his only meal of the day. His mother has left him twenty-five cents for lunch on the dresser. He takes the twenty-five cents and wanders down to the street.

On the corner he finds Chico, who is about his age and also a truant. With Chico is Dice, seventeen, and possessor of a part-time job. Dice has twenty-five cents. Monk and Dice pool this money and get an old wino to buy them a bottle of sneaky pete (cheap wine) for thirty-nine cents. They are too young to make the purchase themselves. They give the wino a drink and down the rest. This puts them into a haze of well-being for a couple of hours. In the afternoon they scare up the price of another bottle of cheap wine. But by 4 P.M. the glow of the wine has long since worn off. Monk and his friends feel bored, mean, depressed and hungry. None of them has eaten all day. They are spoiling for trouble and trouble usually accommodates them.

If the fundamental concept of the Cobras is demesne and its protection, their basic mystique is "heart." Heart is what passes on the street for bravery. Smokey is the leader of the Cobras because of heart. Chico is a respected club member because of heart. Blood, the war counselor, won his post through heart.

So central is this mystique that it comprises the device of the most notorious of all the bopping gangs of New York, the Chaplains. Their motto is "All Chaplains have heart."

Heart as defined by the bopping clubs is not the exact equivalent of courage as, say, Richard Coeur de Lion understood it. For, while curious medieval anachronisms do exist in the bopping world the parallels do not always hold true.

"Heart, well, that's when a bop isn't afraid of anything or anybody," Dice tells you. "He will do absolutely anything. When the chips are down — if he has to fight five he'll fight five. He'll say, 'I'm the butcher, man. I'm the hatchet. If you need anyone to pull the trigger I'll pull the trigger.'

"You take Chico," Dice says. "He has more heart than anyone I ever saw. He's crazy, that boy. Been up to Warwick three times. He don't care what he do. Once we had a rumble with the Chaplains. You know what he did? He went out alone right into Chaplains' turf. In daylight. Just walked in, inviting them to jap him, hoping they would jap him. He'll fight anybody. No matter how many they are. That Chico — he stays drunk all the time. Isn't ever sober. But, man, he sure have heart."

Heart, as the bop defines it, is audacity, devil-may-care disregard for self and consequences. Heart is fourteen-year-old Snake walking up to a patrolman on the corner and making a grab for his pistol. Heart is sixteen-year-old Rocky waiting in ambush outside a school and firing a rifle into a group of teen-agers as they come out, joking and unaware of danger. Heart is Dice taking a dare to jump down three flights of stairs (and only prevented from carrying it out when someone grabs his legs as he leaps).

A boy shows heart by laughing at his attackers when he is japped outside his neighborhood. He shows heart by sounding a street boy bigger and tougher than himself.

The opposite of heart is punking out. When a cool has been on for some time gang leaders may order a "shin fight" (sham battle) between the Little People and the Big People. The shin fight simulates gang combat except that knives and guns are not used and blows are not supposed to be struck below the belt or in the face. A shin battle tests heart and shows which boys will be the most vicious and daring street fighters.

Heart is not the sole criterion for gang leadership. Gang leaders must also have intelligence, insight and knowledge of the world surpassing that of their comrades. Otherwise, the gang will be led into suicidal encounters with larger and more powerful street enemies. It will embark on ventures which bring on fatal encounters with the police.

Smokey, leader of the Cobras, has heart. But he also has more brains than his comrades. The same is true of Vincent, leader of the Silver Arrows. But the leaders of the Apaches are another case. The Apaches are a gang nearing the stage of final dissolution. They are two or three years older than the Cobras or the Arrows. Once they were all-powerful in the neighborhood but that was several years back.

One by one the Apaches left Whitman project. In part this was because of the influx of Negro and Puerto Rican families but mostly it was the product of the violence of the street club. They got into trouble with housing authorities, social workers and the police. Many were expelled from the project and moved into nearby cold-water flats. Conflict between the Apaches and the gangs in the project grew more savage.

"Sometimes," a social worker said, "it seemed as though the Apaches knew in their subconscious that they were bound to lose. After each battle they grew more wild. They were determined to go down in a blaze of violence."

So destructive were the Apaches even when not on the warpath that they were barred from the Neighborhood Center and then from the Catholic Youth Center. Each rebuff stimulated the leaders to new outrages. A street-club worker was assigned to the group, but one evening half a dozen Apaches attacked the man as he stood in friendly conversation with them on a busy street corner. He was sent to the hospital with serious knife wounds. Although they could now muster only a third of the strength of the Cobras and Arrows they deliberately provoked battles in which they inevitably lost more strength. Finally, a dozen Apaches were arrested on charges of possession of concealed weapons. The gang survives but only as a crippled remnant. Obviously its days are numbered. . . .

The structure of the Rovers differs a good deal from that of the Cobras. They have no ritual. Indeed, they deny that they are a street club. No one will admit that he is a leader. It is only when they "go down" or embark on a rumble that the gang structure can be clearly identified. In combat the Rovers act precisely the way their fellow street adolescents do.

But there are differences. One is in style. The Cobras dress like "real diddley bops" — first-class street fighters. Take Blood, the Cobras' war counselor. He has a job and his first week's pay went to buy a twenty-dollar gray alpine-style hat with narrow brim. The hat is decorated with a thick braided gray cord and a neat gray and blue feather. Blood calls this hat a "stenjer." The name derives from the fact that the hat has a "stingy" rather than a "generous" brim.

Blood wears a navy-blue gabardine half coat, peg-top trousers, white and blue longitudinally striped nylon socks, thin-soled black shoes with white-piped welts.

Jimmy, another Cobra with a job, sports a light beige topcoat with black velvet collar. He wears a tight blue beret, silk or dacron shirts, horizontally striped orange-and-black jacket which comes almost to his knees, narrow trousers and thin-soled black woven-leather pumps. He usually displays a large brilliant attached to a fine gold wire in the lobe of his left ear.

Blood and Jimmy dress in what Brooklyn gangs regard as high fashion. However, Central Harlem and lower East Side gang members have abandoned flashy costumes. The Central Harlem youngster has turned to gray flannel suits, regimentally striped neckties, well-cut Harris tweed jackets. He has gone Ivy League with a vengeance. His clothes are cut in Brooks Brothers pattern. Leaders often sport tightly rolled umbrellas with gold gooseneck handles. They have everything but a Madison Avenue brown leather attaché case in which to carry their zip guns. These youngsters seek to create the image of a "cool, cultured, beat-the-rap" type.

The difference in costume between Brooklyn and Manhattan, in the opinion of one observer, represents a cultural lag.

"Brooklyn is about four years behind Manhattan," this man said. "Bedford-Stuyvesant is four years behind Harlem and Williamsburg is four years behind that. Confidentially, Brooklyn is out of this world."

The Rovers display no special peculiarities of every-day dress. They effect the sports shirts and salt-and-pepper odd coats and slacks which are the convention of the high school adolescent throughout the country. Some favor butch haircuts. Others the Sal Mineo spit lock plastered to the forehead. Many wear sideburns long and display ragged Tarzan back bobs in imitation of their beloved Elvis.

But, regardless of style, a street club member is recognizable at a glance by other members of shook-up society.

How this is accomplished is not easy to put down in words. But anyone who has spent much time with teen-age street fighters can spot them at a glance. The gang youngster, whether in his own neighborhood or out, always has a wary eye for enemies. He never feels secure and he betrays this insecurity with quick, darting looks, the stolen glance over the shoulder, the nervous movement of hands (usually held close to the concealed switchblade or zip gun), the almost compulsive twitch of his body. All of these are telltales to other gang members.

The argot in which the youngsters speak is another recognition factor. The argot seems to derive from the world of bebop, jitterbugging and jazz. The street adolescents employ much of the vocabulary of hot music but usually give the words a different connotation. There are no variations in street argot between adolescents of different ethnic background. "They all know the sound," a street club worker said.

Their conversations may not be readily understood by persons unfamiliar with the shook-up generation. When a strange boy walks past the Cobra candy store the following conversation may ensue:

"Who you swinging with, man?"

"Why, I'm swinging with the Bishops, man."

"Good, man. We're tight with the Bishops. We're a brother club. How about dropping a dime, man, and we'll get a bottle of sneaky pete."

"Okay, man. I thought you might be shaking me down."

"Oh, you figured you might have to shuffle, eh?"

"That's what I thought, man. But I'm telling you I got a piece on me. Nobody going to jap me, man."

"I thought you might be a coolie, man."

"You trying to sound me? Let's get that sneaky pete and have us a gig."

Or, in English:

"What street club do you belong to?"

"I belong to the Bishops."

"Good, we're friendly with the Bishops. They are affiliated with our club. How about contributing a dime toward a bottle of wine?"

"Okay, I was afraid you would try to hold me up."

"You thought you might have to fight?"

"Yes, that's why I'm carrying a gun. I'm not letting anyone take me by surprise."

"I thought you might not belong to a gang."

"Don't kid me. Let's get that wine and have a party."

The concept of the coolie is common to all the street gangs. The coolie is a boy who does not belong to a street club. He may be a quiet, retiring youngster who pays a daily tribute of ten cents or a quarter to a gang member who protects him from attack by other teen-agers. Or he may be an outstanding boy in the neighborhood, good in sports, good in school, well liked by other youngsters, who simply stands aside from street activity. Such a boy often is respected and not interfered with by boys dedicated to the bop. Such youngsters can live in a community dominated by street conflict and be untouched by it. In unusual cases they may even be regarded as part of the gang but are tacitly excused from combat.

Much more frequent is the youngster who is "drafted" into the gang. The draft is used by all four gangs in the neighborhood of Whitman Houses — the Cobras, the Arrows, the Rovers and the Apaches.

Smokey, leader of the Cobras, frankly admits that the draft is the only way in which he can maintain his order of battle at full strength.

"There has to be a draft," he says. "There doesn't seem to be any real place in the world for the coolie."

Smokey is unaware how close his remark comes to paralleling those of statesmen pondering the disappearance of national neutrality in the world struggle of great powers.

Application of the draft is very simple. A recruiting squad of three or four boys approaches a coolie.

"Do you want to join the club or do you want a punch in the belly?" they ask. Sometimes, they knock the boy down first and then ask him, just to show they mean business. Few boys refuse to join. If a draftee tries to duck a rumble he is likely to earn new beatings for punking out. Sometimes the beating is inflicted by a formal punishment squad of half a dozen boys. They make the offender run a gantlet while they beat him savagely with brass-studded garrison belts or baseball bats. The next time he goes along on the rumble.

The Cobras have never kicked a member out of the gang although boys have been punished for desertion. It is rare for a boy to be expelled but it sometimes happens when a boy's conduct is so irrational that he repeatedly endangers his fellow members. But since all of the gang are shook-up or disturbed they tolerate much before moving against a comrade.

If a boy is found club hopping (changing sides) or cheesy (guilty of treason) he is in danger of death. If the gang gets its hands on such a boy it will beat him to death or come close to it.

The gang code on treason carries an important escape clause. It is not treason if a member tells something to a street club worker. If a street club worker orders a boy to hand over his zip gun the boy will comply. This is not a violation of gang code. If a street club worker learns of a rumble from a gang member and thwarts the projected fight this is not treason, either. Nor is a gang regarded as punking out if it runs away from the police when they appear on the scene of a planned rumble.

The status of the street club worker is something like that of an International Red Cross representative on the world battlefields. His neutrality and good intentions are recognized by unwritten gang law. No harm accrues to gang members because of contact with him. Intervention of the police is regarded as *force majeure* and thus beyond the control of gang members. Intervention which enables a gang to avoid combat without loss of "rep," or reputation, is secretly welcomed by most boys. . . .

Most youngsters belonging to the seventy-five or one hundred active street fighting gangs in New York City come from lower-income classes. Many are the products of impoverished cultural backgrounds, the plantation economy of South Carolina or the overpopulated areas of Puerto Rico. But not all by any means. Not a few Rovers and Apaches stem from middle-income families. Regardless of economic or cultural differences the similarity in delinquency patterns throughout the country is striking.

The greatest contrast between the Cobras of Brooklyn and the Sportsmen of Jamaica, Long Island, for instance, is technological. The Jamaica boys have access to cars. Theirs is a mobile existence. They hang out not at a neighborhood candy store but at an ice-cream stand out on the highway. In terms of geography their horizon is much wider. They are not confined to a constricted slum area deep within a crowded city.

But geographical freedom does not broaden their ethos. They know the "sound." Their conduct is molded in the same narrow, aggressive antisocial patterns. Their interests outside their own adolescent world are no broader than those of the Cobras. They, too, dream fantasies with a gun. They, too, build their lives on conflict and hostility to other groups and individuals. If their rituals are outwardly more sophisticated they have the same inner emptiness. They judge by the same false standards of "heart" and "punking out." Instead of testing courage in a shin battle they sometimes play "chicken" — the suicidal game in which two drivers race their cars head-on at each other — sixty, seventy, eighty miles an hour. The first to turn aside is chicken — a coward and despised. They treat one another with the same brutal sadism as the Cobras or the Rovers. They live in the same revolt against forces they do not understand. They are in the same sense shook-up.

The cousins of the Jamaica Sportsmen are to be found in Lake Forest, Illinois, or Long Beach, California, or Denver, Colorado. There are, of course, different degrees of being shook-up and regional peculiarities of conduct. In the culturally deprived ghettos of New York the name of the gang and its "rep" may acquire special aura. It may, indeed, serve as a substitute for many things which are lacking in the lives of its members. It may provide a reason for existence, a source of personal satisfaction, a pseudo-purpose for a life which lacks any purpose.

In the gang the street boy feels himself important. Nowhere else does he seem to matter. Not at home (if he has what can be called a home). Not at school, where he can barely read, where there is nothing he can do well enough to give him even a faint glow of achievement. Not on the job, where the boss makes him feel inadequate and inferior.

But with his comrades in his gang he is important. He is needed. He is wanted. He has a place. His gang is his life. As it grows in rep so he grows in rep. He stands taller on the streets. He shows his heart with more reckless abandon. He becomes a Big Man.

There is no essential difference between Chico and Charley. Chico was born in Puerto Rico, brought to the United States by his mother at the age of nine, raised fatherless in the street-fighting grounds of Brooklyn.

Charley, son of moderately well-to-do parents in Philadelphia, brought to Stamford, Connecticut, by his mother after the divorce, was raised in the suburbs of New York.

Chico can hardly read. He doesn't speak English well. He seldom is home. The only place he feels that he belongs is with the Cobras. He drinks every day. His pride is that no one has as much heart as he. He will do anything to show this. Actually, Chico is suicidal. He doesn't care what happens to him. Not after a few drinks.

Charley doesn't read well, either. He reads the comics — the horror comics. Not much else. He hates the home where his mother seldom is and his father never. He drinks every day. The only time he feels himself is with the crowd at the ice-cream joint. His pride is that no one can chicken him on the highway. Actually, Charley is suicidal. He doesn't really care what happens to him. Not after a few drinks.

Chico and Charley are shook-up products of a shook-up world. A world of violence, some of it self-created, some of it not. A world of antagonism and aggression. A world of conflict. A world from which there is no real escape, for, as one of them put it, "A Bishop is always a Bishop, and a Chaplain is always a Chaplain, and there is no such thing as a cool."

Clifton Fadiman

ON THE UTILITY OF U-TALK

ᨆᨆ

Several years ago a book called Noblesse Oblige *appeared in England containing an examination of the distinction between British upper-class and non-upper-class speech (called "U" and "Non-U"). Listing upper-class and non-upper-class ways of talking became, said Russell Lynes, "something of a national parlor game." It played into the*

Reprinted from *Any Number Can Play* by Clifton Fadiman (Cleveland, Ohio: World Publishing Company, 1957), by permission of Fadiman Associates, Ltd. This article also appeared in *Holiday* magazine.

hands of British snobbery. According to Mr. Fadiman, in America despite our insistence on democratic equality we too have class distinctions which are expressed in our talk. Mr. Fadiman begins by characterizing our upper class, providing some context for its language. He then lists U and non-U parallels, such as "long dress" versus "formal." He admits that his U-talk markers are impressionistically gathered. They can be cause for debate.

Last year there appeared an American edition of a book called *Noblesse Oblige*, edited by Nancy Mitford. Our reviewers greeted it with a certain amount of gentle kidding. Having abolished class distinctions by law and retained them in unadmitted actuality, we are naturally forced into a defensive position vis-à-vis the British, who have until recently been franker on the subject. And so, as part of our defense, we laugh at a people who actually dare to be as absorbed in matters of class as we are in something truly important, let us say, the World Series.

The subject of *Noblesse Oblige* is the language, more particularly the vocabulary, used by the English aristocracy. When first published, the little volume kicked up a cloud of dust, some of it not yet laid. The fuss started in Finland. Professor Alan Ross of Birmingham University published in Helsinki for Finnish philologists (I am not making this up) a paper called *U and Non-U: An Essay in Sociological Linguistics*. It was an attempt to define the language used by upper-class (U) Englishmen, language that sets them apart from non-U speakers. Miss Mitford, herself rather aggressively upper class and therefore just a shade non-U, commented wittily in an essay called *The English Aristocracy*. The two essays, with some other related pieces, made up *Noblesse Oblige*.

Why did uproar follow upon its English publication? Because (a) Miss Mitford and Professor Ross let the cat of U-vocabulary out of the closed bag of U-society; (b) according to her peers, Miss Mitford shouldn't have done it, because it is a private cat; (c) England is trying hard to convince itself and the rest of the world that its class system is on the way out; (d) anybody who thinks one way of speaking is better than another is a snob, isn't he, and snobs are bad people, aren't they?

The British tempest in a teapot was not repeated here, when an American edition of *Noblesse Oblige* was published. We should not have expected it to be. For one thing, we are ostensibly less interested in class distinctions — that is, few of us dare to say we are interested. For another, we are less interested in language. For the minority, however, who *may* be interested in language, I should like to set down a few comments on

American U-sage and non-U-sage; and I hope that they will be challenged and corrected by better observers and scholars.

But before so doing I had better come clean and state that I believe there *is* an American U.

The American upper class is the lunatic aunt in the national attic. Both the family and the neighbors know she's there, but neither will own up to it. Superior manners are somehow supposed to betray our political democracy. This is a tenable notion only if we assume that political democracy and bad manners are linked. Governors who campaign with hillbilly bands and presidential aspirants who wear coonskin caps (surmounting tortoise-shell glasses) lend some color to this theory, but not enough for universal persuasion.

Yet a little quiet thought should convince us that ballot-box democracy and an upper class can jog along quite comfortably together. Indeed they have done so ever since the founding of the Republic, an achievement made possible in large part by aristocrats. We would all be a little less touchy on the subject if this simple fact could be taught to children in their first history class. Then, when they grow up to be voters, they may be able to exempt an admittedly U Adlai Stevenson from the admittedly non-U duty of kissing babies that do not belong to him — an example of barbarous manners apparently limited to twenty-five regular appearances per American century.

The present writer is by birth and training drastically non-upper class. That is what permits him to write, in non-U prose, about U's. Upper-class self-contemplation is a bit *infra dig.*, not quite cricket.

Our upper class is not to be confused with our most publicized, our richest, or our most powerful citizens, though it may be sparsely represented in all three groups. In his book *The Power Elite* Professor C. Wright Mills tries to equate this trio with what he thinks of as an emergent upper class. He sees this class — and his argument is often brilliant — as a cohesive, self-perpetuating group largely consisting of our ablest big-corporation executives, certain intelligent (and not necessarily well-publicized) politicians, and the intellectual cream of the admirals and generals. To these he adds a new crowd — the "celebrities" who, he believes, function as a kind of lightning rod to which the attention of the ordinary citizen is harmlessly diverted.

This Power Elite may exist. But even if it does, I do not agree that it runs the country, except intermittently, during the administrations of weak Chief Executives. Furthermore, I do not think it is identical, except to a minor degree, with a *genuine* upper class. To believe it is identical is to confuse ability with character and power with superiority.

Our upper class is less stable than that of England or France. It admits new members more frequently. On the other hand, it tends to lose members more frequently also. The weaker sisters are often seduced by the middle-class Circes of conformity and adjustment. Each such successful seduction decreases the U-will to persistence, for independence, sometimes to the point of arrogance or eccentricity, is a traditional *sine qua non* of a healthy aristocracy.

Is it possible to draw a profile of this upper class? Only roughly, and with many qualifications which the reader is begged to consider I am making in advance. Here perhaps are a few identifiable characteristics:

1. The unit of the uppers is not the individual but the family.

2. By our American standards this family is "old"; perhaps it has been here at least four generations.

3. It is generally of English or Scotch-English stock, or basically so.

4. It has won a certain respect in the community, a respect extended even to its less worthy members.

5. Its male members are usually Ivy League, West Point, or Annapolis.

6. They have not merely attended these schools; they have been educated there. A genuine U may not be mentally brilliant, but he believes, if quite unaggressively, in the value of an intellectual tradition. It is this characteristic alone which makes it impossible for most members of Professor Mills' Power Elite to be uppers.

7. Our *very* richest men are rarely uppers. But in the true U family there is generally *some* money, often inherited. A poverty-stricken upper sooner or later loses his stigmata.

8. Uppers often do nothing and (a faculty the rest of us have lost) do it very well. When they do something it is more apt to be professional than commercial. A few go into politics. Our first six presidents were uppers; the only others, I should think, have been Taft, Wilson, and the two Roosevelts. My own notion of a superb upper is John Quincy Adams, one of the most magnificent and least appreciated human beings ever born on this continent.

9. They are small in number, not generally prominent (in the newspaper sense), and reside in a few large eastern cities and their suburbs — mainly Boston (pre-eminently), New York, Philadelphia, Charleston, Richmond, perhaps San Francisco and New Orleans. Certain cities are by nature non-upper: Los Angeles is the key name here, Detroit is another. Chicago has a few survivals.

10. U's are not effusive and adjustment-mad on the one hand, or competitive on the other. Often highly emotional in their private lives, they do not appear so on the surface. The rest of us call them cold. They do not mind.

11. The final characteristic is the most difficult to phrase. It is even rather difficult to notice, because American uppers are developing a certain anxiety to seem no better (that is, no more distinguishable) than the next fellow. The weaker members of the tribe will often go to great lengths to camouflage those qualities in which they are superior. These qualities

spring from a conscious or unconscious attachment to a dying code of behavior, ultimately derived from eighteenth- or even seventeenth-century England. This behavior is marked by: dislike of publicity; social ease, with "inferiors" as well as equals — uppers are not uppish; avoidance of display and of talk about money; a constant sense, occasionally absurd and boring, of family tradition; gentle manners, but when necessary, arrogant manners, which are not identical with bad manners; the ability, particularly of the women, to converse; the inability to argue, debate, or quote others' views as their own; a marked tendency to say what one thinks, rather than what is fashionable or pleasing; a great interest in physical well-being and strength and grace of body; relatively notable attachment to the past, sometimes exaggerated into a tedious antiquarianism; an almost instinctive capacity to recognize their peers wherever and whenever encountered; and, finally, certain linguistic habits and traditions.

It is these last I should like to discuss briefly.

Let me state at once my awareness of the fact that sufficient usage can eventually make the ugly, the repulsive, the unclear, the evasive, the discordant perfectly correct; and I am not in the least impressed by this circumstance, which seems so greatly to please our professors of linguistics. I am not urging anyone to imitate, let us say, the speech of Adlai Stevenson. It would be foolish and vain to try. I merely say that it is more admirable than certain other kinds of speech, because more efficient, cleanly, and memorable; and for these reasons it is worthy of detached study, study quite unrelated to "snobbery."

I have not known many U-speakers. In one of my trades — entertainment — they are virtually nonexistent, though there are a few English actors resident among us who are genuinely U and several more who are excellent U-mimics, which they should be, as that is part of their business. Writers are usually non-U in their speech and many of the most popular and successful ones are non-U in their writing. (An exception is Mr. John Marquand.) My observations are drawn therefore from limited experience. But this experience is more fruitful than would have been the case had I been U myself, with wider access to U-families. Such families generally are not self-perceptive. The fish does not notice the water. (Miss Mitford is an odd fish indeed.)

Roughly speaking, I would say that American U-sage is marked by:

1. Avoidance (unconscious if upper U, conscious if garden-variety U) of the smart or topical phrase, and of trade jargon and slang. Qualify this last: there is a special U-slang, derived largely from certain U-sports, particularly the hunt. There is also a special U-slang learned in certain Ivy League colleges or gentlemen's preparatory schools.

2. Avoidance of language fidgets. A U does not fiddle with his face. (Observe how many TV speakers are victims of such small tics.) Similarly he does not fiddle with the language. He economizes, often to the point

of sparseness. He does not preface his sentences with "Well . . . ." To say anything a U-speaker will as a general rule use about 20 per cent fewer words than will a non-U.

3. Preference for the direct and simple, even the common or what the non-U speaker would call the vulgar.

4. Often an inability to use *rich* or *striking* language; the wonderful inventiveness of our vernacular (when it *is* wonderful) is entirely non-U. The English of Ring Lardner is, in its coinages, its humor, and its vividness, non-U. However, in its economy and directness it is U. Lardner himself came of a near-U family though most of his later interests and associations were non-U.

5. Certain peculiarities of pronunciation, though not many, as most of our pronunciation differences are matters of region, not of class.

6. Certain minor peculiarities of syllabic accent.

7. Freedom of vocabulary. Longshoremen and U-speakers use Anglo-Saxon monosyllables casually. (So do young American novelists, but for different reasons.) My own class, the middle, is relatively circumspect in its speech.

8. Neatness of enunciation, not to the point of the Oxford or Noel Coward "clipped" accent, but in general an avoidance of drawling and slurring. Except of course in the South — Southern U-families seem to me to speak badly, but that may be because my ears are Northern.

9. A special pitch and tonality, varying with the region, but essentially distinct from that region's non-U. This is a point rather difficult to illustrate without the use of linguistic technicalities. I shall not illustrate it.

Suppose we begin with a few examples as to which there can be little debate. *Black tie* (or often *dress*) is, generally, U, which does not mean it is not also the preferred form of many non-U speakers; whereas *tux* is not only non-U, but perhaps even sub-non-U. *Long dress*, I am told, is more or less U; *formal* is non-U, or perhaps non-U undergraduate jargon, a special non-U subdivision; our great Midwestern and Western colleges are mints of non-U-sage. The simple *how do you do?* is proper and has descended to the rest of us (probably) from U-speakers; *pleased to meet you* and similar unhappy phrases are non-U. U introductions are usually terse and consist of the names of the two principals; *meet the missus, the wife* we need hardly discuss. Jocular introductions (*meet the ball-and-chain*) are sub-non-U. In England, Miss Mitford tells us, *mirror* is non-U as opposed to U *looking glass*; but this usage applies here only among certain conservative New England families. *Curtains* is U, *drapes* non-U, *draperies* is a limbo word. *Pardon me* is vaguely non-U, as is *I beg your pardon*; but I am not sure that *excuse me* or *sorry* are at all decisively U.

Non-U speakers are given to various euphemisms (or perhaps we should say non-U-phemisms) for *bathroom* or *toilet* (this latter word, itself a euphemism, seems hardly to be used at all). *Toilet paper* is in general usage (I do not know quite how to recast that statement), but *toilet tissue* or *bathroom paper* would suggest non-U. In this connection we might note that most advertising copy is non-U, particularly when it is supposed to be exceedingly U. *Rumpus room* and *den* are non-U. *Children* is U as opposed to non-U *kids.* In Hollywood, where only the purest, undefiled non-U is current, a *cook* is generally a *housekeeper.* There is something non-U about *passed away* for *died.*

The most ordinary phrases are often the most crucial. U will often use *woman* where non-U will use *lady;* U *parents,* non-U *folks. Have you got?* and *have you?* are both correct, but the first is a mite non-U. The word *weekend* is interesting: U-speakers often prefer *Friday to Monday* and many who do use *weekend* will accent the second syllable as against non-U *week'end* (either stress is correct). The tendency to accent the first syllable of certain words, by the way, is often a non-U identifier: *cig'arette,* *mag'azine,* are non-U. So are *ice' cream* for *ice cream'* and *Moth'er Goose* for *Mother Goose'.* But *ar'istocrat* seems U as against *arist'ocrat*: either is acceptable.

The scholar-critic Basil Davenport tells me that he feels *commence* is generally non-U as opposed to *begin;* but I think this a bit subtle. I am not sure of the U for *to date* (a girl), but there is no doubt the phrase itself is decisively non-U. *To keep company* used to be non-U, but today one rarely hears the phrase except among elderly non-U's. *To go steady* is perhaps sub-non-U.

The U-speaker avoids like the plague (a phrase he is apt to avoid like the plague) all modish phrases, such as *I couldn't care less, I couldn't agree more, educated guess, calculated risk, I needed that one* (after a drink), *to know the score, 'n stuff, no percentage in it, the psychological moment, I've got news for you, that's for sure, it doesn't add up, you can say that again, out of this world, —— or else!, a fun scarf;* also vogue words: *psychosomatic* and other cheap Freudianisms, *upgrade,* a *character, tycoon, reaction.*

The world of advertising and popular journalism is rife with such phrases, even though many men in these trades are U by birth and education. (It is interesting that the Luce periodicals are managed in large part by U-men, who do their successful utmost to employ and develop a writing style that will conceal their impeccable origins.) Please do not accuse me of political bias when I say that the leaders of our present Administration are prolific users of non-U English. Probably it is part of the homey, cozy honest-American middle-of-the-roadness which is the presumed hallmark of the Republican Party as at present constituted. The late Senator Taft, on the other hand, spoke (for a politician, I mean) relatively U-English.

Vase is interesting. The nearer you are to the correct French pronunciation the more likely you are to be non-U; most U-speakers rhyme the word with *face.* On the other hand, the U-pronunciation of *lingerie* is apt to stick fairly close to the French; non-U is something like *lonjeray.*

I am on debatable ground here but I think U will say *May I have coffee?* whereas non-U will often preface the last word with *my*. A man who orders *a coffee* in a restaurant has probably spent some years in France; but the usage is gaining generally.

To *name* one's country house, particularly jocularly, is a trifle non-U, unless, like Alexander Woollcott's *Wit's End*, the joke is really witty. But a traditional and unexpressive name for a large estate (Mr. Baruch's *Hobcaw*) is England-county-family U.

To call the *maître d'hotel* the *maître D* is blatantly non-U. It is, once again, pure Madison Avenue in origin; all such knowing phrases have a non-U coloration.

To refer to *my wife* is more or less U; *Mrs. Smith* is non-U; *Mrs. S.* sub-non-U.

Professor Ross has an interesting footnote on the phrases used in casual toasting. English U-speakers used to say nothing, which does seem the best form. (In general, when there is no need to say anything, U-speakers say nothing.) *Cheers, down the hatch, bottoms up,* and similar locutions are all perfectly pleasant, perfectly acceptable, and perfectly non-U.

The use of first names among people who have just met each other is increasing among us: it is non-U and probably derived from the entertainment industry.

A U-man will say *view* rather than *viewpoint, good-bye* rather than *'bye now.* Jocularities such as *see you in church* or *don't do anything I wouldn't do* are pathetically non-U and would be repulsive if they were U.

Conference (in business) used to be elegant; then it became non-U and gave way to *meeting.* Unless a businessman is really attending a meeting, *he's busy* would appear the honest U-phrase to be used by the receptionist.

U-talk is often brutal as compared with non-U talk: *poor* is U-sage, *underprivileged* non-U-sage. The jargon of sociology and editorial journalism is responsible for a good deal of this kind of circumlocution.

Non-U's, particularly the ladies, often love the exaggerated phrase: I cannot conceive of a U saying, "I *despise* garlic!" *Tasty*, as applied to food, I find non-U; also the phrase *to go to theater*, perhaps a Yiddishism, as are *this I've got to hear, I told him off, but good,* and similar fashionable locutions.

Our professional students of language have quite properly called upon us to admire the venison richness of our vernacular, the coinages of a Winchell, the inventions of the hard-working journalists of *Time*, the close-to-the-people vocabulary of Ring Lardner. Well and good. But in the excitement of this linguistic Popular Frontism, the quiet, steadying, braking influence of U-speech tends to attract small notice. Concision, understatement, exactness, even conventionality of expression (if the convention is a noble one) are not to be sniffed at. Why not give the underprivileged gentleman a fair shake?

I recollect the exact moment when this became clear to me — the moment that I decided that, despite the New Grammarians, correct usage had its value. As a young man — I was nineteen — I got my first teaching job in a private school. The principal — Herbert W. Smith is now seventy-one, and I should like to record his name here — was interviewing me in his office. He asked my permission to make a necessary telephone call to one of the teachers. To the switchboard operator he said, "May I speak with Miss Jones?" Something about the question struck me as odd. I realized what it was: I would have said "May I speak *to* Miss Jones?" The difference is not unimportant. It is not only a matter of exact meaning, though it is that also. It is a matter of courtesy, even morality. The clearest English is often *good* English, in both senses of the term. It respects the communicatee just as it shows that the communicator respects himself.

My view may seem stiff-necked but here it is: no matter how many people say *to*, *with* is better. And it will remain better even though every English speaker on the face of the earth should reject *with* and embrace *to*.

4 | ✍

SLANG, JARGON, AND ARGOT

"Slang, profoundly consider'd, is the lawless germinal element, below all words and sentences, and behind all poetry, and proves a certain perennial rankness and protestantism in speech." So wrote Walt Whitman eighty years ago. H. L. Mencken saw in slang the same qualities: "a kind of linguistic exuberance, an excess of word-making energy. . . . The best slang is not only ingenious and amusing; it also embodies a kind of social criticism." Emerson said, "The language of the street is always strong. What can describe the folly and emptiness of scolding like the word *jawing*? I feel too the force of the double negative, though clean contrary to our grammar rules. And I confess to some pleasure from the stinging rhetoric of a rattling oath in the mouths of truckmen and teamsters. How laconic and brisk it is by the side of a page of the *North American Review*. Cut these words and they would bleed; they are vascular and alive; they walk and run." For its prodigious vitality, its value as social criticism, and its sheer fascination, slang deserves full consideration in a book on language.

Slang is language in which a great deal is happening all the time. To use slang to describe slang: it's where the action is. The phrase describes slang accurately while at the same time revealing one inherent danger: triteness. Slang reflects the times. Since much of it grows out of the ephemera of any period, it is quick to die. Some slang, however, becomes part of the standard vocabulary. Whether it becomes forgotten or passes into the canon of standard usage, a slang term can reveal the full creative potentiality of language.

Furthermore, because of changes in the attitudes of our society, slang is no longer as disreputable as it once was. We have become freer of censorship. Novelists and scriptwriters, exploring aspects of society more openly, record appropriate dialogue frankly. As the social sciences have increasingly studied outsider groups (criminals, the impoverished, the disaffected), it has become necessary to know their language. The social worker has to know the language of the addict, as the teacher has to know the dialect of the disadvantaged. Nor is slang so threatening to decorum as it once seemed to be. Knowing more about the usage levels, varieties, and appropriateness of language, we feel that we can confront what might have once been unthinkable. We become secure in our sense of the appropriate and flexible in our ability to adjust our language to various social situations. This confidence comes only from experience and knowledge.

The essays in this section radiate into the whole collection. Slang is part of personal life; it mirrors social history; it is an indicator of social forces; it tells something of culture; by its critical attitude, punning, and word-creation it is related to the literary arts. Whitman also said, "Language, be it remember'd, is not an abstract construction of the learn'd, or of dictionary-makers, but is something arising out of the work, needs, ties, joys, affections, tastes, of long generations of humanity, and has its bases broad and low, close to the ground."

Stuart Berg Flexner

AMERICAN SLANG

ᘔᘔ

In the *Dictionary of American Slang*, (DAS), which he compiled with Harold Wentworth, Stuart Berg Flexner asserts that his point of view is the "human element in the formation of slang." He begins by defining some of the categories of language like "standard usage," "colloquialism," and "dialect"; and he adds "cant," "jargon," "argot," and "slang." Mr. Flexner's diagram of the sources of slang illustrates some of the principles upon which our book is based: that each of us belongs to several speech communities, that each community has its own language, that one shifts vocabulary and voice as he moves among communities, that all the communities make contributions to the vital whole. The essay which follows Mr. Flexner's will show the record of the contributions that college students have made to our current stock of slang.

American slang, as used in the title of this dictionary, is the body of words and expressions frequently used by or intelligible to a rather large portion of the general American public, but not accepted as good, formal usage by the majority. No word can be called slang simply because of its etymological history; its source, its spelling, and its meaning in a larger sense do *not* make it slang. Slang is best defined by a dictionary that points out who uses slang and what "flavor" it conveys.

I have called all slang used in the United States "American," regardless of its country of origin or use in other countries.

In this preface I shall discuss the human element in the formation of

Preface to *Dictionary of American Slang*, by Harold Wentworth and Stuart Berg Flexner. Copyright © 1960 by Thomas Y. Crowell Company, New York, publishers.

slang (what American slang is, and how and why slang is created and used)....

The English language has several levels of vocabulary:

Standard usage comprises those words and expressions used, understood, and accepted by a majority of our citizens under any circumstances or degree of formality. Such words are well defined and their most accepted spellings and pronunciations are given in our standard dictionaries. In standard speech one might say: *Sir, you speak English well.*

Colloquialisms are familiar words and idioms used in informal speech and writing, but not considered explicit or formal enough for polite conversation or business correspondence. Unlike slang, however, colloquialisms are used and understood by nearly everyone in the United States. The use of slang conveys the suggestion that the speaker and the listener enjoy a special "fraternity," but the use of colloquialisms emphasizes only the informality and familiarity of a general social situation. Almost all idiomatic expressions, for example, could be labeled colloquial. Colloquially, one might say: *Friend, you talk plain and hit the nail right on the head.*

Dialects are the words, idioms, pronunciations, and speech habits peculiar to specific geographical locations. A dialecticism is a regionalism or localism. In popular use "dialect" has come to mean the words, foreign accents, or speech patterns associated with any ethnic group. In Southern dialect one might say: *Cousin, y'all talk mighty fine.* In ethnic-immigrant "dialects" one might say: *Paisano, you speak good the English,* or *Landsman, your English is plenty all right already.*

Cant, jargon, and *argot* are the words and expressions peculiar to special segments of the population. *Cant* is the conversational, familiar idiom used and generally understood only by members of a specific occupation, trade, profession, sect, class, age group, interest group, or other sub-group of our culture. *Jargon* is the technical or even secret vocabulary of such a sub-group; jargon is "shop talk." *Argot* is both the cant and the jargon of any professional criminal group. In such usages one might say, respectively: *CQ-CQ-CQ . . . the tone of your transmission is good; You are free of anxieties related to interpersonal communication;* or *Duchess, let's have a bowl of chalk.*

Slang[1] is generally defined above. In slang one might say: *Buster, your line is the cat's pajamas,* or *Doll, you come on with the straight jazz, real cool like.*

Each of these levels of language, save standard usage, is more common in speech than in writing, and slang as a whole is no exception. Thus, very few slang words and expressions (hence very few of the entries in this dictionary) appear in standard dictionaries.

---

[1] For the evolution of the word "slang," see F. Klaeber, "Concerning the Etymology of Slang," *American Speech,* April, 1926.

American slang tries for a quick, easy, personal mode of speech. It comes mostly from cant, jargon, and argot words and expressions whose popularity has increased until a large number of the general public uses or understands them. Much of this slang retains a basic characteristic of its origin: it is *fully* intelligible only to initiates.

Slang may be represented pictorially as the more popular portion of the cant, jargon, and argot from many sub-groups (only a few of the sub-groups are shown below). The shaded areas represent only general overlapping between groups.

Eventually, some slang passes into standard speech; other slang flourishes for a time with varying popularity and then is forgotten; finally, some slang is never fully accepted nor completely forgotten. O.K., *jazz* (music), and *A-bomb* were recently considered slang, but they are now standard usages. *Bluebelly, Lucifer,* and *the bee's knees* have faded from popular use. *Bones* (dice) and *beat it* seem destined to remain slang forever: Chaucer used the first and Shakespeare used the second.

It is impossible for any living vocabulary to be static. Most new slang words and usages evolve quite naturally: they result from specific situations. New objects, ideas, or happenings, for example, require new words to describe them. Each generation also seems to need some new words to describe the same old things.

Railroaders (who were probably the first American sub-group to have a nationwide cant and jargon) thought *jerk water town* was ideally descriptive of a community that others called a *one-horse town*. The changes from *one-horse town* and *don't spare the horses* to *a wide place in the road* and *step on it* were natural and necessary when the automobile replaced the horse. The automobile also produced such new words and new meanings (some of them highly specialized) as *gas buggy, jalopy, bent eight, Chevvie, convertible,* and *lube*. Like most major innovations, the automobile affected our social history and introduced or encouraged *dusters, hitch hikers, road hogs, joint hopping, necking, chicken* (the game), *car coats,* and *suburbia*.

The automobile is only one obvious example. Language always responds to new concepts and developments with new words.

Consider the following:

wars: *redcoats, minutemen, bluebelly, over there, doughboy, gold brick, jeep.*

mass immigrations: *Bohunk, greenhorn, shillalagh, voodoo, pizzeria.*

science and technology: *'gin, side-wheeler, wash-and-wear, fringe area, fall-out.*

turbulent eras: *Redskin, maverick, speak, Chicago pineapple, free love, fink, breadline.*

evolution in the styles of eating: *applesauce, clambake, luncheonette, hot dog, coffee and.*

dress: *Mother Hubbard, bustle, shimmy, sailor, Long Johns, zoot suit, Ivy League.*

housing: *lean-to, bundling board, chuck house, W.C., railroad flat, split-level, sectional.*

music: *cakewalk, bandwagon, fish music, long hair, rock.*

personality: *Yankee, alligator, flapper, sheik, hepcat, B.M.O.C., beetle, beat.*

new modes of transportation: *stage, pinto, jitney, kayducer, hot shot, jet jockey.*

new modes of entertainment: *barnstormer, two-a-day, clown alley, talkies, d.j., Spectacular.*

changing attitudes toward sex: *painted woman, fast, broad, wolf, jailbait, sixty-nine.*

human motivations: *boy crazy, gold-digger, money-mad, Momism, Oedipus complex, do-gooder, sick.*

personal relationships: *bunky, kids, old lady, steady, ex, gruesome twosome, John.*

work and workers: *clod buster, scab, pencil pusher, white collar, graveyard shift, company man.*

politics: *Tory, do-nothing, mug-wump, third party, brain trust, fellow traveler, Veep.*

and even hair styles: *bun, rat, peroxide blonde, Italian cut, pony tail, D.A.*

Those social groups that first confront a new object, cope with a new situation, or work with a new concept devise and use new words long before the population at large does. The larger, more imaginative, and useful a group's vocabulary, the more likely it is to contribute slang. To generate slang, a group must either be very large and in constant contact with the dominant culture or be small, closely knit, and removed enough from the dominant culture to evolve an extensive, highly personal, and vivid vocabulary. Teen-agers are an example of a large sub-group contributing many words. Criminals, carnival workers, and hoboes are examples of the smaller groups. The smaller groups, because their vocabulary is personal and vivid, contribute to our general slang out of proportion to their size.

Whether the United States has more slang words than any other country (in proportion to number of people, area, or the number of words in the standard vocabulary) I do not know. Certainly the French and the Spanish enjoy extremely large slang vocabularies. Americans, however, do use their general slang more than any other people.

American slang reflects the kind of people who create and use it. Its diversity and popularity are in part due to the imagination, self-confidence, and optimism of our people. Its vitality is in further part due to our guarantee of free speech and to our lack of a national academy of language or of any "official" attempt to purify our speech. Americans are restless and frequently move from region to region and from job to job. This hopeful wanderlust, from the time of the pioneers through our westward expansion to modern mobility, has helped spread regional and group terms until they have become general slang. Such restlessness has created constantly new situations which provoke new words. Except for a few Eastern industrial areas and some rural regions in the South and West, America just doesn't look or sound "lived in." We often act and speak as if we were simply visiting and observing. What should be an ordinary experience seems new, unique, or colorful to us, worthy of words and forceful speech. People do not "settle down" in their jobs, towns, or vocabularies.

Nor do we "settle down" intellectually, spiritually, or emotionally. We have few religious, regional, family, class, psychological, or philosophical roots. We don't believe in roots, we believe in teamwork. Our strong loyalties, then, are directed to those social groups — or sub-groups as they are often called — with which we are momentarily identified. This ever-changing "membership" helps to promote and spread slang.

But even within each sub-group only a few new words are generally accepted. Most cant and jargon are local and temporary. What persists are the exceptionally apt and useful cant and jargon terms. These become part of the permanent, personal vocabulary of the group members, giving prestige to the users by proving their acceptance and status in the group. Group members then spread some of this more honored cant and jargon in the dominant culture. If the word is also useful to non-group members, it is on its way to becoming slang. Once new words are introduced into the dominant culture, via television, radio, movies, or newspapers, the rapid movement of individuals and rapid communication between individuals and groups spread the new word very quickly.

For example, consider the son of an Italian immigrant living in New York City. He speaks Italian at home. Among neighborhood youths of similar background he uses many Italian expressions because he finds them always on the tip of his tongue and because they give him a sense of solidarity with his group. He may join a street gang, and after school and during vacations work in a factory. After leaving high school, he joins the navy; then he works for a year seeing the country as a carnival worker. He returns to New York, becomes a longshoreman, marries a girl with a German background, and becomes a boxing fan. He uses Italian and German borrowings, some teen-age street-gang terms, a few factory terms, slang with a navy origin, and carnival, dockworker's, and boxing words. He spreads words from each group to all other groups he belongs to. His Italian parents will learn and use a few street-gang, factory, navy, carnival, dockworker's, and boxing terms; his German in-laws will learn some Italian words from his parents; his navy friends will begin to use some of his Italian expressions; his carnival friends a few navy words; his co-workers on the docks some carnival terms, in addition to all the rest; and his social friends, with whom he may usually talk boxing and dock work, will be interested in and learn some of his Italian and carnival terms. His speech may be considered very "slangy" and picturesque because he has belonged to unusual, colorful sub-groups.

On the other hand, a man born into a Midwestern, middle-class, Protestant family whose ancestors came to the United States in the eighteenth century might carry with him popular high-school terms. At high school he had an interest in hot rods and rock-and-roll. He may have served two years in the army, then gone to an Ivy League college where he became an adept bridge player and an enthusiast of cool music. He may then have become a sales executive and developed a liking for golf. This second man, no more usual or unusual than the first, will know cant and jargon terms of teen-age high-school use, hot-rods, rock-and-roll, Ivy League schools, cool jazz, army life, and some golf player's and bridge player's terms. He knows further a few slang expressions from his parents (members of the Jazz Age of the 1920's), from listening to television programs, seeing both American and British movies, reading popular literature, and from frequent meetings with people having completely different backgrounds. When he uses cool terms on the golf course, college expressions at home, business words at the bridge table, when he refers to whiskey or drunkenness by a few words he learned from his parents, curses his next-door neighbor in a few choice army terms — then he too is popularizing slang.

It is, then, clear that three cultural conditions especially contribute to the creation of a large slang vocabulary: (1) hospitality to or acceptance of new objects, situations, and concepts; (2) existence of a large number of diversified sub-groups; (3) democratic mingling between these sub-groups and the dominant culture. Primitive people have little if any slang because their life is restricted by ritual; they develop few new concepts; and there are no sub-groups that mingle with the dominant culture. (Primitive sub-groups, such as medicine men or magic men, have their own vocabularies; but such groups do not mix with the dominant culture and their jargon can never become slang because it is secret or sacred.)

But what, after all, are the advantages that slang possesses which make it useful? Though our choice of any specific word may usually be made from habit, we sometimes consciously select a slang word because we believe that it communicates more quickly and easily, and more personally, than does a standard word. Sometimes we resort to slang because there is no one standard word to use. In the 1940's, *WAC*, *cold war*, and *cool* (music) could not be expressed quickly by any standard synonyms. Such words often become standard quickly, as have the first two. We also use slang because it often is more forceful, vivid, and expressive than are standard usages. Slang usually avoids the sentimentality and formality that older words often assume. Taking a girl to a *dance* may seem sentimental, may convey a degree of formal, emotional interest in the girl, and has overtones of fancy balls, fox trots, best suits, and corsages. At times it is more fun to go to a *hop*. To be *busted* or without a *hog* in one's *jeans* is not only more vivid and forceful than being penniless or without funds, it is also a more optimistic state. A *mouthpiece* (or *legal beagle*), *pencil pusher, sawbones, boneyard, bottle washer* or a course in *biochem* is more vivid and forceful than a lawyer, clerk, doctor, cemetery, laboratory assistant, or a course in biochemistry — and is much more real and less formidable than a legal counsel, junior executive, surgeon, necropolis (or memorial park), laboratory technician, or a course in biological chemistry.

Although standard English is exceedingly hospitable to polysyllabicity and even sesquipedalianism, slang is not. Slang is sometimes used not only because it is concise but just because its brevity makes it forceful. As this dictionary demonstrates, slang seems to prefer short words, especially monosyllables, and, best of all, words beginning with an explosive or an aspirate.[2]

We often use slang *fad* words as a bad habit because they are close to the tip of our tongue. Most of us apply several favorite but vague words to any

---

[2] Many such formations are among our most frequently used slang words. As listed in this dictionary, *bug* has 30 noun meanings, *shot* 14 noun and 4 adjective meanings, *can* 11 noun and 6 verb, *bust* 9 verb and 6 noun, *hook* 8 noun and 5 verb, *fish* 14 noun, and *sack* 8 noun, 1 adjective, and 1 verb meaning. Monosyllabic words also had by far the most citations found in our source reading of popular literature. Of the 40 words for which we found the most quotations, 29 were monosyllabic. Before condensing, *fink* had citations from 70 different sources, *hot* 67, *bug* 62, *blow* and *dog* 60 each, *joint* 59, *stiff* 56, *punk* 53, *bum* and *egg* 50 each, *guy* 43, *make* 41, *bull* and *mug* 37 each, *bird* 34, *fish* and *hit* 30 each, *ham* 25, *yak* 23, *sharp* 14, and *cinch* 10. (Many of these words, of course, have several slang meanings; many of the words also appeared scores of times in the same book or article.)

of several somewhat similar situations; this saves us the time and effort of thinking and speaking precisely. At other times we purposely choose a word because it is vague, because it does not commit us too strongly to what we are saying. For example, if a friend has been praising a woman, we can reply "she's *the bee's knees*" or "she's a real *chick*," which can mean that we consider her very modern, intelligent, pert, and understanding — or can mean that we think she is one of many nondescript, somewhat confused, followers of popular fads. We can also tell our friend that a book we both have recently read is *the cat's pajamas* or *the greatest*. These expressions imply that we liked the book for exactly the same reasons that our friend did, without having to state what these reasons were and thus taking the chance of ruining our rapport.

In our language we are constantly recreating our image in our own minds and in the minds of others. Part of this image, as mentioned above, is created by using sub-group cant and jargon in the dominant society; part of it is created by our choice of both standard and slang words. A sub-group vocabulary shows that we have a group to which we "belong" and in which we are "somebody" — outsiders had better respect us. Slang is used to show others (and to remind ourselves of) our biographical, mental, and psychological background; to show our social, economic, geographical, national, racial, religious, educational, occupational, and group interests, memberships, and patriotisms. One of the easiest and quickest ways to do this is by using counter-words. These are automatic, often one-word responses of like or dislike, of acceptance or rejection. They are used to counter the remarks, or even the presence, of others. Many of our fad words and many student and quasi-intellectual slang words are counter-words. For liking: *beat, the cat's pajamas, drooly, gas, George, the greatest, keen, nice, reet, smooth, super, way out*, etc. For rejection of an outsider (implying incompetence to belong to our group): *boob, creep, dope, drip, droop, goof, jerk, kookie, sap, simp, square, weird*, etc. Such automatic counters are overused, almost meaningless, and are a substitute for thought. But they achieve one of the main purposes of speech: quickly and automatically they express our own sub-group and personal criteria. Counter-words are often fad words creating a common bond of self-defense. All the rejecting counters listed above could refer to a moron, an extreme introvert, a birdwatcher, or a genius. The counters merely say that the person is rejected — he does not belong to the group. In uttering the counter we don't care what the person is; we are pledging our own group loyalty, affirming our identity, and expressing our satisfaction at being accepted.

In like manner, at various periods in history, our slang has abounded in words reflecting the fear, distrust, and dislike of people unlike ourselves. This intolerance is shown by the many derogatory slang words for different immigrant, religious, and racial groups: *Chink, greaser, Heinie, hunkie, mick, mockie, nigger, spik*. Many counters and derogatory words try to identify our own group status, to dare others to question our group's, and therefore our own, superiority.

Sometimes slang is used to escape the dull familiarity of standard words, to suggest an escape from the established routine of everyday life. When slang is used, our life seems a little fresher and a little more personal. Also, as at all levels of speech, slang is sometimes used for the pure joy of making sounds, or even for a need to attract attention by making noise. The sheer newness and informality of certain slang words produces a pleasure.

But more important than this expression of a more or less hidden esthetic motive on the part of the speaker is slang's reflection of the personality, the outward, clearly visible characteristics of the speaker. By and large, the man who uses slang is a forceful, pleasing, acceptable personality. Morality and intellect (too frequently not considered virtues in the modern American man) are overlooked in slang, and this had led to a type of reverse morality; many words, once standing for morally good things, are now critical. No one, for example, though these words were once considered complimentary, wants to be called a *prude* or *Puritan*. Even in standard usage they are mildly derisive.

Moreover, few of the many slang synonyms for drunk are derogatory or critical. To call a person a standard drunk may imply a superior but unsophisticated attitude toward drinking. Thus we use slang and say someone is *boozed up, gassed, high, potted, stinking, has a glow on*, etc., in a verbal attempt to convey our understanding and awareness. These slang words show that we too are human and know the effects of excessive drinking.

In the same spirit we refer to people sexually as *big ass man, fast, John, sex pot, shack job, wolf*, etc., all of which accept unsanctioned sexual intercourse as a matter of fact. These words are often used in a complimentary way and in admiration or envy. They always show acceptance of the person as a "regular guy." They are never used to express a moral judgment. Slang has few complimentary or even purely descriptive words for "virgin," "good girl," or "gentleman." Slang has *bag, bat, ex, gold digger, jerk, money mad, n.g., old lady, square*, etc.; but how many words are there for a good wife and mother, an attractive and chaste woman, an honest, hardworking man who is kind to his family, or even a respected elderly person? Slang — and it is frequently true for all language levels — always tends toward degradation rather than elevation. As slang shows, we would rather share or accept vices than be excluded from a social group. For this reason, for self-defense, and to create an aura (but not the fact) of modernity and individuality, much of our slang purposely expresses amorality, cynicism, and "toughness."

Reverse morality also affects slang in other ways. Many use slang just because it is not standard or polite. Many use slang to show their rebellion against *boobs, fuddy-duddies, marks*, and *squares*. Intellectuals and politicians often use slang to create the "common touch" and others use slang to express either their anti-intellectualism or avant-garde leanings. Thus, for teen-agers, entertainers, college students, beatniks, jazz fans, intellectuals, and other large groups, slang is often used in preference to standard words and expressions. Slang is the "official" modern language of certain vociferous groups in our population.

In my work on this dictionary, I was constantly aware that most American slang is created and used by males. Many types of slang words — including the taboo and strongly derogatory ones, those referring to sex, women, work, money, whiskey,[3] politics, transportation, sports, and the like — refer primarily to male endeavor and interest. The majority of entries in this dictionary could be labeled "primary masculine use." Men belong to more sub-groups than do women; men create and use occupational cant and jargon; in business, men have acquaintances who belong to many different sub-groups. Women, on the other hand, still tend to be restricted to family and neighborhood friends. Women have very little of their own slang.[4] The new words applied to women's clothing, hair styles, homes, kitchen utensils and gadgets are usually created by men. Except when she accompanies her boy friend or husband to *his* recreation (baseball, hunting, etc.) a woman seldom mingles with other groups. When women do mingle outside of their own neighborhood and family circles, they do not often talk of the outside world of business, politics, or other fields of general interest where new feminine names for objects, concepts, and viewpoints could evolve.

Men also tend to avoid words that sound feminine or weak. Thus there are sexual differences in even the standard vocabularies of men and women. A woman may ask her husband to set the table for dinner, asking him to put out the *silver, crystal,* and *china* — while the man will set the table with *knives, forks, spoons, glasses,* and *dishes.* His wife might think the *table linen* attractive, the husband might think the *tablecloth* and *napkins* pretty. A man will buy a *pocketbook* as a gift for his wife, who will receive a *bag.* The couple will live under the same roof, the wife in her *home,* the man in his *house.* Once outside of their domesticity the man will begin to use slang quicker than the woman. She'll get into the *car* while he'll get into the *jalopy* or *Chevvie.* And so they go: she will learn much of her general slang from him; for any word she associates with the home, her personal belongings, or any female concept, he will continue to use a less descriptive, less personal one.

Males also use slang to shock. The rapid tempo of life, combined with

---

[3] It would appear that the word having the most slang synonyms is *drunk.*

[4] Women who do work usually replace men at men's jobs, are less involved in business life than men, and have a shorter business career (often but an interim between school and marriage). The major female sub-groups contributing to American slang are: airline stewardesses, beauty-parlor operators, chorus girls, nurses, prostitutes, and waitresses.

the sometimes low boiling point of males, can evoke emotions — admiration, joy, contempt, anger — stronger than our old standard vocabulary can convey. In the stress of the moment a man is not just in a standard "untenable position," he is *up the creek*. Under strong anger a man does not feel that another is a mere "incompetent" — he is a *jerk*. . . .

Men also seem to relish hyperbole in slang. Under many situations, men do not see or care to express fine shades of meaning: a girl is either a *knockout* or a *dog*, liquor either *good stuff* or *panther piss*, a person either has *guts* or is *chicken*, a book is either *great* or nothing but *crap*. Men also like slang and colloquial wording because they express action or even violence: we *draw pay, pull a boner, make a score, grab some sleep, feed our face, kill time* — in every instance we tend to use the transitive verb, making ourselves the active doer.

The relation between a sub-group's psychology and its cant and jargon is interesting, and the relation between an individual's vocabulary and psychological personality is even more so. Slang can be one of the most revealing things about a person, because our own personal slang vocabulary contains many words used by choice, words which we use to create our own image, words which we find personally appealing and evocative — as opposed to our frequent use of standard words merely from early teaching and habit. Whether a man calls his wife *baby, doll, honey, the little woman, the Mrs.,* or *my old lady* certainly reveals much about him. What words one uses to refer to a mother (*Mom, old lady*), friend (*buddy, bunkie, old man*), the bathroom (*can, John, little boy's room*), parts of the body and sex acts (*boobies, gigi, hard, laid, score*), being tired (*all in, beat*), being drunk (*clobbered, high, lit up like a Christmas tree, paralyzed*), and the like, reveal much about a person and his motivations.[5]

The basic metaphors, at any rate, for all levels of language depend on the five senses. Thus *rough, smooth, touch; prune, sour puss, sweet; fishy, p.u., rotten egg; blow, loud; blue, red, square*. In slang, many metaphors refer to touch (including the sense of heat and cold) and to taste.

Food is probably our most popular slang image. Food from the farm, kitchen, or table, and its shape, color, and taste suggest many slang metaphors. This is because food can appeal to taste, smell, sight, and touch, four of our five senses; because food is a major, universal image to all people, all sub-groups; because men work to provide it and women devote much time to buying and preparing it; because food is before our eyes three times every day.

Many standard food words mean money in nonstandard use: *cabbage, kale, lettuce*. Many apply to parts of the body: *cabbage head, cauliflower ear, meat hooks, nuts, plates of meat*. Many food words refer to people:

---

[5] For just the last example, *clobbered* may indicate that a drinker is punishing himself, *high* that he is escaping, *lit up like a Christmas tree* that he is seeking attention and a more dominant personality, and *paralyzed* that he seeks punishment, escape or death.

apple, cold fish, Frog, fruitcake, honey, sweetie pie. Others refer to general situations and attitudes: to *brew* a plot, to receive a *chewing out,* to find oneself *in a pickle* or something *not kosher,* to be unable to *swallow* another's story, to ask *what's cooking?* Many drunk words also have food images: *boiled, fried, pickled;* and so do many words for nonsense: *applesauce, banana oil, spinach.* Many standard food words also have sexual meanings in slang. The many food words for money, parts of the body, people, and sex reveal that food means much more to us than mere nourishment. When a *good egg brings home the bacon* to his *honey,* or when a *string bean* of a *sugar daddy* takes his *piece* of *barbecue* out to get *fried* with his hard-earned *kale,* food images have gone a long way from the farm, kitchen, and table.

Sex has contributed comparatively few words to modern slang,[6] but these are among our most frequently used. The use of sex words to refer to sex in polite society and as metaphors in other fields is increasing. Sex metaphors are common for the same conscious reasons that food metaphors are. Sex appeals to, and can be used to apply to, most of the five senses. It is common to all persons in all sub-groups, and so we are aware of it continually.

Slang words for sexual attraction and for a variety of sexual acts, positions, and relationships are more common than standard words. Standard non-taboo words referring to sex are so scarce or remote and scientific that slang is often used in referring to the most romantic, the most obscene, and the most humorous sexual situations. Slang is so universally used in sexual communication that when "a man meets a maid" it is best for all concerned that they know slang.[7] Slang words for sex carry little emotional connotation; they express naked desire or mechanical acts, devices, and positions. They are often blunt, cynical and "tough."

The subconscious relating of sex and food is also apparent from reading this dictionary. Many words with primary, standard meanings of food have sexual slang meanings. The body, parts of the body, and descriptions of each, often call food terms into use: *banana, bread, cheese cake, cherry, jelly roll, meat,* etc. Beloved, or simply sexually attractive, people are also often called by food names: *cookie, cup of tea, honey, peach, quail, tomato,* etc. This primary relation between sex and food depends on the fact that they are man's two major sensuous experiences. They are shared by all personalities and all sub-groups and they appeal to the same senses — thus there is bound to be some overlapping in words and imagery. However, there are too many standard food words having sexual meanings in slang

[6] Many so-called bedroom words are not technically slang at all, but are sometimes associated with slang only because standard speech has rejected them as taboo. However, many of these taboo words do have further metaphorical meanings in slang.

[7] On the other hand, Madame de Staël is reported to have complimented one of her favorite lovers with "speech is not his language."

for these conscious reasons to suffice. Sex and food seem to be related in our subconscious.

Also of special interest is the number of slang expressions relating sex and cheating. Used metaphorically, many sex words have secondary meanings of being cheated, deceived, swindled, or taken advantage of, and several words whose primary meaning is cheating or deceiving have further specific sexual meanings: *cheating, make, royal screwing, score, turn a trick*, etc. As expressed in slang, sex is a trick somehow, a deception, a way to cheat and deceive us. To curse someone we can say *screw you*, which expresses a wish to deprive him of his good luck, his success, perhaps even his potency as a man.[8] Sex is also associated with confusion, exhausting tasks, and disaster: *screwed up, snafu*, etc. It seems clear, therefore, that, in slang, success and sexual energy are related or, to put it more accurately, that thwarted sexual energy will somehow result in personal disaster.

Language is a social symbol. The rise of the middle class coincided with the period of great dictionary makers, theoretical grammarians, and the "correct usage" dogma. The new middle class gave authority to the dictionaries and grammarians in return for "correct usage" rules that helped solidify their social position. Today, newspaper ads still implore us to take mail-order courses in order to "learn to speak like a college graduate," and some misguided English instructors still give a good speaking ability as the primary reason for higher education.

The gap between "correct usage" and modern practice widens each day. Are there valid theoretical rules for speaking good English, or should "observed usage" be the main consideration? Standard words do not necessarily make for precise, forceful, or useful speech. On the other hand, "observed usage" can never promise logic and clarity. Today, we have come to depend on "observed usage," just as eighteenth- and nineteenth-century social climbers depended on "correct usage," for social acceptance.

Because it is not standard, formal, or acceptable under all conditions, slang is usually considered vulgar, impolite, or boorish. As this dictionary shows, however, the vast majority of slang words and expressions are neither taboo, vulgar, derogatory, nor offensive in meaning, sound, or

---

[8] See F. P. Wood, "The Vocabulary of Failure," *Better English*, Nov., 1938, p. 34. The vocabulary of failure is itself very revealing. Failure in one's personality, school, job, business, or an attempted love affair are all expressed by the same vocabulary. One gets the *brush off*, the *gate*, a *kiss off*, or *walking papers* in both business and personal relationships. As the previous discussion of counter-words demonstrates, slang allows no distinction or degree among individual failures. Incompetence does not apply to just one job or facet of life — either one belongs or is considered unworthy. This unworthiness applies to the entire personality, there are no alternate avenues for success or happiness. One is not merely of limited intelligence, not merely an introvert, not merely ugly, unknowing, or lacking in aggression — but one is a failure in all these things, a complete *drip, jerk*, or *square*. The basic failure is that of personality, the person is not a mere failure — he is an outcast, an untouchable; he is taboo.

image. There is no reason to avoid any useful, explicit word merely because it is labeled "slang." Our present language has not decayed from some past and perfect "King's English," Latin, Greek, or pre-Tower of Babel tongue. All languages and all words have been, are, and can only be but conventions mutually agreed upon for the sake of communicating. Slang came to America on the Mayflower. In general, it is not vulgar, new, or even peculiarly American: an obvious illustration of this is the polite, old French word *tête*, which was originally slang from a Latin word *testa* — cooking pot.

Cant and jargon in no way refer only to the peculiar words of undesirable or underworld groups. Slang does not necessarily come from the underworld, dope addicts, degenerates, hoboes, and the like. Any cultural sub-group develops its own personal cant and jargon which can later become general slang. All of us belong to several of these specific sub-groups using our own cant and jargon. Teen-agers, steel workers, soldiers, Southerners, narcotic addicts, churchgoers, truck drivers, advertising men, jazz musicians, pickpockets, retail salesmen in every field, golf players, immigrants from every country, college professors, baseball fans — all belong to typical sub-groups from which slang originates. Some of these sub-groups are colorful; most are composed of prosaic, average people.

Many people erroneously believe that a fundamenal of slang is that it is intentionally picturesque, strained in metaphor, or jocular. Picturesque metaphor (and metonymy, hyperbole, and irony) does or should occur frequently in all levels of speech. Picturesque metaphor is a frequent characteristic of slang, but it does not define slang or exist as an inherent part of it. The picturesque or metaphorical aspect of slang is often due to its direct honesty or to its newness. Many standard usages are just as picturesque, but we have forgotten their original metaphor through habitual use. Thus slang's *jerk* and *windbag* are no more picturesque than the standard *incompetent* and *fool*. *Incompetent* is from the Latin *competens* plus the negating prefix *in-* and = "unable or unwilling to compete"; *fool* is Old French, from the Latin *follis* which actually = "bellows or wind bag"; slang's *windbag* and the standard *fool* actually have the same metaphor.

As for picturesque sounds, I find very few in slang. Onomatopoeia, reduplications, harsh sounds and pleasing sounds, even rhyming terms, exist on all levels of speech. Readers of this dictionary will find no more picturesque or unusual sounds here than in a similar length dictionary of standard words. Many slang words are homonyms for standard words.

As has been frequently pointed out, many slang words have the same meaning. There seems to be an unnecessary abundance of counter-words, synonyms for "drunk," hundreds of fad words with almost the same meaning, etc. This is because slang introduces word after word year after year from many, many sub-groups. But slang is a scatter-gun process; many new words come at the general public; most are ignored; a few stick in the popular mind.

Remember that "slang" actually does not exist as an entity except in the minds of those of us who study the language. People express themselves and are seldom aware that they are using the artificial divisions of "slang" or "standard." First and forever, language is language, an attempt at communication and self-expression. The fact that some words or expressions are labeled "slang" while others are labeled "jargon" or said to be "from the Anglo-Saxon" is of little value except to scholars. Thus this dictionary is a legitimate addition to standard dictionaries, defining many words just as meaningful as and often more succinct, useful, and popular than many words in standard dictionaries.

Alan Dundes · Manuel R. Schonhorn

KANSAS UNIVERSITY SLANG
A New Generation

ちち

What follows is a thorough historical study of the slang to be found at one university, with careful cross-referencing to articles about slang at other schools. One aim of the article is to compare the slang of two generations of students. Dundes and Schonhorn explain their unusual method of collecting, a method you might want to put to use locally. In response to their study, however, Professor Henry Kratz has called for a more exact distinction between what can properly be called college slang and what is simply general slang spoken by college students.

Reprinted from *American Speech* **XXXVIII** (October, 1963), pp. 163–177, by permission of Columbia University Press.

In the nineteenth century, the developing concern for the oral as opposed to the written tradition and the romantic attachment to the folk and their idiom resulted in a host of minor but scholarly studies of slang. The remarkable vitality of common speech attracted the attention of both anthropologists and poets. E. B. Tylor, one of the founders of modern anthropology, felt that an analysis of the evolution of slang would reveal those general laws common to the growth of all languages; Walt Whitman, thirty years after the first publication of *Leaves of Grass*, revealed his lifetime preoccupation with American speech in a meaty article covering many of the diverse types of slang, ranging from state soubriquets to hashhouse jargon.[1] The variety of Whitman's examples perhaps indicates the increased awareness of the great number of slang vocabularies employed by different social and occupational groups. The excitement generated by the active recording of American slang is clearly evidenced in the growing number of studies which concentrated upon the characteristic diction of the American undergraduate.

As early as 1851, B. H. Hall presented a compendium of college expressions in use in the New England area.[2] Hall's collection is significant because, though primarily a study of the full range of university experiences, it does contain an abundant amount of student slang. The traditional dismissal of slang as a short-lived linguistic phenomenon is belied by the continuing currency of many of Hall's words and phrases, for example, *cram, crib, cut, flunk,* and *grind.* Perhaps the most scholarly nineteenth-century study of student slang was made by Willard C. Gore in 1895.[3] Gore attempted to find etymological origins, determine morphological changes, and describe the figurative direction of university expressions. Included in Gore's list are: *bone, cram, crib, grind,* and *loaded.* At the turn of the century, the most ambitious project for the collection of American college slang was undertaken by some members of the New York branch of the American Dialect Society.[4] A questionnaire containing some three hundred words was mailed to the heads of the English departments of about four hundred colleges. From the one hundred returns, Eugene H. Babbitt compiled a comprehensive word list of college words and phrases, indicating geographical distribution. This collection demonstrated con-

[1] E. B. Tylor, "The Philology of Slang," *Macmillan's Magazine,* XXIX (1873–74), 502–13; Walt Whitman, "Slang in America," *North American Review,* CXLI (1885), 431–35.

[2] B. H. Hall, *A Collection of College Words and Customs,* rev. ed. (Cambridge, 1856).

[3] Willard C. Gore, *Student Slang,* Contributions to Rhetorical Theory II, ed. Fred Newton Scott (Ann Arbor, [1896]).

[4] E. H. Babbitt, "College Words and Phrases," *Dialect Notes,* II, Part 1 (1900), 3–70. A popular and much abbreviated survey of Babbitt's findings can be found in his article, "College Slang," *The Chautauquan,* XXXI (1900), 22–24.

clusively that most college slang expressions were not peculiar to one institution or to one region. Indeed, Hall's and Gore's *cram* and *crib* were reported no fewer than sixty-three and thirty-six times respectively. Babbitt's comparative and extensive study has not been duplicated. While there have been numerous twentieth-century studies of college slang, few have been comparative and most have been little more than sporadic collectanea. Actually, the first two decades of the century produced no serious study of college slang. Not even articles devoted to collectanea were common in this period.

The enthusiasm for native American themes, following the First World War, as evidenced by the emergence of such journals as *American Speech* and the acceptance of American Literature as an academically respectable area of research, perhaps accounts for the sudden renewed interest in the study of slang in general, and college slang in particular. One of the first collections of college slang was undertaken at the University of Kansas in 1926, by Carl Pingry and Vance Randolph (Randolph has since become probably the leading collector of regional American folklore).[5] In a way, their study is typical of the many compilations which followed. It listed alphabetically the local slang form, but made no attempt to compare and contrast this form with similar materials reported at other institutions. Without such compartive study, it was not possible to show which items were peculiar to the University of Kansas and which were representative of the general American undergraduate speech of the period.

Even so minimal a comparative technique as comparing the slang expressions of a college with earlier expressions from the same college has been sadly neglected. Follow-up studies of the duration and change of undergraduate slang at one institution are rare.[6] The extent to which one generation's slang expressions are understood or utilized by the next has not been accurately determined. This has been one of the aims of the present study, namely, to discover how many of the slang expressions known by the undergraduates at Kansas University in 1926 were understood or utilized in 1962. The study is also comparative in the larger sense: the contemporary slang expressions elicited were checked against a great number of previous collections of college slang.

---

[5] Carl Pingry and Vance Randolph, "Kansas University Slang," *American Speech*, III (1928), 218–21. Randolph's interest in Kansas speech is further illustrated by his study, "Wet Words in Kansas," *American Speech*, IV (1929), 385–89. The material collected by Pingry and Randolph suggests that the alleged attempt in 1912 by the English Department of the University of Kansas to abolish slang was a dismal failure. This early prohibition movement was acclaimed by the editor of *The Nation*: "If the Department of English of the University of Kansas has really begun a campaign against slang, it deserves the thanks of everybody who has ears to hear." For this view and the comments it inspired, see *The Nation*, XCIV (1912), 303, 410, 462.

[6] But see John Ashton Shidler, "More Stanford Expressions," *American Speech*, VII (1932), 434–37, which used as a point of departure an earlier article by William R. Morse, "Stanford Expressions," *American Speech*, II (1927), 275–79.

The following materials were obtained from 123 undergraduates, all of whom were upperclassmen. Because slang is part of the oral tradition, it was thought best to present orally the denotative word or phrase which was intended to elicit a slang response. For each denotative definition, the student was asked to give one or more slang equivalents. Students were urged to be frank and direct. To ensure this, they were instructed to write down the items — some of the girls might have been hesitant about uttering taboo words — and to leave their papers unsigned. Wherever possible, the denotative definitions were taken from those found in the earlier Kansas University slang study. It was felt that the alternative procedure, that of presenting the earlier slang words for purposes of recognition, might have resulted in an unreliable comparison. For example, while students could correctly define a *heel*, one of the earlier slang terms, its contemporary currency is limited and there are other terms for the same referent which students would be much more likely to use.

The slang items in this study are subdivided into two major groupings: (1) academic and (2) social. The format followed supplies first the denotative word or phrase which was used to elicit the slang responses. Next, those responses which occurred at least five times are listed in order of frequency. The frequency, indicated parenthetically, is at best relative, since some of the 123 students did not respond to many of the denotative stimuli.[7] The fact that individual students provided more than one slang response for some items must also be taken into account. In certain cases, where an item appears to be of unusual interest, it has been noted even though its frequency was below the arbitrary cut-off point. Previous notice of individual slang items is indicated in a number of ways. Those items reported in the earlier Kansas study are in small capitals. All items included in the DAS with the same or similar meanings are marked with an asterisk. Finally, items which appear in other collections of college slang are followed by appropriate indications.[8]

[7] The frequency does, however, provide some measure of the relative popularity of individual synonymous slang items. In previous studies, frequencies were not given, thereby making it difficult to ascertain which of several slang choices was the more widely known.

[8] Items appearing in other collections of college slang are indicated by reference to the institution in which the collection was made (with the exception of items mentioned in the article under *General* below). The list of institutions and the sources of the slang material pertaining to them follows:

Albion (College) [Michigan] Dorothy M. Schullian, "College Slang," *School and Society*, LVIII (1943), 169–70.

Brown (University) [Fredson Bowers], "College Slang: A Language All Its Own," *The Literary Digest*, LXXXIV (March 14, 1925), 64–65.

Bryn Mawr (College) Howard J. Savage, "College Slang Words and Phrases from Bryn Mawr College," *Dialect Notes*, V, Part 5 (1922), 139–48.

Colgate (University) Jason Almus Russell, "Colgate University Slang," *American Speech*, V (1930), 238–39.

(The) Citadel R. I. McDavid, Jr., "A Citadel Glossary," *American Speech*, XIV (1939), 23–32.

ACADEMIC

1. To study extremely diligently for an examination:

cram* (82) [Bryn Mawr, General, Johns Hopkins, Missouri, Nebraska, Western Reserve]

bone up* (5) [Bryn Mawr, General, Nebraska, Stanford 1, Stanford 2, Western Reserve]

hit the books* (8) [Florida, Stanford 1, Stanford 2]

book it (5)

(University of) Florida Lalia Phipps Boone, "Gator (University of Florida) Slang," *American Speech*, XXXIV (1959), 153–57.

General (see article for references to specific institutions) E. H. Babbitt, "College Words and Phrases," *Dialect Notes*, II, Part 1 (1900), 3–70.

Johns Hopkins (University) J. Louis Kuethe, "Johns Hopkins Jargon," *American Speech*, VII (1932), 327–38.

Lawrence (College) [Wisconsin] [Mary Ellen Parr], "College Slang," *Science Digest*, XXXVIII, No. 2 (August, 1955), 33–34.

Lincoln (University) [Pennsylvania] Hugh Sebastian, "Negro Slang in Lincoln University," *American Speech*, IX (1934), 287–90.

(University of) Minnesota Nancy Calkin and William Randel, "Campus Slang at Minnesota," *American Speech*, XX (1945), 233–34.

(University of) Missouri Virgina Carter, "University of Missouri Slang," *American Speech*, VI (1931), 203–6.

(University of) Nebraska M. C. McPhee, "College Slang," *American Speech*, III (1927), 131–33.

Stanford (University) 1 William R. Morse, "Stanford Expressions," *American Speech*, II (1927), 275–79.

Stanford (University) 2 John Ashton Shidler, "More Stanford Expressions," *American Speech*, VII (1932), 434–37.

Texas A. & M. [Agricultural and Mechanical College of Texas] Fred Eikel, Jr., "An Aggie Vocabulary of Slang," *American Speech*, XXI (1946), 29–36.

(University of) Virginia 1 Gilmore Spencer, "Current College Slang," *University of Virginia Magazine*, LXXXVII (October, 1926), 16–17.

(University of) Virginia 2 John Wyllie, "Short Dictionary of Slang, Jargon, Cant and Popular Customs," *University of Virginia Alumni News*, XXIV (1936), 80–81.

Wayne [State University] William White, "Wayne University Slang," *American Speech*, XXX (1955), 301–5.

Whitman College William White, "Whitman College Slang," *American Speech*, XVIII (1943), 153–55.

Western Reserve [University] Robert Bolwell, "College Slang Words and Phrases from Western Reserve University," *Dialect Notes*, IV, Part 3 (1915), 231–38.

The following collections of college slang in *American Speech* afforded no parallels for the present study: Lelah Allison, "M. U. Colloquialisms," XVI (1941), 75; Dorothy Carr, "Some Annapolis Slang," XIV (1939), 76–77; George H. Danton, "Americana [Oberlin]," V (1930), 281–82; G. H. D., "College English [Oberlin]," IV (1929), 420; Kenneth L. Daughrity, "Handed-Down Campus Expressions," VI (1930), 129–30; James L. Jackson, "Notes on Air Force Academy Language," XXXVI (1961), 148–49; Klonda Lynn *et al.*, "Gringoisms in Arizona," XXIV (1949), 234–36; M. C. McPhee, "Odd Colloquialisms [Nebraska]," XV (1940), 334–35; William Eben Schultz, "College Abbreviations," V (1930), 240–44; Hugh Sebastian, "Agricultural College Slang in South Dakota," XI (1936), 279–80; and John Shidler and R. M. Clarke, Jr., "Stanfordiana," VII (1932), 232–33. Nor were any parallels found in Margaret L. Farrand "The Slang at Smith," *The Delineator*, XCVII, No. 3 (October, 1920), 119; or in George Monteiro's note on *zapped* in *American Speech*, XXXVII (1962), 71.

2. An easy college course:

pud adj. (99)
snap adj. (22) [Brown, Bryn Mawr,   *breeze* n.* (3)
General, Johns Hopkins, Nebraska,   *gut* adj.* (3)
Stanford 1, Virginia 1]

The term *gut* is extremely popular in Eastern college slang. The few informants in this study who did note the term commented that it had been learned in the East, for example, at Skidmore and Princeton.

3. A difficult college course:

bear (45)   *bastard* (14)
BITCH* (23) [Johns Hopkins, Wayne]

A *bear* at Western Reserve is a professor who overworks his students.

4. To miss class:

cut* (113) [Brown, Bryn Mawr, Gen-   *skip** (18) [General]
eral, Missouri, Texas A. & M., West-
ern Reserve]

5. An unexpected examination:

SHOTGUN* (86)   *pop quiz** (45) [Missouri]

The popularity of the term *shotgun* is indicated by its presence in the punch line of a campus joke: "Do you know what God said to Moses? — Get out your tablet and number from one to ten. We're going to have a shotgun." A possible predecessor of the term *pop quiz* found in Bryn Mawr and General is *drop quiz**.

6. To cheat during an examination:

CRIB* (14) [Bryn Mawr, Colgate,   *fudge** (5) [General]
Florida, General, Missouri, Ne-
braska, Western Reserve]

7. To fail to pass an examination:

flunk*[9] (60) [Brown, General, Mis-   *flag* (28)
souri, Nebraska, Texas A. & M.,   *blow** (5)
Virginia 2]   *bomb** (5)

Some of the more interesting items which occurred but once are: *F'd, get shot out of the saddle, go down the tubes, go out backwards,* and *go out the bottom.*

[9] For a discussion of this term, see Charles H. Livingston, "American English 'Flunk,'" *American Speech,* XXI (1946), 16–18.

8. A student who achieves a high grade on a low-scored examination, thus disturbing the class average:

brain* (11)

fink (7)

d.a.r. [damned average raiser] (2) [Minnesota, Stanford 2, Wayne, Whitman]

9. To acquit oneself creditably in an examination:

ace it (48) [Florida]

bomb it (15)

ace out (7)

Some of the items which occurred once are: breeze out, luck out, and rack out.

10. An extremely poor and dull lecturer:

bore (18) [General]

loser (10) [Wayne]

drag* (6) [Wayne]

bad news (5)

Significantly enough, the denotative term good professor elicited no one response five times. Perhaps this indicates that good professors go unrecorded and unrewarded as far as slang is concerned.[10]

11. To curry favor with a professor:

brown nose* (61) [Citadel, Albion]

brownie* (19)

SUCK* (11) [General, Texas A. & M., Western Reserve]

APPLE POLISH* (8) [Florida, Minnesota, Missouri, Stanford 1, Stanford 2]

butter up* (8)

get brownie points (6)

There were three occurrences of kiss ass and one of the acronym K.A. The noun form inversion A.K. is recorded in Citadel and Florida. Reported once was a curious variant of a traditional phrase: to be an apple knocker.

12. To deprive a student, or to be deprived, of campus privileges:

CAMPUS HIM* (25) [Bryn Mawr, General]

be a social pro* (9)

be on pro* (5)

10 Much the same point is made by Morris Marples in University Slang (London, 1950), his extensive study of the slang of English universities, especially that of Oxford and Cambridge:

the schoolboy is prolific in slang directed against everything unpleasant in school life — hard work, bad food, the school authorities, punishment, his fellows who do not conform to pattern, and so on. He has little to say, in slang terms at any rate, concerning the brighter side of his existence. The undergraduate's slang is modelled on somewhat similar lines. (p. 4)

Some of the very few items in Marples's collection which are common to both American and English universities are: bone, cram, crib, cut, and grind, and such synonyms for drunkenness as blotto and tight.

13. To be called to the Dean's office:

*be called on the carpet** (12)   *be put on the carpet** (12)

The earlier form of *on the carpet* employed *mat** (Nebraska, Western Reserve) instead. Today, this unpleasant experience has given rise to a number of picturesque expressions. The following occurred once: *enter the lion's den, get shot down, go to the snake pit, ride the storm, see the warden* (Nebraska), and *take gas*.

14. The university police force:

campus cops (17) [Texas A. & M.]   *fuzz** (13)

Mildly deprecatory epithets were: *boy scouts* (3), and the following, all reported once: *big gnomes, boy scouts in blue, campus clowns, campus finks, cherry tops, cub scouts, goobies, good humor men, idiot squad, intellects, John Law(s)*, and *mafia*.

15. A college athlete:

jock (81)   *animal* (32)

The word *jock* is an obvious abbreviation of *jockstrap*. The form *strap* occurred but once, with a note as to its eastern geographical provenience. The full synecdoche itself, *jockstrap*, was also reported once. The term *jockstrap* is like *taxicab*, in that each of its constituent morphemes may serve in place of the parent term.

16. A studious classmate:

*brain** (19)   *bookworm* (14)

The term *bookworm* demonstrates the arbitrary and relative nature of definitions of slang. Though no less figurative than *apple polisher*, and though even labelled slang by the students, it nevertheless is part of acceptable standard usage. According to *Webster's New World Dictionary*,[11] *apple polisher* is slang; *bookworm* is not.

The word *grind** (Brown, General, Johns Hopkins, Missouri, Stanford 2, Wayne) so common elsewhere, appeared only once, with the notation that it had been learned at Princeton.

17. An intellectual:

*brain** (51)   *egghead** (15) [Florida]

Informants noted that *brain* was often the honorific term, while *egghead* was usually derogatory.

---

[11] College ed.; Cleveland and New York, 1959.

18. A rather stupid student:

clod* (7)   dope* (5)
loser (6) [Florida, Wayne]   dumb shit* (5)

A term which appeared once, *lunchie*, is probably a derivation of the traditional folk metaphor *to be out to lunch* (Lawrence) meaning 'to have minimal mental capacity' or 'to be temporarily dense.'[12]

19. Wasting time:

goofing off* (28) [Lawrence]   messing around* (5) [Johns Hopkins]
screwing around* (10)   shooting the breeze* (5)
killing time (5)

SOCIAL

1. To go alone to a dance or social function:

stag* (48) [Nebraska, Western   stag it (23) [General]
    Reserve]
go stag* (27)

Although *stag it, v.t.,* is not listed in the DAS, responses indicate that it is used now as it was at the turn of the century.

2. To take one's partner from him in the middle of a dance:

cut in* (58) [Missouri]   cut him out (6)
bird dog* (13)

Informants indicated a distinction between a temporary borrowing for one dance (*cut in*) and a more permanent liaison (*bird dog*) for the entire evening.

3. One who puts a damper on a party:

party pooper*[13] (34) [Wayne]   drag* (12)
wet blanket* (16)   kill-joy* (9)

4. A particularly rough and noisy party:

blast* (52) [Florida, Wayne]   orgy (8)
BRAWL* (8) [Nebraska]

---

12 For the use of the term *lunch* as a synonym for *useless* by University of Buffalo undergraduates, see Robert Ian Scott, " 'Qualm' as Verb, 'Lunch' as Adjective," *American Speech*, XXXVIII (1963), p. 159.

13 The term *party pooper* is noted by Horace Reynolds, "College Words with a Musical Accent," *American Speech*, XXIX (1954), 293, but with no indication as to its specific use at a particular college.

A few of the more colorful expressions appearing once are: *ball**, *bash**, *beer blast, blowout*, boozer,* BUST*, *heller, rocker, shit kicker, shit stomper, smash,* and *swinger.*

5. A poor social evening, a wasted night:

drag* (37) [Wayne]   *bad news* (6)

6. To get away from an unpleasant or undesirable person:

ditch* (23) [Johns Hopkins,   *dump** (5)
   Missouri]
cut out* (12)

7. To break up a campus romance:

to bird dog* (10) [Texas A. & M.]

Many of the responses referring to one party's rejection of another, as, for example, a girl breaking a previously arranged date with a boy, are figurative expressions of excremental activities. A boy so treated is said to have been *dumped on*, flushed,* or *shit on*.* A curious expression is *to get the brown helmet,* which a boy might use to indicate that he had just been *dumped on* by a girl. The phrase may be accompanied by a gesture in which an imaginary helmet is pulled down over the ears.[14]

8. A person who has special influence is said to have:

pull* (51) [Bryn Mawr, General]   *connections* (13)
suck (22) [Texas A. & M.]

The term listed by Pingry and Randolph, *drag* (Albion, Bryn Mawr, Johns Hopkins, Missouri), appeared only once. However, their mention of *sucking crew,* designating a group of students trying to get high grades through personal influence, indicates that *suck* was probably understood in its modern sense at that time.

9. An effeminate young man, a sissy:

queer* (33) [Johns Hopkins]   *fruit** (6)
fairy* (19) [Johns Hopkins]   *pussy** (6)
fink (12)

Some of the less frequent, but more expressive, phrases are: *dink* (cf. General), *dollie daddy, fag** (Johns Hopkins), *faggot** (Johns Hopkins, Lincoln), *homo** (Johns Hopkins), *limp wrist*, mother-o*, music major, pansy** (Johns Hopkins), *pansy-ass, petunia, punk, swish*, twink,* and *weenie.*

[14] For a discussion of the nonbiological figurative uses of sexual or excretory slang, see Edward Sagarin, *The Anatomy of Dirty Words* (New York, 1962).

10. An unusually odd student:

odd ball* (23)   squirrel* (16)
queer (20) [Texas A. & M.]   weird-o (6)
fink (17)

At one institution (Bryn Mawr) in 1915, a stupid or foolish person, a "nut," was termed *squirrel food*.

11. A male student who never engaged in social activities:

fink (10)   squirrel (8)
queer* (10)   twink (6)

Some Dr. Seuss-like terms occurring once were: *furd, gnard, snarf*, and *zonk*.

12. An ill-mannered student with poor, unpolished manners:

clod (23)   fink (5)
slob (13)   hick* (5)
farmer (7)

Of interest is the number of pejorative expressions traditionally directed at the supposedly less sophisticated rural resident: *country bumpkin, dip-shit, farmboy, lout, ox**, and *rube** (General). Even the most earthy response, *clod*, connects the indecorous with the soil.

13. An unpleasant male date:

real loser (22) [Florida]   drag* (7)
squirrel (9)   fink* (7)

14. A noticeably cheap date, one who refuses to spend too much money on a date:

tightwad* (23) [cf. Johns Hopkins]   miser (5)
cheapskate* (9)   skin flint (5)
penny pincher* (6)

15. A concerted effort to impress a girl:

snow job* (69) [Florida, Lawrence]

16. A very pretty female date:

doll* (23)   babe* (5) [Western Reserve]
winner (18)   swinger (5)
chick* (7) [Wayne]

17. A pretty girl who has sex appeal:

*doll** (10)
*babe** (6)

*dolly** (5)
winner (5)

Less common terms include: *bod, body*, cool bod, dish*, hot bod,* KNOCKOUT* (Johns Hopkins, Nebraska, Stanford 1, Stanford 2), *pack the gears, sex box, sex kitten, sex pot** (*Wayne*), and *stacked**. Widely differing temperature indications can designate a common quality, for example, *cool bod* and *hot bod*.[15]

18. An unattractive female date:

*pig** (36) [Florida, Johns Hopkins, Wayne]
loser (29) [Florida]

bad news (8)
*dog** (8)

Ugliness is apparently associated with the animal kingdom and ranges from such general terms as *beast** (Florida, Wayne) to the more specific *bear*, cow*, goose, moose, roach* (Florida), *squirrel*, and *wet fish*. A non-animal phrase rich in irony, used by a girl to comment obliquely on another co-ed's ugliness, is: "The girls all like her; she makes her own clothes."

19. A sorority known for its unprepossessing members:

pigpen (8)

Here too, animal imagery serves as the basis for figurative expression. Noted were: *animal farm, campus pig house, cattle show, dog house, pig house, pig sty, snake house,* and *zoo.*

20. Girls who run around and always date in pairs:

Although no response was recorded five times, several warrant mention: *Bobbsey twins* (4), *Siamese twins* (2), *asshole buddies* (1), *bathtub kids* (1), *chum-buddies* (1), *Gold Dust twins* (1), *package deal* (1), and *sisters* (1).

21. A female who is dated because of her lax sexual habits:

*whore** (18)
slut (11)
*bitch** (9)

*easy make** (9)
punch (6)

The word *punch* may well be a shortened form of *punchboard*, which was recorded twice; the latter usage is current at Indiana University.

---

[15] Just as two apparently contrasting slang terms may have one meaning, so one slang term may have two apparently contradictory meanings. Thus, to *bomb an examination* (see numbers 7 and 9 under *Academic* above) can mean 'to acquit oneself creditably' and 'to fail to pass.' Cf. the same dual use of *bust* in Florida.

22. A co-ed engaged to a young man in a distant college who refuses to date at all while at college:

(she's) true-blue (5)

The following items were recorded once: *cold pussy, ice box, long-distance lover, widow,* and also *(she's) long distancing.* One informant noted that a male in an analogous situation is said to be *pussy whipped,* a term one of the authors recalls having heard in the Navy in 1956.

23. To describe something in the most superlative tones and language is to call it:

great* (15) [Florida, Lawrence]	the most* (11) [Florida, Lawrence, Wayne]
cool* (12) [Wayne]	sharp* (6)

Some of the more novel one-time occurrences are: *fantabulous, hot shit*, neatsie keen, screbolerabins, top drawer*,* and *tremendi.*

24. A good idea or sudden inspiration:

brainstorm* (40) [Johns Hopkins]	flash (14)

25. To go to bed:

sack out* (37) [Florida]	pad out (9)
hit the sack* (33) [Florida]	pad it (8)
hit the hay* (16)	rack out* (7)
hit the pad* (9)	turn in* (5)

An onomatopoetic construction reported four times is *get some Z's,* which in verb form was noted twice as *Z'ing it.* Variants occurring once were: *bagging Z's, copping some Z's, cutting Z's,* and *knocking out Z's.* Also noted once were: *conk out*, flake it** (cf. Florida), *jump in the bag, point toe to heaven,* and *saw wood*.*

26. College meals:

slop (18) [Wayne]	crap (5)
chow* (8)	

Individual items on the college menu include: *barf* 'beef stew,' *beanie-weenies* 'frankfurters and beans,' *beavertail* 'steak,' *grab* 'Sunday supper,' *gristle* 'steak,' *walk-in sauce* 'mayonnaise,' and the ubiquitous military staple *shit on a shingle* (Citadel), which is the old familiar chipped beef on toast probably known to many veterans of the Second World War under the alternate *D.V.O.T.* (Citadel), signifying 'dog vomit on toast.'

27. Drunk:

*soused** (29)
out of it (28)
*stoned** (25) [Florida, Wayne]
bombed (24)
*smashed** (22) [Florida]
out of his mind (18)
plowed (18) [Wayne]
*plastered** (17) [Johns Hopkins]
*high** (13)

*juiced** (9)
*loaded** (9)
*looped** (8)
STEWED* (7) [Bryn Mawr, Nebraska, Virginia 1]
*crocked** (6)
*tight** (5) [Johns Hopkins, Stanford 2]

This question elicited the greatest number of responses. Nearly all of the informants listed at least three slang expressions. Some indicated distinctions in the degree of intoxication. For example, one who is in the more extreme states of drunkenness is referred to as: *plowed, smashed, soused,* and *stoned.* In contrast, the words *happy**, *high,* and *looped* describe a lesser state. Some of the less frequent, but apparently equally traditional, adjectives are: *blotto** (Colgate, Missouri), *boozed**, OILED* (Johns Hopkins), *pickled**, POLLUTED*, *schnockered* (Wayne), *shit-faced, skunked,* and TANKED* (Bryn Mawr, Stanford 1, Whitman).

The above data may some day be used to affirm the commonplace, stating that the slang of our fathers becomes either obsolete or accepted usage. Some of the current Kansas University slang may not survive the present generation; some may become the classicisms of tomorrow. Certainly the slang collections of the past century and a half indicate the remarkable durability of a segment of the university student's private idiom, for example, *cram, crib,* and *flunk*; and at the same time, these collections document the wholesale disappearance of hundreds of expressions. One of the aims of this study was to determine the contemporary Kansas University student's knowledge of the preceding generation's slang as recorded by Pingry and Randolph. The slang surveyed thus far has revealed only thirteen items which were reported in the 1926 collection. However, in order to test more fully the survival and obsolescence of the earlier slang, a more direct approach was employed.

Each of the eighty-five items listed by Pingry and Randolph was read to a new group of thirty-seven upperclassmen who were asked to explain them. Of these eighty-five items, thirty — or more than one third — were either not known at all, or had so changed that their present meanings were completely different from those reported by Pingry and Randolph. For example, the word *eagers,* meaning 'anxiety or haste' in 1926, was completely unknown to students in 1962; *charge,* which formerly was 'a violation of rules of regulations,' has become a synonym for 'thrill.'[16] Of the

[16] The following thirty items listed and defined by Pingry and Randolph were not recognized by thirty-seven informants: *annex baby, bounce, bricks, cellar gang, charge,*

remaining fifty-five items, thirty-nine were recognized by at least five of the thirty-seven members in the new group.[17] This supplementary testing revealed the necessity for distinguishing between the recognition and the actual use of the slang of an earlier generation. More of Pingry and Randolph's expressions were recognized than were used. The first part of the present study, which investigated usage, revealed that thirteen of the earlier items are current. The second part, which tested recognition, indicated that no fewer than fifty-five of the previous expressions were known to some extent. A comparison of the frequencies of occurrence of those few individual items appearing in both sections of this study strengthens the distinction made between recognition and usage. For example, thirty-four out of thirty-seven students defined *apple polish* as 'to curry favor,' whereas only eight out of 123 students gave it as a slang equivalent of 'to curry favor.' Similarly, *knockout* was recognized by thirty-four of the thirty-seven, but was used by fewer than five of the 123 students. Clearly, this indicates that erroneous conclusions could easily have been drawn if only the second technique had been used. One might have assumed, for instance, that *apple polish,* known and used in 1926, was still widely current. However, the results of the first testing indicated its rather infrequent use.

It is obvious, of course, that the controlled-questionnaire approach has disadvantages, as well as advantages. Advantages are that the data obtained from specific questions can be measured with respect to ratio of response, for example, fifty-one of 123 students are familiar with *brain* as a slang designation for intellectual, and furthermore that the relative popularity of synonymous slang alternatives can be approximately gauged, for example, *brain* was used by fifty-one, while *egghead* was used by only fifteen. On the other hand, an inevitable disadvantage is that there is a considerable body of slang which may not be elicited by any one questionnaire. Some current Kansas University slang not obtained through the questionnaire

---

drag, eagers, frig, get a load of pig iron, girk, greased, gripe, hawk, hobnail hop, hot, hot sketch, house, knock off a hoe-down, meat squad, oil can, Phi Beta house, pipe, pop house, right pert, scab, scrim, see a man about a dog, varsity, wet smack, and whiz bitch. There are some surprising historical changes in meaning. For example, see a man about a dog was a Prohibition euphemism for 'buying liquor,' whereas several contemporary students recognized it as a circumlocution for 'visiting a rest room.' See Sagarin, The Anatomy of Dirty Words, p. 71. At Johns Hopkins, the phrase served as an excuse for leaving the scene.

[17] Those items whose present meanings were identical with those of the earlier study include: apple polisher (34), bag (14), blind date (31), brawl (11), broad (34), bull session (32), bust (14), campus (29), catch in the get-along (8), crack a book (31), crib (20), date (33), dirty quiz (12), flat tire (9), get around (9), get going (12), heel (24), hit a quiz (10), horse around (34), hot (6), knock-out (34), mangey (19), mean baby (8), miss a quiz (12), oiled (5), on the hill (25), pass out (21), polluted (15), put out one's pin (22), rate (8), red hot (5), rush (28), rushee (35), shindig (32), shotgun quiz (36), slip me five (5), spike (31), stewed to the gills (34), washout (6), and wow (19).

includes the following. Frequent and time-consuming assignments which appear to be homework for homework's sake are termed *busy work*. An assignment which is regarded as foolish and a waste of time is a *Mickey Mouse*. Popular substitutes for the verb *to eat* include the alliterative *to gobble** groceries and *to snarf down the goodies, snarf* referring, according to one informant, to the act of eating like an animal. An outdoor picnic-party (in the woods) is called a *woodsie*. Local place names also have their slang equivalents. The initials of Gertrude Sellards Pearson, a hall for freshmen women, have given rise to *Girls' State Prison* and *Gertie's Sex Palace*. Again, inter- and intra-fraternity slang has rarely been noted. Yet there are numerous examples of such slang. The Phi Gamma Delta fraternity supposedly houses a large number of athletes. Accordingly the house is termed *Animal Farm* or *The Stables*. A member of Beta Theta Pi may be called a *Beta*, but there are many other terms for members of this fraternity, terms which carry unmistakably homosexual allusions. A *Beta* is also called a *butt*, and his house a *butt hut*. Often, the slang expressions for *Beta* members employ metaphors of flight which are intended to depict their alleged homosexual proclivities. The expression *they fly* is in this vein, as is the epithet *flying squirrels*. Their house has been dubbed *The Aviary* and *Lawrence Municipal Airport*. These few examples suggest that there is a wealth of unmined slang material emanating from fraternity and sorority life.

While this study has concerned itself primarily with the slang of one institution, the materials themselves warrant studies of a more inclusive nature. No doubt many of the slang expressions current at Kansas University are part of the common undergraduate speech at a great many colleges. But in the absence of systematic collections of slang at these colleges, studies of greater scope are well nigh impossible. Ideally, then, thorough and intensive collections of college slang should be made periodically. This would serve the dual purpose of recording the development of slang at individual institutions and of providing a sound basis for comparative studies of college slang generally. Perhaps a comprehensive questionnaire might be devised, similar to that employed by the New York branch of the American Dialect Society more than sixty years ago, to be circulated with additions at regular intervals among American colleges and universities. Only in such a controlled way can the vital idiom of American college youth be accurately preserved.

Robert S. Gold

THE VERNACULAR OF JAZZ

✍✍

So much that is inaccurate and farfetched has been written about the language of jazz that it is good to have this scholarly treatment by Mr. Gold. In his first sentence, he makes a point which we have been developing in the course of this collection — namely, that the study of language can be and should be a careful cultural study also. Mr. Gold makes some observations about the situations out of which the special jargon grew and in which it still flourishes. He examines the "polyglot origins" of jazz in its New Orleans environment, where a people expressed themselves by creating a new music and a new idiom for it. After reading this essay, you might turn your thoughts to further developments of song in our society. For example, what is the language of rock and roll, bluegrass, folksong? What, too, are their origin, impetus, and expression?

The study of the vernacular of the jazz world is necessarily a study in sociology and social psychology as well as in linguistics. For the people who created this peculiarly American idiom did so as a result of the peculiar conditions surrounding the development of modern jazz. Hence, an understanding of their slang is hardly possible without a knowledge of how jazz grew up, who its creators were, and what kind of lives they led. Only then does the language they speak become meaningful.

It is by ignoring the sociological side of the coin that the slick magazines have been able to caricature and patronize the colorful jargon of jazz. *Life, Time, Newsweek, Collier's,* and others have made forays into the field of

220

jazz linguistics to the amusement, if not enlightenment, of their readers. Typical is this caption from *Life*, hardly more accurate in its presentation of jazz speech than in its portrayal of college students:

Voutians (pronounced Vowshuns) are a growing group of United States college students who are uninhibited admirers of Jazz Musician Slim Gaillard, composer of "Cement Mixer Put-ti, Put-ti," "Flat Foot Floogie with the Floy Floy." They play his records, talk his outlandish rhyming language. A pretty girl is a rootie-voutie, or viddle vop. Onions are reetie-pooties. Reeny, roony and aureenie are used as complementary suffixes (hamburgaureenie is a good hamburger).[1]

Accompanying this article are pictures illustrating the "vout handshake," a maneuver requiring a contortionist for its execution (a jazz musician or devotee who tried it would probably meet with serious injury).

So we have that eccentric bane of middle-class existence, the Jazz Musician (*Life's* capitals), poisoning Our Youth (my capitals) with nonconformist speech and greeting. Little surprise, then, that the article provoked letters like this:

Sirs: Physical chastisement may be frowned upon by child psychologists, but it does seem a resounding whack smack with a snap strap on the seat meat of such ants pants as these Voutians would be aurightaureenie. What say, O'Day?
Hopewell, N.J.   R. L. Scharring-Hauser[2]

Scharring-Hauser is no doubt pleased by his own cleverness, but his parody, unknown to him, is more of *Life* than of the ephemeral Voutians, who doubtless vanished at the first sign of a new diversion. The truth is that even by jazz standards Slim Gaillard is an eccentric (but his world is a more tolerant one, and in it, his undisciplined spoofing is taken good-naturedly). Then, too, jazz lingo can hardly be held responsible for university faddism, a runaway horse that has long since departed from the stable of sanity. And, while these shenanigans make delightful copy, one can legitimately object to the editorial irresponsibility which seizes upon the most extravagant jazz parlance and creates the impression that it is the norm. Such exaggerations contribute to the classic slander — that jazz is nothing but a garish art form and its practitioners dope addicts, and that its language proves both points. Gilbert Seldes notes: "I have heard Eddie Condon say that he has never heard and doesn't understand half of the jive language the hepcats are supposed to use."[3] When a noted jazz guitarist who has "gigged around" (worked a variety of jobs) for nearly three decades makes an admission of this sort, it is a sign that much con-

---

[1] *Life*, May 5, 1947, p. 129.
[2] "Letters to the Editor," *Life*, May 26, 1947, p. 7.
[3] *The New York Times Book Review*, July 27, 1947, p. 1.

fusion abounds concerning the language of the jazz world. The air can be cleared only by studying the argot and its speakers concurrently.

Jazz had an imperceptible birth. It did not just happen one fine Louisiana night in a gin mill. It evolved from prior musical forms. In discussing the origins of jazz,

> One can no more neglect the Protestant hymn tune than the Morris dance, no more underestimate the effect of the spiritual on dozens of vaudeville circuits around the United States than the vestiges of African ceremonial in Congo Square, New Orleans. These evidences . . . make clear that New Orleans was the ineluctable starting-point for a story that is orderly for all its academic confusion, American because of its polyglot origins and development — a tapestry of impressions and expressions that becomes the richly textured history of jazz.[4]

Paralleling the "polyglot origins and development" of jazz is the strange amalgam that constitutes the language of the jazz world — the curious mixture of Negro folk expressions with the imagery of the new city life, and the blending of the two with the terms revolving about the music in which these newly freed people found even greater release:

> Jive is one more contribution of Negro America to the United States. White America perpetrated a new and foreign language on the Africans it enslaved. Slowly, over the generations, Negro America, living by and large in its own segregated world, with its own thoughts, found its own way of expression, found its own way of handling English, as it had to find its own way in handling many other aspects of a white, hostile world. Jive . . . may go way back, deep into the bowels of the Negro-American experience, back into the revolutionary times when it was necessary for the Negro to speak, sing, and even think in a kind of code. . . . Jive talk may have been originally a kind of "pig Latin" that the slaves talked with each other . . . when . . . in the presence of whites. Take the word, "ofay."[5] Ninety-nine million white Americans right now probably don't know that that means "a white," but Negroes know it. Negroes needed to have a word like that in their language, needed to create it in self-defense.[6]

So we get a people in rebellion against a dominant majority, but forced to rebel secretly, to sublimate, as the psychologist would put it — to express themselves culturally through the medium of jazz, and linguistically through a code, a jargon. But as the music developed from New Orleans marches and early Dixieland through the blues-and-rhythm cycle and the

---

[4] Barry Ulanov: *A History of Jazz in America* (New York: Viking, 1952), p. 13.

[5] The white man was regarded as a foe. Hence, *ofay* from *foe:* in pig Latin an initial consonant or cluster is dropped and added at the end with an [ei] following it.

[6] Earl Conrad: Introduction to *Dan Burley's Original Handbook of Harlem Jive* (New York, 1944), pp. 5–6.

swing era on into bop and modern, or progressive, jazz, an immense change took place in the life of the Negro. He became more urbanized and the life of the streets peppered his language, and so filtered into jazz parlance, which to this day is highly interrelated with Negro life. Always close (though hardly by choice) to the most squalid aspects of big-city life, the Negro assimilated the jargon of the rackets — dope peddling, prostitution, larceny, gambling — and the more interesting of these terms spilled over into jazz lingo.[7] Then, too, the high frequency of Negro impressment into Southern chain gangs was another, unhappy source of Negro slang, much as it was a source of Negro work songs and folk songs.

The totality of his experience in America stamped the Negro with a psychology demanding not only a unique and rebellious music, but a unique and rebellious way of speaking:

> Jive . . . supplies the answer to the hunger for the unusual, the exotic and the picturesque in speech. It is a medium of escape, a safety valve for people pressed against the wall for centuries, deprived of the advantages of complete social, economic, moral and intellectual freedom. It is an inarticulate protest . . . a defense mechanism, a method of deriving pleasure from something the uninitiated cannot understand. It is the same means of escape that brought into being the spirituals as sung by American slaves; the blues songs of protest that bubble in the breasts of black men and women.[8]

Like most slang, the jazz variety gains sustenance primarily from the uneducated; it is a subjective language, highly colored by the emotional reactions of its users, whose very inadequacy with the standard language prompts and inspires their linguistic inventiveness.

And like slang in general, jazz terms are relegated to the scrap heap with amazing speed, and this frequently makes their etymologies undeterminable. An example is the contradictory information given by different writers on the origin of the word describing the jazz era that grew out of swing around 1945 and evolved into modern, or progressive, jazz about 1952:

> In 1939 . . . [Ella Fitzgerald] scattered around . . . an engaging tune and ended one of her phrases with the word "rebop," undoubtedly the first appearance of the first accredited name for Dizzy Gillespie's and Charlie Parker's music.[9]

> Before it becomes dignified by general acceptance, let us scotch the theory that the terms *bop*, *bebop*, *rebop*, and their derivatives are ono-

---

[7] The often close connection between musicians and racketeers (most often as employee and employer, respectively) receives ample documentation in Mezz Mezzrow's autobiography (with Bernard Wolfe), *Really the Blues* (New York: Random House, 1946).

[8] *Dan Burley's Original Handbook*, p. 71.

[9] Ulanov: *op. cit.*, p. 252.

matopoeic in origin. The jazz musician has merely adopted and assimilated the rhumba-bands' *Arriba, 'riba* (Up, up!), shouted in genuine or feigned excitement at a sudden shift in tempo. . . . *Arriba, 'riba!* has found a home in *Hey, bob a rebop! Oo bop a dah!*[10]

It was at Minton's that the word "bebop" came into being. Dizzy [Gillespie] was trying to show a bass player how the last two notes of a phrase should sound. The bass player tried it again and again, but he couldn't get the two notes. "Be-bop! Be-bop! Be-bop!" Dizzy finally sang.[11]

It is virtually impossible to resolve such a dispute, though a knowledge of jazz makes the first and third explanations more plausible than the second. Many bop phrases seem to derive from the nonsense syllables of scat-singing, q.v., which, in turn, is simply the voice imitating the sound of an instrument, the first known instance of which, so the story goes, occurred when Louis Armstrong dropped his lyric sheet in the middle of a 1926 recording date and was forced to improvise the words.

Among the more unlikely attempts to trace a word origin is this account of the phrase *get hep:*

In the 1890's . . . Joe Hep ran a saloon in Chicago. . . . Although he never quite understood what was going on, he *thought* he did, and considered himself proudly "in" on every "touch" that came off . . . and so Joe Hep's name entered the argot as an ironic appellation for anyone who thought he knew but didn't. The ironic sense has now largely disappeared from elements of the name surviving in the phrases, "to get Joe to" or "to get hep to" something. . . . The term has been sometimes corrupted [sic!] to "hip!"[12]

A more likely effort is this explanation of the origin and evolution of the word *jive:*

Jive is a distortion of that staid, old, respectable English word "jibe." In the sense in which it came into use among Negroes in Chicago about the year 1921, it meant to taunt, to scoff, to sneer — an expression of sarcastic comment. Like the tribal groups of Mohammedans and people of the Orient, Negroes of that period had developed a highly effective manner of talking about each other's ancestors and hereditary traits, a colorful and picturesque linguistic procedure which came to be known as "putting you in the dozens." Later, this was simply called "jiving" someone. Subsequently ragtime musicians picked up the term and it soon came to mean "all things to all men" . . . and since 1930 Jive has been accepted as the trade name for swing music, for the jitterbug population, and as the key to a complete new world in itself.[13]

[10] Maurice Crane: "Bebop," *Word Study*, October, 1954, p. 6.
[11] Richard O. Boyer: "Bop," *The New Yorker*, July 3, 1948, p. 31.
[12] David W. Maurer: "Phrase Origins: Get Hep," *American Mercury*, May, 1947, p. 548.
[13] *Dan Burley's Original Handbook*, p. 71.

The great difficulty in tracing jazz words to their sources stems not only from the dynamic and prolific coinage of the argot, but also from the fact that jazz terms rarely appear in those written records upon which the makers of dictionaries are necessarily so dependent. This is true to some degree, of course, of all highly colloquial language; but it is especially true of the jazz vernacular, which is generated among groups in our society least likely to record their acts and thoughts in writing.

Nonetheless, lexicographers have been all too slow in recording the more permanent jazz phrases, some of which are widely used outside the jazz world (e.g., *blow your top*). For "Negro slang expression, jazz expression, street parlance . . . have entered into the English language to stay, to root themselves, to become part of the orthodox expression of the future."[14]

The language of the jazz world is neither the language of the jazz musician nor the language of the Negro people, but a fusing of the two. It is the language spoken by jazz musicians and appreciators, giving to and receiving from the Negro people new words and phrases. It is a language that would be only partly comprehensible to Negroes not interested in jazz, or to white musicians who play "Mickey Mouse" (i.e., popular music). And it is a language which has always told a great deal about the lives and attitudes of its speakers.

Time says of modern jazz: "The critics like to call it 'music of protest' . . . but the jazz style called modern does not protest against anything very much except dullness."[15] This is an obfuscation of the social roots of jazz, its creators' answer to their disenfranchisement from "highbrow" culture, just as jazz lingo is the impish rebellion of a people largely deprived of formal education.

Time's observation is less truthful than self-revealing. An almost overt hostility has from the beginning characterized jazz reportage, and the jazzman is cynically aware that he is apt to receive notoriety more for his occasional misadventures with the law than for his artistry.

The lives and attitudes of jazzmen have, of course, changed remarkably in the relatively brief history of jazz, but if there is one thing that has remained constant — *Time* and its ilk notwithstanding — it is the essential rebelliousness at the heart of both the music and the speech. This is difficult to demonstrate in the music, which is chiefly non-verbal, though a good case might be made from the lyrics of early blues and of more recent "protest" songs (*Recognition as a Man, Fables of Faubus*, etc.) and from the titles of many jazz compositions (*Gone With What Wind?, Freedom Now Suite*, etc.).

But rejection of or opposition to dominant modes of thinking and feeling *can* be found throughout the history of jazzmen's speech — for example, in

---

[14] Earl Conrad: "The Philology of Negro Dialect," *Journal of Negro Education,* Spring, 1944, p. 150.

[15] *Time,* November 8, 1954, pp. 67, 70.

his deliberate and significant reversal of the conventional connotations of terms such as *mean, dirty,* and *nasty* (all current c. 1900) and more recently, of *bad, tough,* and *terrible.* The logic of jazz usage here lies in the Negro's awareness that conventional white morality, which countenances Negro subservience even while professing egalitarian ideals, is hypocritical and so also must be those terms through which the white man expresses that morality; in addition, the puritanical equation of sex with sin has reinforced the Negro's suspicion that the in-group is supremely mistaken in its judgments of good and bad, and that standard designations of disapproval have been attached to things that are, by sensible standards, perfectly good — for example, earthiness and virility. Hence, the Negro retains the standard terms of designation, but gives to these an interpretation which reverses their value.

Conversely, the favorable connotations of standard terms such as *sweet* and *square* (honest, upright) are reversed by jazzmen by the complementary logic that what the in-group might judge to be good would most likely be merely servile, genteel, or innocuous.

If anything, since the end of World War II the mood of revolt against the conventional has deepened. This is exemplified not only by the highly intricate, often esoteric, character of modern jazz, but also by the fashion in jazz slang of assigning favorable connotations to terms of mental derangement (*crazy, insane, nutty,* etc.), with its obvious suggestion of contempt for normality.

From the outset the Negro's sense of alienation intensified his need for a private vocabulary, both as a defense against hostility and as a reassurance of self-worth. *Ofay* (a white person), as already noted, is derived rather significantly from pig Latin for *foe; I feel a draft,* a relatively new expression, usually means that the Negro speaker suspects hostility or discrimination directed against him by a white; *soul brother* is an honorific phrase used of one Negro by another (it is noteworthy that the locution inevitably carries an implication that the white man's soul has been forfeited by virtue of his long-standing abuse of the Negro); *man* is a term of address to one Negro by another, meant to counteract the debilitating effects on his morale of being called "boy" by whites; etc.

Although the linguistic record is skimpy, one can safely infer from jazz history something about the extent of early jazz slang. First, since a specialized slang does not come into being all at once, it must be that much of the early jazzmen's nonstandard vocabulary consisted of general colloquialisms, Negro folk idiom, and general slang (mostly from underworld speech traditionally synonymous with the word *slang*). The development of a special vocabulary identifiable as jazz slang had to await the growth of a jazz culture which was not merely ancillary to prostitution or the rackets.

Nevertheless, certain locutions arose early either because there was no existing standard term for a phenomenon or, more frequently, because the standard term was either unknown or was too indirect for the users' taste. Special properties of the music, for example, were sometime identified with the musicians' environment: *honkytonk, barrelhouse* and *gutbucket* for the jazz style predominating in taverns; *tailgate* for the New Orleans trombone style, because the trombonist occupied a position in the rear (i.e., close to the tailgate) of New Orleans advertising trucks. Other characteristics of the music, in the absence of standard terms, required fresh identifiers: *blue notes* or *off notes* to describe the in-between pitch most peculiar to jazz.

The emotional content of the music gave rise to a number of terms "formed by metaphor, e.g., by the widespread practice of equating joy with height ('exultation') and grief with depth; or with the colors red and blue, or with fast and slow. Thus the quality most desired in the old blues is that it should be *low-down* or *dragging*."[16] Another early linguistic practice was the designation of rhythmic qualities by kinesthetic association: *ride, rock, roll, swing, romp, stomp,* etc. Unknown to the general public, a number of such terms (e.g., *ride, roll, rock*) derive from sexual collo-quialisms, as does *jazz* itself and most probably *jitterbug* and *boogie-woogie;* the earthiness of the music, then as now, has a linguistic equivalent in the speech of its performers.

A few terms, perhaps because of their simplicity and widespread appli-cability, have survived from the early jazz life. *Hip* (aware, wise, knowl-edgeable) and *gig* (usually a jazzman's job as distinguished from other work) are two such survivors. But, for the most part, jazz parlance has a large and rapid turnover. Since one of the reasons "people talk special kinds of slang [is that] . . . they want to belong to a special group, and to exclude everyone else,"[17] the jazz world has always tended to drop out of its usage such terms as are taken over by the general public. *Cat* (initially a jazzman, now anyone) and *chick* (a young woman) were widespread in the twenties and thirties; *square* (unsophisticated) and *zoot* (flashy) in the thirties and forties; *crazy* and *far out* (both superlatives) in the late forties and fifties — these are just a few of the many terms that have lost ground in jazz circles in almost direct relation to the growth of their popularity with the nonjazz public. The jazz slang speaker's aloofness is tacitly justified by his feeling that only those who are *down with the action* (aware of what is going on) should have access to the speech of those who have *paid their dues* (suffered an apprenticeship in life generally and in the jazz life in particular).

The jazzman's pain, derived in part from the frustrations that normally characterize much of contemporary life, is exacerbated by the inordinate pressure brought to bear on the creative person who must improvise —

[16] Francis Newton: *The Jazz Scene* (London, 1959), pp. 290–91.
[17] Gilbert Highet: *The Anatomy of Slang,* Book-of-the-Month Club transcript of WNYC radio talk, p. 3.

i.e., create on the spot whether he feels like it or not. The quest for release is at least partially responsible for his above-average (though generally exaggerated) addiction to drugs and his customary overindulgence in liquor and marijuana (frequently, although it is not in fact so, classified as an addictive drug by the law and in the public mind). It is inevitable, then, that there should be a considerable number of terms in jazz speech relating to drugs, drug addiction, the effects of stimulants, etc.

Another aspect of the jazz vocabulary that distinguishes it from other specialized slangs is the large number of superlatives, a consequence of a performing art that generally elicits great enthusiasm from its listeners. Currently, in response to an inspired musical performance, a jazz devotee draws from a large storehouse of terms: *crazy, nutty, insane, swinging, groovy, cooking, wailing, burning, smoking, boss, something else, out of sight,* etc. There are also a large number of escapist terms, an obvious response to the depressing realities of much of jazz and Negro life: *send me, out of this world, far out, way out, gone, cloud 9, out of sight, knock out,* etc.

A number of terms applied to human behavior are analogical extensions from properties of the music or musicians. Hence, *riff* and *lick,* originally a musical phrase or idea, are extended to mean any idea, plan, proposal, or situation. A *swinger,* initially an exciting musician, now means anyone who lives excitingly. *I don't dig the tune,* initially an admission on the speaker's part of ignorance as to the melody being played, comes to mean ignorance of whatever is happening.

Contrasting with the extravagant descriptiveness of jazz nouns, adjectives, and adverbs is the spareness of its verbs, most of which are action verbs, e.g., *blow, cook, cop, dig, jump, knock, latch on, make, pick up* and *put down.* Their paucity forces each to carry numerous meanings, e.g., *knock:* to put down, speak, walk, loan, borrow, give, ask, exhibit, etc.

We should perhaps take note of the brief (c. 1935–c. 1940) vogue of rhyming slang in jazz which, unlike the British practice, was based generally on logical similes: e.g., *mellow like a cello; fine as wine; like the bear, I ain't nowhere* (i.e., an extension of the lumbering physical qualities of the animal to the immobilized spiritual state of a man). Although some were of the merely ebullient variety (e.g., *killer-diller:* an extraordinarily good musician or piece of music), characteristically the jazz phrases were formed by semantic association and may be contrasted with the British formations in which the meaningful word, whether slang or standard, is usually replaced by a nonsense rhyming one: e.g., *Kangaroo:* a Jew; *don't make a fuss:* a bus; *down the drains:* brains; *Colney Hatch:* a match.

Logical or not, rhyming slang and much of the older elaborateness were, during the 1940s, frozen out of the language as part of the far-reaching change in the cultural climate of jazz, a change first of all in the consciousness of the jazzman and one which had an enormous effect on his music, his speech, and his self-image. The intellectual *Putsch* of the music called *bop* was a triumph of thought over emotion, of the cerebral over the frenetic, and had a profound effect on the jazz vocabulary.

When swing reached an impasse in the early forties, a group of young Negro musicians created bop. They were rebelling not only against the dead end swing had run into, but against the old-time jazz, ragtime, and Dixieland, which they characterized as "Uncle Tom music," music appropriate to a meeker, less liberated generation of Negroes. The chief contributors to the new music were Negroes — among the more prominent Charlie Parker, Dizzy Gillespie, and Thelonious Monk. Many of the practitioners had a penchant for Mohammedanism, goatees, meerschaum pipes, berets, and shell-rimmed glasses, which seemingly was mere eccentricity or faddism, but actually was emblematic of a proudly conscious separateness.

Bop was more than music. It was the Negro's cultural declaration of independence, a further rejection of white America's conventionality, and it received encouragement by its widespread popularity in France and the Scandinavian countries. The resistance to it by the jazz traditionalists here was considerable:

> Boppers call themselves "the left wing" and their opponents "the right wing." Friends of the older music call the be-boppers "dirty radicals" and "wild-eyed revolutionaries." Boppers are proud of the men that have gone without jobs and meals rather than play music that outraged their convictions, and speak indignantly of "the underground."[18]

But occasionally, backed to the wall by monetary considerations, bopsters would make a partial concession by playing at weddings and other social functions where musical authenticity is held in low esteem. At these times, the linguistic code served a very practical function for "the underground." It enabled them to communicate their disgust to one another in a language the "citizens" could not comprehend, and through this veiled expression of contempt for the watered-down music they were playing, the situation was made somewhat more palatable to them — their feeling of self-betrayal was somewhat mitigated.

The earlier jazzman, despite his courageous musical pioneering, had been socially resigned to his substatus and, sometimes obligingly, sometimes inadvertently, reinforced the white myth of the "happy Negro." The post-World War II jazzman was equally aware of his inability to alter immediately his inferior status; nevertheless, he angrily and militantly insisted on his immediate dignity, and succeeded, at least to the satisfaction of sensitive observers, in shattering the older stereotype. Quiet, thoughtful, musically trained, socially militant, he forged a music of greater complexity, a music that distilled the purely emotional qualities of earlier jazz

[18] Boyer: *op. cit.*, pp. 28–29.

and mixed them with more cerebral qualities; it was a music difficult to play and difficult to follow.

Simultaneously, there entered the jazzman's speech a new spareness and leanness. Typically, the 1930s expression of farewell, *I'll dig you later,* became in the forties *Later!* The thirties expression of weariness or world-weariness, *beat to the socks,* yielded completely to *beat.* Some of the more widely current locutions were deliberately unintelligible, e.g., *eel-yah-dee, oopapada, oobopshebam, oobladee, oolyakoo,* all nonsense syllable words which might mean anything at all. The playful name given to the new music by its innovators, first *be-bop* and then *bop,* is a humorous manifestation of a rebellion that is essentially serious (and one which will doubtless continue for as long as the jazzman feels himself at odds with society).

The great influence of bop on jazz lingo was not so much in changing the vocabulary as in toning it down, in making it as "cool" as the music itself. Much of the earlier jazz vocabulary now seemed too elaborate to the Negro jazzman, whose emerging self-consciousness after World War II militated against speech that would reinforce the old caricature of him. Jazz slang is still humorous, but not extravagant.

Gilbert Seldes has said:

> There are few specifications about slang . . . most people would agree on. The slang word or expression must make its meaning clear; it must add something (novelty, wit, charm) which the common word lacks; it must correspond to the natural genius of the language at the time (being . . . florid in one era, hard and short in another); it must be instinctive rather than cerebral; it must enter quickly into general conversations.[19]

Jazz slang at its best, it seems to me, lives up to these criteria, though it assiduously avoids universality because the music and the lingo are by their very nature in revolt against the dominant culture.

No one, of course, speaks slang all of the time, and the knowledge and use of slang varies greatly among jazzmen; the standard language — its syntax and vocabulary — remains the base for even the slangiest of jazz speakers. Too, there are a considerable number of terms which overlap two or more specialized slangs — e.g., the "Beats," who have evolved a modest slang of their own, have imbibed much of the jazz vocabulary, though their admiration for jazz speech seems to be unrequited. Finally, as has been noted by Ortega y Gasset and others, vocabulary is not the whole of communication: nuance, inflection, gesture, and innuendo will immediately betray the speaker whose intimacy with the vocabulary does not extend to the culture itself.

[19] *The New York Times Book Review,* July 27, 1947, p. 29.

H. L. Mencken

CANT AND ARGOT OF
THE UNDERWORLD

✍✍

A special quality of the work of H. L. Mencken is his own iconoclastic, exuberant delight in the phenomena of language — a quality that comes to us most clearly by means of the profusion of examples embedded in every page of his multi-volumed compilation The American Language. *In this passage, David Maurer, the foremost collector of the argot of criminals, explains that the primary reason for the argot of the underworld is that it gives an isolated group its own sense of solidarity. Mr. Mencken's compilation reveals this secret language and gives us a glimpse of the society of criminals. (This selection is from* The American Language *as abridged and revised by R. I. McDavid, Jr.)*

A century ago the cant of American criminals was still largely dependent upon that of their English colleagues, stretching back for centuries, but though it still shows marks of that influence[1] it is now predominantly on its own. Its chief characteristics, says Maurer, are "its machine-gun staccato, its hard timbre, its rather grim humor, its vivid imagery, and its remarkable compactness."[2] It differs considerably, of course, from specialty to specialty, but within a given specialty "it appears to be well standardized from coast to coast and from the Gulf into Canada." [Subsequently three geographical dialect areas have been tentatively identified — East Coast, Midwest and

[1] For example, in the survival of rhyming slang. An account of the argot of American criminals of the 1900 era is in The Lingo of the Good People, by David W. Maurer, AS, Vol. X, Feb. 1935, pp. 10–23. A great deal of it is now obsolete.
[2] The Argot of the Underworld, AS, Vol. VII, Dec. 1931, pp. 99–118.

West Coast.] It shows the cosmopolitan quality of all American speech, and includes loans from Yiddish, Spanish, German, French, Chinese and even Hindustani. Like slang in general, it is the product, not of the common run of ordinary lawbreakers or amateur criminals, but of the well-established criminal subcultures; it tends to increase in picturesqueness as one goes up the scale of professional rank and dignity. Says Maurer:

> Why do criminals speak a lingo? There are several reasons, perhaps the most widely accepted of which is that they must have a secret language in order to conceal their plans from their victims or from the police. In some instances it is undoubtedly used for this purpose — for instance, *flat-jointers, three-card monte men,* and other *short-con workers*[3] sometimes use it to confuse or deceive their victims. But most professional criminals do not so use it. They speak argot only among themselves, . . . for using it in public would mark them as underworld characters whether or not they were understood. . . . There is a very strong sense of camaraderie among them, a highly developed group-solidarity. . . . A common language helps to bind these groups together and gives expression to the strong fraternal spirit. . . . Professional crime is nothing more than a way of living and working within a great variety of parasitic sub-cultures; hence it is only natural that many of the same factors which operate in the dominant culture and among legitimate craftsmen should affect criminal speech.[4]

The vast upsurge of crime brought in by Prohibition made all Americans familiar with a large number of criminal words and phrases, and many of these, as I have noted, have entered into the everyday speech of the country. How much of the argot of the Volsteadian racketeers was the product of their own fancy and how much was thrust upon them by outside admirers, *e.g.*, newspaper reporters and movie writers, is not easily determined, but Maurer has cited some examples from the latter, including even such apparently characteristic terms as *big shot*. He says[5] that actual

---

[3] *Short-con workers* operate on a modest scale, and are usually content with whatever money the victim has on him at the time he is rooked. They seldom employ the *send* — that is, they seldom send him home for more. [*Short-con* argots have been studied by Maurer in The Argot of the Three-Shell Game, AS, Vol. XXII, Oct. 1947, and The Argot of the Faro Bank, AS, Vol. XVIII, Feb. 1943. Many additional examples of it occur in his The Argot of the Dice Gambler, included in Scarne on Dice, by Clayton Rawson and John Scarne, Harrisburg, Pa., 1945; in his The Argot of the Racetrack, PADS, No. 16, 1951; and in his The Argot of the Professional Dice Gambler, The Annals of the American Academy of Political and Social Science, Vol. 269, May 1950. Most *short-con* games are connected with professional gambling, which has argots so voluminous that they cannot be treated in this work, and which have, in turn, vastly enriched American slang. An excellent survey of gambling, with much argot included, is John Scarne's classic book, Scarne's Complete Guide to Gambling; New York, 1961.]

[4] The Big Con, pp. 270–1 [New York, 1940].

[5] Private communication, Apr. 7, 1940. The anonymous author of The Capone I Knew, *True Detective*, June 1947, p. 80, says that *syndicate*, used by Al to describe his mob, was "picked up from the newspaper stories about him."

members of the *mob* called the brass hats of the profession *wheels* (in the plural). But *trigger man, torpedo, gorilla, pineapple* (bomb), *whiskers* (a federal agent: a reference to Uncle Sam), *hot* (a stolen object or a criminal pursued by the law), *on the lam, to snatch* (to kidnap), *moll* and *racket,* whatever their provenance, were indigenous to the subcultures using them. The gentlemen of the *big con,* i.e., swindlers who specialize in rooking persons of means, constitute the aristocracy of the underworld, and hold aloof from all lesser criminals. They are, taking one with another, of superior intelligence, and not many of them ever land in prison. Their lingo thus shows a considerable elegance and also some humor, e.g., *apple, savage* or *Mr. Bates* for a victim; *big store,* the bogus gambling house or brokerage office to which *apples* are lured; *coarse ones,* large bills; *ear-wigger,* one who tries to eavesdrop; *excess baggage,* a member of a mob who fails to pull his weight in the boat; *to fit the mitt,* to bribe an official; *Joe Hep,* a victim who tumbles (or thinks he does) to what is happening; *larceny,* the itch for illicit money that lures a victim on: "He has *larceny* in his heart"; *to light a rag,* to run away; *to play the C,* to operate a confidence game; *to sting,* to swindle; *sucker word,* a term not used by professionals,[6] and *yellow,* a telegram. The craft is now called the *grift,* not the *graft,*[7] and is characterized by its lack of violence.

At the opposite pole from practitioners of the *big con* are the brutal fellows who follow the *heavy rackets,* i.e., those involving violence. They include some types of burglars, safe blowers (*yeggs*), hijackers, kidnappers, automobile thieves, window smashers, mail robbers, payroll grabbers, bank stick-up men and so on. They had their heyday during the thirteen delirious years of Prohibition, and there was a revival of their art, made much of by the newspapers, following World War II, but on the whole they seem to be declining in prosperity, and the new methods of thief-taking organized by the Federal Bureau of Investigation have landed large numbers of them in prison. They range in professional dignity from the *jug-heavies* or *bank burglars,* who stand at the top, to the mere hoodlums, many of them young neophytes, at the bottom. Among the cant terms of the *jug-heavies* are *bug,* a burglar alarm; *to case,* to spy out; *cutter,* a prosecuting attorney; *dinah* or *noise,* dynamite; *double,* a false key; *forty,* O.K.; *gopher,* an iron safe; *hack,* a watchman; *soup* or *pete,* nitroglycerine; *stiffs,* negotiable securities; *swamped,* surprised and surrounded; and *V,* a safe. Maurer says[8] that there are some regional differences in *jug-heavy* speech; e.g., a bank is a *jug* everywhere but sometimes a *jay* in the Midwest or a *tomb* in the East. [While big-time safecracking disappeared with

[6] I take all these from Maurer.

[7] The glossary in The Big Con is also in The Argot of Confidence Men, *AS,* Vol. XV, Apr. 1940, pp. 113–23, and Confidence Games, by Carlton Brown, *Life,* Aug. 12, 1946, pp. 45–52.

[8] The Lingo of the *Jug-Heavy, Writer's Digest,* Oct. 1931, pp. 27–9.

another generation of experts — new federal laws, improved safes and changes in business practice also had a bearing on the decline of the racket — a large number of smaller safes are still cracked by a younger generation, some of them *turned out* by old-time experts in prisons. Banks to-day are seldom blown, but occasionally some *mob shoots a jug* for a good *score*. The use of *stew* is declining, modern *heavy gees* preferring to use a *stick, ripper* or *can opener* on laminated safes, or specially made tools *to punch the box* or *to pull the combo*. Safes weighing up to half a ton are often trucked away to be opened elsewhere. Present-day *mechanics* are usually expert machinists capable of making such tools as the four-pronged electric vibrator to line up safe-lock tumblers, and possessed of sufficient knowledge of electronics to bypass new alarm systems. Newly invented fiberglass safes which cannot be blown or punched are now literally shaken to pieces by the expert application of precision electronic vibration.] The automobile thieves who once ranged in large and well-organized gangs also had an argot of their own, e.g., *doghouse*, a small garage; *bent one* or *kinky*, a stolen car, and *consent job*, a car stolen with the connivance of an owner eager for the insurance,[9] and so did the hijackers who arose during Prohibition and flourished in the aftermath of World War II, e.g., *baloney*, an automobile tire; *box*, a truck trailer; *to carry the mail*, to drive fast; *crate*, a truck; *dark horse*, a watchman; *girl scout* or *hairpin*, a female associate; *in creeper*, in low gear; *on the I.C.*, on the lookout; *powder wagon* or *blast furnace*, a sawed-off shotgun; *red eye*, a stop signal; *stick*, a crowbar; *toby*, a highway; *traveler*, a hijacker; and *whistler*, a police car.[10] The stick-up men who specialize in robbing pedestrians often operate in pairs. One clasps the victim around the neck from behind and chokes him while the other goes through his pockets. This is often done very violently and sometimes the victim is badly hurt. It is called *mugging* in New York, but *yoking* in most other places.[11]

Forgers (*penmen*), counterfeiters (*designers*) and other such intellectuals have a certain standing in the underworld and even pickpockets are respected more or less as the masters of a difficult art, but they do not rank with the princes of the *big con* nor even with the more daring heroes of the *heavy rackets*. Among forgers, says Maurer,[12] there is a "sharp division of labor." The men who produce forged checks (*makers, designers, scratchers* or *connections*) are usually wholesalers who supply the actual *passers*, but do not tackle the public. The former, like their allies, the counterfeiters, often operate in safety for years on end, but the latter are

[9] I Wonder Who's Driving Her Now, by William G. Shepherd, *Journal of American Insurance*, Feb. 1929, pp. 5–8 (reprinted in *AS*, Vol. V, Feb. 1930, pp. 236–7); Hot Shorts, by T. J. Courtney, *The Saturday Evening Post*, Nov. 30, 1935, pp. 12–13, 72–4.

[10] Hijacker's Argot, Chicago *Tribune*, Jan. 22, 1939.

[11] *Yoking* Means Just That, Baltimore *Evening Sun*, July 16, 1946, p. 32. Ordinarily, *to mugg* means to photograph, especially for the rogues' gallery.

[12] The Argot of Forgery, *AS*, Vol. XVI, Dec. 1941, pp. 243–50.

frequently taken. The *passer* is also called a *paperhanger*, but the colleague who works off counterfeit money is a *paper pusher, pusher* or *shover*. A forged check is *paper, scrip* or a *stiff,* and when it is a cashier's check it is a *jug stiff* or *cert*. *Bouncer* and *rubber check,* both in common use among laymen, do not seem to be in the professional vocabulary. The *paperhanger* does most of his *spread* on Saturday, after the banks close; in consequence he is usually broke by Friday, and he thus calls a dismal countenance a *Friday face.* To him a store detective is a *shamus,* Mr. *Fakus* or *Oscar,* a warrant for his arrest is a *sticker,* a credit manager is a *credie* or a *Joe Goss,* a checkbook is a *damper pad* and the confidence talk which precedes his passing of a bad check is the *business.* Among pickpockets the act of picking a pocket is called the *beat,* the *sting* or a *come-off,* a watch (seldom taken nowadays) is a *toy, thimble, turnip, kettle* or *super,*[13] a policeman is a *buttons, fuzz* or *shamus,* a victim is a *chump, mark, yap* or *hoosier,* the member of a mob who does the actual stealing is a *claw, wire* or *tool,* his assistants are *stalls,* a wallet is a *poke, leather, hide* or *okus,*[14] an empty wallet is a *cold poke, dead skin* or *bloomer,* a ring is a *hoop,* paper money is *rag* or *soft* and an overcoat is a *tog.* All pickpockets are *guns, cannons* or *whiz,* and a lady of the profession is a *gun moll.*[15] *Dip* for a practitioner is now obsolete in America, though it is still used by lay writers upon crime waves and seems to survive in England.[16] Shoplifters, or *boosters,* have some resemblance to pickpockets, but they are much less daring. Many of them are women, and most of the women are amateurs. The professionals often carry a *booster box,* which is a box resembling an ordinary shopper's parcel, but with a trap door for receiving the loot.[17] [Some professional women are highly expert, and can *fork* any object up to the size of a portable TV set — that is, clamp it between the thighs and walk away flat-footed and undetected. All of the good ones know how to make and

---

[13] Says Maurer in *AS,* Vol. XVI, Apr. 1941, p. 154: "Modern thieves call a stolen watch a *super* (or *super and slang* if the chain accompanies it), . . . not realizing that the word is really *souper,* a pun on the older form, *kettle.*"

[14] In Along the Main Stem, *True Detective,* Mar. 1942, p. 73, a writer signing himself The Fly Kid suggested that *okus* (or *hokus*) may have issued from *poke* by way of *hocus-pocus. Hocus-pocus* itself has long been a headache to etymologists. The OED inclines to the theory that it came from the pseudo-Latin patter and assumed name of a juggler during the reign of King James I, but Weekley believes that it may have arisen as a blasphemous perversion of the sacramental blessing, *hoc est corpus (filii).* It has analogues in Norwegian, Swedish and German.

[15] I am indebted here to Everett DeBaun. He tells me that *gun* and *cannon* have nothing to do with artillery. The former is derived from the Yiddish *ganov,* a thief, and *cannon* is simply a more elegant form. During the Golden Age of the Dillingers the newspapers took to calling a racketeer's girl a *gun moll,* but this was an error. [A *gun moll* is simply a female pickpocket, professional.]

[16] In the Argot of the Underworld, by James P. Burke, *American Mercury,* Dec. 1930, pp. 454–8, *catholic* is given as another name for a pickpocket, but without any attempt at an etymology.

[17] I am indebted here to Victor T. Reno, of Los Angeles. See Slick Fingers, by Ralph L. Woods, *Forum,* Dec. 1939, pp. 273–7.

use *booster bloomers* for concealing large numbers of smaller articles beneath a full skirt.]

A large part of the vocabulary of the rum-running mobs of Prohibition days passed into the general speech, *e.g.*, *the real McCoy*,[18] *to take for a ride*,[19] *torpedo*, *triggerman*, *bathtub gin*,[20] *alky*, *to muscle in*, *to cut* (to dilute), *hideout*, *jake* (all right), *to needle* (to add alcohol), *piece* (a share), *tommy gun* and *hijacker*,[21] and some of them seem likely to stick, along with the Yiddish loans that these public servants also made familiar, *e.g.*, *kosher* (reliable), *meshuga* (crazy) and *to yentze* (to cheat). The assorted ruffians who adorned the same glorious era made every American schoolboy aware of the meaning of *to rub out*, *mob*, *to scram*,[22] *G man*,[23] *canary*,[24] *to put the heat on*, *gat*,[25] *on the lam*,[26] — or else, *gangster*, *racketeer*[27] and *public enemy*.[28]

[Although the Mafia has long been deep in the rackets, it is only in recent years that it has been recognized. In fact, the term *Mafia* is such

[18] The origin of this term has been much debated and is still unsettled.

[19] Herbert Asbury says in Gem of the Prairie, New York, 1940, p. 327, that this lovely euphemism was coined by Hymie Weiss, one of the four ranking dignitaries of Chicago gangdom, the others being Johnny Torrio, Al Capone and Dion O'Banion.

[20] Like *big shot*, this one was probably invented by some smart newspaper reporter and imposed upon the racket. Fred Hamann tells me that on the revival of bootlegging during World War II it became *blitz water*, *bang water* or *ceiling buster*.

[21] Said H. K. Croessman in the *American Mercury*, June 1926, pp. 241–2: "The first time I heard *hijacker* was from the lips of an Oklahoman. He explained it as coming from the command customary in holdups: "Stick 'em up high, Jack,' or, more simply, 'Up high, Jack.'"

[22] The first appearance of *to scram* in print seems to have been in Walter Winchell's column, Your Broadway and Mine, Oct. 4, 1928. See *Scram* — a Swell Five-Letter Word, by V. Royce West, AS, Vol. XII, Oct. 1937, pp. 195–202. Partridge says that it reached England via the movies by 1930. Its etymology remains mysterious.

[23] In A Couple of Cops, *The Commonweal*, Jan. 31, 1936, p. 373, Roger Shaw says that the celebrated Machine-Gun Kelly complained of the deadly efficiency of the G men when he was captured at Memphis, Tenn., Sept. 26, 1933, and that "newspapers, fictioneers and the movies took it up." It is from *government man*. [Dr. A. C. Russell, the federal agent who arrested Kelly and guarded him in Memphis, is skeptical of this story, and expressed surprise that the prisoner had held a press conference following his arrest.]

[24] One who *sings*, *i.e.*, confesses to the police.

[25] Apparently from *Gatling gun*. But Booth, before cited, derives it from *catting up*, meaning to rob itinerant workers at pistol point.

[26] Says Peter Tamony in Origin of Words: *Lam*, San Francisco News-Letter and Wasp, Apr. 9, 1939, p. 5: "Its origin should be apparent to anyone who runs over several colloquial phrases for leave-taking, such as *to beat it*, *to hit the trail*. . . . The allusion in *lam* is to *beat*. *Beat it* is old English, meaning to leave."

[27] *Racket*, in the current sense of an anti-social enterprise, appeared in A New and Comprehensive Vocabulary of the Flash Language: London, 1812. But *racketeer* is American.

[28] *Public enemy*, usually followed by a numeral, is said to have been coined by the Hon. Homer S. Cummings, LL.D., Attorney General of the United States, 1933–9. The original *Public Enemy No. 1* was John Dillinger, killed by FBI men in Chicago, July 22, 1934.

a taboo within the Sicilian subculture that many people are unaware — or pretend to be unaware — of its existence, and the organization itself is tightly closed to outsiders. Some terms from the argot are working out, however, among them *capo*, a high-ranking member of the *Mafiosi*, who are also known as *dons, mustachios* or *mustaches* (even though they may be clean-shaven) because the first-generation Mafiosi all wore handle-bar mustaches; *fratuzzi*, the neighborhood folks (little brothers), whom the Mafiosi exploit, though they are supposed to protect them; *ricottari*, the apprentice hoodlums who hope to become Mafiosi someday; *pezzinorante*, the skilled executioners who set up and carry out official (and never solved) murders; *lupara* (literally, *bitch-wolf*), the shot gun loaded with slugs, which is a preferred murder weapon since the slugs are not identifiable ballistically; and *omertà*, the very strict code of the Mafia.]

"One might expect prison slang," says Maurer, "to be a composite of the various specialized argots, but while some bona fide argot crops out in it, it is, on the whole, a separate institutional lingo which differs somewhat from prison to prison." He goes on:

> Relatively few successful professionals *do* much *time*, and when they do they tend to hold themselves somewhat apart from the general run of prisoners. They count upon their strong political connections to secure preferment and often associate with the prison administration on intimate terms. The great bulk of prison populations is composed of amateurs or failures; hence the fallacious belief among some psychologists and criminologists that criminals are subnormal in intelligence. Thorough-going and successful professionals are usually superior in intelligence and have nothing about them to suggest the popular conception of a criminal. If you mixed a hundred of them with an equal number of business and professional men all the statistics of a Hooton or a Lombroso would never set them apart.[29]

But the residuum actually behind the bars is of generally low mentality[30] and in consequence the lingo of the average prison, save insofar as it is reinforced by the inventions of the aloof minority or by contributions from outside, shows little imagination. Its basis, says James Hargan, is "a variety of Anglo-Saxon terms dealing mainly with the sexual and simpler life processes, which have survived the centuries in defiance of the dictionary's refusal to receive them."[31] A large part of it, adds Hargan, shows a "euphe-

[29] Private communication, Apr. 7, 1940.

[30] A survey of all the male inmates of the state prisons of New York showed that 80.2% of them were of less than normal intelligence. My authority here is Dr. H. Curtis Wood, Jr. Dr. James Asa Shield, psychiatrist to the Virginia State Penitentiary at Richmond, reports that among 749 white prisoners examined there in 1935 only 21 showed a mental age of 14 years or over, and that among colored prisoners there were but two.

[31] The Psychology of Prison Language, *Journal of Abnormal and Social Psychology*, Vol. XXXVIII, Oct.–Dec. 1935, pp. 359–65.

mistic, often humorous understatement" by which the prisoner "softens an otherwise too unpleasant reality into something bearable," *e.g.*, *kimono*, a coffin; *dance hall*, the death house; *sleeping time*, a short sentence; *mouse*, a spy or informer; and *bird cage*, a cell. The animal appetites naturally take a major place in his thinking, and much of his humor, such as it is, is devoted to flings at his always monotonous and usually tasteless fare.

This vocabulary has its local variations, but most of it seems to be in general use in American prisons, for the same malefactors move from one to another. A large part of it is identical with the table talk of soldiers and sailors. Milk is *chalk*; macaroni, *dago*; eggs, *cacklers, cackleberries* or *shells*, or, if fried, *red eyes*; potatoes, *spuds*; onions, *stinkers* or *tear gas*; butter, *grease*; catsup, *red lead*; soup, *water*; bread, *duffer* or *punk*; sugar, *sand* or *dirt*; roast beef, *shoe sole, leather* or *young horse*; veal, lamb or mutton, *goat meat*; coffee, *gargle, suds* or *black soup*; sausage, *beagle, dog* or *balloon*; tea, *dishwater*; sauerkraut, *shrubbery* or *hay*; a meatloaf, *mystery* or *rubber heels*; biscuits, *cat heads* or *humpers*; bread and gravy, *poultice*; tapioca, *fish eyes* or *cats' eyes*; and a sandwich, *duki* (from *duke*, the hand). Meat as a whole is *pig* and food in general is *swag, garbage, scoff, chow, chuck* or *peelings*. A waiter is a *soup jockey*. The prison functionaries all have derisive names. The head warden is the *big noise*, the *ball of fire* or *the Man*; the guards are *shields, screws, hooligans, roaches, hacks, slave drivers* or *herders*; the chaplain is a *frocker, goody, psalmer, buck* (if a Catholic priest), *Bible-back* or *the Church*; the doctor is a *croaker, cutemup, sawbones, pill punk, iodine, salts* or *pills*; the barber is a *scraper, chin polisher* or *butcher*.

A new prisoner is a *fish*; a letter smuggled out of prison is a *kite*; a crime is a *trick* or *caper*; a cell, when not a *bird cage*, is a *drum*; a drug addict is a *junker, junkie, hype, whang, hophead* or *snowbird*. A prisoner who goes *stir-crazy* is said to be *on his top, conky, footch, guzzly, beered, loco, blogo, buggy, woody* or *meshuga* (from *meshuggah*). To die is *to go down* or *to slam off*. To escape is *to gut, to mouse, to have the measles, to take* (or *cop*) *a mope, to hang it, to be on the bush, to lam the joint, to go over the wall, to get a bush bond* (or *parole*) or *to crush out*. To finish a sentence is *to get up*. A sentence is a *trick, knock, rap, hitch, bit, stretch* or *jolt*. If short it is *sleeping time*, if for one year it is a *boffo*, if for two a *deuce*, if for five a *five-specker* or *V*, if for twenty a *double sawbuck*, if for life the *book*, the *icebox* or *all*. The prison is the *big house*, the *college* or the *joint*. A pardon or commutation is a *lifeboat*. An arrest is a *fall*, a man is a *gee*, a bed is a *kip*, and the prison morgue is the *greenhouse*. Many euphemisms are in use. At Sing Sing, for example, the death house is *Box Z*, the section for insane convicts is *Box A* and the place where dead inmates are buried is *Box 25*. Not a few of the terms reported smell of the lamp, and certainly did not emanate from the common run of prisoners, *e.g.*, *last mile* for the march to the gallows or electric chair, *Cupid's itch* for venereal disease, *pussy bandit* for a rapist, *gospel fowl* for chicken, *sleigh bells* for silver and *toad hides* for paper money.[32]

Between the world of professional criminals and that of honest folk there is a half-world of part-time, in-and-out malefactors, and to it belongs the army of hoboes, beggars, prostitutes, drug addicts and so on. Most juvenile delinquents are part of it and remain so, for not many of them can ever hope to be promoted from neighborhood gangs to touring mobs. At the bottom of the pile are the poor wretches, mainly aging, who find road life increasingly insupportable, and so gravitate dismally toward the big cities, to become beggars and *mission stiffs.*

It will be recalled that the first investigation of underworld speech in the Fifteenth and Sixteenth Centuries had to do with the talk of such vagrants rather than with the cant of more daring criminals. That speech still excites the interest of the curious, and there is a large literature upon it.[33] In part it is made up of borrowings from criminal cant, in part of loans from the argot of railroad men and in part of what seems to be original inventions. Many of its terms are familiar to most Americans, *e.g., jungles* (usually plural), the camp of vagabonds outside a city, sometimes occupied for years, [to which the modern *asphalt jungle* is related]; *blind,* the front of a baggage car, directly behind the engine tender; *flop,* a place to sleep (*flop house,* a cheap lodging house); *mulligan,* a stew made in the jungles of any food the assembled hoboes can beg, borrow or steal; *slave market,* an employment agency; *main stem* or *drag,* the main street of a town; *crummy,* lousy; *to mooch,* to beg; *handout,* food begged at a house door; *to panhandle; to ride the rods; hoosegow,* a jail; *bughouse,* crazy; *barrelhouse,* a low saloon; *to pound the ties;* and *to rustle a meal.*

Among the more esoteric terms recorded in the literature are *to go gooseberrying,* to rob clothes lines (*gooseberries*); *filling station,* a small

---

[32] I am indebted here to Clinton A. Sanders, Joseph W. Blackwell, Jr., Samuel Meyer and the editors of the *San Quentin News.* I have also made use of My San Quentin Years, by James B. Holohan, published serially in the Los Angeles *Times,* in 1936; Prison Slang, by Clinton T. Duffy, San Quentin, n.d.; Can Cant, by J. Louis Kuethe, Baltimore *Evening Sun,* Dec. 9, 1932 (republished as Prison Parlance, *American Mercury,* Feb. 1934, pp. 25–8); English Behind the Walls, by William H. Hine, *Better Speech,* Dec. 1939, pp. 19–20 (sent to me by Fred Hamann); Convicts' Jargon, by George Milburn, *AS,* Vol. VI, Aug. 1931, pp. 436–42; Prison Phraseology, by Bruce Airey, Montgomery, Ala., 1943; A Prison Dictionary (Expurgated), by Hi Simons, *AS,* Vol. VIII, Oct. 1933, pp. 22–3; Underworld and Prison Slang, by Noel Ersine, Upland, Ind., 1935; Prison Lingo, by Herbert Yenne, *AS,* Vol. II, Mar. 1927, pp. 280–2; More Crook Words, by Paul Robert Beath, *AS,* Vol. VI, Dec. 1930, pp. 131–4; Hipped to the Tip, by Jack Schuyler, *Current History,* Nov. 7, 1940, pp. 21–2; An Analysis of Prison Jargon, by V. Erle Leichty, *Papers of the Michigan Academy of Sciences, Arts and Letters,* Vol. XXX, 1945, pp. 589–600, and the glossaries in Almanac for New Yorkers, 1939, p. 125; Farewell, Mr. Gangster, by Herbert Corey, New York, 1936; The Professional Thief, ed. by Edwin H. Sutherland, Chicago, 1937; Crime as a Business, by J. C. R. MacDonald, Palo Alto, Cal., 1939; [and Statesville Names: A Prison Vocabulary, by Nathan Kantrowitz and Joanne Kantrowitz (in manuscript)].

[33] Many titles are listed in Burke's bibliography.

town (once a *tank town* or *whistle stop*); *bindle,* the hobo's roll of clothes and bedding (if he carries one he is a *bindle stiff*); *scissors bill,* a law-abiding citizen; *rattler,* a freight car; *red ball,* a fast freight; *stash,* a hiding place; *clown,* a rustic policeman; *gay cat,* a newcomer to the road; *jungle buzzard,* one who partakes of a meal in a jungle without contributing anything to it; *skid road* (often *skid row*), a city street frequented by hoboes; *tourist* or *snowfly,* a tramp who goes South in winter to escape the cold weather; *lump* or *poke-out,* a handout (if unwrapped it is a *bald lump*); *locust* or *sap,* a policeman's stick; *to be fanned,* to be awakened by having it applied to the soles of one's feet; *gandy dancer,* a section hand; *hairpin,* a housewife; *pie card,* a union card used as credentials in begging; *shark,* an employment agent; *man catcher,* an employer seeking workers; *stew bum,* a drunkard; *sit-down,* a meal in a house; *hump,* a mountain; *tin cow,* canned milk; *Peoria,* soup;[34] *drag,* a train; *reefer,* a refrigerator car; *shack,* a brakeman; *to put it down,* to get off a train; and *to carry the banner,* to walk the streets all night lacking money for lodging.

The bums who congregate in cities and live by panhandling have special names to designate men whose appeals to charity are helped by various disabilities, real or imaginary. Those who exhibit sores, usually made with acid, are *blisters;* those who throw their bones out of joint are *throw-outs* or *toss-outs,* those who cough dismally are *ghosts* and those who squat in front of churches or other public buildings and pretend to be helpless are *floppers.*[35] Cripples in general are *crips.* Those who repair umbrellas at street corners are *mush fakers* (an umbrella is a *mush*).[36] Those who make and sell objects of wire, *e.g.,* coat hangers, are *qually workers.* Those who gaze longingly into restaurants or bakeshops while they gnaw at prop bread crusts are *nibblers.* Those who dig into garbage cans are *divers.* Those who pretend to have fainted from hunger are *flickers.* Those with hard-luck stories are *weepers.* Those who practice minor con games are *dingoes.*[37] Those who pick up cigar and cigarette butts are *snipe hunters.* Homosexuals are common among hoboes, and have a vocabulary of their own. They are called *wolves* or *jockers* and the boys accompanying them are *guntzels, gazoonies, punks, lambs* or *prushuns.*[38] There are generally recognized hobo nicknames for most towns and many railroads. Chicago is *the Village,* Cincinnati is *Death Valley,* Richmond, Va., is *Grantsville,* Pittsburgh is *Cinders* or *the Burg,* Spokane, Wash., is *the Spokes,* Walla Walla, Wash., is *the Wallows,* Kalamazoo, Mich., is *the Zoo,* Columbus,

---

34 Said to be not from the town name, but from *puree.*

35 I take all these names of specialists from Sister of the Road, by Ben L. Reitman, New York, 1937, pp. 300–1.

36 From *mushroom.* Partridge traces it to 1821 in England.

37 I am indebted here to The Beggars Are Coming, by Meyer Berger, *The New Yorker,* Mar. 11, 1939.

38 See The Language of Homosexuality, by G. Legman, in Sex Variants, by P. W. Henry, New York, 1941, Vol. II, pp. 1149–79.

Ohio, is *Louse Town*, Little Rock, Ark., is *the Rock*, Joliet, Ill., is *Jolly*, Salt Lake City is *the Lake*, Toledo is *T.O.*, Butte, Mont., is *Brass*, Kansas City is *K.C.*, Cleveland is *Yap Town*, Minneapolis is *Minnie*, Washington is *the Cap*, Terre Haute, Ind., is *the Hut* and New York is simply *the City*.[39]

[39] I take these from David W. Maurer's Underworld Place-Names, AS, Vol. XV, Oct. 1940, pp. 340–2, and More Underworld Place-Names, AS, Vol. XVII, Feb. 1942, pp. 75–6.

C. Merton Babcock

THE ECHO OF A WHISTLE

Mr. Flexner's chart shows us two important sources of slang — railroad workers and hoboes. The especially delightful quality of Professor Babcock's article is the way in which he turns a lexicon into paragraphs. He intersperses definitions when needed; he makes meanings and uses clear by context. A sense of hobo life emerges.

The "red ball" freight trains out of Chicago, Cheyenne, Salt Lake, and Rock Springs are running on schedule today, just as they always have. But something is plainly missing. The galloping gondolas are empty. The "jungles" are evacuated. The railroad yards are clean. And the division "bulls" are sitting on their keisters in the station. Because the "bindle-stiffs" are gone.

Up until a few years ago, the itinerant hobo was as much a fixture on the railroad as the blinking semaphores. He was the one sure harbinger of

Reprinted from *Western Folklore* Vol. XIX (1960), pp. 47–51, by permission of the editor.

spring. Before the snow melted off the Tetons up around Jackson Hole, hundreds of "boes," who had "holed up" for the winter somewhere in Dixie, grabbed themselves a "handful of boxcars" and headed for "parts unknown" — some to the Snake River country for work on a government dam, some to Icebox Canyon for the logging operations, some to Oklahoma to follow the harvests straight north to Saskatchewan, some to Skagit County north of Seattle at cherry-picking time, and some to Bellingham to dig for clams. A few "road kids" with "itching feet," of course, went just for the ride — to absorb the scenery, to get an eyeful of America from a "side-door pullman" (boxcar).

The young "punks," or "gay-cats," with more courage than caution, rode "blind baggage" on the passenger runs. That is, until they got "ditched" by the crew. The really daring ones could hold down a flyer like the Twentieth Century Limited all the way from Grand Central Station to La Salle Street, Chicago. This ride was always good for a free bath, too, because the "Twentieth Century" took water on the fly. Getting in proper position to catch a "passenger" at a large terminal like the Union Station in "Chi" (Chicago) was no cinch, because no one could "crash the gate" without a ticket. The "kids" would sometimes crawl down the sides of the overpass from the street above and then drop seven or eight feet to the tracks below. Then they would "hot foot" it along the "off side" of the waiting train, side-stepping mail flunkeys, until they reached an inconspicuous vantage point just opposite the tender. The rest was easy. When the train started moving out, they would walk nonchalantly along with it until it picked up speed. Then they would grab the handrails and hop on.

Nights were for riding passenger trains. After eight or ten hours on a fast express, a "kid" would come off as black as a "shine" (Negro). His own sister couldn't recognize him. He would ride anywhere on the train except the "cushions" (coach seats). Sometimes he would stand secluded in the "first blinds" (just behind the tender). If detected here, he would resort to the "second blinds" (between the first two baggage cars). Kids have been known to ride the "decks" (top), the steps at the rear of the train, the platforms on the Pullmans, and, on rare occasions with a "right" crew, inside the baggage car.

The old sourdough "professionals," who had no particular destination in mind, stuck to the slower but surer "manifests" — the through freights that "high-balled it" past jerkwater towns as if they weren't even on the map. Mostly they preferred the "empties." A few overcautious boes rode the "rods" underneath the train. Some decked themselves on top and ducked for the tunnels. Others rode the "reefers" (refrigerator cars). If worse came to worst, they even resorted to the "bumpers" (couplings between the cars).

Once the "shacks" (crew men) got the train "made up" and gave the "high sign," and the engine blurted out its five long blasts of warning (high-ball), the train began crawling with boes, all clambering for their favorite positions in preparation for a long ride at railroad expense. A few late-comers had to be "histed" aboard the last minute if they could "make the grade." An exceptionally nimble stiff could hook the side ladders, climb to the top, swing into the open door of a boxcar, and land on both feet without mishap.

And then the whole, magnificent affair was under way: snaking across the prairies, boring through the mountains, screaming at the "whistle-stops." Four or five days out of "Chi" and you could dip your "dogs" in the "big drink" (Pacific Ocean). Some of the boes held her down all the way.

But every train was by no means a "gravy train" or a "milk and honey" special. Sometimes the shacks were hostile and forced the boes to "hit the grit" (jump off) even after the train was rolling at top speed. The "yard dicks" and "division bulls" (railroad policemen) were more often than not "lousy sons o' bitches" who hated their own mothers. One or two of them have been known to "sap up" (club) boes within an inch of their lives on the slightest provocation. Some divisions, of course, were worse than others. Stiffs "in the know" (wised up) usually walked around the yards at Cheyenne to avoid a "shakedown" (frisking). A bo could get thirty days in "stir" for trying to snag a mail train. And he could be picked up for "vag" (vagrancy) without batting an eye. Seldom "flush" with coin of the realm, he swore if they were selling locomotives for a nickel apiece he couldn't buy the echo of the whistle.

Probably the most notorious of all the bulls along the "cinder trail" was a piker with the monicker of "Denver Red." He made it standard practice to ride out the trains, shoot off the stiffs, and then quit her himself after she had gained sufficient momentum so nobody could hope to catch her "on the fly." One time, at some dried-up, Nevada water-stop, with a pistol in one hand and a bullwhip in the other, he bounced two hundred tramps off a "cannonball" freight and rode her out alone. The population of the "burg" was quadrupled for twelve hours until the next "drag" (freight) came through. And the "natives" (citizens) locked their doors to save their groceries.

Some of the roads were so rough they could rattle the skin right off your bones. And when the "hogger" (engineer) played crack the whip with a string of empties it sent the boes into such a tailspin they couldn't tell which end was up. "All right, Mack," they would yell in unison, "get this goddam coffee-grinder back on the track."

The boes expressed their private feelings about the various railroad lines by the nicknames they gave them. The Denver and Rio Grande Western Railroad, for example, they named "Damn Rotten Grub." The Milwaukee Road (Chicago, Milwaukee, and St. Paul) was called "Canned Milk and Stale Punk." Houston, Eastern and Western Texas was "Hell Either Way you Take it." The initials of the Delaware, Lackawanna, and Western stood for "Delay, Linger, and Wait." Lake Shore and Michigan Southern was "Less Sleep and More Speed." Fort Worth and Denver meant "Foul Water and Dirty Cars." The Q line (Chicago, Burlington, and Quincy Railroad) suggested "Come Boys and Quit Railroading." Oberlin, Hampton, and Eastern became the "Original Ham and Egg Route." Any slow train was referred to as a "tri-weekly" — goes up one week and tries to get back by the next.

Sitting in the "jungles" (hobo hangout adjacent to the yards), drinking "joe" (jungle coffee), swapping stories, waiting for the trains — this was living. Mulligan — potatoes, meat, vegetables, and whatever "fixings" were at hand — was the staple diet, supplemented, of course, by "handouts" and "lumps" (packages of food) obtained by "slamming gates" or knocking on back doors. You could get a full-scale "set down" (square meal with all the trimmings) for chopping a little wood. And, of course, there was "Salley's" (The Salvation Army), always good for a plate of hash and some "punk and plaster" (bread and butter). But you had to listen to those "mission stiffs" (preachers) and "all that Jesus stuff" (religion). "Panhandling" on the "main stem" (skid row) was good for small change if the "town clowns" (police) didn't interfere. Or you might go to work as a "pearl diver" (dishwasher) in one of the "beaneries" (restaurants) long enough to earn a "feed."

At night, you could "pound your ear" (sleep) in a "flop house" (cheap hotel) for "two bits," but some of those places were simply crawling with "crums" (lice), or "seam squirrels" as they were called. The local "locker" (jail) was a "good deal" except for the midnight "drunks" who couldn't be quieted down with anything short of a "haymaker" to the chin. Or, if you "bedded down" in a "spotted empty" (boxcar likely to be moved at any time), you might wake up in some "starvation siding" where a bo could get so hungry he could see biscuits walking around on crutches.

Then it was high time to go to work, or at least threaten to do so. Taking a job was not nearly as perilous a proposition as it seemed: one could always quit. According to hobo philosophy, a job is never a permanent thing, but an expedient — a means to an end. But the IWW "wobblies" (the "I Won't Work" boys) gave the stiffs a bad name. Most people thought they were all like "Panhandle Pete" from Hangover Hill "who never worked and never will." Somebody started the superstition that hoboes are afraid of work. Nothing could be farther from the truth. I have known boes who could lie down beside a job and go sound to sleep with no apparent apprehension at all. Of course, looking for work was a lot more exciting than actually working. If a couple of thousand miles lay between a bo and a job opportunity, the prospects somehow seemed a lot brighter than if the work was right at hand.

A bo liked to have plenty of time to prepare himself mentally and emotionally for any undertaking involving "elbow grease." He liked to talk matters over with the other stiffs before he committed himself to any ironclad agreement. For one thing, he would count the hoboes going in the opposite direction in order to calculate the odds that the job even existed. Then he would confer with the "boxcar philosophers" (professional tramps) in the jungles. Those birds knew the lay of the land if anyone did, and they were never known to give a buddy a "bum steer" (phony tip). Incidentally, there is a world of difference between a *hobo* and a *bum*. A bona fide hobo is always looking for a job, a bum is usually running away from one.

The way a hobo could predict the weather was positively uncanny. He knew precisely when to "shove off" for his winter quarters in the "sticks" with the "home guard" (people who never left home). "See those snow birds," he would say, "it's time to get back 'over the hump (continental divide).'" In the fall of the year, all birds, of course, were "snow birds." And going "over the hump," even during the summer months, was a cold order. "California blankets" (newspapers) were mighty thin protection in zero weather. Just mention Tennessee Pass to one of the old stiffs, and he will shiver so hard his teeth will rattle.

Well, there it was, Hobohemia, U.S.A., a nether nether world of dreams and dreamers on the outskirts of conventionality and conformity, and nobody anywhere ever enjoyed as much absolutely unadulterated freedom at as little expense as there. Nels Anderson, the famous hobo-sociologist, called it "the one remaining spot of the original Garden of Eden." And now it is gone.

The old boes, once homeless as the smoke the "coal burners" streaked across the sky, are doomed to the dubious delights of domesticity: three "squares" a day and the solid comforts of a double bed. The social workers, in the interests of progress, have detergentized them right out of existence. Very likely some of the stiffs have been reduced to "making a riffle" (earning money) in unemployment benefits. But, for all their new-fangled wonder drugs, the "croakers" (medical men) have yet to put the "kibosh" on "shack fever" (itching feet). There's more to this than meets the naked eye.

I will wager my new "J.B." (Stetson) that, in the spring — come hell or high water — when the ice breaks on the Mississippi, the boes will "hit the road" again, one way or another — even if they have to "pad the hoof" (walk) or "ride the cushions" on one of these jet liners. Wanderlust gets into the blood. Jack London, who confounded the bulls all the way from Hungry Ridge to Kicking Horse Pass, wasn't just "letting off steam" or "blowing his stack" when he said, "Once the road has gripped you, it will never let you go."

5 | 🖎

LANGUAGE IN CULTURE

The concept of culture is all-inclusive. Behavioral scientists continually study its range and limits and its relationship to such terms as *society, civilization,* and *behavior,* terms which are, indeed, often used interchangeably with *culture.* The term *culture* can be used to include patterns of family behavior, social forces, and literary creation — material which we consider in other parts of this book. This section begins with Clyde Kluckhohn's essay on the wide variety of interactions of language and culture. We then continue with some concrete explorations of the role of language in a few selected institutions and systems that are common to our society as a whole and that strongly affect the way we live: advertising, business, law, science, and politics. The time is the present, the place primarily America, although several of the essays apply to the Western world in general.

Language is an essential part of any culture and the chief means by which all other aspects of the culture express themselves. To understand a culture one must, therefore, study the functioning of the language in that culture. What is the degree of the interdependence of language and culture? To what extent does language make thought possible; to what extent is it a straitjacket that restrains thought? Is language the cause of certain kinds of behavior or the result of that behavior? These are very complex questions to which anthropologists, linguists, psychologists, and philosophers are directing more and more attention. The essays in this section consider these questions in the context of several powerful and vital institutions and patterns of behavior in our society.

A major theme of this section is the manipulative power of language. Sir Frederick Pollock and R. W. Maitland, two distinguished legal historians, wrote: "We do not control language; it controls us." In his essay "Politics and the English Language," George Orwell wrote that our language "becomes ugly and inaccurate because our thoughts are foolish, but the slovenliness of our language makes it easier for us to have foolish thoughts." The "venal poetry" of advertising is used to make us buy things we neither need nor want. The jargon of politics and law is used to obscure from us our own best (or worst) interests when we cast our ballots. Men make use of language to confuse, deceive, anaesthetize, and finally control other men.

But men also use language to convey precise descriptions of the world. Does the language of science provide us with the paradigm for clear thought and clear expression that can be applied to other areas of human activity?

Finally, an equally important and insistent corollary theme of this section is that we can develop critical awareness of the roles of language in our culture, and recognize how vulnerable we are to the force of language. This study then gives us the chance to expose and resist dishonest language and to write honestly ourselves.

Clyde Kluckhohn

THE GIFT OF TONGUES

ɬɬ

Anthropologists and linguists have become increasingly aware that the proper study of man demands a broad and incisive scrutiny of the interpenetration of language and experience. The late Clyde Kluckhohn, a distinguished anthropologist, offers many illustrations from different cultures of how the "pie of experience can be sliced in many different ways, and language is the principal directive force in the background." This discussion recalls material and ideas encountered in previous essays: vocabulary reflecting cultural history in the essays by Barfield and Pyles, linguistic practice exposing social structure in Salisbury and Fadiman, language categorizing experience in Flexner and Mencken. It also provides a background for those essays which follow, essays which explore the interplay between various aspects of culture and language.

Our misapprehension of the nature of language has occasioned a greater waste of time, and effort, and genius, than all the other mistakes and delusions with which humanity has been afflicted. It has retarded immeasurably our physical knowledge of every kind, and vitiated what it could not retard.

> A. B. JOHNSON,
> *Treatise on Language*[1]

[1] Alexander Bryan Johnson, *A Treatise on Language*, edited by David Rynin, The University of California Press, 1947.

It's a pity that so few of us have lived down our childhood struggles with grammar. We have been made to suffer so much from memorizing rules by rote and from approaching language in a mechanical, unimaginative way that we tend to think of grammar as the most inhuman of studies. Probably Americans, who dramatize themselves and their independence, have a kind of unconscious resentment against all patterns that are so set as to constitute a gratuitous insult to the principle of free will. For whatever reasons, Americans have been characteristically inept at foreign languages. Like the British, we have expected everybody else to learn English.

Yet nothing is more human than the speech of an individual or of a folk. Human speech, unlike the cry of an animal, does not occur as a mere element in a larger response. Only the human animal can communicate abstract ideas and converse about conditions that are contrary to fact. Indeed the purely conventional element in speech is so large that language can be regarded as pure culture. A Burmese weaver, moved to Mexico, would know at once what a fellow craftsman in Mexico was doing, but would not understand one word of the Nahuatl tongue. No clues are so helpful as those of language in pointing to ultimate, unconscious psychological attitudes. Moreover, much of the friction between groups and between nations arises because in both the literal and the slangy senses they don't speak the same language.

We live in an environment which is largely verbal in the sense that we spend the most of our waking hours uttering words or responding actively or passively to the words of others. We talk to ourselves. We talk to our families and friends — partly to communicate to them and to persuade them, partly just to express ourselves. We read newspapers, magazines, books, and other written matter. We listen to the radio, to sermons, lectures, and movies. As Edward Sapir says:

> Language completely interpenetrates direct experience. For most persons every experience, real or potential, is saturated with verbalism. This perhaps explains why so many nature lovers do not feel that they are truly in touch with nature until they have mastered the names of a great many flowers and trees, as though the primary world of reality were a verbal one, and as though one could not get close to nature unless one first mastered the terminology that somehow magically expresses it. It is this constant interplay between language and experience which removes language from the cold status of such purely and simply symbolic systems as mathematical symbolism or flag signalling.[2]

The dictionaries still say that "language is a device for communicating ideas." The semanticists and the anthropologists agree that this is a tiny,

[2] From "Language," by Edward Sapir, *Encyclopedia of the Social Sciences,* vol. ix. Copyright 1933 by The Macmillan Company.

specialized function of speech. Mainly, language is an instrument for action. The meaning of a word or phrase is not its dictionary equivalent but the difference its utterance brings about in a situation. We use words to comfort and cajole ourselves in fantasy and daydream, to let off steam, to goad ourselves into one type of activity and to deny ourselves another. We use words to promote our own purposes in dealing with others. We build up verbal pictures of ourselves and our motives. We coax, wheedle, protest, invite, and threaten. Even the most intellectual of intellectuals employs only a minute fraction of his total utterance in symbolizing and communicating ideas that are divorced from emotion and action. The primary social value of speech lies in getting individuals to work more effectively together and in easing social tensions. Very often what is said matters much less than that something is said.

To the manipulation of this verbal environment, the anthropological linguist has made some immediately practical contributions. Forced by the absence of written materials and by other circumstances attendant upon work with primitives, he has become an expert on "the direct method." He knows how to learn a language by using it. Though sensitive to the broader implications of subtler, rarer forms of a language, he is skilled in the socially practical. He knows how to dodge the subjunctive when the immediate objective is to get a conversation going. The training of the conventional teacher of languages tempts him to his besetting sin of pre-occupation with the niceties. He loves complicated rules and even more the exceptions to those rules. This is one of the principal reasons that after eight years of instruction in French an American can read a French novel with pleasure but is terrified to ask street directions in Paris. The anthropologist can't look up the rules in the book. He is hardened to making small and large mistakes. His tradition is to break through, to concentrate on the essential, to get on with the talk at all costs.

Since many odd languages were of military significance during World War II, the anthropological linguist had a chance to introduce his method of working directly with the native informant. He prepared educational materials that highlighted anthropological short cuts in learning how to speak languages. The results have influenced the traditional methods of language instruction in the United States. The anthropological linguist has also worked out ways of teaching adults who have no written language and ways of teaching illiterates to write and read their own tongue.

Because anthropological linguists have usually been trained as ethnologists and have often done general field work, they have tended less than other students of language to isolate speech from the total life of the people. To the anthropologist, language is just one kind of cultural behavior with many interesting connections to other aspects of action and thought. Analysis of a vocabulary shows the principal emphases of a culture and reflects culture history. In Arabic, for example, there are more than six thousand different words for camel, its parts, and equipment. The crudity and the special local words of the vocabulary of Spanish-speaking villages in New Mexico reflect the long isolation of these groups from the main stream of Latin culture. The particular archaisms used show that the break with the main continuity of the Spanish language occurred during the eighteenth century. The fact that the Boorabbee Indians of Panama use words like *gadsoot* (gadzooks), *forsoo'* (forsooth), *chee-ah* (cheer), and *mai-api* (mayhap) suggests a possible connection with Elizabethan buccaneers.

A great deal is now known about the history of languages, especially those languages that have been the great carriers of culture: Greek, Latin, Sanskrit, Arabic, Chinese, and English. Certain regularities have been discovered. In contrast to the general course of cultural evolution, languages move from the complex to the simple. Chinese and English have today lost almost all inflections. The uniformities of phonetic change are most encouraging to those who believe that there is a discoverable order in human events. As Bloomfield has said:

> These correspondences are a matter of historical detail, but their significance was overwhelming, since they showed that human action, in the mass, is not altogether haphazard, but may proceed with regularity even in so unimportant a matter as the manner of pronouncing the individual sounds within the flow of speech.[3]

The phonetic side of language beautifully illustrates both the selective nature of culture and the omnipresence of patterning. The sound of the "p" in pin is uttered with a slight puff of breath that is lacking when we sound the "p" in spin. Yet the speakers of English have entered into an unconscious agreement to treat them as the same signals, though they are not acoustically identical. It is like the motorist trained to stop at a light that is any shade of red. If I am investigating an unknown language and discover two sounds that are somewhat similar to those represented by English "b" and "d" but differ in being softly whispered, I can immediately predict that sounds in the new language of "g" type will conform to the same pattern.

Language is as consistently nonrational as any aspect of culture. We cling stubbornly to functionless capital letters. One may also instance our absurd English spelling. "Ghiti" ought to spell fish — gh as in laugh, ti as in ambition. In hiccough, gh has a p sound. "Ghoughteighteau" could be read as potato — figure it out yourself. We say "five houses" when "five house" would be simpler and convey the meaning equally well.

Small peculiarities of linguistic usage are very revealing. It is no accident that French Catholics address the deity with the familiar form of the

[3] Leonard Bloomfield, *Language*, Holt, Rinehart and Winston, Inc., 1933.

personal pronoun (*tu*) and Protestants with the formal (*vous*). In all sectors of French society save the old aristocracy spouses use *tu* to each other. But in the *Faubourg St. Germain* the duke calls his duchess *vous* — it being well understood between them that he reserves *tu* for his mistress.

A whole monograph could well be written on differences in the social structure of European nations as exposed by linguistic habits relating to the second personal pronoun. In France one comes to *tutoyer* few people after adolescence. This familiarity is restricted to immediate relatives and to a few intimate friends of childhood. In the German-speaking world, however, a student who did not soon come to use the familiar *Du* with those whom he saw frequently would be regarded as stuffy. In the army of imperial Austria all officers in the same regiment called each other *Du* regardless of rank. Failure to use the familiar form was equivalent to a challenge to the duel. In Austria and in other European countries the initiation of the familiar usage between adults is formalized in a ceremony. There is an embrace and a drink from each other's glasses. In Spain and Italy the introduction of the *tu* relationship in later life is considerably easier than in France but less frequent than in southern Germany and Austria. In Italy there is the further complication of a special form of respectful address (*Lei*). Choice of *Lei* or the more common formal pronoun became a political issue. The Fascist Party forbade the use of *Lei*. In Sweden also, passions have been aroused over the pronoun *ni* which is used toward those of lower social status — and, in accord with the familiar principle of inverted snobbery,[4] toward royal personages. Clubs were formed to abolish this word. Individuals wore buttons saying, "I don't use *ni* and I hope you don't either." Persons were brought into court for using *ni* toward people who considered themselves the equals or superiors of those who derogated them by using *ni* in address. "You are *ni* to me; I am not *ni* to you."

These are also instances of the intensely emotional symbolism of language. During the course of the development of nationalism and the romantic movement, every tongue was seized upon as the tangible manifestation of each culture's uniqueness. In the earlier part of the nineteenth century Magyar nobles spoke Latin in the Hungarian Parliament because they could not speak Magyar and would not speak German. Magyar, Irish, Lithuanian, and other tongues have been revived within the last hundred years from the category of practically dead languages. This tendency is about as old as written history. In the Bible we learn that the Gileadites slew everyone at the passages of Jordan who said *sibboleth* instead of *shibboleth*.

---

4 Another illustration of the "principle of inverted snobbery": In an American college that is small or struggling for prestige, faculty members who are members of Phi Beta Kappa would as soon appear on the campus without their pants as without their keys. In old well-established universities, ΦBK keys are worn only by a few older professors.

Groups within a culture emphasize their unity by a special language. Criminals have their own argot. So, indeed, do all the professions. One school in England (Winchester) has a language, compounded of medieval Latin and the accretions of the slang of many generations, that is utterly unintelligible to the uninitiated. "The linguistic community" is no meaningless phrase. The use of speech forms in common implies other things in common. The hunting or "county" set in England affects the dropping of final g's as a badge of their being set apart. Understatement is the mark of unshakeable psychological security. If a member of the English upper classes is a member of the Davis Cup team he says, "Yes, I play a little tennis." Individuals of many countries pronounce words in certain ways in order to associate themselves with particular social classes. The extent to which an elderly or middle-aged Englishman is still identifiable as Harrow or Rugby — and not as a Yorkshireman nor even as an Oxonian nor as an army man — proves the identification of distinctive language with social status. You can pretty well place an Englishman by his tie and his accent. Idiomatic turns of speech identify to society at large the special positions and roles of its various members. Cliques and classes unconsciously use this device to prevent absorption into the larger group. "He talks like one of us" is a declaration of acceptance. Euphemisms, special terms of endearment, and slang are class labels.

The essential aroma of each culture or subculture may be caught as a fragrance of language. In the Berlin of 1930, when one met an acquaintance on the street one bowed and stiffly said, "Good day." In Vienna one called out, "I have the honor," to a superior; "May God greet thee (you)," to an intimate; or, "Your servant," to a fellow student or fellow aristocrat. That *gewisse Liebenswürdigkeit* (a certain graciousness) which was the hallmark of Viennese culture came out most clearly and immediately in certain phrases that were not unknown in northern and Protestant Germany but were much less frequent in the stuff of daily conversation: "Live well," "the lady mother," "I kiss the hand, noble lady," and many others. In Austria when the delivery boy brought the groceries to the kitchen he said, "May God greet thee," if the maid received them; "Kiss the hand, noble lady," if the mistress were there.

Although one could press this point of view too far, there is *something* significant in the lists of words from each European language that have become widely current in other languages. From English: gentleman, fair play, week end, sport. From French: *liaison, maitresse, cuisine*. From Italian: *diva, bravo, bel canto*. From German: *Weltschmerz, Sehnsucht, Weltanschauung, Gemütlichkeit*. In *Englishmen, Frenchmen, and Spaniards*, de Madariaga has suggested that the words, fair play, *le droit*, and *el honor* are the keys to the respective cultures. Here is a sample of his discussion of English:

There is deep satisfaction in the thought that English — the language of the man of action — is a monosyllabic language. For the man of action, as we know, lives in the present, and the present is an instant with room for no more than one syllable. Words of more than one syllable are sometimes called in English "dictionary" words, *i.e.*, words for the intellectual, for the bookworm, for the crank, almost for the un-English. They are marvellous, those English monosyllables, particularly, of course, those which represent acts. Their fidelity to the act which they represent is so perfect that one is tempted to think English words are the right and proper names which those acts are meant to have, and all other words but pitiable failures. How could one improve on splash, smash, ooze, shriek, slush, glide, squeak, coo? Who could find anything better than hum or buzz or howl or whir? Who could think of anything more sloppy than slop? Is not the word sweet a kiss in itself and what could suggest a more peremptory obstacle than stop?[5]

Certainly the recurrent turns of phrase, the bromides, of each culture and of different time periods in the same culture are illuminating. They embody in capsule form the central strains and stresses of the society, major cultural interests, the characteristic definitions of the situation, the prime motivations. You can't swear effectively in British to an American audience and vice versa. The Navaho greeting is "All is well"; the Japanese, "There is respectful earliness"; the American, "How do you do?" or "How are you getting on?" Each epoch has its stock phrases. As Carl Becker has written:

> If we would discover the little backstairs door that for any age serves as the secret entranceway to knowledge, we will do well to look for certain unobtrusive words with uncertain meanings that are permitted to slip off the tongue or pen without fear and without research; words which, having from constant repetition lost their metaphorical significance, are unconsciously mistaken for objective realities. . . . In each age these magic words have their entrances and their exits.[6]

In a way there is nothing very new about semantics. The Roman grammarian, Varro, pointed out in a learned treatise that he had discovered 228 distinct meanings for the word "good." His basic point was the same as Aldous Huxley's: "There ought to be some way of dry-cleaning and disinfecting words. Love, purity, goodness, spirit — a pile of dirty linen waiting for the laundress." We are always bringing together by words things that are different and separating verbally things that are, in fact, the same. A Christian Scientist refused to take vitamin tablets on the ground that they were "medicine"; he willingly accepted them when it was explained that they were "food." An insurance company discovered that

[5] S. de Madariaga, *Englishmen, Frenchmen, and Spaniards*, Oxford University Press, 1929.

[6] Carl Becker, *Heavenly City of the Eighteenth Century Philosophers*, Yale University Press, 1935.

behavior toward "gasoline drums" was ordinarily circumspect, that toward "empty gasoline drums" habitually careless. Actually, the "empty" drums are the more dangerous because they contain explosive vapor.

The semantic problem is almost insoluble because, as John Locke said, "So difficult is it to show the various meanings and imperfections of words when we have nothing else but words to do it by." This is one of the reasons that a cross-cultural approach is imperative. Anyone who has struggled with translation is made to realize that there is more to a language than its dictionary. The Italian proverb *"traduttore, tradittore"* (the translator is a betrayer) is all too correct. I asked a Japanese with a fair knowledge of English to translate back from the Japanese that phrase in the new Japanese constitution that represents our "life, liberty, and the pursuit of happiness." He rendered, "license to commit lustful pleasure." English to Russian and Russian back to English transmuted a cablegram "Genevieve suspended for prank" into "Genevieve hanged for juvenile delinquency."

These are obvious crudities. But look at translations into half-a-dozen languages of the same passage in the Old Testament. The sheer difference in length will show that translation is not just a matter of finding a word in the second language that exactly matches a word in the original. Renderings of poetry are especially misleading. The best metrical translation of Homer is probably the fragment done by Hawtrey. The final two lines of the famous "Helen on the wall" passage of the third book in the *Iliad* go as follows:

> So said she; but they long since in earth's soft arms
> > were reposing
> There in their own dear land, their fatherland, Lacedaemon.

Hawtrey has caught the musical effect of Greek hexameter about as well as it is possible to do in English. But the Greek says literally, "but them, on the other hand, the life-giving earth held fast." The original is realistic — Helen's brothers were dead and that was that. The English is sentimental.

Once in Paris I saw a play called "The Weak Sex." I found it charmingly risqué. A year later in Vienna I took a girl to see a German translation of the same play. Though she was no prude, I was embarrassed because the play was vulgar if not obscene in German.

I think I got my first genuine insight into the nature of language when my tutor at Oxford asked me to translate into Greek a few pages from an eighteenth-century British rhetorician which contained the following phrase, "she heaped the utmost virulence of her invective upon him." I struggled with this and finally committed the unforgivable sin of looking up each word in an English-Greek dictionary. My tutor glanced at the resultant monstrosity and looked up at me with mingled disgust, pity, and amazement. "My dear boy," he said, "don't you know that the only possible way you can render that is *deinos aedeitai*, she blamed very strongly?"

Really, there are three kinds of translation. There is the literal or word-for-word variety which is always distorted except perhaps between languages that are very similar in structure and vocabulary. Second, there is the official type where certain conventions as to idiomatic equivalents are respected. The third, or psychological type of translation, where the words produce approximately the same effects in the speakers of the second language as they did in those of the original, is next to impossible. At best, the rendering must be extremely free, with elaborate circumlocutions and explanations. I once heard Einstein make a slip of the tongue that stated the deeper truth. He said, "I shall speak in English this evening, but if I get excited during the discussion I shall break into German and Professor Lindeman will traduce me."

If words referred only to things, translation would be relatively simple. But they refer also to relations between things and the subjective as well as the objective aspects of these relationships. In different tongues relationships are variously conceived. The Balinese word *tis* means not to be cold when it is cold. The Balinese word *paling* designates the state of a trance or drunkenness or a condition of not knowing where you are, what day it is, where the center of the island is, the caste of the person to whom you are talking. The subjective aspects arise from the fact that we use words not only to express things and relationships but to express ourselves; words refer not only to events but to the attitudes of the speakers toward those events.

The words prostitute and whore have exactly the same denotation. The connotation, however, is very different. And a word's connotation is at least as important as the denotation in rousing feeling and producing action. Examine carefully the richest field of modern verbal magic — advertisements.

The same words often don't mean the same thing to different generations within the same culture. Margaret Mead writes:

> Take the word *job*. To the parents a job was something you got when you finished school — the next step, a little grim, a little exciting, the end of carefree school days. A job was something you were going to get, bound to get, something that waited for you at the end of school, just as certainly as autumn follows summer. But job — to those born in 1914, 1915? Something that you might never get, something to be longed for and prayed for, to starve for and steal for, almost — a job. There weren't any. When these two generations talk together and the word *job* is used, how will they understand each other? Suppose the issue is the draft — "A shame a fellow has to give up his job." To the elders this is arrant unpatriotic selfishness. To the young it is obvious sense. They find it strange that older people can see the sacrifice involved when

married men with children must leave their families to go away in the defense service. Yet these same people don't see that any one should mind leaving a job. "Don't they know what a *job* means now, in the thinking of those born in 1915, 1916, 1917? Don't they know that just as among the ancients one was not a man until one had begotten a male child, so today one can't think of one's self as a full human being, without a job? We didn't say a guy wouldn't go because he had a job. We just said it was tough on him. We weren't saying anything they wouldn't say themselves about a man with kids. But gee — how they blew up!"[7]

The British and the Americans are still under the delusion that they speak the same language. With some qualifications this is true as far as denotations are concerned, though there are concepts like "sissy" in American for which there are no precise English equivalents. Connotations, however, are often importantly different, and this makes for the more misunderstanding because both languages are still called "English" (treating alike by words things that are different). An excellent illustration is again supplied by Margaret Mead:

> . . . in Britain, the word "compromise" is a good word, and one may speak approvingly of any arrangement which has been a compromise, including, very often, one in which the other side has gained more than fifty per cent of the points at issue. On the other hand, in the United States, the minority position is still the position from which everyone speaks: the President *versus* Congress, Congress *versus* the President, the State government *versus* the metropolis and the metropolis *versus* the State government. This is congruent with the American doctrine of checks and balances, but it does not permit the word "compromise" to gain the same ethical halo which it has in Britain. Where, in Britain, to compromise means to work out a good solution, in America it usually means to work out a bad one, a solution in which all the points of importance (to both sides) are lost. Thus, in negotiations between the United States and Britain, all of which had, in the nature of the case, to be compromises, as two sovereignties were involved, the British could always speak approvingly and proudly of the result, while the Americans had to emphasize their losses.[8]

The words, then, that pass so readily from mouth to mouth are not entirely trustworthy substitutes for the facts of the physical world. The smooth-worn standard coins are slippery steppingstones from mind to mind. Nor is thinking simply a matter of choosing words to express thoughts. The selected words always mirror social situation as well as objective fact. Two men go into a bar in New York and are overcharged for bad liquor: "This is a gyp joint." The same thing happens in Paris: "The French are a bunch of chiselers."

[7] Margaret Mead, "When Were You Born?" *Child Study,* Spring, 1941.
[8] *Ibid.*

Perhaps the most important contribution of anthropological linguistics has come from the difficulties the anthropologist goes through in trying to express the meanings contained in speech structures completely foreign to the pattern of all European tongues. This study and this experience has forced upon the anthropologist a rather startling discovery which is fraught with meaning for a world where peoples speaking many different idioms are trying to communicate without distortion. Every language is something more than a vehicle for exchanging ideas and information — more even than a tool for self-expression and for letting off emotional steam or for getting other people to do what we want.

Every language is also a special way of looking at the world and interpreting experience. Concealed in the structure of each different language are a whole set of unconscious assumptions about the world and life in it. The anthropological linguist has come to realize that the general ideas one has about what happens in the world outside oneself are not altogether "given" by external events. Rather, up to a point, one sees and hears what the grammatical system of one's language has made one sensitive to, has trained one to look for in experience. This bias is the more insidious because everyone is so unconscious of his native language as a system. To one brought up to speak a certain language it is part of the very nature of things, remaining always in the class of background phenomena. It is as natural that experience should be organized and interpreted in these language-defined classes as it is that the seasons change. In fact the naïve view is that anyone who thinks in any other way is unnatural or stupid, or even vicious — and most certainly illogical.

In point of fact, traditional or Aristotelian logic has been mainly the analysis of consistencies in the structures of languages like Greek and Latin. The subject–predicate form of speech has implied a changeless world of fixed relations between "substances" and their "qualities." This view, as Korzybski has insisted, is quite inadequate to modern physical knowledge which shows that the properties of an atom alter from instant to instant in accord with the shifting relationships of its component elements. The little word "is" has brought us much confusion because sometimes it signifies that the subject exists, sometimes that it is a member of a designated class, sometimes that subject and predicate are identical. Aristotelian logic teaches us that something is or isn't. Such a statement is often false to reality, for both-and is more often true than either-or. "Evil" ranges all the way from black through an infinite number of shades of gray. Actual experience does not present clear-cut entities like "good" and "bad," "mind" and "body"; the sharp split remains verbal. Modern physics has shown that even in the inanimate world there are many questions that cannot be answered by an unrestricted "yes" or an unqualified "no."

From the anthropological point of view there are as many different worlds upon the earth as there are languages. Each language is an instrument which guides people in observing, in reacting, in expressing themselves in a special way. The pie of experience can be sliced in many different ways, and language is the principal directive force in the background. You can't say in Chinese, "answer me yes or no," for there aren't words for yes and no. Chinese gives priority to "how?" and nonexclusive categories; European languages to "what?" and exclusive categories. In English we have both real plurals and imaginary plurals, "ten men" and "ten days"; in Hopi plurals and cardinal numbers may be used only for things that can be seen together as an objective group. The fundamental categories of the French verb are before and after (tense) and potentiality vs. actuality (mood); the fundamental categories of one American Indian language (Wintu) are subjectivity vs. objectivity, knowledge vs. belief, freedom vs. actual necessity.

In the Haida language of British Columbia there are more than twenty verbal prefixes that indicate whether an action was performed by carrying, shooting, hammering, pushing, pulling, floating, stamping, picking, chopping, or the like. Some languages have different verbs, adjectives, and pronouns for animate and inanimate things. In Melanesia there are as many as four variant forms for each possessive pronoun. One may be used for the speaker's body and mind, another for illegitimate relatives and his loincloth, a third his possessions and gifts. The underlying conceptual images of each language tend to constitute a coherent though unconscious philosophy.

Where in English one word, "rough," may equally well be used to describe a road, a rock, or the business surface of a file, the Navaho language finds a need for three different words which may not be used interchangeably. While the general tendency is for Navaho to make finer and more concrete distinctions, this is not inevitably the case. The same stem is used for rip, light beam, and echo, ideas which seem diverse to speakers of European languages. One word is used to designate a medicine bundle with all its contents, the skin quiver in which the contents are wrapped, the contents as a whole, and some of the distinct items. Sometimes the point is not that the images of Navahos are less fluid and more delimited but rather just that the external world is dissected along different lines. For example, the same Navaho word is used to describe both a pimply face and a nodule-covered rock. In English a complexion might be termed "rough" or "coarse," but a rock would never, except facetiously, be described as pimply. Navaho differentiates two types of rough rock: the kind which is rough in the manner in which a file is rough and the kind which is nodule-encrusted. In these cases the differences between the Navaho and the English ways of seeing the world cannot be disposed of merely by saying that the Navaho language is more precise. The variations rest in the features which the two languages see as essential. Cases can indeed be given where the Navaho is notably less precise. Navaho gets along with a single word for flint, metal, knife, and certain other objects of metal. This, to be sure, is due to the historical accident that, after European contact, metal in general and knives in particular took the place of flint.

Navahos are perfectly satisfied with what seem to Europeans rather imprecise discriminations in the realm of time sequences. On the other hand, they are the fussiest people in the world about always making explicit in the forms of the language many distinctions which English makes only occasionally and vaguely. In English one says, "I eat," meaning, "I eat something." The Navaho point of view is different. If the object thought of is actually indefinite, then "something" must be tacked on to the verb.

The nature of their language forces the Navaho to notice and report many other distinctions in physical events which the nature of the English language allows speakers to neglect in most cases, even though their senses are just as capable as those of the Navaho to register the smaller details of what goes on in the external world. For example, suppose a Navaho range rider and a white supervisor see that a wire fence needs repair. The supervisor will probably write in his notebook, "Fence at such and such a place must be fixed." If the Navaho reports the break, he must choose between forms that indicate whether the damage was caused by some person or by a nonhuman agency, whether the fence was of one or several strands of wire.

In general, the difference between Navaho thought and English thought —both as manifested in the language and as forced by the very nature of the linguistic forms into such patterns — is that Navaho thought is ordinarily much more specific. The ideas expressed by the English verb to go provide a nice example. When a Navaho says that he went somewhere he never fails to specify whether it was afoot, astride, by wagon, auto, train, airplane, or boat. If it be a boat, it must be specified whether the boat floats off with the current, is propelled by the speaker, or is made to move by an indefinite or unstated agency. The speed of a horse (walk, trot, gallop, run) is expressed by the verb form chosen. He differentiates between starting to go, going along, arriving at, returning from a point. It is not, of course, that these distinctions *cannot* be made in English, but that they *are not* made consistently. They seem of importance to English speakers only under special circumstances.

A cross-cultural view of the category of time is highly instructive. Beginners in the study of classical Greek are often troubled by the fact that the word *opiso* sometimes means "behind," sometimes "in the future." Speakers of English find this baffling because they are accustomed to think of themselves as moving through time. The Greeks, however, conceived of themselves as stationary, of time as coming up behind them, overtaking them, and then, still moving on, becoming the "past" that lay before their eyes.

Present European languages emphasize time distinctions. The tense systems are usually thought of as the most basic of verbal inflections. However, this was not always so. Streitberg says that in primitive Indo-European a special indicator for the present was usually lacking. In many languages, certainly, time distinctions are only irregularly present or are of distinctly secondary importance. In Hopi the first question answered by the verb form is that of the type of information conveyed by the assertion. Is a situation reported as actuality, as anticipated, or as a general truth? In the anticipatory form there is no necessary distinction between past, present, and future. The English translation must choose from context between "was about to run," "is about to run," and "will run." The Wintu language of California carries this stress upon implications of validity much further. The sentence "Harry is chopping wood" must be translated in five different ways, depending upon whether the speaker knows this by hearsay, by direct observation, or by inference of three degrees of plausibility.

In no language are the whole of a sense experience and all possible interpretations of it expressed. What people think and feel and how they report what they think and feel are determined, to be sure, by their personal history, and by what actually happens in the outside world. But they are also determined by a factor which is often overlooked; namely, the pattern of linguistic habits which people acquire as members of a particular society. It makes a difference whether or not a language is rich in metaphors and conventional imagery.

Our imaginations are restricted in some directions, free in others. The linguistic particularization of detail along one line will mean the neglect of other aspects of the situation. Our thoughts are directed in one way if we speak a language where all objects are classified according to sex, in another if the classification is by social position or the form of the object. Grammars are devices for expressing relations. It makes a difference what is treated as object, as attribute, as state, as act. In Hopi, ideas referring to the seasons are not grouped with what we call nouns but rather with what we call adverbs. Because of our grammar it is easy to personify summer, to think of it as a thing or a state.

Even as between closely related tongues, the conceptual picture may be different. Let us take one final example from Margaret Mead:

> Americans tend to arrange objects on a single scale of value, from best to worst, biggest to smallest, cheapest to most expensive, etc., and are able to express a preference among very complex objects on such a single scale. The question, "What is your favorite color?" so intelligible to an American, is meaningless in Britain, and such a question is countered by: "Favorite color for what? A flower? A necktie?" Each object is thought of as having a most complex set of qualities, and color is merely a quality of an object, not something from a color chart on which one can make a choice which is transferable to a large number of different sorts of objects. The American reduction of complexities to single scales is entirely comprehensible in terms of the great diversity of value systems which different immigrant groups brought to the

American scene. Some common denominator among the incommensurables was very much needed, and over-simplification was almost inevitable. But, as a result, Americans think in terms of qualities which have uni-dimensional scales, while the British, when they think of a complex object or event, even if they reduce it to parts, think of each part as retaining all of the complexities of the whole. Americans subdivide the scale; the British subdivide the object.[9]

Language and its changes cannot be understood unless linguistic behavior is related to other behavioral facts. Conversely, one can gain many subtle insights into those national habits and thought ways of which one is ordinarily unconscious by looking closely at special idioms and turns of speech in one's own and other languages. What a Russian says to an American doesn't really get across just from shuffling words — much is twisted or blunted or lost unless the American knows something about Russia and Russian life, a good deal more than the sheer linguistic skill needed for a formally correct translation. The American must indeed have gained some entrance to that foreign world of values and significances which are pointed up by the emphases of the Russian vocabulary, crystallized in the forms of Russian grammar, implicit in the little distinctions of meaning in the Russian language.

Any language is more than an instrument for conveying ideas, more even than an instrument for working upon the feelings of others and for self-expression. Every language is also a means of categorizing experience. The events of the "real" world are never felt or reported as a machine would do it. There is a selection process and an interpretation in the very act of response. Some features of the external situation are highlighted; others are ignored or not fully discriminated.

Every people has its own characteristic classes in which individuals pigeonhole their experiences. These classes are established primarily by the language through the types of objects, processes, or qualities which received special emphasis in the vocabulary and equally, though more subtly, through the types of differentiation or activity which are distinguished in grammatical forms. The language says, as it were, "notice this," "always consider this separate from that," "such and such things belong together." Since persons are trained from infancy to respond in these ways, they take such discriminations for granted as part of the inescapable stuff of life. When we see two peoples with different social traditions respond in different ways to what appear to the outsider to be identical stimulus situations, we realize that experience is much less an objective absolute than we thought. Every language has an effect upon what the people who use it see, what they feel, how they think, what they can talk about.

[9] Margaret Mead, "The Application of Anthropological Techniques to Cross-National Communication," *Transactions of the New York Academy of Sciences*, February, 1947.

"Common sense" holds that different languages are parallel methods for expressing the same "thoughts." "Common sense," however, itself implies talking so as to be readily understood by one's fellows — in the same culture. Anglo-American "common sense" is actually very sophisticated, deriving from Aristotle and the speculations of scholastic and modern philosophers. The fact that all sorts of basic philosophic questions are begged in the most cavalier fashion is obscured by the conspiracy of silent acceptance which always attends the system of conventional understandings that we call culture.

The lack of true equivalences between any two languages is merely the outward expression of inward differences between two peoples in premises, in basic categories, in the training of fundamental sensitivities, and in general view of the world. The way the Russians put their thoughts together shows the impress of linguistic habits, of characteristic ways of organizing experience, for

> Human beings do not live in the objective world alone, nor alone in the world of social activity as ordinarily understood, but are very much at the mercy of the particular language which has become the medium of expression for their society. It is quite an illusion to imagine that one adjusts to reality essentially without the use of language and that language is merely an incidental means of solving specific problems of communication or reflection. The fact of the matter is that the 'real world' is to a large extent unconsciously built up on the language habits of the group. . . . We see and hear and otherwise experience very largely as we do because the language habits of our community predispose certain choices of interpretation.[10]   —EDWARD SAPIR

A language is, in a sense, a philosophy.

---

[10] Edward Sapir, "The Status of Linguistics As a Science," *Language*, V (1929), pp. 209–10.

Eugene Nida

THORNS AND THISTLES

ɪɪ

The interdependence of language and culture raises the question of the possibility of communication between radically different cultures. Eugene Nida, linguist and Secretary of Translations of the American Bible Society, explores the difficulty of intercultural communication in the context of Bible translation. For instance, in one Latin American language, a literal rendering of "gave breath to the image" (Revelation 13:15) really meant "He made the image stink." While he offers many such examples of the hazards of translating from one culture to another, Mr. Nida does not believe that cultural contrasts prevent translating, for "the more we assimilate of different cultural perspectives the more readily and more fully can we appreciate the idioms of other people."

There is an impression among some people that Bible translating is really quite an easy task, but these persons have not reckoned with the troublesome thorns and thistles which beset the translator at every turn. They presume that all one has to do is to ask natives for the right words and then proceed to write them down, but one can never take anything for granted. One missionary assumed that his helpers were giving him the right words, but in the Beatitudes they failed to understand the meaning of the Spanish *bienaventurados* "blessed," "fortunate," or "lucky"; and as a result the translation into one of the Indian languages of Latin America read literally, "Lucky in gambling are the poor in spirit . . . ; lucky in gambling are those who mourn . . ." etc. The Indian helpers knew the

Spanish word *bienaventurados* in only the one sense of "lucky," and they were happy over the prospects of material rewards for the poor humble hearers of Jesus' words.

Literal translations sometimes turn out ridiculous. In one language of Latin America the translator thought he was describing an image coming to life when he gave a literal rendering of "gave breath to the image" (Revelation 13:15), but what he actually said was, "He made the image stink." In another instance the natives were amazed at the recorded patience and long-suffering of the Lord, for according to the 26th chapter of Matthew in their New Testaments a repentant woman "broke a stone jar of ointment" on Jesus' head. A strange way indeed to express gratitude! In still another case the literal translation of "birthday" (Mark 6:21) meant that Herod threw a drinking party for the leading men of the land on the very day he was born — an incredible stunt, so the people thought, but their mythical heroes were credited with equally amazing exploits at an early age and so they were ready to believe the mistranslation — but only as a fable.

Can you blame one group of Indians in Latin America for being disgusted with Paul when they read in their Scriptures that he talked of "leading a wife around like an ox" (I Corinthians 9:5)? The translator overlooked the right word "to lead by the hand" or "to accompany," and had thoughtlessly used a term which meant only "to lead around like some unruly animal."

Some literal renderings fail to provide the proper meanings, for they are interpreted purely in a material sense. For example, the Valientes of Panama would only understand "stiff-necked people" as those who were afflicted with severe paralysis or rheumatism of the neck. Their equivalent is "holding-back people." That is to say, they constitute the intractable, disobedient people who will not be led, or even pushed — they just hold back in defiance. The San Blas Indians of Panama, a tribe a few hundred miles away from the Valientes, describe similar folks as "people with stopped-up ears." These two different metaphors are two equally good ways of describing rebellious, unco-operative people who insist on their own way.

Some literal translations mean practically nothing. They are incongruous words — nothing more. A translation for the "Holy Spirit" used for some time in one Sudanic language meant only "clean breath," and that meant nothing, for whoever saw a "clean breath"? The translators had looked at their Greek and discovered that the word *pneuma*, meaning "Spirit," also means "breath." They thought that "holy" could best be translated by "clean," since they had an idea that a word describing a state of being physically clean would readily suggest the meaning of holiness. This is an idea which people often embody in the pseudo-Scriptural quotation to the effect that "cleanliness is next to godliness." For this African tribe, being clean was simply unrelated and unrelatable to holiness. But this was not all. The very combination "clean breath" was unthinkable. In order for anything to be clean, these people insisted that it would certainly have to be visible, but a breath is not visible; and hence, how could it be regarded as clean? How could a thing be clean unless it were washable, and whoever heard of washing a breath? Missionaries tried desperately to teach the meaning of this expression, but they completely failed to get across the meaning which they had at first regarded as so immediately evident. So many metaphorical flowers which the translator seeks to grow in the language prove to be thistles and thorns.

To understand a strange culture one must enter as much as possible into the very life and viewpoint of the native people. Otherwise, a person will not realize how ridiculous it is to talk to Indians of southern Mexico about scribes who "devour widows' houses" (Mark 12:40). Their houses are often made with cornstalk walls and grass roofs, and farm animals do eat them when fodder gets scarce, so that people guard against hungry cows breaking in to eat down a house. "Devouring widows' houses" is no bold metaphor in some places, but a real danger. Hence the native reader wonders, "What were these 'scribes' anyway? Was this just a name for starved, ravenous cattle?" In such cases one must translate "destroy widows' houses."

Cultural contrasts do not prevent translating; they only point the direction which the equivalent phrase indicates. One cannot say to the Zanaki people along the winding shores of sprawling Lake Victoria, "Behold I stand at the door and knock" (Revelation 3:20). This would mean that Christ was declaring Himself to be a thief, for in Zanaki land thieves generally made it a practice to knock on the door of a hut which they hope to burglarize; and if they hear any movement or noise inside, they dash off into the dark. An honest man will come to a house and call the name of the person inside, and in this way identify himself by his voice. Accordingly, in the Zanaki translation it is necessary to say, "Behold, I stand at the door and call." This wording may be slightly strange to us, but the meaning is the same. In each case Christ is asking people to open the door. He is no thief and He will not force an entrance; He knocks — and in Zanaki "He calls." If anything, the Zanaki expression is a little more personal than our own.

Cultural parallels at times seem strangely different. On the drying fringe of the vast Sahara desert around the city of Ouagadougou, in French West Africa, the hardy Mossi people know nothing of ships, and certainly nothing of anchors. It would be folly to talk about "a sure and steadfast anchor for the soul" (Hebrews 6:19). To explain the word "anchor" one would need almost a paragraph, and if one insists on "heavy, pronged piece of iron for the soul," this would surely mean a grievous, cruel burden and would have no reference to spiritual safety or security. But the Mossi people have a perfect parallel in the word "picketting-peg." They have prized herds of horses and cattle, and they make it a practice to stake out their animals during the night, tying them to a picketting-peg. Hence the Mossi people read in their New Testament, "A strong and steadfast picketting-peg for the soul." This word "picketting-peg" is especially valuable, for the Mossi people recognize its metaphorical significance. One of their proverbs is, "A man does not tie a good horse to a bad picketting-peg."

In some instances there are simply no cultural parallels. Believe it or not, in some parts of the world people know nothing about gambling. Such a people are to be found among the Shipibos, whose villages are perched on the banks of the broad winding Peruvian tributaries of the Amazon, flowing like tangled, shiny ribbons through endless green. One could search in the Shipibo language forever and still not find a native term for "gamble." There is no such word, for the people do not have games of chance. How then is a person going to translate Mark 15:24, where the soldiers "cast lots" for the clothing of Jesus? One can only describe — even though very inadequately — what possibly happened. Hence, the Shipibo translation reads, "They shook little things to decide what each one should take." Of course, the phrase "shook little things" will need explanation, but this is also true of many things in the Bible.

In places where missionaries have been unaware of the cultural problems involved, serious errors have been made and have caused widespread misunderstanding. One translator in West Africa finally extracted a word which he thought meant "to save." For years he used it, only to discover at last that it meant merely keeping ragged clothes together — scarcely a fitting term to describe the redemptive salvation described in the Bible. To make matters worse, he used a word for "grace" which was used in casting curses upon people. He had explained "grace" as great spiritual power descending upon people, but in many cultures supernatural power is more often fearful and harmful, rather than good. The word which the missionary persisted in using was so taboo that people would utter the word only when others were not listening, for they did not want to be accused of witchcraft. Rather than proclaiming the grace of God, the missionary was extolling the power of black magic and the efficacy of God's curse.

Even more serious, however, than such flagrant mistakes is the tendency to make easy adaptations to native ideas. In one area of West Africa the word for "save" literally meant "to free." This seemed fine, for in the true sense of the word, salvation is a freedom — freedom from the power and guilt of sin. To the practical-minded natives, however, this freedom meant something quite different. Boys who went to school and learned to read and write were not obliged to work on the roads, nor were they forced into jobs as carriers for government officials, and some had no taxes to pay. The converts that worked at the mission station were free from forced labor and free from taxation. Hence, for most people, becoming a Christian and being "freed" had no spiritual significance. They thought only of political and economic freedom, and being associated with the missionary was the best means of obtaining this. For years the earnest preaching of consecrated missionaries had fallen on materialistic ears. These West Africans are essentially like the woman at the well in Sychar, who was interested in the living water in order that she should no longer be obliged to go daily to the well to draw. But Jesus led her from her materialism to an acknowledgment of spiritual need. The gospel message often begins with the expressions for purely physical objects, but it must lead men to spiritual truth. This was, unfortunately, what these missionaries in West Africa were unable to do because they could not speak the native language well enough.

There is a temptation for missionaries to want to manufacture hosts of new words, fashioning them to fit their own ideas. Of course, a great amount of word-forming must be undertaken, but it must not be done in the comfortable isolation of one's study. Words must be tested by constant usage. Otherwise, one may produce such a preposterous expression as occurred in one Indian language in Mexico. The translator wanted to render John 1:14, where the Word is spoken of as "full of grace and truth." He argued with himself that naturally "grace" would be a "gift," but in this context at least it would have to be more than a gift. He would call it "a gift of life," or more literally, "a living gift." However, when his native helper was questioned about this word, he confessed that he did not understand it. Finally he said, "Well, I guess it means 'chicken.'" The point was that the only living (or live) gifts which the people ever exchanged were chickens. Hence, for the natives this passage declared that the Word was "full of chicken and truth."

As a solution to some of the more complicated problems of translating, it is often possible to borrow some technical word from the trade language spoken in the area. But such borrowing cannot be done without careful investigation; for once words have been borrowed, they acquire new meanings from the native culture and not from the culture from which they have come. The Motilone Indians of Venezuela borrowed the Spanish word *purísima* "purest" from the phrase *María purísima* "purest Mary," but the word *purísima* now means "devil" in the Motilone language. It may seem strange that the Motilones should have so altered the meaning of the word *purísima*, but the reason is not difficult to find. These Motilones heard the Spanish speakers using the phrase *María purísima* in precisely the kinds of situations in which they as Motilones would call upon their pagan deities. They could not conceive that the Spanish-speaking people would be calling upon good spirits to aid them in their questionable dealings, and so the Motilones concluded quite reasonably that this word *purísima* was the name of the Spanish devil.

A similar development occurred in one of the tribes on Luzon in the Philippines. The natives borrowed the Spanish word *seguro* "certain, sure" but with the meaning of "perhaps," which they interpreted from the actions of the Spanish-speaking people who used this word *seguro* to back up their very dubious statements.

The superficial veneer of religious terminology in Latin America can be readily recognized when one hears *gluria* (an adapted form of Spanish *gloria* "glory") used in some places to designate a drunken religious festival, or when one discovers that in the Isthmus Zapotec of Mexico the word *dumingu* (a borrowed form of *domingo* "Sunday") really means a dance, or when the Spanish word *ayuno* "fasting" cannot be employed in the Bolivian Quechua translation because it implies religious fasting until noon, to be followed by riotous drinking, all in honor of some local saint.

For those who regard only English as capable of fine distinctions of meaning, it may come as a shock to realize that other languages are often much more explicit about certain things. In the Kpelle language of Liberia the expression "my sheep follow me" (John 10:27) could be translated by three different expressions. However, two of these expressions would bear quite the wrong connotations. One of them would mean "follow me, but at a great distance." This is true enough of many people who claim to be Christians, but this is not what Jesus was saying. Another way of translating this phrase would mean "to stalk" or "to chase after," with the implication of evil intent. The correct translation is the third, which means "follow behind a leader."

By emphasizing the differences between languages it is possible for one to gather the impression that languages never use the same metaphors. This would be quite wrong. A Tarahumara Indian woman in the high mountains of northern Mexico may talk about her husband as "my old man." The Valientes in Panama may say, "He burned him up," when they mean that someone was made angry. Such metaphors sound vividly familiar.

The Shipibo idiom "to have a heart" sounds familiar enough to us, but it not only includes all that would be implied by the corresponding English expression, but goes beyond that and indicates a state of being socially well integrated. For the Shipibos the heart is the center of the personality. In an ideal sense one who possesses a personality should be integrated with others in the tribal unit. In Shipibo society the greatest emphasis is not upon being an outstanding personality, but upon one's ability to blend well into the social structure — making one's contribution without being self-assertive. This ideal is thus expressed in the metaphor "to have a heart."

But what is a person going to do if there are no metaphors and no ready-made expressions? The answer is, "Describe!" This is done in all languages. The Huanuco Quechua language of Peru has no current expression for "do not tempt God" (Matthew 4:7). These people probably never thought of this problem in the Biblical sense, but the present translation admirably describes this situation by saying, "Don't push God to do what you want." This sentence means more than even the English "tempt God," for our word "tempt" implies too much the idea of inducing to sin, and the real point of Matthew 4:7 is that we should not try to force God.

In the Black Thai language of Indo-China there seemed no way of talking about the "new birth." The word "new" simply could not be used with "birth," but the missionaries did solve the problem by using the phrase "birth to receive a new heart." After all, this is the meaning of the "new birth." The emphasis is not upon being born twice, but being born with a new nature.

Missionaries can work out alphabets and analyze grammars in a relatively few years. But it takes many years to enter into the soul of the language — its rich storehouse of idioms. Wooden, soulless translations can be made in a short time, but translations which speak intimately to the people must employ the inner language of the heart — not the outer language of commerce and business. In the Uduk language of the Anglo-Egyptian Sudan it would be possible to translate mundanely the phrase "mind your own business," but the Uduk way of speaking is "sit in the shade of your own hut," that is, do not be a busybody, snooping into others' affairs. In the Ngok Dinka one could translate literally "walk after the fashion of this world" (Ephesians 2:2), but this would be so inferior to the correct equivalent "sitting in the place of this world." The word "walking" has no metaphorical connection with behavior, while sitting does. In the Valiente language one can speak of "after sundown" in translating "evening," but the appropriate Valiente phrase is "the spirit of the day." In Aymara, an Indian language in the wind-swept highlands of Bolivia, the shore of the lake constitutes the "lips of the lake." In Shipibo a "cloud" is literally "sky-smoke," while in the Goajiro language of northern Colombia one speaks of a clear sky as consisting of "blue clouds."

Many native idioms reflect various mythological beliefs. The Mossi in French West Africa say that an eclipse of the moon is "a cat eating the moon," but the Miskitos in Nicaragua insist that "the moon has hold of his mother-in-law" — and is apparently getting the worst of it. We must not imagine, however, that such idioms imply literal belief in such ideas. The San Blas Indians call leprosy "the disease of a serpent bite." They recognize very well indeed that leprosy is not caused by a serpent bite, but this idiom has stuck. Its scientific accuracy is no more defended by them than the expression "devil's food cake" is to be taken literally as reflecting our beliefs. Native idioms are not without a humorous touch. The Uduks, for example, call the Adam's apple "the thing that wants beer."

As we study more and more of a language and interpret it in the light of the culture which it represents and of which it is a living part, we can understand more easily those features of the language which at first may have seemed quite contradictory and impossible. The scattered bands of warring Motilones in the rugged mountains on the frontier of Colombia and Venezuela have a word *etokapa* which they use in three quite distinct senses: (1) to commit suicide, (2) to make corn cakes, and (3) to hatch out eggs. Such meanings apparently bear no relationship to one another, but the Motilone Indians insist, and rightly so, that the word *etokapa* used in these three distinct senses is one and the same word. As we study the Motilone culture, however, it becomes evident that there is a very close relationship between these words, for all three actions involve egg-shaped objects. When a person dies, his body is wrapped up in an egg-shaped package and buried in the floor of the hut to rot. Then after about three years the bones are dug up and are wrapped in another oblong package and stored away in a distant mountain cave. The corn cakes are molded by hand into egg-shaped lumps and then boiled. Of course, the third meaning of hatching out eggs is readily relatable to the first two. The basic meaning of this verb *etokapa* is "an action having to do with egg-shaped objects." Once this is understood, then the relationship of the apparently unrelated meanings becomes obvious.

There is a certain sense in which many languages possess a number of specific, concrete terms but lack general, abstract ones. For instance, in Shipibo there are different names for all kinds of animals but no word for animals in general. On the other hand, aboriginal languages also possess generic terms which include extensive areas of meaning. In Ngok Dinka the word *dhueen* includes everything from "goodness" through "generosity" and up to and including "prestige." Such an almost unbelievable combination of ideas reflects, of course, the Dinka cultural setup, in which one cannot treasure up material possessions, for rotting mold attacks during the humid months of tropical downpours and innumerable rodents pillage the stored grain. Since it is impossible to horde, one is obliged to distribute generously to everyone. Then, in case of need, one may call upon them so as to receive in turn. Wealth and prestige are not dependent upon accumulated possessions, but upon one's capacity to give things away. The one word *dhueen* embraces all of this cultural pattern.

In foreign cultures there are always many features which appear quite contradictory. When we learn that in the Quechua dialect of Bolivia one must speak of the past as being ahead of one and the future as being behind one, we might be inclined to accuse the Quechuas of being stupid or of having a perverted philosophical orientation. Nevertheless, the Quechuas are fully able to defend themselves and their idioms. They argue, "Well, try to imagine, if you will, in your mind's eye the past and the future. Which can you see?" Our only possible answer is that we can see the past and not the future. "Right," they agree, "therefore, the past must be ahead of you and the future behind you." Our interpretation of the past and future is based upon movement; theirs is based on perspective. One is as valid as the other.

But can you talk about a "rectangular circle"? "Of course not!" anyone would say, but the Piro Indians in the jungles of southeastern Peru can use such a phrase and correctly so. The difference is that the geometrical perspective of the Piros is just not ours. They have a word *poprololu* which may be translated either as "square" or "round." What it really means is that the sides of the figures are of equal proportion, whether straight or curved. The word *gitpo* is generally translated "circle," but it primarily defines an object bounded by curved lines. The word *goshpotalu* means a rectangular or oblong object, but generally with right-angle corners. *Goshpotalgitpo* (a compound word made up of the second and third words listed above) does not mean "rectangular circle" as one might suppose at first glance, but identifies an oblong object of symmetrical, curved sides. Actually, none of these terms can be translated by any one term in English because the entire system of identifying geometric shapes is different from ours. Their system is equally as valid as ours and fully adequate to describe their elaborate and intricate designs painted on their pottery, clothing, and faces. The fact that the system is different from ours is no basis for depreciating it.

The more we assimilate of different cultural perspectives the more readily and more fully can we appreciate the idioms of other people. In the Yipounou language of the Gabon the equivalent of "they sent him away empty" (Mark 12:3) is "they sent him away holding his hands." The servant who was sent to carry back to his master some of the fruits of the vineyard was turned away without a thing. One can readily visualize this abused servant departing, holding nothing but his own hands. These are the word pictures which give life to the message.

Some of the word pictures of the Bible have grown dim to us because we no longer understand the culture out of which they have come. The phrase "sealed with the promised Holy Spirit" (Ephesians 1:13) is one of these. To so many persons "sealed" suggests "canned" and "preserved," while the Biblical idea is the confirmation of ownership. The Ngok Dinkas do not employ seals to indicate ownership nor do they confirm an agreement by using sealing wax and a signet ring, but they do mark ownership of their cattle by branding them. When speaking of the Christian's relationship to God, it is not enough to use the words "to brand," but this phrase has been expanded and enriched by the words "in the heart." Accordingly, Ephesians 1:13 reads, "You were branded in the heart by the Holy Spirit who was promised."

Words which in former days included bold figures of speech have often lost their meanings. This is true of the English word "hypocrite," which is a borrowing from Greek and originally meant "an actor." In the Malagasy language, however, the word for a hypocrite is fully understandable in terms of everyday life, for a hypocrite is "one who spreads a clean raffia carpet." The expression arises from the practice of some untidy housekeepers who happen to glance out, and seeing a visitor approaching up the path, hastily take down from the wall a clean raffia carpet and quickly spread it over the dirty, unswept floor. Hypocrites are regarded as specializing in this kind of rapid outward transformation, while remaining at heart their same dirty selves.

Leo Spitzer

AMERICAN ADVERTISING EXPLAINED AS POPULAR ART

𝓚𝓚

You may never have seen the particular advertisement for Sunkist oranges that the late Professor Leo Spitzer explicates in this essay. He evokes the advertisement so fully that you will imagine it clearly anyway. As a result of his sensitive and deep probing into the meanings, implications, and effects of its pictorial and verbal devices, you will come to understand how it and countless advertisements like it reflect "the spirit of our time and of our nation." Not all ads make their appeals in the same way. But Spitzer's approach will work very often and will help you to understand why it pays to study advertising.

The philological method of *explication de texte* is usually applied to works of art and works of great art. But, at all times, there has existed, side by side with great art, that everyday art which the Germans have called

From *Essays on English and American Literature* by Leo Spitzer. Reprinted by permission of the Princeton University Press. Copyright © 1962 by Princeton University Press. Used also by permission of Professor Spitzer's Literary Executor. This essay first appeared in A *Method of Interpreting Literature* (Smith College, 1949), pp. 102–49.

Gebrauchskunst ("applied practical art"): that art which has become a part of the daily routine and which adorns the practical and the utilitarian with beauty. At no time has this type of art played so compensatory a role as is the case today, in the age of machinism, of rationalization, and of the subjection of man to the impersonal necessities of social, economic, and political life. An emphasis on the beautiful has penetrated all levels of fabrication, down to mucilage bottles and matchbooks, and to the packaging of goods; it has also penetrated to the forms of propaganda used to advertise these goods. And the success of such attempts at aesthetic appeal achieved by modern advertising is borne out by the many exhibits of original commercial designs which have attracted a large public. It is also true that particularly novel and clever devices of advertising find an appreciative echo among sophisticated journalists, and there exists today a whole literature devoted to the requirements of effective advertisements. In such treatments, however, the emphasis is generally placed on the psychological element and on the utilitarian efficacy of the propaganda, while little or no attention is paid to the aesthetic as such, to the artistic tradition in which the particular advertisement has its place, to the satisfaction which advertising may offer of contemporary extra-commercial needs, or, finally, to the historical explanation of the phenomenon of advertising, which must, somehow, be related to the American national character and cultural history.[1] Can the linguistically minded literary historian, who harbors no snobbish feelings toward this genre of applied art, give an *explication de texte* of a good sample of modern advertising, in which he would proceed from the exterior features to the "spirit of the text" (and to the spirit of the genre), just as he is accustomed to do with literary texts? Let us try the experiment.

[1] Such a study presupposes that type of "symbolizing" thinking which has been advocated in the introduction to my book, *Linguistics and Literary History* (Princeton University Press, 1948); to see the relationship between an everyday detail which is, all too often, simply taken for granted, and a spiritual entity in itself not unknown, but only vaguely and separately conceived — this is, I believe, to take a step toward the understanding of the well-motivated, coherent, and consistent organism which our civilization is. It is not enough, in the case of American advertising, to admire or savor a new coinage, psychological trick, or strategy, as this may develop in the technique in question: one must try to see the manifold cross-relationships between the detail (the advertisement) and the whole (our civilization) in order that our capacity for feeling at home in this civilization and of enjoying it will be increased. I may say that, in the matter of understanding one's civilization, the French (incidentally, the inventors of the *explication de texte*) have a great advantage over Americans, who, as it seems to me, are less given to probing into the motivation behind the products of their civilization; the French are past masters in establishing (sometimes to excess) relationships between specific aspects of their civilization (French literature or French cuisine) and this civilization itself; they are able to recognize even in the most trivial detail the expression of an implicit national profession of faith. The present writer must confess that it was by applying *explication de texte* to American advertising that he was given the first avenue (a "philological" avenue) leading toward the understanding of the unwritten text of the American way of life.

In undertaking this study, I shall be attempting to apply my method to things American, with which my listeners will be much more familiar than I — a circumstance which, in itself, can only provide a better test of the method. It is needless to state that, in line with this method, I shall here carefully avoid the biographical or pragmatically historical approach: I know nothing about the genesis of the particular advertisement to be discussed, about the persons involved in the choice of the name of the particular product, or about the history of the business firm in question. I shall seek to analyze a given advertisement in the same unbiased manner as I have attempted to do in the case of a poem of St. John of the Cross or of a letter of Voltaire, believing, as I do, that this kind of art, if not comparable in greatness to the texts usually analyzed by the scholar, offers nevertheless a "text" in which we can read, as well in its words as in its literary and pictorial devices, the spirit of our time and of our nation — which are, surely, in their way, "unmittelbar zu Gott."* To adopt a resentful or patronizing attitude toward our time is, obviously, the worst way to understand it. Meditation is needed in the face of things modern as of things ancient. Finally, since the following study is intended as an *explication de texte*, it is hardly necessary to warn the reader that the discussion will be mainly limited to one "text," to one example of one particular type of advertising; there is no intention on my part of offering a general survey of advertising trends.

In the drugstores throughout our country, the brand of oranges known as *Sunkist* was advertised some years ago by the following picture-with-text: on a high mountain range, covered with snow that glistens in the bright sunshine, furrowed by vertical gullies, towering over a white village with its neat, straight rows of orange trees, there rests a huge orange-colored sun, inscribed with the word "Sunkist." In front of this vista, set squarely in the midst of the groves, is a glass of orange-juice which rises to the exact height of the mountain range and whose color exactly matches that of the sun ball. Next to this gigantic glass of juice is a smaller one of the same color, and next to that, a fruit-squeezer on which lies the orange to be squeezed. In the left corner of the advertisement we read, as the only inscription:

From the sunkist groves of California
Fresh for you

The first feature we will observe is that in advertising its *Sunkist* oranges, the firm did not expatiate on the goodness, juiciness, flavor, *etc.*, of this particular "ready-made" type of product, but chose to trace the origin of the product back to the groves which yielded it, so that we may concentrate our attention on the natural beauty of California. From the fruit, our

---

* *Editors' translation:* "a direct route to God."

glance is allowed to pass to the countryside, to the soil, to Nature that grows the fruit — and only to Nature, not to the orange-growers or those who pick the fruit, not the packers who prepare its distribution, not to any human factor. It is Nature that, as by a miracle, brings forth these "sunkist" oranges, brings them "fresh for you," from California. The commercial product (those millions of oranges packed methodically in thousands of cases and transported by the railroads) is shown against the background of its natural environment — indeed, the glass of orange-juice, as we have seen, is set down right in the midst of Nature. In the inscription, there is not even the verbal form "brought" which would suggest human activity: the oranges kissed by the sun are there as an accomplished fact; their transportation over miles and miles of territory is passed over in silence. The elimination of man from this pictorial representation, the concentration on productive Nature and on the miracle of the final appearance of the juice, as we have it before us in our drugstores, represents a highly poetic procedure, since, thereby, our everyday causality (the laws of supply and demand, of mass production and lowered prices) is replaced by other laws (the laws of Nature — and of the miracle); and on our routine reality there is superimposed another, dream-like, reality: the consumer may have the illusion, for a moment, of drinking nectar at the source. And the public accepts willingly the hypocrisy of the artist. It is as though this manifestation of commercial self-expression were denying its essential purpose, that of selling and of profit-making; as though the business world were engrossed only in harvesting what Nature gives and in bringing her gifts to the individual enjoyer — in an Arcadian life harmonious with Nature. In the city drugstore, over whose counter this sunny picture shines, the wall opens up before us like a window on Nature. Business becomes poetic because it recognizes the great grip which poetry has on this modern unpoetic world. It is true that the subtle device of eliminating man is calculated only to bring man back again into the picture; for what, the spectator must ask himself upon reflection, has made possible the miracle of transportation and of transformation, if not the skill, indeed, the magic, of modern industry? And the modest way in which the business firm hides its own tremendous activity behind anonymous Nature will impress us favorably.

Now, when business becomes poetic, for whatever reasons, it must subject itself to the ancient laws of poetry, which remain unshaken by the technical developments of the modern world. We can, then, expect to find in this business art the old, time-honored poetic devices. And, indeed, is the poetically achieved evocation of the natural state of the product of human industry anything but the repetition of a device known to the ancient and the Renaissance poets? We may remember the anonymous inscription (listed in Bartlett's *Familiar Quotations* — 11th ed., p. 1092) discovered on an old violin: *Arbor viva, tacui; mortua, cano.** Or again — why not? — we might think of the lines in Góngora's *Soledades* in which the drowning protagonist rescues himself by means of a floating spar — which is described in terms of the original living pine tree, that once resisted the blasts of the north wind and now resists the floods:

> Del siempre en la montaña opuesto pino
> al enemigo Noto
> piadoso miembro roto
> — breve tabla. . . .**

Similarly, the poet who devised the *Sunkist* advertisement reminds us, when we put a dime down on the counter for a glass of orange-juice, of all the sunshine that went into this refreshing drink: as if we should be able to buy for so small a sum the inexhaustible source of warmth and fecundity, the Sun. We came to the counter for reasons of practical necessity; we walk away, having seen the picture and enjoyed the juice, with an insight into the generosity of Nature and the persistence of its goodness in its smallest yields.

Recourse was had to another ancient poetic and pictorial device when our poet chose to point out a continuous line between the orange-juice and California Nature: he wished to trace a consistent link between the *Sunkist* orange and the orange-juice by use of a motif which shows how Nature plans and man carries out her will: this fusion of man's and Nature's activities manifests itself in the repetition of one motif which has a central part in these activities — the motif of the orange, pictorially represented by means of the unifying orange color. In all, we have the one orange-color motif repeated four times: a natural orange, two glasses of orange-juice, and the "sun" itself (which bears the inscription "Sunkist"); in this representation is offered the symbol of the unity, of the harmony of Nature's and man's concern with the fruit. And, here, modern advertising is returning to a medieval form. On the 11th century portal of the Hildesheim cathedral, in a bas-relief representing the scene of the Fall of Man, we may see four apples which traverse the sculpture in one horizontal line: one is in the mouth of the dragon in the tree, one in Eve's hand, one is figured as the apple of her breast, and one is in the hand of Adam. The central motif in the medieval work of art, the apple, is, of course, the symbol of the forbidden fruit, whereas the central motif in our modern work of *Gebrauchskunst* serves the praise of the natural fruit accessible to all; again, the momentous event of Man's Fall is presented in slow motion, broken up into stages, whereas man's progress in the exploitation of Nature comes to us

---

* *Editors' translation:* "While a live tree, I was silent; dead, I sing."
** *Editors' translation:* "Kind, broken spar, small board of the pine in the mountain, always opposed to its enemy, the North wind."

with an acceleration provided by the technique of the "accomplished fact." Nevertheless, the basic technique, that of the didactically repeated central motif, is the same; modern pantheism has espoused forms of art devised in the religious climate of the Middle Ages.

There may be discerned in this device a subsidiary feature which might appear incongruous with the realism supposedly required in a genre devoted to such practical ends: the "sun-orange" which figures in our picture and which borrows the *exact* shade of coloring from the fruit on which it shines, is a quite violent, surrealistic misrepresentation of reality, apparently symbolical of the powerful attraction exerted by business, which draws all things into its orbit — which puts even the sun to work. Or, perhaps, may we not have to do with the myth of an orange-sun (figured by a sun-orange), which would have the particular function of nurturing orange groves — just as there were ancient *Sondergötter*, particular gods devoted to the growing of wine, of cereals, etc.; just as there are Catholic saints devoted to particular industries and particular natural processes? (A black Madonna caring especially for Negro worshippers is no more startling than is the orange sun which takes its color from the thing it grows.)

As for the gross misrepresentation of size which appears in the gigantic glass of orange-juice in the foreground, which is equal in height to the California mountain range and, despising all laws of proportion, completely overshadows the orange-squeezer, this focuses our attention on the protagonist of the scene, on that glass of juice you will order at the counter — with the same "naïve" technique of the medieval paintings, in which Christ is presented taller than his disciples and these taller than common folk (and which is reflected also in the Nuremberg tin soldiers, whose captain is twice as tall as the common soldier); the significance of a figure is translated into material size. One could, perhaps, think that the huge size of the glass in the foreground is due to a naïve application of the law of the perspective — if it were not for the presence, also in the foreground, of the smaller glass and the fruit-squeezer of normal proportions.

But why does the glass appear twice, as giant and as dwarf, when there is no difference of technical stages between them? Is the glass of normal size a concession to the realism of the beholder, an apology for the colossal glass which had to be honored and magnified as the protagonist? According to this, we should have, along with the fantastic, the criticism thereof — as in the *Don Quijote*, with its double perspective. Thus the element of naïveté would be far from absolute: the naïve and the critical attitudes being juxtaposed. And this twin presentation serves also the more practical aim of attracting "consumer interest": we see first the sun, then the groves of California, then the picked fruit, then the finished product (the glass of orange-juice) — and, finally, in the glass of normal size (the size of the glass to be had at the drugstore counter) we are shown the customer's own personal glass of *Sunkist* orange-juice: by this reduplication in small, the line beginning at the sun is prolonged out from the picture, in the direction of the customer — who, in taking up the glass of orange-juice, puts himself into direct contact with the California sun.[2] In the glass-that-is-the-customer's-glass there is the suggestion to the prospective customer: "*Have* a glass [of this juice]." The imperative which was carefully avoided in the text is insinuated by the picture.

If we now analyze our own analysis, we see that the first general impression was that of a tribute to the fertility of Nature; after reflection, we are made aware of the necessary intervention of man himself (not only the enterprise of the business firm but also the participation of the consumer). We are left, then with the realization that the advertiser has fooled neither us nor himself as to the real purpose of his propaganda. That glass of orange-juice as tall as the mountains of California is a clear testimonial to the businessman's subjective estimation of the comparative importance of business interests. Indeed, when we review the violence done to Nature in our picture (displacement of proportions, surrealistic use of a motif, change of the natural color of objects), we see how, in a very artistic manner, this procedure has served to illustrate, in a spirit, ultimately, of candid self-criticism, the very nature of business which, while associating itself with Nature, subordinates her to its purpose — and to ours. Our picture has used all the attractions of living Nature in order to advertise her commercialized form.

Before concluding the analysis of the pictorial elements of our advertisement, we must note the failure to present graphically the metaphor indicated by the trademark: we do not see the oranges being kissed by the sun. No trace of solar activity is suggested — even in the traditional, schematic form of rays. For this sun is no living entity, it is an emblem, an ideogram created by the advertisers to bear their label. Emblematic poetry uses stereotyped symbols; just as in 16th and 17th century imagery, the arrow of Cupid or the scythe of Death represented ready-made ingredients, the modern industrial labels are (or at least anticipate being) permanent: the *Sunkist* business firm is more interested in propagating its label than in re-enacting the original metaphor. (We are far from the atmosphere of the Greek world where personal gods embrace and beget.) On the other hand, we do not find in the caption of our advertisement the label as such, only a reference to *sunkist groves*. In this way, the reader is cleverly led to retrace

[2] It may be noted that the invitation to drink offered by our advertisement stops short of guaranteeing either the virtue of the product or the happiness in store for the consumer.

If Philip Wylie, in his diatribe, *Generation of Vipers* (1943), 220, is right in indicting "90%" of commercial advertising on the grounds that it promotes a general feeling in the public that material goods can add to their personal happiness and social worth ("cars are, after all, mechanical objects, and nothing else. The rest of the qualities that are attributed to them in the ads . . . belong to *people*. Purchase and possession does not, in itself, do anything to an individual"), then our *Sunkist* advertisement, which promises no transformation of character, would belong to the unimpeached 10%.

the origin of the label. Many years ago the label *Sunkist* had been coined and it had become generally accepted, its pristine freshness lost. With the reference to *sunkist groves* (notice that *sunkist* is not capitalized!) it is as though we were presented with the original situation that inspired the name, with the "pre-proper-name state" or etymology of the trademark.

Now, if we consider the phrase "sunkist groves" from a philological point of view, it is to be noted that this was intended as a poetic expression:[3] it is to be doubted whether millions of Americans have ever read or heard the word "sun-kissed" — except as the denomination of a brand of oranges. At the same time, however, it does not have the flavor of distinguished poetry; the expression "sun-kissed" itself is rather stalely poetic (the only attestation, according to the NED is from a certain E. Brannan: 1873), and the particular form "-kist" is, in addition, a sentimental pastiche of Shakespearian style.[4] It is very interesting to note, however, that this would-be poetic spelling is also reminiscent of the tendency illustrated, for

[3] I do not know the exact date of the coinage of the *Sunkist* trademark, but I assume that it preceded the expansion of the "vitamin myth" as we have this today in America (the word *vitamin* itself was first used by Casimir Funk in 1912). Nevertheless, it is possible that the originally "poetic" term *Sunkist* may have become secondarily attracted into the orbit of that "poetry of science" which has developed from the vision of a world in which longevity and undiminished vigor will be the result of a diet of correctly balanced vitamins. Since oranges, like other citrus fruits, contain the (anti-scorbutic) vitamin C, and since the development of the (anti-rachitic) vitamin D is promoted by the sun (particularly by its ultra-violet rays), and since, too, there is a general tendency on the part of the public to associate loosely all the various vitamins, it would be in line with that poetry of science espoused by the salesman to present the oranges as actually containing the vitamins fostered by the sun: in the advertisement of another firm of orange-growers their fruit-juice is presented as "canned liquid sun." Again, we find, in one of Katherine Anne Porter's short stories, the picture of a travelling salesman of cooking utensils who praises a particular vegetable cooker for its vitamin-preserving qualities, and uses the phrase "those precious sun-lit vitamins" — as if assuming that wherever there are vitamins there the sun must be also. I cannot, of course, be sure how much this secondary flow of scientific poetry has colored, for the minds of the average person who sees the *Sunkist* advertisement, the traditional associations of the all-embracing and all-nurturing sun.

[4] It is obvious that "the poetry of advertising" can never be vanguard poetry: in the period of a Frost it can never be "Frostian," but only Emersonian, Tennysonian, Swinburnian, Elizabethan; it must have a familiar ring, must reproduce the stock poetic devices which the average reader of advertising has been taught to accept as poetic — the folklore of poetry, as it were.

Miss Anna Hatcher has shown in MLN, LXI (1946), 442–47, "Twilight Splendor, Shoe Colors, Bolero Brilliance," that the style of advertising, in borrowing from stock poetic devices, may succeed so completely in acclimatizing these that they are henceforth ruined for poetry. Shakespeare could coin *maiden blushes*, and Keats, *maiden bloom*, but this type is apt to be eschewed in poetry today, when *Maidenform* is the trademark of a brassière.

Incidentally, advertising may set its mark not only on "poetic" patterns but also on phrases common in everyday use: for example, when I wished to conclude a scholarly article with the statement "The reader must be the judge [in this moot question]," I was warned against using a formula current in advertising ("The consumer must be the judge").

One might also mention, in this connection, the verb "to offend," which has become a euphemism for "to smell of perspiration."

example, by the use of *nite* for *night*, or *u* for you (*Uneeda Biscuit*), which is to be found only in arrantly commercial language (and which is due, I have been told, to an economical desire to save space; for myself, however, I am inclined to believe that it is inspired by the more positive desire to create an energetic, streamlined impression of efficiency).[5] We have, that is, to do with a hybrid form, suggestive of two mutually exclusive stylistic environments. And something of this same duality obtains with the compound form consisting of "ablative" + participle: unlike so many compounds, this particular type (*God-given, heaven-blest, man-made, wind-tossed, rain-swept, etc.*) was originally highly literary, and even today it is excluded from colloquial speech. When first introduced into advertising, it represented a literary effort on the part of the writer — though this may no longer be true of all advertising writers, just as it is probably not true of most of their readers, who perhaps are acquainted only with the commercial flavor of the type *oven-baked beans, etc.* As for the particular expression *sunkist*, we are probably justified in assuming a "poetic" intention on the part of the creator of the coinage because of the poetic nature of the concept involved ("kissed by the sun"); at the same time, however, he must have been conscious of its commercial by-flavor; he has been able to play on two chessboards, to appeal to two types of consumers; those who admire a brisk, efficient businesslike style, and those who think that "the sun of Homer, it shineth still on us." Thus our hybrid word, which is without roots in normal speech, is doomed to a homeless existence: *sunkist* is possible only in that No Man's Land where the prosaic is shunned — but the poetic is taken not quite seriously.

And this last fact explains, perhaps, why it can be that businessmen should be so eager to coin, as a technical, commercial term, such a word as *sunkist*, which appeals to poetic imagination in a manner and to a degree quite at variance with their own and their public's speech, and in utter contradiction to what we are supposed to accept as the essential characteristic of business. Psychologists would answer with the concept of "affective appeal," the tendency by which feelings that are aroused by one stimulus will spread and attach themselves to other stimuli. But I fear that the psychologists of advertising oversimplify the psychology of the advertiser — who is not only a businessman but a human being: one who is endowed with all the normal potentialities of emotion and who finds expression of these in the exercise of his profession. In his private life, in his social relations, he has been taught to minimize or even to ridicule the poetic apperception of life; the idea of whiling away his leisure time by composing sonnet sequences, as is quite common with his counterpart in South

[5] How the idea of efficiency and easy functioning may influence the syntax of advertising ("This car parks easily," "This paint applies easily") and, subsequently (if ironically), common speech, has been shown in an article by Professor Hatcher in *MLN*, LVIII (1943), 8–17: "Mr. Howard amuses easy."

America, would be almost unthinkable to him. But his copywriter feels free to indulge in that poetic fancy from which his superior, the business executive, ordinarily shies away (let us not forget that many a copywriter is a thwarted poet whose college dreams have not quite come true). And why does the advertiser, whose mouthpiece is the copywriter, allow himself to be presented before the public as a poet *malgré lui?* Surely it is because he feels himself protected, he feels the fanciful words of the advertisement protected, by invisible "quotation marks" which can ward off the possible ridicule of the public and which exculpate him, in his own eyes, for his daring.

By "quotation marks" I mean to characterize an attitude toward language which is shared by the speaker and his public, and according to which he may use words with the implication: "I have good reasons for saying this — but don't pin me down!" The public, for its part, reacts accordingly: there is on both sides a tacit understanding of the rules of the game (a game which also involves the necessary embellishment by the seller of his products and a corresponding attitude of sales-resistance on the part of the prospect). Thus the word *sunkist* comes to us with its range calculated and delimited, with its impact of reality reduced; this word is noncommittal of reality; it transports the listener into a world of Arcadian beauty, but with no insistence that this world really exists. Of course, the beautiful groves of California which produce excellent oranges do exist, but a world in which they may really be called "sunkist" does not. And everyone knows that, while the advertised goods may be quite first-rate, the better world which the advertiser evokes is a never-never land.[6] Nonetheless, the idealizations of advertising are not wasted upon the listener: though he cannot take up forthwith his dwelling in the paradisiac world filled with

---

[6] The world of optimism and idealism which advertising unfolds before us is reflected in its predilection for the superlative; each of the goods praised is supposedly the finest of its kind, from the tastiest bread in America to the most perfect low-priced car in America. This superlative which rules supreme, and which is not challenged by any factual comparison (since disparaging statements about goods of competitors is prohibited by law) tends to destroy the difference between the superlative and the elative: "the finest . . ." becomes equal to "a very fine . . . ," somewhat equivalent to the Italian elative *buonissimo* (not *il migliore*). The abolition of true comparison ("good" — "better" — "best") is easily understandable in a world containing only "best" things.

As another variety of the advertising elative, we may mention the use of the comparative, which the *New Yorker* has recently defined as the "agency comparative" or the "comparative without comparison": an item is called "better" without any further qualification: "Better than what?" asks the *New Yorker.* (A parallel case is the absolute use in advertising of "different" [even a laxative medicament is called simply "different"], patterned on the popular usage with its slightly snobbish overtones.) Cf. E. K. Sheldon's article on "The Rise of the Incomplete Comparative" in *American Speech,* xx (1945), 161–67.

Incidentally, it is interesting that in a satirical magazine such as the *New Yorker.* where the stories as well as the illustrations and cartoons are intended as a criticism of the easily beautiful and of conventional standards — the advertisements are allowed to provide, unquestioned, the illusory beauty and the snobbism typical of their genre.

fragrant groves where golden fruit slowly ripen under the caress of the sun, his imagination has made the detour through this *word-paradise* and carries back the poetic flavor which will season the physical enjoyment of the orange-juice he will drink for breakfast the next morning. Here, in an unexpected corner of our technologically organized age, and in the service of the most highly rationalized interests, poetry has developed its most miraculous quality: that of establishing a realm of pure, gratuitous, disinterested beauty, which has existence only in the imagination. And the poetic achievement is presented to the public with all sincerity — and with all cautiousness: with overtones of irony which preclude any too-serious commitment.

If we ask ourselves with which historical literary climate we should associate this playful language of advertisement, which is satisfied with feigning gratuitously an ideal *word-world* in empty space, the kinship with certain baroque or *précieux* ways of speech becomes evident: "sunkist" for "oranges" belongs to a poetic "as-if" speech, no different essentially from *conseiller des grâces** for *miroir*.

Préciosité and the parallel baroque styles of euphuism, *Schwulst, marinismo*, and *gongorismo*** (it was not unadvisedly that we quoted above a passage from Góngora) have their cultural roots in a polar tension between life as it is and life as it should be: reality appears on the one hand with all the attractions of beautiful sensuousness and, on the other, beclouded by our consciousness of the futility of these attractions, by the feeling of *desengaño**** — a feeling which prevailed even in France, where only the most "reasonable" variant of the baroque existed. One knows quite well that the mirror cannot always counsel graceful behavior, but one lends it this role in order to create an illusion absolutely unwarranted by reality. The *précieuse* dwells in that borderland of poetry which could "perhaps" be true, but, as she knows, it is not true — this is an example of the same mild form of wishful thinking which is at the bottom of American advertising. The American public, exposed at every moment to the impact of advertising propaganda, easily applies its grain of salt; it does not condemn outright the excesses of *préciosité*, as did Molière's Gorgibus; it can afford to let itself be seduced to a certain point, for it is fully aware of the matter-of-fact reality of the product advertised. Thus, an attitude of *desengaño* would seem to be present here, too; does this represent a general disillusionment, due to particular unfortunate experiences in American history: to the disenchantment of pioneers who had left the Old World in search of a better one — or who, already in this country, had turned to the West in search of gold — and have often seen their hopes frustrated? In view of the

---

* *Editors' translation:* "counselor of graceful behavior."
** *Editors' Note:* These four terms can be applied to a florid, highly ornate style which makes extensive use of elaborate images and metaphors.
*** *Editors' translation:* "disillusionment."

ingrained optimism which still today enables the American to meet each calamity with his hopes of a better deal just around the corner,[7] this hypothesis can hardly endure. Nor can we assume, in the case of the situation of advertising, any actual distrust of the merits of any particular product; there is, undoubtedly, in America an attitude of confidence (supported, it is true, by a whole framework of supervisory regulations) in the factual truthfulness of the claims made by manufacturers. I should say that, in the skeptical, or half-skeptical attitude of the American public[8] in regard to advertising, we may see that basic mistrust of language itself which is one of the most genuine features of the Anglo-Saxon character,[9] as opposed to

[7] It could be said that the American's optimism is also reflected in the abundance of neologisms in advertising: by coining new words one suggests a picture of new and therefore better things to come. This tendency also reveals a special attitude toward language itself as something continuously in flux (as Mencken has repeatedly emphasized) — an attitude which shares with the first a basic "future-mindedness."

Any neologism, however, in the course of time, tends to lose its freshness once it has been accepted by the community — in which case the linguists must speak of "lexicological petrification." The advertisers themselves eventually recognize that the inevitable stage of lexicalization has set in, and are careful thereafter not to stir the ashes of the dead — for any insistence on the symbolic value once possessed by the label would be tedious to the public.

[8] In no language, so far as I know, are there so many prefixes which tend to unmask false values: *pseudo-*, *sham-*, *make-believe-*, *makeshift-*, *mock-*, *would-be-*, *fake-*, *phony-*, *semi-*, *near-*[beer], *baloney-*[dollars], *synthetic-*, *etc.*; it is as though the Anglo-Saxon attitude of distrust of the pretentious would find for itself a grammatically fixed pattern of expression in the language. Americans delight in their impermeability to "bunk" (as is shown by the fertility of the "buncombe" word-family).

[9] It would seem that there is a difference in this regard between the two Anglo-Saxon nations themselves, if we are to believe D. W. Brogan (*The American Character*, New York, 1944), who has been struck by the American love for oratory (p. 131): "In Chambers of Commerce, at Rotary Club meetings, at college commencements, in legislatures, in Congress, speech is treated seriously, according to the skill and taste of the user. There is no fear of boss words or of eloquence, no fear of clichés, no fear of bathos. . . . The British listener, above all the English listener, is surprised and embarrassed by being asked to applaud statements whose truth he has no reason to doubt, but whose expression seems to him remarkably abstract and adorned with flowers of old-fashioned rhetoric." Mr. Brogan gives himself the explanation that Americans "like slogans, like words. They like absolutes in ethics." And the English critic might have brought up the contrast between the American Constitution and the unwritten British Constitution.

On the other hand, I would suggest that there is an English brand of oratory which is slightly alien to the American — for example, the prose of Churchill, which, with its archaisms and periphrastic turns of speech, weaves poetry round the casual concrete happenings of history; by the Americans the "word" is considered less as an artistic than as a moral tool, as abstractly purposeful as the flag. But, even in the realm of absolute morals, the distrust of language is not entirely lacking with Americans; Mr. Brogan himself cannot overlook the fact that many slogans are greeted by Americans with an ironical "Oh, yeah?" or "However you slice it, it's still baloney." How else save by mistrust of the word could one explain the fact that after the exchange of wild abuse indulged in on both sides during an election campaign, Americans, once the election is over, are able to go quietly to work the next day, no attempt being made by the defeated party to start a revolution. The word in itself is not "sacred" and final to the Americans. The difference between the American and the German concepts of the word can be seen in the absence of free speech in Germany: freedom of speech involves a concept of non-finality of speech. In America the human word is thought of only as having a provisionary value. One word can be undone, and outdone, by another.

the trust in words by which the Romance peoples are animated — those *Wortmenschen*, as Schuchardt has called them, whose esthetics Benedetto Croce has formulated in the postulate: "Quello che non è espresso non esiste!"* For the Anglo-Saxon, on the contrary, reality remains ultimately inexpressible. Such a people will, obviously, have a mistrust of poetry because of its too easy, too felicitous finds which cannot be made to square with the complexity of reality. Now since, in the game continually going on between the advertiser and the public, the customer is expected to take the role of skeptic, it is possible for poetry to be given full play; the advertiser does not ask that his words be taken completely at face value, and he must not be held to literal account for the truth of every syllable. Thus the poetry of advertisement can be truly enjoyed because it makes none of the solemn claims of literary poetry. It is precisely because Americans know reality so well, because they ask to face it, and do not like to be hoodwinked, because they are not easily made victims of metaphysical word-clouds as are the Germans, or of word-fulgurations, as are the French, that they can indulge in the *acte gratuit* of the human word in its poetical nowhereness. So fully aware is the advertiser of this discounting attitude on the part of his public that, not infrequently, he anticipates the forthcoming skepticism by the feint of self-indictment — as when Macy's apologizes prettily for its many entrances, but insists, for the reassurance of harassed husbands shopping for their wives, that not *all* subway exits lead to their store. And, in a more pedantic, statistical vein, the well-known claim of "99⁴⁴⁄₁₀₀%" of purity uses a screen of scrupulous precision and self-criticism to advance the claim of what is, after all, an extraordinary degree of near-perfection.

Every work of art is addressed to a public, whether outspokenly or implicitly. A painting on the wall, for example, is an invitation to the beholder to engage in a relationship with it; there are always involved in the painting $n + 1$ elements, with n elements included from the beginning in the work of art itself; and $n + 1$ remains the formula even when there are several beholders. In the case of three persons, for example, the relationships between them and the picture of n elements would be $n + 1^a$, $n + 1^b$, $n + 1^c$ respectively — and in the case of x persons $n + 1^x$. Now we have seen how, in the case of our advertising picture, there has been established, by means of that second glass of normal proportions, a relationship between the groves of California and the ultimate individual consumer. At the same time, this personal relationship is underscored (in a manner unknown to other works of art) by the phrase "fresh *for you*," which every customer must understand as a personal address to himself (incidentally these three words of personal address are printed in script). In this *you* we have, obviously, a device which is not peculiar to the picture in question but is highly representative of the genre itself, and is a quite common feature

---

* *Editors' translation:* "What is not expressed does not exist."

to be found in every page of the daily newspaper. If we would ask ourselves what is involved in the use of this advertising "you," we must first inquire, superfluous and far-fetched as the procedure may seem, into the meaning of this second personal pronoun, according to the philosophy of grammar. "You" is a startling word: it calls up the dormant ego in every human being: "you" is in fact nothing but the ego seen by another; it addresses itself to our feeling that we are a unified person recognizable from the outside; it also suggests someone outside of us who is able to say "you" and who feels akin to "us" as a fellow man. Now, in English, the pronoun "you" enjoys an ambiguity to a degree unknown in the main European languages, which are characterized by greater inflection; it is equally applicable to a singular or a plural audience, and, in advertising, this double reference is fully exploited: the advertiser, while preparing his copy for the general public, thinks the "you" as an "all of you" — but intends it to be interpreted as a "you personally," applicable to the individual A, B, or C. In the case of our advertisement A translates the algebraic X of the "you" as "fresh for *me* has the orange been brought here from California"; and B and C do the same. Though he is only one of millions, every single individual is individually addressed and flattered.

Jules Henry

ADVERTISING AS A PHILOSOPHICAL SYSTEM

☙☙

Leo Spitzer's approach to advertising, as seen in the previous essay, is basically objective; he is not explicitly concerned with the morality of advertising. But Jules Henry says that the book from which the following selection is excerpted "is not an objective description of

America, but rather a passionate ethnography . . . . Since I have an attitude toward culture, I discuss data as illustrative of a viewpoint and as a take-off for expressing a conviction." One of these convictions is that ours is a driven culture, a culture which generates the continuous urge for expansion, competition, and achievement. Advertising is a prime agency in fostering these drives, a system whose first commandment is CREATE NEW DESIRE. *Mr. Henry studies the language of this system to reveal how it accomplishes its ends.*

Advertising is an expression of an irrational economy that has depended for survival on a fantastically high standard of living incorporated into the American mind as a moral imperative. Yet a moral imperative cannot of itself give direction; there must be some institution or agency to constantly direct and redirect the mind and emotions to it. This function is served for the high-rising living standard by advertising which, day and night, with increasing pressure reminds us of what there is to buy; and if money accumulates for one instant in our bank accounts, advertising reminds us that it must be spent and tells us how to do it. As a quasi-moral institution advertising, like any other basic cultural institution anywhere, must have a philosophy and a method of thinking. The purpose of this chapter is to demonstrate the character of advertising thought, and to show how it relates to other aspects of our culture. In order to make this relationship manifest at the outset I have dubbed this method of thought *pecuniary philosophy.*

THE PROBLEM

Since the problem of truth is central to all philosophy, the reader is asked to ask himself, while perusing the following advertising, "Is it literally true that . . ."

. . . everybody's talking about the new *Starfire* [automobile]?

. . . *Alpine* cigarettes "put the men in menthol smoking"?

. . . a woman in *Distinction* foundations is so beautiful that all other women want to kill her?

. . . *Hudson's Bay Scotch* "is scotch for the men among men"?

. . . if one buys clothes at Whitehouse and Hardy his wardrobe will have "the confident look of a totally well-dressed man"?

. . . *Old Spice* accessories are "the finest grooming aides a man can use"?

. . . 7 *Crown* whiskey "holds within its icy depths a world of summertime"?

... "A man needs *Jockey* support" because *Jockey* briefs "give a man the feeling of security and protection he needs"?

... one will "get the smoothest, safest ride of your life on tires of *Butyl*"?

... the new *Pal Premium Injector* blade "takes the friction out of shaving" because it "rides on liquid ball bearings"?

... *Pango Peach* color by Revlon comes "from east of the sun ... west of the moon where each tomorrow dawns" ... is "succulent on your lips" and "sizzling on your finger tips (And on your toes, goodness knows)" and so will be one's "adventure in paradise"?

... if a woman gives in to her "divine restlessness" and paints up her eyelids with *The Look* her eyes will become "jungle green ... glittery gold ... flirty eyes, tiger eyes"?

... a "new ingredient" in *Max Factor Toiletries* "separates the men from the boys"?

... when the Confederate General Basil Duke arrived in New York at the end of the Civil War "*Old Crow* [whiskey] quite naturally would be served"?

... *Bayer* aspirin provides "the fastest, most gentle to the stomach relief you can get from pain"?

Are these statements, bits of advertising copy, true or false? Are they merely "harmless exaggeration or puffing"[1] as the Federal Trade Commission calls it? Are they simply para-poetic hyperboles — exotic fruits of Madison Avenue creativity? Perhaps they are fragments of a new language, expressing a revolutionary pecuniary truth that derives authority from a phantasmic advertising universe. In the following pages I try to get some clarity on this difficult and murky matter by teasing out of the language of advertising some of the components of pecuniary philosophy I perceive there.

Pecuniary Pseudo-Truth. No sane American would think that literally everybody is "talking about the new *Starfire*," that Alpine cigarettes literally "put the men in menthol smoking" or that a woman wearing a *Distinction* foundation garment becomes so beautiful that her sisters literally want to kill her. Since he will not take these burblings literally, he will not call them lies, even though they are all manifestly untrue. Ergo, a new kind of truth has emerged — *pecuniary pseudo-truth* — which may be defined as a false statement made as if it were true, but not intended to be believed. No proof is offered for a pecuniary pseudo-truth, and no one looks for it. Its proof is that it sells merchandise; if it does not, it is false.

Para-Poetic Hyperbole. 7 *Crown* whiskey's fantasies of icy depths, Revlon's rhapsodies on *Pango Peach*, *The Look's* word pictures of alluring

---

[1] An expression used by the Federal Trade Commission in dismissing a complaint against a company for using extreme methods in its advertising.

eyes, and similar poesies are called para-poetic hyperbole because they are something like poetry, with high-flown figures of speech, though they are not poetry. Note, however, that they are also pecuniary pseudo-truths because nobody is expected to believe them.

Pecuniary Logic. When we read the advertisements for *Butyl* and *Old Crow* it begins to look as if *Butyl* and *Old Crow* really *want* us to believe, for they try to prove that what they say is true. *Butyl,* for example, asserts that "major tire marketers . . . are now bringing you tires made of this remarkable material"; and *Old Crow* says that the reason it "would quite naturally be served" to General Duke in New York was because he "esteemed it 'the most famous [whiskey] ever made in Kentucky.' " When one is asked to accept the literal message of a product on the basis of shadowy evidence, I dub it *pecuniary logic.* In other words, pecuniary logic is a proof that it is not a proof but is intended to be so for commercial purposes.

There is nothing basically novel in pecuniary logic, for most people use it at times in their everyday life. What business has done is adopt one of the commoner elements of folk thought and use it for selling products to people who think this way all the time. This kind of thinking — which accepts proof that is not proof — is an *essential* intellectual factor in our economy, for if people were careful thinkers it would be difficult to sell anything. From this it follows that in order for our economy to continue in its present form people must learn to be fuzzy-minded and impulsive, for if they were clear-headed and deliberate they would rarely put their hands in their pockets; or if they did, they would leave them there. If we were all logicians the economy could not survive, and herein lies a terrifying paradox, for *in order to exist economically as we are we must try by might and main to remain stupid.*

The problem has now been stated and briefly illustrated: pecuniary thinking can be analyzed into component parts each one of which serves a specific purpose in marketing in our own peculiarly constructed economy. In the next section, I shall present some of the tribulations of the pecuniary system of thought and then go on to a more extensive analysis of its complexities.

PITFALLS TO PECUNIARY PHILOSOPHY

Like all philosophies pecuniary philosophy has its limitations. The central issue in the viability of philosophies is the truth they assume and what they try to explain. Every philosophy must work in its own backyard, so to speak; that is why Buddhism, for example, has no place in a physics laboratory or logical empiricism in a Buddhist temple. When one philosophy "encroaches" on the "territory" of another's universe it runs into difficulties. Now pecuniary philosophy may be satisfactory for selling cosmetics or whiskey but when it tries to "sell" health or any other form of human welfare it becomes vulnerable to attack by the more traditional logical methods. At such a point the question, "Does aspirin *really* provide the fastest relief for pain, and is its effect on the digestive tract literally gentler than that of any other pain-killer?" cannot be answered by a logic whose only test is whether the product sells, but must be answered by the more traditional truth-logic. Pecuniary philosophy has two problems here. In the first place, human suffering is at issue; in the second place, terms like "relief," "fast," and "gentle" have specific, identifiable physiological referents, and physiology is the province of true scientific research and discovery. Each has its own sphere, and traditional logic and science are as inappropriate for selling nail polish in American culture as pecuniary reasoning is for selling medicine. When medicine is to be sold the canons of traditional reasoning must be respected; when one is selling whiskey or electric razors "folk-think" and pecuniary logic will, perhaps, serve. Put another way, government, with the connivance of the people, permits the exploitation of wooly-mindedness up to a certain point, in the interests of maintaining an irrational economy; but this cannot be allowed if it results in obvious physical suffering, since the right to seek, without trammel or deceit, relief from physical anguish, has become an inviolable value of the American people. . . .

PECUNIARY TRUTH

Most people are not obsessive truth-seekers; they do not yearn to get to the bottom of things; they are willing to let absurd or merely ambiguous statements pass. And this undemandingness that does insist that the world stand up and prove that it is real, this air of relaxed wooly-mindedness, is a necessary condition for the development of the revolutionary mode of thought herein called *pecuniary philosophy*. The relaxed attitude toward veracity (or mendacity, depending on the point of view) and its complement, pecuniary philosophy, are important to the American economy, for they make possible an enormous amount of selling that could not otherwise take place.

Every culture creates philosophy out of its own needs and ours has produced traditional philosophies based on truths verifiable by some primordial objective or supernatural criteria, and another, pecuniary philosophy, derived from an irrational need to sell. The heart of truth in our traditional philosophies was God or His equivalent, such as an identifiable empirical reality. The heart of truth in pecuniary philosophy is contained in the following three postulates:

Truth is what sells.
Truth is what you want people to believe.
Truth is that which is not legally false.

The first two postulates are clear, but the third probably requires a little explaining and a good example. A report in *Science* on the marketing practices of the *Encyclopaedia Britannica* is just what we need at this point.

> One of the tasks of the Federal Trade Commission, according to the Encyclopaedia Britannica, is to order business organizations to stop using deceptive advertising when such organizations are found to be so engaged. A few weeks ago Encyclopaedia Britannica, Inc., was ordered by the Federal Trade Commission to stop using advertising that misrepresents its regular prices as reduced prices available for a limited time only. . . .
>
> Some of the company's sales practices are ingenious. The FTC shows, for example, how the prospective customer, once he has gained the impression that he is being offered the Encyclopaedia and accessories at reduced prices, is led to believe that the purported reduced prices are good only for a limited time. This is done by two kinds of statements, each one being true enough if regarded separately.
>
> The first kind of statement, which appears in written material, says such things as "This offer is necessarily subject to withdrawal without notice."[2]

Science explains that the second kind of statement is made by the salesman when he applies pressure to the prospective customer by telling him he will not return. The Federal Trade Commission, in enjoining the *Encyclopaedia Britannica* from using this kind of sales technique, argued that the first statement plus the second created the impression in the customer's mind that if he does not buy now he will lose the opportunity to buy at what he has been given to think is a reduced price. Actually, *Science* points out, it is not a reduced price, for the price has not changed since 1949. Since it is literally true that a business has the right to raise prices without advance notice, the *Britannica* advertisement is not legally false, even though it reads like a warning that prices will go up soon. I have coined the term *legally innocent prevarication* to cover all statements which, though not legally untrue, misrepresent by implication. . . .

PARA-POETIC HYPERBOLE AND THE BRAIN BOX

Revlon, manufacturer extraordinary of cosmetics, often picks for the central figure in its advertisements in *Life* magazine a woman with the good looks of a lower-middle-class working girl dressed up for a place she will never get to; a destination *sans merci*, an empty port on the technicolor Sea of Lower-Middle-Class Dreams. Sales clerks, routine office workers, lower-middle-class housewives can identify with these average looking females in fancy costumes floating on a Saturday night cloud. Para-poetic

[2] *Science*, July 14, 1961.

hyperbole thus begins with the hyperbolic picture, as the advertisement zeroes in on a deprived target (the lower-middle-class working girl or house-wife) who started life with a Self but lost it somewhere along the way. Revlon will fix all that, for Revlon is medicine man and magician to the soul. Consider the advertisement for *Pango Peach,* a new color introduced by Revlon in 1960. A young woman leans against the upper rungs of a lad-der leading to a palm-thatched bamboo tree-house. *Pango Peach* are her *sari,* her blouse, her toe and finger nails, and the cape she holds. A sky of South Pacific blue is behind her, and the cape, as it flutters in the wind, stains the heavens *Pango Peach.* "From east of the sun — west of the moon where each tomorrow dawns . . ." beckons the ad, in corny pecuniary lingo. But when you are trying to sell nail polish to a filing clerk with two years of high school you don't quote Dylan Thomas! The idea of the ad is to make a woman think she is reading real poetry when she is not, and at the same time to evoke in her the specific fantasy that will sell the product. Millions will respond to poetry as a value and feel good when they think they are responding to it, and this process of getting people to respond to pseudo-values as if they were responding to real ones is called here *pecuniary distortion of values.*

In the ad *Pango Peach* is called "A many splendoured coral . . . pink with pleasure . . . a volcano of color!" It goes on to say that "It's a full ripe peach with a world of difference . . . born to be worn in big juicy slices. Succulent on your lips. Sizzling on your fingertips. . . . Go Pango Peach . . . your adventure in paradise." Each word in the advertisement is carefully chosen to tap a particular yearning and hunger in the American woman. "Many-splendoured," for example, is a reference to the novel and movie *Love Is a Many Splendored Thing,* a tale of passion in an Oriental setting. "Volcano" is meant to arouse the latent wish to be a volcanic lover and to be loved by one. The mouthful of oral stimuli — "ripe," "succulent," "juicy" — puts sales resistance in double jeopardy because mouths are even more for kissing than for eating. "Sizzling" can refer only to *l'amour à la folie;* and, finally, "Your adventure in paradise," is an invitation to love everlasting with a dark-skinned man in a tree-house on the island of Pango.

Whether anybody reads such advertisements is really not my concern, although the fact that Revlon repeats them year after year suggests that women do read them.[3] What is most interesting is Madison Avenue's opinion of the females to whom these ads are addressed, for what this and other Revlon advertisements project is a female who does not believe in herself, has yearnings toward a sexuality which she holds back within her like a rumbling volcano, and who has fantastic dreams. Is this indeed the mask that looks at us from the Revlon ads? Is this girl of fragile poise,

---

[3] Revlon sales increased from $33,604,000 in 1954 to $110,363,000 in 1958 (*New York Times,* November 5, 1959, p. 28). Some of this increase is due, of course, to Revlon's rigged TV quiz shows.

tricked out in pecuniary scenery, the one that leans on the boy friend's arm on Saturday night on all the subways, on all the Main Streets across the land? Are these in their millions mothers of Americans? Could it be true?

Advertising helps while it profits by this female, for some new cosmetic may make her imagine for a moment that she *is* something. But such "help," such *product therapy*, is merely palliative at best and lethal at worst; for products in fancy dress sustain and support underlying flaws, while assuring these girls that they have nothing to offer a man but allure. So again a culturally patterned defect, as Fromm would call it, becomes the maid of all work for the economy, for this girl will buy almost anything that will make her feel good.

> Fill her wanting eye
> with wishes, her will-
> ing ear with answers.
> She will never be more
> open-to-buy.
> *The same thing that*
> *makes her buy . . . pure*
> *emotion.*
> *They feel be-*
> *fore they think,* they
> perceive before they
> see, *they buy more on*
> *impulse than on purpose,*
> *they do more on inspiration than*
> *by plan.*

says *Glamour*[4] talking intimately to its Madison Avenue brethren and other businessmen.

When you dress up a girl, surround her with tropical scenery, and put her in a bamboo tree-house on the island of Pango, it makes sense to talk about volcanoes, sizzling finger tips, and adventures in paradise, for you have manufactured a dream for a sex that is *scenery-prone*. Industry spends billions exploiting the capacity of American women to lend themselves to unreality. Since our culture gives women no firm role except an erotic one, but rather surrounds them with ambiguities, they fit readily into tree-houses or any other kind of commercial fantasy. Men are more intractible in this regard; it is more difficult to metamorphose them into make-believe creatures because their roles are more real. Hence there is a poverty of hyperbole in the advertisements addressed to men. Hence also the monotony of the appeal, playing constantly on the tired themes of virility and status. Only occasionally does hyperbole appear, like a fresh rosy neon light. The

[4] In the *New York Times,* October 3 and 5, 1961.

following advertisement for *Excello* shirts is one of the rare examples of para-poetic hyperbole in the masculine vein: A picture of the upper body of a broad-shouldered, ruggedly handsome, deeply troubled and rather driven-looking man occupies almost all of the frame. He is between thirty-five and forty years old and wears a somewhat rumpled but clean shirt and a tie. His brows are knit, his arms and shoulders are disposed in dynamic tension, and the veins on his right hand bulge. In a sense, he is what every man who can afford "quality" shirts would like to be and fears he may not be: drive-packed, masculine, achieving. The copy burbles in purest para-poetic hyperbole:

> A shirt is the day's beginning, a special semaphore signaling the forward thrust of endeavor. A shirt is the morning mood of man, his ebbing effort at evening. A shirt is Excello.

The *New York Times*, May 17, 1961, says of the ad

> The Meyers [advertising] agency believes that the contrast of emotion and realism will produce psychological undertones that "should gain increased attention for the product."

Well, what are the emotions and what are the "psychological undertones" (sometimes referred to by others as "unconscious motivations") that Meyers is reaching for here? I think that in the first place they are trying to transmute commonplace and even somewhat unpleasant things, like going to work in the morning and going out in the evening when you are tired and would rather stay home, into something vibrant; they are attempting to convert industrial time and its inexorable demands into a poetic thing. This conversion I call *hyperbolic transformation*. In the second place I think they want men to identify with the executive-appearing male wearing the rumpled shirt, while they say to us, "You are just like this man of high drive, for whom morning is a forward thrust of endeavor and evening a time when, exhausted from his driving labor, he, with his last ebbing effort, dons a fresh shirt to go out and relax." This is *pecuniary identification*.

The *Excello* advertisement adeptly exploits the mood-meanings of time — morning mood and evening mood — and the desire for status. What emotions American men experience on starting out in the morning and what yearnings toward or satisfactions they may have in the executive position, are spun by the advertising copy into a para-poetic statement tying them to shirts. This is what I would like to call the *monetization* of time and status, and I shall use the term *monetization* where cultural factors not usually thought of as entering the processes of production and sale are used to make money. Another example of monetization would be the exploitation of women's feeling that they have nothing to offer but allure, for this transmutes feelings of inadequacy into cash.

MONETIZATION

Since values like love, truth, the sacredness of high office, God, the Bible, motherhood, generosity, solicitude for others, and so on are the foundation of Western culture, anything that weakens or distorts them shakes traditional life. The traditional values are part of traditional philosophy, but pecuniary philosophy, far from being at odds with them, appears to embrace them with fervor. This is the embrace of a grizzly bear, for as it embraces the traditional values pecuniary philosophy chokes them to death. The specific choking mechanism is *monetization*.

Let us consider the following advertisement for a popular women's magazine: Against a black sky covering almost an entire page in the *New York Times* of June 2, 1960 is chalked the following from the New Testament: "Children, love ye one another." Below, the advertising copy tells us that *McCall's* magazine will carry in its next issue parables from five faiths, and that

> Such spiritual splendor, such profound mystical insight, seem perfectly at home in the pages of *McCall's*, where the editorial approach is all-inclusive, universal, matching the infinite variety of today's existence.

Guilt by association is familiar enough to the American people through the work of various sedulous agencies of Government. *McCall's*, however, has discovered its opposite — *glory* by association, or, in the language of this work, pecuniary transfiguration. Since "spiritual splendor" and "mystical insight" are traits of holy books, and since examples of these are printed in *McCall's*, it is by that fact a kind of holy book. This is what I mean by the use of values for pecuniary purposes; this is value distortion through monetization. . . .

The following are examples of frenzied monetization of values by different women's magazines:

> "M is for *motherhood*. . . . M is also for *McCall's*. This week, when everybody, including the sophisticated, is out shopping for Mother's Day, we urge you to do the following for the mother of your choice. Kiss her. Tell her you *love* her. Either get her a subscription to *McCall's* or give her enough money to buy it at the newstand for a year."[5]

A large picture of a woman of about eighteen to twenty-two years of age shows her looking tenderly at a cake she has just baked. Above her in large type it says, "½ Pillsbury [flour] — ½ *Mother Love*." Below, the copy reads, ". . . the making and serving of food is not a chore, but an act of *love* that daily restates the *devotion* of *Mother* to *family*. . . . It is understanding this attitude, and editing our food pages 'with *love*,' that makes them so much more meaningful. . . ."[6]

[5] *New York Times*, May 5, 1960.
[6] *Ibid.*, October 30, 1959.

The copy reads: "In women's language, *love* of a *child*, of an *ideal*, of a *purpose*, is often expressed in the negative; as a refusal of permissiveness that would seem easy and relaxed — but would be in fact an act of unloving. So it is with *Good Housekeeping*. Because this magazine is woman-like in its *caring*, it must often reject what might be glitteringly attractive on the surface, but dangerous or *impure* in its nature or its ultimate effects."[7]

A pair of enormous, clinking glasses of champagne dominates the page, and above them the copy reads "To the most wonderful woman in the world!" Below and in between the glasses it says, "(and 6,000,000 more just like her). At the beginning of the new year, we would like to lift our glass to the millions of women who read *Ladies' Home Journal*. We would like to salute, first off, their *wisdom*. They know that a magazine's mission is more than to be 'a physical and neutral carrier of advertising messages.' Much more. Our readers prove it by their special *loyalty* to the *Journal*. In November when readers of the three leading women's magazines were asked which magazines they liked best, 50% more of them chose the *Journal* than either of the other two. We *thank* them for this *affection*. We also cheer our readers' *zest* for living. A *Journal* reader, we have discovered, is a very *special sort of person*. For one thing she's *younger* — a whole year younger — than readers of other women's magazines. She has a higher income. She's better *educated*. She *cares* more about her life and the world around her, and spends more in time and money on her *home* and *family*. And we toast our readers' *loyalty* — which gives *Ladies' Home Journal* the largest average circulation of any woman's magazine on earth. A Happy New Year to you all."[8] [Italics supplied.]

In these passages, bubbling with monetization, the monetized values have been italicized by me. The advertisements suggest a law: *the more intense competition between claims becomes, the greater the extent of monetization*. This is probably valid regardless of what the product is. The *law of competition and monetization* makes clear the fact that unbridled competition among products increases monetization, saps values, and imperils the foundations of our society.

Now, the reader may urge, nobody reads these ads and no one is gulled by this nonsense. I would urge, on the contrary, that since the three magazines quoted above have a combined circulation of about 20 million there must be some attractive power in their approach, and that this consists in a shrewd capacity to exploit woman's unmet need to be loved and to feel she is a loving, wise, caring, pure, forever young, motherly, idealistic, loyal being. What is monetized and exploited is the American woman's idealization of herself — a further example of her ability to lend herself to unreality. On the island of Pango we saw her in a house of bamboo *scenery*; here she is in a house of bamboo *values*.

[7] *Ibid.*, January 21, 1961.
[8] *Ibid.*, January 4, 1960.

Consequences of Monetization. Well, perhaps one takes all this too seriously and perhaps my embarrassment at the magazines' utilization of emotional hunger to push sales is just a quaint personality distortion of my own, quite unbecoming in an objective scientist. Perhaps, who knows, the number of women who read the copy — instead of merely responding to the name of the magazine — is very, very small, and perhaps many of those who read do not grasp what is said. So in the end the advertisements have really not *hurt* anybody. Who could prove they have? But this is really not my central concern. What I argue is that advertising will exploit sacred values for pecuniary ends, that the transition from relatively *harmless* distortion to relatively *harmful* is gradual, and that most pecuniary philosophers cannot tell the difference. . . .

Dwight Macdonald

Taken From

THE PHILANTHROPOIDS

 KK

Giving away money is a very big business in the United States, and the Ford Foundation is the biggest in the business of giving away money. The directors of foundations manage money and to this extent are like the managerial executives who control our major corporations. Dwight Macdonald, anatomist of American culture, examines the Ford Foundation's activities, habitat, rituals, and (in this excerpt) language. He describes two types of language, esoteric and exoteric. The first is the self-effacingly earnest argot of the foundation's inner workings. The second is the jargon of its official public utterances, always serious, indirect, and inoffensive. This essay was written over ten years ago. What are your impressions of the current spread and location of Macdonald's key examples?

Taken from "Foundation—III—The Philanthropoids," *The New Yorker*, XXXI (Dec. 10, 1955). Reprinted by permission; Copr. © 1955 The New Yorker Magazine, Inc.

The Ford Foundation, which is to other foundations as a whale is to a school of tuna fish, has its headquarters at 477 Madison Avenue, at Fifty-first Street, in the heart of the account-executive territory. Its offices, designed by the firm of Skidmore, Owings & Merrill, which did Lever House, are in the most discreetly expensive modern style. Chastity is carried to the point of antisepsis, with gray and beige the dominant colors. All the offices, and even the corridors, are carpeted — an arrangement that is at once sumptuous and democratic, and thus a true expression of the Foundation's personality. (It is also painful, for the carpet causes every door handle to administer a slight, waspish shock of static electricity.) Some members of the staff feel that this elegance is not appropriate to a foundation that deals with scholars, scientists, and other persons of modest income, and would prefer a more run-down setting in a less glittering quarter of the city, or even in some outlying college town. But the Ford Foundation is a $2,500,000,000 proposition, and it is hard for so much money not to dress the part.

The crucial decisions in the Foundation's work — namely, who or what will get slices of the more than $60,000,000 it gives away each year — are made by a group of about fifty people, consisting of its twelve trustees and some forty philanthropoids. A philanthropoid — the term was first given currency by the late Frederick P. Keppel, while he was president of the Carnegie Corporation — is the middleman between the philanthropist and the philanthropee. His profession is the giving away of other people's money, and he is the key figure in most of today's great foundations, now that the original donors are safely dead. Some two hundred and thirty people are employed by the Ford Foundation — a small payroll, considering its size. Thirty work in "the field," staffing the overseas offices in the Near and Far East — in Karachi, Rangoon, New Delhi, Beirut, and Djakarta. Of the two hundred who work in New York, thirty are on the payroll of "Omnibus," the Foundation's television show, and about a hundred and thirty are office workers below the decision-making level. This leaves the forty-odd philanthropoids, who, for all practical purposes, are the Ford Foundation. They screen the thousands of applications for grants that come in every year; they look into new fields for spending; they think up problems worth solving (the first problem a foundation faces is what *is* the problem) and select the institutions or the people to try to solve them; they carry on the negotiations, often protracted, and the inquiries, often delicate, that may or may not lead to a grant, and they follow up the grants that are made; they dictate the systolic flow of memoranda that is the blood stream of a modern foundation. Through all these activities, and always subject to the final vote of the trustees, the philanthropoids determine that this enterprise of benevolence or scholarship shall be nourished with Ford money, while that one shall not.

The typical Ford philanthropoid is youngish, earnest, sincere (as social workers, rather than advertising men, use the term), unpretentious, and, above all, friendly. He shakes your hand firmly, looks you straight in the eye, and does not conceal his pleasure at meeting you or his hope that he can be of some help. His dress strikes a mean between academic dowdiness (sharply pressed pants and gleaming shoes are uncommon, tie clips are not) and Madison Avenue chic (his suits, though unpampered, are of conservative cut). An atmosphere of strict informality prevails in his office. A Ford philanthropoid is not at ease until he has got on a first-name basis with a visitor, which may take as much as five minutes. (He is already on a first-name basis with his immediate boss and his boss's boss; even the boss of all bosses, Chairman Henry Ford II, is "Henry" around head-quarters, at least in indirect discourse.) He is, in short, a far cry from the sedate elder statesmen of philanthropy who used to predominate in founda-tions thirty years ago, gazing down patronizingly on aspiring grantees from their million-dollar ramparts. These gentlemen would not have understood a recent observation of a Ford executive — "We've got to be humble. After all, it's not our money and we don't do the work. The grantees do." The old genus is practically extinct now. "They [the endowers of foundations] and their administrators continue to insist that wealth is a private possession and that the possessor may dispose of it as he pleases," Eduard C. Linde-man wrote in his book on the American foundation, "Wealth & Culture," published in 1936. At that time, many foundations didn't even issue reports, and of the some three hundred Mr. Lindeman tried to cover in his study, two-thirds refused to give him any information at all. "My first surprise was to find that those who managed foundations and trusts did not wish to have these instruments investigated," he wrote. "Had it occurred to me then that it would require eight years of persistent inquiry . . . to disclose even the basic quantitative facts required, I am sure that the study would have been promptly abandoned." The attitude of present-day phi-lanthropoids is quite different. "It is the policy of the Ford Foundation and the other major foundations to report fully on all they do," H. Rowan Gaither, Jr., the president of the Ford Foundation, told the Economic Club of Detroit last month. "We welcome and need responsible criticism and debate, for this is a valuable guide in improving our philanthropic services." Today, most large foundations not only issue regular reports but also submit willingly to journalistic inquiries into their workings. The Ford Foundation has a conscientious Office of Reports, the sole function of which is pro-viding information to whoever wants it. The Office is headed by Porter McKeever, who is youngish, earnest, sincere, unpretentious, and friendly, and whose previous jobs have included serving as chief press officer of the American delegation to the United Nations and as publicity director of Citizens for Stevenson during the 1952 campaign. Mr. McKeever's — or, rather, Porter's — office takes its title seriously enough to have distributed 60,000 copies of the Ford Foundation's Annual Report for 1954.

The usual philanthropoidal background is academic, but at Ford the prevailing type is more likely to have been connected with the government or with one of the committees, commissions, councils, agencies, associations, societies, institutes, boards, and bureaus without which Americans seem unable to do anything except make money. Some representative former jobs of Ford philanthropoids are program director of the Committee for the International Trade Organization, chief of the Division of International Security Affairs of the State Department's Bureau of United Nations' Affairs, president of the Alaska Rural Rehabilitation Corporation, director of the Chicago Council on Foreign Relations, research director of the Bureau of Applied Social Research at Columbia University, director of the Labor Office of the Office of Price Administration, and field director of the Division of Program Surveys in the Bureau of Agricultural Economics of the United States Department of Agriculture. As this sort of background might suggest, and as Mr. Westbrook Pegler gloomily suspects, the Ford philanthropoid is of a liberal turn politically, habituated to collective, non-profit enterprise, and inclined more toward internationalism than isolationism. He appears to be serious, even idealistic, about his work, and he gives every evidence of enjoying it; the cynicism prevalent elsewhere on Madison Avenue has not infected the Ford Foundation. And, indeed, his work combines the moral glow of a Worthy Cause with a salary that is comfortable, if not luxurious. A hundred dollars is about the same in his personal life as a million is to him professionally; when he has lunch — at Schrafft's — with colleagues from other foundations, he is used to such kidding as, "Have you spent your million for today yet?" His living standards perk up when he travels on an expense account, and thus comes more directly into the Foundation's well-heeled orbit; so do those of his grantees and consultants, who sometimes feel guilty about being permitted, and even encouraged, to take taxis, engage clerical help, and otherwise spend "as much as you need to do a good job." One professor who was brought to New York for a week by the Foundation and established in the Hotel Pierre found it impossible to overcome his ingrained habits of thrift. "I'll bet I'm the only man in town who's living at the Pierre and eating at Nedick's," he remarked to a friend.

The philanthropoids at Ford communicate with each other in a special jargon, the lingua franca of the foundation world; it is a scholarly jive, with traces of the argot of the surrounding account-executive region. At times, its purpose is to relax and reassure, to make it clear that the speaker is not on a higher intellectual level than the most modestly endowed of his audience — as, indeed, he usually is not. "Now, I'm not quite sure how the discussion ought to roll," the chairman of a round table will begin, and, in fact, has begun on at least one occasion. "But let's just bat it around a little and see where the ball comes out. No holds barred and we *do* want to have a real meeting of minds." At other times, quite to the contrary, it is a professional shorthand, comprehensible only to fellow-initiates. When a Ford philanthropoid defines the ideal project as one that (a) is self-liquidating, (b) has plenty of leverage, and is both (c) programmed from within and (d) a response to a felt need, he means (a) that it will either be completed or taken over by someone else after a reasonable period, (b) that it stimulates others to put in money, too, (c) that the members of the staff didn't merely open their mail but thought up the project themselves, and (d) that it is something the beneficiaries feel they need, as opposed to something they just passively accept. Some key terms in the language are "grass roots;" "perspective" ("He's been away long enough to get some perspective on it"); "pinpoint" ("I want to pinpoint the factor of variability in these estimates" — a sentence in which either "highlight" or "showcase" may be substituted for "pinpoint," all three expressions being examples of a tendency in modern foundation jargon to use nouns as verbs in an effort to achieve forcefulness, however spurious); "grass roots;" "think through" ("I wonder if Don has really thought through the implications of his proposal"); "tailor" ("The program is tailored to the felt needs of the community"); "built-in" ("Can we keep an eye on progress through some built-in evaluation procedures?"); "topflight" ("a well-rounded group of topflight men in the field" — cf. "I'm flying low today," meaning "I'm not feeling very well today"); "grass roots;" "brief" ("We're briefing him on local conditions"); "challenge" (this word, as in "What confronts us here is a stimulating challenge to us all," has a peculiar attraction, or challenge, for philanthropoids, to whom life is real, earnest, and full of problems); "germinal" ("A small grant might have germinal possibilities," from which it follows that a terminal grant is a germinal grant gone to seed); "maximize" ("We'll bring together some topflighters and maximize their experiences"); "rundown," "button up," "kick off" ("Let's give the project a final rundown tomorrow, button it up by Friday, and then kick off the field survey"); "grass roots;" "spearhead" ("a subcommittee to spearhead the attack on the problem"); "bird-dog" ("I can't find that evaluation report, Jack. Will you bird-dog it for me in the files?"); "to get mileage out of" (to make use of, as "The Nobel people certainly get a lot of mileage, publicity-wise, out of their $200,000 a year!"); "frame of reference;" "develop a clearer picture;" and, of course, "grass roots," which is an interesting example of an attempt to compensate in language for what is felt to be lacking in reality.

This is the esoteric language, for use among philanthropoids in their inter-office memoranda and in the staff and committee meetings at which they spend a great deal of their time. (When a philanthropoid's secretary says he is in conference, she generally means it, poor fellow.) There is also an exoteric language, for communication with the outside world, which is developed most fully in the Annual Report, a literary product that is some-what more readable than the phone book and somewhat less so than the collected sermons of Henry Ward Beecher. This language — foundationese — is, like Latin, a dead language, written rather than spoken, and designed for ceremony rather than utility. Its function is magical and incantatory — not to give information or to communicate ideas or to express feelings but to reassure the reader that the situation is well in hand. A cardinal principle is to accentuate the positive. Thus, President Gaither, a master of foundationese, writes in his latest Annual Report, apropos of the trustees' decision to cut the annual rate of support for the Fund for the Advancement of Education from $10,000,000 to $3,000,000, "In adopting this course, the Trustees acknowledged the encouraging results of the Fund's efforts in a relatively short period and reaffirmed their belief that the Fund's assistance to education showed exceptional promise for the future [Translation: The trustees are cooling off toward the Fund and have decided to spend most of their educational money themselves in the future]." Similarly, when he writes in the Report, "The Foundation and the Fund [for Adult Education] have undertaken a comprehensive study of the facilities and requirements of adult education, to provide guidance for future activities," he means that the Foundation wonders how much future activity there should be. Another principle of foundationese is not to go to undue lengths — or, in fact, to any lengths at all — to avoid the obvious, since foundationese is committee language and is therefore ever seeking the lowest denominator that everybody will agree on. Sometimes this is well below sea level:

> It is apparent to the trustees that the problems confronting people everywhere are vast in number. While important efforts to solve these problems are being made by government, industry, foundations, and other institutions, the needs far transcend the present total effort. In the opinion of the trustees, new resources, such as those of the Ford Foundation, can result in significant contributions to the understanding and solution of these problems if properly employed. The potential social value of the foundation rests on its ability to locate the areas where additional efforts toward the solution of major problems are most needed.

Henry Ford II handed the above to the press in 1948, but these heavy-breathing periods are not his natural style of expression, which is sensible and direct; he was merely entangled in the toils of foundationese. The same thing happens to President Gaither, who talks perfectly rationally but adorns his Annual Reports with observations like the following: "The Foundation attempts to administer its funds in ways that strengthen its grantees and enhance their ability to accomplish the purposes for which the grants were made." (As against, presumably, foundations that try to weaken their grantees and lessen their ability to make good use of their grants.) Or "The Trustees of the Ford Foundation believe [any sentence beginning this way is bound to be disappointing] that a healthy economy is essential if American democracy is to function effectively." Or "The Ford Foundation believes that the advancement of human welfare depends on the partnership in progress of all free men." The virtuosity of President Gaither in handling foundationese becomes apparent when one considers that not only do the last two sentences mean nothing as they stand (that is, without a lengthy explication of almost every term) but also the gist of them is reversible, like a trench coat, thus: "Democracy is essential if a healthy economy is to function effectively" and "The partnership in progress of all free men depends on the advancement of human welfare." Gives just as good wear either way. . . .

David Mellinkoff

TOWARD A MORE INTELLIGIBLE LANGUAGE OF THE LAW

↙↙

Justice Oliver Wendell Holmes, Jr., in one of his Supreme Court decisions, wrote: "A word is not a crystal, transparent and unchanged; it is the skin of a living thought and may vary greatly in color and content according to the circumstances and the time in which it is used." David Mellinkoff, an attorney, became so interested in the problems of precision and imprecision, stability and change in legal language that he gave up his practice to devote full attention to the study of it. His encyclopedic book "tells what the language of the law is, how it got that way, and how it works out in practice." In this excerpt Mr. Mellinkoff concentrates on various kinds of unintelli-

Reprinted from *The Language of the Law* by David Mellinkoff (Boston: Little, Brown and Company, 1963), by permission of the publisher. Copyright, ©, 1963 by David Mellinkoff.

gibility — some habitual and unthinking, some sinister and calculated — all of which can have the effect of manipulating and misleading laymen and even lawyers themselves.

The areas of misunderstanding

Intelligible and *unintelligible* have an overpowering sound of absoluteness that limits their usefulness in discussion of the language of the law. It is a very empty phrase that someone, somewhere, cannot squeeze a drop of sense from, yet some glittering nonsense discourages the effort. Take this specimen, spawned by a current vogue for legislation about emergency calls on party lines:

> In every telephone directory . . . there shall be printed in type not smaller than any other type appearing on the same page, a notice preceded by the word "warning" printed in type at least as large as the largest type on the same page, . . .

This is no misprint. It had models in the laws of sister states, and in turn has become a model for others. Take comfort that some draftsmen have refused to buy this pre-wrapped shoddy, stopping the word flow when they had had enough for law, for good English, and for people — after the word *warning*. Take comfort too that complete gibberish is not the typical instance of language mangling by lawyers.

It is still aiming too low to be satisfied with language that is only "capable of being understood," the standard definition of *intelligible*. The general antipathy to absolutes has for centuries split *intelligible* into degrees, and as used in this book it means "easily understood," what some mean by clear or plain. Its opposite — *unintelligible* — covers the full muddy spectrum available to lawyers. From the shortest nonsense — *ss*.[1] Through long rows of unnecessarily unclear words and constructions, variously distinguished as obscure, vague, ambiguous, and in other circles called doubletalk, officialese, gobbledygook, federal prose, etc. Down into the scraps of language which at best are not easily understood, such as *and/or* and *or/and*.

This breadth of range is a further reminder that intelligibility is not synonymous with brevity, though verbosity does make it easier for the writer to lose himself while losing his reader.

Likewise, intelligibility is not dependent upon precision, which sometimes must be sacrificed for quick understanding, as in the traffic signs which tell pedestrians to WAIT (without saying for how long), and to WALK

---

[1] *Editors' Note:* ss abbreviates the Latin *scilicet* (to wit). Of such abbreviations Mr. Mellinkoff writes, "[They] are not precise in form or in meaning, and serve no good purpose at all."

(without adding, "if you want to"). The sacrifice of precision for intelligibility needs mention, not to encourage sloppiness but appropriateness, and to offset the single-minded teaching which reverses the rites — making intelligibility always the goat. There are still times when magic words make a legal difference — e.g., *consideration for the lease* (instead of *prepaid rent*), or the weaker magic of *liquidated damages* (instead of *forfeiture* or *penalty*). Even so, there is little legal prose of any sort which cannot be made more intelligible than it usually is.

Once the draftsman starts with a clear understanding of what it is he wants to say, making himself understood is more a matter of how than of what. If the simplest truth goes in fuzzy, it will come out that way. And if complexity goes in clear, it can come out that way — gospel or not. Even ". . . Holmes was sometimes clearly wrong; but . . . when this was so he was always wrong clearly."

Any legal prose can be made more intelligible if the draftsman is striving for intelligibility, but even the careful draftsman sometimes finds more pressing concerns — some legitimate. There is, for example, the deliberate use of language which everyone recognizes as being easily misunderstood, accepted for the sake of quick agreement. This sort of *calculated ambiguity* is left for later. Also left for later is the deliberate use of language which though not always easily understood is quickly felt, the language of ceremony and persuasion.

On the blacker side is the art of planned confusion, which has its advocates, its gray and off-white shadings, and above all its patterns for identification. The patterns are so strong that at times the "planned" aspect has dropped deep into the inner lawyer, to become merely habitual without taint of sinister purpose.

Planned confusion takes two major forms: (1) saying-nothing and making it look like something, and (2) saying-something and making it look like nothing, or like something else. The law has no monopoly on either form, but as wholesale dealers in words lawyers have found the patterns too useful.

At its mildest, nonprofessional saying-nothing takes the form of small talk, the polite lying that is the mark of civilized society. Thus,

we say	*instead of*
I find it stimulating	Absolute nonsense
Most interesting	What a bore
Very stately	Real ugly
We must get together soon	Thank God, you're leaving town

Related to this is the lawyer's

"progress" letter	*instead of*
Your matter is being given due consideration in the light of the pertinent statutes and case law, and you will be further advised in due course.	Right now it looks like you're stuck. But don't go shopping for another lawyer.

A more widespread malady of nothingness at the bar is the *one-legged subjunctive*. Its most prevalent forms are *it would seem* and *it may well be*, which make no more sense when joined together like this:

> It would seem also that a further and more far reaching effect of the instant judgment may well be to encourage other persons to breach their obligations . . .

Variants are *one might wish* and the emphatically spurious *it may very well be*.

Unlike the bald fraud of *yes and no*, these phrases equivocate even on being equivocal. *It would seem* (that is the appearance of things, says the writer) — and you wait in vain for the other shoe to drop. Not *it would seem to be, but the fact is*, just way up in the air, *it would seem*. So that the writer can never be called to account. Not what I thought or believed or what the fact was, just what it seemed to be. And then again, *it may well be* something completely different or *it may well not be*. I'm not sure or won't say; at least I haven't said.

The lawyer's addiction to *it would seem* is related to the old and continuing law use of French *semble* (it seems). But that is a technical expression of uncertainty and lack of authority which still has a place (in footnotes), and should be kept there. A more intelligible statement of guess is *one of the possibilities is*, and a candid *I don't know* would win the law some friends.

A more vicious way of saying-nothing is the lawyer's *agreement to agree*, or — as it frequently appears by design or accident — *subject to change by mutual consent*. Of course. It always is. Like the *whereas* recital, this phrase gives the hurried bargainer the false impression that something has been taken care of. It is eyewash or worse.

One step deeper into bad morals is saying-something calculated to mislead. This is a species of unintelligibility related to the practice of using fine print to make contracts illegible. The object of each is the same — to force law on the victim without arousing suspicion that it is there. Various paths lead to the same sinkhole.

One of them is using words so ordinary in appearance that the reader thinks he understands. Here is a sample. Without counsel, the citizen in the hurried sanctuary of the voting booth ponders "Yes" or "No" on a —

Ballot	*Meaning*
ASSESSMENT OF GOLF COURSES. Assembly Constitutional Amendment No. 29. Establishes manner in which non-profit golf-courses should be assessed for purposes of taxation.	Private golf courses shall be taxed less than other private property.

These ballot words are carefully designed to produce a "yes" vote (which they did). First, they speak of the "manner" of *doing something* — "assessment," "establishes," "assessed," "taxation." So that attention is diverted from the fact that the words are consistent with a way of *not doing something* — not assessing, not taxing. Second, they speak of *non-profit*, which (if it means anything to the voter) has a vaguely charitable sound, unconnected with expensive memberships. Yet on the statute books, the words will mean what they mean to lawyers — ". . . not designed primarily to pay dividends . . ." If the ballot measure had said what it meant, the issue would have been clear and the vote in doubt.

Another form of saying-something is the disarmingly disingenuous letter agreement. Here boring repetition and amiable fairness combine to mask the one sharp tooth:

> We agree to pay all bills in full promptly as they come in, including without limitation of the generality of the foregoing all bills for labor, services, and materials, supplies, utilities, taxes, permits, fees, royalties, and everything else directly or indirectly for or used in connection with the construction of your building, you of course to reimburse us for everything spent for labor, services, and materials, supplies, utilities, taxes, permits, fees, royalties, overhead, and everything else directly or indirectly for or used in connection with the construction of your building.

*   *   *

To make the language fit

After hours, lawyers talk just like people. The off-duty lawyer will tell you, as any other citizen might, that he *needs help fast when his life or property* (in that order) *is in danger*. But let him sit down at the office desk to put the same thing into law. He switches on the dictating machine. The bell rings. He commences to salivate and to gibber. Somehow it gets all mushed up, like this:

> "Emergency" as used in this section means a situation in which property or human life is in jeopardy and the prompt summoning of aid is essential.

What happened?

It is a lawyer's rather than a Marxian explanation for the precedence of *property over human life*. If you said *human life or property*, this might also be understood to say *human property*, which even to a lawyer is nonsense. But why *human life* at all? Well, to the precisionist there was a fleeting glimpse of a *dog's life*, and the glimpse was too fleeting to let the possibility rest in the concept of *property*. And — come to think of it — there are other possibilities. No one is going to drive a wild jackass through my statute!

And *jeopardy?* It has a lawyerly sound, though here it serves no lawyer's purpose. It diverts the lawyer's attention to more accustomed thoughts of *double jeopardy* and danger-of-being-convicted, which are his proper uses of the word. It also slows down the layman. His *property* would be in *danger,* and he would think it an *emergency* if an outhouse were on fire, but he would let it burn to the ground before saying "My privy is in jeopardy."

The phrase *the prompt summoning of aid is essential* has its syntactic roots in Bentham's "substantive-preferring principle," no contribution to intelligibility. The individual words as used here have no precise legal meaning: *prompt* (fast or quickly), *aid* (help), *essential* (need fast, i.e., "demanding maximum attention"), and *summoning* (calling) — which is incidental to the help that is needed.

The draftsman — as he approached a legal subject — had vague stirrings of conscience that somehow he must "talk like a lawyer," his ferment fed by the myth that he is dealing with a language that is precise. If he does not write in this obscure way, perhaps he will be suspected of not holding a union card. So he prefers the roundabout and the uncommon, which the law does not require nor bless as "precise." He uses words and phrases that have a legal flavor, language that stops the ordered progress of eye and mind to make lawyers and laymen ponder whether some special meaning is hinted at. The draftsman ends up by being less intelligible even to lawyers.

There is no inherent vice in the law which requires it be written unintelligibly. (That sentence should be a platitude but it isn't.) And it can be demonstrated that the evil is in the mind of the beholder.

Observe two lawyers putting the same bit of law into words, and see if you misunderstand both of them. You will be at once suspicious when you find that though they cover the same ground, they do not say the same things. One starts your mind running in several directions at once, and (if you have the time) you will reread more than once to make sure that there is indeed a central theme. Everything is hedged but the obvious, and that well documented. Oftener than not the grammar is dubious, the sentences long ones — with words to spare. There are so many obstacles to quick comprehension that it will be startling to discover that another has said it so easily.

Take for example the hoary dogma that *an appellate court will affirm when a judgment rests on the credibility of witnesses.* If it needs saying, it can be said like that — hornbook style — and like this:

> Inasmuch as the issues arising out of this contention are mainly factual, almost every material part of the testimony is in dispute, and plaintiff relies only on the evidence favorable to her, we point up the fundamental rule that this court has "no power to judge of the effect or value of the evidence, to weigh the evidence, to consider the credibility of the witnesses, or to resolve conflicts in the evidence or in the reason-

able inferences that may be drawn therefrom" (*Overton v. Vita-Food Corp.*, 94 Cal. App. 2d 367, 370 [210 P.2d 757]), nor may it substitute its deductions for those of the trial court (*Grainger v. Antoyan*, 48 Cal. 2d 805 [313 P.2d 848]). Thus, the presumption being in favor of the judgment we view the evidence in the light most favorable to the defendant giving him the benefit of every reasonable inference and resolving all conflicts in favor of the judgment. (*Crawford v. Southern Pacific Co.*, 3 Cal. 2d 427 [45 P.2d 183]; *Estate of Bristol*, 23 Cal. 2d 221 [143 P.2d 689]). Over 1100 pages of testimony produced 11 witnesses and numerous exhibits, all of which resulted in considerable conflict. The trial judge heard and observed the witnesses; and that the circumstances occurred over 20 years ago in a foreign country, interpreters were needed by some witnesses and others were unavailable or testified by way of deposition, the claim involved extensive property and was vigorously tried, and some of the witnesses showed more than the ordinary bias, were all factors for the judge's consideration in determining that which was worthy of belief. Further, when a finding is attacked for insufficiency of the evidence, "the power of an appellate court *begins* and *ends* with the determination as to whether there is any substantial evidence *contradicted* or *uncontradicted* which will support the finding of fact. [Citations.]" (*Primm v. Primm*, 46 Cal. 2d 690, 693 [299 P.2d 231].) (Emphasis added.)

And it can also be said most intelligibly like this:

> I do not profess to understand the reasoning of the magistrate; but, as he saw the defendant and heard him cross-examined, it would be impossible for us to say that there was no evidence on which he could come to his conclusion of fact. . . .

No lawyer likes to be reminded that it was his witness who was not believed, but every lawyer has long learned the rule of law that these opinions deal with. The second opinion applies the rule, making its factual basis comprehensible to anyone. The first opinion repeats the rule with ruffles and flourishes, so unnecessary and so involved that the reader loses himself trying to figure out which comes first, the witness or his testimony. Nothing is gained in restating the rule for lawyers, nor in hiding it from laymen. For the proposition that the law discusses here is old and simple in the common experience of all men — a distrust of liars.

But suppose the law itself is uncertain. What is *commerce?* a *reasonable doubt? proximate cause?* an *accident?* It is less a rebuke to either language or law than to the writer that the uncertainty of a legal concept results in language that is unintelligible. The gobbledygook comes when the writer does not know that the concept is uncertain or pretends that it is certain.

Extreme cruelty is about as uncertain as you could wish for. The words are flabby individually and get no support by leaning upon each other.

A statute which says that

> Extreme cruelty is the wrongful infliction of grievous bodily injury, or grievous mental suffering, . . .

does tell us that cruelty can be physical or mental, but beyond that it talks uncertainly about uncertainty. *Wrongful* begs the question, and *grievous* is as indefinite as *extreme*. This is no definition at all, and other attempts to firm it up make no improvement. For example:

> . . . any unjustifiable and long practiced course of conduct . . . which utterly destroys the legitimate ends and objects of matrimony . . .

Worse yet:

> . . . that degree of cruelty, either actually inflicted or reasonably inferred, which endangers the life or health of the aggrieved party, or renders his or her life one of such extreme discomfort and wretchedness as to incapacitate him or her, physically or mentally, from discharging the marital duties.

If there could be agreement on what *destroys* a marriage, or *utterly destroys* what is left of its redundant *ends and objects*, then *destroy* could be the ground of divorce rather than the catchphrase *extreme cruelty*. So too with a life of *extreme discomfort and wretchedness*, which ventures further into the nuance of sensibility that defies definition. Better to recognize that *extreme cruelty* is a ground for divorce, see what he did, and see if it bothers you.

For example. A Gay Nineties court takes a decree away from a wife — a bitter woman whose drunken husband called her "whore," "damned bitch," and "damned bitch from hell." Does that bother you? Either the conduct of husband or of court? This language of the dissenter would apply to both:

> And while extreme cruelty of either kind [i.e., physical or mental] cannot, in the very nature of things, be accurately defined, there is often misconduct so far outside of and beyond that produced by the ordinary weaknesses and passions of men that the common judgment of mankind pronounces it extremely cruel.

That is no definition either, and it doesn't make *extreme cruelty* a solid legal concept. But it is the sort of uncertainty that all men live with every day. "How was it?" you ask. The old man shakes his head and says, "It was real bad." *Extremely cruel.*

Jurors don't often have to be bothered with divorce, but if they did, even a juror could understand language like that, or like this charge:

There is but little difficulty in deciding whether certain facts do or do not amount to extreme cruelty, but there is great difficulty in giving a general definition of extreme cruelty; perhaps, however, it may be said to be such conduct on the part of one of the parties, whether manifested by words alone, or by personal violence, or by both, as by the common understanding and judgment of mankind, living in civilized societies, ought not to be borne or tolerated by the other, which is probbably [*sic*] as near a definition as the court can give, to aid you in coming to a conclusion upon the point.

The law was uncertain; it remains uncertain; and the language says so. The language is more certain than the law. That is intelligible enough.

In these samplings — an appellate court affirming and *extreme cruelty* — nothing is discussed that requires language peculiar to the law. The language is customarily addressed more to lawyers than to laymen, but there is no reason why the intelligent of each species should not understand all of it. No reason to accentuate the trend of our age to shut off intelligent beings from intelligible communication. No reason for lawyers to strive after differences that don't help anyone. . . .

The party line emergency statutes — bad enough in a lawyer's library — also invade the sanctity of the home. They require a notice in telephone books explaining the law to laymen. This is a part of one notice:

California Penal Code section 384 makes it a misdemeanor for any person who shall wilfully refuse to immediately relinquish a telephone party-line when informed that such line is needed for an emergency call to a fire department or police department or for medical aid or ambulance service. Also, any person who shall secure the use of a telephone party-line by falsely stating that such line is needed for an emergency call, shall be guilty of a misdemeanor.

With almost the same statute to work from, another draftsman has tailored the same part of the notice to his audience, striving to eliminate the frightening lawyer smell:

New York State law requires you to hang up the receiver of a party line telephone immediately when told the line is needed for an emergency call to a fire department or police department or for medical aid or ambulance service. It is unlawful to take over a party line by stating falsely that the line is needed for an emergency.

The California draftsman has taken the easy way — following the language of the statute, thus passing on to laymen technicality they don't need and words they don't understand. The New Yorker gives as much as the layman needs. He has avoided repetitions and chosen the ordinary, the direct, rather than the strange and roundabout. This is how he did it:

California	New York
Penal Code section 384 makes it a misdemeanor	State law requires
for any person who	you
shall willfully refuse to immediately relinquish a telephone party line	to hang up the receiver of a party line telephone immediately
when informed	when told
that such line	the line
is needed for an emergency call . . .	is needed for an emergency call . . .
Also, any person who	It is unlawful
shall secure the use of a telephone party line	to take over a party line
by falsely stating	by stating falsely
that such line	that the line
is needed for an emergency call	is needed for an emergency.
shall be guilty of a misdemeanor.	. . . .

There is a small terroristic value in California's brandishing of the words *Penal Code, section 384, guilty, misdemeanor.* But for most citizens it is enough to learn from a telephone directory that conduct is against the law. Beyond the level of the parking ticket, when a layman needs to weigh the specific consequences of law-breaking, he is on his way to a lawyer or to prison. The New York draft is both shorter and more intelligible, with nothing essential lost.

Theodore H. Savory

THE CHARACTER OF THE
LANGUAGE OF SCIENCE

✌ ✌

*This essay and the following one present two languages of science.
The first is the language of taxonomy, the language required for the
scrupulous naming and classifying of the almost infinite variety of
natural phenomena. Theodore Savory, a zoologist, describes this language with its enormous, unambiguous vocabulary, its comfortable
limitation of choice, its absence of humor, its eschewal of grace and
poetic associations. Resigned to the limitations on the expressive
power of scientific language, Mr. Savory exults in its precision, its
logic, and its freedom from the restraint of taboos.*

Until now our concern has been with the words of science, treated separately as symbols and without consideration of their contributions to the
sentences into which they can be made or the prose of which these sentences are the units. This must now be done.

It was shown that among the characteristics of the words of science were
their constancy of meaning, their ugliness and their emotional neutrality.
It might therefore be argued that the language of science must show the
same qualities as its constituent words and must be unchanging, ugly,
insensitive. This is true only within limits. There is a holism about language, an emergence of new qualities in the whole over and above the
qualities of its components, which gives to a sentence something not found

Reprinted from *The Language of Science* by T. H. Savory (London: Andre Deutsch
Ltd., 1953) by permission of the publisher.

313

in its separate words, and to a page something not present in a single sentence.

The words which the scientist borrows, imports and invents are intended, like all the other words of all other men, both for the writer who uses them in composition, and for the reader to whom they supply the only means of ascertaining the scientist's thoughts. The two uses are complementary and are closely allied, but an attempt, perhaps artificial, will be made to separate them.

The successful composition of English prose is a difficult art, which, like mathematics and sculpture, is more difficult for some men than for others. Fundamentally it involves a selecting of words, and secondarily it involves an arranging of words, and since they are nearly always alternatives both in choice and in pattern, it is very necessary that the writer should be clear about the reasons behind the final solutions of his problems.

The character of a sentence or a paragraph in English prose or verse arises from at least three different features of each separate word in it. Nearly forty years ago Mr John Bailey, in a study of Milton's poetry, determined that Milton used words which best provided him with three qualities: 'the exact expression of the meaning needed for the purpose in hand, the associations fittest to enhance or enrich that meaning, the rhythmical or musical effect required for the verse'. Although . . . scientists do not write in the manner of Milton, the same attributes must be considered by every writer if he wishes to compose a satisfying sentence and one which is in harmony with the general effect that he is trying to produce.

Much might be said, and something must be said, about each of these qualities of a word. Reference has already been made to the fact that in ordinary speech a word may have more than one meaning, but it is also true that the same meaning may often be expressed by different words:

I usually finished the work by twelve o'clock;
I often completed the task by noon.

These two sentences have as nearly the same meaning as any pair which could easily be found. Yet in science, just as one word has, or should have, one meaning only, so also there is usually only one word to express any particular meaning. Even so simple a statement as, 'total internal reflection occurs if the angle of incidence is greater than the critical angle', cannot, I think, be expressed in any other words, except, of course, by using absurd explanatory periphrases. Total internal reflection has no other name, nor have the angle of incidence and the critical angle. It follows that this statement, which incidentally expresses a fact of considerable importance, is likely to be made in the same words, whoever the author may be. He may be able to write our language with the incomparable skill of John Ruskin, or only with the moderate competence of a schoolboy; he is unlikely to cast the statement into any other form.

Writers about the English language often emphasize the fact that no two words have exactly the same meaning. Because of this much care is necessary in choosing the words which most closely express the exact shade of meaning which the writer wishes to convey, and the writing of clear, precise, unambiguous prose demands both care and practice. It appears that in this matter the scientific author is to be envied, for, provided that he knows what he wants to say, there should be few alternatives in his choosing of his words. Ideally there should be no alternatives, only one selection of words should be admissible. This would seem to suggest that the writing of scientific prose should be comparatively easy.

I think that it is a matter of experience that, in general, this is true; but it is true only in so far as one's paragraph is rigidly scientific. Here is an example:

> The prosoma of the Chelonethi is covered by a carapace, quadrate or triangular in shape, and almost certainly formed by a fusion of the primitive sclerites. Sometimes there are no transverse furrows, but often these are present, and divide the carapace into four regions. The first of these, anterior to the eyes, is known as the cucullus. It is morphologically the same as the usually perpendicular clypeus of Araneae and is probably homologous with the distinct hinged cucullus of the Ricinulei.

Such a paragraph is easy to write. I quote it from my own book *The Arachnida,* and therefore I know that, in fact, it was; and it is clear that this was so because the paragraph was rigidly scientific in the sense that it was intended for zoologists only. Hence no doubt arose in the mind of the writer that his readers would understand the meanings of such words as sclerites, cucullus and clypeus. To rewrite the paragraph so that it should be equally informative to an athlete, an archdeacon or an accountant would be difficult, and would take much time and thought — certainly far more than its effect on the minds of any of these readers would justify.

★　★　★

But although this constancy of meaning among scientific words makes science comparatively easy to write, it also makes it dull, and the writer of scientific prose is condemned if not to dullness at least to being unoriginal. The sentence about total reflection, quoted above, is one example of this. Suppose, alternatively, that a chemist wishes to record the fact that when a solution of any chloride is added to a solution of a lead salt, lead chloride is precipitated and can be purified by filtering, redissolving and crystallising. In this statement the words solution, precipitate, filter and crystallise cannot be displaced by any others; no other words have the same meanings. A well-known dictionary of English synonyms was found on consultation not to mention one of them, save only precipitate in its irrelevant sense as an adjective.

In consequence the scientific writer must abandon all hope of being interestingly original in style and can but cherish a faint hope that he may show some originality in the arrangement or treatment of his matter. Before he begins to write his book he must accept the fact that to a very large extent it is going to be just like all other books on the same subject.

The more elementary the book the more conspicuously will this be true. Prof. J. R. Partington has dealt with this fact in the preface to a book on elementary chemistry — and there are surely more introductions to chemistry more closely resembling each other than any other kind of scientific text. Admitting that he is about to deal with very familiar matters, he says that every author should be allowed his chance to find the ideal way of presenting them to the young student. He seeks justification in a parallel. Almost every novel, he says, deals with the same theme, but everyone agrees that successive generations of novelists should be allowed to treat it in the way that seems best to each separate author. But the two kinds of book are not exact parallels. The emotions that are occasioned by the meeting of a man and a woman may be described in a wide variety of words, and phrases can be attuned to varying intensities with which these feelings exert themselves. This is not true of the preparation of nitric acid or the action of chlorine on caustic potash.

With this inevitable uniformity in his choice of words, the scientist is debarred, more by convention than necessity, from using any of the devices that lead to graciousness in writing. These devices, commonly called figures of speech, are the accepted ornaments of literary composition, and are wholly absent from scientific prose. The scientist does not write in metaphors; metonomy or satire might mar the clearness he prizes so highly; his facts do not lend themselves to arrangement in climax or bathos; he seldom allows himself even the indulgence of a mild alliteration. However amazing his phenomena may be, he never permits a hint of hyperbole. The action of a beakerful of hot nitric acid on half a pound of sugar is one of the fantastic sights in elementary chemistry and to watch it is an astonishing experience: I have known it to interrupt a nearby game of lawn-tennis, but I have never seen it described in a text-book in any words more exciting than 'a copious evolution of nitrogen peroxide'. Surely the scientist, besides being tone-deaf, lacks something that would testify to common humanity.

For again, the language of science makes no provision for the slightest gleam of humour. Perhaps this is inevitable, a consequence of the fact that science is really a serious business in which levity has no place. And yet very few departments of human thought can really be said to possess no openings at which cheerfulness may break in; so that the absence of humour from science must be due to its deliberate exclusion by the scientists themselves. They work in an atmosphere in which determinism is the rule and surprises are the exception, and surprise more than anything else is the cause of the smiles that brighten the humdrum lives of men. It is necessary to search for a long time before one can find a passage in which a scientist has allowed himself to recognise a lighter side implied by the facts he is discussing, and the example given here should be regarded as a rarity and valued accordingly.

Dr A. R. Jackson describing a collection of Arctic spiders in 1934, came upon a male Coryphoeolanus thulensis in which the palpal organ was fully extended, an unusual occurrence in preserved specimens. He suggested that this mild satyriasis might be due to the chance that the animal had been captured when close to a female or to the effect of the alcohol in which it had been preserved, and added the simple and not unnatural comment, 'women and wine, in fact'. The amount of critical correspondence which this called forth surprised both author and editor, and seemed to show that scientists are unduly sensitive to any suspicion of light-heartedness in serious journals.

★   ★   ★

The sound of words is the origin of all the balance and rhythm of a sentence. A writer who wishes his sentences to possess these desirable qualities is helped by reading his sentencs aloud; and if he is successful the result may be surprising in its unexpected attractiveness. Sometimes such sentences appear, as it were by chance, in the course of otherwise plain and unremarkable pages. I quote, as an example, from a recent novel:

> Lord Fingleton rode out to meet them in a flurry of golden retrievers, and they made a rakish cavalcade — the young horses, the excited dogs, the bouncing trap, the two large men and the girl in the silly hat.

A scientist very seldom tries to write like this; he is more likely to produce this:

> It has been shown that in electrolysis those metals whose use as cathode require the highest voltages in order to bring about liberation of hydrogen yield hydrogen of the greatest activity.

I picked this sentence quite by chance, opening a well-known chemistry text-book at random and reading the first sentence that caught my eye. I might, therefore, have found uglier ones with a little search; but here is a typical specimen which even carries the hall-mark of the careless writer, a grammatical mistake. 'Use' is the singular subject of the plural verb 'require'.

The sounds of words or sentences seem to make no appeal to the scientist. There are so many words in the vocabulary of science which are undeniably ugly that this must, in the main, be true; nor is it easy to recall an instance of a scientist's objection to a new word on the grounds that its ugliness would mar the acceptance of the principle which needed its use, or even that the reader's pleasure would suffer as he met it.

When it is realised that such words as onchosphere, siphonoglyph, telo-lethical and dozens and scores of others as cacophonous, and many that are worse, such as Anomomeristica and mitoschisis, have been proposed and used, it can only be imagined that scientists are tone-deaf, and that they read silently without inward appreciation of the sounds of the printed words.

The point is one to which we shall return: for the present it seems that the care for sound which must be taken by any writer of literary English, and taken far more scrupulously by a poet, is simply not existent in the writing of science. The meaning is the only matter of importance.

Of course it is easy enough to show that in ordinary language the meaning of a word, impressed on us by long use, is of greater power than its actual sound. An excellent example of this is found in the story of the two cricketers who, in an attempt to improve the close understanding which existed between them and enabled them to steal many short runs, sought to confuse the fielding side by calling to each other 'No' with the implica-tion 'Yes', and 'Yes' with the implication 'No'. They found that they so often reacted to the customary meanings, instead of listening to and interpreting the sounds, that they invariably ran one another out.

★   ★   ★

Discussion of the scientist's concern with the sound of his words has occupied less space than the discussion of his greater concern with their meanings, but his concern with their associations will occupy a little more. In ordinary speech the associations which a word acquires in the course of its life are of overwhelming importance and the choice of any particular word from among a number of alternatives is more strongly influenced by its associations than by anything else. So supreme is this power that it can change the apparent meaning of a sentence — compare the words:

Her boy has recently come into the house

with its almost exact paraphrase:

Her son has just come home.

Again, association can supply an apparent meaning where otherwise there would be none. Shelley wrote:

The cloud which rested on that cone of flame was cloven. . . .

and to a purely scientific reader the impression given by this sentence is that it is nonsense. He will argue that heat of combustion will so quickly evaporate drops of liquid that a cloud cannot rest on a flame; but for the poetically minded reader the associations of cloud, flame and cloven so thickly surround the words that their meanings do not have to be con-sidered; an impression is produced, which is most likely to be the one which the poet sought to convey, and is almost certainly not that of impossibility which the scientist notices.

There are some words which have manifest associations in ordinary speech and which are often used by scientists. These words seem to shed their associations completely when they are found in a scientific environment. Examples are purity, truth and strength. Put them together into two sentences:

> The purity of her nature and the truth of her ideals gave her a strength that could not be mistaken.

> The purity of his reagents and the truth of his balance give him the strength of the solution without an error.

It can be seen that the three words concerned are used in the second sentence solely because of their meanings, and their associations have no influence on the impression which the statement produces.

Again, scientific words seem to have a property which inhibits the formation of associations. Words such as 'diathermanous' or 'anisotropic' repel associative accretions because they have no emotional content.

Further, any facet of human thought which might introduce an emotion can generally be expressed in the warmer tones of ordinary human speech, the use of which leaves the scientific terms in their untouched untouchable purity; just as the visitors who concentrate themselves about Broadway leave the rest of the Cotswolds to the enjoyment of others. For example, a physiologist may speak or write of the mammary glands of the female with a frigidity that is almost incredible to the lover who is thinking of the breasts of his mistress; and yet it is a fact that reference is being made by both to precisely the same objects.

This, then, is the position. The scientist is to be envied because he does not have to select his words from among groups of alternatives, and is then criticised because the sentences over which he can exercise so little control are not aesthetically pleasing to the ear of the reader. What can the scientist do? He can do very little, and his usual way out of the difficulty is not to recognise it, and to regard himself as immune from the problems which beset other writers. He uses the language of science according to his ability and is, or should be, grateful that its qualities make his task so easy.

★   ★   ★

A language whose first qualities are precision and lucidity should be a language of great power, power not over men's hearts and emotions but over their minds and efforts. It should be the ideal language in which to explain abstruse concepts so that readers should have the least possible difficulty in grasping ideas that are strange to their accustomed modes of thought. In other words the language of science possesses great powers of penetration, carrying its readers to the core of a problem and, once there, expounding the difficulties encountered and to come. Generally it does this successfully and it is a fact that no scientific concept has ever been made easier to understand by attempts to express it in unscientific language.

Moreover, the scientist while writing science can write as he could never do in ordinary literary work, because he can use scientific and emotionally neutral words. The custom of writers, as of speakers, is to avoid direct statements of anything that has painful, fearful or shameful associations, and such ordinary biological events as death and reproduction are mentioned only in protective periphrases. The scientific writer has no need to use these methods; he can describe these happenings with outspoken plainness of speech because his scientific words are free from all misunderstanding, free from all the associations which have grown about Anglo-Saxon words with identical meanings. The language of science overturns the illogical attitude of the ordinary man, defies his spirit of taboo, permits no evasions and countenances no sniggerings. This conquest of the habitual mode of thought, if thought it be, of the average man is one of the greatest triumphs that must be credited to the language of science.

★   ★   ★

When the language of science fails it does so not from its own weakness but because of the limitations of the mind of man. Many of the ideas of the scientists are far from being simple ones, and words, even the special words of the scientists' vocabulary, cannot express them shortly. Long phrases clog the mind, which in consequence can but imperfectly develop ideas which trail so much verbiage behind them. As an example of this one may quote the statement: 'If there are more cows in the world than there are hairs in the tail of any one cow, there must be some cows with the same number of hairs in their tails.' This fact is undoubtedly true, but when it is presented in a form which necessitates thirty-three words and even when the important ones are short homely words like cow, hair and tail, the mind of the reader fails to penetrate immediately to the central facts. He may ask for time to think it over, or even for a careful explanation, taken slowly, step by step, until at last the light breaks through and the principle is accepted as obvious.

But if this is the reception given to relatively simple statements, what can be expected of more complex ones? Obviously they will be so cumbersome as to be quite unwieldy. The only hope of progress is to replace the wordy phrases by something that can be more easily manipulated, to have a symbol instead of a mass of words. Thus even a child soon learns to begin the solving of an algebraic problem by suggesting that, shall we say, the speed of the cyclist in miles per hour on his outward journey shall be shortened to the single symbol 'x'. A simplification like this makes the problem much easier; the mind can do things with 'x' which it cannot do with the words 'the outward speed of the cyclist'. In fact, for purposes of investigation symbols are often better than words.

The comparison between the symbolic words of science and the symbols of the mathematician has been made before, and has been mentioned above, in connection with individual words. The symbolic language written by the mathematician has certain characteristics which it is helpful to investigate. First of all it has, like other languages, to be learnt before it can be used; a young student, at what is to-day called the Ordinary Level, is expected to be able to show that he has begun to learn it. He may be asked to express in symbolic form some such statement as: 'Twice the product of any two consecutive numbers is less by unity than the sum of their squares.' When he does so, and writes

$$2x \, (x + 1) = x^2 + (x + 1)^2 - 1$$

he is, in effect, translating the statement from English words into algebraic symbols, just as if he were translating it into French, or any other language. There is, in fact, an algebraic language, the chief characteristics of which are its brevity and its many possible applications.

The use of symbols, or the habit of making use of symbolic statement of facts, is an essential part of the scientific language. It reaches its highest development in mathematical physics. In this realm of science symbols first displace words, then render the words unnecessary or forgettable, and finally surpass them. In the very simple example about consecutive numbers which has just been given, symbols displace the words, or, as we said, translate them. Still within the limits of elementary knowledge, a familiar formula like $\sin (A + B) = \sin A \cos B + \cos A \sin B$ can be used without the smallest need to think of the words in which sines and cosines are defined. If one tried to explain the meaning behind a symbolic statement of this kind to an intelligent adult who had never read enough mathematics to know what a sine or a cosine was, one would be amazed at the very large number of words that would be needed, and one would perceive how far a symbolic statement may be removed from its original ideas.

There is in consequence little reason to be surprised when it is detected that in the hands of a genius the manipulation of symbols may carry the manipulator beyond the realms in which the implications of the formula he has deduced can be expressed in words. Many of the formulae derived and used in the theory of relativity are of this ultra-translatable type; and so justify conclusively the contention that symbolic expression is an integral part of the language of science.

In the language of chemistry formulae are indispensable, for their short symbols include so much information. If, for example, one can imagine a chemist who had not previously heard the word aniline, the name would tell him nothing about the compound in question (unless his Arabic were good enough to suggest its origin in indigo). But the formula $C_6H_5NH_2$ would tell him the elements of which it was composed, carbon, hydrogen, nitrogen, the proportions in which they were present, $72 : 7 : 14$, and would also enable him to foretell several of its reactions with other substances. In the same way a simple equation like $CuSO_4 + BaCl_2 = BaSO_4 + CuCl_2$ contains so much information about atoms, radicles and molecules, about the composition of the compounds concerned, and about the quantities in which they react or are produced, that to set it all out in full would take twelve or fifteen lines of print. . . .

The whole of this chapter may perhaps be summarised by saying quite shortly that the writer of the language of science must from the outset abandon all thoughts or hopes of achieving eloquence; that is to say he can scarcely attain that appeal to the emotions which is the ambition of the orator. But in the sense of fitness for his purpose, the sense, that is to say, expounded by Cicero in the paragraph quoted in Chapter 1,* the scientist should have the power to achieve distinction. He runs a much smaller risk of using the wrong word.

Accepting this possibility of an unemotional eloquence based on an exact fitness of words, we should therefore say, perhaps, that the scientist cannot write what in other kinds of literature is sometimes known as the 'purple passage'. Scientific excerpts do not often find places in anthologies of prose, unless these anthologies have been compiled not for their literary but for their scientific interest. In the latter case they cannot be read for pleasure, but only because they illustrate the development of scientific thought.

Finally, let me quote a short passage from the biological works of Professors Geddes and Thompson, which can lay claim to eloquence; it was written during a brief period of hope that science might be able to do something to alleviate the disillusion that followed the First World War.

> And as the psychologists are now bringing their own organ-building into fuller adjustment with that of biology, new voluntaries increasingly appear until even in the more idealist of these we may hear anew the vox Coelestis jubilate, however may, in these sad days, the vox humana wail.

My purpose in quoting it is to point out that its claim to notice rests on its use of a musical metaphor, and not on its science.

---

* *Editors' Note:* In brief: "Eloquence will be his . . . who can adapt his style to whatever his theme may be."

Anatol Rapoport

THE LANGUAGE OF SCIENCE
Its Simplicity, Beauty, and Humor

🙶🙶

For Anatol Rapoport, a mathematical biologist and semanticist, the notion of the language of science as consisting of an esoteric vocabulary or a completely prosaic one is incomplete. In the areas of physics and mathematics, simple, common words — *group, field, limit, neighborhood, force, mass* — are used to denote extremely complex notions which do not require concrete visualization. According to Rapoport, the advantage that science has over other areas which also use "abstract visualizeable concepts" but which often require large and complex vocabularies — psychology, philosophy, and theology, for example — is that science builds up "simple concepts into complex ones by clearly prescribed rules." In philosophy, no mathematical formula can prescribe the connection between *honesty, virtue,* and *happiness.* However, when science does turn to metaphor to provide visualization for its concepts, as examples in this essay show it frequently does, these metaphors stem from insights which, unlike those of poetry, "are rooted not in personal or cultural perceptions of relatedness but in the actual structure of the world to the extent that this structure reflects itself in the mathematical description of reality." An empathetic attitude may allow the non-scientist some appreciation of the beauty of this structure, but he will insist on asking nevertheless how much humanity is contained within this structure.

Reprinted from ETC.: A Review of General Semantics, Vol. XVI, No. 4 (Summer, 1959) by permission of the editor.

The most advanced branches of science, namely, the physical, have developed their own special languages, such as the mathematics of theoretical physics and the molecular structure symbolism of chemistry. Even in these highly formalized sciences there is a residue of "ordinary" language; and, of course, many sciences are still written entirely in the general purpose idiom. My remarks will be largely concerned with this vernacular component of the language of science.

There are two widely held notions about the language of science: first, that the vocabularly of this language consists largely of words difficult to spell and to pronounce; second, that it is an extremely prosaic language, a language of factual reports, one that excludes both sentiment and imagery. These two notions are held by most non-scientists — both by those who hold the language of science in disdain and those who are awed by it. The anti-intellectuals, when they ridicule scientific vocabulary, often accuse the scientist of deliberately obscuring his language, either because of snobbism or exhibitionism. They say that the long, difficult expressions are often no more than needlessly complicated ways of saying simple things, such as can be frequently demonstrated in translations from Federalese and Legalese.

In rebuttal, the defenders of scientific terminology point out that the scientist must make distinctions which are of little consequence to the layman. For example, when the layman says "grouse," the ornithologist must say *Lagopus scoticus* or *Lyrurus tetrix* or *Bonasa umbellus*, because all of these grouse do not even belong to the same genus, and the distinctions are important to the ornithologist. Since there are hundreds of thousands of known species of animals and plants, the vocabulary of the naturalist must be immense. To avoid further confusion, Latin has been adopted as the universal language of biological taxonomy. The necessity for the long and difficult vocabulary is thus demonstrated in this instance. The argument, however, is not immune to a counter-rebuttal, which is not without justification. Many examples of academic discourse can be cited where precision of meaning or fineness of distinction are not at all in evidence but an obscure vocabulary is very much so. However, we shall leave this argument at this point and turn to the other widespread notion about the language of science, namely, that it is dry and matter of fact.

Paul H. Oeser in his charming article entitled "The Lion and the Lamb: An Essay on Science and Poetry" (*American Scientist*, XLIII [1955], 89–96) offers this dramatic example of contrast between prose and poetry. The first is from Henry S. Canby's *Definitions: Second Series*:

> Tail nearly as long as to slightly longer than wing, more or less rounded, flat (not vaulted), the retrices relatively broad, with broadly rounded tips. Tarsus less than one-fourth to about one-third as long as wing, the acrotarsium with a single row of large transverse scutella, the planta tarsi usually with a single row of small scutella along outer side

and smaller, irregular scutella on inner side; lateral toe reaching to or slightly beyond . . .

Contrasted with this is a stanza by Lew Sarett on the common loon (*Gavia immer*):

> With mournful wail from dusk to dawn
> He gibbered at the taunting stars —
> A hermit-soul gone raving mad,
> And beating at his bars.

Again we recall the familiar attacks upon and the defenses of the language of science. The attackers point to scientific description as dessicative, as something that acts like a destroyer of spiritual meanings. I suppose these people find a similarity between the language of science and that perversion of the commercial mentality which is aware of the price of everything and of the value of nothing.

And, of course, there are the standard defenses. We must separate knowledge from sentiment. Recall that compassion may comfort the sick, but it will never cure them as prosaic medical knowledge will. In politics, sentiment leads to demagogy, while dispassionate analysis encourages statesmanship, etc.

Here, too, both sides have a point. Unquestionably to gain and communicate knowledge a language of detachment is indispensable. But often a language which excludes affect also excludes insight, an important ingredient of all knowledge that matters.

My concern will not be with the issue of whether the often outlandish vocabulary and the graceless style of scientific writing is a good or a bad thing. Instead I will make a case against the assumptions made both by the foes and by many of the friends of the scientific attitude, namely, that the language of science necessarily depends on a large and esoteric vocabulary and that this language is necessarily devoid of poetry. I will argue that just in those areas of science where the richest and the most profound insights abound, the reverse is true: (1) vocabularies are small and consist of short, commonly used words; (2) the elements of poetry, such as symmetry of expression, figures of speech, and rich imagery abound.

I am referring to mathematics and physics, which certainly deserve to be viewed as the epitome of scientific achievement, not only in themselves but for their increasing influence upon the methodology of all natural science and increasingly even upon social science. The character of scientific language varies widely among the disciplines, but it is certainly defensible to take the language of mathematics and physics as important manifestations of the language of science.

The key terms in the vocabulary of modern higher algebra are words like *group, ring, field, ideal, trace, norm, normal, simple.* The vocabulary of analysis (another of the main branches of mathematics) depends heavily on words like *limit, function, converge, continuous, regular, analytic, pole.* In topology we have different kinds of *sets*, for example, *open, closed,* and *perfect;* different kinds of *spaces,* for example, *compact, ordered,* and *separable.* A term of crucial importance in topology is *neighborhood.* Fundamental words in physics are *force, mass, work, power, action, energy, field, charge, current, potential, flux, heat, pressure, temperature, nucleus, particle, orbit, spin.*

Certainly none of these words appear to have been designed to impress or intimidate anyone. However, here is the rub. It is impossible to explain the meaning of a single one of the words in the mathematical list and of most of the words in the physics list to anyone who has not had literally years of certain kinds of experience.

As an example, there is no practical way even to begin to explain to a non-mathematician the meaning of the homely word *neighborhood* as it is used in topology. The usual way to explain the meaning of a word is "backwards," that is, in terms of other words believed to be more directly related to experience. If these are still not understood, one continues the regression until words linked to experience are reached. But if such a process were started with *neighborhood* in its topological sense, the chain of reduction would have to go on and on. Before commonly understood terms were reached, the explanation would become so long that its beginning would be forgotten.

There remains only the "forward" type of explanation. That is, one starts with commonly understood mathematical terms and compounds their meanings into more complicated notions to which one then gives names. Then one compounds these notions into still more complex ones, etc., until the term to be defined is reached. This chain will, of course, be just as long as the "backward" chain, but one can hope that in the forward process, the intervening concepts will be digested or, to change the metaphor, will be used as successive springboards. But this is nothing but training. At the end of the process, the trainee with his internalized compounded concepts will have become a mathematician. Therefore one must conclude that the meaning of terms like *neighborhood* can be imparted only to mature mathematicians. Exactly the same situation exists with respect to the word *simple* as it used in the theory of linear algebras, and with most of the other "easy" words which make up the vocabulary of higher mathematics.

Thus it appears that in important areas of science, far from using complicated words to denote simple notions (as many believe) the language of science uses very simple words to denote exceedingly complex notions. Moreover, the compounding of notions makes large vocabularies unnecessary. The latter point is easy to illustrate in the language of physics. The logic of the language of physics is the logic of mathematical operation. In this respect it is quite unlike the logic to which our aristotelian heritage has accustomed us, namely, the logic of taxonomy. In the latter, newly defined terms stand largely for intersections of classes, and classes are defined by syndromes of properties. Thus in classical logic horses are defined as quadrupeds with certain equine properties, and human beings as bipeds with certain anthropoid properties, etc.

Most of the terms in physics are defined not by classification but by mathematical operation. *Mass* is *force* divided by *acceleration; power* is *work* divided by *time; action* is *energy* multiplied by *time,* etc. To someone who thinks only in terms of classificatory logic these definitions must seem strange. True, we tend to become used to them, exposed as many of us are to elementary engineering and to mass production (who has not heard of "man-hours"?). But just because we are becoming used to this sort of thinking we often fail to realize what a profound difference in semantics the operational language of exact science has brought about.

Think for a moment about *acceleration.* A car salesman tells you that the car he is selling will attain a speed of 60 miles per hour from dead start in 11 seconds. Its acceleration during this period is therefore 88 feet per second per 11 seconds, or eight feet per second per second. Instead of using the awkward expression "per second per second," the physicist says "per second squared." In my school days I remember a bold and honest boy in the physics class who asked the teacher just what he meant by a "square second." The teacher's sarcastic reply indicated that he did not know.

It is, of course, foolish to try to evoke an "image" of a square second. But that is just the point. The literal-minded are inevitably stymied, because they insist on thinking in terms of visual images and cannot get rid of a feeling that what cannot be visually imagined is not quite real. I am not referring to the dullards and to those who sacrifice imagination on the altar of so-called hard-headed realism. I am referring to the best minds in classical Greece, the first honest-to-goodness mathematicians in the Western World. They *could* think mathematically, but almost exclusively in terms of visualized geometry. To them a "square" *was* a square, not the result of a mathematical operation. Therefore the cube of a quantity might still have made sense to them, because it could be represented as a real cube. But a fourth power would have appeared as unreal to the Greek geometer as the fourth dimension appears to the layman of today. Neither is translatable into a visual image.

Here, then, is the first tremendous conceptual innovation which we owe to the language of science. Science has freed the intellect from dependence on concrete visualizable conceptualizations — largely through introducing mathematical operation as a generator of concepts. It is this semantic device which makes a comparatively small vocabulary sufficient for physics. Indeed the technical glossary of the physicist is quite small, and the majority of terms in it are borrowed from common usage. The vast complexity of the language of physics stems from the richness of mathematical manipulation, which makes the coinage of new and complicated terms largely unnecessary. One might say that truly scientific terms are to common language words as the letters of the alphabet are to ideograms. The letters are simpler, more abstract, and endowed with far greater potential for combinations.

There are certainly other areas of thought where abstract unvisualizable concepts abound, for example, depth psychology, philosophy, and theology. These areas, however, are by no means characterized by simple vocabularies, as physics is. I believe this is because the discipline of strictly operational definition, the compounding of simple concepts into complex ones by clearly prescribed rules, is lacking in these areas. Consequently, meanings and distinctions are not clear and a great proliferation of terminology, even of private jargons, clutters the language of those areas. The esoteric languages of the speculative disciplines are, in a way, the very antithesis of the characteristic language of science.

I shall now argue against the other prevalent notion, namely, that the language of science is prosaic. Examples supporting this view, such as excerpts from handbooks and catalogues, are well known. Examples to the contrary are hardly known at all. This is not surprising. If science has a language of its own, its poetry is also its own. This poetry speaks to the initiates, and, like most poetry and indigenous humor, it does not lend itself well to translation. Nevertheless I will try, at the risk of sacrilege, to translate some instances of scientific poetry and of scientific humor.

Poetry, I suppose, is a mixture of music, imagery, and metaphor. I will begin by giving an example of a scientific metaphor. First consider the notion of a *spectrum* as it is used in optics. Light, as is generally known, is pictured in physics as electromagnetic vibrations in a certain range of frequency. Monochromatic light consists of a single frequency, describable by a simple sine wave. Combinations of sine waves of different frequencies and amplitudes characterize the actual light of our experience. A beam of such light, passed through a prism, will decompose into the constituent monochromatic parts, i.e., into different pure colors. These colors (i.e., wave lengths) with their associated amplitudes make up the spectrum of the beam. Mathematically speaking, the spectrum is a table in which each of the frequencies of which a beam of light is composed is associated with its amplitude. To the eye, a spectrum appears as a gradation of colors in space. In particular, a rainbow is a spectrum. Here it would seem, the contrast between the prose of scientific language and poetry is particularly crass, for the rainbow is usually held to be a poetic object, and its reduction to a table of numbers is conventionally viewed as a debasement of esthetic value. But please follow me further.

It is shown mathematically that any periodic vibration is analyzable into constituent frequencies with associated amplitudes. Indeed, the frequencies of a strictly periodic process must all be whole number multiples of a single fundamental frequency. A musical tone is just such a process. Every musical tone, therefore, has a *spectrum*, perceived by the ear as the "quality" of the tone, that which makes the difference between the tone of the oboe and that of a flute, or the difference between the violin tone of a beginner and that of a master. In every musical tone, the frequencies are all simple multiples of a single fundamental frequency. The spectra of such tones (called discrete spectra) are therefore particularly simple. A noise, however, is not a strictly periodic process and so cannot be broken up into a series of evenly spaced frequencies. The spectrum of a noise is a continuous one, in which all the frequencies, not just the multiples of a fundamental, may be represented.

Now the spectrum of white light is also a continuous one, specifically one in which *all the frequencies have the same amplitude*. In view of all these analogies, one can justify the metaphor "white noise," i.e., *a noise whose frequency spectrum contains all the frequencies with equal amplitudes*.

But time-dependent processes are not confined to light and sound. Electric current or the motion of an object can also be expressed as mathematical functions. If the mathematical functions are periodic, the associated spectra are discrete; otherwise they are continuous. In particular, *any* process whose frequency spectrum has the same mathematical form as the spectrum of white light can be christened "white noise" — a term much used in modern communication engineering, a truly interdisciplinary metaphor, whose parentage stems from optics and acoustics respectively, but whose general meaning now implies a precise *mathematical* definition of "chaos." It is "chaos" because it can be shown that a white noise process is one where it is most difficult to guess on the basis of what has happened what is going to happen next!

Now you may well ask why this example is offered as an illustration of poetry in the language of science. To answer this question, let us recall that the effectiveness of a metaphor is gauged by two things: by the degree of superficial diversity and the degree of inherent similarity of the things identified. If a metaphor is extremely far-fetched but at the same time calls attention to a profound relatedness of two phenomena, it is a powerful metaphor. A poetic metaphor is supposed to impart insight — the insight of recognition. And one of the principal functions of poetry is to impart such insights, which poetry does largely through inspired uses of metaphor. I submit that the language of science does just this.

Science, we see, has its own peculiar method of metaphor construction. Like the metaphors of poetry, those of science stem from insights. But these insights, unlike those of poetry, are rooted not in personal or cultural perceptions of relatedness but in the actual structure of the world to the extent that this structure reflects itself in the mathematical description of reality.

One more example of this sort is instructive, because the metaphor it gives rise to is so far-fetched as to seem humorous. Several years ago workers concerned with the statistical characteristics of verbal output discovered striking regularities in the relationship between the frequency with which words occur in large samples of verbal output and the number of different words associated with each frequency. Thus the words which are used with the greatest frequency like "the," "of," and "to" have the fewest representatives, while words which occur least frequently have the most representatives. To put it another way, of the words that occur frequently, there are few; of the words that occur rarely, there are many.

Bénoit Mandelbrot showed that these statistical regularities in the frequency of words are just what one would expect to find if one assumed that the users of language used it in such a way as to convey the most "information" at a given fixed average "cost" per word. Here "information" is used in the technical sense of the communication engineer, and "cost" is analogous to the energy expended in encoding, producing, or decoding a word. It was also shown by workers concerned with the mathematical theory of information (particularly by Claude E. Shannon and Norbert Wiener) that the communication engineer's measure of information is mathematically analogous to what is known as entropy in thermodynamics. The statistics of verbal output approaching its equilibrium (in the evolution of language) then becomes entirely analogous to the statistical behavior of a physical system, say a gas, approaching its equilibrium. There too, the greatest possible entropy (analogous to information) is attained under the restraint of constant total energy (or average energy per molecule), i.e., the temperature of the gas. The mathematical isomorphism of the two mathematical theories being complete, it becomes possible to identify a parameter in the formula describing the frequency distribution of words in a given sample with the parameter describing the temperature of a gas which has reached equilibrium. Indeed, Mandelbrot makes just such a metaphorical identification. He speaks of the "temperature" of a language sample. It turns out that one of the "hottest" examples of English prose is Joyce's *Ulysses*, while the language of children or schizophrenics turns out to be characteristically "cool"!

I think these examples match some of the weirdest identifications to be found in poetry, and I suppose they serve a somewhat similar purpose. They are forms of play, but in the case of the mathematical metaphor, they are strictly disciplined play.

Nor does the language of science lack ordinary metaphors, whose function is simply to add to the vividness of discourse. In mathematics one finds an *osculating* curve, one which has very close-fitting contact with another. (*To osculate* means, of course, *to kiss*.) One finds in mathematics also *pathological* functions, i.e., relations among variables with bizarre paradoxical properties. The language of American electronic technology is full of slang with its *feedbacks, dashpots, choppers,* and *pip-trappers.* The engineer has also introduced the *black box,* the hidden inner arrangement of a system, which must be inferred by observing the relations between the inputs and the outputs. The psychologist has enthusiastically embraced this term, for it fits his own methodological problem. He observes the stimuli and the responses of an organism; what happens between them is shut in a *black box,* the organism's nervous system.

Threshold is a common term in neurophysiology. It has become so common that we forget its metaphorical origin. The physicist speaks of a *degenerate gas,* a metaphor borrowed from the mathematical metaphor *degenerate curve,* a curve characterized by a special value of a parameter which reduces it to a more primitive curve. The word *primitive* is, of course, also a metaphor, related to a hierarchy of complexity in mathematical expression. The biologist speaks of *mutation pressure* and of *selection pressure,* which are not pressures at all in the literal physical sense but which produce effects analogous to those of pressure, and of an *adaptation landscape,* over whose *hills* and *valleys* a population can be said to *wander* as its genetic make-up undergoes evolutionary changes. *Pay-off,* whose origin is possibly rooted in underworld jargon, is today a key term in the highly sophisticated mathematical theory of games.

As we pass to psychiatry, the metaphors of its technical discourse become, as is well known, so profuse that one wonders whether this language has not already crossed the boundary between science and poetry.

It is most difficult to speak of those esthetic qualities of the language of science which are most directly related to direct perception of beauty, difficult in the same sense as it is for a European to explain to a non-European wherein lies the haunting charm of a Schubert song. Some of the grandest generalizations of theoretical physics appear remarkably symmetrical when expressed in mathematical equations. For example, Hamilton's magnificent summary of the entire scope of Newtonian mechanics looks like this:

$$\frac{\partial H}{\partial q_j} = \dot{p}_j$$

$$\frac{\partial H}{\partial p_j} = -\dot{q}_j$$

As with the "easy" words of advanced mathematics, it is useless to explain the meaning of the symbols. Just to understand H requires thorough familiarity with advanced theoretical physics. Therefore nothing is gained by identifying the p_j with the momentum of the j-th particle of a system, the q_j with a generalized spatial coordinate, and the dot as a symbol of differentiation with respect to time. The words in the definition are equally meaningless to one not at home in the language of physics. However, an empathetic attitude may lead one at least to a faint understanding of the sort of feeling which a scientist might have in contemplating the almost perfectly symmetrical arrangement of the symbols on the page ("almost" because of the minus sign, which appears in the second equation only), while he ponders on the fact that the knowledge accumulated over twenty-four centuries is concentrated in those symbols. Perhaps the Chinese philosopher, contemplating the exquisite calligraphic expression of an ancient aphorism on the printed page experiences a similar emotion.

In summary, I have tried to emphasize not the well-known aspects of the language of science, namely, its precision, its algorithms of deduction, its ideal of objectivity, but rather the characteristics not so widely appreciated: its pithiness (rather than verboseness of which it is often accused), and its esthetic qualities.

The semanticists often say that our language does our thinking for us. This is true, of course, of the language of science. Our language is also a source of erotic activity — I take erotic here in its generalized sense of playful creativeness. The expressive richness of dialects, slangs, and jargons attests to this. The language of science is by no means lacking in such elements. It even gives birth to its own special jokes. To appreciate these one needs a sense of humor rooted in an intimacy with the special situations and states of mind which occur in scientific activity.

I will now tell three jokes and will violate the ethics of humor by explaining them. The explanations will kill the jokes, but this cannot be helped. Vivisection is sometimes a necessary evil.

The first is an example of the vilest form of humor, the pun. One can only say in its defense that this one is a quadruple pun. On releasing the animals from the ark, Noah bid them to go forth and multiply. Suddenly two little snakes spoke up, "But we can't multiply — we are adders." Thereupon Noah constructed a table from rough-hewn lumber and said, "Here is a log table. Now you adders can multiply."

The puns on "adders" and "multiply" are obvious. However there are two more puns, barbs aimed at the viscera of the mathematician: "log table," i.e., a logarithmic table is a device which reduces multiplication to addition.

The next joke, in the form of a wisecrack definition, is more sophisticated mathematically. "A topologist is a guy who doesn't know the difference between a coffee cup and a doughnut." The definition hits at the very essence of topology, in which all configurations are considered equivalent if they can be deformed into each other without "tearing." A little reflection reveals that coffee cups and doughnuts belong to the same topological genus (the "torus"), which distinguishes them from baseballs (a lower genus) and lidless teapots (a higher one).

The last joke concerns the mental patient who was convinced that he was dead. The psychiatrist, intent on trying the rational approach, got the patient to admit that dead men don't bleed and then pricked the patient's finger and pointed triumphantly to the emerging drop of blood. The patient's response was, "I was wrong, doctor. Dead men apparently do bleed." This joke, of course, needs no explanation. But it may be pertinent to point out that its humor taps a most profound question of scientific philosophy — the metaphysical underpinnings of the language of science: where is the border between knowledge and faith?

Arthur Schlesinger, Jr.

A PLAGUE OF GOBBLEDYGOOK

ϟϟ

"Let the word go forth from this time and place, to friend and foe alike, that the torch has been passed to a new generation of Americans. . . ." So spoke President Kennedy at his inauguration. Among the men of this new generation whom the President brought into government were the economist John Kenneth Galbraith and the historian Arthur Schlesinger, Jr. Kennedy's advisers were impatient with those whose fidelity to the past made them cling to old programs, old attitudes, and tired clichés. They distrusted the automated response and its accompanying prefabricated language. Note the exact parallel between Schlesinger's description of the talking and writing of the State Department and Macdonald's account of the language of foundations. From Mr. Schlesinger, we get this close-up view of the constant struggle, too often a vain one, to cut through the rigidity of language so as to avoid rigidity of policy.

Reprinted from A *Thousand Days* by Arthur Schlesinger, Jr. (Boston: Houghton Mifflin Company, 1965), by permission of the publisher.

. . . One almost concluded that the definition of a Foreign Service officer was a man for whom the risks always outweighed the opportunities. Career officers had always tended to believe that the foreign policy of the United States was their institutional, if not their personal, property, to be solicitously protected against interference from the White House and other misguided amateurs; and by 1961 those favored in the Dulles years added to this proprietary instinct an immovable devotion to the attitudes of the past, whether good or bad. The hardest thing of all was to change anything — attitudes, programs, clichés. No one was more annoyed by this fidelity to the past, or more poignant in expressing his annoyance, than Galbraith. "You have no idea," he wrote me from New Delhi in 1961, "how difficult it is to control one's reaction over the smug pursuit of what experience has already shown to be disastrous policies." The situation led Galbraith's more philosophical associate, the social analyst Mark Epernay, to point out that, for the sophisticated man, the wisdom of policy naturally mattered far less than its stability. "Few things more clearly mark the amateur in diplomacy than his inability to see that even the change from the wrong policy to the right policy involves the admission of previous error and hence is damaging to national prestige." This insight stimulated Epernay to design a "fully automated foreign policy" guaranteed to produce the proper response to every crisis. So, if Khrushchev threatened to sign a peace treaty with East Germany, the electronic computer could immediately type out the appropriate reply: "We stand willing to negotiate but we cannot act under threat or pressure and we must not make concessions. The reunification of Germany is essential but we do not thereby concede the existence of East Germany. We support the brave people of West Berlin."*

At times, it almost seemed that we had achieved the fully automated foreign policy. Thus I spent three years in the White House in a plaintive and unavailing effort to beg the State Department to stop using the phrase 'Sino-Soviet bloc.' This was a typical Foreign Service expression — barbarous in form (the parallelism would be 'Russo-Chinese' or, if absolutely necessary, 'Sino-Russian') and obsolescent in content. In a memorandum to the State Department Secretariat in January 1963, I wrote:

> Whatever substance [the phrase] might once have had as referring to a unified Russo-Chinese operation has surely been trickling away rather fast in recent months. Today the phrase is in most instances simply absurd. It suggests that those who use it don't know what is going on in the world. I assume that this is not the case.

Again in July, when the feud between Moscow and Peking seemed beyond all possibility of denial:

* Mark Epernay, *The McLandress Dimension* (Boston, 1963), 61, 67.

In view of what is going on currently in Moscow, could not the Department bring itself to abolish the usage 'Sino-Soviet bloc'? The relationship of that phrase to reality grows more tenuous all the time.*

This dedication to the past found its ultimate sanction in what seemed the Service's unshakable determination to protect those who, if wrong, were wrong in the right way and to penalize those who, though right, were right out of channels or out of cadence. The Foreign Service operated as a sort of benevolent society, taking care of its worst as well as — sometimes better than — its best. The promotion system was in effect a conspiracy of the conventional against the unconventional. J. Graham Parsons, having drastically misconceived the situation in Laos, was made ambassador to Sweden. His successor as Assistant Secretary for Far Eastern Affairs, a blameless but unimaginative career officer, having displayed no initiative in Washington, was sent as ambassador to a pivotal Asian state.

On the other hand, zeal for good, but new, policies at the expense of bad, but established, ones was likely to gain an officer the reputation for causing trouble and — under the system where the challenged officer wrote the 'efficiency reports' — a place at the bottom of his Foreign Service class. When Kennedy ended the unrelenting American opposition to the center-left coalition in Italy, the Deputy Chief of Mission in Rome, who had been single-handedly responsible for the prolongation of that policy long after it had become obsolete, became ambassador to Czechoslovakia; while an intelligent junior officer who had fought prematurely for the new policy in the Rome Embassy was marked down for insubordination, his offense having been that of carrying the case past the D.C.M. to the ambassador. This man was saved only by White House intervention from being 'selected out' (a phrase apparently adapted from Samuel Goldwyn) of the Service. Another young officer had served in an Iron Curtain capital. Visiting his country some years before, I had been impressed not only by his insight into the country but by his skill in the language and his exceptional range of acquaintances among writers, journalists and scholars. I ran into him again in 1962 and noted: "His is the all too familiar story. His independence and originality of mind brought him into conflict with his superior. . . . They denounced him as insubordinate; he was rated in the bottom five per cent of his class by the selection board; and is now slated for a consulship in [an Asian country] — obviously a punitive assignment." As Harriman told the Jackson Subcommittee in 1963, "I have noted that men because they haven't gotten along with one individual have been given very low ratings, when others have given them high ratings. . . . Men with a

* It was a losing fight. As I write — on May 9, 1965 — I note Thomas C. Mann, Under Secretary of State for Economic Affairs, running on in an interview with the *New York Times* about "instruments of Sino-Soviet military power" and "orders from the Sino-Soviet military bloc."

spark and independence of expression are at times held down, whereas caution is rewarded."

Caution even smothered the Department's relations with its own envoys abroad. In Western Europe after the Bay of Pigs one ambassador after another asked me in varying tones of perplexity and anguish what in hell had happened. On my return I called for the cable files and found that Washington had confined itself to sending around bland official 'explanations' couched in language suitable for public release. For what had really happened American diplomats overseas did better to rely on *Newsweek* and *Time*. Even though the Attorney General interested himself in the problem, we were never able to persuade State to level with its own embassies on this matter. This sort of thing was all too common. Galbraith, after receiving a similarly useless 'explanation' of policy, sent a crisp cable to the Department suggesting that in the future the confidential communications of the State Department not be used for purposes of "internal bemusement." The suggestion was unavailing.

The intellectual exhaustion of the Foreign Service expressed itself in the poverty of the official rhetoric. In meetings the men from State would talk in a bureaucratic patois borrowed in large part from the Department of Defense. We would be exhorted to 'zero in' on 'the purpose of the drill' (or of the 'exercise' or 'operation'), to 'crank in' this and 'phase out' that and 'gin up' something else, to 'pinpoint' a 'viable' policy and, behind it, a 'fall-back position,' to ignore the 'flak' from competing government bureaus or from the communists, to refrain from 'nit-picking' and never to be 'counterproductive.' Once we were 'seized of the problem,' preferably in as 'hard-nosed' a manner as possible, we would review 'options,' discuss 'over-all' objectives, seek 'breakthroughs,' consider 'crash programs,' 'staff out' policies — doing all these things preferably 'meaningfully' and 'in depth' until we were ready to 'finalize' our deliberations, 'sign on to' or 'sign off on' a conclusion (I never could discover the distinction, if any, between these two locutions) and 'implement' a decision. This was not just shorthand; part of the conference-table vocabulary involved a studied multiplication of words. Thus one never talked about a 'paper' but always a 'piece of paper,' never said 'at this point' but always 'at this point in time.'

Graceless as this patois was, it did have a certain, if sometimes spurious, air of briskness and efficiency. The result was far worse when the Department stopped talking and started writing. Whether drafting memoranda, cables or even letters or statements for the President, the Department fell into full, ripe dreariness of utterance with hideous ease. The recipe was evidently to take a handful of clichés (saying something in a fresh way might create unforeseen troubles), repeat at five-minute intervals (lest the argument become clear or interesting), stir in the dough of the passive voice (the active voice assigns responsibility and was therefore hazardous) and garnish with self-serving rhetoric (Congress would be unhappy unless we constantly proclaimed the rectitude of American motives).

After the Bay of Pigs, the State Department sent over a document entitled "The Communist Totalitarian Government of Cuba as a Source of International Tension in the Americas," which it had approved for distribution to NATO, CENTO, SEATO, the OAS and the free governments of Latin America and eventually for public release. In addition to the usual defects of Foggy Bottom prose, the paper was filled with bad spelling and grammar. Moreover, the narrative, which mysteriously stopped at the beginning of April 1961, contained a self-righteous condemnation of Castro's interventionist activities in the Caribbean that an unfriendly critic, alas! could have applied, without changing a word, to more recent actions by the United States. I responded on behalf of the White House:

> It is our feeling here that the paper should not be disseminated in its present form. . . .
>
> Presumably the document is designed to impress, not an audience which is already passionately anti-Castro, but an audience which has not yet finally made up its mind on the gravity of the problem. Such an audience is going to be persuaded, not by rhetoric, but by evidence. Every effort to heighten the evidence by rhetoric only impairs the persuasive power of the document. Observe the title: 'The Communist Totalitarian Government of Cuba . . .' This title presupposes the conclusion which the paper seeks to establish. Why not call it 'The Castro Regime in Cuba' and let the reader draw his own conclusions from the evidence? And why call it both 'Communist' and 'totalitarian'? All Communist governments are totalitarian. The paper, in our view, should be understated rather than overstated; it should eschew cold war jargon; the argument should be carried by facts, not exhortations. The writing is below the level we would hope for in papers for dissemination to other countries. The writing of lucid and forceful English is not too arcane an art.

The President himself, with his sensitive ear for style, led the fight for literacy in the Department; and he had the vigorous support of some State Department officials, notably George Ball, Harriman and William R. Tyler. But the effort to liberate the State Department from automatic writing had little success. As late as 1963, the Department could submit as a draft of a presidential message on the National Academy of Foreign Affairs a text which provoked this resigned White House comment:

> This is only the latest and worst of a long number of drafts sent here for Presidential signature. Most of the time it does not matter, I suppose, if the prose is tired, the thought banal and the syntax bureaucratic; and, occasionally when it does matter, State's drafts are very good. But sometimes, as in this case, they are not.

A message to Congress is a fairly important form of Presidential communication. The President does not send so many — nor of those he does send, does State draft so many — that each one cannot receive due care and attention. My own old-fashioned belief is that every Presidential message should be a model of grace, lucidity and taste in expression. At the very least, each message should be (a) in English, (b) clear and trenchant in its style, (c) logical in its structure and (d) devoid of gobbledygook. The State Department draft on the Academy failed each one of these tests (including, in my view, the first).

Would it not be possible for someone in the Department with at least minimal sensibility to take a look at pieces of paper designed for Presidential signature before they are sent to the White House?

It was a vain fight; the plague of gobbledygook was hard to shake off. I note words like "minimal" (at least not "optimal") and "pieces of paper" in my own lament. I can only testify with what interest and relief the President and the White House read cables from ambassadors who could write — Galbraith from New Delhi with his suave irony, David Bruce from London with his sharp wit, Kennan from Belgrade with his historical perspective and somber eloquence, John Bartlow Martin from Santo Domingo and William Attwood from Guinea with their vivid journalistic touch.

Theodore H. White summed it all up in a letter he sent me from the Far East in the summer of 1961 — a dispatch the President read with great interest. "The State Department and its competitive instruments," White wrote, "have in the years since I worked with them become so tangled as to be almost unfit for any policy-making purpose or decision. . . . Somewhere there exists in the State Department a zone, or a climate, or inertia, which prevents it from thinking in terms of a new kind of politics, new departures in technique, an inertia which binds it rigidly to the fossil routine of conferences, negotiations, frozen positions. What must be changed must be changed first in Washington, at the center." . . .

Herbert Marcuse

THE CLOSING OF THE UNIVERSE OF DISCOURSE

Ɫ Ɫ

A one-dimensional society, according to Herbert Marcuse, Professor of Politics and Philosophy, is one in which advanced industrial technology is so pervasive and so successful that it determines "not only the socially needed occupations, skills, and attitudes, but also individual needs and aspirations." In one-dimensional man there is no "opposition between the private and public existence, between individual and social needs." The language of this society and this man is a one-dimensional discourse which is so blatantly assertive in reconciling the irreconcilable (as in terms like "clean bomb" and "harmless fall-out") that it seals out distinction, criticism, and protest. In this essay, we examine once again the problem of the interdependence between thought and language, and we confront the possibility that the closed discourse of a closed society may render man helpless to change his condition substantially.

"*Dans l'état présent de l'Histoire, toute écriture politique ne peut que confirmer un univers policier, de même toute écriture intellectuelle ne peut qu'instituer une para-littérature, qui n'ose plus dire son nom.*"

"In the present state of history, all political writing can only confirm a police-universe, just as all intellectual writing can only produce para-literature which does not dare any longer to tell its name."

ROLAND BARTHES

From *One-Dimensional Man* (Boston: Beacon Press, 1964). Reprinted by permission of the Beacon Press, copyright © 1964 by Herbert Marcuse.

The Happy Consciousness — the belief that the real is rational and that the system delivers the goods — reflects the new conformism which is a facet of technological rationality translated into social behavior. It is new because it is rational to an unprecedented degree. It sustains a society which has reduced — and in its most advanced areas eliminated — the more primitive irrationality of the preceding stages, which prolongs and improves life more regularly than before. The war of annihilation has not yet occurred; the Nazi extermination camps have been abolished. The Happy Consciousness repels the connection. Torture has been re-introduced as a normal affair, but in a colonial war which takes place at the margin of the civilized world. And there it is practiced with good conscience, for war is war. And this war, too, is at the margin — it ravages only the "under-developed" countries. Otherwise, peace reigns.

The power over man which this society has acquired is daily absolved by its efficacy and productiveness. If it assimilates everything it touches, if it absorbs the opposition, if it plays with the contradiction, it demonstrates its cultural superiority. And in the same way the destruction of resources and the proliferation of waste demonstrate its opulence and the "high levels of well-being"; "the Community is too well off to care!"[1]

The Language of Total Administration

This sort of well-being, the productive superstructure over the unhappy base of society, permeates the "media" which mediate between the masters and their dependents. Its publicity agents shape the universe of communication in which the one-dimensional behavior expresses itself. Its language testifies to identification and unification, to the systematic promotion of positive thinking and doing, to the concerted attack on transcendent, critical notions. In the prevailing modes of speech, the contrast appears between two-dimensional, dialectical modes of thought and technological behavior or social "habits of thought."

In the expression of these habits of thought, the tensions between appearance and reality, fact and factor, substance and attribute tend to disappear. The elements of autonomy, discovery, demonstration, and critique recede before designation, assertion, and imitation. Magical, authoritarian and ritual elements permeate speech and language. Discourse is deprived of the mediations which are the stages of the process of cognition and cognitive evaluation. The concepts which comprehend the facts and thereby transcend the facts are losing their authentic linguistic representation. Without these mediations, language tends to express and promote the immediate identification of reason and fact, truth and established truth, essence and existence, the thing and its function.

[1] John Kenneth Galbraith, *American Capitalism* (Boston: Houghton Mifflin, 1956), p. 96.

These identifications, which appeared as a feature of operationalism,[2] reappear as features of discourse in social behavior. Here functionalization of language helps to repel non-conformist elements from the structure and movement of speech. Vocabulary and syntax are equally affected. Society expresses its requirements directly in the linguistic material but not without opposition; the popular language strikes with spiteful and defiant humor at the official and semi-official discourse. Slang and colloquial speech have rarely been so creative. It is as if the common man (or his anonymous spokesman) would in his speech assert his humanity against the powers that be, as if the rejection and revolt, subdued in the political sphere, would burst out in the vocabulary that calls things by their names: "head-shrinker" and "egghead," "boob tube," "think tank," "beat it" and "dig it," and "gone, man, gone."

However, the defense laboratories and the executive offices, the governments and the machines, the time-keepers and managers, the efficiency experts and the political beauty parlors (which provide the leaders with the appropriate make-up) speak a different language and, for the time being, they seem to have the last word. It is the word that orders and organizes, that induces people to do, to buy, and to accept. It is transmitted in a style which is a veritable linguistic creation; a syntax in which the structure of the sentence is abridged and condensed in such a way that no tension, no "space" is left between the parts of the sentence. This linguistic form militates against a development of meaning. I shall presently try to illustrate this style.

The feature of operationalism — to make the concept synonymous with the corresponding set of operations — recurs in the linguistic tendency "to consider the names of things as being indicative at the same time of their manner of functioning, and the names of properties and processes as symbolical of the apparatus used to detect or produce them."[3] This is technological reasoning, which tends "to identify things and their functions."[4]

As a habit of thought outside the scientific and technical language, such reasoning shapes the expression of a specific social and political behaviorism. In this behavioral universe, words and concepts tend to coincide, or rather the concept tends to be absorbed by the word. The former has no other content than that designated by the word in the publicized and standardized usage, and the word is expected to have no other response than the publicized and standardized behavior (reaction). The word becomes

[2] *Editors' Note:* To show what is meant by "operationalism" Marcuse quotes P. W. Bridgman's statement that "we mean by any concept nothing more than a set of operations."

[3] Stanley Gerr, "Language and Science," in *Philosophy of Science*, April 1942, p. 156.

[4] *Ibid.*

cliché and, as cliché, governs the speech or the writing; the communication thus precludes genuine development of meaning.

To be sure, any language contains innumerable terms which do not require development of their meaning, such as the terms designating the objects and implements of daily life, visible nature, vital needs and wants. These terms are generally understood so that their mere appearance produces a response (linguistic or operational) adequate to the pragmatic context in which they are spoken.

The situation is very different with respect to terms which denote things or occurrences beyond this noncontroversial context. Here, the functionalization of language expresses an abridgment of meaning which has a political connotation. The names of things are not only "indicative of their manner of functioning," but their (actual) manner of functioning also defines and "closes" the meaning of the thing, excluding other manners of functioning. The noun governs the sentence in an authoritarian and totalitarian fashion, and the sentence becomes a declaration to be accepted — it repels demonstration, qualification, negation of its codified and declared meaning.

At the nodal points of the universe of public discourse, self-validating, analytical propositions appear which function like magic-ritual formulas. Hammered and re-hammered into the recipient's mind, they produce the effect of enclosing it within the circle of the conditions prescribed by the formula.

I have already referred to the self-validating hypothesis as propositional form in the universe of political discourse. Such nouns as "freedom," "equality," "democracy," and "peace" imply, analytically, a specific set of attributes which occur invariably when the noun is spoken or written. In the West, the analytic predication is in such terms as free enterprise, initiative, elections, individual; in the East in terms of workers and peasants, building communism or socialism, abolition of hostile classes. On either side, transgression of the discourse beyond the closed analytical structure is incorrect or propaganda, although the means of enforcing the truth and the degree of punishment are very different. In this universe of public discourse, speech moves in synonyms and tautologies; actually, it never moves toward the qualitative difference. The analytic structure insulates the governing noun from those of its contents which would invalidate or at least disturb the accepted use of the noun in statements of policy and public opinion. The ritualized concept is made immune against contradiction.

Thus, the fact that the prevailing mode of freedom is servitude, and that the prevailing mode of equality is superimposed inequality is barred from expression by the closed definition of these concepts in terms of the powers which shape the respective universe of discourse. The result is the familiar Orwellian language ("peace is war" and "war is peace," etc.), which is by no means that of terroristic totalitarianism only. Nor is it any less Orwellian if the contradiction is not made explicit in the sentence but is enclosed in the noun. That a political party which works for the defense and growth of capitalism is called "Socialist," and a despotic government "democratic," and a rigged election "free" are familiar linguistic — and political — features which long predate Orwell.

Relatively new is the general acceptance of these lies by public and private opinion, the suppression of their monstrous content. The spread and the effectiveness of this language testify to the triumph of society over the contradictions which it contains; they are reproduced without exploding the social system. And it is the outspoken, blatant contradiction which is made into a device of speech and publicity. The syntax of abridgment proclaims the reconciliation of opposites by welding them together in a firm and familiar structure. I shall attempt to show that the "clean bomb" and the "harmless fall-out" are only the extreme creations of a normal style. Once considered the principal offense against logic, the contradiction now appears as a principle of the logic of manipulation — realistic caricature of dialectics. It is the logic of a society which can afford to dispense with logic and play with destruction, a society with technological mastery of mind and matter.

The universe of discourse in which the opposites are reconciled has a firm basis for such unification — its beneficial destructiveness. Total commercialization joins formerly antagonistic spheres of life, and this union expresses itself in the smooth linguistic conjunction of conflicting parts of speech. To a mind not yet sufficiently conditioned, much of the public speaking and printing appears utterly surrealistic. Captions such as "Labor is Seeking Missile Harmony,"[5] and advertisements such as a "Luxury Fall-Out Shelter"[6] may still evoke the naïve reaction that "Labor," "Missile," and "Harmony" are irreconcilable contradictions, and that no logic and no language should be capable of correctly joining luxury and fall-out. However, the logic and the language become perfectly rational when we learn that a "nuclear-powered, ballistic-missile-firing submarine" "carries a price tag of $120,000,000" and that "carpeting, scrabble and TV" are provided in the $1,000 model of the shelter. The validation is not primarily in the fact that this language sells (it seems that the fall-out business was not so good) but rather that it promotes the immediate identification of the particular with the general interest, Business with National Power, prosperity with the annihilation potential. It is only a slip of the truth if a theater announces as a "Special Election Eve Perf., Strindberg's *Dance of Death*."[7] The announcement reveals the connection in a less ideological form than is normally admitted.

[5] *New York Times,* December 1, 1960.
[6] *Ibid.,* November 2, 1960.
[7] *Ibid.,* November 7, 1960.

The unification of opposites which characterizes the commercial and political style is one of the many ways in which discourse and communication make themselves immune against the expression of protest and refusal. How can such protest and refusal find the right word when the organs of the established order admit and advertise that peace is really the brink of war, that the ultimate weapons carry their profitable price tags, and that the bomb shelter may spell coziness? In exhibiting its contradictions as the token of its truth, this universe of discourse closes itself against any other discourse which is not on its own terms. And, by its capacity to assimilate all other terms to its own, it offers the prospect of combining the greatest possible tolerance with the greatest possible unity. Nevertheless its language testifies to the repressive character of this unity. This language speaks in constructions which impose upon the recipient the slanted and abridged meaning, the blocked development of content, the acceptance of that which is offered in the form in which it is offered.

The analytic predication is such a repressive construction. The fact that a specific noun is almost always coupled with the same "explicatory" adjectives and attributes makes the sentence into a hypnotic formula which, endlessly repeated, fixes the meaning in the recipient's mind. He does not think of essentially different (and possibly true) explications of the noun. Later we shall examine other constructions in which the authoritarian character of this language reveals itself. They have in common a telescoping and abridgment of syntax which cuts off development of meaning by creating fixed images which impose themselves with an overwhelming and petrified concreteness. It is the well-known technique of the advertisement industry, where it is methodically used for "establishing an image" which sticks to the mind and to the product, and helps to sell the men and the goods. Speech and writing are grouped around "impact lines" and "audience rousers" which convey the image. This image may be "freedom" or "peace," or the "nice guy" or the "communist" or "Miss Rheingold." The reader or listener is expected to associate (and does associate) with them a fixated structure of institutions, attitudes, aspirations, and he is expected to react in a fixated, specific manner.

Beyond the relatively harmless sphere of merchandising, the consequences are rather serious, for such language is at one and the same time "intimidation and glorification."[8] Propositions assume the form of suggestive commands — they are evocative rather than demonstrative. Predication becomes prescription; the whole communication has a hypnotic character. At the same time it is tinged with a false familiarity — the result of constant repetition, and of the skillfully managed popular directness of the communication. This relates itself to the recipient immediately — without distance of status, education, and office — and hits him or her in the informal atmosphere of the living room, kitchen, and bedroom.

[8] Roland Barthes, *Le Degré zéro de l'écriture* (Paris: Editions du Seuil, 1953), p. 33.

The same familiarity is established through personalized language, which plays a considerable role in advanced communication.[9] It is "your" congressman, "your" highway, "your" favorite drugstore, "your" newspaper; it is brought "to you," it invites "you," etc. In this manner, superimposed, standardized, and general things and functions are presented as "especially for you." It makes little difference whether or not the individuals thus addressed believe it. Its success indicates that it promotes the self-identification of the individuals with the functions which they and the others perform.

In the most advanced sectors of functional and manipulated communication, language imposes in truly striking constructions the authoritarian identification of person and function. *Time* magazine may serve as an extreme example of this trend. Its use of the inflectional genitive makes individuals appear to be mere appendices or properties of their place, their job, their employer, or enterprise. They are introduced as Virginia's Byrd, U.S. Steel's Blough, Egypt's Nasser. A hyphenated attributive construction creates a fixed syndrome:

> "Georgia's high-handed, low-browed governor . . . had the stage all set for one of his wild political rallies last week."

The governor,[10] his function, his physical features, and his political practices are fused together into one indivisible and immutable structure which, in its natural innocence and immediacy, overwhelms the reader's mind. The structure leaves no space for distinction, development, differentiation of meaning: it moves and lives only as a whole. Dominated by such personalized and hypnotic images, the article can then proceed to give even essential information. The narrative remains safely within the well-edited framework of a more or less human interest story as defined by the publisher's policy.

Use of the hyphenized abridgment is widespread. For example, "brush-browed" Teller, the "father of the H-bomb," "bull-shouldered missileman von Braun," "science-military dinner"[11] and the "nuclear-powered, ballistic-missile-firing" submarine. Such constructions are, perhaps not accidentally, particularly frequent in phrases joining technology, politics, and the military. Terms designating quite different spheres or qualities are forced together into a solid, overpowering whole.

The effect is again a magical and hypnotic one — the projection of images which convey irresistible unity, harmony of contradictions. Thus the loved and feared Father, the spender of life, generates the H-bomb for the annihilation of life; "science-military" joins the efforts to reduce anxiety

[9] See Leo Lowenthal, *Literature, Popular Culture, and Society* (Prentice-Hall, 1961), p. 109 ff. and Richard Hoggart, *The Uses of Literacy* (Boston: Beacon Press, 1961), p. 161 ff.

[10] The statement refers, not to the present Governor, but to Mr. Talmadge.

[11] The last three items quoted in *The Nation*, Feb. 22, 1958.

and suffering with the job of creating anxiety and suffering. Or, without the hyphen, the Freedom Academy of cold war specialists,[12] and the "clean bomb" — attributing to destruction moral and physical integrity. People who speak and accept such language seem to be immune to everything — and susceptible to everything. Hyphenation (explicit or not) does not always reconcile the irreconcilable; frequently, the combine is quite gentle — as in the case of the "bull-shouldered missileman" — or it conveys a threat, or an inspiring dynamic. But the effect is similar. The imposing structure unites the actors and actions of violence, power, protection, and propaganda in one lightning flash. We see the man or the thing in operation and only in operation — it cannot be otherwise.

Note on abridgment. NATO, SEATO, UN, AFL-CIO, AEC, but also USSR, DDR, etc. Most of these abbreviations are perfectly reasonable and justified by the length of the unabbreviated designata. However, one might venture to see in some of them a "cunning of Reason" — the abbreviation may help to repress undesired questions. NATO does not suggest what North Atlantic Treaty Organization says, namely, a treaty among the nations on the North-Atlantic — in which case one might ask questions about the membership of Greece and Turkey. USSR abbreviates Socialism and Soviet; DDR: democratic. UN dispenses with undue emphasis on "united"; SEATO with those Southeast-Asian countries which do not belong to it. AFL-CIO entombs the radical political differences which once separated the two organizations, and AEC is just one administrative agency among many others. The abbreviations denote that and only that which is institutionalized in such a way that the transcending connotation is cut off. The meaning is fixed, doctored, loaded. Once it has become an official vocable, constantly repeated in general usage, "sanctioned" by the intellectuals, it has lost all cognitive value and serves merely for recognition of an unquestionable fact.

This style is of an overwhelming *concreteness*. The "thing identified with its function" is more real than the thing distinguished from its function, and the linguistic expression of this identification (in the functional noun, and in the many forms of syntactical abridgment) creates a basic vocabulary and syntax which stand in the way of differentiation, separation, and distinction. This language, which constantly imposes *images*, militates against the development and expression of *concepts*. In its immediacy and directness, it impedes conceptual thinking; thus, it impedes

---

[12] A suggestion of *Life* magazine, quoted in *The Nation*, August 20, 1960. According to David Sarnoff, a bill to establish such an Academy is before Congress. See John K. Jessup, Adlai Stevenson, and others, *The National Purpose* (produced under the supervision and with the help of the editorial staff of *Life* magazine; New York, Holt, Rinehart and Winston, 1960), p. 58.

thinking. For the concept does *not* identify the thing and its function. Such identification may well be the legitimate and perhaps even the only meaning of the operational and technological concept, but operational and technological definitions are specific usages of concepts for specific purposes. Moreover, they dissolve concepts in operations and exclude the conceptual intent which is opposed to such dissolution. Prior to its operational usage, the concept *denies* the identification of the thing with its function; it distinguishes that which the thing *is* from the contingent functions of the thing in the established reality. . . .

George Orwell

THE PRINCIPLES
OF NEWSPEAK

Marshall McLuhan has remarked that 1984 should really have been called 1934. In 1949, when Orwell published his novel, Oceania had a nightmarish recognizability which certainly has not lessened since then. The similarities between Newspeak and the one-dimensional discourse that Marcuse describes with examples from the real world, our world, are self-evident. Indeed, Newspeak, the language that makes certain modes of thought impossible, that diminishes the range of feeling and discrimination, that destroys precision, and that makes speech as nearly as possible independent of consciousness, bears significant resemblances to the language that many of the writers in this section have been describing and analyzing.

Newspeak was the official language of Oceania and had been devised to meet the ideological needs of Ingsoc, or English Socialism. In the year 1984 there was not as yet anyone who used Newspeak as his sole means of communication, either in speech or writing. The leading articles in the *Times* were written in it, but this was a tour de force which could only be carried out by a specialist. It was expected that Newspeak would have finally superseded Oldspeak (or Standard English, as we should call it) by about the year 2050. Meanwhile it gained ground steadily, all Party members tending to use Newspeak words and grammatical constructions more and more in their everyday speech. The version in use in 1984, and embodied in the Ninth and Tenth Editions of the Newspeak dictionary, was a provisional one, and contained many superfluous words and archaic formations which were due to be suppressed later. It is with the final, perfected version, as embodied in the Eleventh Edition of the dictionary, that we are concerned here.

The purpose of Newspeak was not only to provide a medium of expression for the world-view and mental habits proper to the devotees of Ingsoc, but to make all other modes of thought impossible. It was intended that when Newspeak had been adopted once and for all and Oldspeak forgotten, a heretical thought — that is, a thought diverging from the principles of Ingsoc — should be literally unthinkable, at least so far as thought is dependent on words. Its vocabulary was so constructed as to give exact and often very subtle expression to every meaning that a Party member could properly wish to express, while excluding all other meanings and also the possibility of arriving at them by indirect methods. This was done partly by the invention of new words, but chiefly by eliminating undesirable words and by stripping such words as remained of unorthodox meanings, and so far as possible of all secondary meanings whatever. To give a single example. The word *free* still existed in Newspeak, but it could only be used in such statements as "This dog is free from lice" or "This field is free from weeds." It could not be used in its old sense of "politically free" or "intellectually free," since political and intellectual freedom no longer existed even as concepts, and were therefore of necessity nameless. Quite apart from the suppression of definitely heretical words, reduction of vocabulary was regarded as an end in itself, and no word that could be dispensed with was allowed to survive. Newspeak was designed not to extend but to *diminish* the range of thought, and this purpose was indirectly assisted by cutting the choice of words down to a minimum.

Newspeak was founded on the English language as we now know it, though many Newspeak sentences, even when not containing newly created words, would be barely intelligible to an English-speaker of our own day. Newspeak words were divided into three distinct classes, known as the A vocabulary, the B vocabulary (also called compound words), and the C vocabulary. It will be simpler to discuss each class separately, but the grammatical peculiarities of the language can be dealt with in the section devoted to the A vocabulary, since the same rules held good for all three categories.

The A vocabulary. The A vocabulary consisted of the words needed for the business of everyday life — for such things as eating, drinking, working, putting on one's clothes, going up and down stairs, riding in vehicles, gardening, cooking, and the like. It was composed almost entirely of words that we already possess — words like *hit, run, dog, tree, sugar, house, field* — but in comparison with the present-day English vocabulary, their number was extremely small, while their meanings were far more rigidly defined. All ambiguities and shades of meaning had been purged out of them. So far as it could be achieved, a Newspeak word of this class was simply a staccato sound expressing *one* clearly understood concept. It would have been quite impossible to use the A vocabulary for literary purposes or for political or philosophical discussion. It was intended only to express simple, purposive thoughts, usually involving concrete objects or physical actions.

The grammar of Newspeak had two outstanding peculiarities. The first of these was an almost complete interchangeability between different parts of speech. Any word in the language (in principle this applied even to very abstract words such as *if* or *when*) could be used either as verb, noun, adjective, or adverb. Between the verb and the noun form, when they were of the same root, there was never any variation, this rule of itself involving the destruction of many archaic forms. The word *thought*, for example, did not exist in Newspeak. Its place was taken by *think*, which did duty for both noun and verb. No etymological principle was followed here; in some cases it was the original noun that was chosen for retention, in other cases the verb. Even where a noun and verb of kindred meaning were not etymologically connected, one or other of them was frequently suppressed. There was, for example, no such word as *cut*, its meaning being sufficiently covered by the noun-verb *knife*. Adjectives were formed by adding the suffix *-ful* to the noun-verb, and adverbs by adding *-wise*. Thus, for example, *speedful* meant "rapid" and *speedwise* meant "quickly." Certain of our present-day adjectives, such as *good, strong, big, black, soft*, were retained, but their total number was very small. There was little need for them, since almost any adjectival meaning could be arrived at by adding *-ful* to a noun-verb. None of the now-existing adverbs was retained, except for a very few already ending in *-wise*; the *-wise* termination was invariable. The word *well*, for example, was replaced by *goodwise*.

In addition, any word — this again applied in principle to every word in the language — could be negatived by adding the affix *un-*, or could be strengthened by the affix *plus-*, or, for still greater emphasis, *doubleplus-*. Thus, for example, *uncold* meant "warm," while *pluscold* and *doubleplus-cold* meant, respectively, "very cold" and "superlatively cold." It was also possible, as in present-day English, to modify the meaning of almost any word by prepositional affixes such as *ante-*, *post-*, *up-*, *down-*, etc. By such methods it was found possible to bring about an enormous diminution of vocabulary. Given, for instance, the word *good*, there was no need for such a word as *bad*, since the required meaning was equally well — indeed, better — expressed by *ungood*. All that was necessary, in any case where two words formed a natural pair of opposites, was to decide which of them to suppress. *Dark*, for example, could be replaced by *unlight*, or *light* by *undark*, according to preference.

The second distinguishing mark of Newspeak grammar was its regularity. Subject to a few exceptions which are mentioned below, all inflections followed the same rules. Thus, in all verbs the preterite and the past participle were the same and ended in *-ed*. The preterite of *steal* was *stealed*, the preterite of *think* was *thinked*, and so on throughout the language, all such forms as *swam, gave, brought, spoke, taken*, etc., being abolished. All plurals were made by adding *-s* or *-es* as the case might be. The plurals of *man, ox, life* were *mans, oxes, lifes*. Comparison of adjectives was invariably made by adding *-er, -est* (*good, gooder, goodest*), irregular forms and the *more, most* formation being suppressed.

The only classes of words that were still allowed to inflect irregularly were the pronouns, the relatives, the demonstrative adjectives, and the auxiliary verbs. All of these followed their ancient usage, except that *whom* had been scrapped as unnecessary, and the *shall, should* tenses had been dropped, all their uses being covered by *will* and *would*. There were also certain irregularities in word-formation arising out of the need for rapid and easy speech. A word which was difficult to utter, or was liable to be incorrectly heard, was held to be ipso facto a bad word; occasionally therefore, for the sake of euphony, extra letters were inserted into a word or an archaic formation was retained. But this need made itself felt chiefly in connection with the B vocabulary. *Why* so great an importance was attached to ease of pronunciation will be made clear later in this essay.

The B vocabulary. The B vocabulary consisted of words which had been deliberately constructed for political purposes: words, that is to say, which not only had in every case a political implication, but were intended to impose a desirable mental attitude upon the person using them. Without a full understanding of the principles of Ingsoc it was difficult to use these words correctly. In some cases they could be translated into Oldspeak, or even into words taken from the A vocabulary, but this usually demanded a long paraphrase and always involved the loss of certain overtones. The B words were a sort of verbal shorthand, often packing whole ranges of ideas into a few syllables, and at the same time more accurate and forcible than ordinary language.

The B words were in all cases compound words.* They consisted of two or more words, or portions of words, welded together in an easily pronounceable form. The resulting amalgam was always a noun-verb, and inflected according to the ordinary rules. To take a single example: the word *goodthink*, meaning, very roughly, "orthodoxy," or, if one chose to regard it as a verb, "to think in an orthodox manner." This inflected as follows: noun-verb, *goodthink*; past tense and past participle, *goodthinked*; present participle, *goodthinking*; adjective, *goodthinkful*; adverb, *goodthinkwise*; verbal noun, *goodthinker*.

The B words were not constructed on any etymological plan. The words of which they were made up could be any parts of speech, and could be placed in any order and mutilated in any way which made them easy to pronounce while indicating their derivation. In the word *crimethink* (thoughtcrime), for instance, the *think* came second, whereas in *thinkpol* (Thought Police) it came first, and in the latter word *police* had lost its second syllable. Because of the greater difficulty in securing euphony, irregular formations were commoner in the B vocabulary than in the A vocabulary. For example, the adjectival forms of *Minitrue*, *Minipax*, and *Miniluv* were, respectively *Minitruthful*, *Minipeaceful*, and *Minilovely*, simply because *-trueful*, *-paxful*, and *-loveful* were slightly awkward to pronounce. In principle, however, all B words could inflect, and all inflected in exactly the same way.

Some of the B words had highly subtilized meanings, barely intelligible to anyone who had not mastered the language as a whole. Consider, for example, such a typical sentence from a *Times* leading article as *Oldthinkers unbellyfeel Ingsoc*. The shortest rendering that one could make of this in Oldspeak would be: "Those whose ideas were formed before the Revolution cannot have a full emotional understanding of the principles of English Socialism." But this is not an adequate translation. To begin with, in order to grasp the full meaning of the Newspeak sentence quoted above, one would have to have a clear idea of what is meant by *Ingsoc*. And, in addition, only a person thoroughly grounded in Ingsoc could appreciate the full force of the word *bellyfeel*, which implied a blind, enthusiastic acceptance difficult to imagine today; or of the word *oldthink*, which was inextricably mixed up with the idea of wickedness and decadence. But the special function of certain Newspeak words, of which *oldthink* was one, was not so much to express meanings as to destroy them. These words, necessarily few in number, had had their meanings extended until they contained within themselves whole batteries of words which, as

* Compound words, such as *speakwrite*, were of course to be found in the A vocabulary, but these were merely convenient abbreviations and had no special ideological color.

they were sufficiently covered by a single comprehensive term, could now be scrapped and forgotten. The greatest difficulty facing the compilers of the Newspeak dictionary was not to invent new words, but, having invented them, to make sure what they meant: to make sure, that is to say, what ranges of words they canceled by their existence.

As we have already seen in the case of the word *free*, words which had once borne a heretical meaning were sometimes retained for the sake of convenience, but only with the undesirable meanings purged out of them. Countless other words such as *honor, justice, morality, internationalism, democracy, science,* and *religion* had simply ceased to exist. A few blanket words covered them, and, in covering them, abolished them. All words grouping themselves round the concepts of liberty and equality, for instance, were contained in the single word *crimethink*, while all words grouping themselves round the concepts of objectivity and rationalism were contained in the single word *oldthink*. Greater precision would have been dangerous. What was required in a Party member was an outlook similar to that of the ancient Hebrew who knew, without knowing much else, that all nations other than his own worshiped "false gods." He did not need to know that these gods were called Baal, Osiris, Moloch, Ashtaroth, and the like; probably the less he knew about them the better for his orthodoxy. He knew Jehovah and the commandments of Jehovah; he knew, therefore, that all gods with other names or other attributes were false gods. In somewhat the same way, the Party member knew what constituted right conduct, and in exceedingly vague, generalized terms he knew what kinds of departure from it were possible. His sexual life, for example, was entirely regulated by the two Newspeak words *sexcrime* (sexual immorality) and *goodsex* (chastity). *Sexcrime* covered all sexual misdeeds whatever. It covered fornication, adultery, homosexuality, and other perversions, and, in addition, normal intercourse practiced for its own sake. There was no need to enumerate them separately, since they were all equally culpable, and, in principle, all punishable by death. In the C vocabulary, which consisted of scientific and technical words, it might be necessary to give specialized names to certain sexual aberrations, but the ordinary citizen had no need of them. He knew what was meant by *goodsex* — that is to say, normal intercourse between man and wife, for the sole purpose of begetting children, and without physical pleasure on the part of the woman; all else was *sexcrime*. In Newspeak it was seldom possible to follow a heretical thought further than the perception that it *was* heretical; beyond that point the necessary words were nonexistent.

No word in the B vocabulary was ideologically neutral. A great many were euphemisms. Such words, for instance, as *joycamp* (forced-labor camp) or *Minipax* (Ministry of Peace, i.e., Ministry of War) meant almost the exact opposite of what they appeared to mean. Some words, on the other hand, displayed a frank and contemptuous understanding of the real nature of Oceanic society. An example was *prolefeed,* meaning the rubbishy entertainment and spurious news which the Party handed out to the masses. Other words, again, were ambivalent, having the connotation "good" when applied to the Party and "bad" when applied to its enemies. But in addition there were great numbers of words which at first sight appeared to be mere abbreviations and which derived their ideological color not from their meaning but from their structure.

So far as it could be contrived, everything that had or might have political significance of any kind was fitted into the B vocabulary. The name of every organization, or body of people, or doctrine, or country, or institution, or public building, was invariably cut down into the familiar shape; that is, a single easily pronounced word with the smallest number of syllables that would preserve the original derivation. In the Ministry of Truth, for example, the Records Department, in which Winston Smith worked, was called *Recdep,* the Fiction Department was called *Ficdep,* the Teleprograms Department was called *Teledep,* and so on. This was not done solely with the object of saving time. Even in the early decades of the twentieth century, telescoped words and phrases had been one of the characteristic features of political language; and it had been noticed that the tendency to use abbreviations of this kind was most marked in totalitarian countries and totalitarian organizations. Examples were such words as *Nazi, Gestapo, Comintern, Inprecorr, Agitprop.* In the beginning the practice had been adopted as it were instinctively, but in Newspeak it was used with a conscious purpose. It was perceived that in thus abbreviating a name one narrowed and subtly altered its meaning, by cutting out most of the associations that would otherwise cling to it. The words *Communist International,* for instance, call up a composite picture of universal human brotherhood, red flags, barricades, Karl Marx, and the Paris Commune. The word Comintern, on the other hand, suggests merely a tightly knit organization and a well-defined body of doctrine. It refers to something almost as easily recognized, and as limited in purpose, as a chair or a table. *Comintern* is a word that can be uttered almost without taking thought, whereas *Communist International* is a phrase over which one is obliged to linger at least momentarily. In the same way, the associations called up by a word like *Minitrue* are fewer and more controllable than those called up by *Ministry of Truth.* This accounted not only for the habit of abbreviating whenever possible, but also for the almost exaggerated care that was taken to make every word easily pronounceable.

In Newspeak, euphony outweighed every consideration other than exactitude of meaning. Regularity of grammar was always sacrificed to it when it seemed necessary. And rightly so, since what was required, above all for political purposes, were short clipped words of unmistakable meaning which could be uttered rapidly and which roused the minimum of echoes in the speaker's mind. The words of the B vocabulary even gained in force from the fact that nearly all of them were very much alike. Almost invariably these words — *goodthink, Minipax, prolefeed, sexcrime, joycamp, Ingsoc, bellyfeel, thinkpol,* and countless others — were words of two or three syllables, with the stress distributed equally between the first syllable and the last. The use of them encouraged a gabbling style of speech, at once staccato and monotonous. And this was exactly what was aimed at. The intention was to make speech, and especially speech on any subject not ideologically neutral, as nearly as possible independent of consciousness. For the purposes of everyday life it was no doubt necessary, or sometimes necessary, to reflect before speaking, but a Party member called upon to make a political or ethical judgment should be able to spray forth the correct opinions as automatically as a machine gun spraying forth bullets. His training fitted him to do this, the language gave him an almost foolproof instrument, and the texture of the words, with their harsh sound and a certain willful ugliness which was in accord with the spirit of Ingsoc, assisted the process still further.

So did the fact of having very few words to choose from. Relative to our own, the Newspeak vocabulary was tiny, and new ways of reducing it were constantly being devised. Newspeak, indeed, differed from almost all other languages in that its vocabulary grew smaller instead of larger every year. Each reduction was a gain, since the smaller the area of choice, the smaller the temptation to take thought. Ultimately it was hoped to make articulate speech issue from the larynx without involving the higher brain centers at all. This aim was frankly admitted in the Newspeak word *duckspeak,* meaning "to quack like a duck." Like various other words in the B vocabulary, *duckspeak* was ambivalent in meaning. Provided that the opinions which were quacked out were orthodox ones, it implied nothing but praise, and when the *Times* referred to one of the orators of the Party as a *doubleplusgood duckspeaker* it was paying a warm and valued compliment.

The C vocabulary. The C vocabulary was supplementary to the others and consisted entirely of scientific and technical terms. These resembled the scientific terms in use today, and were constructed from the same roots, but the usual care was taken to define them rigidly and strip them of undesirable meanings. They followed the same grammatical rules as the words in the other two vocabularies. Very few of the C words had any currency either in everyday speech or in political speech. Any scientific worker or technician could find all the words he needed in the list devoted to his own speciality, but he seldom had more than a smattering of the words occurring in the other lists. Only a very few words were common to all lists, and there was no vocabulary expressing the function of Science as a habit of mind, or a method of thought, irrespective of its particular branches. There was, indeed, no word for "Science," any meaning that it could possibly bear being already sufficiently covered by the word *Ingsoc*.

From the foregoing account it will be seen that in Newspeak the expression of unorthodox opinions, above a very low level, was well-nigh impossible. It was of course possible to utter heresies of a very crude kind, a species of blasphemy. It would have been possible, for example, to say *Big Brother is ungood*. But this statement, which to an orthodox ear merely conveyed a self-evident absurdity, could not have been sustained by reasoned argument, because the necessary words were not available. Ideas inimical to Ingsoc could only be entertained in a vague wordless form, and could only be named in very broad terms which lumped together and condemned whole groups of heresies without defining them in doing so. One could, in fact, only use Newspeak for unorthodox purposes by illegitimately translating some of the words back into Oldspeak. For example, *All mans are equal* was a possible Newspeak sentence, but only in the same sense in which *All men are redhaired* is a possible Oldspeak sentence. It did not contain a grammatical error, but it expressed a palpable untruth, i.e., that all men are of equal size, weight, or strength. The concept of political equality no longer existed, and this secondary meaning had accordingly been purged out of the word *equal*. In 1984, when Oldspeak was still the normal means of communication, the danger theoretically existed that in using Newspeak words one might remember their original meanings. In practice it was not difficult for any person well grounded in *doublethink* to avoid doing this, but within a couple of generations even the possibility of such a lapse would have vanished. A person growing up with Newspeak as his sole language would no more know that *equal* had once had the secondary meaning of "politically equal," or that *free* had once meant "intellectually free," than, for instance, a person who had never heard of chess would be aware of the secondary meanings attaching to *queen* and *rook*. There would be many crimes and errors which it would be beyond his power to commit, simply because they were nameless and therefore unimaginable. And it was to be foreseen that with the passage of time the distinguishing characteristics of Newspeak would become more and more pronounced — its words growing fewer and fewer, their meanings more and more rigid, and the chance of putting them to improper uses always diminishing.

When Oldspeak had been once and for all superseded, the last link with the past would have been severed. History had already been rewritten, but fragments of the literature of the past survived here and there, imperfectly censored, and so long as one retained one's knowledge of Oldspeak it was possible to read them. In the future such fragments, even if they chanced to survive, would be unintelligible and untranslatable. It was impossible to translate any passage of Oldspeak into Newspeak unless it either referred to some technical process or some very simple everyday action, or was already orthodox (*goodthinkful* would be the Newspeak expression) in tendency. In practice this meant that no book written before approximately 1960 could be translated as a whole. Prerevolutionary literature could only be subjected to ideological translation — that is, alteration in sense as well as language. Take for example the well-known passage from the Declaration of Independence:

We hold these truths to be self-evident, that all men are created equal, that they are endowed by their Creator with certain inalienable rights, that among these are life, liberty and the pursuit of happiness. That to secure these rights, Governments are instituted among men, deriving their powers from the consent of the governed. That whenever any form of Government becomes destructive of those ends, it is the right of the People to alter or abolish it, and to institute new Government . . .

It would have been quite impossible to render this into Newspeak while keeping to the sense of the original. The nearest one could come to doing so would be to swallow the whole passage up in the single word *crimethink*. A full translation could only be an ideological translation, whereby Jefferson's words would be changed into a panegyric on absolute government.

A good deal of the literature of the past was, indeed, already being transformed in this way. Considerations of prestige made it desirable to preserve the memory of certain historical figures, while at the same time bringing their achievements into line with the philosophy of Ingsoc. Various writers, such as Shakespeare, Milton, Swift, Byron, Dickens, and some others were therefore in process of translation; when the task had been completed, their original writings, with all else that survived of the literature of the past, would be destroyed. These translations were a slow and difficult business, and it was not expected that they would be finished before the first or second decade of the twenty-first century. There were also large quantities of merely utilitarian literature — indispensable technical manuals and the like — that had to be treated in the same way. It was chiefly in order to allow time for the preliminary work of translation that the final adoption of Newspeak had been fixed for so late a date as 2050.

6 | ✍

LANGUAGE AND LITERATURE

Epictetus said, "Style? What is style? First I ask myself if what I am about to say is true. Then I say it as clearly as I can in the light of truth. I go not with those who dance around the image of truth less out of honor for her than to display their own skill and address." The literary artist, with his integrity of vision and his sensitivity to language, helps us find the image of truth in ourselves and in our society. F. L. Lucas says that the problems of style are the problems of personality. Style "is personality clothed in words, character embodied in speech." In each choice of word, an author reveals character as well as idea.

What the editors of this book have tried to do is to assemble essays that will increase the reader's consciousness of language, train him to see language in its many facets, provide him with a vocabulary suitable for talking about language, and prepare him to read, write, and think about literary art with understanding and perception.

One path of development in American literature has been the vernacular style in which Hemingway and Salinger have followed the lead of Whitman and Twain. The ear must be keen for the words and patterns of human speech. It is a style suitable for the informal essay also, as Montaigne realized: "I speak to my paper as I speak to the first person I meet." Or for poetry, as Frost said: "We must go out into the vernacular for tones that haven't been brought to book. We must write with the ear on the speaking voice."

There are other styles, however, that employ not only the spoken language but also additional resources of vocabulary and structure. Allen Tate has pointed out how Emily Dickinson uses two features of the diction of English: the Anglo-Saxon for perceptions, the Latinate for ideas. She juxtaposes them imaginatively, provocatively, and startlingly.

No one has ever used language more imaginatively than Shakespeare. Living in the free atmosphere of the Renaissance, he made daring experiments in word-borrowing and word-creation. He had a vocabulary in excess of 20,000 words, or about 10 percent of what was available to him in the lexicon of Elizabethan English and probably more than that of any other creative writer. The vocabulary of his time was rich not only in Anglo-Saxon monosyllables, but also in words of all length, complexity, and variety from French, Spanish, Italian, and Latin. In addition, he used the resources of syntax to create new words, turning nouns into verbs and verbs into nouns, interchanging other parts of speech, and employing constructions that one might call ungrammatical, except that they serve his poetic purposes. His vocabulary, lastly, is strikingly adapted to the demands of characterization — high as the court, low as the alehouse.

The critic George Steiner believes that in our time there has been a "thinning out of language" which "has condemned much of modern literature to mediocrity." He says, "The brute snobbish fact is that men who die speaking as does Macbeth are more tragic than those who sputter platitudes in the style of Willy Loman." But a number of modern writers have attempted a counterattack against "the diminution of language." James Joyce was the most revolutionary of them. In this collection Margaret Schlauch discusses some of his expansions of language, as well as those of other writers.

Just as writers strive to reach the limits of experience, so they attempt to find a language to express what may never yet have been said. They prevent our anesthetization by making the environment visible. They share with us their personal experience, their sense of history, their creativity. They renovate, rejuvenate, rebuild.

The essays on Dickinson and on Shakespeare explore the problem of what language can and cannot do. Thus we confront, to use Walker Gibson's phrase, "the limits of language." But the sense of limitation seems to deter few people from making the effort to say what must be said. Amid all the difficulties, we continue to try to say what we mean as best we can, not only because we remember the pleasure and delight in the experience of language, but also because we *must* communicate with each other.

F. L. Lucas

WHAT IS STYLE?

Is style the man, as a famous epigram asserts it is? Mr. Lucas believes so. One is always expressing himself, giving something of himself away "in whatever he does, and certainly in whatever he writes." Thoreau noted: "Nothing goes by luck in composition. It allows of no tricks. The best you can write will be the best you are. . . . The author's character is read from title-page to end." Mr. Lucas shows us how we can discuss style in the most particular way. Considering the power of words, we have an obligation to develop the best style we can. Mr. Lucas has eight or ten recommendations. He begins with the necessity for honesty and courtesy, but also suggests bringing language alive through metaphor. Such a detailed analysis makes it possible for us to recognize our own style, and to achieve a proud identity in words.

When it was suggested to Walt Whitman that one of his works should be bound in vellum, he was outraged — "Pshaw!" he snorted, "— hangings, curtains, finger bowls, chinaware, Matthew Arnold!" And he might have been equally irritated by talk of style; for he boasted of "my barbaric yawp" — he would *not* be literary; his readers should touch not a book but a man. Yet Whitman took the pains to rewrite *Leaves of Grass* four times, and his style is unmistakable. Samuel Butler maintained that writers who bothered about their style became unreadable but he bothered about his own. "Style" has got a bad name by growing associated with precious and superior persons who, like Oscar Wilde, spend a morning putting in a comma, and

Reprinted from *Holiday* magazine, XXVII, (March, 1960), by permission of the author.

the afternoon (so he said) taking it out again. But such abuse of "style" is misuse of English. For the word means merely "a way of expressing oneself, in language, manner, or appearance"; or, secondly, "a *good* way of so expressing oneself" — as when one says, "Her behavior never lacked style."

Now there is no crime in expressing oneself (though to try to *im*press oneself on others easily grows revolting or ridiculous). Indeed one cannot help expressing oneself, unless one passes one's life in a cupboard. Even the most rigid Communist, or Organization-man, is compelled by Nature to have a unique voice, unique fingerprints, unique handwriting. Even the signatures of the letters on your breakfast table may reveal more than their writers guess. There are blustering signatures that swish across the page like cornstalks bowed before a tempest. There are cryptic signatures, like a scrabble of lightning across a cloud, suggesting that behind is a lofty divinity whom all must know, or an aloof divinity whom none is worthy to know (though, as this might be highly inconvenient, a docile typist sometimes interprets the mystery in a bracket underneath). There are impetuous squiggles implying that the author is a sort of strenuous Sputnik streaking round the globe every eighty minutes. There are florid signatures, all curlicues and danglements and flamboyance, like the youthful Disraeli (though these seem rather out of fashion). There are humble, humdrum signatures. And there are also, sometimes, signatures that are courteously clear, yet mindful of a certain simple grace and artistic economy — in short, of style.

Since, then, not one of us can put pen to paper, or even upon his mouth, without giving something of himself away to shrewd observers, it seems mere common sense to give the matter a little thought. Yet it does not seem very common. Ladies may take infinite pains about having style in their clothes, but many of us remain curiously indifferent about having it in our words. How many women would dream of polishing not only their nails but also their tongues? They may play freely on that perilous little organ, but they cannot often be bothered to tune it. And how many men think of improving their talk as well as their golf handicap?

No doubt strong silent men, speaking only in gruff monosyllables, may despise "mere words." No doubt the world does suffer from an endemic plague of verbal dysentery. But that, precisely, is bad style. And consider the amazing power of mere words. Adolf Hitler was a bad artist, bad statesman, bad general, and bad man. But largely because he could tune his rant, with psychological nicety, to the exact wave length of his audiences and make millions quarrelsome-drunk all at the same time by his command of windy nonsense, skilled statesmen, soldiers, scientists were blown away like chaff, and he came near to rule the world. If Sir Winston Churchill had been a mere speechifier, we might well have lost the war; yet his speeches did quite a lot to win it.

No man was less of a literary aesthete than Benjamin Franklin; yet this tallow-chandler's son, who changed world history, regarded as "a principal means of my advancement" that pungent style which he acquired partly by working in youth over old *Spectators*; but mainly by being Benjamin Franklin. The squinting demagogue, John Wilkes, as ugly as his many sins, had yet a tongue so winning that he asked only half an hour's start (to counteract his face) against any rival for a woman's favor. "Vote for you!" growled a surly elector in his constituency. "I'd sooner vote for the devil!" "But in case your friend should not stand . . .?" Cleopatra, that ensnarer of world conquerors, owed less to the shape of her nose than to the charm of her tongue. Shakespeare himself has often poor plots and thin ideas; even his mastery of character has been questioned; what does remain unchallenged is his verbal magic. Men are often taken, like rabbits, by the ears. And though the tongue has no bones, it can sometimes break millions of them.

"But," the reader may grumble, "I am neither Hitler, Cleopatra, nor Shakespeare. What is all this to me?" Yet we all talk — often too much; we all have to write letters — often too many. We live not by bread alone but also by words. And not always with remarkable efficiency. Strikes, lawsuits, divorces, all sorts of public nuisance and private misery, often come just from the gaggling incompetence with which we express ourselves. Americans and British get at cross-purposes because they use the same words with different meanings. Men have been hanged on a comma in a statute. And in the valley of Balaclava a mere verbal ambiguity, about *which* guns were to be captured, sent the whole Light Brigade to futile annihilation.

Words can be more powerful, and more treacherous, than we sometimes suspect; communication more difficult than we may think. We are all serving life sentences of solitary confinement within our own bodies; like prisoners, we have, as it were, to tap in awkward code to our fellow men in their neighboring cells. Further, when A and B converse, there take part in their dialogue not two characters, as they suppose, but six. For there is A's real self — call it A_1; there is also A's picture of himself — A_2; there is also B's picture of A — A_3. And there are three corresponding personalities of B. With six characters involved even in a simple tête-à-tête, no wonder we fall into muddles and misunderstandings.

Perhaps, then, there are five main reasons for trying to gain some mastery of language:

We have no other way of understanding, informing, misinforming, or persuading one another.

Even alone, we think mainly in words; if our language is muddy, so will our thinking be.

By our handling of words we are often revealed and judged. "Has he written anything?" said Napoleon of a candidate for an appointment. "Let me see his *style*."

Without a feeling for language one remains half-blind and deaf to literature.

Our mother tongue is bettered or worsened by the way each generation uses it. Languages evolve like species. They can degenerate; just as oysters and barnacles have lost their heads. Compare ancient Greek with modern. A heavy responsibility, though often forgotten.

Why and how did I become interested in style? The main answer, I suppose, is that I was born that way. Then I was, till ten, an only child running loose in a house packed with books, and in a world (thank goodness) still undistracted by radio and television. So at three I groaned to my mother, "Oh, I *wish* I could read," and at four I read. Now travel among books is the best travel of all, and the easiest, and the cheapest. (Not that I belittle ordinary travel — which I regard as one of the three main pleasures in life.) One learns to write by reading good books, as one learns to talk by hearing good talkers. And if I have learned anything of writing, it is largely from writers like Montaigne, Dorothy Osborne, Horace Walpole, Johnson, Goldsmith, Montesquieu, Voltaire, Flaubert and Anatole France. Again, I was reared on Greek and Latin, and one can learn much from translating Homer or the Greek Anthology, Horace or Tacitus, if one is thrilled by the originals and tries, however vainly, to recapture some of that thrill in English.

But at Rugby I could *not* write English essays. I believe it stupid to torment boys to write on topics that they know and care nothing about. I used to rush to the school library and cram the subject, like a python swallowing rabbits; then, still replete as a postprandial python, I would tie myself in clumsy knots to embrace those accursed themes. Bacon was wise in saying that reading makes a full man; talking, a ready one; writing, an exact one. But writing from an empty head is futile anguish.

At Cambridge, my head having grown a little fuller, I suddenly found I *could* write — not with enjoyment (it is always tearing oneself in pieces) — but fairly fluently. Then came the War of 1914–18; and though soldiers have other things than pens to handle, they learn painfully to be clear and brief. Then the late Sir Desmond MacCarthy invited me to review for the *New Statesman*; it was a useful apprenticeship, and he was delightful to work for. But I think it was well after a few years to stop; reviewers remain essential, but there are too many books one *cannot* praise, and only the pugnacious enjoy amassing enemies. By then I was an ink-addict — not because writing is much pleasure, but because not to write is pain; just as some smokers do not so much enjoy tobacco as suffer without it. The positive happiness of writing comes, I think, from work when done — decently, one hopes, and not without use — and from the letters of readers which help to reassure, or delude, one that so it is.

But one of my most vivid lessons came, I think, from service in a war department during the Second War. Then, if the matter one sent out was too wordy, the communication channels might choke; yet if it was not absolutely clear, the results might be serious. So I emerged, after six years of it, with more passion than ever for clarity and brevity, more loathing than ever for the obscure and the verbose.

For forty years at Cambridge I have tried to teach young men to write well, and have come to think it impossible. To write really well is a gift inborn; those who have it teach themselves; one can only try to help and hasten the process. After all, the uneducated sometimes express themselves far better than their "betters." In language, as in life, it is possible to be perfectly correct — and yet perfectly tedious, or odious. The illiterate last letter of the doomed Vanzetti was more moving than most professional orators; 18th Century ladies, who should have been spanked for their spelling, could yet write far better letters than most professors of English; and the talk of Synge's Irish peasants seems to me vastly more vivid than the later style of Henry James. Yet Synge averred that his characters owed far less of their eloquence to what he invented for them than to what he had overheard in the cottages of Wicklow and Kerry:

> *Christy.* "It's little you'll think if my love's a poacher's, or an earl's itself, when you'll feel my two hands stretched around you, and I squeezing kisses on your puckered lips, till I'd feel a kind of pity for the Lord God is all ages sitting lonesome in His golden chair."
> *Pegeen.* "That'll be right fun, Christy Mahon, and any girl would walk her heart out before she'd meet a young man was your like for eloquence, or talk at all."

Well she might! It's not like that they talk in universities — more's the pity.

But though one cannot teach people to write well, one can sometimes teach them to write rather better. One can give a certain number of hints, which often seem boringly obvious — only experience shows they are not.

One can say: Beware of pronouns — they are devils. Look at even Addison, describing the type of pedant who chatters of style without having any: "Upon enquiry I found my learned friend had dined that day with Mr. Swan, the famous punster; and desiring *him* to give me some account of Mr. Swan's conversation, *he* told me that *he* generally talked in the Paronomasia, that *he* sometimes gave in to the Plocé, but that in *his* humble opinion *he* shone most in the Antanaclasis." What a sluttish muddle of *he* and *him* and *his!* It all needs rewording. Far better repeat a noun, or a name, than puzzle the reader, even for a moment, with ambiguous pronouns. Thou shalt not puzzle thy reader.

Or one can say: Avoid jingles. The B.B.C. news bulletins seem compiled by earless persons, capable of crying round the globe: "The enemy is re-

ported to have seized this im*port*ant *port,* and reinforcements are hurrying up in sup*port*." Any fool, once told, can hear such things to be insupportable.

Or one can say: Be sparing with relative clauses. Don't string them together like sausages, or jam them inside one another like Chinese boxes or the receptacles of Buddha's tooth. Or one can say: Don't flaunt jargon, like Addison's Mr. Swan, or the type of modern critic who gurgles more technical terms in a page than Johnson used in all his *Lives* or Sainte-Beuve in thirty volumes. But dozens of such snippety precepts, though they may sometimes save people from writing badly, will help them little toward writing well. Are there no general rules of a more positive kind, and of more positive use?

Perhaps. There *are* certain basic principles which seem to me observed by many authors I admire, which I think have served me and which may serve others. I am not talking of geniuses, who are a law to themselves (and do not always write a very good style, either); nor of poetry, which has different laws from prose; nor of poetic prose, like Sir Thomas Browne's or De Quincey's, which is often more akin to poetry; but of the plain prose of ordinary books and documents, letters and talk.

The writer should respect truth and himself; therefore honesty. He should respect his readers; therefore courtesy. These are two of the cornerstones of style. Confucius saw it, twenty-five centuries ago: "The Master said, The gentleman is courteous, but not pliable: common men are pliable, but not courteous."

First, honesty. In literature, as in life, one of the fundamentals is to find, and be, one's true self. One's true self may indeed be unpleasant (though one can try to better it); but a false self, sooner or later, becomes disgusting — just as a nice plain woman, painted to the eyebrows, can become horrid. In writing, in the long run, pretense does not work. As the police put it, anything you say may be used as evidence against you. If handwriting reveals character, writing reveals it still more. You cannot fool *all* your judges *all* the time.

Most style is not honest enough. Easy to say, but hard to practice. A writer may take to long words, as young men to beards — to impress. But long words, like long beards, are often the badge of charlatans. Or a writer may cultivate the obscure, to seem profound. But even carefully muddied puddles are soon fathomed. Or he may cultivate eccentricity, to seem original. But really original people do not have to think about being original — they can no more help it than they can help breathing. They do not need to dye their hair green. The fame of Meredith, Wilde or Bernard Shaw might now shine brighter, had they struggled less to be brilliant; whereas Johnson remains great, not merely because his gifts were formidable but also because, with all his prejudice and passion, he fought no less passionately to "clear his mind of cant."

Secondly, courtesy — respect for the reader. From this follow several other basic principles of style. Clarity is one. For it is boorish to make your reader rack his brains to understand. One should aim at being impossible to misunderstand — though men's capacity for misunderstanding approaches infinity. Hence Molière and Po Chu-i tried their work on their cooks; and Swift his on his menservants — "which, if they did not comprehend, he would alter and amend, until they understood it perfectly." Our bureaucrats and pundits, unfortunately, are less considerate.

Brevity is another basic principle. For it is boorish, also, to waste your reader's time. People who would not dream of stealing a penny of one's money turn not a hair at stealing hours of one's life. But that does not make them less exasperating. Therefore there is no excuse for the sort of writer who takes as long as a marching army corps to pass a given point. Besides, brevity is often more effective; the half can say more than the whole, and to imply things may strike far deeper than to state them at length. And because one is particularly apt to waste words on preambles before coming to the substance, there was sense in the Scots professor who always asked his pupils —"Did ye remember to tear up that fir-r-st page?"

Here are some instances that would only lose by lengthening:

It is useless to go to bed to save the light, if the result is twins. (Chinese proverb.)

My barn is burnt down —
Nothing hides the moon. (Complete Japanese poem.)

Je me regrette. (Dying words of the gay Vicomtesse d'Houdetot.)

I have seen their backs before. (Wellington, when French marshals turned their backs on him at a reception.)

Continue until the tanks stop, then get out and walk. (Patton to the Twelfth Corps, halted for fuel supplies at St. Dizier, 8/30/44.)

Or there is the most laconic diplomatic note on record: when Philip of Macedon wrote to the Spartans that, if he came within their borders, he would leave not one stone of their city, they wrote back the one word — "If."

Clarity comes before even brevity. But it is a fallacy that wordiness is necessarily clearer. Metternich when he thought something he had written was obscure would simply go through it crossing out everything irrelevant. What remained, he found, often became clear. Wellington, asked to recommend three names for the post of Commander-in-Chief, India, took a piece of paper and wrote three times — "Napier." Pages could not have been clearer — or as forcible. On the other hand the lectures, and the sentences, of Coleridge became at times bewildering because his mind was often "wiggle-waggle"; just as he could not even walk straight on a path.

But clarity and brevity, though a good beginning, are only a beginning. By themselves, they may remain bare and bleak. When Calvin Coolidge, asked by his wife what the preacher had preached on, replied "Sin," and, asked what the preacher had said, replied, "He was against it," he was brief enough. But one hardly envies Mrs. Coolidge.

An attractive style requires, of course, all kinds of further gifts — such as variety, good humor, good sense, vitality, imagination. Variety means avoiding monotony of rhythm, of language, of mood. One needs to vary one's sentence length (this present article has too many short sentences; but so vast a subject grows here as cramped as a djin in a bottle); to amplify one's vocabulary; to diversify one's tone. There are books that petrify one throughout, with the rigidly pompous solemnity of an owl perched on a leafless tree. But ceaseless facetiousness can be as bad; or perpetual irony. Even the smile of Voltaire can seem at times a fixed grin, a disagreeable wrinkle. Constant peevishness is far worse, as often in Swift; even on the stage too much irritable dialogue may irritate an audience, without its knowing why.

Still more are vitality, energy, imagination gifts that must be inborn before they can be cultivated. But under the head of imagination two common devices may be mentioned that have been the making of many a style — metaphor and simile. Why such magic power should reside in simply saying, or implying, that A is like B remains a little mysterious. But even our unconscious seems to love symbols; again, language often tends to lose itself in clouds of vaporous abstraction, and simile or metaphor can bring it back to concrete solidity; and, again, such imagery can gild the gray flats of prose with sudden sun-glints of poetry.

If a foreigner may for a moment be impertinent, I admire the native gift of Americans for imagery as much as I wince at their fondness for slang. (Slang seems to me a kind of linguistic fungus; as poisonous, and as short-lived, as toadstools.) When Matthew Arnold lectured in the United States, he was likened by one newspaper to "an elderly macaw pecking at a trellis of grapes"; he observed, very justly, "How lively journalistic fancy is among the Americans!" General Grant, again, unable to hear him, remarked: "Well, wife, we've paid to see the British lion, but as we can't hear him roar, we'd better go home." By simile and metaphor, these two quotations bring before us the slightly pompous, fastidious, inaudible Arnold as no direct description could have done.

Or consider how language comes alive in the Chinese saying that lending to the feckless is "like pelting a stray dog with dumplings," or in the Arab proverb: "They came to shoe the pasha's horse, and the beetle stretched forth his leg"; in the Greek phrase for a perilous cape — "step-mother of ships"; or the Hebrew adage that "as the climbing up a sandy way is to the feet of the aged, so is a wife full of words to a quiet man"; in Shakespeare's phrase for a little England lost in the world's vastness — "in a great

Poole, a Swan's-nest"; or Fuller's libel on tall men — "Ofttimes such who are built four stories high are observed to have little in their cockloft"; in Chateaubriand's "I go yawning my life"; or in Jules Renard's portrait of a cat, "well buttoned in her fur." Or, to take a modern instance, there is Churchill on dealings with Russia: "Trying to maintain good relations with a Communist is like wooing a crocodile. You do not know whether to tickle it under the chin or beat it over the head. When it opens its mouth, you cannot tell whether it is trying to smile or preparing to eat you up." What a miracle human speech can be, and how dull is most that one hears! Would one hold one's hearers, it is far less help, I suspect, to read manuals on style than to cultivate one's own imagination and imagery.

I will end with two remarks by two wise old women of the civilized 18th Century.

The first is from the blind Mme. du Deffand (the friend of Horace Walpole) to that Mlle. de Lespinasse with whom, alas, she was to quarrel so unwisely: "You must make up your mind, my queen, to live with me in the greatest truth and sincerity. You will be charming so long as you let yourself be natural, and remain without pretension and without artifice." The second is from Mme. de Charrière, the Zélide whom Boswell had once loved at Utrecht in vain, to a Swiss girl friend: "Lucinde, my clever Lucinde, while you wait for the Romeos to arrive, you have nothing better to do than become perfect. Have ideas that are clear, and expressions that are simple." (*"Ayez des idées nettes et des expressions simples."*) More than half the bad writing in the world, I believe, comes from neglecting those two very simple pieces of advice.

In many ways, no doubt, our world grows more and more complex; sputniks cannot be simple; yet how many of our complexities remain futile, how many of our artificialities false. Simplicity too can be subtle — as the straight lines of a Greek temple, like the Parthenon at Athens, are delicately curved, in order to look straighter still.

Weller Embler

FIVE METAPHORS FROM
THE MODERN REPERTORY

꾼꾼

Weller Embler *tells us that metaphors give order to our thoughts,
enabling us to find a way of saying something significant about
our world. One handbook (A Handbook to Literature edited by
Thrall, Hibbard, and Holman) defines metaphor as "an implied
analogy which imaginatively identifies one object with another and
ascribes to the first one or more of the qualities of the second or
invests the first with emotional or imaginative qualities associated
with the second." Aristotle gave first place to metaphor-making as the
ability that identifies the poet. But metaphor is everywhere, in the
everyday speech of non-poets, also. Frost said, "All thinking is metaphorical." Sometimes metaphor is just a yoking of two words, but
occasionally the term is used to describe larger constructions. Mr.
Embler discusses metaphors small and large, calling our attention to
the way larger metaphors have given us several broad images of our
present human condition.*

When we wish to say something about ourselves or our environment, we
choose a *way* of ordering our thoughts, a way which will be, we hope,
meaningful to ourselves and to our listeners, a way which will do justice
to the eager activity of our minds. Metaphor appears to be a very effective

way of making meaning, if we may judge from the extensive and successful use of it by poets. Yet metaphor consists of something more than airy nothing. Rather, it "gives to airy nothing / A local habitation and a name." One part of the metaphor exists in everyday reality, the transitory portion, while the other part, the enduring portion, is a thought, an intuition, an airy nothing. When we join the transitory image with the enduring thought, we create a metaphor, a way of uttering an insight about ourselves and our world.

I. THE PRISON

The transitory portion of a metaphor is often selected from among prevailing images of one's time, from among those particulars which affect us emotionally and impress people of the time as having unusual power and meaning. For example, the prison has been a powerful reality in many societies, and notable works of literature and art have employed the image of the prison to give substance to a thought or feeling. It must have been very real and powerful to Plato, and he chose it more than once as the perfect apt transitory portion of the metaphor he creates to express the philosophy of idealism. In the *Phaedo* Socrates says, "Those too who have been preeminent for holiness of life are released from this earthly prison, and go to their pure home which is above, and dwell in the purer earth." The allegory of the cave is also based on the prison metaphor, its enduring portion the ascent of the soul out of the cave or prison of human imperfection and misery into intellectual freedom where all things beautiful and right are seen in the light of a great vision.

The prison or dungeon was a bitter reality in the eighteenth and nineteenth centuries and appears often in the works of European writers and artists of the time. There were, for example, the engravings of Giovanni Battista Piranesi, Beethoven's *Fidelio*, Dumas' *The Count of Monte Cristo*, Victor Hugo's *Les Misérables*, and of course that symbol of all prisons of all time, the Bastille.

In the works of the English romantic poets the prison metaphor continued to assist tellingly in the revelations of Platonic idealism.[1] For Blake "A robin redbreast in a cage / Puts all heaven in a rage"; after the death of his brothers, the prisoner of Chillon in Byron's poem says, "And the whole earth would henceforth be / A wider prison unto me"; the fireside is a prison to Wordsworth when he is melancholy, a prison from

[1] One wonders what images a Platonist *could* use if there were no prisons in his society and he had no knowledge of "stone walls and iron bars." On the other hand it is interesting to ask whether some intuition of confinement in the world has not perhaps given men the idea of a similar incarceration in a man-made jail for purposes of worldly punishment. Opposed to the prison in the imagination of man are the heavens — home of that romantic symbol of perfect freedom, the skylark — even the hills, age-old images of emancipation from the fetters and restraints of the earthbound.

which he is released only by the glad song of the thrush. But of the metaphors of the English romantic poets the one which comes first to mind is found in Wordsworth's "Ode on the Intimations of Immortality":

> Our birth is but a sleep and a forgetting
> The Soul that rises with us, our life's Star,
>   Hath had elsewhere its setting,
>   And cometh from afar:
>   Not in entire forgetfulness,
>   And not in utter nakedness,
> But trailing clouds of glory do we come
>   From God, who is our home:
> Heaven lies about us in our infancy!
> Shades of the prison-house begin to close
>   Upon the growing Boy,
> But he beholds the light and whence it flows,
>   He sees it in his joy;
> The Youth, who daily farther from the east
>   Must travel, still is Nature's priest
>   And by the vision splendid
>   Is on his way attended;
> At length the Man perceives it die away,
> And fade into the light of common day.

The prison image is a pervading fantasy in western literature. Inspired by a theme from Dante's Inferno, Eliot brings the metaphor of the prison into the twentieth century when in *The Waste Land* the protagonist of that poem watches the crowd of people flowing over London Bridge and says, "I had not thought death had undone so many." Indeed, this passage in the poem suggests a similarity between crowds of people moving in a city and convicts moving in a prison yard: "Sighs, short and infrequent, were exhaled, / And each man fixed his eyes before his feet."[2] The representation of the world as a vast purgatorial prison has persevered for more than two thousand years, and it is revealing that one of the most celebrated of modern poems should revive the idea that life in this world is death, a death from which one may be delivered only through the mystery of spiritual rebirth. In the last section of *The Waste Land* Eliot uses the metaphor again in a somewhat more modern interpretation. Following the voice of thunder and the exhortation to sympathy, the poem expresses human loneliness and isolation in the modern world through the image of the prison — "each in his prison / Thinking of the key" — of the key of

[2] From T. S. Eliot, *Collected Poems.* Copyright, 1936, by Harcourt, Brace and Company, Inc.

sympathy which will open the door and release us from the bondage of our selfishness.[3]

As the philosophers of the seventeenth century observed, so long as men live in society they will have to give up some of their freedoms to the social contract. Laws and restraints are inevitable in any social order, and images of the prison will occur in literature to express the *feeling* of restriction — in some ages and societies strong, as in our own, perhaps because of the density of modern bureaucratic organization, in some weak or non-existent. The image also expresses the feeling of immense loneliness, a characteristic feeling, apparently, of our time.

We meet the prison metaphor in full modern dress in Jean Paul Sartre's *No Exit*. However much one may wish to fly away, however one may delude himself into thinking he is free as a skylark, in sober moments, we suspect we are most subtly "trapped," that there is no escape from this small room, the world, in which we are doomed to live with other people.[4] Hell is not fire and brimstone and red-hot pokers, says Garcin in *No Exit*. "Hell is — other people!" Metaphorically, then, we are imprisoned in the world and compelled to live out our lives suffering from the wounds inflicted by other people. *No Exit* brings up to date the mutual hatred and repulsion of the traitors in Dante's lowest circle of Hell. The metaphor of "no exit" appears aptly chosen as a modern expression of the *feeling* of incarceration, especially since the transitory portion of the metaphor is drawn from the image of the enclosed theatre or multiple dwelling which purposely holds a number of people. To be captive in a small space with other people in a state of panic with no exit is indeed to suffer greatly at their hands.[5]

If we were *alone* in the world, we should be truly free — we are inclined

[3] Compare the prison metaphors in W. H. Auden's poem, "In Memory of W. B. Yeats." ("And each in the cell of himself is almost convinced of his freedom.") One of the most anguished cries in modern literature is this aphorism from Franz Kafka's "Notes from the Year 1920": "He feels imprisoned on this earth, he feels constricted; the melancholy, the impotence, the sickness, the feverish fancies of the captive afflict him; no comfort can comfort him, since it is merely comfort, gentle head-splitting comfort glazing the brutal fact of imprisonment. But if he is asked what he actually wants he cannot reply, for — that is one of his strongest proofs — he has no conception of freedom." (From *The Great Wall of China* [New York, 1946], p. 265.)

[4] Our persistent, impassioned desire to get to the moon may well be a strategy by which we hope to circumvent the sentence of imprisonment in the world, especially since the world's room is shrinking daily in apparent size. Sails on the horizon were once thought of as images of freedom; the astronaut cruising through the illimitable in his spacecraft may become a modern image of freedom, though his vehicle suggests a more severe confinement than the erstwhile sailing vessel, open as it was to the then wide world. Even in the swift airliners of today one has the feeling of being in captivity, literally strapped in, far more than one has when he is traveling on a train or boat.

[5] The image of the "wall" as barrier — often as death — is vivid and meaningful in the twentieth century and is used by poets and writers from Robert Frost through Sartre and John Hersey, with luminous irony in Kafka's *The Great Wall of China*.

to think. But we are not alone in the world, and for Sartre, the only realistic freedom is acceptance of full responsibility for our behavior.[6] For the most part we tend to think of freedom today as the opportunity for the uninhibited expression of our own individuality, largely through freedom of movement. When, then, we discover the NO EXIT sign lit by day and night for our information, we tend to despair; for to many people in the modern world it sometimes *seems* as though there were "no way out," unless perhaps through the now not so illimitable space to the stars above.

Walls, prisons, guards, keys, the trial, the conviction, the sentence, the shutting of the door, the confinement, and the escape — all the realities and fantasies of imprisonment occur so frequently in Western World literature there can scarcely be any doubt that the prison image describes with emotional intensity the feelings and thoughts which people have about freedom, not necessarily freedom from the literal jail but the nature of freedom itself, what it is for, how to define it. The metaphysical contrarieties in the thought of our time are not better illustrated than in this aphorism from Kafka's "Notes":

> He could have resigned himself to a prison. To end as a prisoner — that could be a life's ambition. But it was a barred cage that he was in. Calmly and insolently, as if at home, the din of the world streamed out and in through the bars, the prisoner was really free, he could take part in everything, nothing that went on outside escaped him, he could simply have left the cage, the bars were yards apart, he was not even a prisoner.[7]

---

[6] Walter Kaufmann in his *The Faith of a Heretic* (Garden City, New York, 1961) has dealt severely with the confusions that surround the concept of commitment as interpreted by the existentialists. As a man of reason he feels that commitment is often very unreasonable, fanaticism in effect, and that much which was unholy has been done in its name. His commentary on Kierkegaard's concept of faith may not be quite just, however. The story of Abraham and Isaac should, perhaps, be read as a parable, that is, a metaphor, an exaggerated way of talking about or describing "faith," a powerful transitory image of the *idea* of faith, not to be taken literally but imaginatively as expressive of the burning desire of all men to believe, to trust. The compelling *wish* to believe and the enduring hope that the good will come true in spite of commanding appearances to the contrary are existential facts of human experience.

At times the romantic poets were unexpectedly sophisticated in their interpretation of imprisonment, recognizing necessity and consenting, even eagerly, to earthly bondage, turning it to account as a fact not without use and value. For the prisoner of Chillon, the prison becomes a "second home," a "hermitage" for the solitary soul, a place of refuge. In Wordsworth's sonnet "Nuns Fret Not At Their Convent's Narrow Room" the poet says that for those "Who have felt the weight of too much liberty," the prison unto which they doom themselves "no prison is," as with the nuns who fret not at their convent's narrow room, the hermit who is contented with his cell, the student in his citadel, the weaver at his loom, the bee in the foxglove bell, and the poet bound "Within the Sonnet's scanty plot of ground."

[7] *Op. cit.*, p. 264. Compare the following from "Spiritual Autobiography" by Simone Weil: "I fell in love with Saint Francis of Assisi as soon as I came to know him. I always believed and hoped that one day Fate would force upon me the condition of a vagabond and a beggar which he embraced freely. Actually I felt the same way about

II. THE WASTELAND

In literature, probably the most widely known metaphor of our time is the metaphor of the "wasteland" from the poem by T. S. Eliot. When *The Waste Land* was first published in 1922, general critical judgment pronounced it so ridiculously complex and recondite as to be unreadable. But the genius of T. S. Eliot and the relevance of his poem to the condition of the modern world have since become evident and celebrated. Eliot appears to be one of those writers whom literary historians select as the genius speaking for his age.

Eliot's intuitive understanding of the world of his time coincides with the silent feelings of his contemporaries; and he articulates their mood in the compressed and impassioned language of poetry. Or better, the poet identifies the malaise and gives it meaning through a symbol or image which turns out to be wholly acceptable.

However, when an all-encompassing image enters the public domain, it is usually accompanied by a considerable retinue of literary and historical servants. The mythic image of a wasteland which is found in the legends of the Sangraal and the Arthurian stories gives a local habitation and a name to the idea of spiritual aridity. And the pilgrimage or quest, the seeking out of that which is concealed, the search for the Holy Grail, the search for salvation, appears to be a basic fact of existence.

The master metaphor of the Middle Ages is the pilgrimage as a quest for salvation, the literal journey, perhaps, to the holy place, or simply everyman's journey, his going forth toward an unknown destination in search of a mysterious something not revealed to him. The pilgrim knows only that he must seek and continue to seek with single-minded purpose until, if he is devout and faithful, he is vouchsafed the reason for his journey in the beatific vision which is the consummation of all his wandering and questing. The metaphor of the pilgrimage or journey is found in the Arthurian legends in the search for the Holy Grail, is expressed with great beauty in "Sir Gawain and the Green Knight," is the religious motive of the historical Crusades, and is the artless natural framework of *The Canterbury Tales*.

In *The Waste Land*, Eliot concentrates on the decay of the modern world, on its wasteland character, on the spiritual aridity of our times rather than on the image of the journey or pilgrimage. Indeed, it is because the will is atrophied, because spiritual purpose is infirm and hesitant that no quest is undertaken in the twentieth century. The emphasis in the poem is on the lack of spiritual determination, on the spiritual sickness of our time.

---

prison." Like Kafka, Simone Weil longs for a condition which is positive (even if it has to be the lowest — categorical, perhaps, because it is the lowest), a well-marked condition, explicit, and not, as it were, an ambiguous condition of being half in and half out. (From *Waiting for God* by Simone Weil [New York, 1951], p. 65).

Though he does not use the term "wasteland" in the descriptive passage which opens Chapter II of *The Great Gatsby* (1925), F. Scott Fitzgerald may well have had T. S. Eliot's famous image in mind when he wrote the following:

> About half way between West Egg and New York the motor road hastily joins the railroad and runs beside it for a quarter of a mile, so as to shrink away from a certain desolate area of land. This is a valley of ashes — a fantastic farm where ashes grow like wheat into ridges and hills and grotesque gardens; where ashes take the forms of houses and chimneys and rising smoke and, finally, with a transcendent effort, of ash-gray men who move dimly and already crumbling through the powdery air. Occasionally a line of gray cars crawls along an invisible track, gives out a ghastly creak, and comes to rest, and immediately the ash-gray men swarm up with leaden spades and stir up an impenetrable cloud, which screens their obscure operations from your sight.
>
> But above the gray land and the spasms of bleak dust which drift endlessly over it, you perceive, after a moment, the eyes of Doctor T. J. Eckleburg. The eyes of Doctor T. J. Eckleburg are blue and gigantic — their retinas are one yard high. They look out of no face, but, instead, from a pair of enormous yellow spectacles which pass over a non-existent nose. Evidently some wild wag of an oculist set them there to fatten his practice in the borough of Queens, and then sank down himself into eternal blindness, or forgot them and moved away. But his eyes, dimmed a little by many paintless days, under sun and rain, brood on over the solemn dumping ground.[8]

The brooding Dr. Eckleburg is, perhaps, Fitzgerald's depiction of the legendary sick Fisher King who plays so large a role in *The Waste Land*.

The image of the modern world as a spiritual wasteland now appears to be an apt and fitting figure. Though the social revolution of the 1930's sought to repudiate the wasteland metaphor and to replace it with images of fertility and the fellowship of the common man, the desolation caused by World War II gave a new rightness to the "wasteland" analogy. In any event, Eliot's metaphor has prevailed for forty years as a literary description of an anarchic and spiritually desiccated modern world.

III. THE MONSTER

Though human beings in society may have little control, individually, over their predicament (existing in the world *and* in society), each thinks of himself *as* something — a "human being," for instance. What, then, is a human being. Everyone knows what a human being is, or at least what a human being is not. A human being is *not* an insect — there are demonstrable differences. But a human being may be said to be *like* an insect.

[8] This selection is taken from the volume entitled *The Last Tycoon*, which includes *The Great Gatsby* (New York, 1941).

Even if we do not know what we *are*, we may say we know what we are *like*; and it is what we say we are like that makes all the difference in our attitude toward ourselves and our neighbors. Man is like a machine. Man is like an angel. Man is like an insect. Man is a rhinoceros. Man is a trapped animal. Man is garbage.

In Franz Kafka's celebrated short story "Metamorphosis," Gregor Samsa, the central character, thinks of himself as an enormous insect, repulsive, disgusting. Although here and there in the history of European literature authors have pointed sharply to the similarity between some of their characters and vicious or contemptible animal creatures, their purpose was to show explicitly the ample distance between noble human beings and, say, despicable quadrupeds. The comparison was made for the purpose of elevating the human. But much of modern literature seems intent upon identifying the human with the beastly. It is doubtful that even Swift thought of human beings as in a class with baboons. He made it perfectly clear that in his estimation his friends were not yahoos. But the swine in George Orwell's *Animal Farm* bear a striking resemblance to all human beings whether they are one's friends or one's enemies. Indeed, at the end of the story, while the farm animals gazed upon their animal leaders (pigs) and their human neighbors, they saw that something had happened to the faces of the pigs. "The creatures outside looked from pig to man and from man to pig, and from pig to man again; but already it was impossible to say which was which."[9]

The image of man as a "human being" was given its modern definition during the Renaissance. This is the image we have in mind when we deplore the non-humanistic trends of our time. Clinging to this image, we are sickened by the appalling idea that we may not be "human" at all, but enormous insects or brainy pigs. In general we still *say* that man is Renaissance man. But what appears to trouble our sleep is the suspicion that the Renaissance ideal was only another piece of self-delusion and that man is really, at best, a "despicable biped" and at worst a pig, an enormous insect, or a field creature (as in Kafka's "The Burrow") pitifully erecting his flimsy defences against an unseen and unnameable enemy, consumed by a very understandable anxiety. Shakespeare's Dogberry is a monument of majesty compared to Gregor Samsa.

The image of man created by the Renaissance centered upon the concepts of personality and character. These are exalted ideas and are sub-

[9] George Orwell, *Animal Farm* (New York, 1946), p. 118.

Eugene O'Neill writes allegorically about the emotional clashes consequent upon the ambiguities in the human predicament. In *The Hairy Ape* (1922), the main character, Yank, is described in the beginning as having the appearance of "Neanderthal Man," not quite man and not quite gorilla; and the irony of the last scene is unrelieved as the caged Gorilla of the Zoo crushes Yank "in a murderous hug," throws the dying man's body in the cage, and shuts the door. "*Perhaps,*" says O'Neill in the last words of the play, "*Perhaps, the Hairy Ape at last belongs.*"

sumed under the master concept of the richly endowed individuality. The dignity of man derives from the integrity which is his and which is expressed through his unique personality and through his self-discipline which we recognize as character. He is a special creature singled out for glory. This image of man is not, of course, new with the Renaissance; indeed, it is very ancient, a characteristic of pagan as well as of Christian beliefs. Man in his fullness is a nature, that is, a human nature, or better, a human spirit, an ideal form, a central beautiful form against the prepared and ideal form of the landscape, against a framed space which dotes upon and admires its lovely human figures, a madonna in a painting by Raphael, a David in a sculpture by Michelangelo.

The new image of man as portrayed by several distinguished contemporary painters and sculptors is forcefully presented in a single text by Peter Selz in *New Images of Man,* published by the Museum of Modern Art in connection with its exhibition "New Images of Man" in 1959. There can be no doubt of the range and creative power of the new imagination. These figures cast in bronze or painted on canvas distinctly *resemble* human beings, but seldom human beings as we are accustomed to seeing them. They are powerful impressions of the mood of modern man, plastic evocations of the way he feels. Rather than recognizable as everyday persons, they are self-conscious figures, evolving *out* of their "human" form into another form, tormented and suffering in the contemplation of their own new image.

Writing about the sculpture of Kenneth Armitage, Selz says: "Like Gregor in Kafka's *Metamorphosis,* these human figures with their thin extremities are turned into helpless bugs." Of the sculpture of Reg Butler, Selz observes that his sculpture "always relates to the human figure," but resembles "bird and insect forms." Jean Dubuffet's painting *Woman with Furs* "is a conglomeration of lichens or organisms seen under a microscope." Willem de Kooning's *Woman I* has the look of a predatory beast, enfanged, lusting after prey with single-minded intensity. (There is something to be said for the modern artist's verisimilitude. At least we often come to see people as the modern artist shows them to us.) "After the initial shock of her appearance wears off," says the art critic Thomas B. Hess of the de Kooning Woman, "she sits next to us on a bus, or is seen waving at someone behind us in a restaurant."[10]

Man has been called a variety of names in the history of the Western World — a creature like unto the Olympian gods, a political animal, a rational being, the temple of the Holy Spirit. At the moment he is sometimes seen as a human monster, less companionable than the legendary

[10] Thomas B. Hess, *Willem de Kooning* (New York, 1959), p. 29.

wivern of heraldry. In *New Images of Man,* he is a prodigy of distortion, by turns sinister and pathetic, threatening and corroded with decay.[11]

Yet there is method in this madness. Dwelling as so many sculptors and painters do on the "despoiled and debauched" image of the human figure, they still believe, I suspect, with Leonard Baskin that "The forging of works of art is one of man's remaining semblances to divinity." These ogres, in addition to having their own personalities, are reflections of a modern state of mind, a state of mind characterized by repulsion and by longing. Self-conscious before the "cracked mirror" of the world, these figures are waiting to be born again into something they can at least understand and accept. As Paul Tillich says in his Prefatory Note to *New Images of Man,* if there is anxiety and despair, there is also longing and hope, "a reaching out into the unknown."

IV. THE MACHINE

Though at first glance it might seem that the machine metaphor is a common form of expression today, it is no longer, I believe, taken seriously as revelation of the human condition in the second half of the twentieth century. But from the late eighteenth century until, one might say, Chaplin's film *Modern Times* in 1936, the machine idea exercised a potent influence over the human mind. There was, for example, the all-encompassing image in the eighteenth century of the universe as a vast clock running according to unalterable mechanical law; and in 1820 Napoleon Bonaparte could say with conviction, "We are a machine made to live. . . . Our body is a watch, intended to go for a given time." Dickens speaks of "this machine called Man!" and someone referred to Daniel Webster as "a steam-engine in trousers." Karl Marx in *Capital* condemns "the intellectual desolation artificially produced by converting immature human beings into mere machines," and Havelock Ellis, later in the nineteenth century, was convinced that the "greatest task before civilization at present is to make machines what they ought to be, the slaves, instead of the masters of men." In 1922, when T. S. Eliot described in *The Waste Land* the "human engine" waiting "Like a taxi throbbing waiting," there was still considerable vitality in the image, but when, in 1938, Sartre's hero, Roquentin, in *Nausea* feels his body "at rest like a precision machine," the meaning in the similarity has diminished very nearly, I think, to the status of cliché.

In his famous chapter "The Dynamo and the Virgin" in *The Education of Henry Adams,* Henry Adams presented the dynamo as the greatest force in the Western World, standing for power, inexorable law, organization,

---

[11] In Samuel Beckett's play *Endgame,* a moving tragic drama of the human condition in the modern world, two of the characters, an old man and an old woman, appear to "live" in garbage cans. Their names are Nagg and Nell.

productivity (if not fertility). Yet "All the steam in the world," he said, "could not, like the Virgin, build Chartres." Instead, together with the dynamo, it was steam that built the modern world, whatever opinion one may have of either. Modern metaphorical use of the machine is found in Eugene O'Neill's *Dynamo* (New York, 1929) where the dynamo is represented in the mind of the protagonist as the "Divine Image on earth" of the "Great Mother of Eternal Life, Electricity." "Her power houses are the new churches!" It may very well have been that O'Neill was inspired by Adams' "The Dynamo and the Virgin." In any event, it is interesting to read in that chapter that "Everyone, even among Puritans, knew that neither Diana of the Ephesians nor any of the Oriental goddesses was worshipped for her beauty. She was goddess because of her force; she was the animated dynamo; she was reproduction — the greatest and most mysterious of all energies; all she needed was to be fecund." For comparison, it is instructive to quote from one of the stage directions in O'Neill's *Dynamo*: "The oil switches, with their spindly steel legs, their square, crisscrossed steel bodies (the containers inside looking like bellies), their six cupped arms stretching upward, seem like queer Hindu idols tortured into scientific supplications."[12]

The urge to create a "mechanical" man has challenged the imagination since Mary Shelley's *Frankenstein* was published in 1817. *R.U.R.*, for instance, by Karel Capek, first produced in Prague in 1920, is the story of the robot who becomes master over man but cannot survive because he lacks life and soul. For the most part, the use of the image of the mechanical man in modern literature has been humanistic, that is to say, critical of the thought that man is nothing but a machine or a cog in a machine, and Chaplin's *Modern Times* was a powerful satire on the idea of man as machine, suggesting distinctly and in characteristic Chaplinesque style that human beings are human *individuals* and should not be regimented by the world of machines. The machine is the machine and Charlie Chaplin is the man, and the two are quite different.

But as I observed at the outset of this section, the machine metaphor appears to have lost its vigor of expression in the literature of today. The computing machine is said to be "like" the human brain, but the metaphor is not emotionally significant, and a statement of the following kind appeals to us as rather more amusing than instructive:

The normal healthy brain puts out "remarkable mileage." It consumes 1 teaspoon of sugar per hour. Using the terminology of industry, total operating costs are remarkably low. Energy output per hour is equal to that of a 20-watt light bulb. It is remarkable that while the combined brain energy of the group of men who worked on the atomic bomb did not equal the electrical energy consumed by the lights in an

---

[12] Act III, Scene 2.

average office, nevertheless, they released atomic energy which is now being measured in megatons. Thus the brain is the control organ that directs the power flow of modern industry.[13]

If the metaphor of the machine stirs our feelings at all today, it would seem to be in terms of the sick machine, or the machine destroying itself, as in objects created by the sculptor, Jean Tinguely. But again, in these displays, the effect, if not the intention, is apparently more comic than tragic.[14]

V. THE HOSPITAL

Although Freud warned against graphic representations of psycho-analytical hypotheses, it is meaningful that the "unconscious" should have lent itself so readily to interpretation in the popular imagination as a secret subterranean "place" where repressed wishes are kept in captivity, a dungeon for unruly and wicked thoughts. Naturally, the sole aim of the repressed desire or impulse is freedom, and on occasions, at night, like the ghost of Hamlet's father, it is allowed (under surveillance of the censor and clad in suitable ghostly garments) to venture into the upper world and there unfold its tale, though forbidden to tell *all* "the secrets of the prison-house." But by the middle of the twentieth century the Freudian theories came to be expressed more in terms of the "hospital" than of the prison, and the "unconscious" becomes the place of "sick" rather than of wicked or criminal thoughts, even a place of refuge from the brutalities of the world.

Though there are many philosophies offered for our inspection in the modern world, one is conspicuous by its absence. There appears to be no positive Philosophy of Health. One remembers that in ages past there were, for instance, the ideals of the healthy mind in a healthy body, and earlier, in classical antiquity, of the beautiful mind in a beautiful body. Though scarcely an ideal, today's philosophy of health appears ironically often to be the notion that modern man is a sick mind in a sick body. Witness the multitude of "sick" jokes, the statistical evidence of wide-spread mental illness, and the continuous building of new and larger hospitals everywhere. An amusing cartoon which I saw recently, but unfortunately cannot document, pictures two heavily bearded young men standing on a city street observing a third heavily bearded young man walking past them with his head down upon his chest in a mood of despair. One of the observers says in evident disgust as he watches the passerby, "What bugs me is this sicker-than-thou attitude."

---

[13] From "The Management Team — Its Selection and Development" by Robert K Burns, in the *Year Book* of the American Iron and Steel Institute (New York, 1955).

[14] There is probably some relation today between the machine metaphor and "junk" sculpture where iron monsters display strong evidence of suffering under the burden of their existence; and it must be said that some pieces are emotionally very moving.

Popular expressions of the "sick" modern might be merely comic correctives to too much faddish despair and sophomoric melancholy. We could let it go at that except for the deeper evidence of "sickness" which is to be found in many first-rate pieces of contemporary imaginative literature.

What *is* sickness? The question is in a sense unanswerable unless one has a positive philosophy of health. Such a philosophy was on the way to being built in the 1930's. "A quart of milk every day on every doorstep" was a vigorous popular image; but the forces inimical to man of the twentieth century swept like a tidal wave over the concept of green pastures and still waters. I should like in this essay to present only those metaphors which seem especially meaningful in what they say about the modern world; and I find that the metaphor of the "hospital" is widespread and apparently one of the most acceptable. So far as I know, the metaphor of the world-as-a-hospital was first used in the modern sense by Baudelaire.[15] The prose poem "Anywhere Out of the World" opens with these lines:

> Life is a Hospital, in which every
> patient is possessed by the desire to change his bed.
> This one would prefer to suffer in front of the stove,
> and that one believes he would get well if he were placed
> by the window.

In the poem "Reversibility" Baudelaire calls upon the angels of gaiety, goodness, health, beauty, joy and asks each if they have known their opposite:

> Angel full of health, have you known the Fevers,
> That along the walls of hospitals go sagging,
> Like exiles who seek the sun, find hell's retrievers,
> Who move their lips, foot after tired foot dragging?
> Angel full of health, have you known the Fevers?

In his introduction to *Baudelaire, Rimbaud, Verlaine*, Joseph M. Bernstein observes that when we ask about Baudelaire's greatness, we insist on stressing his modernity, "his direct and unusually vibrant appeal to modern man." And it is, I think, in Baudelaire's preoccupation with "sickness" that his modernity lies, in his anticipation of the anguish of modern man, "a divided man often at odds with himself and with life." In any event, the hospital metaphor has persevered into the literature of our time, and, as one might suspect, forcefully in some of the poems of T. S. Eliot. There is, for example, the variation on the theme in "The Love Song of J. Alfred Prufrock" in the first three lines:

[15] The quotations from Baudelaire are taken from *Baudelaire, Rimbaud, Verlaine, Selected Verse and Prose Poems*, ed. Joseph Bernstein, trans. Arthur Symons (New York, 1947).

> Let us go then, you and I,
> When the evening is spread out against the sky
> Like a patient etherised upon a table.[16]

The metaphor is used more explicitly in *Four Quartets* in the poem "East Coker" where section IV is developed almost entirely in terms of sickness — in the first stanza the use of "surgeon," in the second "nurse," in the third "The whole earth is our hospital," in the fourth "chill" and "fever," in the fifth the irony of our delusion that we like to think, in spite of the spiritual malaise, "That we are sound, substantial flesh and blood."[17]

It is in the plays of Tennessee Williams that the sickness metaphors come prominently before the contemporary audience. In *A Streetcar Named Desire* the theme of sickness is vivified by the appearance of the "strangers," the doctor and the nurse, who come for Blanche to take her away to the place of sanctuary, the hospital. The strangers enter the play like "gods out of the machine," and Blanche, in one of the most pathetic lines in the modern theatre, appeals to their mercy saying, "I have always depended on the kindness of strangers." There is scarcely a play of Williams' which does not have as its major theme the theme of sickness both physical and mental, but in *Period of Adjustment* the world as hospital is given an optimistic turn when the unhappy newlywed Isabel, who is a nurse, comforts her husband, who suffers from nervous "shakes."

> Inside or outside, they've all got a nervous tremor of some kind, sweetheart. The world is a big hospital, and I am a nurse in it, George. The whole world's a big hospital, a big neurological ward and I am a student nurse in it. I guess that's still my job![18]

Moving indeed is this timorous and faint hope that with gentle care the sick may be healed after all.

Jean Paul Sartre's novel *Nausea*[19] is a work which will probably last a long time as a relentless commentary on the tormented mind of modern man. The title is intended, I suppose, as an imaginative summary of human life in the twentieth century. Roquentin, the hero of *Nausea*, is sickened by an acute awareness of the realities around him (the purple suspenders of the bartender, the chocolate-colored wall of the cafe), is sickened by his intellectual encounter with existence and the stickiness, the "sweetish" taste, the "gelatinous slither" of the "naked World." The transitory portion of Sartre's metaphor is the literal nausea ("I wanted to

[16] T. S. Eliot, *op. cit.*

[17] T. S. Eliot, *Four Quartets*, Harcourt, Brace and Company, New York. Copyright, 1943, by T. S. Eliot.

[18] Tennessee Williams, *Period of Adjustment* (New York, 1960), Act III.

[19] Sartre (Norfolk, Connecticut, 1959). *La Nausée* was first published in 1938 by Librairie Gallimard.

vomit"), the revolt of the stomach. The enduring portion of the metaphor is the metaphysical anguish by which modern man is oppressed through the discovery of his freedom and the anxiety aroused by the dawning awareness of his being in a world where there are no signs to tell him who he is or where to go or what to do.

In the famous scene in the park where Roquentin in a mystical adventure finds the key to Existence, Roquentin says, "I would so like to let myself go, forget myself, sleep. But I can't. I'm suffocating: existence penetrates me everywhere, through the eyes, the nose, the mouth. . . . The Nausea has not left me and I don't believe it will leave me soon; but I no longer have to bear it, it is no longer an illness or a passing fit: it is I."

At the expense of (and oversimplifying, of course) Sartre's extraordinarily penetrating insights, one might venture the emendation: I am sick, therefore I exist; or — I exist, ergo I am sick! There is something of this, though, in existential philosophy — perhaps that is why it seems to say so much about modern man and his predicament. Roquentin's "fascination" with the root of the chestnut tree explains his nausea, the nausea that follows the invasion of existence, that attends the slow awareness of being, of being which is simply *there*, outside "the world of explanations and reasons" and which weighs "heavily on your heart like a great motionless beast."

But with Sartre, as I observed earlier, there is a cure for this illness. The sickness is not quite unto death. Sartre's philosophy of health lies in the leap or act of commitment. Sickness and suffering come of aimlessness, and existence is aimless except as man gives it aim and purpose. To be well, then, is to be committed, to be bound, if only within, as Wordsworth said, the scanty limits of the sonnet. Whether the cure is effective or not, or whatever we may think of the cure or the sickness as Sartre presents it, modern man, in a great deal of modern literature, is, figuratively and literally, one way or another, unmistakably "ill."[20]

[20] It is revealing that Thomas Mann should have chosen a sanitarium as the setting for his best known novel, *The Magic Mountain*, one of the great works of our time. It is significant also that widespread sickness is the framework for an important contemporary European novel, *The Plague* by Albert Camus.

Margaret Schlauch

LANGUAGE AND POETIC
CREATION

ᛕᛕ

*When Margaret Schlauch says, "Everybody starts out as a potential
artist in words," and speaks of the large number of children who show
impulses of inventiveness in language, she brings back to our minds
such essays as those about the lore of the schoolyard or about the
word-creation of American frontiersmen. After making that initial
observation, Miss Schlauch turns to the most creative users of language, the poets and novelists, and shows how they use the history of
words and make new words in their search for the expression of the
modern temper. As we recognize what they are doing, we gain a
heightened responsiveness to the potentialities of language.*

Pleasurable Aspects of Speech

We may know very little about the origin of human speech, but it is
probably safe to assume that men found pleasure as well as use in it from
the very beginning. Like other means employed to make life increasingly
bearable in a practical way, it was adapted also to aesthetic satisfactions.
Pitch and stress, qualities of vowel and consonant, tempo and dynamics
were present in spoken sentences and offered the raw material for artistic
creation. We may assume that as long as men have been human they have
been aware that one way of saying a thing might be more pleasing than
another. We have no reason to suppose that they have ever been mere
animated machines, content to enunciate a wishful statement with the

utmost of curt efficiency. If the earliest pottery shows a striving for design, early sentences probably did too.

Language is different from the other media which may be used for artistic purposes. It has some noteworthy advantages — which upon closer examination turn out to be handicaps to the aspiring apprentice in the poetic art. Conversely, of course, there are media in which the initial difficulties may be subdued to downright advantage.

For one thing, the process of learning your mother tongue occurs early, and is performed by all normally functioning members of the community. It is a painless act when compared with the struggles over raw materials in the other arts. Everybody, so to speak, starts out as a potential artist in words. And an extraordinarily large number of children show at least some impulse towards this form of aesthetic expression if they are given encouragement. To put the situation simply: you have to be very good to rise above the average high level of achievement which is the rightful prerogative of every speaking human being, not to mention the occasional outstanding accomplishments of average citizens under emotional stress. This is one way in which your initial advantage turns against you.

Words as Symbols

For another thing, you are operating with a highly symbolic medium when you put words together. The word is not the thing, as we are frequently reminded. A pot may be a pot *plus* something more imponderable: an expression of aspiration, let us say, or of squat complacent solidity. But the word is *nothing but* that imponderable plus, the symbol. Like ambition (as described by Rosencrantz in *Hamlet*) the word is of so airy and light a quality that it is but a shadow's shadow. Its meaning, as we have observed repeatedly, is purely conventional and exists only by tacit consent on the part of the community as a whole. To elevate it to higher significance is a correspondingly difficult feat. There must be a second, added aura of symbolism to provide the aesthetic element. This is not meant to imply anything too pretentious. Perhaps a simple example will explain.

The single word "rain" is a sentence — a presentative sentence — insofar as it announces or presents the appearance of a familiar form of precipitation of moisture from the heavens. Yet there is nothing in the sounds of [ɪein] to compel their relationship in our minds with falling water. That is due to habitual association. An inflection of the voice may suggest pleasure in the rain, but still present it as an everyday experience. The individual sounds in the word, if pronounced by a pleasingly modulated voice, may have aesthetic quality, in and of themselves. But the symbol stands alone as a factual sign. There has been no organization of elements (sounds as parts of symbols) with the primary intent to convey aesthetic experience. And aesthetic experience requires meaningful organization of a medium, according to principles of unity, diversity, balance, imbalance (and so on), which have been found by experience to add effective elements of emotive power to ordinary experience.

The word "rain" as ordinarily used is a jaded symbol. It evokes no tactile memories of stinging impact, cool envelopment, or warm spraying diffusion; no lively visual memories of slanting silver wire; no auditory memories of dull thudding heavy drops or the sharp battering on slate roofs. If an artist wishes to make you relive the experience of rain by sharing in his word-stimuli, he must operate consciously on the medium and galvanize you into fresh awareness, the more powerfully since words are so much a part of your everyday experience. If he does this one thing alone he has conveyed a certain higher symbolic meaning to "rain" in merely causing you to relive it thus in terms of verbal symbols. He has put a frame about the image and thus heightened its meaning, for frames add to the sense of what they enclose merely by setting it off.

This may be worth doing for itself. The imagists were content with this accomplishment. But the word-artist may be engaged in a more exalted act of patterning his elements. He may be evoking the experience of rain as part of a much more complex creative effort in organization of the medium. The rain may contribute to a larger mood, and at the same time put forward the plot of a story by its effect on the characters. Finally it may itself suggest more elusive analogous meanings of an abstract order while it accomplishes the concrete re-creation of physical experience. It is thus that Joyce treats snow in "The Dead," the last story of his incomparable *Dubliners*. Here the verbal symbols are used in the erection of higher order symbolism, as is frequently the case in Dante.

Linguistics and Poetry

To investigate the methodology of all this would be to attempt a new handbook of poetics. But that is not the purpose of this chapter. Instead I wish merely to indicate briefly the uses of some practical linguistic knowledge in studying literature, particularly the work of modern poets reputed to be "difficult" for technical reasons. Philology may be a humble follower in the train of the Muses, but she is of some assistance in gaining you an introduction to the loftier handmaids of Apollo. The thorny path traveled in some of our earlier chapters may lead you direct to pleasures of the Pierean spring — or at least help to speed you on your way.

In the first place, certain concessions are necessary from the unpracticed and possibly impatient reader. Since the idiom of much contemporary writing (especially in verse) is special and alien, readers tend to assume over-hastily that it expresses nothing at all. They label it nonsense and so have done with it. To do so is to barricade comprehension effectively. A more fruitful attitude is to assume that something is actually being said. The comprehension of it may require several types of effort, including a fresh approach to language. In the end you may decide that the effort was not worth making. The content may not, in your opinion, justify the technical difficulties put in your way. But if it does, the effort of collaboration with the author will have intensified your eventual appreciation. The discovery must at least precede the judgment. Remembering the basic handicap of language as a medium, you are asked to consent to innovations which will help to surmount it. And among one of the most urgent demands put upon you is the obligation to look at words afresh.

The following are some of the most stimulating techniques to be observed in contemporary writing.

Semantic Rejuvenation

We have seen in the discussion of compound words, that some of the most abstract terms in the language are really faded metaphors. On examination it turns out that an earlier meaning, now forgotten, is often lively in the extreme. Hence an obvious means of invigorating our jejune vocabulary is to fall back on those lively older meanings. True enough, the average speaker does not know that they ever existed. He is not *reminded* that "express" once meant, literally and physically, "to press out." But he can learn it instantaneously from a context. It may be that only the archaic literal sense is intended, or it may be that both the physical and the metaphorical are to be grasped simultaneously. In any event, the impact of the divergent use on an attentive reader forces him to a new experience of the word, without sacrificing comprehension. An example of the use of "express" in this revivified fashion will be found in Emily Dickinson:

> Essential oils are wrung;
> The attar from the rose
> Is not expressed by suns alone,
> It is the gift of screws.

In the age of Shakespeare, intensive classical education had shaped a reading public (among the few, of course) who could sense the older meaning with less effort than many feel today. The plays offer repeated vivid uses of etymological rejuvenation of words. Horatio's "Season thy admiration for a while with an attent ear" makes use of the Latin sense of *admirāri*, "to wonder at" something and of "attent" in the sense of "stretched." "Hast thou no *speculation* in those eyes?" recalls the literal meaning of *speculāre*, "to gaze, look upon." "Occulted guilt" means guilt covered over, or hidden. When Troilus says "there's no maculation in thy heart" he reminds us of the concrete meaning of *macula*, namely "spot (of dirt)," and when he refers to his "sequent protestation" it is in the concrete sense of "my calling on witness, which now follows." Hamlet's injunction "Let it be tenable in your silence still" evokes the basic meaning of Latin *tenēre*, "to hold" — not merely "to maintain a theoretical position." So when Laertes warns his sister that "nature, crescent, does not grow alone in thews and bulk," the adjective reminds us that *crescrere* meant "to grow," to mature in a physical sense. In *Troilus and Cressida* Ulysses can speak of "deracinating" a political state and thus call upon us to think of *racine,* a root, so that the meaning of "uproot" is conveyed in an unaccustomed startling manner. The usual word having lost emphasis, the learned one infuses new life by causing us to share in the original metaphoric synthesis.

Sophisticated writers still impose the etymological task upon their readers as part of the aesthetic experience. It may be said, in fact, that etymology is one of the devices by which readers are now called upon to share in the creative act. The enormous influence of English metaphysical poets of the seventeenth century on modern writers — notably the influence of Donne — has accentuated this etymological awareness. The reason for a return to metaphysical poets as a source of inspiration is not our subject here. But a consequence of it is certainly a recourse to similar linguistic devices.

James Joyce, for instance, has evinced etymological preoccupations throughout his entire work. When he says that one pugilist's fist is "proposed" under the chin of another, he intends the word as Latin *proponere,* "to place under"; and he is capable of using "supplant" as "to plant under" in describing the Gracehoper (i.e., Grasshopper) of *Finnegans Wake:* "he had a partner pair of findlestilts to *supplant* him." T. S. Eliot expects the same etymological collaboration from his readers in his simile from "The Love Song of J. Alfred Prufrock":

> Streets that follow like a tedious argument
> Of insidious intent
> To lead you to an overwhelming question. . . .

Like Shakespeare, he wishes you to remember that "intent" means a thing that is taut and stretched for action, and that "insidious" (Latin *insidiae,* "sitting or lurking within") means "ambushed" against an enemy. At the same time the literal metaphor of warfare is merged in the image of a verbal argument. In "Preludes" there is another figure of the many he evokes from the streets of a city:

> The conscience of a blackened street
> Impatient to assume the world.

Here it is necessary to remember that "assume" means "to take on" (*adsumere*) and hence "to play the part of." In his epithet "maculate giraffe" ("Sweeney among the Nightingales") he is doing exactly as Shakespeare did: reminding us that our faded theological term "immaculate conception" contains a sharp visual image of literal, physical spots.

So C. D. Lewis makes use of both the literal and figurative senses of "derelict mills" in "You that love England." He means lonely and abandoned mills, of course, but also mills that have simply and unmetaphorically been "left behind" (*de-linqui*) by those who formerly worked in them. And W. H. Auden, speaking in "Sir, No Man's Enemy" of "the distortions of ingrown virginity," surely intends us to feel the root meaning of "twist, physical bending from the norm" under the abstract "distortion." When he uses the expression "trains that *fume* in the station" he evokes the literal visual image "to smoke" as well as the later extended meaning "to be impatient."

Hart Crane's strange vigor is in part derived from the reminder of root meanings. Here are a few examples. In a description of an airplane flying over Mount Hatteras, the pilot is thus addressed:

> Remember, Falcon-Ace,
> Thou hast there in thy wrist a Sanskrit charge
> To conjugate infinity's dim marge —
> Anew . . . !

If the general sense is the quasi-magic power of dominating the horizons of infinity, the root meaning of "conjugate" is still felt as "to put a yoke on," rather than "to inflect a verb." In "Garden Abstract" the opening lines are

> The apple on its bough is her desire, —
> Shining suspension, mimic of the sun.

The abstract word "suspension" is to be interpreted as "the thing which is hung." In the haunting phrase "the silken skilled transmemberment of song" there is an enormous heightening of effect when the trite word "trans-formation" (passing of one form into another) is replaced by "transmemberment" (passing of one member into another). This particular instance shows how readily an acquired skill in etymological rejuvenation will pass into creative independence in handling words. It is but a step to

Word Formation

out of elements already known or guessed. There is less downright creation of words, even by the boldest innovators, than is popularly supposed. Hart Crane's "thunder is galvothermic" (from "The Tunnel") creates a word not registered in the dictionaries: but its component parts make clear the sense of "electrically warm." (The fuller form "galvanothermic" would have been more conventional.) Thomas Hardy subdues language to his purposes when he writes verbs like "to unbe," "unillude," or "unbloom," and nouns like "unease" and "lippings" (meaning "talk"). James Joyce has experimented in the creation of new word forms to meet special needs, especially adapted to the passages of interior monologue in *Ulysses*. In this he diverges conspicuously from the example of his predecessor Dujardin, whose novel of interior monologue, *Les Laurier sont coupés*, does not contain any linguistic innovations and is written in conventional French.

Joyce tried to approximate the stuff of our flowing wakeful consciousness by reproducing in speech the leaps, combinations, and blurring of word and image characteristic of our private thoughts. Only certain parts of the novel are composed in this fashion. Cutting across these are sharp word-images recording the sounds and sights of the objective world. Onomatopoeia shapes some of the new formations of words. A long-held note of a song, a "longindying call," is said to dissolve in "endlessnessnessness"; a woman's hair is "wavyavyeavyheavyeavyevyevy"; the sound of passing horses' hoofs becomes "steelhoofs ringhoof ring." The mundane sound of body gases accompanies the hero's solemn meditation: "Then, not till then, my eppripfftaph. Be pfrwritt." Disjointed meditation is indicated by clipped forms: "He saved the situa. Tight trow. Brilliant ide," for "He saved the situation. Tight trousers. Brilliant idea." But it is noteworthy that the most audacious coiners of verbal currency are limited to units capable of conveying sense — and therefore meaningful because they are in some degree familiar.

Punning

is a technique now being exploited once more in all seriousness after centuries of disrepute. It is made possible by the existence of homonyms in a language: words identical in spoken form but having different meanings, often different origins. The spelling may or may not differ. In French there are two words *louer*: one, meaning "to praise," from Latin *laudāre*; the other meaning "to rent" from Latin *locāre*. The identity of forms today makes it possible to construct a witty compliment to a landlord in French, using a single phrase to indicate that a house is both praiseworthy and rentable. *"Je loue votre maison parceque je la loue!"* In Shakespeare's day this double use of homonyms was considered a legitimate adjunct of superbly serious style. It was not limited, although it was also applied, to joking frivolous discourse. In *Julius Caesar* the words of Mark Antony spoken alone over the dead body in the Senate —

> O world, thou wast the forest to this *hart*,
> And this indeed, O world, the very *heart* of three —

were not meant to elicit smiles. The conscious balancing of the two homonyms was felt to heighten the intensity of Antony's tribute because it offered an auditory bond, "hart: heart," for the linking of two very serious metaphors.

Among modern writers James Joyce is again the most conspicuous exploiter of the pun. He uses it as part of his general attempt to widen the scope of language. There are tentative trial instances in *Ulysses*: "She rose and closed her reading rose of Castille," or "With the greatest alacrity,

Miss Douce agreed. With grace of alacrity . . . she turned herself." On the opening pages of *Finnegans Wake* we find the following double meanings:

> doublin = Dublin, doublin'
> retaled = retailed, re-taled (i.e., told again)
> erse solid man = Erse solid, arse-solid
> wills = wills (n.) and wills (vb., opposite to "won'ts")
> Finnegan = Finnegan, Finn again
> half = halve, have
> wan = wan, one
> lean on = lean on, lien on

If foreign words may be included the list may be lengthened:

> bygmester = big master, Danish *Byggmester* (master builder)
> violer d'amores = *viola d'amore*, violator of loves
> wallhall = wall hall, Walhalla
> one eyegonblack = *ein Augenblick*; a blackened eye
> fern = fern (the plant), *fern* (distant)
> far = far (adv.), Danish *Far* (father) (*cf.* p. 628)
> mere = only, *Meer* (ocean) (p. 628)

Verbal and Phrasal Distortions

In many of the punning expressions of Joyce, there is use of words not strictly homonymous. Two words not precisely alike in sound are related to each other by a slight distortion of one of them which brings them closer together. This is employed far more widely than straight punning in *Finnegans Wake*. The purpose is to extend the application of a single word or phrase by evoking simultaneously another one also pertinent to the occasion although in an entirely different fashion. The allusions are not limited to English. As with the simple puns, the phrases are so treated as to include references to other languages.

> dontelleries = *dentelleries* (French for lace-adorned objects); also discreet, intimate garments which "don't tell"
> erigenating = originating; also Erigena-ting (from Duns Scotus Erigena, the "Erin-born" philosopher)
> venissoon after = very soon after; venison after; Venus' son after
> eroscope = horoscope; Eros-scope; hero-scope
> Fiendish Park = Phoenix Park; Park of Fiends
> museyroom = museum; musing room
> Champ de Mors = Champ de Mars; Field of Death (Mors)
> herodotary = hereditary; hero-doter; Herodotus(?)
> pigmaid = made like a pig; pigmied

Whole phrases are made to evoke others at the same time, so that a simple statement is paralleled by another heard in overtones:

and of course all chimed din width the eatmost boviality = and of course all chimed in with the utmost joviality (implications of noise, expansiveness, beefy appetite)

honeys wore camelia paints = Honey swore Camelia paints; also *honi soit qui mal y pense*

haloed be her eve, her singtime sung, her rill be run, unhemmed as it is uneven! = the Lord's prayer transferred to a mythological goddess-river

when ginabawdy meadabawdy = gin-bawdy, mead-bawdy; also "gin a body meet a body"

sware by all his lards porsenal = pig's fat; Lars Porsena

a king off duty and a jaw forever = a thing of beauty and a joy forever; also a bore

Are you not danzzling on the age of a vulcano? = dancing on the edge; also, dazzled in a volcano-like age (also, Vulcan-like).

Polyphonic Sentences

The purpose of Joyce is the achievement of the effects of polyphonic music in verbal writing. Hitherto it has seemed impossible for literature to approximate the advantage of music: namely an ability to have the ear apprehend, simultaneously and yet distinctly, two or more themes being unfolded at once. Joyce substitutes for melodies polysemantic verbal patterns realized by means of distortions. The intonation of the phrase is important in establishing the secondary motif. This is not the place to discuss the value or aesthetic justifications for Joyce's experiment. It may be pointed out, however, that the curious and ambiguous linguistic medium is employed to treat a subject-matter derived largely from the subconscious: a dream state.

There is an aptness in the occasion, at any rate. The material of the "story" is the dream of a Dublin citizen, with lapses into nightmare, interruptions, and starts into half-consciousness, throughout a long night. The author tries to penetrate beneath the most inclusive recordings of a flow of waking consciousness, and to express in this new literary medium the flow of subconscious imagery in a dream. The attempts appears at first sight to result in little more than a private, non-communicable gibberish. A page of these multiple simultaneous themes, replete with unconventional punctuation and capitalization, looks like strange nonsense to the uninitiated. But it does yield to patient analysis.

To be sure a properly equipped reader is expected to be unprecedentedly polyglot and widely read. Very few, presumably, are in a position to decipher the text. And there are all sorts of questions which may be legitimately raised about the ultimate value of the significant content which may underlie all the verbal distortions. Nevertheless the sheer virtuosity of Joyce's performance is beyond comparison. Even a slight experiment in interpretation of it will be found to be linguistically exhilarating. At the very least a reader will emerge newly alert to the resources of language as more ordinary people use it.

Concretes to Express Abstractions

There is another way of refreshing verbal concepts besides reminding readers of the component parts of abstract terms. It is to make bold substitution of entirely concrete simple terms for the vaguer abstract ones which are actually intended. "Protection" is a chilly, colorless word. It becomes more vivid if you are reminded that it means a covering-over (*tegere*) in behalf of (*pro*) someone. It becomes poignantly immediate if it is translated into the still more concrete image of "*roofing* over" (*tectum*). The disadvantage is, however, that the implied abstraction, although still essential to the meaning, may be lost entirely from the image. Width of scope may be sacrificed to immediacy. "He gave me the roofing over me" is a heart-warming statement, but it may fail to convey the general and inclusive function of protection-in-general. It may be taken as a bald statement of a mere night's shelter — limited, literal, and unsymbolic.

Gerard Manley Hopkins is a master of the successful transposition of abstract into concrete. The implications of generality, even of universality, are never missed when he intends to suggest them through a tangible word. In "Felix Randall," the priest speaks of the large and handsome body of the man who has just died — "his moult of man" — "pining, pining, till time when reason *rambled* in it." The errancy of thought during delirium is brought close by the concrete term. Of God it is said, "He *fathers-forth* whose beauty is past change," a vivid transmutation of theological terminology about divine creation. The acceptance of castigation is expressed:

> I did say yes
> O at lightning and lashed rod.

The grandeur and sweep of the adjoining images prevent any misunderstanding of the unpretentious first four words. Less skilfully placed they might have failed, because of over-simplicity, to convey the complex metaphysical act to be designated. This would have defeated half of the intent. Vigor would have been gained at the price of significance. . . .

Abstractions to Express the Concrete

If the use of a limited concrete word heightens vivid immediacy, the use of an abstract one for a concrete situation will heighten the general sense of importance and significance in the situation. Much of the vague awe and reverence attendant upon the religious vocabulary in English is due to its formation out of Latin abstract nouns with no homely connotations in ordinary speech. In other languages with a more homogeneous vocabulary this may not be true. A German child learning the term *unbeflecktes*

Empfängnis may recognize in the first word the humble word *Flecke*, "spot," which he first learned when he spattered mud or grease over his clothes. The correlation will help clarify the semantic situation for him, but it may somewhat reduce his sense of awe. An English-speaking child has no similar experience to fall back on when he learns the august phrase "immaculate conception." The vagueness of the connotations may therefore heighten his sense of mystery in dealing with the phrase. Emily Dickinson employs occasional abstractions in order to give transcendent value to poignant homely situations.

> Go not too near a house of rose,
> The *depredation* of a breeze
> Or *inundation* of a dew
> Alarm its walls away;
> Nor try to tie the butterfly;
> Nor climb the bars of *ecstasy*.
> In *insecurity* to lie
> Is *joy's* insuring *quality*.

Instances can be found in contemporary poets too. The shift from defined situation to an abstraction often marks the end of a poem. This is in line with the transmutation of significance implied in an abstract term. Robert Graves, concluding a brief sketch of a "Quayside," refers to the spaces at sea for contrast, where

> ships are few, each on its proper course,
> With no occasion for *approach* or *discourse*.

In a poem called "O Love in me," he presents first graphic images of the impact of existence, and then concludes:

> Take your delight in *momentariness*,
> Walk between dark and dark, a shining space
> With the grave's *narrowness*, though not its *peace*.

Two examples from Auden:

> You are alone, alone, O imaginary song,
> Are unable to say an existence is wrong,
> And pour out your *forgiveness* like a wine.
>
> ("The Composer")

> May I, composed like them   [i.e., the Just]
> Of Eros and of dust,
> Beleaguered by the same
> *Negation* and *despair*
> Show an affirming flame.
>
> ("September 1, 1939")

The effect of abstractions is exploited in connection with the concrete theme of moonlight: "This lunar beauty has no history. . . ."

There is sustained use of abstractions implanted among particulars in the following stanza of Ben Belitt, describing "Battery Park: High Noon":

> Suddenly
> Between flint and glitter, the leant leaf
> The formal *blueness*, blooming over slate.
> Struck into glass and plate,
> The public tulips, treading *meridian glare*
> In bronze and whalebone by the statue bases
>> Elude the Battery Square,
>>> Turn, with a southern gesture, in remembered air,
>>> And claim a loved *identity*, like faces. . . .

Hart Crane is as bold with abstractions as with their opposites. In fact it may be said that much of his verbal effect comes from swift alternation of stingingly concrete images with abstract terms. The illustrations are easy to find: "A boy runs with a dog before the sun, straddling/*Spontaneities* that form their independent orbits. . . ." (p. 67); "Smutty wings flash out *equivocations*" (p. 93); "from palms to the severe/Chilled albatross's white *immutability*" (p. 105); "Infinite consanguinity it bears — /This tendered theme of you. . . ." (p. 104); "Expose vaunted validities that yawn/Past *pleasantries.* . . ." (p. 130). To paraphrase these is to spoil the effect Crane deliberately strove for. Still, some periphrasis is required, since Crane challenges the intellectual participation as much as sensuous appreciation, quite in the manner of the complex metaphysical poets. It will be noticed that in these quotations the effect of the abstractions is heightened by emplacement near extremely vivid words. "Smutty wings" and "equivocations" heighten each other by contrast, as do "validities" and "yawning." This leads to the general question of semantic enrichment by means of another technique: juxtapositions.

Juxtapositions

We have seen in the chapter on semantics that all words are surrounded by an aura of connotations in addition to the precise denotations. When two words with similar connotative spheres are put together they strengthen each other so far as factual information is concerned, but they do not offer a challenge to the attention or a marked stimulus to the imagination. It is otherwise when two words are juxtaposed out of different connotative spheres. The element of conflict enriches the expression. A simple form of the usage has long been practiced by English poets. It consists in placing together two words belonging to two different realms of physical sense.

Milton's "blind mouths" is an example. E. E. Cummings speaks of "eyes which mutter thickly" (*is 5*, Three, iv), of something "noisecolored" (*W*, or *Viva*, p. 3), and a "rolypoly voice" (*is 5*, One, i).

The general device is being widely employed today. T. S. Eliot is a past master of this technique, which harmonizes with his larger purpose of contrasting moods and cultures deliberately by way of satiric commentary. The technique is epitomized in the sentence from "Whispers of Immortality": ". . . her friendly bust/Gives promise of pneumatic bliss," where the derisive adjective conflicts with the traditionally "poetic" noun. In a more abstract way Gertrude Stein does the same thing; witness her titular expression "Tender Buttons." The satirical intent is lacking in such a pairing off; what you receive is rather a verbal shock producing an effect so diffuse that it can scarcely be used to serve a wider purpose. Eliot, of course, goes much farther than simple combinations of words. The balance may involve parts of a sentence. In

> I have measured out my life with coffee spoons.

the caesura of the line marks the break between the two antithetical elements. The same poem, "The Love Song of J. Alfred Prufrock," contains an extended example of phrasal juxtaposition.

> There will be time to murder and create,
> And time for all the works and days of hands
> That lift and drop a question on your plate;
> Time for you and time for me,
> And time yet for a hundred indecisions,
> And for a hundred visions and revisions,
> Before the taking of a toast and tea.

Here the first imposing line — held in suspense in your mind while you read the next five — is contrasted with the mundane ordinariness of the last. Within this enclosing envelope of juxtaposition there are smaller units: "murder" put beside "create," the abstract "question" beside the concrete "plate." And there is also a case of etymological rejuvenation. The juxtaposition of "revisions" beside "visions" reminds you that the word once meant "seeing for a second time." Here you are supposed to grasp both the literal and metaphorical meanings simultaneously. . . .

Levels of Discourse

Comparable to the juxtaposition of words with conflicting connotations is the abrupt change from one level of discourse to another. . . . Languages like ours exist in several strata, according to the economic and cultural positions occupied by different speakers. To pass from one to another in the

"The Love Song of J. Alfred Prufrock" from *Collected Poems 1909–1962* by T. S. Eliot. Reprinted by permission of Harcourt, Brace & World, Inc., Publishers.

confines of a single poem is to give the reader another type of stimulating shock: a rhetorical one. John Dos Passos, interrupting lyrical passages in his novels with snatches of popular song, journalistic headlines, and colloquialisms, made sustained use of this variety in his novels. A German example, also in prose, is Alfred Döblin's *Berlin Alexanderplatz*. The alternation of styles may be found in poems like Horace Gregory's "Columbo Dominico" and "Longface Mahoney Discusses Heaven." Archibald MacLeish makes judicious use of the admixture of colloquial in lofty context in *Frescoes for Mr. Rockefeller's City*. Edgar Lee Masters tried the abrupt shift in some poems of his *Spoon River Anthology*, though here it was images rather than locutions which were put into bizarre juxtaposition.

Some contemporary poets are conducting experiments in the total use of substandard colloquial speech for lyrical purposes. John Weaver did so, some time ago, in his poems *In American*. Kenneth Fearing is exploring the possibilities today. E. E. Cummings sometimes produces a mystifying example of his own special type of "phonetic" writing on this level. Of course it is not phonetic. It takes liberties with the sounds really used on this level, presumably in order to satisfy the inner ear of Mr. Cummings, and it indulges in a curious vivisection of words to conform to his rhythmical desires. Here is an example:

> oil tel duh woil doi sez
> dooyuh unnurs tanmih eesez pullih hizmus tah oi
> dough un giv uh shid oi sez. . . .
>
> . . . Fur Croi saik
>
> ainnoughbudih gutnutntuhplai?

You may decipher this readily enough if you read it aloud without regarding the divisions of words.

Evocation of the Unsaid

Because we learn words and phrases in contexts, each fresh use of them tends to recall the original association. In expressions frequently employed, like proverbs, the initial word or two will be sufficient to recall the whole. An allusive and pregnant style results when discourse is made up of the minimum verbal signals necessary to recall an entire statement. No one is puzzled by the fragmentary "A word to the wise." The equivalent statement in Latin is even more pregnant, since it can be reduced to two words: "*Verbum sapienti.*" Writers who attempt to record a stream of consciousness use fragmentary allusion generously, since it corresponds in some sort to the rapid short-cuts we make in thinking without elaborate verbalization, especially on the emotive level.

Here again a considerable burden is placed on the reader. The difference between complete understanding and complete mystification may depend on knowledge of one incomplete allusion. So in the otherwise clear character sketch by E. E. Cummings:

yonder deadfromtheneckupgraduate of a
somewhat obscure to be sure university spends
her time looking picturesque under

the as it happens quite
erroneous impression that he

nascitur.

The task of supplying punctuation is not difficult, but the whole point
of the sketch is lost if you fail to recall the Latin saying, *Poeta nascitur
non fit,* "A poet is born, not trained." If you do remember, you will
realize that "he" must be a poet. The self-conscious young lady graduate
spends her time posturing for "him" under the illusion that he is a poet
and will immortalize her. (The same proverb is alluded to in another of
Cummings' lines: "Each dream nascitur, is not made. . . .") Without
knowledge of the unsaid, that which is said usually conveys little or no
meaning.

Shift of Grammatical Category

Since the Renaissance, poets have been making use of the elasticity of
English grammar. There is nothing to distinguish many verbs from the
nouns derived from them; adverbs are often identical with adjectives or
with prepositions in outward form. This being so, a creative writer is
easily led to increase the elasticity of ordinary speech when he transforms
it for his higher ends. Shakespeare uses an adjective as a verb when he says
"*sicklied* o'er with the pale cast of thought" or "*violenteth* in a sense as
strong"; a noun as a verb when he says "Lord Angelo dukes" it well. It is
quite usual to hear "but me no buts" in ordinary speech; and most school
children will recall Tennyson's "Diamond me no diamonds," and "Prize
me no prizes" from the *Idylls of the King.*

The moderns furnish plenty of instances; in fact one is embarrassed by
the multiplicity of them. Of course when writers abandon formal grammar
temporarily it is hard to tell how much shifting is going on, and you are
presumably at liberty to interpret the syntax (if any) as you please. This
is only true, however, in the most esoteric passages of writers like Stein.
Elsewhere a little reflection will clear up a seeming snarl of relationships.

Occasionally Gerard Manley Hopkins permits himself a daring shift in
parts of speech. He refers to the ocean in "The Deutschland" as "widow-
making unchilding unfathering deeps." Not only are two nouns here made
into verbs, but they are provided with unprecedented negative forms. In
the same poem an adverbial phrase becomes a noun: "dandled the to and
fro." Joyce has made two similar adverbial expressions into verbs. "The
hitherandthithering waters" of the Liffey River conveys the effect of cur-
rents and eddies; a dog "almosting" a bone indicates strain and frustrated

"yonder deadfromtheneckupgraduate" from *Poems 1923–1954* by E. E. Cummings.
Reprinted by permission of Harcourt, Brace & World, Inc., Publishers.

effort better than the usual expression because it embodies the central transitive idea in the verb where it belongs. ("Get" has become as colorless as "is.") An adjective is treated the same way in the phrase "warm sunshine merrying over the sea." Here again the conventional expression "making merry" is ineffective because the verb — which should be important in a verbal idea — is lacking in color. A pronoun becomes a noun in Cummings's "the feline she with radish red legs." An adverb sprouts unorthodox suffixes in the phrase "hoop returns fasterishly." In Auden's

> Sir, no man's enemy, forgiving all
> But will his negative inversion, be prodigal,

the noun "inversion" appears to be used as a verb, with the object preceding. This is not certain, however. There is similar doubt about the construction of the sentence in his *Double Man*, lines 194–99, which hinge on the ambiguous words "frowns the young Rimbaud guilt demands." The hesitation engendered by such innovations may delay the current of the reader's attention in a salutary manner. But this is true only if the arrested flow serves to underscore a genuinely significant thought.

Enjoyment of Poetry

The best heritage of poetry belongs, like the best of all the arts, to all the people who can enjoy it. Under more favorable circumstances I am convinced that this would include vast numbers who never hear about their heritage today. The chorus of snobs and cynics will say: "Ah, but the people as a whole are congenitally incapable of appreciating the work of those choice spirits known as poets. Such things are not for them. They *prefer* the cheap and vulgar sensations offered them by press, movies, and radio. Artists and critics must turn their backs on the profane herd to save themselves." Certain of the illuminati enjoy thinking this, as they are thus proved to be the rarer souls by contrast.

Such judgment is found in various forms, variously disguised. It involves sociology as well as literary criticism. Social attitudes are of course always closely related to literary dicta. If a critic believes that limits and stultification and indifference in the reading public have something to do with malnutrition, poverty, unemployment, and despair; with low vitality and the conscious commercial debauchery of literary taste, he will not conclude that innate human bestiality is the prime cause for a limited circulation of the classics. He will not echo Horace's *Odi profanum vulgus et arceo*. He may instead wonder optimistically how the barriers to culture may be broken down and the fertile tide released. Even the most "spiritual" of literary critics may have noted that he is himself temporarily disqualified to some degree from professional activity if he has allowed extreme hunger to bring on a headache. Conversely, he may therefore concede that food, light, air, and sleep may transform seeming dullards into alert people.

It is no magic, only elemental human bio-chemistry. And it is a process which we now know is capable of realization. The conditions for doing so have been explored and tested.

How then, if in addition illiteracy were to be abolished, the specter of insecurity banished, and the arts of recreation so presented as to refine the public's sensibilities instead of corrupting them? The luminous possibilities can only be dimly imagined in our age of Hollywood films and venal journalism, not to speak of the actual bleak analphabetism of hundreds of thousands of our fellow-citizens. If deep-lying biological factors of inheritance have indeed worsened some part of our stock beyond repair, there is no need to assume that this is true of most of it, and certainly none to cause us to adjust all popular arts to the least talented of men and women among us.

All of this has some bearing on the material of this chapter. You will have noticed that I have expressed from time to time a certain doubt as to the enduring value of some of the authors cited. Naturally we cannot know which writings of today will earn the enduring affections of posterity. Even where great gifts indubitably exist, as with James Joyce, we have reason to doubt whether they have been applied to themes and techniques of perennial value. But one thing is sure: if the value *is* there, mere technical difficulty will not keep it alien to the reading public of the future. It is their heritage and they will enjoy it. Technical obscurities have a way of disappearing within the span of a generation. Some of us have the courage to hope that the first real age of human Enlightenment may succeed the contemporary horror. If science is at last permitted to serve the public's physical needs as it could do, art may minister to the spiritual solace of all as never before. For such readers of the future the technical devices of poetry here surveyed will no doubt appear much more transparent than now in our own day.

And even now there is no reason why they should mystify as many as they do. Within the limited circle of our own reading public, as it is called, there are many already waiting for the small amount of guidance needed towards the comprehension of beauties they vaguely surmise in the current offering of literature. It is a genuine pity, I think, that critical interpretation offers so little help. The radio alone, with its direct aural appeal, could be used to foster a tremendous renascence of poetry and the appreciation of poetry. Many of the appeals described in this chapter could better be explained by a speaking voice than by printed words.

An elementary knowledge of linguistics, then, could aid in the cultural enrichment of all our people. Even this forbidding science has its humane applications, too long neglected. I should like to see the study of language pursued, not only as an esoteric end in itself, but also as an auxiliary to aesthetic enjoyment. . . .

Leo Marx

THE VERNACULAR STYLE
IN AMERICAN LITERATURE

✍✍

We have studied the history of the English language in Britain and in America. During the colonial period and even for several decades after the Revolution, writers looked to Europe for leadership in literature. But after the achievement of political confidence, a cry arose for literary independence also, most notably in Emerson's address called "The American Scholar." In the essay that follows, Professor Marx discusses the revolution in language that Whitman and Twain effected to solve the problem of finding an American style to go with the new American subject.

From the beginning writers have had much less trouble finding an American subject than a mode appropriate to its expression. In 1620 William Bradford recognized an inevitable subject even before he stepped off the *Mayflower*. Gazing toward the forbidding shore he asked, in effect, "What is to be the fate of civilized man in this prehistoric landscape?" Later the question was reformulated. Writers like James Fenimore Cooper, Nathaniel Hawthorne, and Henry James asked, "What does it mean to be an American?" Around this theme they elaborated an infinitely complex art. To get at the meaning of American experience they submitted the native character to the test of Europe. They created a drama of cultural contrast. What

Reprinted from *Studies in American Culture*, edited by Joseph J. Kwiat and Mary C. Turpie (Minneapolis: University of Minnesota Press, 1960), by permission of Leo Marx and of *Die Neueren Sprachen* (Germany), in which this essay originally appeared.

gave their work its American stamp was their vivid awareness of certain cultural differences.

And yet, having said all that, we are not satisfied that we have settled the old problem: what *is* different, after all, about American literature? Granted that the "international theme" is American, can a particular subject ever make for a lasting distinction between one national literature and another? If we ask what is different about German writing, we know very well the first answer to expect: it is written in German. But the language of Cooper is not all that different from the language of Scott, and with Cooper's generation the boundary between British and American literature remains uncertain. When we come to "Song of Myself" or *Huckleberry Finn*, however, the line is much more distinct. That may explain why Walt Whitman and Mark Twain are so widely respected, nowadays, as the two great seminal figures of modern American writing. They establish, once and for all, the literary usefulness of the native idiom. With it they fashioned a vernacular mode or, if you will, a national style. This style marks a major difference between English and American literature, and it is the one I propose to consider here.

However, I do not mean to suggest, as many contemporary critics do, a violent opposition between two strains in American writing. In *The Complex Fate*, for example, Marius Bewley deplores the influence of Whitman and Twain, seeing in it a narrow chauvinism, a kind of literary isolationism in marked contrast to the scope and subtlety of Hawthorne and James. My own view is quite different. The style of Whitman and Twain seems to me to serve as a measure, even an embodiment, of the very cultural differences that preoccupy Hawthorne and James. The image of America that we find in the work of Hawthorne and James, though depicted from another angle, is really the same image we find in Whitman and Twain. All these writers were concerned with what it means to be an American; all felt — though in different degrees to be sure — the tension between the possibilities and the dangers of the new society. And not one was a narrow chauvinist. Much of Mr. Bewley's contempt for the work of Whitman and Twain derives, I believe, from a mistaken conception of the vernacular tradition.

To see what is contained in that tradition — if the word can be used to describe so rebellious a state of mind — let us first consider Walt Whitman.

When Whitman's first poems were taking shape, America was preoccupied with the slavery problem — another rather special American subject. Whitman's contemporaries turned out a large volume of poetry about slavery. Here is a fair sample by the most popular poet of the age, Henry Wadsworth Longfellow:

THE SLAVE IN THE DISMAL SWAMP

In dark fens of the Dismal Swamp
 The hunted Negro lay;
He saw the fire of the midnight camp,
And heard at times a horse's tramp
 And a bloodhound's distant bay.

Where will-o'-the wisps and glow-worms shine,
 In bulrush and in brake;
Where waving mosses shroud the pine,
And the cedar grows, and the poisonous vine
 Is spotted like the snake;

Where hardly a human foot could pass,
 Or a human heart would dare,
On the quaking turf of the green morass
He crouched in the rank and tangled grass,
 Like a wild beast in his lair.

A poor old slave, infirm and lame;
 Great scars deformed his face;
On his forehead he bore the brand of shame,
And the rags, that hid his mangled frame,
 Were the livery of disgrace.

All things above were bright and fair,
 All things were glad and free;
Lithe squirrels darted here and there,
And wild birds filled the echoing air
 With songs of Liberty!

On him alone was the doom of pain,
 From the morning of his birth;
On him alone the curse of Cain
Fell, like a flail on the garnered grain,
 And struck him to the earth!

Now let us set beside Longfellow's poem these lines from Section 10 of "Song of Myself":

The runaway slave came to my house and stopt outside,
I heard his motions crackling the twigs of the woodpile,
Through the swung half-door of the kitchen I saw him limpsy
 and weak,

And went where he sat on a log and led him in and assured him,
And brought water and fill'd a tub for his sweated body
   and bruis'd feet,
And gave him a room that enter'd from my own, and gave
   him some coarse clean clothes,
And remember perfectly well his revolving eyes and
   his awkwardness,
And remember putting plasters on the galls of his neck and ankles;
He staid with me a week before he was recuperated and
   pass'd north,
I had him sit next me at table, my fire-lock lean'd in the corner.

One might easily use this comparison to demonstrate the difference between good and bad poetry. But that is not my purpose. The point is that Longfellow's poem was written in a shopworn literary language then still thought to be poetic in America. To get near his subject Whitman felt it necessary to dispense with the entire apparatus of such poetry: not only the diction, but the meter and rhyme as well. Indeed, he went further than that; he dispensed with the poet. By this I mean that in Longfellow's poem the traditional calling of the man of letters is obtrusive. The words carry our thoughts not to a slave in a swamp, but to a man using the special equipment reserved for men of letters when they write poems. In Whitman's lines, on the contrary, the poet disappears. Like Huckleberry Finn, the "I" of Whitman's poem is at once the hero and the poet. That is to say, both Whitman and Twain resorted to the old device of the persona — the first-person narrator; and the result was a new sort of immediacy. The American subject was brought up closer than it ever had been before. If the device was old, the particular persona was new. Whitman's hero is the product of a new sort of culture, and appropriately enough, he speaks a new language.

There is no need to insist that Whitman's language literally was the spoken language of his time. Indeed, we can be sure that it was not. What matters is that at his best he succeeds in creating the illusion that a certain kind of man is speaking. In his case the illusion probably stems from the cadence, and the absence of traditional meter and rhyme, rather than from the diction. In any event, his poetry is nearer to the spoken language of Americans than our poetry had ever got before. I do not mean to imply that there is any absolute value in using the spoken language in poetry. That depends upon the particular aims of the writer. But given Whitman's problem, his desire to convey ideas and emotions for which the standard manner of poetry was inappropriate, the vernacular was a source of immense vitality. To see this one only has to compare Whitman with Longfellow:

> In dark fens of the Dismal Swamp
> The hunted Negro lay;

> I heard his motions crackling the twigs of the woodpile,
> Through the swung half-door of the kitchen I saw him limpsy
>   and weak.

What is most striking here is the extraordinary sense of immediacy that the vernacular mode conveys. We see Longfellow's subject through a murk of tired images: "like a wild beast in his lair"; to Whitman he is a man with "sweated body and bruis'd feet." Everyone knows that the more specific image is likely to be the more evocative. But why does one writer seize it while another avoids it? Longfellow says of the slave, "great scars deformed his face." Whitman says, "And remember putting plasters on the galls of his neck and ankles." The fact is that Whitman imagines a completely different relation to the Negro, and it takes us back of language to something more fundamental, to the kind of persona Whitman felt impelled to employ. He is a man "hankering, gross, mystical, nude." He is aggressively ungenteel, and he thinks about the slave in a very different way than Longfellow does.

> In all people I see myself, none more and not one a barley-corn less,
> And the good or bad I say of myself I say of them.

Given this sort of hero, Whitman can introduce details once thought to lie outside the bounds of respectable poetry. Among other things, the vernacular made possible a long step forward in the candor of modern writing, as in Whitman's daring treatment of physical love.

There is another kind of immediacy that results from the use of the vernacular narrator. That is the way meaning comes to us here by what Whitman called "indirection" rather than by use of personification, abstraction, or, for that matter, direct statement. Longfellow finds it necessary to tell us of the slave, "on him alone the curse of Cain/Fell . . ." Whitman avoids comment. He describes the relations between his mythic hero and the slave, and then at the end he casually mentions the gun in the corner. The image *is* the meaning; it is a perfect expression of the democratic hero's relaxed but militant egalitarianism. Right here, incidentally, Whitman anticipates that mode of ironic understatement that was to become a dominant accent of twentieth-century American poetry.

But it must not be thought that a mere technical device enables Whitman to convey so much in so little. If he does not need to proclaim the solidarity between the two men, it is because he can describe it so vividly. That is, the style has been called forth as a fitting expression of something else, an ideal human situation, indeed a kind of model society. The slave and the hero exemplify the egalitarian community of Whitman's imagination. It is a society that stands in relation to the actual society as the vernacular language to the stock elevated language of poetry. All of Whitman's poetry exalts this conception. It is the same sort of community, as a matter of fact, that Mark Twain later sets up aboard a Mississippi raft. Here is the core of the American vernacular. It is not simply a style, but a style with a politics in view. The style is a vehicle for the affirmation of an egalitarian faith so radical that we can scarcely credit it today. It sweeps aside received notions of class and status — and literature. In Whitman's mind all of these inherited forms are identified with Europe.

This is where the problem of chauvinism arises. There can be no question that Whitman celebrates America at the expense of Europe and the past. Of course the notion that stylistic elegance was the literary counterpart of European political oppression arose in America long before Whitman. In 1787, for example, Royall Tyler had expressed this prejudice in his play *The Contrast*; speaking of aristocratic titles, ornaments, and manners, Tyler said:

> Our free-born ancestors such arts despis'd;
> Genuine sincerity alone they priz'd;
> Their minds, with honest emulation fir'd,
> To solid good — not ornament — aspir'd . . .

Constance Rourke has shown how this "contrast theme" runs through our tradition of native humor. By Whitman's time the animus against a European style of life had been strengthened by the repeated European sneer against the crudities of American culture. To establish his identity the American is impelled to defy tradition:

> I too am not a bit tamed, I too am untranslatable,
> I sound my barbaric yawp over the roofs of the world.

Now granted that as a view of human experience there are serious limitations to this Whitmanian yawp, it does not seem to me that chauvinism is one of them. Whitman does not celebrate the vernacular hero because he is an American, but the other way around. It is because he is "untranslatable" that the American must be allowed to have his say in his own idiom. He is a new kind of man, and the social conditions which brought him into being may (at least theoretically) be reproduced anywhere. In reality the vernacular character is of an international cast. Hence Whitman's attitude is not to be confused with what Mr. Bewley calls "literary isolationism." To see that, one has only to read what Whitman had to say later when he thought that America was betraying the egalitarian ideal. Like Hawthorne and James, he put his country to a severe test. It was not the same test they used, but it was exacting nevertheless. In point of fact it proved finally to be too exacting.

Curiously enough, Whitman represents that side of the vernacular tradition which drew its inspiration from Europe in the first place. We know that he was inspired by Emerson, who recognized what American poets needed to do, even if he was not the man to do it. And behind Emerson, of course, we are led directly to England, and the revolution in poetry Wordsworth had announced fifty-five years before *Leaves of Grass*, in the Preface to the second edition of *Lyrical Ballads* in 1800. I do not mean to imply that in Whitman we have a simple case of delayed literary influence, of what is sometimes called "cultural lag." Whitman went much further than Wordsworth, and he did so largely because American conditions imparted a special intensity to Wordsworthian doctrine. Was it a good thing for poets to escape the refinements of civilization, to catch impulses from the vernal wood? Then how lucky to be an American poet! Was it true that Wordsworth's country neighbors spoke a language more vivid and precise, hence more poetic than the language of cultivated men? Again, this idea touched an American in ways unimaginable to an English poet. In America the exaltation of what Wordsworth called "humble and rustic life" could not be received as a mere program for poetry. By Whitman's time it had already become something like a national ethos. In the defiant accent of Whitman's hero we recognize how far we have come from Wordsworth's simple peasants.

> Who goes there? hankering, gross, mystical, nude;
> How is it I extract strength from the beef I eat?
> What is a man anyhow? what am I? what are you?
>
> .   .   .   .
>
> I wear my hat as I please indoors or out.
> Why should I pray? why should I venerate and be ceremonious?
> Having pried through the strata, analyzed to a hair, counsel'd
>   with doctors and calculated close,
> I find no sweeter fat than sticks to my own bones.

This boast is a self-portrait of Whitman's democratic man. It is a revealing and ironic fact that the average American reader preferred Longfellow's poetry. Whether this had anything to do with Whitman's style, his success or failure in catching the popular tone of voice, is a question that is probably unanswerable. But in any event Whitman was never persuaded that he was speaking the truly distinctive native idiom, and what is more, he had a good idea where that idiom was likely to arise. "Today," he wrote in 1871, "doubtless, the infant genius of American poetic expression . . . lies sleeping far away, happily unrecognized and uninjur'd by the coteries, the art-writers, the talkers and critics of the saloons, or the lecturers in the colleges — lies sleeping, aside, unrecking itself, in some western idiom . . . ."

This brings me to Mark Twain and the other or frontier side of the vernacular tradition. His mature style, the very essence of his humor, is grounded in a sensitivity to language as an index of cultural difference. He felt that the distinguishing trait of the American story was its emphasis upon *manner* rather than matter. That also explains why Mark Twain was so exasperated by the work of James Fenimore Cooper. For him reading Cooper was like listening to a tone-deaf man trying to sing. "He keeps near the tune," said Twain, "but it is *not* the tune. . . . you perceive what he is intending to say, but you also perceive that he doesn't *say* it." In other words Cooper, like Longfellow, had spoiled a fine subject by encasing it in a foreign idiom. As it happens it was Twain's chosen subject, so he had a special reason for wanting to dispose of Cooper. Fitness of language to subject was a cardinal point in the literary ethic of Mark Twain. He felt that Cooper achieved his blurred effect by virtue of his unfailing instinct for the *approximate* word. As his best work suggests, the *precise* word for Twain was the word spoken by his native hero himself.

Twain's feeling for language was in large measure derived from the oral tradition of the West. The frontiersman was a celebrated boaster. He screamed his barbaric yawp to call attention to his strength, and his many triumphs over nature. The vocabulary of the boast was itself a form of triumph. He used it to display his dexterity and ingenuity with language: "Mister . . . I can whip my weight in wild cats, and ride straight thro' a crab apple orchard on a flash of lightening — clear meat axe disposition — the best man, if I an't, I wish I may be tetotaciously exfluncated." The western man's idiom made him conspicuous, and sometimes it made him feel a fool. Actually, he was sensitive about it, and his tall tale was in part an effort to get his own back from those who mocked his barbaric speech. We see this clearly in T. B. Thorpe's classic, "The Big Bear of Arkansas" (1841) — a story which belongs to the long line of American hunting fantasies which include Melville's *Moby Dick*, Faulkner's "The Bear," and Hemingway's *Old Man and the Sea*. Here the western narrator introduces his tale with a brief account of his visit to the big city, from which he is returning. There he had met some gentlemen who interrogated him about his home state, Arkansas. But they did not speak his language, and when they asked him about "game" in Arkansas he mistook them and told about "poker, and high-low-jack." They laughed at him, and called him green. "Strangers," he says he told them, "if you'd asked me *how we got our meat* in Arkansaw, I'd a told you at once . . . Game, indeed, that's what city folks call it . . ." With this prelude, he launches his boastful story. Of course he tells it in the same vernacular idiom that had marked him for a rustic dolt in the eyes of gentlemen. But he has learned that his speech is his identity, and now he will use it to glorify himself at the expense of those who patronize him. Here again is the hostility, the defiance of what pretends to be a superior culture that so often animates the vernacular style.

In *Huckleberry Finn* Mark Twain exploits similar misunderstandings on the part of his western hero for similar purposes. For example, in reporting the king's funeral oration, Huck says that he "slobbers out a speech, all full of tears and flapdoodle, about its being a sore trial for him and his poor brother to lose the *diseased*, and to miss seeing *diseased* alive." Clearly, this joke has two edges. We are intended to laugh at Huck's ignorance, to be sure; the real butt, however, is the pompous euphemism, the respectable burial rhetoric which he does not recognize for what it is. This is a minor example of the satiric device that Mark Twain uses throughout. In the magnificent description of the Grangerford house he turns it against all the pretensions of refinement associated with the sort of people Huck calls the "quality." He has never been in such a nice house before, and he is impressed. He admires everything from the brass door knob to Emmeline Grangerford's poetry. But at the same time his keen eye makes it possible for us to see how spurious it all is: "On the table in the middle of the room was a kind of a lovely crockery basket that had apples and oranges and peaches and grapes piled up in it, which was much redder and yellower and prettier than real ones is, but they warn't real because you could see where pieces had got chipped off and showed the white chalk, or whatever it was, underneath."

Huck is less certain about the pictures on the walls: "They was different from any pictures I ever see before — blacker, mostly, than is common. One was a woman in a slim black dress, belted small under the armpits, with bulges like a cabbage in the middle of the sleeves, and a large black scoop-shovel bonnet with a black veil, and white slim ankles crossed about with black tape, and very wee black slippers, like a chisel, and she was leaning pensive on a tombstone on her right elbow, under a weeping willow, and her other hand hanging down her side holding a white handkerchief and a reticule, and underneath the picture it said 'Shall I Never See Thee More Alas.'" In conclusion, Huck says: "These was all nice pictures, I reckon, but I didn't somehow seem to take to them, because if ever I was down a little they always give me the fan-tods." (When reading these words to a European audience one feels the need to provide a gloss on "fan-tods." Not that Americans necessarily can define the word with precision. It is not even to be found in the *Dictionary of Americanisms*. But a native audience can be relied on to get the point.) The passage contains the recurrent pattern of the book: Huck knows how he is supposed to feel about many things, but he cannot always feel that way.

Much the same thing happens to his feelings about Jim and obedience to the laws enforcing the slave system. He knows that he should pray for divine help to return Jim to his "rightful owner," and occasionally this knowledge takes possession of his will, as in the moral crisis of the book — when he writes to Miss Watson to tell her of Jim's presence. But having written the letter, Huck says: "[I] got to thinking over our trip down the river; and I see Jim before me all the time: in the day and in the night-time, sometimes moonlight, sometimes storms, and we a-floating along, talking and singing and laughing. But somehow I couldn't seem to strike no places to harden me against him, but only the other kind. I'd see him standing my watch on top of his'n, 'stead of calling me, so I could go on sleeping; and see him how glad he was when I come back out of the fog . . . and at last I struck the time I saved him by telling the men we had smallpox aboard, and he was so grateful, and said I was the best friend old Jim ever had in the world, and the *only* one he's got now; and then I happened to look around and see that paper. It was a close place. I took it up and held it in my hand. I was a-trembling, because I'd got to decide, forever, betwixt two things, and I knowed it." Here, at the level of social morality, is the same distinction Huck had felt in the Grangerford house. Indeed, the respectable values of society prove to be like the lovely crockery basket of fruit that "warn't real because you could see where pieces had got chipped off and showed the white chalk, or whatever it was, underneath." In the crisis Huck finally is forced to choose between two things: the demands of the crockery culture and those of the egalitarian community he and Jim have established aboard the raft.

In the background we can still discern the contrast theme in slightly modified form. Here the young barbarian is compared to a spurious local culture. But in the moral geography of America, this sentimental elegance is associated with the culture of the eastern seaboard, which in turn is but an American extension of European civilization. Here the vernacular humor also is used against the old European targets. The two rogues, the Duke and the Dauphin, are the crockery royalty that serves to expose the real thing:

"Don't it s'prise you [Jim asks] de way dem kings carries on, Huck?"
"No," I says, "it don't."
"Why don't it, Huck?"
"Well, it don't, because it's in the breed. I reckon they're all alike."
"But, Huck, dese kings o' ourn is reglar rapscallions; dat's jist what dey is; dey's reglar rapscallions."
"Well, that's what I'm a-saying; all kings is mostly rapscallions, as fur as I can make out."
"Is dat so?"

Mark Twain pushes this republican piety right back to the genesis of the contrast theme, the American Revolution itself: "You don't know kings, Jim, but I know them; and this old rip of ourn is one of the cleanest I've struck in history. Well, Henry he takes a notion he wants to get up some trouble with this country. How does he go at it — give notice? — give the country a show? No. All of a sudden he heaves all the tea in Boston Harbor overboard, and whacks out a declaration of independence, and dares them to come on. That was *his* style — he never give anybody a chance."

So far I have talked about the vernacular mode of *Huckleberry Finn* in its negative aspect, that is, the aggressive use of the style. But in this book we also find an affirmation, the hero's self-exaltation: "Well," says Huck, "the days went along, and the river went down between its banks again; and about the first thing we done was to bait one of the big hooks with a skinned rabbit and set it and catch a catfish that was as big as a man, being six foot two inches long, and weighed over two hundred pounds." Actually, there is not much of this sort of thing in *Huckleberry Finn*. The reason is that the entire book, in its total conception, is a westerner's boast. He is telling the story in his own idiom, hence the tale is a celebration of his point of view from beginning to end. Like Whitman's hero, Huck is a rebellious, democratic barbarian. He lies, he steals, he prefers magic to religion, he identifies his interests with those of escaped slaves, and above all he speaks the vernacular. The largest boast of *Huckleberry Finn* is reserved for the language itself — its capacity to take on the dignity of art, to replace the elevated style of Longfellow or Cooper.

The vernacular style bears many marks of its plebeian origin. For example, it has been peculiarly useful in expressing a preoccupation with process, with the way things are done. By its very nature a genteel style implies an invidious distinction between intellectual and manual work. But the vernacular hero does not honor the distinction, and moreover his very language seems to deny its significance: "Well, last I *pulled* out some of my hair, *and blooded* the ax good, *and stuck* it on the back side, *and slung* the ax in the corner. Then I *took* up the pig *and held* him to my breast with my jacket (so he couldn't drip) till I got a good piece below the house *and then dumped* him into the river. Now I thought of something else. So *I went and got* the bag of meal and my old saw out of the canoe, *and fetched* them to the house. *I took* the bag to where it used to stand, *and ripped* a hole in the bottom of it with the saw . . ." What we have here is a meticulous rendering, one by one, of physical actions or manipulations. A series of verbs (here italicized) is strung together, largely by the word "and," and the total effect is an immediate impression of a process. The writer takes it for granted that we are as interested in *how* he does things as *what* he does. From this passage one can make a direct link to the style of many of our modern writers, say Ernest Hemingway describing in the same way how he baits a fishhook.

Vernacular narration is the key to Mark Twain's style just as it is the key to Whitman's. Twain uses a naive character and his naive language to convey a highly complicated state of mind. But the point of view and the idiom finally are inseparable: together they form a style. And it is this style that lends immediacy to the affirmation without which the book would be morally empty. Huck compresses his whole conception of felicity into one sentence: "It's lovely," he says, "to live on a raft." Actually there are two separate but analogous ideals implied in Huck's pastoral emotion here. The first is a relation between men (it is in a sense political), while the other is a relation between man and nature (it is religious or, if you will, metaphysical).

The political ideal is freedom, freedom *from* the oppression of society, and freedom *to* establish the egalitarian community. The escaped slave and the son of the village drunkard set up their model society on the raft. "What you want," says Huck, "above all things, on a raft, is for everybody to be satisfied, and feel right and kind toward the others." This sort of community only can exist on the river, insulated from the surrounding culture, and even there it is terribly vulnerable. Rogues take over the raft, a steamboat smashes into it, and the river's current carries it steadily toward the slave society its occupants want to escape. But vulnerability, after all, is appropriate to what is essentially a utopian conception. The anarchic impulse that leads the vernacular hero to renounce the existing society is much stronger, needless to say, than the impulse to create a new one.

Although the vernacular ideal of the raft turns upon human solidarity, it derives its ultimate support from another sort of solidarity — one which is given to us only indirectly, by way of the lyrical strain in the book: "Sometimes we'd have that whole river all to ourselves for the longest time. Yonder was the banks and the islands, across the water; and maybe a spark — which was a candle in a cabin window; and sometimes on the water you could see a spark or two — on a raft or a scow, you know; and maybe you could hear a fiddle or a song coming over from one of them crafts. It's lovely to live on a raft. We had the sky up there, all speckled with stars, and we used to lay on our backs and look up at them, and discuss about whether they was made or only just happened." In such passages Mark Twain manages to convey a feeling of belonging to the physical universe comparable to the feeling of community aboard the raft. That is, he suggests a grand analogy between the political and metaphysical relations within the novel. The vernacular thereby receives its final sanction from nature itself. It is a fitting sanction for a literary style developed in a new society in a prehistoric landscape.

The vernacular style is a distinctive achievement of American culture. But this is not to say that it has served to convey anything like an adequate view of experience, or that it has yet given America a great literature. Its creativity came from the radical program of freedom it affirmed, but like any such program, it demands an exceptional discipline. The writer who works in the vernacular takes great risks. To see this we have only to recall those excesses of uncontrolled improvisation that mar the work of Whitman and Twain. This literary barbarism follows from the rejection of inherited forms and theories. It is of course a symptom of primitivism, and along with it we get what is perhaps the chief defect of the vernacular mode — its unremitting anti-intellectualism. This seems to me a more valid point of attack than chauvinism. In defying the constraints and oppression identified with the European past, our writers also have tended to ignore the achievements of the trained intellect. This familiar primitivist bias has retained its affinity to the mode in our time. It seems to have followed the style from Walt Whitman to Carl Sandburg, from Mark Twain to Ernest Hemingway.

But it is one thing to charge the vernacular with an anti-intellectual bias, and quite another to think it (as Mr. Bewley does) "uncritically acceptant" of America. In Hawthorne and James criticism arose from a comparison of America to tradition, to the past. In Whitman and Twain, on the other hand, the criticism was based on utopian standards. It came from a comparison of an actual America with an ideal vision of the nation's destiny. That is what led to the writing of such uncompromising works as *Democratic Vistas, A Connecticut Yankee*, and "The Man That Corrupted Hadleyburg." My point has been that from the beginning the vernacular was more than a literary technique — it was a view of experience. When the style first emerged it was nourished by an egalitarian faith that we can scarcely imagine nowadays. Since that time the history of the vernacular has been a history of its fragmentation. The technique has been separated from the belief it originally was designed to affirm. But that is another story.

Harry Levin

OBSERVATIONS ON THE
STYLE OF ERNEST HEMINGWAY

✍ ✍

The vernacular style of Whitman and Twain continued in the work
of Sherwood Anderson, Gertrude Stein, Ernest Hemingway, and
others. Hemingway carried further what Mr. Levin calls a purgation
of genteel language and rhetorical oratory. The wounded soldier of
World War I cannot believe any longer in the big abstractions like
"glory" and "honor": "All our words from loose using have lost their
edge," said Hemingway. Mr. Levin teaches us how to move from
analysis of style to general statements about the attitudes and values
of a writer. One begins with observations about the range and choices
of vocabulary, the use of adjectives, the limitations on verbs; he studies
the handling of syntax and the disposition of subordinate ideas. Such
an analysis provides an answer to the question, "What is behind the
unexampled dynamics of Hemingway's style?" Mr. Levin can then
make statements about Hemingway's beliefs.

I

Hemingway's hatred for the profession of letters stems quite obviously
from a lover's quarrel. When Richard Gordon is reviled by his dissatisfied
wife in *To Have and Have Not*, her most embittered epithet is "you
writer." Yet Hemingway's writing abounds in salutes to various fellow
writers, from the waitress' anecdote about Henry James in *The Torrents of
Spring* to Colonel Cantwell's spiritual affinity with D'Annunzio. And from

Nick Adams, who takes Meredith and Chesterton along on fishing trips, to Hemingway himself, who arranges to be interviewed on American literature in *Green Hills of Africa*, his heroes do not shy away from critical discussion. His titles, so often quoted from books by earlier writers, have been so apt that they have all but established a convention. He shows an almost academic fondness, as well as a remarkable flair, for epigraphs: the Colonel dies with a quotation on his lips. Like all of us, Hemingway has been influenced by T. S. Eliot's taste for Elizabethan drama and metaphysical poetry. Thus Hemingway's title, "In Another Country," is borrowed from a passage he elsewhere cites, which he might have found in Marlowe's *Jew of Malta* or possibly in Eliot's "Portrait of a Lady." A *Farewell to Arms*, which echoes Lovelace's title, quotes in passing from Marvell's "To His Coy Mistress," echoed more recently by Robert Penn Warren, which is parodied in *Death in the Afternoon*. Hemingway is no exception to the rule that makes parody the starting point for realistic fiction. Just as Fielding took off from Richardson, so Hemingway takes off from Sherwood Anderson — indeed his first novel, *The Torrents of Spring*, which parodies Anderson's *Dark Laughter*, is explicit in its acknowledgments to *Joseph Andrews*. It has passages, however, which read today like a *pastiche* of the later Hemingway:

> Yogi was worried. There was something on his mind. It was spring, there was no doubt of that now, and he did not want a woman. He had worried about it a lot lately. There was no question about it. He did not want a woman. He couldn't explain it to himself. He had gone to the Public Library and asked for a book the night before. He looked at the librarian. He did not want her. Somehow she meant nothing to him.

A recoil from bookishness, after a preliminary immersion in it, provided Fielding's master, Cervantes, with the original impetus for the novel. In "A Banal Story" Hemingway provides us with his own variation on the theme of *Don Quixote*, where a writer sits reading about romance in a magazine advertisement, while in far-off Madrid a bullfighter dies and is buried. The ironic contrast — romantic preconception exploded by contact with harsh reality — is basic with Hemingway, as it has been with all novelists who have written effectively about war. The realism of his generation reacted not only against Wilsonian idealism, but against Wilsonian rhetoric. Hence the famous paragraph from the Caporetto episode describing Frederic Henry's embarrassment before such abstract words as "glory" and "honor," which seem to him obscene beside the concrete names of places and numbers of roads. For a Spaniard, Hemingway notes in *Death in the Afternoon*, the abstraction may still have concreteness: honor may be "as real a thing as water, wine, or olive oil." It is not so for us: "All our words from loose using have lost their edge." And "The Gambler, the Nun, and the Radio" brings forward a clinching example: "Liberty, what we believed in, now the name of a Macfadden publication." That same story trails off in a litany which reduces a Marxist slogan to meaninglessness: "the opium of the people" is everything and nothing. Even more desolating, in "A Clean, Well-Lighted Place," is the reduction of the Lord's prayer to nothingness: "Our nada who art in nada . . ." Since words have become inflated and devalued, Hemingway is willing to recognize no values save those which can be immediately felt and directly pointed out. It is his verbal skepticism which leads toward what some critics have called his moral nihilism. Anything serious had better be said with a smile, stranger. The classic echo, "irony and pity," jingles through *The Sun Also Rises* like a singing commercial.

There is something in common between this attitude and the familiar British habit of understatement. "No pleasure in anything if you mouth it too much," says Wilson, the guide in "The Short, Happy Life of Francis Macomber." Yet Jake, the narrator of *The Sun Also Rises*, protests — in the name of American garrulity — that the English use fewer words than the Eskimos. Spanish, the language of Hemingway's preference, is at once emotive and highly formal. His Spanish, to judge from *Death in the Afternoon*, is just as ungrammatical as his English. In "The Undefeated" his Spanish bullfighters are made to speak the slang of American prizefighters. Americanisms and Hispanisms, archaic and polyglot elements are so intermingled in *For Whom the Bell Tolls* that it calls to mind what Ben Jonson said of *The Faerie Queene*: "Spenser writ no language." Hemingway offers a succinct example by translating "*Eras mucho caballo*" as "Thou wert plenty of horse." It is somewhat paradoxical that a writer, having severely cut down his English vocabulary, should augment it by continual importation from other languages, including the Swahili. But this is a facet of the larger paradox that a writer so essentially American should set the bulk of his work against foreign backgrounds. His characters, expatriates for the most part, wander through the ruins of Babel, smattering many tongues and speaking a demotic version of their own. Obscenity presents another linguistic problem, for which Hemingway is not responsible; but his coy ways of circumventing the taboos of censorship are more of a distraction than the conventional blanks. When he does permit himself an expression not usually considered printable, in *Death in the Afternoon*, the context is significant. His interlocutor, the Old Lady, requests a definition and he politely responds: "Madam, we apply the term now to describe unsoundness in abstract conversation or, indeed, any overmetaphysical tendency in speech."

For language, as for literature, his feeling is strongly ambivalent. Perhaps it could be summed up by Pascal's maxim: "True eloquence makes fun of eloquence." Like the notorious General Cambronne, Hemingway feels that one short spontaneous vulgarism is more honest than all those grand-iloquent slogans which rhetoricians dream up long after the battle. The disparity between rhetoric and experience, which became so evident during the First World War, prompted the 'twenties to repudiate the genteel stylistic tradition and to accept the American vernacular as our norm of literary discourse. "Literary" is a contradiction in terms, for the resultant style is basically oral; and when the semiliterate speaker takes pen in hand, as Hemingway demonstrates in "One Reader Writes" — as H. L. Mencken demonstrated in "A Short View of Gamalielese" — the result is even more artificial than if it had been written by a writer. A page is always flat, and we need perspective to make it convey the illusion of life in the round. Yet the very fact that words mean so much less to us than the things they represent in our lives is a stimulus to our imaginations. In "Fathers and Sons" young Nick Adams reads that Caruso has been arrested for "mash-ing," and asks his father the meaning of that expression.

> "It is one of the most heinous of crimes," his father answered. Nick's imagination pictured the great tenor doing something strange, bizarre, and heinous with a potato masher to a beautiful lady who looked liked the pictures of Anna Held on the inside of cigar boxes. He resolved, with considerable horror, that when he was old enough he would try mashing at least once.

The tone of this passage is not altogether typical of Hemingway. Rather, as the point of view detaches itself affectionately and ironically from the youth, it approximates the early Joyce. This may help to explain why it suggests a more optimistic approach to language than the presumption that, since phrases can be snares and delusions, their scope should be limited to straight denotation. The powers of connotation, the possibilities of oblique suggestion and semantic association, are actually grasped by Hemingway as well as any writer of our time. Thus he can retrospectively endow a cheap and faded term like "mashing" with all the promise and poetry of awaken-ing manhood. When Nick grows up, foreign terms will hold out the same allure to him; like Frederic Henry, he will seek the actuality that resides be-hind the names of places; and Robert Jordan will first be attracted to Spain as a professional philologist. But none of them will find an equivalence between the word and the thing; and Hemingway, at the end of *Death in the Afternoon*, laments that no book is big enough to do final justice to its living subject. "There was so much to write," the dying writer realizes in "The Snows of Kilimanjaro," and his last thoughts are moving and memo-rable recollections of some of the many things that will now go unwritten. Walt Whitman stated this challenge and this dilemma, for all good writers, when he spoke of expressing the inexpressible.

II

The inevitable compromise, for Hemingway, is best expressed by his account of Romero's bullfighting style: "the holding of his purity of line through the maximum of exposure." The maximum of exposure — this throws much light upon the restlessness of Hemingway's career, but here we are primarily concerned with the holding of his purity of line. It had to be the simplest and most flexible of lines in order to accommodate itself to his desperate pursuit of material. His purgation of language has aptly been compared, by Robert Penn Warren, to the revival of diction that Wordsworth accomplished with *Lyrical Ballads*. Indeed the question that Coleridge afterward raised might once again be asked: why should the speech of some men be more real than that of others? Today that question restates itself in ideological terms: whether respect for the common man necessitates the adoption of a commonplace standard. Everyone who writes faces the same old problems, and the original writers — like Wordsworth or Hemingway — are those who develop new ways of meeting them. The case of Wordsworth would show us, if that of Hemingway did not, that those who break down conventions tend to substitute conventions of their own. Hemingway's prose is not without precedents; it is interesting to recall that his maiden effort, published by *The Double Dealer* in 1922, parodied the King James Bible. He has his forerunners in American fiction, from Cooper to Jack London, whose conspicuous lack was a style as dynamic as their subject-matter. The ring-tailed roarers of the frontier, such as Davy Crockett, were Colonel Cantwell's brothers under the skin; but as contrasted with the latter's tragic conception of himself, they were mock-heroic and serio-comic figures, who recommend themselves to the reader's condescension. Mark Twain has been the most genuine influence, and Hemingway has acknowledged this by declaring — with sweeping generosity — that *Huckleberry Finn* is the source of all modern American literature.

But Mark Twain was conducting a monologue, a virtual *tour de force* of impersonation, and he ordinarily kept a certain distance between his narrative role and his characters. And among Hemingway's elder contemporaries, Ring Lardner was a kind of ventriloquist, who made devastating use of the vernacular to satirize the vulgarity and stupidity of his dummies. It remained for Hemingway — along with Anderson — to identify himself wholly with the lives he wrote about, not so much entering into them as allowing them to take possession of him, and accepting — along with their sensibilities and perceptions — the limitations of their point of view and the limits of their range of expression. We need make no word-count to be sure that his literary vocabulary, with foreign and technical exceptions, consists of relatively few and short words. The corollary, of course, is that every word sees a good deal of hard use. Furthermore, his syntax is informal to the point of fluidity, simplifying as far as possible the already simple system of English inflections. Thus "who" is normally substituted for "whom," presumably to avoid schoolmarmish correctness; and "that," doing duty for "which," seems somehow less prophetic of complexity. Personal pronouns frequently get involved in what is stigmatized, by teachers of freshman composition, as faulty reference; there are sentences in which it is hard to tell the hunter from his quarry or the bullfighter from the bull. "When his father died he was only a kid and his manager buried him perpetually." So begins, rather confusingly, "The Mother of a Queen." Sometimes it seems as if Hemingway were taking pains to be ungrammatical, as do many educated people out of a twisted sense of *noblesse oblige.* Yet when he comes closest to pronouncing a moral, the last words of Harry Morgan — the analphabetic hero of *To Have and Have Not* — seem to be half-consciously fumbling toward some grammatical resolution: "A man . . . ain't got no hasn't got any can't really isn't any way out. . ."

The effectiveness of Hemingway's method depends very largely upon his keen ear for speech. His conversations are vivid, often dramatic, although he comes to depend too heavily upon them and to scant the other obligations of the novelist. Many of his wisecracks are quotable out of context, but as Gertrude Stein warned him: "Remarks are not literature." He can get his story told, and still be as conversational as he pleases, by telling it in the first person. "Brother, that was some storm," says the narrator, and the reader hears the very tone of his voice. In one of Hemingway's critical digressions, he declares that he has always sought "the real thing, the sequence of motion and fact which [sic] made the emotion. . ." This seems to imply the clear-cut mechanism of verbal stimulus and psychological response that Eliot formulates in his theory of the objective correlative. In practice, however, Hemingway is no more of a behaviorist than Eliot, and the sharp distinction between motion and emotion is soon blurred. Consider his restricted choice of adjectives, and the heavy load of subjective implication carried by such uncertain monosyllables as "fine" and "nice." From examples on nearly every page, we are struck by one which helps to set the scene for *A Farewell to Arms:* "The town was very nice and our house was very fine." Such descriptions — if we may consider them descriptions — are obviously not designed for pictorial effect. When the Colonel is tempted to call some fishing-boats picturesque, he corrects himself: "The hell with picturesque. They are just damned beautiful." Where "picturesque" might sound arty and hence artificial, "beautiful" — with "damned" to take off the curse — is permissible because Hemingway has packed it with his own emotional charge. He even uses it in *For Whom the Bell Tolls* to express his esthetic appreciation of gunfire. Like "fine" and "nice," or "good" and "lovely," it does not describe; it evaluates. It is not a stimulus but a projected response, a projection of the narrator's euphoria in a given situation. Hemingway, in effect, is saying to the reader: *Having wonderful time. Wish you were here.*

In short, he is communicating excitement; and if this communication is received, it establishes a uniquely personal relationship; but when it goes astray, the diction goes flat and vague. Hemingway manages to sustain his reputation for concreteness by an exploring eye for the incidental detail. The one typescript of his that I have seen, his carbon copy of "The Killers" now in the Harvard College Library, would indicate that the arc-light and the tipped-back derby hat were later observations than the rest. Precision at times becomes so arithmetical that, in "The Light of the World," it lines up his characters like a drill-sergeant: "Down at the station there were five whores waiting for the train to come in, and six white men and four Indians." Numbers enlarge the irony that concludes the opening chapter of *A Farewell to Arms* when, after a far from epic invocation, a casual introduction to the landscape, and a dusty record of troops falling back through the autumn, rain brings the cholera which kills "only seven thousand." A trick of multiplication, which Hemingway may have picked up from Gertrude Stein, is to generalize the specific episode: "They always picked the finest places to have the quarrels." When he offers this general view of a restaurant — "It was full of smoke and drinking and singing" — he is an impressionist if not an abstractionist. Thence to expressionism is an easy step: ". . . the room whirled." It happens that, under pressure from his first American publishers, the author was compelled to modify the phrasing of "Mr. and Mrs. Elliot." In the original version, subsequently restored, the title characters "try to have a baby." In the modified version they "think of having a baby." It could be argued that, in characterizing this rather tepid couple, the later verb is more expressive and no more euphemistic than the earlier one; that "think," at any rate, is not less precise or effectual than "try." But, whereas the sense of effort came naturally, the cerebration was an afterthought.

If we regard the adjective as a luxury, decorative more often than functional, we can well understand why Hemingway doesn't cultivate it. But, assuming that the sentence derives its energy from the verb, we are in for a shock if we expect his verbs to be numerous or varied or emphatic. His usage supports C. K. Ogden's argument that verb-forms are disappearing from English grammar. Without much self-deprivation, Hemingway could get along on the so-called "operators" of Basic English, the sixteen monosyllabic verbs that stem from movements of the body. The substantive verb *to be* is predominant, characteristically introduced by an expletive. Thus the first story of *In Our Time* begins, and the last one ends, with the story-teller's gambit: "there was," "there were." In the first two pages of *A Farewell to Arms* nearly every other sentence is of this type, and the third page employs the awkward construction "there being." There is — I find the habit contagious — a tendency to immobilize verbs by transposing them into gerunds. Instead of writing *they fought* or *we did not feel*, Hemingway writes "there was fighting" and "there was not the feeling of a storm coming." The subject does little more than point impersonally at its predicate: an object, a situation, an emotion. Yet the idiom, like the French *il y a*, is ambiguous; inversion can turn the gesture of pointing into a physical act; and the indefinite adverb can indicate, if not specify, a definite place. Contrast, with the opening of A *Farewell to Arms*, that of "In Another Country": "In the fall the war was always there, but we did not go to it any more." The negative is even more striking, when Frederic Henry has registered the sensations of his wound, and dares to look at it for the first time, and notes: "My knee wasn't there." The adverb is *there* rather than *here*, the verb is *was* rather than *is*, because we — the readers — are separated from the event in space and time. But the narrator has lived through it, like the Ancient Mariner, and now he chooses his words to grip and transfix us. *Lo!* he says. *Look! I was there.*

III

Granted, then, that Hemingway's diction is thin; that, in the technical sense, his syntax is weak; and that he would rather be caught dead than seeking the *mot juste* or the balanced phrase. Granted that his adjectives are not colorful and his verbs not particularly energetic. Granted that he commits as many literary offenses as Mark Twain brought to book with Fenimore Cooper. What is behind his indubitable punch, the unexampled dynamics of Heminway's style? How does he manage, as he does, to animate this characteristic sentence from "After the Storm"?

> I said "Who killed him?" and he said "I don't know who killed him but he's dead all right," and it was dark and there was water standing in the street and no lights and windows broke and boats all up in the town and trees blown down and everything all blown and I got a skiff and went out and found my boat where I had her inside of Mango Key and she was all right only she was full of water.

Here is a good example of Hemingway's "sequence of motion and fact." It starts from dialogue and leads into first-person action; but the central description is a single clause, where the expletive takes the place of the observer and his observations are registered one by one. Hence, for the reader, it lives up to Robert Jordan's intention: "you . . . feel that all that happened to you." Hemingway puts his emphasis on nouns because, among parts of speech, they come closest to things. Stringing them along by means of conjunctions, he approximates the actual flow of experience. For him, as for Marion Tweedy Bloom, the key word is *and*, with its renewable promise of continuity, occasionally varied by *then* and *so*. The rhetorical scheme is *polysyndeton* — a large name for the childishly simple habit of linking sentences together. The subject, when it is not taken for granted, merely puts us in touch with the predicate: the series of objects that Hemingway wants to point out. Even a preposition can turn this trick as "with" does in this account of El Sordo waiting to see the whites of his enemy's eyes:

> Come on, Comrade Voyager . . . Keep on coming with your eyes forward . . . Look. With a red face and blond hair and blue eyes. With no cap on and his moustache is yellow. With blue eyes. With pale blue eyes. With pale blue eyes with something wrong with them. With pale blue eyes that don't focus. Close enough. Too close. Yes, Comrade Voyager. Take it, Comrade Voyager.

Prose gets as near as it can to physical conflict here. The figure enlarges as it advances, the quickening impression grows clear and sharp and almost unbearable, whereupon it is blackened out by El Sordo's rifle. Each clipped sentence, each prepositional phrase, is like a new frame in a strip of film; indeed the whole passage, like so many others might have been filmed by the camera and projected on the screen. The course of Harry Morgan's launch speeding through the Gulf Stream, or of Frederic Henry's fantasy ascending the elevator with Catherine Barkley, is given this cinematographic presentation. *Green Hills of Africa* voices the long-range ambition of obtaining a fourth and fifth dimension in prose. Yet if the subordinate clause and the complex sentence are the usual ways for writers to obtain a third dimension, Hemingway keeps his writing on a linear plane. He holds the purity of his line by moving in one direction, ignoring sidetracks and avoiding structural complications. By presenting a succession of images, each of which has its brief moment when it commands the reader's undivided attention, he achieves his special vividness and fluidity. For what he lacks in structure he makes up in sequence, carefully ordering visual impressions as he sets them down and ironically juxtaposing the various items on his lists and inventories. "A Way You'll Never Be" opens with a close-up showing the debris on a battlefield, variously specifying munitions, medicaments, and left-overs from a field kitchen, then closing in on the scattered papers with this striking montage-effect: ". . . group postcards showing the machine-gun unit standing in ranked and ruddy cheerfulness as in a football picture for a college annual; now they were humped and swollen in the grass. . . ." It is not surprising that Hemingway's verse, published by *Poetry* in 1923, is recognizably imagistic in character — and perhaps his later heroics are foreshadowed by the subject of one of those poems, Theodore Roosevelt.

In her observant book, *L'Age du roman américain*, Claude-Edmonde Magny stresses Hemingway's "exaltation of the instant." We can note how this emphasis is reflected in his timing, which — after his placing has bridged the distance from *there* to *here* — strives to close the gap between *then* and *now*. Where Baudelaire's clock said "remember" in many languages, Robert Jordan's memory says: "Now, *ahora, maintenant, heute.*"

When death interrupts a dream, in "The Snows of Kilimanjaro," the ultimate reality is heralded by a rising insistence upon the word "now." It is not for nothing that Hemingway is the younger contemporary of Proust and Joyce. Though his time is neither *le temps perdu* nor the past nostalgically recaptured, he spends it gathering roses while he can, to the ever accelerating rhythm of headlines and telegrams and loud-speakers. The act, no sooner done than said, becomes simultaneous with the word, no sooner said than felt. Hemingway goes so far, in "Fathers and Sons," as to render a sexual embrace by an onomatopoetic sequence of adverbs. But unlike Damon Runyon and Dickens, he seldom narrates in the present tense, except in such sporting events as "Fifty Grand." Rather, his timeliness expresses itself in continuous forms of the verb and in his fondness for all kinds of participial constructions. These, compounded and multiplied, create an ambiance of overwhelming activity, and the epithets shift from El Sordo's harassed feelings to the impact of the reiterated bullets, as Hemingway recounts "the last lung-aching, leg-dead, mouth-dry, bullet-spatting, bullet-cracking, bullet-singing run up the final slope of the hill." More often the meaning takes the opposite turn, and moves from the external plane into the range of a character's senses, proceeding serially from the visual to the tactile, as it does when the "Wine of Wyoming" is sampled: "It was very light and clear and good and still tasted of the grapes."

When Nick Adams goes fishing, the temperature is very tangibly indicated: "It was getting hot, the sun hot on the back of his neck." The remark about the weather is thereby extended in two directions, toward the distant source of the heat and toward its immediate perception. Again in "Big Two-Hearted River," Nick's fatigue is measured by the weight of his pack: ". . . it was heavy. It was much too heavy." As in the movies, the illusion of movement is produced by repeating the same shot with further modification every time. Whenever a new clause takes more than one step ahead, a subsequent clause repeats it in order to catch up. Repetition, as in "Up in Michigan," brings the advancing narrative back to an initial point of reference. "Liz liked Jim very much. She liked it the way he walked over from the shop and often went to the kitchen door to watch him start down the road. She liked it about his moustache. She liked it about how white his teeth were when he smiled." The opaque verb "like," made increasingly transparent, is utilized five more times in this paragraph; and the fumbling preposition "about" may be an acknowledgment of Hemingway's early debt to Gertrude Stein. The situation is located somewhere between a subjective Liz and an objective Jim. The theme of love is always a test of Hemingway's objectivity. When Frederic kisses Catherine, her responses are not less moving because they are presented through his reflexes; but it is her sentimental conversation which leaves him free to ask himself: "What the hell?" At first glance, in a behavioristic formula which elsewhere recurs, Colonel Cantwell seems so hard-boiled that motions are his only emotions: "He saw that his hand was trembling." But his vision is blurred by conventionally romantic tenderness when he contemplates a heroine whose profile "could break your . . . or anyone else's heart." Hemingway's heroines, when they aren't bitches, are fantasies — or rather, the masculine reader is invited to supply his own, as with the weather in Mark Twain's *American Claimant*. They are pin-up girls.

If beauty lies in the eye of the beholder, Hemingway's purpose is to make his readers beholders. This is easily done when the narration is conducted in the first person; we can sit down and drink, with Jake Barnes, and watch Paris walk by. The interpolated chapters of *In Our Time*, most of them reminiscences from the army, employ the collective *we*; but, except for "My Old Man," the stories themselves are told in the third person. Sometimes, to strengthen the sense of identification, they make direct appeal to the second person; the protagonist of "Soldier's Home" is "you" as well as "he" — and, more generally, "a fellow." With the exception of Jake's confessions, that is to say *The Sun Also Rises*, all of Hemingway's novels are written in the *style indirect libre* — indirect discourse which more or less closely follows the consciousness of a central character. An increasing tendency for the author to intrude, commenting in his own person, is one of the weaknesses of *Across the River*. He derives his strength from a power to visualize episodes through the eyes of those most directly involved; for a page, in "The Short, Happy Life of Francis Macomber," the hunt is actually seen from the beast's point of view. Hemingway's use of interior monologue is effective when sensations from the outer world are entering the stream of a character's consciousness, as they do with such a rush at El Sordo's last stand. But introspection is not Hemingway's genre, and the night-thoughts of *To Have and Have Not* are among his least successful episodes. His best are events, which are never far to seek; things are constantly happening in his world; his leg-man, Nick Adams, happens to be the eye-witness of "The Killers." The state of mind that Hemingway communicates to us is the thrill that Nick got from skiing in "Cross Country Snow," which "plucked Nick's mind out and left him only the wonderful, flying, dropping sensation in his body."

IV

If psychological theories could be proved by works of fiction, Hemingway would lend his authority to the long contested formula of William James, which equates emotion with bodily sensation. Most other serious writers, however, would bear witness to deeper ranges of sensibility and more complex processes of motivation than those he sees fit to describe. Some of them have accused Hemingway of aggressive anti-intellectualism: I am thinking particularly of Aldous Huxley. But Huxley's own work is so pure an example of all that Hemingway has recoiled from, so intellectual in the airiest sense, and so unsupported by felt experience, that the argument has played into Hemingway's hands. We have seen enough of the latter to know that he doesn't really hate books — himself having written a dozen, several of which are, and will remain, the best of their kind. As for his refusal to behave like a man of letters, he reminds us of Hotspur, who professes to be a laconic philistine and turns out — with no little grandiloquence — to be the most poetic character in Shakespeare's play. Furthermore, it is not Hemingway, but the slogan-mongers of our epoch, who have debased the language; he has been attempting to restore some decent degree of correspondence between words and things; and the task of verification is a heavy one, which throws the individual back on his personal resources of awareness. That he has succeeded within limits, and with considerable strain, is less important than that he has succeeded, that a few more aspects of life have been captured for literature. Meanwhile the word continues to dematerialize, and has to be made flesh all over again; the first-hand perception, once it gets written down, becomes the second-hand notation; and the writer, who attains his individuality by repudiating literary affectation, ends by finding that he has struck a new pose and founded another school.

It is understandable why no critique of Hemingway, including this one, can speak for long of the style without speaking of the man. Improving on Buffon, Mark Schorer recently wrote: "[Hemingway's] style is not only his subject, it is his view of life." It could also be called his way of life, his *Lebenstil*. It has led him to live his books, to brave the maximum of exposure, to tour the world in an endless search for wars and their moral equivalents. It has cast him in the special role of our agent, our plenipotentiary, our roving correspondent on whom we depend for news from the fighting fronts of modern consciousness. Here he is, the man who was there. His writing seems so intent upon the actual, so impersonal in its surfaces, that it momentarily prompts us to overlook the personality behind them. That would be a serious mistake; for the point of view, though brilliantly intense, is narrowly focused and obliquely angled. We must ask: who is this guide to whom we have entrusted ourselves on intimate terms in dangerous places? Where are his limitations? What are his values? We may well discover that they differ from our assumptions, when he shows us a photograph of a bullfighter close to a bull, and comments: "If there is no blood on his belly afterwards you ought to get your money back." We may be ungrateful to question such curiosity, when we are indebted to it for many enlargements of our vicarious knowledge; and it may well spring from the callowness of the tourist rather than the morbidity of the *voyeur*, from the American zest of the fan who pays his money to reckon the carnage. When Spain's great poet, García Lorca, celebrated the very same theme, averting his gaze from the spilling of the blood, his refrain was *"Que no quiero verla!"* ("I do not want to see it!").

Yet Hemingway wants to see everything — or possibly he wants to be in a position to tell us that he has seen everything. While the boy Nick, his seeing eye, eagerly watches a Caesarian childbirth in "Indian Camp," the far from impassive husband turns away; and it is later discovered that he has killed himself. "He couldn't stand things . . ." so runs the diagnosis of Nick's father, the doctor. This, for Nick, is an initiation to suffering and death; but with the sunrise, shortly afterward, youth and well-being reassert themselves; and the end of the story reaffirms the generalization that Hazlitt once drew: "No young man ever thinks he shall die." It is easy enough for such a young man to stand things, for he is not yet painfully involved in them; he is not a sufferer but a wide-eyed onlooker, to whom the word "mashing" holds out mysterious enticements. Hemingway's projection of this attitude has given his best work perennial youthfulness; it has also armed his critics with the accusation that, like his Robert Cohn, he is "a case of arrested development." If this be so, his plight is generalized by the Englishman Wilson, who observes that "Americans stay little boys . . . all their lives." And the object of Wilson's observation, Francis Macomber, would furnish a classic case history for Adler, if not for Freud — the masculine sense of inferiority which seeks to overcome itself by acts of prowess, both sanguinary and sexual. Despite these two sources of excitement, the story is a plaintive modulation of two rather dissonant themes: *None but the brave deserves the fair* and *The female of the species is more deadly than the male*. After Francis Macomber has demonstrated his manhood, the next step is death. The world that remains most alive to Hemingway is that stretch between puberty and maturity which is strictly governed by the ephebic code: a world of mixed apprehension and bravado before the rite of passage, the baptism of fire, the introduction to sex.

Afterward comes the boasting, along with such surviving ideals as Hemingway subsumes in the word *cojones* — the English equivalent sounds more skeptical. But for Jake Barnes, all passion spent in the First World War, or for Colonel Cantwell, tired and disgruntled by the Second, the aftermath can only be elegiac. The weather-beaten hero of *Across the River*, which appears in 1950, is fifty years old and uneasily conscious of that fact; whereas "the childish, drunken heroics" of *The Sun Also Rises* took place just about twenty-five years ago. From his spectacular arrival in the 'twenties, Hemingway's course has paralleled that of our century; and now, at its midpoint, he balks like the rest of us before the responsibilities of middle age. When, if ever, does the *enfant du siècle*, that *enfant terrible*, grow up? (Not necessarily when he grows a beard and calls himself "Mr. Papa.") Frederic Henry plunges into the Po much as Huck Finn dived into the Mississippi, but emerges to remind us even more pointedly of Fabrice del Dongo in Stendhal's *Chartreuse de Parme*, and of our great contemporary shift from transatlantic innocence to old-world experience. Certain intimations of later years are present in Hemingway's earlier stories, typically Ad Francis, the slap-happy ex-champ in "The Battler." Even in "Fifty Grand," his most contrived tale, the beat-up prizefighter suffers more than he acts and wins by losing — a situation which has its corollary in the title of Hemingway's third collection, *Winner Take Nothing*. The ultimate article of his credo, which he shares with Malraux and Sartre, is the good fight for the lost cause. And the ultimate protagonist is Jesus in "Today Is Friday," whose crucifixion is treated like an athletic feat, and whose capacity for taking punishment rouses a fellow-feeling in the Roman soldiers. The stoic or masochistic determination to take it brings us back from Hemingway to his medium, which — although it eschews the passive voice — is essentially a receiving instrument, especially sensitized for recording a series of violent shocks.

The paradox of toughness and sensitivity is resolved, and the qualities and defects of his writing are reconciled, if we merely remember that he was — and still is — a poet. That he is not a novelist by vocation, if it were not revealed by his books, could be inferred from his well-known retort to F. Scott Fitzgerald. For Fitzgerald the rich were different — not quantitatively, because they had more money, but qualitatively, because he had a novelistic interest in manners and morals. Again, when we read André Gide's reports from the Congo, we realize what *Green Hills of Africa* lacks in the way of social or psychological insight. As W. M. Frohock has perceived, Hemingway is less concerned with human relations than with his own relationship to the universe — a concern which might have spontaneously flowered into poetry. His talents come out most fully in the texture of his work, whereas the structure tends to be episodic and uncontrived to the point of formlessness. *For Whom the Bell Tolls*, the only one of his six novels that has been carefully constructed, is in some respects an over-expanded short story. Editors rejected his earliest stories on the grounds that they were nothing but sketches and anecdotes, thereby paying incidental tribute to his sense of reality. Fragments of truth, after all, are the best that a writer can offer; and, as Hemingway has said, ". . . Any part you make will represent the whole if it's made truly." In periods as confusing as the present, when broader and maturer representations are likely to falsify, we are fortunate if we can find authenticity in the lyric cry, the adolescent mood, the tangible feeling, the trigger response. If we think of Hemingway's temperamental kinship with E. E. Cummings, and of Cummings' "Buffalo Bill" or "Olaf glad and big," it is easy to think of Hemingway as a poet. After the attractions and distractions of timeliness have been outdated, together with categorical distinctions between the rich and the poor, perhaps he will be remembered for a poetic vision which renews our interrupted contact with the timeless elements of man's existence: bread, wine, bed, music, and just a few more of the concrete universals. When El Sordo raises his glance from the battlefield, he looks up at the identical patch of the blue sky that Henry Fleming saw in *The Red Badge of Courage* and that looked down on Prince Andrey in *War and Peace*.

Donald P. Costello

THE LANGUAGE OF
"THE CATCHER IN THE RYE"

ౡౡ

This essay illustrates the kind of analysis of language that critics commonly exercise on poetry but have only recently begun to apply to prose. Professor Costello operates very close to his material. The Catcher in the Rye, narrated by 16-year-old Holden Caulfield, is a good record of teenage speech of the 1950s. Mr. Costello studies the relationship between speech habits and characterization. Holden's use of language reflects his education, his social background, and finally his view of the world. Like Hemingway's narrator-hero in A Farewell to Arms, Holden purges his language to avoid all phoniness, yet he believes in love and loyalty where he honestly finds them.

A study of the language of J. D. Salinger's *The Catcher in the Rye* can be justified not only on the basis of literary interest, but also on the basis of linguistic significance. Today we study *The Adventures of Huckleberry Finn* (with which many critics have compared *The Catcher in the Rye*) not only as a great work of literary art, but as a valuable study in 1884 dialect. In coming decades, *The Catcher in the Rye* will be studied, I feel, not only as a literary work, but also as an example of teenage vernacular in the 1950s. As such, the book will be a significant historical linguistic

Reprinted from *American Speech*, XXXIV (October 1959), pp. 172–181, by permission of the author.

record of a type of speech rarely made available in permanent form. Its linguistic importance will increase as the American speech it records becomes less current.

Most critics who looked at *The Catcher in the Rye* at the time of its publication thought that its language was a true and authentic rendering of teenage colloquial speech. Reviewers in the Chicago *Sunday Tribune*, the London *Times Literary Supplement*, the *New Republic*, the New York *Herald Tribune Book Review*, the New York *Times*, the *New Yorker*, and the *Saturday Review of Literature* all specifically mentioned the authenticity of the book's language. Various aspects of its language were also discussed in the reviews published in *America*, the *Atlantic*, the *Catholic World*, the *Christian Science Monitor*, the *Library Journal*, the Manchester *Guardian*, the *Nation*, the *New Statesman and Nation*, the New York *Times Book Review*, *Newsweek*, the *Spectator*, and *Time*.[1] Of these many reviews, only the writers for the *Catholic World* and the *Christian Science Monitor* denied the authenticity of the book's language, but both of these are religious journals which refused to believe that the 'obscenity' was realistic. An examination of the reviews of *The Catcher in the Rye* proves that the language of Holden Caulfield, the book's sixteen-year-old narrator, struck the ear of the contemporary reader as an accurate rendering of the informal speech of an intelligent, educated, Northeastern American adolescent.[2]

In addition to commenting on its authenticity, critics have often remarked — uneasily — the 'daring,' 'obscene,' 'blasphemous' features of

---

[1] See reviews in *America*, LXXV (August 11, 1951), 463, 464; *Atlantic*, CLXXXVIII (1951), 82; *Catholic World*, CLXXIV (1951), 154; Chicago *Sunday Tribune*, July 15, 1951, Part 4, p. 3; *Christian Science Monitor*, July 19, 1951, p. 9; *Library Journal*, LXXVI (1951), 1125; *Times* [London] *Literary Supplement*, September 7, 1951, p. 561; Manchester *Guardian*, August 10, 1951, p. 4; *Nation*, CLXXIII (September 1, 1951), 176; *New Republic*, CXXV (July 16, 1951), 20, 21; *New Statesman and Nation*, XLII (August 18, 1951), 185; New York *Herald Tribune Book Review*, July 15, 1951, p. 3; New York *Times Book Review*, July 15, 1951, p. 5; New York *Times*, July 16, 1951, p. 19; *New Yorker*, XXVII (August 11, 1951), 71–76; *Newsweek*, XXXVIII (July 16, 1951), 89, 90; *Saturday Review of Literature*, XXXIV (July 14, 1951), 12, 13; *Spectator*, CLXXXVII (August 17, 1951), 224; *Time*, LVIII (July 16, 1951), 96, 97.

[2] If additional evidence of the authenticity of the book's language is required, one need only look at the phenomenal regard with which *The Catcher in the Rye* is held by today's college students, who were about Holden's age at the time the book was written. In its March 9, 1957, issue, the *Nation* published a symposium which attempted to discover the major influences upon the college students of today. Many teachers pointed out the impact of Salinger. Carlos Baker, of Princeton, stated: 'There is still, as there has been for years, a cult of Thomas Wolfe. They have all read J. D. Salinger, Wolfe's closest competitor.' Stanley Kunitz, of Queens College, wrote: "The only novelist I have heard praised vociferously is J. D. Salinger.' Harvey Curtis Webster, of the University of Louisville, listed Salinger as one of the 'stimulators.' R. J. Kaufman, of the University of Rochester, called *The Catcher in the Rye* 'a book which has complexly aroused nearly all of them.' See 'The Careful Young Men,' *Nation*, CLXXXIV (March 9, 1957), 199–214. I have never heard any Salinger partisan among college students doubt the authenticity of the language of their compatriot, Holden.

Holden's language. Another commonly noted feature of the book's language has been its comic effect. And yet there has never been an extensive investigation of the language itself. That is what this paper proposes to do.

Even though Holden's language is authentic teenage speech, recording it was certainly not the major intention of Salinger. He was faced with the artistic task of creating an individual character, not with the linguistic task of reproducing the exact speech of teenagers in general. Yet Holden had to speak a recognizable teenage language, and at the same time had to be identifiable as an individual. This difficult task Salinger achieved by giving Holden an extremely trite and typical teenage speech, overlaid with strong personal idiosyncrasies. There are two major speech habits which are Holden's own, which are endlessly repeated throughout the book, and which are, nevertheless, typical enough of teenage speech so that Holden can be both typical and individual in his use of them. It is certainly common for teenagers to end thoughts with a loosely dangling 'and all,' just as it is common for them to add an insistent 'I really did,' 'It really was.' But Holden uses these phrases to such an overpowering degree that they become a clear part of the flavor of the book; they become, more, a part of Holden himself, and actually help to characterize him.

Holden's 'and all' and its twins, 'or something,' 'or anything,' serve no real, consistent linguistic function. They simply give a sense of looseness of expression and looseness of thought. Often they signify that Holden knows there is more that could be said about the issue at hand, but he is not going to bother going into it:

> . . . how my parents were occupied and all before they had me (5)[3]
> . . . they're *nice* and all (5)
> I'm not going to tell you my whole goddam autobiography or anything. (5)
> . . . splendid and clear-thinking and all (6)

But just as often the use of such expressions is purely arbitrary, with no discernible meaning:

> . . . he's my *brother* and all (5)
> . . . was in the Revolutionary War and all (6)
> It was December and all (7)
> . . . no gloves or anything (7)
> . . . right in the pocket and all (7)

Donald Barr, writing in the *Commonweal*, finds this habit indicative of Holden's tendency to generalize, to find the all in the one:

[3] Whenever *The Catcher in the Rye* is substantially quoted in this paper, a page number will be included in the text immediately after the quotation. The edition to which the page numbers refer is the Signet paperback reprint.

Salinger has an ear not only for idiosyncrasies of diction and syntax, but for mental processes. Holden Caulfield's phrase is 'and all' — 'She looked so damn *nice*, the way she kept going around and around in her blue coat and all' — as if each experience wore a halo. His fallacy is *ab uno disce omnes*; he abstracts and generalizes wildly.[4]

Heiserman and Miller, in the *Western Humanities Review*, comment specifically upon Holden's second most obvious idiosyncrasy: 'In a phony world Holden feels compelled to reenforce his sincerity and truthfulness constantly with, "It really is" or "It really did." '[5] S. N. Behrman, in the *New Yorker*, finds a double function of these 'perpetual insistences of Holden's.' Behrman thinks they 'reveal his age, even when he is thinking much older,' and, more important, 'he is so aware of the danger of slipping into phoniness himself that he has to repeat over and over "I really mean it," "It really does." '[6] Holden uses this idiosyncrasy of insistence almost every time that he makes an affirmation.

Allied to Holden's habit of insistence is his 'if you want to know the truth.' Heiserman and Miller are able to find characterization in this habit too:

> The skepticism inherent in that casual phrase, 'if you want to know the truth,' suggesting that as a matter of fact in the world of Holden Caulfield very few people do, characterizes this sixteen-year-old 'crazy mixed up kid' more sharply and vividly than pages of character 'analysis' possibly could.[7]

Holden uses this phrase only after affirmations, just as he uses 'It really does,' but usually after the personal ones, where he is consciously being frank:

> I have no wind, if you want to know the truth. (8)
> I don't even think that bastard had a handkerchief, if you want to know the truth. (34)
> I'm a pacifist, if you want to know the truth. (44)
> She had quite a lot of sex appeal, too, if you really want to know. (53)
> I was damn near bawling, I felt so damn happy, if you want to know the truth. (191)

These personal idiosyncrasies of Holden's speech are in keeping with general teenage language. Yet they are so much a part of Holden and of the flavor of the book that they are much of what makes Holden to be Holden. They are the most memorable feature of the book's language.

[4] Donald Barr, 'Saints, Pilgrims, and Artists,' *Commonweal*, LVXII (October 25, 1957), 90.

[5] Arthur Heiserman and James E. Miller, Jr., 'J. D. Salinger: Some Crazy Cliff,' *Western Humanities Review*, X (1956), 136.

[6] S. N. Behrman, 'The Vision of the Innocent,' *New Yorker*, XXVII (August 11, 1951), 72.

[7] Heiserman and Miller, *op. cit.*, p. 135.

Although always in character, the rest of Holden's speech is more typical than individual. The special quality of this language comes from its triteness, its lack of distinctive qualities.

Holden's informal, schoolboy vernacular is particularly typical in its 'vulgarity' and 'obscenity.' No one familiar with prep-school speech could seriously contend that Salinger overplayed his hand in this respect. On the contrary, Holden's restraints help to characterize him as a sensitive youth who avoids the most strongly forbidden terms, and who never uses vulgarity in a self-conscious or phony way to help him be 'one of the boys.' *Fuck*, for example, is never used as a part of Holden's speech. The word appears in the novel four times, but only when Holden disapprovingly discusses its wide appearance on walls. The Divine name is used habitually by Holden only in the comparatively weak *for God's sake, God,* and *goddam.* The stronger and usually *more offensive for Chrissake* or *Jesus* or *Jesus Christ* are used habitually by Ackley and Stradlater; but Holden uses them when he feels the need for a strong expression. He almost never uses *for Chrissake* in an unemotional situation. *Goddam* is Holden's favorite adjective. This word is used with no relationship to its original meaning, or to Holden's attitude toward the word to which it is attached. It simply expresses an emotional feeling toward the object: either favorable, as in 'goddam hunting cap'; or unfavorable, as in 'ya goddam moron'; or indifferent, as in 'coming in the goddam windows.' *Damn* is used interchangeably with *goddam*; no differentiation in its meaning is detectable.

Other crude words are also often used in Holden's vocabulary. *Ass* keeps a fairly restricted meaning as a part of the human anatomy, but it is used in a variety of ways. It can refer simply to that specific part of the body ('I moved my ass a little'), or be a part of a trite expression ('freezing my ass off'; 'in a half-assed way'), or be an expletive ('Game, my *ass.*'). *Hell* is perhaps the most versatile word in Holden's entire vocabulary; it serves most of the meanings and constructions which Mencken lists in his *American Speech* article on 'American Profanity.'[8] So far is Holden's use of *hell* from its original meaning that he can use the sentence 'We had a helluva time' to mean that he and Phoebe had a decidedly pleasant time downtown shopping for shoes. The most common function of *hell* is as the second part of a simile, in which a thing can be either 'hot as hell' or, strangely, 'cold as hell'; 'sad as hell' or 'playful as hell'; 'old as hell' or 'pretty as hell.' Like all of these words, *hell* has no close relationship to its original meaning.

Both *bastard* and *sonuvabitch* have also drastically changed in meaning. They no longer, of course, in Holden's vocabulary, have any connection with the accidents of birth. Unless used in a trite simile, *bastard* is a strong word, reserved for things and people Holden particularly dislikes, especially

[8] See H. L. Mencken, 'American Profanity,' *American Speech,* XIX (1944), 242.

'phonies.' *Sonuvabitch* has an even stronger meaning to Holden; he uses it only in the deepest anger. When, for example, Holden is furious with Stradlater over his treatment of Jane Gallagher, Holden repeats again and again that he 'kept calling him a moron sonuvabitch' (43).

The use of crude language in *The Catcher in the Rye* increases, as we should expect, when Holden is reporting schoolboy dialogue. When he is directly addressing the reader, Holden's use of such language drops off almost entirely. There is also an increase in this language when any of the characters are excited or angry. Thus, when Holden is apprehensive over Stradlater's treatment of Jane, his *goddams* increase suddenly to seven on a single page (39).

Holden's speech is also typical in his use of slang. I have catalogued over a hundred slang terms used by Holden, and every one of these is in widespread use. Although Holden's slang is rich and colorful, it, of course, being slang, often fails at precise communication. Thus, Holden's *crap* is used in seven different ways. It can mean foolishness, as 'all that David Copperfield kind of crap,' or messy matter, as 'I spilled some crap all over my gray flannel,' or merely miscellaneous matter, as 'I was putting on my galoshes and crap.' It can also carry its basic meaning, animal excreta, as 'there didn't look like there was anything in the park except dog crap,' and it can be used as an adjective meaning anything generally unfavorable, as 'The show was on the crappy side.' Holden uses the phrases *to be a lot of crap* and *to shoot the crap* and *to chuck the crap* all to mean 'to be untrue,' but he can also use *to shoot the crap* to mean 'to chat,' with no connotation of untruth, as in 'I certainly wouldn't have minded shooting the crap with old Phoebe for a while.'

Similarly Holden's slang use of *crazy* is both trite and imprecise. 'That drives me crazy' means that he violently dislikes something; yet 'to be crazy about' something means just the opposite. In the same way, to be 'killed' by something can mean that he was emotionally affected either favorably ('That story just about killed me.') or unfavorably ('Then she turned her back on me again. It nearly killed me.'). This use of *killed* is one of Holden's favorite slang expressions. Heiserman and Miller are, incidentally, certainly incorrect when they conclude: 'Holden always lets us know when he has insight into the absurdity of the endlessly absurd situations which make up the life of a sixteen-year-old by exclaiming, "It killed me." '[9] Holden often uses this expression with no connection to the absurd; he even uses it for his beloved Phoebe. The expression simply indicates a high degree of emotion — any kind. It is hazardous to conclude that any of Holden's slang has a precise and consistent meaning or function. These same critics fall into the same error when they conclude that Holden's use of the adjective *old* serves as 'a term of endearment.'[10] Holden appends this word

[9] Heiserman and Miller, *op. cit.*, p. 136.
[10] *Ibid.*

to almost every character, real or fictional, mentioned in the novel, from the hated 'old Maurice' to 'old Peter Lorre,' to 'old Phoebe,' and even 'old Jesus.' The only pattern that can be discovered in Holden's use of this term is that he usually uses it only after he has previously mentioned the character; he then feels free to append the familiar *old*. All we can conclude from Holden's slang is that it is typical teenage slang: versatile yet narrow, expressive yet unimaginative, imprecise, often crude, and always trite.

Holden has many favorite slang expressions which he overuses. In one place, he admits:

> 'Boy!' I said. I also say 'Boy!' quite a lot. Partly because I have a lousy vocabulary and partly because I act quite young for my age sometimes. (12)

But if Holden's slang shows the typically 'lousy vocabulary' of even the educated American teenager, this failing becomes even more obvious when we narrow our view to Holden's choice of adjectives and adverbs. The choice is indeed narrow, with a constant repetition of a few favorite words: *lousy, pretty, crumby, terrific, quite, old, stupid* — all used, as is the habit of teenage vernacular, with little regard to specific meaning. Thus, most of the nouns which are called 'stupid' could not in any logical framework be called 'ignorant,' and, as we have seen, *old* before a proper noun has nothing to do with age.

Another respect in which Holden was correct in accusing himself of having a 'lousy vocabulary' is discovered in the ease with which he falls into trite figures of speech. We have already seen that Holden's most common simile is the worn and meaningless 'as hell'; but his often-repeated 'like a madman' and 'like a bastard' are just about as unrelated to a literal meaning and are easily as unimaginative. Even Holden's nonhabitual figures of speech are usually trite: 'sharp as a tack'; 'hot as a firecracker'; 'laughed like a hyena'; 'I know old Jane like a book'; 'drove off like a bat out of hell'; 'I began to feel like a horse's ass'; 'blind as a bat'; 'I know Central Park like the back of my hand.'

Repetitious and trite as Holden's vocabulary may be, it can, nevertheless, become highly effective. For example, when Holden piles one trite adjective upon another, a strong power of invective is often the result:

> He was a goddam stupid moron. (42)
> Get your dirty stinking moron knees off my chest. (43)
> You're a dirty stupid sonuvabitch of a moron. (43)

And his limited vocabulary can also be used for good comic effect. Holden's constant repetition of identical expressions in countless widely different situations is often hilariously funny.

But all of the humor in Holden's vocabulary does not come from its unimaginative quality. Quite the contrary, some of his figures of speech are entirely original; and these are inspired, dramatically effective, and terribly funny. As always, Salinger's Holden is basically typical, with a strong overlay of the individual:

> He started handling my exam paper like it was a turd or something. (13)
> He put my goddam paper down then and looked at me like he'd just beaten the hell out of me in ping-pong or something. (14)
> That guy Morrow was about as sensitive as a goddam toilet seat. (52)
> Old Marty was like dragging the Statue of Liberty around the floor. (69)

Another aspect in which Holden's language is typical is that it shows the general American characteristic of adaptability — apparently strengthened by his teenage lack of restraint. It is very easy for Holden to turn nouns into adjectives, with the simple addition of a -y: 'perverty,' 'Christmasy,' 'vomity-looking,' 'whory-looking,' 'hoodlumy-looking,' 'show-offy,' 'flitty-looking,' 'dumpy-looking,' 'pimpy,' 'snobby,' 'fisty.' Like all of English, Holden's language shows a versatile combining ability: 'They gave Sally this little blue butt-twitcher of a dress to wear' (117) and 'That magazine was some little cheerer upper' (176). Perhaps the most interesting aspect of the adaptability of Holden's language in his ability to use nouns as adverbs: 'She sings it very Dixieland and whorehouse, and it doesn't sound at all mushy' (105).

As we have seen, Holden shares, in general, the trite repetitive vocabulary which is the typical lot of his age group. But as there are exceptions in his figures of speech, so are there exceptions in his vocabulary itself, in his word stock. An intelligent, well-read ('I'm quite illiterate, but I read a lot'), and educated boy, Holden possesses, and can use when he wants to, many words which are many a cut above Basic English, including 'ostracized,' 'exhibitionist,' 'unscrupulous,' 'conversationalist,' 'psychic,' 'bourgeois.' Often Holden seems to choose his words consciously, in an effort to communicate to his adult reader clearly and properly, as in such terms as 'lose my virginity,' 'relieve himself,' 'an alcoholic'; for upon occasion, he also uses the more vulgar terms 'to give someone the time,' 'to take a leak,' 'booze hound.' Much of the humor arises, in fact, from Holden's habit of writing on more than one level at the same time. Thus, we have such phrases as 'They give guys the ax quite frequently at Pency' and 'It has a very good academic rating, Pency' (7). Both sentences show a colloquial idiom with an overlay of consciously selected words.

Such a conscious choice of words seems to indicate that Salinger, in his attempt to create a realistic character in Holden, wanted to make him aware of his speech, as, indeed, a real teenager would be when communicating to the outside world. Another piece of evidence that Holden is conscious of his speech and, more, realizes a difficulty in communication, is found in his habit of direct repetition: 'She likes me a lot. I mean she's quite fond of me' (141), and 'She can be very snotty sometimes. She can be quite snotty' (150). Sometimes the repetition is exact: 'He was a very nervous guy — I mean he was a very nervous guy' (165), and 'I sort of missed them. I mean I sort of missed them' (169). Sometimes Holden stops specifically to interpret slang terms, as when he wants to communicate the fact that Allie liked Phoebe: 'She killed Allie, too. I mean he liked her, too' (64).

There is still more direct evidence that Holden was conscious of his speech. Many of his comments to the reader are concerned with language. He was aware, for example, of the 'phony' quality of many words and phrases, such as 'grand,' 'prince,' 'traveling incognito,' 'little girls' room,' 'licorice stick' and 'angels.' Holden is also conscious, of course, of the existence of 'taboo words.' He makes a point of mentioning that the girl from Seattle repeatedly asked him to 'watch your language, if you don't mind' (67), and that his mother told Phoebe not to say 'lousy' (160). When the prostitute says 'Like fun you are,' Holden comments:

> It was a funny thing to say. It sounded like a real kid. You'd think a prostitute and all would say 'Like hell you are' or 'Cut the crap' instead of 'Like fun you are.' (87)

In grammar, too, as in vocabulary, Holden possesses a certain self-consciousness. (It is, of course, impossible to imagine a student getting through today's schools without a self-consciousness with regard to grammar rules.) Holden is, in fact, not only aware of the existence of 'grammatical errors,' but knows the social taboos that accompany them. He is disturbed by a schoolmate who is ashamed of his parents' grammar, and he reports that his former teacher, Mr. Antolini, warned him about picking up 'just enough education to hate people who say, "It's a secret between he and I"' (168).

Holden is a typical enough teenager to violate the grammar rules, even though he knows of their social importance. His most common rule violation is the misuse of *lie* and *lay*, but he also is careless about relative pronouns ('about a traffic cop that falls in love'), the double negative ('I hardly didn't even know I was doing it'), the perfect tenses ('I'd woke him up'), extra words ('like as if all you ever did at Pencey was play polo all the time'), pronoun number ('it's pretty disgusting to watch somebody picking their nose'), and pronoun position ('I and this friend of mine, Mal Brossard'). More remarkable, however, than the instances of grammar rule violations is Holden's relative 'correctness.' Holden is always intelligible, and is even 'correct' in many usually difficult constructions. Grammatically speaking, Holden's language seems to point up the fact that

English was the only subject in which he was not failing. It is interesting to note how much more 'correct' Holden's speech is than that of Huck Finn. But then Holden is educated, and since the time of Huck there had been sixty-seven years of authoritarian schoolmarms working on the likes of Holden. He has, in fact, been overtaught, so that he uses many 'hyper' forms:

> I used to play tennis with he and Mrs. Antolini quite frequently. (163)
> She'd give Allie or I a push. (64)
> I and Allie used to take her to the park with us. (64)
> I think I probably woke he and his wife up. (157)

Now that we have examined several aspects of Holden's vocabulary and grammar, it would be well to look at a few examples of how he puts these elements together into sentences. The structure of Holden's sentences indicates that Salinger thinks of the book more in terms of spoken speech than written speech. Holden's faulty structure is quite common and typical in vocal expression; I doubt if a student who is 'good in English' would ever create such sentence structure in writing. A student who showed the self-consciousness of Holden would not *write* so many fragments, such afterthoughts (e.g., 'It has a very good academic rating, Pency' [7]), or such repetitions (e.g., 'Where I lived at Pency, I lived in the Ossenburger Memorial Wing of the new dorms' [18]).

There are other indications that Holden's speech is vocal. In many places Salinger mildly imitates spoken speech. Sentences such as 'You could tell old Spencer'd got a big bang out of buying it' (10) and 'I'd've killed him' (42) are repeated throughout the book. Yet it is impossible to imagine Holden taking pen in hand and actually writing 'Spencer'd' or 'I'd've.' Sometimes, too, emphasized words, or even parts of words, are italicized, as in 'Now *shut up*, Holden. God damn it — I'm *warning* ya' (42). This is often done with good effect, imitating quite perfectly the rhythms of speech, as in the typical:

> I practically sat down on her *lap*, as a matter of fact. Then she *really* started to cry, and the next thing I knew, I was kissing her all over — *any*where — her eyes, her *nose*, her forehead, her eyebrows and all, her *ears* — her whole face except her mouth and all. (73)

The language of *The Catcher in the Rye* is, as we have seen, an authentic artistic rendering of a type of informal, colloquial, teenage American spoken speech. It is strongly typical and trite, yet often somewhat individual; it is crude and slangy and imprecise, imitative yet occasionally imaginative, and affected toward standardization by the strong efforts of schools. But authentic and interesting as this language may be, it must be remembered that it exists, in *The Catcher in the Rye*, as only one part of an artistic achievement. The language was not written for itself, but as a part of a greater whole. Like the great Twain work with which it is often compared, a study of *The Catcher in the Rye* repays both the linguist and the literary critic; for as one critic has said, 'In them, 1884 and 1951 speak to us in the idiom and accent of two youthful travelers who have earned their passports to literary immortality.'[11]

[11] Charles Kaplan, 'Holden and Huck: the Odysseys of Youth,' *College English*, XVIII (1956), 80.

Donald E. Thackrey

THE COMMUNICATION
OF THE WORD

ᎦᎦ

At her death in 1886, Emily Dickinson left 1775 poems, of which she had allowed only seven to be published in her lifetime. She never married and rarely left her home. For image and subject this recluse drew upon her garden, friends, religion, deprivations, love, and sense of death. Thackrey speaks of her manipulations of words, of their hypnotic power for her. She constantly wrote about words. Out of this fascination with words and reverence for them, she achieved the shocks and surprises in her poems. When Thackrey's impressive description of Miss Dickinson's love of words reaches its climax (about midway), it then takes an unexpected turn; he reveals that she also considered words hazardous and finally impotent to express fully what she thought and felt. The result was "a meaningful silence" and "powerful poems confessing their powerlessness."

Reprinted from *Emily Dickinson's Approach to Poetry* by Donald E. Thackrey by permission of University of Nebraska Press, 1954.

In the beginning was the word." Emily Dickinson probably would have accepted a literal interpretation of this opening phrase of the Gospel of St. John. Language and communication exercised an almost hypnotic fascination over her; the power of the individual word, in particular, seems to have inspired her with nothing less than reverence. Such an attitude toward words is an important aspect of Emily Dickinson's approach to poetry in that it partially accounts for her method of composition and helps explain her use of poetic composition to discipline the mystical intuitions which involved her in both ecstasy and suffering of extreme intensity. This chapter is devoted to discovering the essential viewpoints of Emily Dickinson in regard to the power for communication of the individual word.

It seems certain that Emily Dickinson approached the writing of poetry inductively — that is, through the combining of words to arrive at whatever conclusion the word pattern seemed to suggest, rather than using words as subordinate instruments in expressing a total conception. Her amazing inconsistency of intellectual position may have resulted in part from the practice of starting with individual words and manipulating them into brilliant patterns regardless of the direction of thought, instead of always orienting her poems within an integrated philosophy. One notices how many of her poems seem less concerned with a total conception than with expressing a series of staccato inspirations occurring to her in the form of individual words. The following poem is remarkable in its use of words; its meaning, however, is somewhat obscured by the constant impact of words which seem to be separate entities refusing to assume a subordinate position in the poem.

> A nearness to Tremendousness
> An Agony procures,
> Affliction ranges Boundlessness.
> Vicinity to laws
> Contentment's quiet suburb, —
> Affliction cannot stay
> In acre or location —
> It rents Immensity.[1]

The poem contrasts contentment with affliction. One is orderly, secluded, innocuous; the other is unrestrained, passionate, infinite. However, the

[1] *Poems*, p. 453, No. cxxx. [Martha Dickinson Bianchi and Alfred Leete Hampson, eds., *Poems by Emily Dickinson* (Boston: Little, Brown and Co., 1937). Reprinted here by permission of Little, Brown and Company.]

excessive weight of such words as *Tremendousness, Boundlessness, Immensity* together with the extraordinary implications of the words *procures, ranges, suburb, rents,* all overflowing one small stanza is more than a reader can grasp without dividing the poem into its elements and studying each word individually.

Emily Dickinson herself gives us ample warrant for studying her poems a word at a time. Her constant practice of compiling a thesaurus of word choices for a single line, while constituting grave editorial difficulty, is at least an indication that each word was a veritable dynamo of implication and associations. Mrs. Bingham gives an interesting account in *Ancestors' Brocades* of the abundant presence of alternative words in the Dickinson manuscripts. She cites an example occurring in the poem "The Bible is an antique volume" of which the final lines read in manuscript:

> Had but the tale a thrilling, typic,
> > hearty, bonnie, breathless, spacious,
> > tropic, warbling, ardent, friendly,
> > magic, pungent, winning, mellow
> > teller
> All the boys would come —
> Orpheus's sermon captivated,
> It did not condemn.[2]

Each of the variant adjectives apparently occurred to her as refined gradations or aspects of her total conception. Her consequent reluctance to choose a single word now poses the almost insuperable editorial problem of determining which word she probably would have preferred. In the above instance, *warbling* was selected out of the possible fourteen choices. Many of the published poems themselves exhibit a similar concern with individual words. Note the accumulation of verbs in the following stanza.

> 'Tis this invites, appals, endows,
> Flits, glimmers, proves, dissolves,
> Returns, suggests, convicts, enchants —
> Then flings in Paradise![3]

Emily Dickinson wrote one poem specifically about the choice of words.

---

[2] Millicent Todd Bingham, *Ancestors' Brocades: The Literary Debut of Emily Dickinson* (New York: Harper & Brothers, 1945), p. 314. [Reprinted here by permission of Houghton Mifflin Company.]

[3] *Poems,* p. 352, No. cxxxii. [Reprinted here by permission of Little, Brown and Company.]

"The Bible is an antique volume" from *The Life and Letters of Emily Dickinson,* edited by Martha D. Bianchi. Reprinted by permission of the publisher, Houghton Mifflin Company.

"Shall I take thee?" the poet said
To the propounded word.
"Be stationed with the candidates
Till I have further tried."

The poet probed philology
And when about to ring
For the suspended candidate,
There came unsummoned in

That portion of the vision
The word applied to fill.
Not unto nomination
The cherubim reveal.[4]

This poem is extremely instructive in indicating Emily Dickinson's actual method of composition and in suggesting the relationship between rational labor and inspiration. The two instances of the numerous word "candidates" partly fulfill the poet's intention but also suggest new words which more aptly represent further aspects of the total conception. Soon the train of "candidates" has exhausted every facet and implication of the idea, and in doing so has securely established the fully developed idea in the poet's mind. But still no one word is adequate to the idea. As the poet attempts to choose the best alternative, the "cherubim" of artistic inspiration reveal the precise word which completes the "vision." It is significant that the revealed word comes "unsummoned" in a flash of intuition. Such a word admits of no hesitation or doubt in the poet's mind. And yet the implication of the poem is that the revealing of the word must be preceded by the preparatory, conscious, rational effort of probing philology. Perhaps we can assume that the long series of "nominations" with no indicated choice which occur in some of her manuscript poems represent occasions when a portion of the vision was not filled by the revelation of the cherubim. She herself was well aware that inspiration, while all-sufficient when present, seldom came even to a great poet.

Your thoughts don't have words every day,
They come a single time
Like signal esoteric sips
Of sacramental wine,
Which while you taste so native seems,
So bounteous, so free,

[4] *Bolts of Melody*, p. 228, No. 436. [Mabel Loomis Todd and Millicent Todd Bingham, eds., *Bolts of Melody: New Poems of Emily Dickinson* (New York: Harper & Brothers, 1945). Reprinted here by permission of The President and Fellows of Harvard College and The Trustees of Amherst College.]

You cannot comprehend its worth
Nor its infrequency.[5]

Even in friendly letters Emily Dickinson apparently could never escape the significance and implication of the words she used. In a letter in which she wrote the sentence, "Thank you for remembering me," there is the reflection immediately following it, "Remembrance — mighty word."[6] So conscious of particular words was she that the use of an especially significant word in a letter stimulated a parenthetical exclamation written perhaps with the desire to share with her friend something of her own intoxication with words.

The most evident characteristic of words, as far as Emily Dickinson was concerned, is their startling vitality. Her poems indicate that she regarded words as organic — separate little entities with a being, growth, and immortality of their own.

> A word is dead
> When it is said,
> Some say.
> I say it just
> Begins to live
> That day.[7]

The life of the spoken word does not depend upon the duration of sound vibrations but is an inextricable part of the experience and being of the speaker and those to whom he speaks. Thus a word, no matter how simple, may be charged with imperishable significance because of its intimate relationship with human minds and souls. Connotations and symbolic extensions of meaning become inseparable from the word, so that its pronouncement will forever stimulate an entire "circumference" of meaning in addition to its denotative definition. In the following poem the idea of the immortality of words which are expressions of and inevitable associations with significant experience is clearly stated.

> A little overflowing word
> That any hearing had inferred
> For ardor or for tears,
> Though generations pass away,
> Traditions ripen and decay,
> As eloquent appears.[8]

[5] *Ibid.*, p. 228, No. 435. [Reprinted here by permission of The President and Fellows of Harvard College and The Trustees of Amherst College.]

[6] *Letters*, p. 248. [Mabel Loomis Todd, *The Letters of Emily Dickinson* (Cleveland: The World Publishing Co., 1951).]

[7] *Poems*, p. 42, No. lxxxix.

[8] *Ibid.*, p. 269, No. cxxxvi. [Reprinted here by permission of Houghton Mifflin Company.]

Eloquence, of course, did not mean for Emily Dickinson long-winded-ness, or unusual figures of speech, or any formal consideration; it meant the effective thrust of meaning stripped of everything that might qualify, ornament, or weaken it. Much of her imagery chosen to describe the effect of a word upon him who hears it supports the contention that, for her, communication consisted in transmitting or perceiving an immediate, over-powering vision.

> There is a word
> Which bears a sword
> Can pierce an armed man.
> It hurls its barbed syllables, —
> At once is mute again.[9]

Communication is a *sword*. It *pierces*. *Barbed* syllables are *hurled*. There is no room here for slow comprehension, perception aided by illustration and analogy, and understanding based on a cautious consideration and analysis of a statement. There is only the overpowering immediacy of the piercing word. The sword imagery is elaborated in the following stanza.

> She dealt her pretty words like blades,
> As glittering they shone,
> And every one unbared a nerve
> Or wantoned with a bone.[10]

Emily Dickinson testified that the concept of the "sword eloquence" of words was not a theoretical speculation for her, but was a personal, vivid reality. Consider, for example, how the sound of her lover's name affected her.

> I got so I could hear his name
> Without —
> Tremendous gain! —
> That stop-sensation in my soul,
> And thunder in the room.[11]

Eloquence, however, even in the sharpened sense in which she used the term, was not the real nature of words for Emily Dickinson. The eloquence was only the flash of light a calm ocean surface reflects. Deeper than light penetrates there is the turbulence of an unseen tide. Words seemed to her to embody some terrifying, mysterious power which approached omni-potence. She knew that such power was not suspected by most people who ordinarily used words glibly and thoughtlessly. And she apparently believed

[9] *Ibid.*, p. 148, No. xliv.
[10] *Ibid.*, p. 290, No. xxix. [Reprinted here by permission of Little, Brown and Company.]
[11] *Ibid.*, p. 370, No. clxvi. [Reprinted here by permission of Little, Brown and Company.]

that even she herself could only sense the existence of this power and never fully perceive its extent.

> Could any mortal lip divine
> The undeveloped freight
> Of a delivered syllable,
> 'Twould crumble with the weight.[12]

The power of words, while a great source of wonder and delight for her, was not regarded as wholly beneficial. No great power is entirely hazardless. "What a hazard an accent is! When I think of the hearts it has scuttled or sunk, I almost fear to lift my hand to so much as a punctuation."[13] And in one poem she even compares words with malignant germs.

> A word dropped careless on a page
> May stimulate an eye,
> When folded in perpetual seam
> The wrinkled author lie.
>
> Infection in the sentence breeds;
> We may inhale despair
> At distances of centuries
> From the malaria.[14]

Emily Dickinson seems fascinated with the thought that words once expressed assume an existence of their own and can never be recalled by their "wrinkled author." In a letter she warns, "We must be careful what we say. No bird resumes its egg."[15] She then copies the first stanza of the poem just quoted, replacing the word *stimulate* with the word *consecrate* and the word *dropped* with the word *left*. The meaning of the stanza is now different but the fundamental expression of the potency and endurance of "a word" remains unchanged.

An interesting aspect of Emily Dickinson's reverence for words is the way in which she frequently uses terms of language and communication to describe or symbolize something entirely different from communication in the ordinary sense of the term. For instance in a poem beginning, "Step lightly on this narrow spot!" she says that a certain dead person's name is told as far as "fame export / Her deathless syllable."[16] In another poem the concept of love is symbolized by the phrases of endearment between lovers which eclipse all other communication.

---

12 *Ibid.*, p. 45, No. xcv.

13 *Letters*, p. 364.

14 Millicent Todd Bingham, "Poems of Emily Dickinson: Hitherto Published Only in Part," *New England Quarterly*, XX (March, 1947), 15. [Reprinted here by permission of The President and Fellows of Harvard College and The Trustees of Amherst College.]

15 *Letters*, p. 233.

16 *Poems*, p. 176, No. xliv.

Many a phrase has the English language, —
I have heard but one

. . . .

Breaking in bright orthography
On my simple sleep;

. . . .

Say it again — Saxon!
Hush — only to me![17]

Even natural objects were described in terms implying human communication.

The hills in purple syllables
The day's adventures tell
To little groups of continents
Just going home from school.[18]

Occasionally she uses language terms in writing about death. The mystery of death has often been called "a riddle" by poets, but Emily Dickinson endows that word with unusual power by making it a separate, vital entity — a technique characteristic of her emphasis upon the individual word. One poem begins, "I have not told my garden yet," and the last stanza reads:

Nor lisp it at the table,
Nor heedless by the way
Hint that within the riddle
One will walk to-day![19]

The "riddle" becomes an existing locality or condition — something into which one can walk. After stepping within the riddle, Emily Dickinson suggests, one is still helpless without the power and the grace of the Divine. Such power is inevitably described in terms of language.

The quiet nonchalance of death
No daybreak can bestir;
The slow archangel's syllables
Must awaken her.[20]

And in "Tis whiter than an Indian pipe," Emily Dickinson describes the awakened spirit as a "limitless hyperbole."[21] In the same type of metaphor

---

[17] *Ibid.*, p. 422, No. lxxvii. [Reprinted here by permission of Little, Brown and Company.]
[18] *Bolts of Melody*, p. 92, No. 166. [Reprinted here by permission of The President and Fellows of Harvard College and The Trustees of Amherst College.]
[19] *Poems*, p. 178, No. xlviii.
[20] *Ibid.*, p. 159, No. v.
[21] *Ibid.*, p. 201, No. c.

she pictures herself as a syllable in the poem beginning, "I could suffice for Him."

> "Would I be whole?" He sudden broached.
> My syllable rebelled . . .[22]

Her answer, or more generally, her powers of communication are identified with herself.

It seems likely that Emily Dickinson would have devoted herself to individual words if only because she keenly realized their vital power in both of its aspects — the sudden lightning flash, and the deep, undeveloped freight. Apparently she delighted in words for their own sake, as most of us do only as children. She admittedly was childlike in many respects and indeed consciously sought to maintain in herself the eagerness and wonder of a child. Thus it is not inconsistent with her attitude and general approach to experience that she should savor the sounds and meanings of words just as a child experiments and practices with his first syllables.

However, Emily Dickinson had a more serious objective in experimenting with words than the delight which this afforded. She was concerned with language as an instrument for communication. Her capacity to perceive the significant and her desire to express her perceptions in poetic form made this concern inevitable. To a mind brimming with acute impressions, observations, and speculations, the ambiguity of ordinary language must have seemed intolerable. The evidence is clear that she gave great care to the evaluation of not only lines but the very syllables of each word. In this way she apparently hoped to achieve a skill in the use of language which would preclude ambiguity and verbosity. Hypothetically, we can trace the reasoning which led her to her unique way of using words.

The tendency of human minds to interpret words in the light of their own prejudices, ignorances, and inclinations is easily apparent. Therefore the fewer words one used, the less opportunity he provided for misinterpretation — that is, if the words were chosen which in their denotative meanings and their connotative associations would most exactly convey one's intentions. Thus Emily Dickinson attempted to develop a shorthand system of poetic language which would combine the advantage of conciseness with the capability of connoting a rich complex of suggestions.

In conjunction with the development of a shorthand language arose an unshakable attachment to *frugality, economy, conciseness, reticence* and *simplicity.* Any reader of the Dickinson poems will recognize these concepts as typical and often recurring themes. One suspects that she admired frugality not only for its usefulness in poetic communication but also as a compelling concept in itself. At any rate, her poems show *economy* to have been a constant watchword. Even a rat is described as having "con-

---

[22] *Ibid.,* p. 425, No. lxxxii. [Reprinted here by permission of Little, Brown and Company.]

cise" characteristics and as being "a foe so reticent."[23] Valuable or awe-some things — books, lover's words, nature, death — are all described in terms of frugality, simplicity, and reticence.[24] The human being in particular achieved stature and power in proportion to his reserve.

> I fear a man of scanty speech,
> I fear a silent man,
> Haranguer I can overtake
> Or babbler entertain —
>
> But he who waiteth while the rest
> Expend their inmost pound,
> Of this Man I am wary —
> I fear that He is Grand.[25]

She felt, truly enough, that she herself was liberally endowed with the supreme virtue of reticence. In some poems she symbolically identifies her own existence as a form and practice of some type of economy.

> Alone and in a circumstance
> Reluctant to be told,
> A spider on my reticence
> Deliberately crawled . . .[26]

Twice she refers to "my frugal eyes."[27] And the following poem has auto-biographical overtones even if she were not specifically talking about herself.

> Superiority to fate
> Is difficult to learn.
> 'Tis not conferred by any,
> But possible to earn
>
> A pittance at a time,
> Until, to her surprise,
> The soul with strict economy
> Subsists till Paradise.[28]

In respect to Emily Dickinson's concept of economy, one can trace the progression of her thinking from a reverence for words to a realization that

[23] *Poems*, p. 84, No. xxxv.
[24] *Ibid.*, p. 46, No. xcix; p. 83, No. xxxi; p. 233, No. xxxiv; and *Bolts of Melody*, p. 192, No. 356.
[25] *Poems*, p. 277, No. i. [Reprinted here by permission of Little, Brown and Company.]
[26] *Bolts of Melody*, p. 102, No. 181. [Reprinted here by permission of The President and Fellows of Harvard College and The Trustees of Amherst College.]
[27] *Poems*, p. 47, No. cii; and p. 173, No. xxxvi.
[28] *Ibid.*, p. 41, No. lxxv.

"scanty speech" is the most effective means of communicating and to an emphasis upon the concept of frugality as a value in itself. "Oneness" is the essence of meaningful experience.

> One and One are One,
> Two be finished using,
> Well enough for schools,
> But for inner choosing,
> Life — just, or Death —
> Or the Everlasting.
> Two would be too vast,
> For the Soul's comprising.[29]

From this position it was inevitable that Emily Dickinson would proceed to the logical conclusion that if economy and reticence of expression were more meaningful than the effusiveness and carelessness of most ordinary speech, then still more significant would be *silence*. This conclusion was apparently her final and unwavering position in regard to the efficacy of words and became one of her most pervasive themes. Two aspects of her experience supported such a conviction and probably contributed to its genesis.

First she saw that the most awe-inspiring and significant things experienced in the external world are wrapped in silence and mystery.

> Aloud
> Is nothing that is chief,
> But still.[30]

Faced with this fact, Emily Dickinson could only adopt a "reverential face" and, in her idiom, not profane the time with the symbol of a word.[31]

> My best acquaintances are those
> With whom I spoke no word;
> The stars that stated come to town
> Esteemed me never rude
>
> Although to their celestial call
> I failed to make reply,
> My constant reverential face
> Sufficient courtesy.[32]

---

[29] *Ibid.*, p. 356, No. cxl. [Reprinted here by permission of Little, Brown and Company.]

[30] *Bolts of Melody*, p. 249, No. 485. [Reprinted here by permission of The President and Fellows of Harvard College and The Trustees of Amherst College.]

[31] *Poems*, p. 133, No. xiii.

[32] *Bolts of Melody*, p. 122, No. 225. [Reprinted here by permission of The President and Fellows of Harvard College and The Trustees of Amherst College.]

The essential element in this poem is Emily Dickinson's avowal that non-speaking, inanimate "things" are her best acquaintances. In this category would fall the sublime aspects of nature such as the volcano:

> The reticent volcano keeps
>   His never slumbering plan;
> Confided are his projects pink
>   To no precarious man.[33]

And the sea which

> Develops pearl and weed,
> But only to himself is known
> The fathoms they abide.[34]

And Nature as a total phenomenon:

> We pass and she abides;
> We conjugate her skill
> While she creates and federates
> Without a syllable.[35]

> Nature is what we know
> But have no art to say,
> So impotent our wisdom is
> To Her simplicity.[36]

Emily Dickinson's "best acquaintances" also included such intangible concepts as Melody:

> The definition of melody is
> That definition is none.[37]

Life:

> A still volcano — Life —
> That flickered in the night
> When it was dark enough to show
> Without endangering sight.[38]

[33] *Poems*, p. 49, No. cvii.
[34] *Ibid.*, p. 136, No. xvii.
[35] *Bolts of Melody*, p. 51, No. 92. [Reprinted here by permission of The President and Fellows of Harvard College and The Trustees of Amherst College.]
[36] *Poems*, p. 233, No. xxxiv. [Reprinted here by permission of Little, Brown and Company.]
[37] *Ibid.*, p. 310, No. lvii. [Reprinted here by permission of Little, Brown and Company.]
[38] *Ibid.*, p. 292, No. xxxiii. [Reprinted here by permission of Little, Brown and Company.]

the Future:

> The Future never spoke,
> Nor will he, like the Dumb,
> Reveal by sign or syllable
> Of his profound To-come.[39]

Divinity:

> Divinity dwells under the seal.[40]

or God:

> Our little secrets slink away
> Beside God's "will not tell" . . .[41]

the Heavens:

> The Heavens with a smile
> Sweep by our disappointed heads,
> But deign no syllable.[42]

and of course — Death:

> The Living tell
> The Dying but a syllable;
> The coy Dead — none.[43]

> Like Death,
>   Who only shows his
>   Marble disc —
> Sublimer sort than speech.[44]

All these "best acquaintances" have in common the characteristic, extremely significant for Emily Dickinson, of existing on levels incomprehensible to the human mind, of never yielding the secret of their nature. As I have already observed, Emily Dickinson probably concluded that the withdrawal from communication manifested by the mightiest things conceivable to the human mind was worth emulating, in so far as possible, by the mightiest human minds.

---

[39] *Ibid.*, p. 232, No. xxxi. [Reprinted here by permission of Little, Brown and Company.]

[40] *Bolts of Melody*, p. 249, No. 485.

[41] *Ibid.*, p. 280, No. 560. [Reprinted here by permission of The President and Fellows of Harvard College and The Trustees of Amherst College.]

[42] *Poems*, p. 321, No. lxxx. [Reprinted here by permission of Little, Brown and Company.]

[43] *Ibid.*, p. 447, No. cxvii. [Reprinted here by permission of Little, Brown and Company.]

[44] *Poems*, p. 271, No. cxlii. [Reprinted here by permission of Little, Brown and Company.]

The second aspect of her experience which led her to a worshipful attitude toward silence was her intimate knowledge of human experience. She, perhaps as much as any other human being, was aware of the profound complexities of experience which accompany, like the submerged mass of an iceberg, the apparent superficiality and simplicity of daily life. These complexities, she knew, defied the limits of communication and made inevitable the fact that the essential nature of human beings must always remain secreted in the lonely isolation of the individual.

> Growth of Man like growth of Nature
> Gravitates within,
> Atmosphere and sun confirm it
> But it stirs alone.
>
> Each its difficult ideal
> Must achieve itself,
> Through the solitary prowess
> Of a silent life.[45]

Emily Dickinson noticed that it was the most significant aspects of the human being which seemed most removed from communication.

> Best things dwell out of sight —
> The pearl, the just, our thought . . .[46]
>
> Speech is a symptom of affection,
> And Silence one,
> The perfectest communication
> Is heard of none . . .[47]

Of the two symptoms of affection Emily Dickinson's preference is clearly for silence — not an empty, passive silence but one made electric by the energy of a powerful restraint.

> There is no silence in the earth so silent
>   As that endured
> Which, uttered, would discourage nature
> And haunt the world.[48]

The significance of silence is not comprised in a lack of something but in a tremendous excess existing within the human being. Extremes of emo-

---

[45] *Ibid.*, p. 282, No. xiv. [Reprinted here by permission of Little, Brown and Company.]

[46] *Bolts of Melody*, p. 274, No. 543. [Reprinted here by permission of The President and Fellows of Harvard College and The Trustees of Amherst College.]

[47] *Poems*, p. 261, No. cx. [Reprinted here by permission of Little, Brown and Company.]

[48] *Bolts of Melody*, p. 250, No. 488. [Reprinted here by permission of The President and Fellows of Harvard College and The Trustees of Amherst College.]

tion such as joy or grief, for instance, often underlie a meaningful silence. Emily Dickinson knew from her own experience that verbalization is hopelessly inadequate beyond a certain point to express joy:

> If I could tell how glad I was,
> I should not be so glad,
> But when I cannot make the Force
> Nor mould it into word,
> I know it is a sign
> That new Dilemma be
> From mathematics further off,
> Than from Eternity.[49]

Or grief:

> Best grief is tongueless —[50]

Her observation of other people indicated that the same was true for them.

> Give little anguish
> Lives will fret.
> Give avalanches —
> And they'll slant,
>
> Straighten, look cautious for their breath,
> But make no syllable —
> Like Death,
>   Who only shows his
>   Marble disc —
> Sublimer sort than speech.[51]
>
> The words the happy say
> Are paltry melody;
> But those the silent feel
> Are beautiful.[52]
>
> She was mute from transport,
> I, from agony![53]

Emily Dickinson asked herself why it was that words, which ordinarily seemed almost infinitely capable of expressing thought and emotion,

[49] *Poems,* p. 267, No. cxxviii. [Reprinted here by permission of Little, Brown and Company.]

[50] *Bolts of Melody,* p. 252, No. 493.

[51] *Poems,* pp. 270 f., No. cxlii. [Reprinted here by permission of Little, Brown and Company.]

[52] *Bolts of Melody,* p. 249, No. 487. [Reprinted here by permission of The President and Fellows of Harvard College and The Trustees of Amherst College.]

[53] *Poems,* p. 176, No. xlv.

should on occasion become pitifully inadequate. "Is it that words are suddenly small, or that we are suddenly large, that they cease to suffice us to thank a friend? Perhaps it is chiefly both."[54] Apparently she regarded the expressive power of words and the perceptiveness of the human being as associated in an almost organic relationship. The increase of awareness in a person which made him "suddenly large" was accompanied by an apparent decrease in the effectiveness of words to express the newly acquired excess of thought or emotion. However, even though the deepest thought and emotion dwelled in inexpressible depths, there was, as Emily Dickinson knew, no reason to deny its real existence.

> Gratitude is not the mention
> Of a tenderness,
> But its still appreciation
> Out of plumb of speech.
>
> When the sea return no answer
> By the line and lead
> Proves it there's no sea, or rather
> A remoter bed?[55]

The conclusion, then, to which Emily Dickinson came was that words, powerful as they are, cannot encompass what is truly significant. As a result of this conclusion, her position as a poet who was concerned with molding thought and experience into language was indeed strange. The apparently logical thing to do would be to withdraw from all attempts at language communication and devote herself to a mystical experiencing of truth. Such a course of action would not have been foreign to her nature or inclination. Few persons have so completely withdrawn from human society as she did. However, Emily Dickinson was apparently not the type of person who could attain a completely mystical approach to life. She seemed to feel a desperate need for language communication, or at least the need to organize her experience to such a degree that it could be expressed on paper if only for herself to read. Thus, fully aware that she was attempting the exact thing which she considered impossible, she tried to find phrases for her thoughts.

> I found the phrase to every thought
> I ever had, but one;
> And that defies me, — as a hand
> Did try to chalk the sun

---

[54] *Letters*, p. 324.
[55] Bingham, "Poems of Emily Dickinson: Hitherto Published Only in Part," *op. cit.*, p. 38. [Reprinted here by permission of Houghton Mifflin Company.]

"Gratitude is not the mention" from *Emily Dickinson Face to Face*, edited by Martha D. Bianchi. Reprinted by permission of the publisher, Houghton Mifflin Company.

To races nurtured in the dark; —
How would your own begin?
Can blaze be done in cochineal,
Or noon in mazarin?[56]

This poem usually is interpreted as expressing Emily Dickinson's extreme confidence in her ability to express everything except perhaps the concept of immortality. And of course it is evident that she did possess great self-confidence in the use of words; however, this one poem should not make us forget her conviction, expressed repeatedly, that the truly significant things in human experience dwelled in the realm of silence and secrecy. The poem quoted above, furthermore, is not so much a contradiction as a confirmation of her position regarding the impotency of words. In the first place she is speaking of a specific, significant thought — most likely the concept of immortality which she habitually describes in terms of *blaze, noon, sun.* To emphasize the gigantic stature and inaccessibility of this concept, she uses a contrast based upon the clearest, most concise distinction possible — a sharp dichotomy between the concept of immortality and all other concepts. The poem would lose much of its direct-ness and power if she had made a general statement to the effect that she had difficulty expressing the thoughts which concerned her most. Secondly, the exaggeration in the first two lines is too apparent to be taken as literal truth. The one thought she could not express should be considered a symbol of the realm of thoughts which are too intrinsically a part of the human soul to be severed from it. Since such a realm of thoughts would naturally be associated with and probably epitomized by the concept of immortality, it was logical for Emily Dickinson to think of it as the repre-sentative "one" thought to which she could not find a phrase. Her desire to be concise, specific, and economic in poetry will inevitably lead her to this solution of a poetic problem.

I have shown how Emily Dickinson's attitude toward words was some-thing of a paradox. Her intellect and intuitive imagination told her that human communication was unavailing before the greatness of the universe and the complexity of man's experience within it. But her emotional nature, her delight in a struggle, and her unlimited courage bade her make the attempt regardless of its futility. As long as her poetry could at least suggest the infiniteness and wonder of the universe, she thought the effort was justified. And if nothing else, she could vividly call attention to poetry's inadequacy for the most significant communication by, paradox-ically enough, communicating that very idea as profoundly as she could to any possible reader of her poems. Thus the awe-inspiring mysteries with which Emily Dickinson was concerned would be dramatically focused in the reader's mind through a striking incongruity: powerful poems confess-

[56] *Poems*, p. 17, No. xxxi.

ing their powerlessness. The paradox inherent in such a situation is the result of the poet's attempt to bridge the gap between a mortal and super-human consciousness.

It should be noted that Emily Dickinson did not regard the impotency of words as a total disadvantage. There was an attraction, even a fascination, in the imperfection of human language, for if communication was necessarily incomplete and vague, the human imagination was thus allowed more scope, given more importance, and developed more extensively. All poets by the nature of their calling depend upon and revere the imagination, and Emily Dickinson was no exception. She preferred the world of her own creation to the objective world of observable fact. The lady in the following poem knows that the "image" has advantages over the "interview."

> A charm invests a face
> Imperfectly beheld, —
> The lady dare not lift her veil
> For fear it be dispelled
>
> But peers beyond her mesh,
> And wishes, and denies, —
> Lest interview annul a want
> That image satisfies.[57]

In another poem on the same theme Emily Dickinson uses erotic imagery in a highly unusual context.

> Did the harebell loose her girdle
> To the lover bee,
> Would the bee the harebell hallow
> Much as formerly?
>
> Did the paradise, persuaded,
> Yield her moat of pearl,
> Would the Eden be an Eden,
> Or the earl an earl?[58]

[57] *Ibid.*, p. 142, No. xxviii.

[58] *Ibid.*, p. 142, No. xxvii. Richard Chase (*Emily Dickinson* ["The American Men of Letters Series"; William Sloan Associates, 1951], p. 139) comments on this poem as follows:

"The poem beginning 'Did the harebell loose her girdle' asks, in terms of a rather confused nature allegory, whether female creatures (the category seems extensive) lose caste by yielding to their lovers, and also whether the lovers lose caste (for 'Eden' read 'the innocent sexuality of women,' and for 'earl' read 'lover'): [Mr. Chase quotes here the second stanza of the poem.] There is no specific idea of sin in this poem. The specification is of status, though the exact kind of status in question is, as frequently happens, not very clear."

Why not accept the obvious meaning of "Eden" and "earl" as Heaven and God? Emily Dickinson frequently used terms of royalty to designate God, and she used the words "Eden," "Paradise," "Heaven," "Eternity" as more or less synonymous. See, for example, *Poems*, p. 191, No. lxxiii, and p. 216, No. cxxxvi; pp. 295 f., No. xxxvii, and pp. 309 f., No. lvii.

An image of a maiden who maintains her alluring mystery and attractiveness by preserving her chastity is here applied to a harebell, and then in a daring extension to Heaven itself. Heaven and God, if perceived and understood by men, would not retain their present status in men's thoughts and imagination. The implication is that incommunicableness in this case is a distinct advantage.

Perhaps Emily Dickinson's viewpoint concerning the inadequacy of the word to express the poet's deepest intuitions, and yet the value, notwithstanding, of struggling to express the inexpressible is summed up in the following poem.

> To tell the beauty would decrease,
> To state the Spell demean,
> There is a syllableless sea
> Of which it is the sign.
>
> My will endeavours for its word
> And fails, but entertains
> A rapture as of legacies —
> Of introspective mines.[59]

[59] *Poems*, p. 266, No. cxxiv. [Reprinted here by permission of Little, Brown and Company.]

M. M. Mahood

SHAKESPEARE'S WORLD OF WORDS

ᴋᴋ

One special value of the concluding selection of our book is that it summarizes some basic theoretical aspects of language. It is concerned with the philosophical problem of the meaning of meaning — that is, with the effort to come to a understanding of the relationship between words and things. It also returns our thinking to several points with

Reprinted from *Shakespeare's Wordplay* by M. M. Mahood (London: Methuen & Co., Ltd., 1957), by permission of the publisher.

which this book began: to the ritual of naming, to the conjuring power of language, to the activity of wordplay, to the history of words. By means of Professor Mahood's essay we re-enter the Elizabethan age, a period of great linguistic creativity. The work of Shakespeare reflects not only the Elizabethan search for new lands but also its explorations into the world of words. The Elizabethans trusted — and yet distrusted — words. Both attitudes appear in Shakespeare's plays. For instance, Shakespeare's treatment of the word honor in Henry IV illustrates two views of language and experience. For Falstaff, honor is but air; for Prince Hal, it is "full of connotative life"; each character is made to act upon his conception of honor's meaning and overtones. Professor Mahood examines Shakespeare's language in Julius Caesar, King Lear, and other plays, too. She suggests that the life of language can pass through stages of skepticism and confidence. The example of Shakespeare is instructive: he could exploit both the tensions and the accommodations between the world of words and the world of fact.

No one could play so long and brilliantly with words as Shakespeare did without asking himself: what is the relationship of words to things — the meaning of meaning? Nor was he the only Elizabethan to pose the question 'What's in a name?' to which one answer was provided by the great linguistic revolution of the seventeenth century. It is the nature of drama to raise questions rather than to answer them. So much of Shakespeare's dramatic writing is, however, concerned with the truth and power of words, that I think it is possible to trace his changing views of language through the sequence of his plays to something very like a conclusive answer to the problem, in as far as it affected him as a poet, in his final comedies.

1

The Elizabethan attitude towards language is assumed rather than stated, and is therefore much easier to feel than to define. Like Plato, the Elizabethans believed in the truth of names, but whereas, according to Socrates in the *Cratylus*, these right names had been given by 'the legislators', to sixteenth-century ways of thinking the right names of things had been given by God and found out by Adam. In a play on the Creation acted at Florence early in the seventeenth century, Adam takes a very long time to name the property trees, stars, and the like. It is tedious for the modern reader, but clearly it was exciting for the contemporary spectators when they heard Adam guess all the names right. Even after the seventeenth century as a whole had decided that names were arbitrary and conventional, the Cabalists went on hunting for the natural language of Adam; and this notion of a natural language was alive and meaningful for Coleridge, who enjoyed the anti-materialist, anti-rationalist undercurrents of late seventeenth-century thought. Names, then, seemed true to most people in the sixteenth century because they thought of them as at most the images of things and at least the shadows of things, and where there was a shadow there must be a body to cast it. This view of language has died hard. The argument of sixteenth-century astronomers that no new star could be discovered because there would be no name to call it by, seems less fantastically remote from our ways of thinking when we recall that, in the present century, there were doctors who refused to accept Freud's clinical proof that men could have hysteria on the grounds that the word was derived from ὑστέρα and could therefore only apply to women. The Elizabethan faith in the rightness of words is perhaps best seen in the way their preachers handle their texts. A simple piece of poetic parallelism is developed into two topics on the assumption that where there are two words there are two things. If a word has several meanings they are shown, through the serious punning which so exasperated a later generation, to bear a kind of transcendental relationship to one another. Name puns were serious for the Elizabethans on the same principle. The bearer of a name was everything the name implied; a notion not unknown among modern parents.

Given this belief in the truth of names, a belief in the power of words through sympathetic magic followed. Where there was a name there was a thing; therefore names could conjure up things. There was, moreover, religious sanction for this traditional belief in the efficacy of words. The verbal authority given to the apostles by the Incarnate Word lived on in the Church's power to bind or loose. 'For curs wol slee — right as assoillyng savith' says Chaucer, and I think we are wrong to read our modern verbal scepticism into his words. The Word of Scripture retained the same magical power; *in principio* was, significantly, the beginning of exorcisms, and we still hold an oath on the Bible to be the most binding. Magic relied on the direct efficacy of words for spells, curses and incantations, and the superstition of dead-naming is a powerful theme of some sagas and ballads. Verbal authority passed to the king at his coronation, so that just as Christ had dubbed the apostles,[1] the king could create knights. In their turn, nobility and knighthood gave their holders the power to make their words good in challenge or vow. In the legal sphere too, the king's word was immediately effective, and so were the words spoken by those to whom he deputed legal authority, since an *act*, a *sentence*, a *deed*, were all forms of words that implied action. There is one further aspect of this belief in the efficacy of words. When Elizabethan

---

[1] See Skeat's note on *Piers Plowman* II, 102 (C text).

rhetoricians spoke of the power and force of words, their meaning may have been as much literal as metaphorical. They may have thought of their words going home by physical and physiological means. Just as a glance from his lady's eye darted into the poet's eye and thence travelled down with dire results into his heart, so Hamlet's words could wring his mother's heart or cleave it in twain.

Alongside this dominant linguistic realism there had always been a certain linguistic scepticism. In the *Cratylus*, Socrates is said to be refuting the opinions of Hermogenes and of many others who declare names to be conventional. In Shakespeare's day, an abundance of popular proverbs, such as 'fine words fill not a firlot', voice the same doubt. Linguistic scepticism is also to be found in popular tales like the one of the false miracle at St Albans, about the man whose pretence of having regained his sight after lifelong blindness was exposed by his calling the king's cloak red. Shakespeare's version of the incident, in the second part of *Henry VI*, is based on the Chronicles, but it was also told to Sir Thomas More by his father. The Chronicles, too, record a number of prophecies which came true in word and not in fact, and these stories suggest a popular ironic distinction between the world of events and the conceptual world of words. Finally, linguistic scepticism of a learned kind had once flourished among the English nominalists, and their habits of thought may never have been entirely suppressed.

The first reasoned protest against the magic of names was made in the soft and insidious voice of Francis Bacon. Bacon's technique for introducing a new idea was, by his own admission, to pour new meanings into old words, and this in itself constitutes a sceptical attitude to language. He is wary of a direct break with the traditional notion that words are the images of things, since this has the backing of Plato, but his project for the advancement of learning includes an impartial enquiry, to be made without deference to the Ancients, into the relationship of words to things. His own linguistic position is stated in the first book of *The Advancement of Learning*, when he says: 'Words are but the images of matter: and except they have life of reason and invention, to fall in love with them is all one as to fall in love with a picture.'[2] What is here implicit is finally made explicit by Hobbes: the look-say element of a word tells us nothing about the thing it stands for, but is a quite arbitrary mark or sign of our concept of that thing. By the 1640's, Hobbes was able to assume in his readers the same notion of the arbitrary and conventional nature of words: 'But seeing names ordered in speech (as is defined) are signs of our conceptions, it is manifest that they are not signs of the things themselves; for that the sound of this word *stone* should be the sign of a stone, cannot be understood in any other sense but this, that he that hears it collects that he that pro-

---

[2] *Philosophical Works*, ed. John M. Robertson (1905), p. 54.

nounces it thinks of a stone. And, therefore, that disputation, whether names signify the matter or form, or something compounded of both, and such like subtleties of the *metaphysics*, is kept up by erring men, and such as understand not the words they dispute about.'[3] Something like this theory of communication is suggested by Bacon's phrase about words' 'life of reason and invention'. But on the whole, Bacon, whose ideal of communication is demonstration in a laboratory, tends to speak of turning men's minds from the quirks of words to the subtleties of things as if communication could be made without words. Several of Bacon's scientific followers saw what he had ignored, the relationship of words to things through concepts, and strove to carry out the Baconian object of cultivating 'a just . . . familiarity between the mind and things' by treating concepts simply as the string to connect the label-word with its object. Independent concepts had to be eliminated, if necessary by an act of parliament forbidding metaphorical speech. 'The Light of human minds', writes Hobbes in *Leviathan*, 'is Perspicuous Words, but by exact definitions first snuffed and purged from ambiguity.' Coleridge speaks of 'certain focal words . . . which heat and burn', but Hobbes's ideal of language is light without heat. 'Perspicuous' is a favourite word with the linguistic reformers. Language was to be translucent, displaying objects clearly, and not prismatic, reflecting back a whole spectrum of meanings. Something of this ideal underlies the poetic diction of the Augustans. A word like 'bird' could put up a series of different concepts in one mind, and different concepts in different minds, but a phrase like 'feathered tribe', which may seem to us an obfuscation, appealed to them as clarity itself, because it produced the same single, generalised concept of birdness in everyone's mind.

The *reductio ad absurdum* of linguistic scepticism is sometimes held to have been reached in 1668 when John Wilkins published his *Essay towards a Real Character and a Philosophical Language*, in which he invented a series of symbols to indicate the genus, species, subspecies and nature of everything in existence. Wilkins became a bishop in the same year, so everything in existence included the facts of the Apostles' Creed, which he wrote out for his readers in the Real Character; but it did not include fairies and fauns, for which no symbols are provided. Wilkins's project is certainly the butt of Swift, whose Lagodan School of Languages got rid of words altogether by inducing people to carry about instead the objects they wished to discuss. Any physical disadvantage in this method was outweighed — metaphorically, at any rate — by its being a really universal language. Wilkins, however, did not degrade language, so much as abandon language as a means of scientific communication. This he did because he understood better than Hobbes the true nature of words. It was a fact that words related to concepts before things — that was why Wilkins

3 *English Works*, ed. Molesworth (1839), I, p. 17.

invented his hieroglyphs in an effort to by-pass concepts; but it was not true that concepts were the mere connections between words and things. Words have a conceptual life of their own which has nothing to do with the existence or non-existence of the things they signify.

Words heat and burn with a connotative energy. For this reason, a rose could not smell as sweet by any other name. Were it called a grump it would smell as sweet as a rose only if the gardens of our childhood had been full of grumps and if poets had always likened their loves to red, red grumps. We respond to the invitation 'Do smell this rose' with all the associations of delight the word has gathered in our previous experience, of which reading is a major part. While the linguistic sceptics of the seventeenth century rightly showed there was no direct relationship between words and things, they abused the very nature of language in trying to rob words of their independent conceptual life. If a man stops when bidden to do so in the Prince's name, he does so not because the word has conjured him to a standstill, but because he has previously encountered the Prince's name in contexts which have ensured for it a response of respect and awe. Of course, if the connotations of the word have changed, it is probable that 'a will not stand'. In Shakespeare's lifetime the old hierarchy of delegated verbal authority was breaking up, and many words which had once seemed to hold magical efficacy were losing their connotative power. In the phrase of Richard of Bordeaux, men set the word against the word: the immediately realisable word of chivalry or the excommunicative power of the Pope against the decrees of absolute monarchy, the new Protestant reliance upon the word of Scripture against the traditional authority of the Church. The second Murderer of Clarence sets the word of the King's warrant against the word of the commandment to do no murder; and in the most exciting scene of *King John*, Philip's agreement with John is undermined by his previous word of promise to Constance, by her potentially effective curses, and by the papal legate's threat of excommunication. It is typical of Shakespeare's own linguistic scepticism in the early History plays that in each case the conflict is settled by expediency — that daily break-vow, Commodity. Neither the Murderer's fealty nor his faith weighs anything against the word *reward* — which has a more immediate and tangible referent than either the King's warrant or the tables of the law.

At the time he wrote these two plays, Shakespeare's experience with words had shown him that the existence of a name did not necessitate the existence of the thing named. And because the Elizabethan belief in the power of words was dependent on a belief in their truth, Shakespeare remains for a time profoundly sceptical of that power. But from his own practice as a poet comes an understanding of the conceptual power of words which has nothing to do with their rightness as names. In the great tragedies, disbelief in the truth of words is balanced by a recognition of their connotative power: and in the last plays, Shakespeare's own insight as a poet into that connotative power restores him to faith in the rightness of words. The conceptual world of words built by poetry has its own validity and truth.

2

Love's Labour's Lost is the first play in which Shakespeare boldly questions the truth of words. A repeated quibble upon *light* points to the play's central theme that words, for all their witty sparkle, are without weight or substance. In the King's opening speech, reputation, an enduring name, is the reward offered to those who will remain with him in Navarre's academy, 'Still and contemplatiue in liuing Art'. 'Living art' is an ominous phrase. It suggests *tableaux vivants,* a substitute for that experience which alone could teach the *ars vivendi.* To the will o' the wisp intellectual pretensions of the King and his companions, Berowne opposes the light of nature. The learning of the Academy is the kind that darkens counsel by words without knowledge — 'Light seeking light, doth light of light beguile'. It may enable its scholars to become 'earthly Godfathers of heauens lights', but it will not give them any real knowledge of the stars they name. He is no less sceptical of the oaths imposed upon the academicians; and before long the Princess and her ladies have proved Berowne's mistrust of words to be justified. The facts of nature prove stronger than verbal resolves, and the courtiers are forced to explain away their *perjury* (a keyword of the play) with 'Vowes are but breath, and breath a vapour is'. The words and antics of the Humour characters are brought into line with this theme. Holofernes and Armado both draw out the thread of their verbosity finer than the staple of their argument. Moth's 'how easie it is to put yeres to the word three, and study three yeeres in two words, the dancing horse will tell you' parodies the attempt of the Navarre courtiers to bring things into existence by words. In the same way Costard's quibbling efforts to stave off the charges against him parody the sophistries of Berowne when he tries to prove that he and his companions are not forsworn. The play's best source of laughter is in this sleight of tongue in the verbal sceptic Berowne, as with the cry of 'O who can giue an oth? Where is a booke?' he proceeds to prove black white, and the swarthy Rosalind beautiful.

The Princess and her companions, for all the brilliance of their word-play, are sceptical of words from the start. To prove afresh the frailty of speech, they trick their lovers into breaking a new set of vows, those of constancy:

> Now to our periurie, to adde more terror,
> We are againe forsworne in will and error.   (V.ii.471–2)

and once the tersely-worded fact of the French king's death has brought to an end their wit-contests, they have no ear even for russet yeas and honest kersey noes. Only deeds can speak now:

> Your oth I will not trust: but go with speed
> To some forlorne and naked Hermitage . . .   (802–3)

and Berowne is dispatched to discover the hollowness of words by jesting in a hospital. The great feast of language vanishes to the sound of harpies' wings. There is no substance in speech.

In the plays that follow this, Shakespeare questions every kind of power attributed to language. Prophecies come true in word alone: the promise that he shall die in Jerusalem which Henry IV cherishes as the very hope of his salvation has only a quibbling fulfilment. Spells do not work: Hotspur jeers at Glendower's boast that he can call spirits from the vasty deep. Characters curse, but the stars shine still: the gardener in *Richard II* is unmoved by the Queen's malediction on his plants. Nor is there any magic in baptismal names: Hero's does not ensure that she will be the type of faithful love, since 'Hero itself can blot out *Hero's* virtue'. And all Shakespeare's kings know the vanity of what were called *additions*:

> Thinks thou the fierie Feuer will goe out
> With Titles blowne from Adulation?
> (*Henry* V, IV.i.273–4)

Shakespeare's verbal scepticism can be very sweeping in these comedies and histories written in the 1590's. Yet it never comprises the whole of his thought and feeling about language. Even in the instances I have given, scepticism was not always justified. Berowne's praise of Rosalind makes beauty the gift of the lover's words. However the thick-spoken Hotspur may jeer, the eloquent Glendower *is* able to call up music from the air. The Queen's curse in *Richard II* does not blight a single flower, but in so far as the garden is meant to stand for England, misfortune blights the country throughout the reign of the usurper Bolingbroke. Finally, there is something in a name in *Much Ado*, since Leander's Hero could not be more loyal than Claudio's Hero is finally proved to be. The ambivalence of Shakespeare's attitude to language at this stage in his career is most clearly seen in *Richard II*. The play might be summed up in Hobbes's aphorism: 'Words are wise men's counters, but the money of fools.' But if, from this point of view, Bolingbroke is the wise man and Richard the fool, from another, dramatically valid viewpoint, Bolingbroke is the villain and Richard the hero. Behind the sympathetic portrayal of the defeated and deposed king at Pomfret, turning over the gilt counterfeits of speech which he had once taken for true gold, we feel Shakespeare's conviction that it is better to have had and lost a faith in words than never to have surrendered to their magic.

The Henry IV plays are also deeply concerned with the truth and power of words. Here Shakespeare's flying thoughts on language all settle round the notion of Honour, a Good Name. The extreme of verbal scepticism is reached at the end of Part One by the arch-liar Falstaff: 'what is honor? a word, what is in that word honor? what is that honour? aire.'[4] In a

---

[4] Quoted from the Quarto.

sense, Shakespeare means Falstaff to be right. Glorious war is strongly satirised when, after all Hotspur's rhodomontade about plucking honour from the pale-faced moon, Falstaff turns over the body of Sir William Blunt to contemplate its grinning honour. But it is worth noticing that Falstaff does to the word *honour* exactly what the inventors of Newspeak, in George Orwell's totalitarian state, did to the word *free*. Because it was mere breath to them, they set to work to rob it of its emotive force for others, by restricting its use to such material and negative contexts as 'the dog is free from lice'; until, as a result of this brainwashing, a sentence such as 'All men are born free' came to seem meaningless. But for Prince Hal, the word *honour* is full of connotative life, so that he responds to its associations with honourable deeds of his own; and the final parting of Hal from Falstaff shows that Shakespeare himself believed honour to be more than a breath. In *All's Well* he goes even further and, in the King's speech upon honour and virtue, reverts to an almost magical idea of meaning. Bertram, who too easily takes the word for the thing, as his deception by Parolles indicates, will not accept Hellena as wife because she lacks a noble name. Perversely, he regards the titular honour the King is prepared to confer on Hellena as breath, a mere word. The King's long speech at this point shows, however, that, as befits a divinely appointed monarch, he regards his power to bestow honours as an extension of the original *fiat*. The inheritors of honoured names may dishonour them, but if meaning could be lost, meaning could also be found. By recognising true virtue and honour in his bestowal of titular honours, the King keeps alive the conceptual reality of the words. In giving Hellena a title of honour, he gives her her right name:

> that is honours scorne,
> Which challenges it selfe as honours borne,
> And is not like the sire: Honours thriue,
> When rather from our acts we them deriue
> Then our fore-goers: the mere words, a slaue
> Debosh'd on euerie tombe, on euerie graue:
> A lying Trophee, and as oft is dumbe,
> Where dust, and damn'd obliuion is the Tombe.
> Of honour'd bones indeed, what should be saide?
> If thou canst like this creature, as a maide,
> I can create the rest: Vertue, and shee
> Is her owne dower: Honour and wealth, from mee.
> (II.iii.140–51)

This word *honour* has a special fascination for Shakespeare at this stage of his life's work because the tension between its shallow and deeper meanings corresponds to his own dilemma between linguistic scepticism and faith in the power of words. It is particularly effective as Isabella uses it five times over to Angelo in *Measure for Measure*: 'Heauen keepe your honor.' At first this seems a piece of direct, negative irony; Angelo's honour is merely his title as judge, and does not correspond to any real quality in his character. But if honour is a mere scutcheon to Angelo in the depths of his self-discovery, it is for Isabella the concept which preserves them both. Her conventional phrase is also a prayer which is answered when the Duke, in his Providential aspect, preserves Angelo from the seduction of Isabella and from the murder of her brother. In the second scene between Isabella and Angelo, the word is set against the word — not destructively, as in *King John*, but creatively, as in the third book of *Paradise Lost*: mercy against justice, the redemptive promise against the harshness of the law. And the play's conclusion sustains this by upholding the power of the Word; more particularly, of the Sermon on the Mount.

There is here strong indication of a renewed faith in language. But meanwhile, in the series of great tragedies, scepticism prevails. The stage Shakespeare's thought about language had reached towards the turn of the century can best be seen in *Julius Cæsar*. The dramatic conflict of that play is above all a conflict of linguistic attitudes. At one extreme there is Caesar himself, a superstitious man, who believes in the magic of his own name which is 'not liable to fear', and who tries to conjure with it by always speaking of himself in the third person. At the other extreme is the sceptic Cassius:

> *Brutus* and *Cæsar*: What should be in that *Cæsar*?
> Why should that name be sounded more than yours
> Write them together: Yours, is as faire a Name:
> Sound them, it doth become the mouth as well:
> Weigh them, it is as heauy: Coniure with 'em,
> *Brutus* will start a Spirit as soone as *Cæsar*.
> (I.ii.141–6)

For both Cassius and Brutus, words are arbitrary symbols without properties of their own. Brutus so mistrusts the effective power of words, that he will have no oaths between the conspirators. Events at first justify the scepticism of Cassius, since Caesar's name proves no talisman to him. But there is an ominous irony in Brutus's words:

> We all stand vp against the spirit of Cæsar,
> And in the Spirit of men there is no blood.
> O that we then could come by Cæsars Spirit,
> And not dismember Cæsar!   (II.i.167–70)

Words, the breathing spirit of men, are in fact the cause of much bloodshed in the remainder of the play, since the evocative power of Caesar's name is not dismembered but lives on as 'Caesarism'. The statement that '*Brutus* will start a Spirit as soone as *Cæsar*', coming from Cassius, is probably intentional irony, for he does not believe either name to have any magical power. But it is also negative dramatic irony. Brutus can *not* start a spirit because he lacks both Caesar's faith in the magic of words and Antony's knowledge of the connotative power of words. Brutus's address to the citizens approaches the Baconian ideal of establishing a just relationship between the mind and things: it is a pithy appeal to look at the facts. Its utter failure is indicated by the man in the crowd who cries out 'Let him be Cæsar.' Antony, on the contrary, has the skill not only to play upon the connotations of the word *Caesar* but also, in the course of his oration, to strip the epithet *honourable* of all its normal connotations as it is applied to Brutus. Moreover, Caesar's word lives on in Caesar's will, and thus inflames the citizens to avenge his murder. The odd episode of Cinna the poet being lynched in error for Cinna the conspirator seems irrelevant, but in fact sums up a main theme of the play. There is everything in a name — for the ignorant and irrational. The fact that none of the characters in *Julius Cæsar*, with the exception of Brutus, is morally 'placed' suggests that, while Shakespeare has cleared his thinking on language to the point where he knows words have no inherent magic but have immense connotative powers, the moral implications of this discovery, already suggested in *Richard II*, have yet to be explored. That exploration follows in the major tragedies, where the discovery that words are arbitrary signs and not right names is made by the heroes and the knowledge that the life of words is in their connotations is put to use by the villains.

3

For all Shakespeare's tragic heroes, words lose their meaning. The verbal rules and principles, the moral code by which they have lived, have ceased to correspond to things-as-they-are. The mood is that of Edmund Blunden's 'Report on Experience':

> I have been young, and now am not too old;
> And I have seen the righteous forsaken,
> His health, his honour and his quality taken.
> This is not what we were formerly told.

Given the Elizabethan belief in the rightness of words, the authoritative words of Scripture and of the moral philosophers constituted a map of experience. But for Shakespeare's tragic heroes, the map no longer corresponds to the terrain. Where a fat land was indicated there are found to be quagmires and monsters.[5] *Timon of Athens* depicts this experience with heavy moral satire, in its story of how Timon is awakened from a verbal dream in which his protestations of generosity make him rich and his guests' protestations of gratitude make them grateful. At the end of *Troilus*

---

[5] For a discussion of the tragic hero's 'journey without maps' see F. G. Butler: *An Aspect of Tragedy* (Grahamstown, 1953).

and Cressida two kinds of good name — the Virtue of Cressida, the Honour of Achilles — are found to be meaningless: 'Words, words, meere words, no matter from the heart.' The play ends where *Hamlet* begins, with the hero sustaining a shock that takes the matter out of words; at the Ghost's revelation, Hamlet wipes from his memory all 'saws of books', the commonplaces of moral philosophy. They are now 'words, words, words' — the kind of platitude spoken by Polonius, the occasional excellent moral advice of Claudius, without any relationship to the actual world of evil that has opened into Hamlet's experience.

In these three plays the discovery of facts shatters the heroes' faith in words. In other tragedies, villainy needs only words for this work. Iago himself knows words to be arbitrary signs without inherent meaning, but he makes use of the associative strength words hold for anyone as verbally credulous as Othello. A good name, reputation, is to Iago 'a most false imposition', but he plays fiendishly on Othello's belief that a good name is the immediate jewel of the soul. Othello's trust in the power of words shows itself in the white magic of an eloquence that can quell a brawl or enchant a Desdemona. This eloquence would be the sign of his nobility to the average Elizabethan, but to Shakespeare, who is a more than average Elizabethan, it is also a sign of his weakness. His insistence on his parts, his titles and his perfect soul suggests that he is bolstering up some funda- mental uncertainty — about Desdemona's love, or about his place in this alien society — with the reassurance of his own rhetoric. Iago recognises this weakness. 'I neuer yet did heare: That the bruized heart was pierc'd through the eares' says Brabantio, a little before we see just this happen. Othello protests 'It is not words that moues me thus', when in fact it is nothing else. By the verbal black magic which Granville Barker neatly calls 'poetic practice bedevilled', Iago makes use of ambiguities to insert a wedge between the word and the fact for Othello. His use of *think* racks Othello between its uncertain meaning (as in 'I think it's nearly four') and its meaning of certainty based on knowledge ('I think she's a fool'). So with *seems*: 'men should be what they seem' may use *seems* as we do when we say 'it seems she is going away' or as in 'he seems better than he is'. The result of this on Othello is that words fail him in every meaning of the phrase. His splendidly assured rhetoric, in which each word was backed by fact or by the power to make it fact, breaks down into gibberish, and then is built up by Iago into a high-sounding façade of speech behind which Othello himself is in ruins.

In *King Lear*, different attitudes to the problem of language are dis- tinguished in the wordplay upon *nothing*. When Cordelia uses the word to reply to the question 'What can you say, to draw A third, more opilent then your Sisters?' she implies that only good actions could, to her way of thinking, gain such results, and a good word is not a spell to produce a good action — it is, in fact, no *thing*. The soft words of Goneril and Regan correspond to no thing in subsequent events, but they draw a delegated power in this first scene from the associations they hold for Lear. Subsequently, Lear, like the other tragic heroes, discovers that words are no things. He has dressed himself in flattery, only to find, like Richard of Bordeaux, that the additions of a king are mere lendings. The disillusionment is so complete that at first Lear's identity seems to be lost with his titles: 'Who is it that can tell me who I am?' The Fool supplies the answer: 'now thou art an O without a figure, I am better then thou art now, I am a Foole, thou art nothing.' It is not just the voice of the child-like Fool telling the emperor he has no clothes on. It is Lear's shadow, his own insight, speaking out of his disillusionment in words; there is no reality to correspond to signs, and he himself is only a cipher.

The good, then, are wrong about words for they have, in Bacon's phrase, fallen in love with a picture; and the bad are right about them, for they know they relate to concepts, not things, and they turn this knowledge to their own advantage. Can we distinguish in the tragedies any other linguistic attitude which might lead Shakespeare out of this impasse? I think that in each major tragedy there is the hint of a reconciliation between the world of words and the world of facts — with the exception of *Macbeth* where the villain-hero ends by finding life a meaningless tale. In *King Lear*, Cordelia tries to preserve the bond of nature by giving all her words the validity of her actions. In consequence of this, she is able to bring Lear back from the despair in which he was an O without a figure, and man a poor bare forked animal, to that sober approximation of words with facts in which he sees himself as a foolish, fond old man. Othello, too, is restored to some belated faith in words by the discovery that Desdemona was true to her vows. Iago's abuse of words is finished — 'From this time forth I neuer will speake word' — but with 'Soft you; a word or two before you go', Othello holds his hearers spellbound until his purpose is accomplished, and so revives for us the nobly eloquent Othello of the first two acts. *Hamlet* offers, as I have tried to show, yet another reconciliation of the world of words and that of facts, when Hamlet finds that his conviction that the world of common speech and intercourse is a make-believe world does not free him from the necessity to play his part on this great stage. Just as the Murder of Gonzago caught the conscience of the king, so Hamlet's performance of the conventional role of the Avenger may have its effect upon the world of evil revealed to him in his mother's conduct and the Ghost's disclosures.

When the seeming truth of things is found to be fiction, fiction may be the only way to the truth. Hamlet's use of the players points to a discovery Shakespeare was making about his own art. The consolation of a Shakespearean tragedy is ultimately to be found, not in any explicit statement that all is best, nor yet in the events of the play, but in the existence of the play itself. The inadequacy of words to express things has been explored and expressed in words. The poet has not only that power over words, abused by Shakespeare's villains, of playing upon the associations they hold for other people. He has also power to restore the truth of words, to ensure that where there is a word there is a thing; for in the theatre, the conceptual life of words is brought by the actors as near as it may be to actuality, so that it becomes for the audience a valid part of their experience. The golden world of Navarre is none the less real to our experience because it is shattered by the brazen fact of Mercade's message. In crying against the truth of words, Shakespeare was crying out against his own succession as a poet; and a full realisation of this seems to come in his last comedies.

4

In *The Winter's Tale* and *The Tempest*, Shakespeare's battling thoughts on language come in for the last round. The conflict of the earlier plays, between linguistic faith and linguistic scepticism, had widened, in the tragedies, into an opposition between those who have had, but lost, faith in commonplaces, the axioms of philosophy, and those who on the other hand live by no verbal principles but can always cite Scripture for their ill purposes. The final conflict is between Shakespeare's self-doubts and his faith in his own achievement; between mistrust of poetry as a mere world of words and the vindication of poetry as the only creative mode of language.

With his greatest achievement behind him, it was natural for Shakespeare in his retirement to ask himself if it had been worth doing and if it would endure, or if the best in this kind were but shadows, less valuable and less durable than the actions of life itself. As the problem of *mimesis* this had been fought out by the Ancients, and by the critics of the Renaissance in their own variations upon the *Poetics*. The debate between Perdita and Polixenes in Act IV of *The Winter's Tale* can be matched, in its use of the grafting image, by quotation from the Italian Danielli, the Frenchman Peletier and the English Puttenham.[6] Perdita will have no streaked gilly-flowers:

> For I haue heard it said,
> There is an Art, which in their pidenesse shares
> With great creating-Nature.

POLIXENES: Say there be:
> Yet Nature is made better by no meane,
> But Nature makes that Meane: so ouer that Art,
> (Which you say addes to Nature) is an Art
> That Nature makes. (IV.iv.86–92)

[6] See Harold J. Wilson: 'Nature and Art in *The Winter's Tale* IV.iv.86 following', *Shakespeare Association Bulletin*, 1943.

The meaning of this last phrase is uncertain; it could mean that Nature makes Art, but it can also mean that Art makes Nature because, in Sir Thomas Browne's phrase, Nature is the Art of God. The same problem of the inferiority or superiority of art to nature teases Keats out of thought when he looks at the Grecian Urn, too cold and motionless to satisfy as a perpetuation of the life it depicts. Is the lifeless permanence of art better than the transience of 'all breathing human passion'? Hokusai can still a breaking wave for the pleasure of many centuries, but his wave does not still move. But here Shakespeare has the advantage over the painter and even over the craftsman whose Chinese jar, in T. S. Eliot's phrase 'Still moves perpetually in its stillness'. As soon as he has shown that the relationship of art to nature cannot be solved by the hen-and-egg argument of Perdita and Polixenes, he gives us one resolution of the problem in Perdita's dance and in Florizel's description of her dancing:

> When you do dance, I wish you
> A waue o'th Sea, that you might euer do
> Nothing but that: moue *still, still* so:
> And owne no other Function.   (140–3)

Drama comes nearest to life of all forms of *mimesis* because it is continually reanimated by living actors; and in acknowledgement of this Shakespeare entrusts the weight of the play's meaning at this climax to a boy-actor's silent mimetic art. When Perdita dances, the old antagonism of art and nature disappears, for there is no way in which we can tell the dancer from the dance.

This is Shakespeare's first statement in *The Winter's Tale* of the interdependence of art and nature, and his first claim for drama's power to reconcile them as it is represented in Perdita's make-believe of Queen of the Feast. The whole scene of the sheep-shearing feast is one of the finest celebrations in English Renaissance literature of the plenitude and renewing vigour of 'great creating Nature'. It is matched only by Spenser's myth of the Garden of Adonis in Book III of *The Faerie Queene*. In one way the resemblance of the two passages is very close. In each the poet seems to be seeking, but failing to find, the satisfaction of a personal desire. The exiled Spenser craves a stability which is not to be found even in 'the first seminary of all things':

> For all that liues, is subject to that law:
> All things decay in time, and to their end do draw.

Time is the troubler of Spenser's garden, just as Time, in the person of the wintry Polixenes, tramples Perdita's flowers. Perdita is a nature spirit, the symbol of the renewing seasons, welcome to her father even before her recognition 'As is the Spring to th'Earth'. But because Nature is at the mercy of Time, Leontes' renewal through Perdita's return is only a token rejuvenation; the life of the next generation is their own, not ours.

The past, however, is restored to Leontes in the person of Hermione, whose revival is Shakespeare's second statement of drama's power to reconcile art and nature. I have suggested earlier that Perdita represents natural goodness. In this aspect of Nature she helps in the regeneration of Everyman Leontes but she cannot accomplish it alone; the priestess-like Paulina must invoke for him the Grace of Heaven as it is represented in the rejected but faithful Hermione. Hermione represents also the graces of art which must be added to the delights of nature before Leontes is restored to a full and good life. When Hermione plays at being a statue that comes to life, Shakespeare is not just trifling with a piece of stage-business borrowed from the masque. The scene is Shakespeare's affirmation of his faith as a dramatist that the best in this kind are much more than shadows. Art, represented by the play-acting Hermione, replaces the destroyed illusion of Leontes by 'a new truth' bringing with it

> a new peace, having heard the solemn
> Music strike and seen the statue move
> To forgive our illusion.[7]

Auden's words recall *The Winter's Tale*, but they define the ultimate mood of *The Tempest*, in which Shakespeare once again questions and vindicates the value of the poet's work. The contention in *The Winter's Tale* is between Art and Nature; in *The Tempest*, it is rather between Art and Action. A self-doubt as dark as that of the later Ibsen makes itself felt at several points in the play. Prospero is haunted by the recollection of how he lost his dukedom by neglecting worldly business for the bookish world of words. Within the play, he nearly loses his life when, absorbed in the presentation of his masque for the lovers, he forgets the plot of Caliban and his confederates; but with the intrusion of reality into Prospero's beating mind the whole spectacle of plenty, harmony and fertility vanishes into thin air.

Yet the truth of poetry, the validity of the conceptual life in words, is reasserted after a struggle against thoughts such as these. Prospero's neglect of life for art is more than atoned for in his use of his magician's art to set all to rights in the courts of Naples and Milan. Caliban's warning to the conspirators:

> Remember
> First to possesse his Bookes; for without them
> Hee's but a Sot, as I am,   (III.ii.102–4)

is, by its truth and untruth, the play's first vindication of art. The second comes when Prospero himself likens the vanished masque to the fading

---

[7] W. H. Auden, *The Sea and the Mirror*, p. 25 (in *For the Time Being*, 1945).

pageant of nature; for we feel that, in some Aristotelian sense of *mimesis*, the shadow of a shadow may well be nearer to a substantial reality than is the fading vicissitude it imitates. The final and the strongest vindication of Prospero's art is spoken at the end of the play by Gonzalo:

> In one voyage
> Did Claribell her husband finde at Tunis,
> And Ferdinand her brother, found a wife,
> Where he himselfe was lost: Prospero, his Dukedome
> In a poor Isle: and all of vs, our selues,
> When no man was his owne.   (V.i.208–13)

The world of words had once seemed to Shakespeare tragically incompatible with the world of things. Now he finds in the world built from Prospero's words of magic the truth of what we are. Belief in words is foremost among the lost things which are found again in Shakespeare's final comedies.